"I highly recommend this introduction to Matthew's Gospel. It is well-informed regarding introductory issues and conversant with a range of Matthean scholarship in multiple languages. Moreover, few scholars could rival Bauer's skill in inductive close reading of the text."

Craig S. Keener, author of *The IVP Bible Background Commentary: New Testament*

"The fruit of decades of research and teaching the Gospel according to Matthew, David Bauer's new introduction proves a sure-footed pathway for initiates while providing plenty of food for thought for those who think themselves already well-traveled. This will be the scholarly orientation to Matthew for the next generation."

Garwood P. Anderson, president and provost of Nashotah House Theological Seminary

"*The Gospel of the Son of God* is an incredibly rich and comprehensive resource examining the historical, literary, and theological dimensions of Matthew. Bauer proves himself to be a highly knowledgeable, judicious, and insightful guide. There is now no better introduction to the Gospel of Matthew."

Nijay K. Gupta, associate professor of New Testament, Portland Seminary

"Like a cartographer who knows the terrain, David Bauer maps the Gospel according to Matthew with deftness and clarity, giving both the student and the expert the lay of the land. He covers the ground well, providing an orientation (methods), interpretation (message), and reflection (theology) of the first Gospel. Informed by recent scholarship, Bauer's introduction is accessible and substantive, helpful to the novice and enjoyable for the frequent traveler to Matthew's literary world. Highly recommended."

Rodney Reeves, author of *Matthew* in the Story of God Bible Commentary Series

"This book is a masterful treatment of the Gospel of Matthew. I know of none like it. It will become 'must' reading of interpreters of Matthew. It is carefully written in a style that is accessible to the reader. It reflects a thorough knowledge of the scholarly literature pertaining to Matthew and of the history of its interpretation. Against the background of a treatment of other methods scholars have used to interpret the Gospel, Bauer chooses the inductive approach. . . . A welcome characteristic is that Bauer does not press evidence beyond what it will bear and evaluates alternative attempts to deal with such evidence. . . . In all, Bauer's interpretation of the Gospel of Matthew proves to be both comprehensive and persuasive. Scholars, pastors, and students will read it with profit."

Jack Dean Kingsbury, Aubrey Lee Brooks Professor of Biblical Theology Emeritus at Union Presbyterian Seminary

"David Bauer has labored long in the vineyard known as Matthew's Gospel and knows full well the range of issues and possibilities that this Gospel presents to us. This was the most copied and used Gospel in the earliest church period, which is in part why it is the first Gospel presented in the New Testament. David presents a careful, clear, and concise introduction to this crucial early Christian document. Highly recommended!"

Ben Witherington III, Amos Professor for New Testament Doctoral Studies, Asbury Theological Seminary

"David Bauer has written an eminently readable and useful introduction to the Gospel of Matthew that covers all the complex matters of background, setting, interpretation, main themes, and theological reflections. It is informed by research, undertakes sober exegesis of the text, and offers genuine insights on how Matthew matters for us today."

Michael F. Bird, academic dean and lecturer in theology at Ridley College, Melbourne, Australia

THE GOSPEL OF THE SON OF GOD

AN INTRODUCTION TO MATTHEW

DAVID R. BAUER

An imprint of InterVarsity Press
Downers Grove, Illinois

InterVarsity Press
P.O. Box 1400, Downers Grove, IL 60515-1426
ivpress.com
email@ivpress.com

©2019 by David R. Bauer

All rights reserved. No part of this book may be reproduced in any form without written permission from InterVarsity Press.

InterVarsity Press® is the book-publishing division of InterVarsity Christian Fellowship/USA®, a movement of students and faculty active on campus at hundreds of universities, colleges, and schools of nursing in the United States of America, and a member movement of the International Fellowship of Evangelical Students. For information about local and regional activities, visit intervarsity.org.

All Scripture quotations, unless otherwise indicated, are the author's own translation.

Cover design and image composite: David Fassett
Interior design: Daniel van Loon
Images: Jesus and the Resurrection © Yoeml / iStock / Getty Images Plus

ISBN 978-0-8308-5232-1 (print)
ISBN 978-0-8308-7342-5 (digital)

InterVarsity Press is committed to ecological stewardship and to the conservation of natural resources in all our operations. This book was printed using sustainably sourced paper.

Library of Congress Cataloging-in-Publication Data

Names: Bauer, David R., author.
Title: The gospel of the son of God : an introduction to Matthew / David R. Bauer.
Description: Downers Grove, Illinois : IVP Academic, an imprint of InterVarsity Press, [2019] | Includes bibliographical references and index.
Identifiers: LCCN 2019029421 (print) | LCCN 2019029422 (ebook) | ISBN 9780830852321 (paperback) | ISBN 9780830873425 (ebook)
Subjects: LCSH: Bible. Matthew—Introductions.
Classification: LCC BS2575.52 .B38 2019 (print) | LCC BS2575.52 (ebook) | DDC 226.2/06—dc23
LC record available at https://lccn.loc.gov/2019029421
LC ebook record available at https://lccn.loc.gov/2019029422

P	25	24	23	22	21	20	19	18	17	16	15	14	13	12	11	10	9	8	7	6	5	4	3	2	1
Y	37	36	35	34	33	32	31	30	29	28	27	26	25	24	23	22	21	20	19						

To

Christopher, my son

CONTENTS

Preface	*ix*
Acknowledgments	*xiii*
Abbreviations	*xv*
Introduction	1
PART 1 · ORIENTATION	**7**
1 Form and Genre	9
2 Approach and Method	25
3 Circumstances of Composition	42
4 Shape of Composition	95
PART 2 · INTERPRETATION	**137**
5 Interpretation of Matthew 1:1–4:16	139
6 Interpretation of Matthew 4:17–16:20	162
7 Interpretation of Matthew 16:21–28:20	195
PART 3 · REFLECTION	**235**
8 Jesus: The Christological Titles	237
9 Jesus: Additional Aspects of Christology	259
10 God	276
11 Salvation History and Eschatology	285
12 Discipleship	309
Bibliography	329
Author Index	355
Scripture Index	360

PREFACE

THIS VOLUME REPRESENTS THE FRUIT of nearly forty years of research and teaching on the Gospel of Matthew. I can testify that every day I have spent with this remarkable Gospel has been a joy. In the preparation of this book I have once again been impressed with the richness, complexity, and interpretive challenges that Matthew's Gospel offers.

But these considerations do not in themselves justify the appearance of this, yet another, book on the Gospel of Matthew. Such justification requires an explanation of the ways in which this volume differs from most other studies on Matthew's Gospel. Here I mention three particulars. First, with regard to the matters treated and the organization of their treatment, this book seeks to be holistic and integrative. It gives attention to the Gospel's setting, centers on its interpretation, and culminates in its theology. Accordingly, the book contains three sections, orientation, interpretation, and (theological) reflection; and each section (with the obvious exception of the first) builds upon that which precedes. These sections reflect the threefold character of Matthew's Gospel: historical, literary, and theological. These three aspects intersect; and thus even though each is targeted in the section that pertains specifically to it, in the final analysis they cannot be treated in complete isolation. It is my conviction that a holistic understanding of the Gospel requires attention to all three of these components.

Second, with regard to methodology, this volume espouses an inductive approach, which means essentially that we allow the character of the Gospel of Matthew itself to determine how we go about reading and understanding it. In recent years biblical scholarship has often adopted hermeneutical programs that give priority to the reader. According to these programs, the interests or decisions of readers define the proper approach to the study of books. This contemporary predilection is an understandable reaction against the earlier, long-standing neglect of the role of the reader in the interpretive process. And, in addition, it marks a realistic acknowledgment of the significance of the context and experiences of the interpreter and interpretive communities.

Yet the most fundamental reality of the phenomenon of reading is the sense of a transpersonal, and even transcommunity, presence, viz., the reality of a text that is separate from ourselves (or our group), in which we encounter a voice that is not collapsible into our own. This profound sense of the other, of a separate reality that confronts us from outside of ourselves, representing a distinctive point of view, spoken into a particular historical moment that (in the case of the Gospel of Matthew) we no longer share, invites us to approach this Gospel according to *its* own set of expectations. The very presence of this Gospel before us, with its own agglomeration of characteristics, demands that we reflect on the specific ways in which the Gospel itself determines the most appropriate process for its study.

This kind of methodological reflection has not always been obvious in Matthean scholarship. Scholars have often simply assumed that an understanding of the Gospel is reducible to the identification of literary sources and an analysis of the evangelist's adaptation of these sources, or to a reconstruction of the social and religious setting of the Gospel. Attention to these matters is critical, in that they address certain broad realities that pertain to Matthew's Gospel. But for the study of the Gospel of Matthew as such their role is subordinate to a concentration on the Gospel itself as it has actually come to us. We must constantly keep in mind the necessarily tentative character of any reconstruction of realities that lie behind the text. And we must remember, too, that an understanding of the Gospel itself is not coterminous with conclusions regarding matters of historical background. Accordingly, I have adopted a text-centered, yet not text-exclusive, methodological program; and I have attempted to argue for the validity of the method herein adopted. Consequently, I focus upon the Gospel of Matthew itself within its historical setting, attentive to its ultimately theological purpose.

The third way in which this present volume is at least somewhat distinct has to do with the range of audience. Although I have written with university and seminary students primarily in mind, I have hope that the book will prove helpful to informed pastors and even certain laypersons, on one side, and, on the other side, that it will contribute to current scholarship on Matthew's Gospel.

I have written this book with a recognition that any biblical interpreter must acknowledge his or her limitations and thus remain open to new insights and correction from others. I have no illusions of infallibility. My desire is that each reader will fairly consider what I have written and assess it critically in light of the data in and surrounding the Gospel of Matthew. And my hope is that this book will make at least a modest contribution as it joins the ongoing conversation in the church and the academy about the character and especially the message of the Gospel of Matthew. For it is out of such a conversation that real progress in understanding will come.

ACKNOWLEDGMENTS

I AM DEEPLY GRATEFUL to all those who have made this book a reality. I wish to thank, first, the editors and staff at InterVarsity Press, and particularly Mr. Daniel Reid and Ms. Anna Gissing. It has been a joy to work with them. I appreciate especially their informed and sage judgements, their openness and flexibility, their professionalism, and their attentiveness to quality at every step in the process. I cannot adequately express the high regard in which I hold them. Second, I thank Asbury Theological Seminary for granting to me the sabbatical during which I wrote the bulk of this volume. The seminary's generous sabbatical policy reflects its serious commitment to minister to the academy and the church around the world through the research and publications of its faculty. Third, I thank Professor Jack Dean Kingsbury for carefully reading the manuscript and offering his characteristically insightful comments and thoughtful suggestions. And, finally, I thank my son, Christopher, who compiled the author index. But, most importantly, I am grateful for his presence in my life. Accordingly, I have lovingly dedicated this book to him.

ABBREVIATIONS

1QpsDan A (4Q246)	Apocryphon of Daniel
1QSa	Rule of the Congregation
4QFlor	Florilegium, also Midrash on Eschatology
ABD	*Anchor Bible Dictionary*, ed. D. N. Freedman. 6 vols. New York. 1992.
ABRL	Anchor Bible Reference Library
AJ	*Asbury Journal*
AmJT	*American Journal of Theology*
AnBib	Analecta Biblica
b. Sanh.	Babylonian Talmud: Sanhedrin
b. Shab.	Babylonian Talmud: Shabbat
BDAG	Bauer, W., F. W. Danker, W. F. Arndt, and F. W. Gingrich. *Greek-English Lexicon of the New Testament and Other Early Christian Literature*. 3rd ed. Chicago: University of Chicago Press, 2000.
BECNT	Baker Exegetical Commentary of the New Testament
BETL	Bibliotheca Ephemeridum Theologicarum Lovaniensium
BibInt	*Biblical Interpretation*
BNTC	Black's New Testament Commentary
BTB	*Biblical Theology Bulletin*
BW	*Biblical World*
BZ	*Biblische Zeitschrift*
BZNW	Beihefte zur Zeitschrift für die neutestamentliche Wissenschaft

CBQ	*Catholic Biblical Quarterly*
CBQMS	Catholic Biblical Quarterly Monograph Series
CCT	Chalice Commentaries Today
ConcC	Concordia Commentary
CSCD	Cambridge Studies in Christian Doctrine
ETL	*Ephemerides Theologicae Lovanienses*
ExpTim	*Expository Times*
GBS	Guides to Biblical Scholarship
GuL	*Geist und Leben*
HNT	Handbuch zum Neuen Testament
HThKNT	Herders Theologischer Kommentar zum Neuen Testament
HTR	*Harvard Theological Review*
IBC	Interpretation: A Bible Commentary for Teaching and Preaching
IBS	*Irish Biblical Studies*
ICC	International Critical Commentary
Int	*Interpretation*
JAAR	*Journal of the American Academy of Religion*
JBL	*Journal of Biblical Literature*
JCT	Jewish and Christian Texts
JETS	*Journal of the Evangelical Theological Society*
JIBS	*Journal of Inductive Biblical Studies*
JSNT	*Journal for the Study of the New Testament*
JSNTSup	Journal for the Study of the New Testament Supplement Series
JTS	*Journal of Theological Studies*
KNT	Kommentar zum Neuen Testament
LNTS	Library of New Testament Studies
LTQ	Lexington Theological Quarterly
LXX	Septuagint
m. ʾAbot	Mishnah Avot
m. Ber.	Mishnah Berakhot
MNTC	Moffat New Testament Commentary
NAC	New American Commentary

NCB	New Century Bible
NCBC	New Cambridge Bible Commentary
NICNT	New International Commentary on the New Testament
NIGTC	New International Greek Testament Commentary
NovT	*Novum Testamentum*
NovTOA	Novum Testamentum Orbis Antiquus
NovTSup	Novum Testamentum Supplement Series
NRSV	New Revised Standard Version
NSBT	New Studies in Biblical Theology
NTL	New Testament Library
NTS	*New Testament Studies*
PNTC	Pillar New Testament Commentaries
RB	*Revue Biblique*
SBibApL	Studies in Biblical Apocalyptic Literature
SBLAcBib	Society of Biblical Literature Academia Biblica
SBLDS	Society of Biblical Literature Dissertation Series
SBLMS	Society of Biblical Literature Monograph Series
SBLSS	Society of Biblical Literature Symposium Series
ScEs	*Science et esprit*
ScrMin	Scripta Minora Regiae Societatis Humaniorum Litterarum Lundensis
SHBC	Smyth & Helwys Bible Commentary
SNTSMS	Society of New Testament Studies Monograph Series
SNTW	Studies of the New Testament and Its World
SUNT	Studien zur Umwelt des Neuen Testaments
TD	*Theology Digest*
TDNT	*Theological Dictionary of the New Testament*. Edited by G. Kittel and G. Friedrich. Translated by G. W. Bromiley. 10 vols. Grand Rapids: Eerdmans, 1964–1976.

TDOT	*Theological Dictionary of the Old Testament.* Edited by G. Johannes Botterweck, Helmer Ringgren, and Heinz-Josef Fabry. Translated by David E. Green. 15 vols. Grand Rapids: Eerdmans, 1974-2006.
TJ	*Trinity Journal*
TynBul	*Tyndale Bulletin*
WBC	Word Biblical Commentary
WUNT	Wissenschaftliche Untersuchungen zum Neuen Testament
ZAW	*Zeitschrift für die alttestamentliche Wissenschaft*
ZECNT	Zondervan Exegetical Commentary on the New Testament
ZNTW	*Zeitschrift für Neutestamentliche Wissenschaft*
ZNW	*Zeitschrift für die neutestamentliche Wissenschaft und die Kunde der älteren Kirche*

INTRODUCTION

ALONG WITH PAUL'S EPISTLE TO THE ROMANS, the Gospel of Matthew is the most significant Christian writing in existence. The Gospels stand at the center of the New Testament canon, functioning as "foundation documents" that present the story and teaching of Jesus and thus form the presupposition for the apostolic ministry (Acts) and the apostolic teaching (the epistles and the Revelation) that constitute the remainder of the New Testament.[1] And among the Gospels Matthew has exercised the greatest influence.

It is typical for books dealing with the Gospel of Matthew to begin by making the claim that, at least for the first eighteen centuries, the Gospel of Matthew has exercised a privileged position as "the church's Gospel."[2] In his examination of the use of the Gospel of Matthew in the earliest church, Edouard Massaux has demonstrated that when the Fathers quoted or otherwise cited the Gospel tradition it was usually the Gospel of Matthew to which they turned.[3] Martin Hengel insists that of all the Gospels "only the Gospel of Matthew enjoyed a high reputation almost everywhere very soon

---

[1] I use *apostolic* in the broad sense of ministry and teaching that stands in continuity with the apostles. Clearly, the ministry described in the Book of Acts is not confined to the twelve apostles; and almost all the epistles were written by those who do not qualify as apostles, at least according to the criteria set forth in Acts 1:21-26.

[2] See, e.g., recently, Ian Boxall, *Discovering Matthew: Content, Interpretation, Reception* (Grand Rapids: Eerdmans, 2014), 1-5.

[3] Edouard Massaux, *The Influence of the Gospel of St. Matthew in the Christian Literature Before St. Irenaeus*, ed. A. J. Bellinzoni (Macon, GA: Mercer, 1990).

after it was introduced."[4] Even in our contemporary church experience it is the Matthean version of the beatitudes and the Lord's Prayer with which Christians are most familiar. Ernst von Dobschütz puts the matter succinctly: "This Gospel more than any has determined people's ideas and . . . it has been normative for both the outline of the life of Jesus and the individual form of the Lord's deeds and words."[5]

The reasons for the dominance of the Gospel of Matthew are ready at hand. For one thing, before the scholarly consensus that formed in the middle of the nineteenth century around the priority of Mark's Gospel, almost everyone assumed that the Gospel of Matthew was the first Gospel to be produced and that it was written by the apostle who bore that name. It was believed, therefore, to be the only synoptic Gospel that came directly from the hand of an apostle, and thus from someone who had experienced the ministry of Jesus; Mark and Luke were thought to bear only indirect apostolic testimony, derived from Peter in the case of Mark and from Paul in the case of Luke.[6] The emergence of the hypothesis of Markan priority may have dislodged the Gospel of Matthew from its perch in scholarly circles, at least for a time, but that has not undermined its exalted position in the church at large because of additional bases of its influence.[7]

One of these additional bases of the Gospel of Matthew's significance is the canonical ordering. Since the second century it has been customary to

---

[4]Martin Hengel, *Studies in the Gospel of Mark* (Philadelphia: Fortress, 1985), 82.
[5]Ernst von Dobschütz, "Matthew as Rabbi and Catechist," in *The Interpretation of Matthew*, ed. Graham Stanton (Philadelphia: Fortress, 1983), 19.
[6]The word *synoptic* derives from the Greek and means essentially "to see together." In NT studies it pertains to the first three Gospels (Matthew, Mark, and Luke), which see, or present, the life of Jesus in basically the same way, i.e., according to the same general outline and with much of the same material, over against the Gospel of John, which is distinct, both in the ordering of events and in many of its details. The tradition that Mark contains the memoirs of Peter that Mark recorded from Peter's preaching stems from the testimony of the second-century Syrian father Papias, found in Eusebius, *Ecclesiastical History* 3.39.15. For additional discussion of patristic testimony, see Hengel, *Studies*, 2-6. On Luke and Paul, see the "we" sections in Acts, where the author speaks in the first-person plural and which naturally suggest that the author (Luke) was a sometime companion of Paul (Acts 16:10-17; 20:5-15; 21:1-18; 27:1–28:16; cf. Col 2:14). Paul was presumably not an eyewitness of the Jesus events; but Luke insists that his account was based on eyewitness testimony (Lk 1:1-4).
[7]In the first three-quarters of the twentieth century Mark received relatively more attention than did the Gospel of Matthew. But in recent years we have seen a resurgence of interest in Matthean studies. See, e.g., David L. Turner, *Matthew*, BECNT (Grand Rapids: Baker, 2008), 2-3.

place the Gospel of Matthew first among the Gospels.⁸ This practice no doubt reflects the assumption of its apostolic authorship, but it was also natural since the Gospel of Matthew, more than any of the others, makes connection with the Old Testament, and indeed begins with the genealogy of Jesus which Matthew traces back to Abraham through David (1:1-17).⁹ The Gospel of Matthew thus serves as a kind of pivot for the Christian biblical canon, functioning as a bridge between the testaments.

A further basis for the popularity of the Gospel of Matthew in the church is its orderly character. In terms of the narrative, Matthew, like Luke but unlike Mark, includes an account of Jesus' birth and infancy. Hence, readers experience a sense of wholeness in the presentation of Jesus which is in some measure absent in Mark. And although Matthew's narrative lacks the chronological smoothness that we expect from modern biographies, readers of the Gospel of Matthew sense a developmental flow from event to event that distinguishes it from Luke's relatively choppy or more "episodic" feel. In terms of discourse or teaching material, Matthew generally groups the teaching of Jesus into extended passages or blocks of discourse that deal with common topics,¹⁰ over against the tendency in Mark and especially Luke to sprinkle small bits of Jesus' teaching throughout the narrative. The church has thus found the Gospel of Matthew more useful for liturgy and for catechesis than the other Gospels.¹¹

These observations pertaining to the supreme importance of the Gospel of Matthew, especially within the church, lead naturally to considerations regarding the most effective way to engage the Gospel of Matthew, that is,

---

⁸For brief discussions of the Gospel of Matthew's priority in the canonical order, see R. T. France, *Matthew: Evangelist and Teacher* (Grand Rapids: Zondervan, 1989), 13-14; and Bruce M. Metzger, *The Canon of the New Testament* (Oxford: Clarendon, 1987), 296-97. Theodor Zahn, *Geschichte des neutestamentlichen Kanons. II. Urkunden und Belege zum ersten und dritten Band, 1 Hälfte* (Erlangen und Leipzig: A Deichert, 1890), 364-75, lists several ways in which the Gospels were ordered in the earliest period, but the Gospel of Matthew is normally first, though sometimes John assumes the primary position. From Irenaeus on, the Gospel of Matthew is consistently first.

⁹Throughout I will refer to the author of the Gospel of Matthew as "Matthew," out of custom, but without any bias regarding the apostle Matthew being the author of the Gospel.

¹⁰This "grouping" is found especially in the five great discourses (Mt 5–7; 10; 13; 18; 24–25), but also in other passages throughout the Gospel (e.g., Mt 11:2-19; 22:1-45; 23:1-39).

¹¹Regarding liturgy, see, e.g., G. D. Kilpatrick, *The Origins of the Gospel According to St. Matthew* (Oxford: Clarendon, 1946); M. D. Goulder, *Midrash and Lection in Matthew* (London: SPCK, 1974). Regarding catechesis, see von Dobschütz, "Matthew as Rabbi and Catechist" and Paul S. Minear, *Matthew: The Teacher's Gospel* (New York: Pilgrim, 1982).

the method to be pursued in grasping the message of this most influential book. The primary conviction of the present volume is that hermeneutical method, that is, the specific strategy for reading and interpreting material, must correspond to the character of that which is being studied.[12] In other words, the very nature of the Gospel of Matthew should provide us with the framework or mode for its study. It is my contention that, in terms of form, the Gospel of Matthew is *literary*; in terms of content, it is *theological*; and in terms of context, it is *historical*. Therefore, the focus of our study ought properly to be literary, theological, and historical.

These convictions regarding the character of the Gospel of Matthew will also determine the contours and the substance of the present volume. This volume falls into three main sections: **orientation, interpretation,** and **reflection.**

Part one ("**Orientation**") will provide a framework for readers to study and understand the Gospel of Matthew, providing also background to the **interpretation** and (indirectly) **reflection** sections. This first section contains four chapters. Chapter one ("Form and Genre") will explore the importance of identifying a genre for the reading of any book, and particularly for an understanding of the Gospel of Matthew. It will examine the major possibilities for the form and genre of Matthew, including a brief history of the various ways the Gospel of Matthew's genre has been understood, the difference these generic determinations make in the reading and understanding of the Gospel of Matthew, and the best option for the identification of the genre of this Gospel on the basis of an examination of the text itself.

The issue of the genre of the Gospel of Matthew leads naturally into an examination of the most appropriate way to approach the reading and interpretation of the Gospel of Matthew, that is, method. Chapter two ("Approach and Method") will present the major methodological approaches that have been employed, noting the advantages and disadvantages/limitations of each. I will contend that a holistic inductive approach that

---

[12]This conviction pertains to what we might call the principle of suitability, according to which method is understood as that process which is most appropriate or suitable to the task being pursued. For a discussion of the principle of suitability in biblical study, see David R. Bauer and Robert A. Traina, *Inductive Bible Study: A Comprehensive Guide to the Practice of Hermeneutics* (Grand Rapids: Baker Academic, 2011), 13-15; see also Howard Tillman Kuist, *These Words Upon Thy Heart: Scripture and the Christian Response* (Richmond: John Knox, 1947), 47-48.

incorporates certain perspectives and insights from the various specific methods with a view toward a literary/theological reading of the Gospel is the most effective way to proceed.

Chapter three ("Circumstances of Composition") will discuss various issues involved in the construction of the Gospel of Matthew. I will examine the sources that Matthew employed in compiling his Gospel, the authorship of the Gospel of Matthew, the intended audience, the date of composition, and the place of composition.

Chapter four ("Shape of Composition") will explore the literary structure of the Gospel of Matthew, evaluating proposals for the Gospel's structure in terms of alignment with the text of the Gospel of Matthew. I will argue for an understanding of literary structure that focuses on the final form of the text and recognizes that this book is primarily a story about Jesus. And I will present a proposal for the plan of the Gospel of Matthew that best accounts for all the data within the text. Moreover, I will argue that structure involves more than plan (or linear development) but also "organizational systems" (e.g., contrast, comparison, climax) that are employed by the author to relate major elements within the text to each other and thereby to build meaning.

Part two ("Interpretation") will lead the reader through the text of the Gospel of Matthew, on the basis of the literary structure of the Gospel of Matthew in the large as well as the structure of divisions, sections, and segments within it. It will not involve a verse-by-verse commentary but rather will discuss the structure and meaning of larger blocks of the Gospel of Matthew, and within these larger blocks it will discuss the meaning of particular segments. The interpretation will emphasize the meaning of passages within their literary context(s) and employ additional exegetical considerations as appropriate to the interpretive demands the text itself places on the reader—for instance, syntax, lexical background, historical background, and canonical intertextuality. Certain individual passages or motifs will receive more detailed examination, as appropriate to understanding the most significant theological aspects of the Gospel of Matthew. This section includes chapters five through seven, which broadly reflect the linear division of the Gospel of Matthew (Mt 1:1–4:16; 4:17–16:20; 16:21–28:20).

Part three ("Reflection") will synthesize and develop some of the major theological issues emerging from the **interpretation** section. Chapters eight and nine will treat the person and work of Jesus Christ (Christology). Here I will argue that the Gospel of Matthew is profoundly Christocentric and therefore every other theological issue or claim stems from and is an expression of its Christology. These chapters will treat the major christological categories (e.g., Son of Man, Son of David, Son of God) but also move beyond christological titles to explore the ways the Gospel of Matthew builds an understanding of Jesus that transcends the narrow confines of titles.

Chapter ten ("God") will note that while Jesus is the primary concern of the content of the Gospel of Matthew, God is the ultimate reality in the world of the Gospel of Matthew. We will see that, in terms of theological structure, Jesus is subordinate to God (the Father) and that he and his actions or work are to be understood, assessed, and evaluated in terms of God. Therefore, a rather specific and definite understanding of God in the Gospel of Matthew emerges.

In chapter eleven ("Salvation History and Eschatology") we will see that Matthew's understanding of salvation history and eschatology are inextricably related. Here I will discuss such key issues as fulfillment, the kingdom of heaven/God, and the consummation.

Finally, chapter twelve ("Discipleship") will acknowledge that while the central concern of the content of the Gospel of Matthew is Jesus Messiah, arguably the purpose of the Gospel of Matthew involves discipleship. Here I will explore Matthean discipleship both in terms of the expectations for discipleship that we find in the Gospel of Matthew but also in terms of the way in which the presentation of Jesus himself and of the disciples illumines Matthew's theology of discipleship. Within this chapter I will discuss also Matthean ecclesiology and mission.

Throughout the volume all biblical quotations represent my own translation, unless I specifically identify an English version.

PART ONE

ORIENTATION

Any final interpretation of the Gospel of Matthew necessarily assumes certain positions on such matters as the genre of the book, the most appropriate way in which to approach the study of the book, and the historical setting of the author and intended readers. For this reason, our examination of the Gospel will begin with a discussion of these matters.

1

FORM AND GENRE

COMMUNICATION IS IMPOSSIBLE WITHOUT GENRE. Every piece of writing employs a literary form, or genre.[1] In short, genre is a repeated and therefore familiar combination of material content and the arrangement of that content. Or as James Bailey puts it: "Genres are the conventional and repeatable patterns of oral and written speech, which facilitate interaction among people in specific social situations."[2] In each culture or subculture certain genres are recognizable and their characteristics are known. A genre represents a kind of agreement between writers and readers.

Thus a genre is actually an implicit code by which the writer directs the audience to adopt reading strategies that are appropriate to that genre and discourages those reading strategies that may be proper to other genres but unsuitable to the one being employed. Persons living in a certain culture are naturally familiar with the genres available and under most circumstances will almost subconsciously recognize a genre and read according to its implicit set of expectations. But it is possible that readers who confront

---

[1] It is possible to differentiate literary form and genre. Sometimes "genre" is applied to whole books or at least larger blocks of material (e.g., novel, biography, apocalypse) and "literary form" to what we find in smaller passages (e.g., pronouncement story, miracle story). See, e.g., James L. Bailey and Lyle D. Vander Broek, *Literary Forms in the New Testament* (Louisville: Westminster John Knox, 1992). At other times these two terms are used interchangeably; see, e.g., James L. Bailey, "Genre Analysis," in *Hearing the New Testament: Strategies for Interpretation*, ed. Joel B. Green (Grand Rapids: Eerdmans, 1995), 197n1. For the sake of simplicity, we will use these terms interchangeably.

[2] Bailey, "Genre Analysis," 200.

literature produced in another culture, with its own pool of genres, will misidentify the genre and read that literary product in ways that contradict its generic intentions. This consideration points to the importance of our identifying the genre of the Gospel of Matthew and utilizing insights from that generic determination to interpret it.

THE GENRE OF THE GOSPELS

The similarity of content and arrangement among the four canonical Gospels suggests that they share a common genre, and such has been the general consensus throughout the past two hundred years.[3] But this period has also witnessed disagreement regarding precisely what that genre is. We may identify three stages in the scholarly debate on this question.[4]

As for the first stage, scholarly attention to the issue of the Gospels' genre began in the nineteenth century. That century saw the emergence of the modern biography, and it was natural that nineteenth-century readers, including scholars, would construe the Gospels according to this popular literary form. Scholars often produced their own biographies or lives of Jesus and treated the Gospels as earlier manifestations of that same genre; indeed, scholars mined the Gospels for their own nineteenth-century reconstructions. But even scholars who did not produce their own biographies of Jesus approached the Gospels along the lines established by modern biographies. The forging of such a connection between the Gospels and the modern biographical movement was to be expected since the Gospels focus on the person of Jesus and present an account of his deeds and teachings. Some of these scholars, notably Ernst Renan and Clyde Weber Votaw, attempted to compare the Gospels with works of ancient biography roughly contemporary to our Gospels; yet even in these cases a tendency existed to assume more continuity between ancient biographical works and modern biography than was warranted.[5]

---

[3]This has been the view of most readers and indeed of most scholars over the centuries. See, e.g., Werner Georg Kümmel, *Introduction to the New Testament*, rev. ed. (Nashville: Abingdon, 1975), 200; Richard A. Burridge, *What Are the Gospels? A Comparison with Graeco-Roman Biography*, 2nd ed. (Grand Rapids: Eerdmans, 2004), 213-32.

[4]Our discussion on the history of the question pertaining to the Gospels' genre follows the careful and authoritative account by Burridge, *What Are the Gospels?*, 3-24.

[5]Ernst Renan, *Life of Jesus* (London: Kegan Paul, 1893; original 1863). The comment of Burridge, *What Are the Gospels?*, 6, is apt: "Renan sees his own *Life of Jesus*, nineteenth-century ideas of

Form and Genre

But scholars increasingly realized that serious differences existed between modern biographies and the Gospels. For example, modern biographies typically present the life of the subject by reporting all the significant events of that subject's life in strict chronological sequence, while the Gospels pass over whole periods of Jesus' life. Indeed, Mark and John tell us nothing of Jesus' birth and early life but rather begin with Jesus' adulthood, and Matthew and Luke skip over the period from Jesus' infancy to his adulthood with the exception of only one vignette offered by Luke (Lk 2:41-51). And the evangelists typically chart the events of Jesus' life in a chronologically loose way, usually with only vague connectives,[6] thus often making it difficult for those who are accustomed to the explicit development of a subject's life in modern biographies to note the precise relationship of individual events to one another within the Gospels.[7]

In addition, modern biographies are characterized by careful attention to the psychological, social, and moral development of the subject, and the factors that contributed to such development. But these considerations are conspicuously absent in our Gospels. We learn little of the influences that contributed to Jesus' character. In fact, the Gospels contain no reference to any sort of personal, moral, or spiritual development in Jesus.[8]

Finally, modern biographers tend to limit attention to empirically verifiable phenomena, that is, to those things that can be observed on the human-historical plane, while our Gospels embrace the perspective that the ultimate actor in history, including and especially the history of Jesus, is God. Correspondingly, our Gospels are written from a strong theological perspective. In other words, according to the Gospels, transcendent theological realities are ultimately determinative for understanding the life of Jesus; and

---

biography, and Graeco-Roman Lives as all being the same thing." Clyde Weber Votaw, "The Gospels and Contemporary Biographies," *AmJT* 19 (1915): 45-73; reprinted (with an introduction by John Reumann) as *Gospels and Contemporary Biographies in the Graeco-Roman World* (Philadelphia: Fortress, 1970).

[6]The exceptions here are the passion narratives, which have a higher degree of plot connection than the rest of the Gospel accounts. But the passion narratives account for only around 18 to 20 percent of the content of our Gospels.

[7]Jack Dean Kingsbury, *Matthew*, 3rd ed. (Nappanee, IN: Evangel, 1998), 5-6, points out that nineteenth-century scholars felt it necessary to fill in the details left by voids in the Gospel accounts, and they did so with speculation that often reflected their own personal or cultural biases.

[8]Luke's comment that "Jesus increased in wisdom and in years, and in divine and human favor" (Lk 2:52) is an exception that proves the rule, and this very general remark is indicative of the lack of specificity when it comes to Jesus' development.

in the Gospels the story of Jesus is shaped by these theological interests. For the most part, then, nineteenth-century scholarship filtered out these transcendent and theological elements in their reading of the Gospels, or at least in their reconstruction of the life of Jesus from their examination of the Gospels.[9]

This understanding of the Gospels in terms of biography as historical reportage thus eventually proved untenable,[10] and at the beginning of the twentieth century a significant reconsideration of the genre of the Gospels occurred. This shift marks the second stage of scholarly work on the Gospels' genre. The differences between the Gospels and modern biographies or ancient biographies construed more or less along the lines of modern biographies led scholars to abandon the notion that the Gospels shared the genre of biography. Rather, they viewed the Gospels either as folk literature that emerged from an oral, storytelling tradition and thus lacked the literary sophistication that made any genre identification useful,[11] or as constituting a unique genre (*sui generis*). The notion that the Gospels represent a unique genre that emerged as an outgrowth of the earliest Christian preaching, or *kerygma*, and thus were not formally comparable to any other writing, became the increasingly dominant position.[12]

This view of the Gospels as *sui generis* held sway until approximately 1980 when the third stage of scholarly investigation into the Gospels' genre took hold with a series of books that argued, in different ways and with varying degrees of success, that the Gospels belong to the genre of ancient biography. In contrast to the nineteenth-century advocates of the biographical genre, the authors of these more recent works attended seriously to the differences

---

[9]Some more conservative nineteenth-century NT scholars did accept the transcendent theological perspective of the Gospels, including Theodor Zahn, *Das Evangelium des Matthäus*, 3rd ed. KNT (Leipzig: A Deichert, 1910); Adolf Schlatter, *Der Evangelist Matthäus*, 5th ed. (Stuttgart: Calwer, 1959); and Marie-Joseph LaGrange, *Évangile selon Saint Matthieu*, 7th ed. (Paris: Gabalda, 1948).

[10]Kingsbury, *Matthew*, 1-9.

[11]See especially Martin Dibelius, *From Tradition to Gospel* (London: James Clarke, 1971 [1919]); and Karl Ludwig Schmidt, *Der Rahmen der Geschichte Jesu* (Berlin: Trowitzsch und Sohn, 1919). Dibelius and Schmidt introduced the distinction between *Kleinliteratur* (subliterary works) and *Hochliteratur* (works of literature) and identified the Gospels with the former.

[12]Rudolf Bultmann, *The History of the Synoptic Tradition*, rev. ed. (Oxford: Blackwell, 1972), especially 371-78; see also his "The Gospels (Form)," in *Twentieth Century Theology in the Making*, ed. Jaroslav Pelikan (London: Fontana, 1969), 1:86-92; Donald Guthrie, *New Testament Introduction*, 4th ed. (Downers Grove, IL: InterVarsity Press, 1990), 21.

Form and Genre

between modern and ancient biography. Moses Hadas and Morton Smith argued that the Gospels are aretalogies, a subcategory of ancient biography which described the miraculous deeds of a hero or a god in such a way as to urge readers to emulate him and follow his teachings.[13] Philip Shuler insisted that the Gospels, and in particular the Gospel of Matthew, are an example of "laudatory biography," or *encomium*, which was produced to heap praise on the subject.[14] Unfortunately, these scholars were unable to identify compelling examples in the ancient world of such specific genres. More significant was Charles Talbert's 1977 volume *What Is a Gospel? The Genre of the Canonical Gospels*, in which he argued that our Gospels represent various versions of ancient biography.[15] Yet in the judgment of many all three of these works lacked an adequate theory of genre and made claims regarding ancient biographical writings that failed to bear up under scrutiny.

This critique was made especially by Richard A. Burridge, who sought to address these shortcomings in his monumental study, *What Are the Gospels? A Comparison with Graeco-Roman Biography*. On the basis of a sophisticated theory of genre and a careful comparison of ancient biographies to the Gospels, he argued that the Gospels belong to the genre of ancient biography in general and cannot be identified with any more specific subcategory of biography.[16] According to Burridge, the Gospels share by far the majority of the characteristics found in ancient biographies, or βίοι. This broad, though not absolute, correspondence is sufficient to establish the Gospels as biographies, since genre classification allows for some flexibility and does not demand absolute conformity at each point; we cannot expect any one ancient biography to exhibit all the standard characteristics of the genre. Indeed, the Gospels diverge no more from the several standard characteristics of ancient biographies than do a number of ancient documents which were clearly and explicitly considered βίοι. This book is probably the most

---

[13] Moses Hadas and Morton Smith, *Heroes and Gods: Spiritual Biographies in Antiquity* (London: Routledge & Kegan Paul, 1965).

[14] Philip L. Shuler, *A Genre for the Gospels: The Biographical Character of Matthew* (Philadelphia: Fortress, 1982).

[15] Charles H. Talbert, *What Is A Gospel?: The Genre of the Canonical Gospels* (Philadelphia: Fortress, 1977).

[16] Although Burridge does allow that the Gospels might be said to belong to the subgenre "religious or philosophical βίοι"; Burridge, *What Are the Gospels?*, 240, 243. Dirk Frickenschmidt, *Evangelium als Biographie: Die vier Evangelien im Rahmen antiker Erzählkunst* (Tübingen: Francke, 1997), came to generally the same conclusions as Burridge.

significant treatment ever produced on the topic of the Gospels' genre. Since its publication a scholarly consensus has formed that the Gospels belong to the genre of ancient biography.[17]

THE GENRE OF MATTHEW

In the volume just described Burridge identified eighteen characteristics of ancient biography and insisted that our Gospels share by far the majority of these characteristics, which are more than enough to establish a "family resemblance."[18] We turn now to the Gospel of Matthew and note the specific ways it reflects the generic characteristics of ancient biography.

Title. Ancient biographies usually included a title which identified the genre (βίοι) and the name of the writer, typically in the genitive. Such a title is lacking in the Gospel of Matthew. The title "The Gospel According to Matthew" (εὐαγγέλιον κατά Μαθθαῖον), along with the comparable titles of the other three Gospels, was added later, probably around AD 100.[19] Moreover, in these titles the name does not appear in the genitive but in the accusative within a prepositional phrase, thus "according to Matthew" (κατά Μαθθαῖον). Here then we have a distinction between the Gospel of Matthew and that which we usually find in ancient biographies.

Opening formula/prologue/preface. Ancient biographies often begin with a preface or prologue, or at least mention the name of the subject at the very beginning of the book. Although Luke's Gospel contains a prologue (Lk 1:1-4) it is not clear that such is the case with the Gospel of Matthew. The genealogy of Jesus in Matthew 1:1-17 may serve as a prologue,[20] but as we will see below in our discussion of the structure of the Gospel of Matthew it is more likely that the genealogy belongs to the whole of Matthew 1:1–4:16 as a structural unity. Yet Matthew mentions Jesus explicitly at the very beginning of his Gospel (Mt 1:1).

---

[17]See Burridge, *What Are the Gospels?*, 253-307 for responses and reactions to the first edition (1992) of Burridge's work. Some have not been convinced, e.g., Norman Peterson, "Can One Speak of a Gospel Genre?" *Neotestamentica* 28 (1994): 137-58; W. D. Davies and Dale C. Allison Jr., *The Gospel According to Saint Matthew*, ICC (New York: T&T Clark, 1997), 3:707-18, consider Matthew to contain an "omnibus" of genres, among which biography is one; Ulrich Luz, *Studies in Matthew* (Grand Rapids: Eerdmans, 2004), 31-32.

[18]Burridge, *What Are the Gospels?*, 211-12.

[19]See Martin Hengel, *Studies in the Gospel of Mark* (Philadelphia: Fortress, 1985), 64-84, for a helpful discussion of the titles affixed to our Gospels.

[20]Burridge, *What Are the Gospels?*, 188-89.

Subject of the verbs. In ancient biographies the person who is the subject of the biography is usually also the grammatical subject of a proportionately larger number of verbs than anyone else mentioned in the book. The Gospel of Matthew qualifies according to this criterion, since Jesus is the subject of 17.2 percent of the verbs, versus the disciples who are the subject of 8.8 percent and the religious leaders who are the subject of 4.4 percent of the verbs.[21]

Allocation of space. Ancient biographies may give a disproportionate amount of space to certain periods in the subject's life, especially to the death (and events consequent to the death) of the subject. According to this criterion, the fact that Matthew passes over the many years between Jesus' infancy and his baptism (Mt 3:1) while devoting approximately 40 percent of the total narrative to the last several weeks of Jesus' ministry through his death and resurrection is entirely within the realm of expectation for ancient biographies.[22]

Mode of presentation. Ancient biographies are written in prose narrative, yet often with the inclusion of other forms at points. Clearly the Gospel of Matthew is prose narrative, presenting a continuous story from beginning to end, while repeatedly introducing blocks of teaching. All of this is clearly in line with the expectations of ancient biography.

Size. Ancient biographies are typically between five thousand and thirty thousand words in length. With 18,305 words the Gospel of Matthew is clearly in the middle of this range.[23]

Structure. Ancient biographies are typically structured according to a broad chronological sequence from beginning to end, though sometimes with the inclusion of topical sections. Again, the Gospel of Matthew is the story of Jesus from birth and infancy, through ministry and growing conflict with the religious and political leadership, to his suffering, death, and resurrection. In this way too the Gospel of Matthew qualifies as ancient biography.

Scale. Ancient biographies focus on the one person who is the subject of the biography. Manifestly every passage in the Gospel of Matthew centers

---

[21]Burridge, *What Are the Gospels?*, 190-91.
[22]The space from Mt 19:1 to Mt 28:20 is 42.4 percent, according to Burridge, *What Are The Gospels?*, 191.
[23]Word count is per Robert Morgenthaler, *Statistik des neutestamentlichen Wortschatzes* (Zurich: Gotthelf, 1958), 164.

on Jesus. The disciples have significance because they are followers of *Jesus*. The religious and political authorities are mentioned precisely because of their opposition to *Jesus*. And the significance of the blocks of teaching in the Gospel of Matthew is that it is *Jesus* who is uttering the instruction.[24]

Literary units. Ancient biographies include various types of literary units, for instance, individual stories or anecdotes, legends, discourses, or sayings. I have just mentioned the bodies of teaching, or discourses, throughout the Gospel of Matthew. I might add the plethora of individual sayings (e.g., Mt 8:20, 22; 9:12-13, 15-17; 15:10-11; 17:20-21) and parables (e.g., Mt 12:43-45; 13:1-52; 20:1-15; 21:28-43). And we might note that a large portion of the narrative consists of individual stories (see, e.g., Mt 8:1–9:1; 12:1-50; 19:1-30).[25]

Use of sources. Ancient biographies typically employ sources for their material, which involves the biographer's decision to include or to omit source material at his disposal. Although the Gospel of Matthew makes no explicit references to earlier sources employed, source criticism and form criticism have identified a rich employment of both written and oral sources; and redaction criticism has emphasized the evangelist's intentional and creative work in weaving this source material together into a unified narrative.

Methods of characterization. In ancient biographies characterization, that is, the presenting of the character traits of the subject of the biography, is accomplished not by direct authorial comment but rather through the description of the characters' deeds and speech. In the Gospel of Matthew we find no direct statement from the evangelist regarding Jesus' physical, mental, moral, or spiritual characteristics. Nevertheless, we come away from the Gospel of Matthew with a significant picture of Jesus' moral and spiritual character on the basis of Matthew's story of Jesus. We know, for example, that Jesus is merciful since, among the beatitudes, he declares "Blessed are the merciful, for they will receive mercy" (Mt 5:7); he twice announces that God "desires mercy and not

---

[24]Note that the concluding formula at the end of each of the five major discourses always explicitly mentions Jesus (Mt 7:28-29; 11:1; 13:53; 19:1; 26:1).

[25]For classifications of the various individual stories in the Gospels, including Matthew, see, e.g., Martin Dibelius, *From Tradition to Gospel*; Bultmann, *History of the Synoptic Tradition*; Vincent Taylor, *The Formation of the Gospel Tradition* (London: Macmillan, 1960).

sacrifice" (Mt 9:13; 12:7); he tells a parable that condemns an "unmerciful servant" (Mt 18:23-35); and he repeatedly heals those who call on him for mercy (Mt 9:27; 15:22; 17:15; 20:30-31).

Settings. In ancient biographies the various settings, be they geographical or dramatic, are centered on the subject of the biography. Also in the case of the Gospel of Matthew Jesus is consistently the center of attention. The geographical settings are always places where Jesus is or where events that are significant for Jesus take place (e.g., Mt 2:1-8; 3:1-12; 12:4; 14:1-12; 27:3-10, 62-66; 28:11-15); the geographical locations are not important in themselves but derive their importance through the person of Jesus. As far as dramatic settings are concerned, all interactions among people in the Gospel of Matthew focus on Jesus. When he is actively participating in the interaction he is at the center, and when he is absent the interaction still centers on him.[26]

Topics. Ancient biographies typically included topics such as ancestry, birth, adolescence and education, heroic or miraculous acts, and death (and consequences of death). Although Matthew mentions nothing of Jesus' youth or education, he does include a genealogy of Jesus (Mt 1:1-17), an account of his birth and infancy (Mt 1:18–2:23),[27] many miraculous deeds (e.g., Mt 8–9), and a relatively detailed account of his death and resurrection (Mt 26–28).

Style. Ancient biographies were often written in a sophisticated, formal style characteristic of the higher classes, but could assume a more popular form. Although Matthew employs fine Greek, his style is of a more popular variety that one would expect among the nonelite. Here again, the Gospel of Matthew falls within the range of expectations of ancient biography.

Atmosphere. Ancient biographies often expressed an atmosphere of seriousness or reverence, although some were characterized by a more lighthearted feel. With its emphasis on the momentous and indeed transcendently significant person of Jesus and the events surrounding the

---

[26]When Jesus is at the center: e.g., Mt 8:1–9:34; 12:1-8, 22-50; 15:1-28; 16:13-20; 19:1-29; 26:57–27:26; when Jesus is absent: e.g., Mt 1:18–2:23; 3:1-12; 9:10-11; 12:14; 14:1-12; 26:14-16; 27:3-10; 28:11-15.

[27]If, indeed, Matthew employed Mark as one of his sources, a possibility we will discuss below, Matthew's addition of the genealogy and the birth/infancy narrative may have augmented Mark in such a way as to create a Gospel that reflects in greater measure the expectation of the biographical genre.

inauguration of the kingdom of God in Jesus' person, the Gospel of Matthew is characterized by extreme sobriety.

Quality of characterization. Ancient biographies tended to present their subjects in stereotypical fashion, emphasizing certain stock characteristics, yet often with anecdotes or stories that provided a sense of reality and individual distinctiveness. Insofar as the Matthean Jesus is entirely virtuous and exemplary, with no moral or spiritual faults or shortcomings, he is representative of a stereotypical presentation. But the conglomeration of individual stories, which portray Jesus as speaking and acting in a variety of specific situations, express a realism and even a certain complexity in his personality.

Social setting and occasion. Most of the ancient biographies that have come down to us appear to have arisen from within an educated and upper-class social setting, but often the occasion of the reading of the biography was a public event. The fact that these biographies were often read in a public setting may suggest that the intended audience was relatively broad. The Gospel of Matthew gives no explicit indication of the social level of its audience or of the evangelist and offers few clear hints.[28] We simply do not have enough information to reach a conclusion on this matter. Nor can we state with any certainty the specific occasions or settings in which the Gospel of Matthew was intended to be read.

Authorial intention or purpose. Ancient biographies reflect a number of specific purposes, including encomium (praise of the subject), exemplification (presenting the subject of the biography as an example), information, entertainment, instruction, and apology or polemic. Some ancient biographies were written with only one of these purposes in mind, whereas others were written for multiple purposes. Most of these purposes may be inferred from the Gospel of Matthew. Matthew certainly emphasizes the praiseworthy character of Jesus; he is the Christ, the Son of God (e.g., Mt 16:13-18), whose teaching is more authoritative than even the law of Moses (Mt 4:21-48), and who is worthy to be worshiped (Mt 2:11; 14:33;

---

[28]The literary and linguistic style of the Gospel of Matthew, unadorned and straightforward, may favor an audience that had a basic Hellenistic education with little exposure to the literary artistry of the upper classes. See Richard A. Burridge, "Gospel Genre and Audiences," in *The Gospels for All Christians: Rethinking the Gospel Audiences*, ed. Richard Bauckham (Grand Rapids: Eerdmans, 1998), 140.

Form and Genre

28:17) even as God is worshiped (Mt 4:10). Matthew also presents Jesus as an example to be followed, for as we shall see below Matthew repeatedly draws a comparison between Jesus, as he is presented in this Gospel, and the expectations for his followers, the disciples. The Gospel of Matthew also provides significant information regarding Jesus, including some information that is missing in other Gospels;[29] yet it is unclear that this is a major purpose for the Gospel, since it seems to have been written primarily to Christians who would presumably have already known at least the contours and probably also many of the details of Jesus' life and teaching. Given the seriousness of the subject matter and the sober treatment it receives at the hands of Matthew it seems unlikely that entertainment factors as a purpose for the Gospel of Matthew. In contrast, the presence of large amounts of teaching, including the five major discourses (Mt 5–7; 10; 13; 18; 24–25),[30] and the consideration that the Gospel of Matthew ends with the exalted Christ commissioning his disciples to make disciples by "teaching them to observe all that I have commanded you" (Mt 28:20) leaves little doubt that a major purpose of the Gospel of Matthew is didactic. Although the Gospel of Matthew seems to be directed primarily, if not exclusively, to a Christian audience, it does contain a number of apologetic features, that is, elements designed to offer a defense of Jesus and of the Christian movement (e.g., Mt 1:1-17; 5:17-48; 12:22-29; 27:62-66; 28:11-15; to which we might add the "fulfillment quotations" in, e.g., Mt 1:22-23; 4:14-16). And many scholars have argued that Matthew employs the strong denunciation of the Jewish leaders to engage in a polemic against the Jewish leadership of the synagogue which had set itself in opposition to the Matthean community.[31]

From the foregoing comparison we can see that the Gospel of Matthew manifests entirely fifteen of the eighteen identifying characteristics of the

---

[29]See Burnett Hillman Streeter, *The Four Gospels: A Study of Origins* (London: Macmillan, 1924), 198, for a list of passages that are peculiar to Matthew.

[30]I shall argue below that the content of these five great discourses pertains to post-Easter discipleship in general and are not directed primarily to the twelve disciples during Jesus' earthly ministry.

[31]G. D. Kilpatrick, *The Origins of the Gospel According to St. Matthew* (Oxford: Clarendon, 1946), 100-23; Reinhart Hummel, *Die Auseindersetzung zwischen Kirche und Judentum im Matthäusevangelium* (München: Kaiser, 1963); Ulrich Luz, *The Theology of the Gospel of Matthew* (New York: Cambridge University Press, 1995), 9, 18-19, 65-66; Graham Stanton, *A Gospel for a New People: Studies in Matthew* (New York: T&T Clark, 1992), 116-68.

genre of ancient biography. And in the remaining three cases (title, opening formula/prologue/preface, and social setting/occasion), it partially corresponds to the characteristics. We may conclude, then, that the judgment of Burridge regarding the ancient biographical character of the Gospels in general obtains specifically for the Gospel of Matthew. But if the Gospel of Matthew belongs to the genre of ancient biography, what difference does it make? Does this conclusion contain an interpretive payoff, and if so, what is it?

The very flexibility of genre may limit the interpretive value of genre identification. Once we grant that no one book necessarily participates in all the characteristics of its genre classification, we cannot simply assume that because a text—for example, the Gospel of Matthew—belongs to a given genre everything that is generally true of that genre necessarily obtains for our document. For example, the fact that ancient biography is characterized by the presence of a prologue or preface at the beginning of the book does not warrant the assumption that such a prologue or preface is necessarily present in our particular ancient biography, and we must be careful not to construe a passage as a prologue or preface if the text resists such a construal. This caution will prevent us from reading a certain typical generic feature into our text when the text itself gives no indication that this feature is present.

Nevertheless, so long as we keep these limitations and potential dangers in mind, the identification of the Gospel of Matthew as ancient biography can assist in our understanding of the Gospel of Matthew.[32] Viewing the Gospel of Matthew as ancient biography establishes a set of expectations with which to approach the text and provides an opportunity to determine if these genre expectations are present and, if so, how they function. This concern for genre, then, invites a critical comparison between genre expectations and the data in and surrounding the text.

One value of understanding the Gospel of Matthew as ancient biography is that such identification prevents us from reading the Gospel of Matthew according to other genres to which the Gospel of Matthew does not belong.[33]

---

[32] For a commentary on the Gospel of Matthew specifically written from the perspective of ancient biographical genre see Craig S. Keener, *A Commentary on the Gospel of Matthew* (Grand Rapids: Eerdmans, 1999).

[33] Kingsbury, *Matthew*, 12.

It directs us away from reading the Gospel of Matthew as a lectionary, or as a catechism, or as a manual for teachers, with all the implications from these alternative generic designations.[34] It warns us also against treating Matthew's Gospel as a modern biography, attempting to discern such things as Jesus' inner thoughts, or his "God-consciousness," the development of his character, or his early influences, which would necessarily involve us in imaginative speculation.

Identifying the Gospel of Matthew as ancient biography alerts us also to the absolute centrality of Jesus in it. Everything else described in the Gospel of Matthew, whether it be the disciples, the religious and political leaders, or the various geographical locations, have significance because of their relationship to Jesus, the subject of the biography.[35] Indeed, the Gospel of Matthew is ultimately not even about God; as far as the narrative dynamic is concerned the presentation of God is subordinate to the portrayal of Jesus. Christology, then, is Matthew's main concern; and issues of discipleship, conflict, power, and even theology in the narrow sense of the doctrine of God are finally derived from Christology and gain their meaning in reference to Jesus Christ.

A recognition of the ancient biographical character of the Gospel of Matthew may also suggest that the original audience, or intended readership, of the Gospel of Matthew was not limited to one small house church, or even to a narrow group of house churches in a single city, as has often been assumed,[36] but rather was directed to Christians in general, or at least to Christians scattered over a broad region.[37] This conclusion stems from the observation that ancient biographies, especially those whose subjects were

---

[34]For a reading of the Gospel of Matthew as a lectionary, see Kilpatrick, *Origins*, 59-100; M. D. Goulder, *Midrash and Lection in Matthew* (London: SPCK, 1974); as a catechism, see Ernst von Dobschütz, "Matthew as Rabbi and Catechist," in *The Interpretation of Matthew*, ed. Graham Stanton (Philadelphia: Fortress, 1983); Gottfried Schille, "Bemerkungen zur Formgeschichte des Evangeliums. II. Das Evangelium des Matthäus als Katechismus," *NTS* 4 (1957/58): 101-68; as a manual for teachers, see Krister Stendahl, *The School of St. Matthew and its Use of the Old Testament* (Philadelphia: Fortress, 1968); Paul S. Minear, *Matthew: The Teacher's Gospel* (New York: Pilgrim, 1982).

[35]Burridge, *What Are the Gospels?*, 247-50, 289-94.

[36]Such was the (largely unexamined) assumption of almost all Matthean scholarship in the last half of the twentieth century. See Richard Bauckham, "For Whom Were the Gospels Written?," in Bauckham, *Gospels for All Christians*, 9-22.

[37]Stanton, *Gospel for a New People*, 51-53, and "Revisiting Matthew's Communities," in *SBL 1994 Seminar Papers*, ed. Eugene H. Lovering Jr. (Atlanta: Scholars, 1994), 9-23.

religious or philosophical leaders, were typically written for broad dissemination and not for specific groups or communities.[38]

The observations that the ancient biographical genre of the Gospel of Matthew points to the centrality of Jesus and to the likelihood of a general audience or readership over against a small community in one narrow geographical area together raise serious questions about the obsession in recent Matthean scholarship to reconstruct the "community of Matthew" and to interpret the Gospel of Matthew in light of that community reconstruction. The consideration that the Gospel of Matthew centers on Jesus argues against a hermeneutical process that assumes that the Gospel of Matthew is essentially a window into the Matthean community, and that the various characters are "transparent" for persons or groups in Matthew's community. According to this understanding, the disciples in the Gospel of Matthew represent Christians or factions of Christians in Matthew's church, and the religious authorities stand for the leaders of the synagogue who oppose Matthew's Christian community. Such an enterprise takes for granted that the Gospel of Matthew is primarily about Matthew's church rather than about Jesus himself. Indeed, Francis Watson has referred to this approach as a form of allegorization, since it construes the Gospel of Matthew from the perspective that the various elements of the story, though apparently literal, actually "stand for" other realities; thus, according to this view, the Gospel of Matthew *seems* to be about Jesus, but it is really about Matthew's community.[39]

A recognition of the ancient biographical character of the Gospel of Matthew suggests also that the Gospel of Matthew was meant to be read as a continuous narrative at one sitting rather than in snippets or small blocks as is often done today in worship or liturgical settings, or even in personal devotions. We have seen above that one of the markers of ancient biography is a continuous narrative in which the (perhaps originally) separate anecdotes and sayings have been woven together into a developing story, climaxing in the death (and consequences of death) of the subject. Moreover, Burridge has shown that the social setting of the

---

[38]Burridge, *What Are the Gospels?*, 294-99, and Burridge, "About People, by People, for People: Gospel Genre and Audiences," in Bauckham, *Gospels for All Christians*, 145.
[39]Francis Watson, "Toward a Literal Reading of the Gospels," in Bauckham, *Gospels for All Christians*, 195-217.

reading of ancient biographies was typically in public festivals or after-dinner events at which the biography would be read orally in its entirety.[40] This insight accords with the character of the Gospel of Matthew itself, as W. D. Davies indicated: "There are documents which are so closely knit that their parts can only be adequately understood in light of the whole. Such is the Fourth Gospel, and such also is Matthew. It reveals not only a meticulous concern, numerically and otherwise, in the arrangements of its details, but also an architectonic grandeur in its totality."[41] Indeed, intentional structuring of the whole is a mark of ancient biography.[42] This consideration gives warrant for our careful analysis of the structure of the entire Gospel as essential for understanding not only the Gospel as a whole but its individual parts.

A final implication from the ancient biographical genre of the Gospel of Matthew is that the reader is expected to accept the reportage of the biography as historically reliable, while at the same time recognizing that the writer may have modified certain details for the sake of bringing out the deeper significance of the subject or the events described, especially as this deeper significance may speak to the needs or circumstances of the audience.[43] After a painstaking analysis of ancient biographies, Craig S. Keener has demonstrated that such biographies differed materially from novels or romances in that the former were concerned to relate the actual deeds and teachings of the subject; yet these biographies reflected the biases of the biographer in a measure that goes beyond what we would typically expect in modern biographies, and they sometimes embellished their sources,

---

[40]Burridge, *What Are the Gospels?*, 298-99; Burridge, "About People," 140-42. While Burridge insists that the length of the Gospels (including the Gospel of Matthew) made them ideal for reading at one sitting, Stanton (*Gospel for a New People*, 75) draws the opposite conclusion when he argues that a three-hour reading would be too long and that therefore the Gospels were read in smaller sections. But Stanton gives no evidence that the Gospels were considered too long to be read at one sitting, and his opinion seems to reflect the limited attention span of modern audiences rather than the considerably longer attention span of ancient ones.

[41]William D. Davies, *The Setting of the Sermon on the Mount* (New York: Cambridge University Press, 1966), 14.

[42]Craig S. Keener, *The Historical Jesus of the Gospels* (Grand Rapids: Eerdmans, 2009), 73-74.

[43]This claim does not contradict the argument above that our Gospels may not have been written to specific narrow Christian communities but rather to the church as a whole or at least to broad cross-sections of first-century Christians, since the evangelists may have had in mind needs or concerns of Christians in general or of certain groups of Christians that would be represented in many congregations throughout the Mediterranean world.

especially in terms of details. All of this was acceptable and expected in ancient biography and did not compromise the assumption that one could place confidence in the account.[44] These conclusions actually accord well with the results of much redaction-critical study of the Gospel of Matthew.[45]

---

[44]Keener, *Historical Jesus*, 73-84, 110-11, 123, 125; Craig S. Keener, "Introduction," in *Biographies and Jesus: What Does It Mean for the Gospels to Be Biographies?* ed. Craig S. Keener and Edward T. Wright (Lexington, KY: Emeth, 2016), 1-45. See also Michael R. Licona, "Viewing the Gospels as Ancient Biographies Resolves Many Perceived Contradictions," in Keener and Wright, *Biographies and Jesus*, 323-28.

[45]See, e.g., Robert H. Gundry, *Matthew: A Commentary on His Handbook for a Mixed Church Under Persecution*, 2nd ed. (Grand Rapids: Eerdmans, 1994), 623-40.

2

APPROACH AND METHOD

HAVING DISCUSSED IN THE PREVIOUS CHAPTER the nature of the Gospels, and more specifically of the Gospel of Matthew, it is appropriate now to address the issue of the method with which we should approach the study of the Gospel of Matthew. I have argued elsewhere that method is the best specific procedure for doing anything, and "best" is defined as that which is most appropriate to the object of study.[1] Applied to the Gospel of Matthew, this principle means that the proper method for studying the Gospel of Matthew is that strategic process which accords with the very nature of the Gospel of Matthew. Certainly, the determination that the Gospel of Matthew is of the genre of ancient biography will affect our methodological decisions. But additional aspects of the nature of the Gospel of Matthew will also play a role in decisions regarding method. Thus I will assess the value of the various methods that have been applied to the Gospel of Matthew on the basis of their congruence with its character, and I will set forth a methodological proposal that accords best with its nature.

The modern study of the Gospels runs from the middle of the nineteenth century to the present and involves a series of six methodological phases. In each of the first five phases a particular method held dominance for a time, only to be succeeded by the next in the series. In each case the dominant

---

[1]David R. Bauer and Robert A. Traina, *Inductive Bible Study: A Comprehensive Guide to the Practice of Hermeneutics* (Grand Rapids: Baker Academic, 2011), 14-15.

method was followed by one that built on it but attempted to address aspects of the Gospel tradition that the earlier method(s) had neglected. These various methods focused on the several stages of the Gospel tradition. As we shall see below, at the present time no one method for studying the Gospels stands out as dominant.

Historical Criticism

The earliest stage of the Gospel tradition is that of the historical Jesus, which involves both Jesus' actions and speech as he traversed Galilee and Judea. Scholars refer to this stage as the *Sitz im Leben Jesu*, "the setting in the life of Jesus." The critical method that arose in order to address this stage is historical criticism. Although "historical criticism," or the "historical-critical method," is often used in the broad sense of any attempt to understand the Bible according to an "objective"[2] application of modern historical inquiry,[3] I am employing it here in the narrow sense of reconstructing the life and teachings of the earthly Jesus. This enterprise was a dominant force from approximately 1850 until 1900 but reemerged as a prominent movement at least twice in the twentieth century.

In the nineteenth century it took the form of the "quest for the historical Jesus," now referred to as the "first quest." Scholars scoured the Gospels to locate information about the earthly Jesus, and in some cases these scholars made their findings the basis for their various "lives of Jesus." This first quest ended with the publication of Albert Schweitzer's *The Quest for the Historical Jesus*, in which he demonstrated that these "lives of Jesus" reflected nineteenth-century European cultural and religious predilections rather than the Jesus who actually strode the shores of Galilee. According to Schweitzer, the Jesus whom the Gospels describe is a strange figure, a thoroughly Jewish eschatological prophet whose mission ended

---

[2] I place "objective" in quotation marks because scholars have become increasingly aware that no historical study is completely objective; it is naïve to think otherwise. Hans-Georg Gadamer, *Truth and Method* (New York: Crossroad, 1988), 460-91; Edgar V. McKnight, "Presuppositions in New Testament Study," in *Hearing the New Testament: Strategies for Interpretation*, ed. Joel B. Green (Grand Rapids: Eerdmans, 1995), 278-300; Markus Bockmuehl, *Seeing the Word: Refocusing New Testament Studies* (Grand Rapids: Baker, 2006), 44-45.
[3] Richard N. Soulen and R. Kendall Soulen, *Handbook of Biblical Criticism*, 3rd ed. (Louisville: Westminster John Knox, 2001), 78-80; cf. Edgar Krentz, *The Historical-Critical Method*, GBS (Philadelphia: Fortress, 1975).

in failure.⁴ The implication was that such a Jesus had little to say to the modern world.

Yet interest in the historical Jesus reemerged in the 1950s and 1960s with the "second quest." Chastened by the failure of the nineteenth-century lives of Jesus, the second quest forsook the attempt to reconstruct the life of Jesus from beginning to end and pursued the more modest task of establishing certain details pertaining to Jesus' life and especially to his teaching.⁵ The "third quest" emerged toward the end of the twentieth century and continues to the present. It seeks to take advantage of the great strides in recent historical, archaeological, and sociological studies pertaining to the first-century Palestinian world in order to construct a portrait of Jesus as a Jewish eschatological prophet in a critically accurate fashion.⁶

Historical criticism, then, views the Gospels as material for providing evidence pertaining to the life and teachings of Jesus. Since Gospel scholarship generally accepts the thesis that Mark is the earliest Gospel, these historical critics give the lion's share of attention to Mark; for the most part they are interested in Matthew and Luke only insofar as these Gospels contain certain teaching material from Jesus which is absent from Mark.

I mentioned above that we can identify a succession of dominant methods, one following after the other. In fact, however, this historical criticism that seeks to reconstruct the life and teachings of Jesus serves as something of an exception, since it has repeatedly played a prominent role throughout the

---

⁴Albert Schweitzer, *The Quest of the Historical Jesus: A Critical Study of Its Progress from Reimarus to Wrede* (New York: Macmillan, 1968 [1906]); Johannes Weiss, *Jesus' Proclamation of the Kingdom of God*, ed. Richard H. Hiers and D. Larrimore Holland (Philadelphia: Fortress, 1971 [1892]), reached many of the same conclusions at about the same time as Schweitzer and independently of him.

⁵See James M. Robinson, *A New Quest for the Historical Jesus* (London: SCM, 1959); Ernst Käsemann, "The Problem of the Historical Jesus," in *Essays on New Testament Themes* (Philadelphia: Fortress, 1982), 15-47; Günther Bornkamm, *Jesus of Nazareth* (New York: Harper & Row, 1960).

⁶This description of Jesus as an "eschatological prophet" pertains to most works emanating from the third quest, e.g., E. P. Sanders, *Jesus and Judaism* (Philadelphia: Fortress, 1985); N. T. Wright, *Jesus and the Victory of God* (Minneapolis: Fortress, 1996); John P. Meier, *A Marginal Jew: Rethinking the Historical Jesus*, 5 vols. ABRL (New York: Doubleday, 1987-2015); Dale C. Allison Jr., *Jesus of Nazareth: A Millenarian Prophet* (Minneapolis: Fortress, 1998); Geza Vermes, *Jesus in the Jewish World* (London: SCM, 2010); but cf. John Dominic Crossan, *The Historical Jesus: The Life of a Mediterranean Jewish Peasant* (San Francisco: Harper, 1991) for a portrait of Jesus as essentially a cynic. For an accessible survey of the three quests, see Mark Allan Powell, *Jesus as a Figure in History: How Modern Historians View the Man from Galilee* (Louisville: Westminster John Knox, 1998).

modern period. It dominated the last half of the nineteenth century, and it has experienced periods of resurgence and is even today a significant aspect of the study of the Gospels.

Yet it is clear that historical criticism cannot be the primary way in which we approach the Gospel of Matthew. For one thing, serious questions exist regarding the level of confidence we may have in any historical reconstruction of Jesus. The attempt to reconstruct the life of Jesus distinct from the portrayal in our Gospels necessarily involves a significant element of speculation. In fact, the only Jesus we have is the Jesus who comes to us in the Gospels.[7] Consequently, scholars must fill in many gaps and engage in a tenuous exercise of connecting the events which they deem occurred in Jesus' life into what amounts to a new narrative. Moreover, as I have pointed out, historical criticism is much more interested in the Gospel of Mark than in the Gospel of Matthew. It gives little attention to the Gospel of Matthew, with the exception of certain sayings and perhaps a very few narratives that are unique to it. Yet even more importantly, historical criticism does not deal with any of our Gospels, including the Gospel of Matthew, in themselves, but approaches them rather as fields of recollections from which we can mine information about realities that are reported in the Gospels but are separate from the Gospels in that these realities lie behind the Gospels.

SOURCE CRITICISM

Insofar as nineteenth-century historical criticism utilized our Gospels as source material for the historical Jesus, it is understandable that the rise of historical criticism coincided with scholarly interest in the earliest written sources behind our Gospels. The critical discipline that seeks to reconstruct these written sources is "source criticism," a method that held sway in Gospel studies from around 1860 to 1920. Although the dominance of source criticism was generally contemporaneous with the first quest for the historical Jesus, we may still consider it the second phase of modern Gospel research.

Source criticism received impetus from the emergence of a consensus regarding the literary sources behind our Gospels. The consensus ran like

---

[7] At most we have two possible references to Jesus in Josephus (*Antiquities of the Jews* 20.9.1; *Testimonium Flavianum* 18.3.3); cf. James D. G. Dunn, *Jesus Remembered*, Christianity in the Making, vol. 1 (Grand Rapids: Eerdmans, 2003), 141. Suetonius, *Claudius* 25, may also mention Jesus, referring to a certain "Chrestus." But these passages add nothing to our knowledge of Jesus.

Approach and Method

this: the literary relationship among the synoptic Gospels as it pertains to their origin ("the synoptic problem") is best answered by the "two-source hypothesis," that is, that Matthew and Luke made use of two sources—Mark and a hypothetical sayings source usually dubbed "Q."[8] Thus, Mark was the first Gospel, and Matthew and Luke composed their Gospels by combining material from Mark and Q. Burnett Hillman Streeter gave classic expression to this view in his influential book, *The Four Gospels: A Study in Origins*, in which he developed the two-source hypothesis further into a four-source hypothesis; in addition to their use of Mark and Q Matthew and Luke employed also sources that were unique to each of them, M (Matthew) and L (Luke). The confident identification of these sources led naturally to the practice of dissecting Matthew (and Luke) so as to locate in each passage the specific sources employed and to reproduce the sources that lie behind the Gospel with a view toward establishing a sure foundation for reconstructions of the life of Jesus. Thus source criticism primarily served the purpose of historical criticism.

As we saw in the case of historical criticism, so also source criticism is of limited value for interpreting the Gospel of Matthew itself. If the conclusions of source criticism can be established it does assist us in understanding the development of the Gospel tradition and the origins of the Gospel of Matthew, which in turn may provide at least indirect insight into the nature of the Gospel of Matthew and its message. Nevertheless, the focus of source criticism is not the Gospel of Matthew itself but the written sources that presumably lie behind the Gospel of Matthew.

Form Criticism

The search for traditions behind our Gospels eventually led scholars to recognize that before the emergence of and also contemporaneous with the written sources, stories about Jesus and reports of his teachings circulated in oral form. This recognition resulted in the attempt to reconstruct the Gospel tradition at its oral stage; this attempt pertains to the third phase of Gospel studies, "form criticism," which dominated Gospel studies from 1920 to around 1946.[9]

---

[8] So named because the first letter of the German word for source (*Quelle*) is Q.
[9] Edgar V. McKnight, *What Is Form Criticism?*, GBS (Philadelphia: Fortress, 1969). The leading form critics were Rudolf Bultmann, *The History of the Synoptic Tradition*, rev. ed. (Oxford:

Form critics believed that in the years immediately following Jesus' resurrection those in the church made use of the oral traditions of Jesus' deeds and speech as they engaged in preaching, teaching, and controversies with both Jews and Gentiles. In the process the various Christian communities adapted these Jesus traditions to the tasks and situations they were facing. Form critics insisted that these oral traditions took on stereotypical forms (hence "form" criticism) that reflect the situation of the churches that made use of them. Thus form critics were confident that by examining the various forms of the oral stage of the tradition they could recreate the situation and beliefs of the early Christian communities. Unlike source critics and historical critics, for the most part form critics were interested not in the *Sitz im Leben Jesu*, but the *Sitz im Leben Kirche* ("setting in the life of the church").[10] So far as form critics were concerned, the Gospel tradition could not tell us much if anything about the historical Jesus, but only about the faith of the early Christian communities.[11] Besides, the demise of the first quest for the historical Jesus with the work of Schweitzer led them to conclude that Jesus as a historical figure had little relevance for modern persons. Thus both the impossibility of knowing anything substantial from the Gospels about the person of Jesus and the irrelevance of the historical figure of Jesus led these form critics to shift their focus away from Jesus and to the faith of the earliest Christian communities.

But these form critics were not only disinterested in the historical figure of Jesus, they also had no interest in our Gospels as holistic compositions. As far as form critics were concerned, the Gospels were not unified narratives, but simply a collection of individual stories and sayings. Nor were the evangelists real authors but rather "cut and paste" editors who strung together the various stories and teachings of Jesus without having an

---

Blackwell, 1972); Karl Ludwig Schmidt, *Der Rahmen der Geschichte Jesu* (Berlin: Trowitzsch und Sohn, 1919); Martin Dibelius, *From Tradition to Gospel* (London: James Clarke, 1971 [1919]); and Vincent Taylor, *The Formation of the Gospel Tradition* (London: Macmillan, 1960).

[10]It is true that scholars sometimes employed form criticism in their attempt to move back to the earliest stages of the Gospel tradition as the basis for historical Jesus research. See McKnight, *What is Form Criticism?*, 57-78.

[11]Robert Henry Lightfoot, *History and Interpretation in the Gospels* (London: Hodder and Stoughton, 1935); Lightfoot's work actually serves as a bridge between form criticism and redaction criticism (see below). Also Rudolf Bultmann, *Jesus and the Word* (New York: Scribner's, 1934).

overarching purpose that they wished to achieve through the literary arrangements of materials.

Like source criticism, form criticism tended to deal more with Mark than with Matthew (or Luke), since form criticism focused on the earliest written sources as the basis for moving backward to the oral stage of the tradition. Therefore, although some studies of specific Matthean passages employed form criticism,[12] virtually no commentaries on the Gospel of Matthew were written from a thoroughgoing form-critical perspective, such as Vincent Taylor's commentary on Mark.[13] More generally, of all the critical methods discussed in this chapter, form criticism is the one that has had little enduring significance in New Testament studies. This sad reality is due to the fact that form criticism's repudiation of the significance of the historical figure of Jesus has rendered it generally useless not only to history-of-Jesus research but increasingly also to Gospel studies. As we saw above, recent studies have emphasized that our Gospels are in the form of ancient biography, and ancient biographies were concerned with the historical realities pertaining to the subject of the biography. But form criticism was out of step with the developing trends in Gospel studies in yet another way, for immediately after the Second World War scholars increasingly recognized that our evangelists were real authors who were intentional in communicating their theology through the composition of their Gospels. This recognition led to the rise of redaction criticism.

REDACTION CRITICISM

Redaction criticism, which forms the fourth phase of modern Gospel studies, rejected form criticism's notion that our Gospels are little more than mere compilations of isolated traditions in favor of the view that the Gospels are carefully constructed compositions produced by real authors who communicated their message through purposeful and meticulous editing of the sources at hand. Indeed, *redaction* stems from the German word for editing. Yet redaction criticism did accept form criticism's interest in using Gospel materials to reconstruct the character and beliefs of the Christian communities. But whereas form criticism focused on the oral stage of the

---

[12]E.g., Jean Daniélou, *The Infancy Narratives* (New York: Herder and Herder, 1968).
[13]Vincent Taylor, *The Gospel According to St. Mark: The Greek Text with Introduction, Notes, and Indexes* (London: Macmillan, 1952).

tradition, redaction criticism analyzed the evangelist's redaction of traditional materials in order to establish a picture of the faith community of the evangelist. Thus redaction criticism operates on the basis of three claims: 1) each evangelist was an intentional, careful, and creative editor of received tradition to the extent that he functioned essentially as the author of his Gospel; 2) an analysis of the evangelist's editorial processes will reveal the theology of the evangelist; and 3) an examination of the evangelist's editorial processes may also reveal the complexion and beliefs of the community to which the Gospel was written.[14]

Redaction criticism was dominant in Gospel studies from 1946 to around 1980, although what came to be known as redaction criticism was practiced by a few scholars in earlier years.[15] The pioneer redaction critic in Matthew was Günther Bornkamm.[16] Redaction critics focus on the changes, additions, and omissions the evangelists made to their sources, inferring from these redactional modifications the theology of the evangelists and the characteristics of their communities. Of course, considerations regarding the evangelists' editing of sources assumes a certain source theory, and virtually all redaction critics accept the two (four)-source hypothesis as presented by Streeter.[17] Redaction critics note, for example, that Matthew: *changes* Mark 9:40 "Whoever is not against us is for us," to "Whoever is not with me is against me" (Mt 12:30), *adds* the phrase "if you would be perfect" at Matthew 19:21 to his Markan source (cf. Mk 10:21), *adds* the phrase "in spirit" to his Q source (Mt 5:3; cf. Lk 6:20), *omits* the exorcism story found in Mark 1:23-27, and *replaces* Mark's parable of the seed growing secretly (Mk 4:26-29) with the parable of the weeds (Mt 13:24-30).

The early redaction critics tended to see significance only in the editorial modifications introduced by the evangelists, deemphasizing and sometimes even ignoring the traditional materials an evangelist incorporated without

---

[14]Norman Perrin, *What Is Redaction Criticism?*, GBS (Philadelphia: Fortress, 1969).

[15]E.g., Lightfoot, *History and Interpretation*; Benjamin Wisner Bacon, *Studies in Matthew* (New York: Henry Holt, 1930).

[16]Günther Bornkamm, "The Stilling of the Storm in Matthew," in *Tradition and Interpretation in Matthew*, ed. Günther Bornkamm, Gerhard Barth, and Heinz Joachim Held, NTL (Philadelphia: Westminster, 1963), 52-57.

[17]It is possible to engage in redaction criticism while espousing another view of the synoptic problem; e.g., William R. Farmer, *Jesus and the Gospel: Tradition, Scripture, and Canon* (Philadelphia: Fortress, 1982), who pursues redaction-critical study with the assumption of the Griesbach hypothesis that Matthew was the earliest Gospel, followed by Luke and finally Mark.

modification.[18] This narrow focus was clearly a problem, since when an evangelist included traditional material into his Gospel the evangelist embraced that traditional material and it became part of his Gospel; it made its own contribution to his comprehensive theological program. Later redaction critics addressed this problem by broadening their investigations to include not only redactional modifications that the evangelist has made to received tradition but also the entire composition of both individual passages as well as the Gospel as a whole. This later iteration of redaction criticism has been dubbed "composition criticism."[19]

Even with the move toward a compositional orientation within redaction criticism, which addressed the problem of attending almost exclusively to alterations the evangelist may have introduced, certain continuing weaknesses of redaction criticism have become apparent. For one thing, scholars have become increasingly uncomfortable with redaction criticism's necessary dependence on a specific theory of synoptic relationships. Although most scholars continue to hold to the two (four)-source hypothesis as the most likely explanation of Gospel origins, other source theories have been reasserted, and the emergence of other ways of understanding Gospel origins has led scholars to acknowledge weaknesses in the two (four)-source hypothesis that have long been ignored and to recognize the tentative character of any hypothesis attempting to address the synoptic problem. Thus many scholars have been inclined to consider methods of interpreting the Gospels that are not, like redaction criticism, bound to a particular view of Gospel sources.

For another thing, redaction criticism assumes a role for the reader that is questionable.[20] Redaction criticism of the Gospel of Matthew assumes a reader who has the Gospel of Matthew in front of him,[21] with a copy of Mark

---

[18]This principle which was implicitly adopted by almost all the early redaction critics is explicitly articulated by Joachim Rohde, *Rediscovering the Teaching of the Evangelists*, NTL (Philadelphia: Westminster, 1968), 91.

[19]This term was introduced by William G. Thompson, *Matthew's Advice to a Divided Community: Mt. 17:22-18:35*, AB (Rome: Biblical Institute Press, 1970); cf. William G. Thompson, "Reflections on the Composition of Mt 8:1-9:34," *CBQ* 33 (1971): 365-88; and Jack Dean Kingsbury, *Matthew*, 3rd ed. (Nappanee, IN: Evangel, 1998), 17-18.

[20]For the role of the reader in hermeneutics, see Kevin J. Vanhoozer, "The Reader in New Testament Interpretation," in *Hearing the New Testament*, ed. Joel B. Green (Grand Rapids: Eerdmans, 1995), 301-28.

[21]The portrait of the reader ("implied reader") of the Gospel of Matthew is a male (note, e.g., the masculine participle at Mt 24:15); thus I use the male pronoun.

on one side and a copy of Q on the other, whose eyes constantly dart back and forth in an effort to compare Matthew with Mark and Q with a view toward deriving meaning from Matthew's alterations of Mark and Q. This is exactly the process modern redaction critics employ in their interpretation of the Gospel of Matthew. But did any ancient reader pursue this kind of process, and, even more importantly, does the text of the Gospel of Matthew assume or encourage this kind of reading? It is, in fact, unclear that the original readers of the Gospel of Matthew would have known Mark or Q.[22] And, even if they were acquainted with these documents, the Gospel of Matthew does not mention or suggest recourse to any other Gospel text.[23] Indeed, according to its nature as a continuous, unified narrative, the Gospel of Matthew encourages a construal on the basis of the single text of the Gospel of Matthew read as a continuous narrative. The Gospel of Matthew envisages a reader who construes its meaning on the basis of the narrative itself. This observation does not deny the legitimacy and potential helpfulness of comparing a passage in the Gospel of Matthew with its

---

[22] I am not persuaded by the suggestion that because Matthew (presumably) used Mark and Q therefore we can be confident that the members of his community would have known these sources and would have read Matthew over against them as a foil; cf. Warren Carter, *Matthew: Storyteller, Interpreter, Evangelist* (Peabody, MA: Hendrickson, 1996), 55-70. As we will see below, the two-source hypothesis that claims that Matthew used Mark and Q is at best the most probable solution to the synoptic problem, but by no means certain. Moreover, even if Matthew used Mark it does not follow that all or even most of his intended readership would have known Mark, particularly if one posits a universal (Bauckham) or broadly extended group of churches (Stanton) as the intended audience. Finally, it is an open question, debated by scholars, whether Matthew's production of a new Gospel, presumably on the basis of Mark, was intended to supplement or to replace Mark. For the replacement theory, see Burnett Hillman Streeter, *The Four Gospels: A Study of Origins* (London: Macmillan, 1924), 507; David C. Sim, "Matthew's Use of Mark: Did Matthew Intend to Supplement or to Replace His Primary Source?" *NTS* 57 (2011): 176-92. For the supplement theory, see Graham Stanton, "The Fourfold Gospel," *NTS* 43 (1997): 341; Ulrich Luz, *Studies in Matthew* (Grand Rapids: Eerdmans, 2004), 35. Nor do I find it compelling that Matthew's intended audience would necessarily have possessed all the canonical Gospels and would therefore have read/heard Matthew in light of the others; see Bauckham, "For Whom Were the Gospels Written?," in Bauckham, *Gospels for All Christians*, 47-48, who considers this issue "open," though cf. Bauckham, "John for Readers of Mark," in Bauckham, *Gospels for All Christians*, 147-71. Even if, as Bauckham argues, the Gospels were intended for all Christians it does not follow that Matthew could have assumed that Mark would have circulated and become known to virtually all who read/heard the Gospel of Matthew before the Gospel of Matthew reached them.

[23] Although Q was not technically a "Gospel," I refer to it, along with Mark, as a "Gospel text," because Q (if it existed) did contain Gospel tradition. I specify that Matthew does not mention other *Gospel* texts, because (as I shall discuss below) the Gospel of Matthew does mention OT texts.

parallel in another Gospel, but to do so would involve using such comparison heuristically, that is, as a means of noticing certain features in the Matthean text that are certainly present there but which might have been missed save for this synoptic comparison. Such a process of synoptic comparison would not form the basis for the *determination* of the meaning of the Matthean passage but would involve a *discovery* of elements in the text whose meaning and significance may then be construed on the basis of the Gospel of Matthew itself.

Moreover, although it has often been maintained that redaction criticism deals with the final form of the text, that is, the text as we have it, over against earlier stages of the tradition that lie behind the final form, in fact redaction criticism does not focus on the text itself but rather concerns itself with the intentions and interests of the evangelists and with the character and complexion of the communities to which the Gospels were addressed. In other words, like the other critical methods described above, redaction criticism attends to matters that lie "behind the text" rather than purely with those embedded "within the text."

Narrative Criticism

In order to take full advantage of the insight from redaction criticism that our evangelists are truly authors of their respective Gospels, and in order to avoid dependence on any one specific source theory, many recent scholars have embraced narrative criticism, which constitutes the fifth methodological phase of modern Gospel studies.[24] Narrative criticism differs in two ways from all the previous methods discussed. First, whereas each of the methods described above dominated Gospel studies for a set period of time, narrative criticism does not hold the kind of sole prominence that, for example, redaction criticism enjoyed during its reign from 1946 until 1980. Indeed, at the present time no single method exercises that degree of prominence. Narrative criticism is now popular, but it is not dominant. Second, whereas all the methods discussed above were unique to biblical studies, narrative criticism was imported into biblical scholarship from secular literary studies, which pursued "literary criticism." In fact, what we now call

---

[24]For introductions to New Testament narrative criticism, see Mark Allan Powell, *What Is Narrative Criticism?*, GBS (Minneapolis: Fortress, 1990); and James L. Resseguie, *Narrative Criticism of the New Testament: An Introduction* (Grand Rapids: Baker, 2005).

"narrative criticism" was originally introduced into biblical studies as literary criticism. Both secular literary criticism and biblical narrative criticism focus on the meaning that the text itself generates on the basis of its own form and content.[25] Indeed, narrative critics insist that whenever someone writes a narrative, that person creates a "narrative world," which is a more or less self-contained system; consequently, we must interpret that piece of literature on the basis of its internal system.

The pioneers of narrative criticism in the Gospels include David Rhoads and Donald Michie on Mark, Jack Dean Kingsbury on Matthew, Robert Tannehill on Luke, and R. Alan Culpepper on John.[26] These pioneers, and most subsequent New Testament narrative critics, employ categories drawn from literary theorist Seymour Chatman and Russian formalist Boris Uspensky.[27]

Chatman insists that all narratives contain two elements: story ("what is told") and discourse ("how it is told").[28] The story consists of events, characters, settings, and plot.[29] "Events" refer to the incidents in the story, for instance, Jesus' baptism (Mt 3:1-17) or crucifixion (Mt 27:27-54). These incidents are set in successive order, and the order of these events forms the plot. The plot is the chain-like causal progression from one event to the next, which marks the development of the story. The plot of Matthew's story runs from the birth of Jesus to his resurrection. "Characters" are the various persons who are mentioned in the narrative. Characters are "round" if they

---

[25]Secular literary studies do not use the expression "narrative criticism," which is employed only within biblical studies. Nevertheless, biblical narrative criticism overlaps significantly with what university departments of literature call "literary criticism."

[26]David Rhoads and Donald Michie, *Mark as Story: An Introduction to the Narrative of a Gospel* (Philadelphia: Fortress, 1982). Jack Dean Kingsbury, *Matthew as Story* (Minneapolis: Fortress, 1986); "The Figure of Jesus in Matthew's Story: A Literary-Critical Probe," *JSNT* 21 (1984): 3-36; and "The Developing Conflict Between Jesus and the Jewish Leaders in Matthew's Gospel: A Literary-Critical Study," *CBQ* 49 (1987): 57-73; Robert C. Tannehill, *The Narrative Unity of Luke-Acts: A Literary Interpretation, Volume One: The Gospel According to Luke* (Philadelphia: Fortress, 1986); R. Alan Culpepper, *The Anatomy of the Fourth Gospel: A Study in Literary Design* (Philadelphia: Fortress, 1983). For a history of the rise of NT narrative criticism, see Powell, *What Is Narrative Criticism?*, 1-6.

[27]Seymour Chatman, *Story and Discourse: Narrative Structure in Fiction and Film* (Ithaca, NY: Cornell University Press, 1978); Boris Uspensky, *A Poetics of Composition: The Structure of the Artistic Text and Typology of a Compositional Form* (Berkeley, CA: University of California, 1973).

[28]Chatman, *Story and Discourse*, 19-42; Kingsbury, *Matthew as Story*, 3.

[29]For a helpful discussion of these three aspects of story in NT narratives, see Resseguie, *Narrative Criticism*, 87-165, 197-240.

possess several traits, such as Jesus in the Gospel of Matthew; they are "flat" if they possess just a few traits, such as the religious leaders in Matthew's story; and they are "stock" if they possess only a single trait, as, for example, the scribe in Matthew 8:19-20. A whole group of persons can actually function as a character, which we refer to as "character groups," if they possess a single set of traits. In the Gospel of Matthew the religious leaders and the Jewish crowds are such character groups. "Settings" refer to the contexts in which events take place; narratives contain spatial settings, such as the temple in which Jesus teaches in Matthew 21:23–23:39, or temporal settings, such as the reference to first day of the week in Matthew 28:1. These two examples from the Gospel of Matthew indicate that settings can have symbolic or cultural/religious significance that informs interpretation.

The discourse of a narrative consists of the implied author, implied reader, and point of view.[30] The implied author is the version of the author that we can infer (hence "implied") from the text.[31] The implied author is not identical to the flesh-and-blood person who composed the document but rather the writer as he presents himself in the text.[32] As I have discussed elsewhere, the implied author is at the same time both larger and smaller than the flesh-and-blood writer.[33] The person who composed the Gospel of Matthew no doubt knew much more about Jesus than what he included within his Gospel, and he had perceptions and convictions about Jesus that did not find their way into the Gospel he produced; thus, the implied author is smaller than the flesh-and-blood writer. On the other hand, the implied author may be larger than the flesh-and-blood author. The meaning of certain passages in the Gospel of Matthew may transcend what the physical author of the Gospel consciously intended to say. Every text, particularly an extended

---

[30] Narrative critics will often add to this list "rhetorical features" such as irony or metonymy. Although such features are proper to a literary, or narrative, study of the text, they are not unique to narrative criticism. See Powell, *What Is Narrative Criticism?*, 27-31; Resseguie, *Narrative Criticism*, 41-86.

[31] The notion of the implied author has been part of literary thought for a long time, but the idea was developed and the term coined by Wayne Booth, *The Rhetoric of Fiction* (Chicago: University of Chicago Press, 1961). For a helpful discussion on the implied author, see Meir Sternberg, *The Poetics of Biblical Narrative: Ideological Literature and the Drama of Reading* (Bloomington: Indiana University Press, 1987), 32-35, 58-85, 127, 412-13.

[32] Scholars agree that the authors of our Gospels present themselves as male; hence I employ the masculine pronoun for the implied author.

[33] Bauer and Traina, *Inductive Bible Study*, 43.

narrative, has meaning potential that goes beyond the conscious intention of the writer.[34] The writer of the Gospel of Matthew, living well before the church had the opportunity to reflect deeply about all the ramifications of the relationship between God the Father and Jesus the Son could not be expected to possess a full-blown doctrine of the Trinity; yet the implied author of our Gospel may have presented Jesus in such a way as to accord with at least significant aspects of later trinitarian thought.

Corresponding to the implied author is the implied reader. The implied reader is the image of the reader that we infer from the text, that is, the kind of reader the text assumes. Narrative critics sometimes refer to the implied reader as the "ideal reader," the reader who recognizes all the clues the implied author gives and possesses just the right kind of background information and thus construes the meaning of the text in perfect accord with the intentions of the implied author. The implied reader is not identical to any actual historical reader, even the original intended audience, since no flesh-and-blood reader construes any narrative perfectly, that is, entirely in accord with its own communicative signals.[35]

The third aspect of discourse is "point of view," which involves the relationship between the perspective of the implied author and that of various characters within the narrative.[36] Although Chatman discusses point of view, most narrative critics adopt the taxonomy of point of view developed by Boris Uspensky.[37] He describes four types of point of view, the most significant of which is *evaluative* point of view—the beliefs and values of the implied author and the various characters as he presents them. The implied reader is urged to assess or make judgments about the various characters on the basis of the relationship between their evaluative point of view and that of the implied author.

---

[34]E. D. Hirsch Jr., *Validity in Interpretation* (New Haven: Yale University Press, 1967), 6-9. Hirsch differentiates between "meaning," which is what the flesh-and-blood writer consciously intended to say, and "significance," which is what the text implies beyond what the writer may have consciously had in mind. The latter pertains to the implied author.

[35]For an illuminating comparison of the concept of the reader of the Gospel of Matthew in redaction and narrative criticism, see Jack Dean Kingsbury, "Reflections on 'the Reader' of Matthew's Gospel," *NTS* 34 (1988): 442-60.

[36]For discussions of point of view in NT narratives see Resseguie, *Narrative Criticism*, 167-96; and Gary Yamasaki, *Watching a Biblical Narrative: Point of View in Biblical Exegesis* (New York: T&T Clark, 2007).

[37]Upensky, *Poetics of Composition*.

Narrative criticism has rightly taken the fundamentally literary character of our Gospels seriously and has developed effective processes to analyze the various literary features of the text so as to lead readers to a fuller and at times more accurate interpretation of the Gospels. Yet some scholars have complained that narrative criticism draws too heavily on literary criticism that was designed to deal with fiction,[38] while our Gospels are concerned to present actual historical events.[39] But Mark Allan Powell has rightly pointed out that the narrative character of historical reportage renders it formally so similar to fiction that we can properly interpret it according to the same standards and processes.[40] Yet one might register a deeper critique here. The identification of our Gospels as ancient biography implies that they have a referential purpose, that is, to refer the reader to historical events that have significance precisely in their historical happened-ness. While narrative criticism does not deny the existence of this referential purpose, it does not in itself have the resources to address this aspect of the Gospels. This critique does not involve a fundamental flaw in narrative criticism, but it does point to a limitation.[41]

Additional Contemporary Methods

I mentioned above that since redaction criticism was deposed from its methodological perch around 1980, no one specific way of approaching the Gospels has achieved the dominance that it enjoyed. On the contrary, Gospel studies are today characterized by a range of methods such as reader-response criticism, various "advocacy criticisms" (for instance, feminist[42] or postcolonial[43] interpretations), and social-scientific criticism (which actually addresses sociological and cultural aspects of historical background),[44] each

---

[38] E.g., the subtitle of Chatman's book is *Narrative Structure in Fiction and Film*.
[39] E.g., Raymond E. Brown, *Introduction to the New Testament* (New York: Doubleday, 1997), 25-26.
[40] Powell, *What Is Narrative Criticism?*, 93-94.
[41] For additional objections to narrative criticism, with rejoinder, see Powell, *What Is Narrative Criticism?*, 91-101.
[42] E.g., Elaine M. Wainwright, *Towards a Feminist Critical Reading of the Gospel According to Matthew*, BZRG (Berlin: deGruyter, 1991); Janice Capel Anderson, "Matthew: Gender and Reading," *Semeia* 28 (1983): 3-27.
[43] See, e.g., Yonghan Chung, "A Postcolonial Reading of the Great Commission (Matt 28:16-20) with a Korean Myth," *ThTo* 72 (2015): 276-88. Cf. David R. Bauer, "Inductive Biblical Study: History, Character, and Prospects in a Global Environment," *AJ* 68 (2013): 6-35.
[44] See, e.g., David L. Balch, ed., *Social History of the Matthean Community: Cross-Disciplinary Approaches* (Minneapolis: Fortress, 1991); Jerome H. Neyrey, *Honor and Shame in the Gospel of*

of which has value but focuses on only a certain aspect of the Gospels. I have given specific attention to one of these methods, narrative criticism, because it is the most natural successor to redaction criticism, and because it represents a kind of text-centered approach such as I have adopted in this volume. The value of narrative criticism is that it focuses on what the Gospel of Matthew essentially is: a literary document. The limits of space prevent me from giving attention to the many other contemporary methods that scholars apply to the Gospel of Matthew.[45]

Methodological Approach Adopted in the Present Study

We have seen that throughout the modern period and into the present time several methods have been employed in the interpretation of the Gospel of Matthew. We have seen, too, that each of these methods addresses but one aspect of the Gospel. Moreover, we have noted that, with the exception of narrative criticism, they all deal largely with matters that lie either behind the text (e.g., source criticism) or in front of the text, that is, with later readers (reader-response criticism), rather than with the text itself.

This multiplicity of methods may be viewed as a positive circumstance, allowing various interpreters to choose the method that best fits their needs or preferences. But such a methodological smorgasbord, with the several alternatives available, does not provide a consensual way of reading the Gospel of Matthew, that is, a way of reading the book that all, or at least most, interpreters can agree on. A consensual manner of reading the Gospel of Matthew is not synonymous with a consensual interpretation of the Gospel of Matthew, for a common way of reading the Gospel of Matthew does not guarantee agreement on the meaning of individual passages. But a consensual interpretive approach is necessary for interpreters to talk meaningfully with each other about the meaning of the Gospel of Matthew.

Matthew (Louisville: Westminster John Knox, 1998); Bruce J. Malina and Jerome H. Neyrey, *Calling Jesus Names: The Social Value of Labels in Matthew*, FFSF (Sonoma, CA: Polebridge, 1988).

[45] For a discussion of some of these contemporary methods and their application to the Gospel of Matthew, see Mark Allan Powell, ed., *Methods for Matthew* (New York: Cambridge University Press, 2009); cf. Steven L. McKenzie and John Kaltner, eds., *Recent Approaches to Biblical Criticism and Their Applications* (Louisville: Westminster John Knox, 2013).

In the face of these various methodological options I wish to offer an approach to the interpretation of the Gospel of Matthew that can fulfil such a consensual role. I call it an inductive approach, since it operates on the principle that interpretive method should arise from and reflect the very character of that which is studied, namely, for our present purpose, the Gospel of Matthew. In other words, we must allow the realities that belong to the Gospel of Matthew itself to determine the best procedure for its interpretation. The methodological approach I adopt will be a holistic enterprise that seeks to address the various realities that pertain to the Gospel of Matthew. Therefore, aspects of the critical methods that I have discussed above will be represented in this synthetic approach. Note that I use the phrase "inductive approach" rather than "inductive method," for this is not one method alongside others, but rather a holistic, synthetic approach that seeks to hear the message of the Gospel of Matthew on its own terms, and which, in the process, incorporates in the most optimal way elements from every legitimate method.

This inductive procedure involves, specifically 1) a focus on the final form of the text; 2) an emphasis on the way in which attention to the literary structure of the book and of individual passages enables us to ascertain the meaning of the Matthean text; 3) attention to the ways in which the history that bounded the composition of the Gospel of Matthew may illumine the Gospel; 4) employment at relevant points of narrative-critical categories such as characterization and point of view; 5) an attempt to interpret every individual passage in light of its function within the entire book; 6) a commitment to interpret every passage Christocentrically though not Christonomistically, that is, noting always the christological concerns while recognizing that some passages deal with issues which, though related to Jesus, are distinct in some measure from him, such as discipleship or mission; 7) care to identify, when helpful, points of continuity and discontinuity between the Matthean text on the one hand and other New Testament materials, especially Mark and Luke, on the other; 8) attention to matters of intertextuality, especially Old Testament passages quoted or alluded to, for, as we shall see, the implied reader of the Gospel of Matthew knows the Old Testament and is intended to interpret the Gospel of Matthew in light of the Old Testament.

3

CIRCUMSTANCES OF COMPOSITION

THIS CHAPTER AND THE NEXT BOTH deal with the composition of the Gospel of Matthew. In the present chapter I discuss the circumstances, or the historical situation, surrounding the writing of the Gospel of Matthew. Here I am using "composition" with an emphasis on the verbal aspect of the word: what the writer did in composing the book, and how the historical setting of the evangelist informed his work of composition. In the following chapter I will explore the shape of the composition, that is, the literary structure of the Gospel of Matthew. There I will use "composition" with an emphasis on its nominal (noun) aspect: what the writer produced, that is, how the book comes to us as a composition, a unified and integrated whole. It is natural to move from the situation of writing to the shape or structure of the written document, especially since much scholarly discussion of the structure of the Gospel of Matthew has depended on prior conclusions regarding the evangelist's use of sources. More specifically, in this chapter I will address the following questions: (1) What sources did the writer use to compile the Gospel of Matthew? (2) Who was the writer responsible for the composition of the Gospel of Matthew? (3) Who was the intended audience for the composition? (4) What was the date of composition? (5) What was the place of composition?

What Sources Did the Writer Use to Compile His Gospel?

The question of the sources that Matthew used in compiling his Gospel goes beyond the study of the Gospel of Matthew itself. It necessarily involves all three synoptic Gospels and their relationship to one another, that is, the "synoptic problem"; for the combination of similarities and differences between the synoptic Gospels makes clear that some sort of literary relationship exists between them. Almost from the very beginning this fact has been acknowledged. The only question is the precise nature of that relationship.

The history of the church's attempts to address the synoptic problem has been described fully elsewhere, and I direct interested readers to consult those discussions for a more detailed treatment.[1] From the time of the Fathers until the nineteenth century a consensus held sway that the Gospel of Matthew was the first Gospel written, followed by Mark and later Luke. This ordering is indicated clearly in Irenaeus, Origen, and Jerome.[2] For example, Irenaeus claimed that

> Matthew also issued a written Gospel among the Hebrews in their own dialect, while Peter and Paul were preaching at Rome, and laying the foundations of the Church. After their departure [deaths], Mark, the disciple and interpreter of Peter, also handed down to us in writing what had been preached by Peter. Luke also, the companion of Paul, recorded in a book the Gospel preached by him.[3]

Yet these Fathers did not discuss the literary relationship among the synoptic Gospels. The first to do so was Augustine who, on the basis of his analysis of Gospel relationships which he conducted in preparing his *Harmony of the Gospels*, concluded:

---

[1] See especially Werner Georg Kümmel, *The New Testament: The History of the Investigation of Its Problems* (Nashville: Abingdon, 1972), 144-61; William R. Farmer, *The Synoptic Problem: A Critical Analysis* (New York: Macmillan, 1964), 1-198; R. T. France, *Matthew: Evangelist and Teacher* (Grand Rapids: Zondervan, 1989), 20-22, 24-46; Robert H. Stein, *The Synoptic Problem: An Introduction* (Grand Rapids: Baker, 1987).
[2] Origen is cited by Eusebius, *Ecclesiastical History* 6.25; Jerome, *Preface to the Four Gospels*. Clement of Alexandria is an exception in that he adopted the order Matthew-Luke-Mark, which anticipates the Griesbach Hypothesis, discussed below. Yet Clement describes only the order of the Gospels, not their literary interdependence. Clement's statements are recorded by Eusebius, *Ecclesiastical History* 6.14.5-7.
[3] Irenaeus, *Against Heresies* 3.1.1 in *Ante-Nicene Fathers*, ed. Alexander Roberts and James Donaldson (repr., Peabody, MA: Hendrickson, 1994).

> Now those four evangelists . . . are believed to have written in the order which follows: first Matthew, then Mark, thirdly Luke, lastly John. . . . Of these four . . . only Matthew is reckoned to have written in the Hebrew language; the others in Greek. . . . For Matthew is understood to have taken it in hand to construct the record of the incarnation of the Lord according to the royal lineage, and to give an account of most part of his deeds and words as they stood in relation to this present life of humans. Mark follows him closely, and looks like his attendant and epitomizer.[4]

We note that Irenaeus and Augustine explicitly mention that the Gospel of Matthew was written in Hebrew, by which they presumably mean Aramaic. Here they are following the tradition of Papias, which I will discuss below, to the effect that Matthew composed his Gospel in "the Hebrew dialect." Indeed, throughout this period almost everyone believed that the Gospel of Matthew was the first Gospel to be written, that it was produced by the apostle Matthew and had as its source reminiscences from his firsthand experience of the ministry of Jesus, and that it was composed in Hebrew/Aramaic.

This notion that the first Gospel to be composed came from the hand of Matthew and was written in Aramaic eventually gave rise to the hypothesis put forward by G. E. Lessing and J. G. Eichhorn that a now lost Aramaic Gospel of Matthew (which they believed Papias was referencing) is the ultimate source of all four of our canonical Gospels, including our (Greek) Gospel of Matthew. This view (the "primitive Gospel hypothesis") began to take hold in the beginning of the nineteenth century,[5] along with the "Griesbach hypothesis," which held that the Gospel of Matthew was the first Gospel produced, followed by Luke, which was dependent on Matthew, with Mark "abbreviating" both the Gospels of Matthew and Luke.[6]

By the middle of the nineteenth century the consensus regarding the synoptic problem had begun to break down. This situation was soon addressed by a series of studies that argued for the priority of Mark.[7] But it was

---

[4]Augustine, *Harmony of the Gospels* 1.3-4 in *Nicene and Post-Nicene Fathers*, ed. Philip Schaff, trans. S. D. F. Salmond (repr., Peabody, MA: Hendrickson, 1994).
[5]Farmer, *Synoptic Problem*, 1-35.
[6]Griesbach published his views regarding the synoptic problem in 1783-90.
[7]These include the studies by Gottlob Christian Storr, *Über den Zweck der evangelischen Geschichte und der Briefe Johannes* (Tübingen: Heerbrandt, 1786); Karl Lachman, "De ordine narrationum in evangeliis synopticis," *Theologische Studien und Kritiken* (1835): 570-90 (English translation:

through the work of Christian Hermann Weiss in 1838 and especially the monumental study by Heinrich Julius Holtzmann in 1863 that the two-source hypothesis was forged.[8] These scholars combined the notion of the priority of the Gospel of Mark with the idea of a "sayings source," both of which were used by Matthew and Luke to form their Gospels. Although Matthean priority continued to be argued by a few scholars in the nineteenth and early twentieth centuries, notably Theodor Zahn, Marie-Joseph Lagrange, and Adolf Schlatter, the two-source hypothesis became the new orthodoxy.[9] It was Burnet Hillman Streeter who in 1924 put forward the fullest and most convincing argument for the two (four)-source hypothesis; his work remains the classic expression of this dominant view regarding Gospel origins.[10]

Yet, into the consensus of the two (four)-source hypothesis, two alternative theories have been put forth. In fact, these theories represent the reemergence of earlier hypotheses. Some scholars, most notably John Chapman and Benjamin C. Butler, have attempted to revive the Augustinian hypothesis (Matthew-Mark-Luke).[11] Yet this view has garnered almost no support.[12] But the reemergence of the Griesbach hypothesis (Matthew-Luke-Mark),

---

N. H. Palmer, "Lachmann's Argument," *NTS* 13 [1967]: 368-78). Lachman did not explicitly urge Markan priority but prepared the way for it (see Farmer, *Synoptic Problem*, 16); Christian Gottlob Wilke, *Der Urevangelist, oder exegetisch kritische Untersuchung über das Verwandtschaftsverhältnis der drei ersten Evangelien* (Dresden: Gerhard Fleischer, 1838), who actually argued for the order Mark-Luke-Matthew ("Matthean posteriority").

[8]Christian Hermann Weiss, *Die evangelische Geschichte*, 3 vols. (Leipzig: Breitkopf und Härtel, 1838); Heinrich Julius Holtzmann, *Die Synoptischen Evangelien: Ihr Ursprung und Geschichtlicher Charakter* (Leipzig: Wilhelm Enselmann, 1863). On Holtzmann, see Kümmel, *New Testament*, 151-56; Farmer, *Synoptic Problem*, 36-47.

[9]Theodor Zahn, *Introduction to the New Testament*, 3 vols. (New York: T&T Clark, 1909 [1897]), 2:601-17, and *Das Evangelium des Matthäus*, KNT, 3rd ed. (Leipzig: A Deichert, 1910), 1-32; Marie-Joseph LaGrange, *Évangile selon Saint Matthieu*, 7th ed. (Paris: Gabalda, 1948); Adolf Schlatter, *Der Evangelist Matthäus*, 5th ed. (Stuttgart: Calwer, 1959). Zahn and Schlatter actually argued that the Aramaic Matthew was the earliest Gospel, which was adopted by Mark as his source; our Greek Gospel of Matthew, then, was based on both the Aramaic Matthew and the Greek Mark. For the history of the two-source hypothesis, see H.-H. Stoldt, *History and Criticism of the Marcan Hypothesis* (New York: T&T Clark, 1980).

[10]Burnett Hillman Streeter, *The Four Gospels: A Study of Origins* (London: Macmillan, 1924), 151-98.

[11]John Chapman, *Matthew, Mark and Luke: A Study in the Order and Interrelation of the Synoptic Gospels* (London: Longmans, Green, 1937); Benjamin C. Butler, *The Originality of St. Matthew* (New York: Cambridge University Press, 1951); also John Wenham, *Redating Matthew, Mark, and Luke: A Fresh Assault on the Synoptic Problem* (Downers Grove, IL: InterVarsity Press, 1992).

[12]For arguments against the Augustinian hypothesis, see Farmer, *Synoptic Problem*, 211-32.

particularly under the vigorous labors of William R. Farmer, has created a major reexamination of the synoptic problem.[13]

I have elsewhere offered a critical assessment of the arguments presented by Streeter for the two (four)-source hypothesis and the arguments from Farmer for the Griesbach hypothesis, indicating that each of these proposals has strengths and weaknesses.[14] This consideration has given rise to other theories regarding Gospel origins. For example, some scholars have rejected the notion of simple stages of literary dependence among the canonical Gospels in which later canonical Gospels are directly dependent on earlier one(s) in favor of complex and reciprocal sharing among the canonical Gospels or in favor of the view that each evangelist made use of a number of written and oral traditions (perhaps in addition to one or more of the canonical Gospels), some of which are no longer available to us. We might refer to this cluster of proposals as the "multiple interaction hypothesis." Some scholars who adopt this view posit elaborate and complex interconnections among our canonical Gospels or between now extinct sources and our canonical Gospels. But others simply insist that some such process is likely responsible for our Gospels even though we cannot now describe the specific form that it may have taken.[15]

But these proposals are even more complicated and speculative than the two (four)-source or the Griesbach hypotheses. And in many cases they fail to take seriously the close similarities in both order and wording among the canonical Gospels. Yet the multiple interaction hypothesis, while not entirely convincing, is a viable alternative to the two (four)-source and Griesbach hypotheses. In addition, Robert MacEwan has recently urged a consideration of Matthean posteriority, which is the view

---

[13] See especially Farmer, *Synoptic Problem*, 199-232; also Stoldt, *History and Criticism*; J. B. Orchard, *Matthew, Luke, and Mark* (Manchester: Koinonia, 1977).

[14] David R. Bauer, "Streeter Versus Farmer: The Present State of the Synoptic Problem as Argument for a Synchronic Emphasis in Gospel Interpretation," *JIBS* 6 (2019), 7-28.

[15] Antonio Gaboury, *La Structure des Evangiles synoptique* (Paris: Desclée, 1970), discussed and critiqued in Stephen Hultgren, *Narrative Elements in the Double Tradition: A Study of Their Place Within the Framework of the Gospel Narrative* (Berlin: De Gruyter, 2002), 138-69; Pierre Benoit and M.-E. Boismard, *Synopse des quartres Evangiles en français*, Tome II (Paris: le Cerf, 1972); John M. Rist, *On the Independence of Matthew and Mark* (New York: Cambridge University Press, 1978); Bo Reicke, *The Roots of the Synoptic Gospels* (Philadelphia: Fortress, 1986); Jeffrey A. Gibbs, *Matthew 1:1–11:1*, ConcC (St. Louis: Concordia, 2006), 21; E. P. Sanders, *The Tendencies of the Synoptic Tradition* (New York: Cambridge University Press, 1969); E. P. Sanders and Margaret Davies, *Studying the Synoptic Gospels* (London: SCM, 1989), 51-119.

that Matthew made use of Mark and Luke in the production of his Gospel.[16] Yet even he does not argue that this is the best solution but only that it deserves attention.

The present state of the scholarly discussion on this matter is somewhat fluid. The major contenders are the two (four)-source hypothesis, which continues to enjoy the majority of scholarly support, and to a lesser extent the Griesbach hypothesis. In my judgment, the fundamental issue in deciding between these two proposals is the consideration that it is very difficult to account for Mark's redaction of Matthew and Luke on the basis of the Griesbach hypothesis. In the final analysis, it is unclear what kind of community situation or theological, pastoral, or literary purpose would have led Mark to create his Gospel out of Matthew and Luke. For example, when one considers the verbosity of Mark's Gospel, it is difficult to understand why, on the theory of Matthean priority, Mark would have enlarged individual passages which he found in the Gospel of Matthew with the addition of unnecessary details only to omit so much of Jesus' teaching material, even though Mark describes Jesus as a teacher and makes mention of his teaching activity more often than Matthew. On the other hand, the extensive redaction-critical study that has been conducted on the basis of the two (four)-source hypothesis has demonstrated the reasonableness of such redactional activity on the part of Matthew and Luke on their Markan *Vorlage* (source-text). But reasonableness is not certainty and significant arguments exist against the two (four)-source hypothesis.

In my judgment, the two (four)-source hypothesis is more likely than the competing proposals; but we can no longer think of it as an "assured result" of New Testament criticism. Unless additional evidence surfaces or revolutionary new ways of construing the evidence emerge, the scholarly pursuit of Gospel origins has reached an impasse. Further endeavor will likely yield little fruit.

What, then, is the significance of this rather ambiguous conclusion regarding the synoptic problem for the study of the Gospel of Matthew?

---

[16]Robert MacEwen, *Matthean Posteriority: An Exploration of Matthew's Use of Mark and Luke as a Solution to the Synoptic Problem*, LNTS 501 (New York: T&T Clark, 2015). A form of Matthean posteriority was proposed by some earlier scholars, e.g., Ernst von Dobschütz, "Matthew as Rabbi and Catechist," in *The Interpretation of Matthew*, ed. Graham Stanton (Philadelphia: Fortress, 1983), 26; George Kennedy, cited in W. D. Davies and Dale C. Allison Jr., *The Gospel According to Saint Matthew*, ICC (New York: T&T Clark, 1997), 1:14.

Certainly one of the most important purposes for adopting a specific source theory is that such a theory serves as the basis for redaction-critical study of the Gospels.[17] Any redaction-critical study must assume knowledge of the sources employed by the evangelist. A lack of firm confidence in any given solution to the synoptic problem, then, renders redaction-critical study at least somewhat tentative. The time has come to acknowledge the debatable foundation on which a thoroughgoing redaction-critical study of the Gospel of Matthew is built and rather to adopt a process that examines the Gospel on its own terms, while considering its differences from Mark and Luke as indications of Matthean emphases rather than necessarily expressions of deliberate editorial decisions.[18] The church especially requires an interpretation of Gospel materials that is based on the foundation of firm data rather than on a tentative framework of scholarly reconstruction. Inevitably differences in interpretation of the Gospels will emerge, but it is important that a solid agreement exist with regard to the data that are to be interpreted. We ought to agree to focus on the Gospels themselves over against putative redactional processes that are based on particular scholarly theories of Gospel origins.

Who Was the Writer Responsible for the Composition of This Gospel?

The external evidence points exclusively to the apostle Matthew as the author of the Gospel of Matthew. Possibly the earliest connection between this Gospel and Matthew comes with the title "According to Matthew" (κατά Μαθθαῖον) or "The Gospel According to Matthew" (εὐαγγέλιον κατά Μαθθαῖον),[19] which was not original to the document but was added, along

---

[17]Stein, *Synoptic Problem*, 143-51, 237-63.

[18]This approach is sometimes referred to as "new redaction criticism." See Marc Goodacre, *The Case Against Q: Studies in Markan Priority and the Synoptic Problem* (New York: T&T Clark, 2002), 108; Joel B. Green, "Narrative and New Testament Interpretation: Reflections on the State of the Art," LTQ 39 (2004): 162-63; Roland Meynet, *Le fait synoptique reconsidéré*, (Rome: Gregorian and Biblical Press, 2014). Although he does not use the expression "new redaction criticism," this approach seems to be employed by R. T. France, *The Gospel of Matthew*, NICNT (Grand Rapids: Eerdmans, 2007). David D. Kupp, *Matthew's Emmanuel: Divine Presence and God's People in the First Gospel*, SNTSMS 90 (New York: Cambridge University Press, 1996), 6, adopts a similar approach.

[19]I say "possibly" because some question exists regarding whether the title to the Gospels or Papias's testimony to the origin of Mark and Matthew is earlier. Typically scholars consider, on

with the titles to the other Gospels, probably between AD 120 and 160, although Hengel has argued that they may have arisen soon after the production of the Gospels, between AD 60 and 100.[20] Yet the title is not necessarily intended to indicate authorship. It was typical in ancient documents for the name of the author to appear first, in the genitive, followed by a description of the subject of the book.[21] As Richard Burridge states, "Κατά plus the accusative [which is the construction of the title to the Gospel of Matthew] is not to be seen as equivalent to the normal genitive of the author."[22] The title indicates some connection between this Gospel and Matthew, but the connection is not clear. It may involve an ascription of authorship, but it may suggest only a connection between Matthew and some of the traditions that have been incorporated into the Gospel,[23] although even this possibility is not certain.[24]

The earliest discussion of the Gospel of Matthew, or what might seem to be the Gospel of Matthew, comes from Papias, the Syrian Bishop of Hierapolis who wrote sometime between AD 100 and 150.[25] Fragments of his work "Exposition of the Lord's Oracles" (Λογίων κυριακῶν ἐξήσηως) are reproduced by Eusebius in his fourth-century *Ecclesiastical History*. Papias's testimony regarding Matthew reads as follows: "Matthew set in order the *logia* in (the) Hebrew dialect, and each interpreted them as he was able."[26]

---

the basis of the manuscript tradition, that the shorter form of the title was the earlier, whereas "The Gospel According to Matthew" was a somewhat later development.

[20]Martin Hengel, *Studies in the Gospel of Mark* (Philadelphia: Fortress, 1985), 64-84.

[21]Hengel, *Studies*, 65.

[22]Richard A. Burridge, *What Are the Gospels? A Comparison with Graeco-Roman Biography*, 2nd ed. (Grand Rapids: Eerdmans, 2004), 186; G. D. Kilpatrick, *The Origins of the Gospel According to St. Matthew* (Oxford: Clarendon, 1946), 137-38, is of the opinion that the author of the Gospel of Matthew was responsible for the title and for the change of "Levi" (Mk 2:13-14) to "Matthew" (Mt 9:9) and the addition of "tax collector" at Mt 10:3 in order to ascribe the Gospel pseudonymously to Matthew the apostle. This view is problematic given the observations that 1) the title did not reflect the form that was typically used to indicate authorship, and 2) the form of the title is found in all four canonical Gospels, and almost certainly arose not from the Gospel of Matthew but rather from Mark 1:1 and its reference to the "gospel" (εὐαγγέλιον).

[23]Perhaps Q or M if one accepts Streeter's proposal. Many scholars have taken this position, e.g., Alfred Wikenhauser, *Introduction to the New Testament* (New York: Herder and Herder, 1958), 178-82; Donald A. Hagner, *Matthew 1-13*, WBC (Dallas: Word, 1993), lxxvi.

[24]John Nolland, *The Gospel of Matthew*, NIGTC (Grand Rapids: Eerdmans, 2005), 4.

[25]Most scholars date Papias around AD 135, but Gundry has argued for a date prior to AD 110; cf. Robert H. Gundry, *Matthew: A Commentary on His Handbook for a Mixed Church Under Persecution*, 2nd ed. (Grand Rapids: Eerdmans, 1994); see also Robert W. Yarbrough, "The Date of Papias: A Reassessment," *JETS* (1983): 181-91.

[26]Eusebius, *Ecclesiastical History* 3.39.16.

Papias may depend here on tradition delivered to him by "John the elder,"[27] referring either to a certain John who was a hearer of the apostles or to John the apostle.[28] But the exact meaning of Papias's statement is debatable. Two points in his testimony deserve comment.

First, Papias speaks of the *logia* (λόγια), which typically means "sayings," rather than "story" or "narrative." When Luke wishes to describe his Gospel, he uses διήγησις, usually translated "narrative" (Lk 1:1). Many have therefore taken Papias's statement to refer not to the Gospel of Matthew but rather to a collection of Jesus' sayings, perhaps similar to *The Gospel of Thomas*. Possible candidates are the hypothetical document Q, which is understood to include almost exclusively Jesus' sayings, or a collocation of scriptural testimonies, perhaps represented in the "fulfillment quotations" throughout Matthew. Yet the fact that Papias elsewhere uses λόγια to refer to the Gospel of Mark suggests that he may be using the same word to describe the Gospel of Matthew. Moreover, Papias employs the same word in the title to his work, "Expositions (Λογίων) of the Oracles of the Lord," which manifestly pertained not just to Jesus' sayings but to the accounts of his deeds as well.

Second, Papias speaks of the "Hebrew dialect." By Hebrew Papias almost certainly meant Aramaic, since Aramaic and not Hebrew was spoken in first-century Palestine and since the New Testament (including the Gospels) preserves isolated Aramaic expressions used by Jesus (e.g., Mt 6:24; 27:46). The problem is that a careful linguistic and literary analysis of the Gospel of Matthew indicates it was probably originally written in Greek and is not a translation from an Aramaic original.[29] Some have attempted to address this

---

[27]Papias credits John the Elder for his testimony concerning Mark (Eusebius, *Ecclesiastical History* 3.39.15), which appears immediately before his testimony concerning Matthew in Eusebius, yet Eusebius separates these two fragments from Papias: "Such was the account of Papias, respecting Mark. Of Matthew he had stated as follows." Because Eusebius is presenting fragments of Papias's work, and because he separates the fragments pertaining to Mark and those relating to Matthew, it remains unclear whether Papias is ascribing his testimony regarding Matthew to John the Elder. In addition, it is possible that Papias is depending on Polycarp (AD 60–155), for Irenaeus claimed that Papias was also a companion to Polycarp (Irenaeus, *Against Heresies* 3.3.4).

[28]Eusebius distinguishes between "John the Elder" and the apostle John. But Gundry, *Matthew*, 611-16, argues that Eusebius was in error and that Papias meant "John the Elder" to refer to the apostle John.

[29]The originally Greek character of the Gospel of Matthew is almost universally accepted by scholars today. See the helpful summary in France, *Evangelist and Teacher*, 62-64. Cf. C. F. D. Moule, *The Birth of the New Testament*, 3rd ed. (London: A. and C. Black, 1981), 276-80; James Hope Moulton and Nigel Turner, *A Grammar of New Testament Greek* (repr., New York: T&T Clark, 2000), 4:31-44. But see the discussion in Davies and Allison, *Matthew*, 1:7-17, for

difficulty by positing that "Hebrew dialect" (διαλέκτῳ) here means "a Hebrew or Semitic style," rather than the Hebrew language, pointing out that in Papias this noun has no definite article, and therefore may be understood to be indefinite, and that the noun was sometimes used, especially among ancient rhetoricians, to refer to literary style.³⁰ These scholars must then take ἡρμήνευσον ("interpret") in the sense of "explain" rather than "translate." But διαλέκτος almost always referred to a language, and in the New Testament it pertains exclusively to a spoken language. Further, in Greek an anarthrous noun (that is, one lacking the definite article) is not necessarily to be understood as indefinite. Indeed, the fact that Papias joins διαλέκτος with ἡρμήνευσεν points strongly to the conclusion that Papias is referring not to a Semitic style but to the Hebrew (that is, Aramaic) language.³¹ We should note in this regard that Papias suggests some difficulty in the task he describes: "Each one interpreted them *as he was able.*" Presumably it would be more difficult to translate from one language to another than to "explain" the text.³²

Thus Papias may not be referencing our Gospel of Matthew at all but another document originally produced in Hebrew or Aramaic. Insofar as Gospels written in Hebrew and Aramaic and ascribed to Matthew circulated in the early church (which were known at least by the second and third centuries), some have insisted that Papias is referring to one of them.³³ And insofar as Q contained the teachings or λόγια of Jesus and was probably originally composed in Aramaic, some have insisted that Papias is referring to Q.³⁴ Still others conjecture that Papias may have in mind Matthew's

---

warnings regarding too hasty conclusions on this point and the one regarding Papias intending Aramaic rather than Hebrew, as they contend that Hebrew was spoken in first-century Palestine. While their cautions are well taken, the preponderance of evidence is in favor of the majority scholarly opinion. An exception to the *opinio consensus* is Paul Gaechter, *Die Literarische Kunst im Matthäus-Evangelium* (Stuttgart: Katholisches Bibelwerk, 1966) and *Das Matthäus Evangelium: Ein Kommentar* (Innsbruch: Tyrolia-Verlog, 1963), who claims that the Gospel of Matthew was written by Matthew in Hebrew.

³⁰E.g., Gundry, *Matthew*, 619-20; cf. Josef Kürzinger, "Das Papiaszeugnis und die Erstgestalt des Matthäusevangeliums," *BZ* 4 (1960): 19-38.

³¹France, *Evangelist and Teacher*, 57.

³²See Hagner, *Matthew 1-13*, xlv.

³³Among these are the Gospel According to the Hebrews, the Gospel of the Ebionites, and the Gospel of the Nazoreans. See Hagner, *Matthew 1-13*, xlv.

³⁴Friedrich Schleiermacher, "Über die Zeugnisse des Papias von unsern beiden ersten Evangelien," *Theologische Studien und Kritiken* 5 (1892): 735-68; T. W. Manson, *The Sayings of Jesus*, 2nd ed. (London: SCM, 1949), 28-30; pace J. Armitage Robinson, *The Study of the Gospels* (London:

special material (Streeter's M).³⁵ Since it is quite conceivable that the apostle Matthew may have been responsible for collecting Jesus' sayings in Aramaic into Q or M, the inclusion of this material into the Gospel of Matthew would account for the association in the early church of the Gospel of Matthew with the apostle Matthew. Over a century ago Willoughby C. Allen presented a specific and plausible explanation as to how the incorporation of sayings material, originally composed in Aramaic by the apostle Matthew, may explain the connection of this Gospel with Matthew.³⁶

Later patristic statements essentially agree with Papias's testimony, insofar as his declarations are assumed to refer to the Gospel of Matthew. I quoted the testimony of Irenaeus above to the effect that Matthew published his Gospel among the Hebrew people in Hebrew while Peter and Paul were founding the church in Rome. This statement actually goes beyond Papias in providing external evidence for the date and provenance of the Gospel of Matthew, which we will examine below.

Tertullian makes brief reference to "John and Matthew" as "those who first instill faith in us" apparently through their apostolic authorship of their respective Gospels.³⁷ According to Origin, "The first [Gospel] to be written was according to Matthew, a one-time tax-collector and later an apostle of Jesus Christ; he produced it for those who had come to [Christian] faith from Judaism, and it was written in Hebrew letters."³⁸ Here Origen clearly declares the Gospel of Matthew to be the first and identifies the author as Matthew the tax-collector. He agrees with Irenaeus that it was written in Hebrew on behalf of Jewish Christians.

Eusebius references one Panaenus, a missionary to India, who "found his own arrival [in India] preceded by some who were acquainted with the

---

Longmans, Green, 1902), 68-70. For a discussion of the relationship between Papias's λόγια and Q, see Hultgren, *Narrative Elements*, 12-18.

³⁵E.g., Hagner, *Matthew 1-13*, xlvi.

³⁶Willoughby C. Allen, *A Critical and Exegetical Commentary on the Gospel According to S. Matthew*, 3rd ed. ICC (Edinburgh: T&T Clark, 1912), lxxx-lxxxi. Streeter, *Four Gospels*, 500-501, provides a specific explanation for the change from "Levi" (Mark and Luke) to "Matthew" (Matthew) on the assumption that our Gospel came to be associated with the apostle Matthew by the inclusion of material from the apostle Matthew (Q). Many scholars, including evangelical ones, have accepted this explanation of the origin of the connection of the Gospel of Matthew with the apostle Matthew; e.g., Hagner, *Matthew 1-13*; Ralph P. Martin, *New Testament Foundations: A Guide for Christian Students* (Grand Rapids: Eerdmans, 1975), 1:239-40.

³⁷Tertullian, *Against Marcion* 4.2; cf. 4.5.

³⁸Quoted by Eusebius, *Ecclesiastical History* 6.25.3-6.

Gospel of Matthew, to whom Bartholomew, one of the apostles, had preached and left them the Gospel of Matthew in Hebrew, which is also preserved until the present time."[39] Eusebius himself declares that of the apostles only Matthew and John left Gospels, which he dubs "memoirs" or remembrances (ὑπομνήματα). He adds that the Gospel of Matthew represents Matthew's preaching in Hebrew, and its production was necessitated by his ministry among the nations (apparently in compliance with Mt 28:18-20?).[40] This series of patristic testimony reaches a culmination in Jerome: "Matthew, who is also called Levi, a former tax-collector and then an apostle, first produced a gospel of Christ in Judea, on behalf of those who had come to faith from among the circumcision, in Hebrew letters and words. It is uncertain who later translated it into Greek. The Hebrew text itself is still preserved to this day in the library at Caesarea."[41]

It is clear that each of these patristic witnesses develops the tradition regarding the Gospel of Matthew beyond the earlier one(s). It is also clear why most scholars believe that Irenaeus, who knew Papias's tome, based his claims on Papias, and that it is likely that subsequent witnesses expanded what they had learned from Irenaeus by adding elements that for the most part could be surmised from the Gospel of Matthew, although a few of their claims may represent independent tradition. It is arresting that all these patristic testimonies refer to the Gospel of Matthew as written in Hebrew, and that the last of these fathers, Jerome, insisted that a copy of the Hebrew text existed in Jerome's hometown of Caesarea. Since it is indubitable that the Gospel of Matthew was composed in Greek, these references to a Hebrew Matthew are probably inferences from the statement of Papias and from the Jewish character of the Gospel of Matthew combined with confusion of our Greek Gospel of Matthew with other Gospels, written in Aramaic and believed to have come from Matthew's hand, and thus assumed to lie behind and serve as the basis for the Gospel of Matthew.[42]

While it is important to examine and properly interpret external testimony, and particularly early testimony, regarding authorship, it is even more critical to assess the evidence for the authorship of the Gospel of

---

[39] Eusebius, *Ecclesiastical History* 5.10.3.
[40] Eusebius, *Ecclesiastical History* 24.5.6.
[41] Jerome, *On Illustrious Men* 3.
[42] France, *Evangelist and Teacher*, 64-66.

Matthew from internal evidence within and surrounding it. For in the final analysis, the Gospel of Matthew itself is the most reliable witness to authorship.

Does the internal evidence align with the external testimony, or does it point to an alternative regarding authorship? As we saw above, it is possible that the author of the Gospel of Matthew used Mark as one of his main sources and, more specifically, may have adopted Mark's framework for his own Gospel. One of the most commonly repeated arguments made against Matthean authorship is that it is inconceivable that an apostle would rely so heavily on the work of a non-apostle. On the surface, such a practice on the part of an apostle does seem odd. Yet if it is the case that Mark compiled his Gospel on the basis of the recollections of Peter, as Papias testified, it is perhaps a bit more understandable that Matthew may have followed the Gospel which contained the recollections of Peter, the first disciple to be called (Mt 4:18-19; cf. Mt 10:2, where Peter is called "first"), one of Jesus' "inner circle" (Mt 17:1-8; 26:37-45; cf. also Mk 5:35-39), who especially in the Gospel of Matthew repeatedly functions as the spokesperson and representative for the disciples (Mt 8:14-17; 14:28-33; 16:16-20, 22-23; 17:24-27; 18:21-22; 19:27; 26:31-35, 40; 27:57-75). We should also remember that although the two (four)-source hypothesis may be the most likely explanation of Gospel origins, it is by no means certain. Therefore, it is problematic to allow this appeal to Markan priority to have a determinative bearing on the issue of authorship.

We note too that the apostle Matthew plays a slightly more significant role in our Gospel than in the others. Mark and Luke record the calling of a tax collector named Levi to discipleship (Mk 2:13-14, where he is described as the "son of Alphaeus"; Lk 5:27-28), while they do not mention Levi at all in the list of disciples (Mk 3:13-19; Acts 1:13-14). But our evangelist identifies this man as "Matthew" (Mt 9:9) and, in contrast to Mark and Luke, describes Matthew in the list of apostles at Matthew 10:2-4 as "the tax collector." Some have suggested that this variation found in the Gospel of Matthew reflects an autobiographical touch on the part of the author: he preferred the name Matthew, perhaps a new name given to him by Jesus, to his original name, Levi. But this explanation is highly speculative and probably would not have occurred to anyone if not for the association of Matthew with this Gospel in the church's tradition. The evidence surrounding Matthew 9:9 and Matthew 10:2-4 is inconclusive for the issue of authorship.

The fact that, according to the Gospel of Matthew, the apostle Matthew was originally a tax collector raises the question of the likelihood that a man with this kind of background was responsible for this Gospel. Clearly Matthew was a toll collector whose "tax office" was located near Capernaum, probably on the border of Galilee, ruled by Herod Antipas, and the Decapolis, ruled by Philip. Since toll collectors were chosen from the local population, Matthew would have been a Galilean Jew who had elected, probably out of motives of financial gain, to align himself with the Herods and ultimately with Rome, thus incurring resentment on the part of his Jewish compatriots. Such a person would have been literate and would have been conversant in both Aramaic and Greek, a consideration that accords well with the relatively high quality of Greek that characterizes the Gospel of Matthew.[43] Although some have tried to argue that the several specific references to money that are unique to this Gospel (e.g., Mt 17:24-27; 26:14-15; 27:3-10; 28:11-15) support the notion that it was penned by a former tax collector, money does not feature any more prominently in our Gospel than in the other Synoptics (although in general Matthew makes mention of larger denominations of money), and even if it did, such a consideration would not necessarily point to a tax collector as the author. Indeed, von Dobschütz and Goulder have made a convincing case that several passages unique to the Gospel of Matthew as well as the writer's method of composition indicate that its author may well have had scribal, and perhaps rabbinical scribal, training.[44] A Jewish scribe, or even someone well acquainted with Jewish

---

[43]Almost all scholars agree that the Greek of the Gospel of Matthew is basically good, though not elegant or exceptional. See, e.g., Davies and Allison, *Matthew*, 1:72-73; Moule, *Birth*, 278-80; Benjamin Wisner Bacon, *Studies in Matthew* (New York: Henry Holt, 1930), 498-504.

[44]Von Dobschütz, "Matthew as Rabbi and Catechist," 20-26; Kilpatrick, *Origins*, 137-38; M. D. Goulder, *Midrash and Lection in Matthew* (London: SPCK, 1974), 1-27; Francis Wright Beare, *The Gospel According to Matthew* (San Francisco: Harper & Row, 1981), 7-13; Georg Kümmel, *Introduction to the New Testament*, rev. ed. (Nashville: Abingdon, 1975), 121. Von Dobschütz's claim that our evangelist may have earlier been a disciple of Rabbi Jochanan ben Zachai is, however, highly speculative. Many who have refused to go so far as von Dobschütz to argue that the author was a converted rabbi still find a decided scribal interest on the part of the writer and even suggest that the reference to a "scribe trained for the kingdom of heaven" (Mt 13:52) is autobiographical. See O. Lamar Cope, *Matthew: A Scribe Trained for the Kingdom of Heaven*, CBQMS 5 (Washington, DC: Catholic Biblical Association of America, 1976); Krister Stendahl,

scribal traditions, as the writer of the Gospel of Matthew almost certainly was, would have occupied a place at the opposite end of Jewish society from a tax collector.

Even if one is not prepared to go so far as to say that the author was a converted rabbi, the evidence from the Gospel of Matthew is overwhelming that the author was a Jewish Christian. Many have rightly described the Gospel of Matthew as the most Jewish book in the New Testament. For example,

- Matthew begins his Gospel with a genealogy in which he traces Jesus' lineage through David to Abraham (Mt 1:1-17), thus indicating that Jesus is to be understood fundamentally in terms of his relationship to Israel and its history. In this regard Matthew's genealogy stands in contrast to that which is presented by Luke, who traces Jesus' lineage to Adam (Lk 3:23-38), suggesting that Jesus is to be understood primarily in terms of his relation to humanity.

- The Gospel of Matthew contains indications that our evangelist knew Hebrew.[45] For example, he is apparently responsible for a play on words pertaining to the name Jesus (Ἰησοῦς), which is a transliteration of the shortened form of the Hebrew *Yehoshua* (יהושע). The writer links the meaning of the Hebrew name behind this Greek transliteration ("Yahweh is salvation") to Jesus' mission, "to save his people from their sins." In addition, scholars have long recognized that the scriptural quotations and allusions that are unique to the Gospel of Matthew often depart from the Septuagint (LXX) in the direction of a "mixed text," that manifests acquaintance with the Hebrew (proto-Masoretic) text.[46]

The School of St. Matthew and its Use of the Old Testament (Philadelphia: Fortress, 1968), 30; David E. Orton, *The Understanding Scribe: Matthew and the Apocalyptic Ideal* (New York: T&T Clark, 1989), 165-76.

[45]See Davies and Allison, *Matthew*, 1:33; Beare, *Matthew*, 10.

[46]See Stendahl, *School*; Nolland, *Gospel of Matthew*. Robert H. Gundry, *The Use of the Old Testament in St. Matthew's Gospel with Special Reference to the Messianic Hope*, NovTSup 18 (Leiden: Brill, 1967), also notes that uniquely Matthean scriptural quotations and allusions are of a mixed text type, reflecting knowledge of Hebrew, but insists that this mixed text is typical of synoptic quotations and allusions in general (and came originally from the apostle Matthew), and it is only those scriptural citations that Matthew derives from Mark that are drawn from the LXX. A more nuanced conclusion is offered by M. J. J. Menken, *Matthew's Bible: The Old Testament Text of the Evangelist*, BETL 173 (Leuven: Peeters, 2004), who insists that all the Matthean quotations

- The Gospel of Matthew shows greater interest in a number of themes that were especially at home in a Jewish context, such as righteousness (δικαιοσύνη, five times in the Gospel of Matthew [Mt 3:15; 5:6, 10, 20; 6:1, 33; 21:32], once in Luke, absent in Mark), the role of the law in daily life (Mt 5:17-48; 7:12; 12:5; 15:6; 22:36-40; 23:23-26), and judgment (Mt 3:7-12; 5:29-30; 7:13-27; 8:11-13; 10:15, 28; 11:20-24; 12:36-37; 13:24-28, 47-50; 16:27-28; 18:5-35; 25:31-46).[47]

- The Gospel of Matthew is characterized by the Jewish practice of substituting "heaven" for "God," reflected in Matthew's preference for "kingdom of heaven" over "kingdom of God."[48]

- Matthew refers to Jerusalem in typical Jewish fashion as "the city of the great king" (Mt 5:35) and as "the holy city" (Mt 27:53).

- Only the Matthean Jesus describes the three major forms of Jewish piety: almsgiving, prayer, and fasting (Mt 6:1-18).

- The material unique to the Gospel of Matthew repeatedly describes Jewish rituals and practices (Mt 5:21-26; 17:24-27; 23:1-7, 13-28; 24:20; 27:6-10).

- The Gospel of Matthew's unique material typically describes Gentiles as outsiders (Mt 5:47; 6:7, 32; 10:5, 18; 20:25).

Given the popular notion that the Gospel of Matthew is Jewish in character it may seem unnecessary to demonstrate through specific evidence that the author most likely was a Jew. But in fact several scholars have posited that a Gentile author is responsible for the Gospel of Matthew, at least in its final form.[49] Among other things, they point to Matthean passages where

---

(including the fulfillment quotations) represent a revised LXX which Matthew has at times altered to bring them into greater conformity with the Hebrew.

[47]Cf. Daniel Marguerat, *Le Jugement dans L'Évangile de Matthieu*, La Monde de la Bible (Geneva: Labor et Fides, 1981), 16-63. This theme is part of the broader Matthean emphasis on apocalyptic eschatology. See David C. Sim, *Apocalyptic Eschatology in the Gospel of Matthew*, SNTSMS 88 (New York: Cambridge University Press, 1996).

[48]See "kingdom of heaven" at Mt 3:2; 4:17; 7:21; 8:11; 11:11, 12; 13:24, 31, 33, 44, 45, 47, 52; 16:19; 18:1, 3-4, 23; 19:12, 14, 23; 20:1; 22:2; 23:13; 25:1, and "kingdom of God" at Mt 12:28; 19:24; 21:31, 43. See Jonathan Pennington, *Heaven and Earth in the Gospel of Matthew*, NovTSup 126 (Leiden: Brill, 2007) for a different understanding of the role of "kingdom of heaven."

[49]Kenneth W. Clark, "The Gentile Bias in Matthew," *JBL* 66, no. 2 (1947): 165-72; Poul Nepper-Christensen, *Das Matthäusevangelium: Ein juden-christliches Evangelium?* (Aarhus: Universitetsforlaget, 1958); Rolf Walker, *Die Heilsgeschichte im ersten Evangelium* (Göttingen: Vandenhoeck &

Gentiles are presented more positively than Jews (Mt 8:5-13; 15:21-28; 21:23, where "nation" [ἔθνος] may be understood as "Gentiles;" cf. Mt 12:18-21). They also note that the passages unique to Matthew contain a generally condemnatory attitude toward Jewish leaders and even to some extent the Jewish crowds (Mt 3:7-10; 5:17-48; 6:1-18; 12:33-37; 21:28-32; 23:1-36; 27:3-10, 25, 62-66; 28:11-15), and they cite passages in which the writer demonstrates misunderstanding of the Jewish context of Jesus' day and thus demonstrates his ignorance of things Jewish.[50]

An examination of these "errors," however, shows that they are not mistakes at all but rather reflect Matthew's theological purposes.[51] And it is quite possible that a Jewish writer might be harshly critical of the Jewish leadership and masses who have rejected the man he considered to be God's chosen Messiah.[52] Moreover, although Matthew speaks positively of some Gentiles and anticipates a future mission to Gentiles, his Gospel still presents Gentiles in a generally negative way (Mt 5:47; 6:7, 32; 10:5; 18:17; 20:19, 25).

These scholars have pointed out certain tensions in the Gospel of Matthew and have attempted to address them by claiming dissonance between Matthew's sources and the editorial work of the final redactor. According to them, the final writer incorporated earlier (Jewish) traditions, but his own redactional additions reveal a Gentile Christian. But the assumption that a redactor would simply incorporate into his Gospel earlier traditions with which he disagreed and allow them to stand, side by side, with his actual perspective reflects an earlier, problematic stage of redaction criticism. Rather, we should understand that when a writer incorporates material, he

---

Ruprecht, 1967); Ernest L. Abel, "Who Wrote Matthew?" *NTS* 17 (1970-71): 138-52; Sjef van Tilborg, *The Jewish Leaders in Matthew* (Leiden: Brill, 1972); Lloyd Gaston, "The Messiah of Israel as Teacher of the Gentiles: The Setting of Matthew's Christology," *Int* 29 (1975): 24-40; Hubert Frankemölle, *Jahwe-Bund und Kirche Christi: Studien zur Form- und Traditionsgeschichte des "Evangeliums" nach Matthäus*, Neutestamentliche Abhandlungen/Neue Folge 10 (Münster: Aschendorff, 1974); Georg Strecker, *Der Weg der Gerechtigkeit* (Göttingen: Vandenhoeck & Ruprecht, 1975); John P. Meier, *Law and History in Matthew's Gospel* (Rome: Biblical Institute Press, 1976), and *The Vision of Matthew: Christ, Church, and Morality in the First Gospel* (New York: Paulist, 1979), 17-25.

[50]E.g., Meier, *Vision of Matthew*, 19-22.

[51]See the thorough response to the claim of Gentile authorship in Davies and Allison, *Matthew*, 1:28-58.

[52]France, *Evangelist and Teacher*, 102-8; Graham Stanton, *A Gospel for a New People: Studies in Matthew* (New York: T&T Clark, 1992), 146-68.

makes that material, and its point of view, his own, and the final composition together expresses the perspective of the author.

Further, this theory of competing perspectives raises problems regarding the notion of the reader. Are we to imagine a reader who is expected to discern the message of the Gospel of Matthew by separating out the evangelist's editorial additions and changes from earlier traditions and who accepts only the former as the meaning that is herein communicated? This conclusion lacks plausibility and introduces an inadequate theory of reading. Yet these scholars have done Matthean studies a service by highlighting complexities and apparent contradictions within the Gospel of Matthew that deserve serious consideration and that we should take into account in the interpretation of the Gospel of Matthew. But as far as the present question is concerned, I can find no sufficient reason to believe that the author of the Gospel of Matthew was a Gentile.

How, then, are we to understand the authorship of the Gospel of Matthew? On the basis of the internal evidence of the Gospel of Matthew we conclude that he was a Jewish Christian who possessed knowledge of Hebrew, Greek, and Aramaic and who probably had scribal training (perhaps rabbinical). In spite of external evidence, he was probably not the tax collector Matthew (although the possibility of Matthean authorship for the Gospel of Matthew cannot be entirely excluded). Yet we are obliged to take seriously the patristic mention of Matthew, particularly from Papias, given the primitive character of the tradition he cites and the fact that the title that connects Matthew to the Gospel of Matthew is early. When we consider the precise wording of Papias it is likely that he was referencing a collection of Jesus sayings that our evangelist included within his Gospel, and it was perhaps because of the inclusion of that Matthean material that the Gospel of Matthew came to be associated with the apostle Matthew. This explanation is much more probable than the suggestion that the need to associate the Gospel with an apostle led an unknown early Christian to link it to the name of Matthew.[53] Matthew was too obscure an apostle to be thus selected. Indeed, if my surmise is accurate, in a sense the Gospel of Matthew is a product of the apostle Matthew.

---

[53] E.g., Kilpatrick, *Origins*, 137-39. The suggestion, often made, that the apostle came to be associated with the Gospel of Matthew because of his connection with the church to which the Gospel of Matthew was originally addressed is pure guesswork.

Clearly, the tentative conclusion that the Gospel of Matthew, in its final form, may not come from the hand of an apostle does not pose a theological problem. The Gospel of Matthew is, after all, anonymous. And the church's acceptance of Luke and Mark, which manifestly were produced by non-apostles, as canonical Scripture indicates that legitimate canonicity is not at stake. And without question, the Gospel tradition found in the Gospel of Matthew is early and by all accounts reliable. We turn now to the issues of the audience, date, and provenance of the Gospel of Matthew.

Who Was the Intended Audience for the Composition?

Closely related to the question of authorship is the question of the recipients or audience. As we saw above, the fact that the Gospel of Matthew is cast in the genre of ancient biography may suggest that, like many other ancient biographies, it was not directed to a particular group (church), but rather written for a general audience, intended to be read by Christians throughout the world or at least by those scattered throughout a wide geographical area. If this is the case, it would be impossible to say anything very specific regarding the intended audience. This is the view pressed by Richard Bauckham and other scholars who contributed along with him to the influential volume, *The Gospel for All Christians: Rethinking the Gospel Audiences*.[54] But even if the Gospel of Matthew is in the form of ancient biography, it does not follow that it shares absolutely all the characteristics of that genre.

Bauckham and others have made a strong case against an easy assumption that our Gospels, like the epistles, were written to specific churches to address the needs of those churches, with the corollary that we can tease out the situation of the original readers from our Gospel texts. Yet two considerations warrant caution toward abandoning completely the notion of discernable Gospel audiences. First, the relationship between the Gospel of John and the Johannine epistles strongly suggests that John's Gospel, at least, was directed to a specific Christian community in order to address situational challenges. Second, the Gospel writers certainly had purposes for writing, which surely involved addressing perceived needs among the

---

[54]Richard Bauckham, ed. *The Gospels for All Christians: Rethinking the Gospel Audiences* (Grand Rapids: Eerdmans, 1997).

readership. Those perceptions of audience needs would be shaped by each evangelist's experience with his own church or churches. Consequently, even if the Gospel of Matthew was not directed to just one specific community but to a wider group of churches, either universal or broadly regional, Matthew wrote out of some perception of intended audience which was shaped by his own community or communities.

But if we should hesitate to abandon entirely the notion of discernable Gospel audiences, we should also avoid the tendency of many redaction critics to view our Gospels as "transparent" of the communities addressed in the sense that elements in the Gospel story essentially stand for or represent persons or situations in the church to which the Gospel is written. To do so would be to fail to take seriously the narrative character of the Gospels, that is, to read them according to their character as story rather than allegory.[55]

The most effective way forward, then, is to consider how Matthew's presentation of the story of Jesus and the assumptions Matthew makes regarding the readers may reveal the character and situation of Matthew's audience, or at least the audience as Matthew perceived it. When I mention Matthew's perception of his audience I am speaking of the implied reader of the Gospel of Matthew, the reader that we can discern from the text. Although this implied reader, being a construct of the text, is distinct from the flesh-and-blood audience to which the Gospel of Matthew was addressed, it is likely that some real connection exists between the implied reader and the actual original intended audience. Thus Kingsbury helpfully argues that the implied reader can serve as an "index" to the audience of the Gospel of Matthew.[56]

Who, then, is the reader that the Gospel of Matthew envisages? First, the reader is a Jewish Christian. Many of the indications, discussed above, of the Jewishness of the author pertain also to the audience. In addition, we note that the audience understands Jesus in characteristically Jewish categories. He is the Son of Abraham, the Son of David, the king of the Jews who ushers in God's end-time rule, and Emmanuel.[57] The audience not only

---

[55] Francis Watson, "Toward a Literal Reading of the Gospels," in Bauckham, *Gospels for All Christians*, 207-17.

[56] Jack Dean Kingsbury, "Reflections on 'the Reader' of Matthew's Gospel," *NTS* 34 (1988): 458-59, and *Matthew as Story* (Minneapolis: Fortress, 1986), 147-60.

[57] Son of Abraham (Mt 1:1-2, 17); son of David (Mt 1:1, 4, 17, 20; 9:27; 12:23; 15:22; 20:30-31; 21:9, 15; 22:42, 45); the king of the Jews (Mt 1:6; 2:2, 9; 3:2; 4:23; 5:19-20; 6:10, 33; 7:21; 8:11; 9:35; 11:11, 12;

knows the Old Testament, which might be said of most Gentile Christians in the early church,[58] but is expected to recognize the significance of obscure persons and passages in the Old Testament as well as subtle allusions to numerous Old Testament passages.[59] They understood typical Jewish ways of using the Old Testament Scriptures and arguing from them.[60] They were acquainted with the structure of the synagogue, including its "council" (Mt 5:22). They were aware of the practice of sacrificing in the temple (Mt 5:23-24), and of temple oaths (Mt 23:16-22), as well as the temple tax (Mt 17:24-27). They considered Jerusalem to be "the holy city" (Mt 4:5; 27:53) and "the city of the great King" (Mt 5:35). They were aware of the character and marginal role within Jewish society of tax collectors (Mt 5:46; 18:17; 21:32). They embraced almsgiving, prayer, and fasting as the three major forms of Jewish piety (Mt 6:1-18). They even recognized that "sound the trumpet" referred to trumpets heralding worship on the sabbath and that "pray at the street corners" recalled the practice of pious Jews standing and praying where they were at the hour of prayer.[61] They needed no explanation of the "tradition of the elders" (Mt 15:1-6) or of "phylacteries" and "fringes" (Mt 23:5).

The audience obviously knew Greek, but it is unclear whether they knew Hebrew or Aramaic. The writer translates the Hebrew *Emmanuel* (Mt 1:21) as "God with us," but perhaps does so for literary and theological reasons to connect it with Jesus' statement at the end of the Gospel, "I am with you always to the end of the age" (Mt 28:20). And the reader is aware of the etymological significance of the name of Jesus, which, as we saw, is the

---

12:25, 26, 28; 13:17-19, 24, 31, 33, 38, 41, 43-45, 47, 52; 16:19, 28; 17:25; 18:1, 3-4, 23; 19:12, 14, 23-24; 20:1, 21; 21:31, 43; 22:2; 23:13; 24:14; 25:1, 40; 26:29; 27:11, 29, 37, 42); Emmanuel (Mt 1:21-23).

[58]Note, e.g., the great reliance on specific argumentation from the OT in Galatians, whose audience was exclusively, or at least almost exclusively, Gentile.

[59]We find this feature throughout the Gospel of Matthew, but especially in Mt 1:18–2:23. The allusions in this passage are so subtle and so numerous that many have questioned whether even an intelligent and informed Jew would be able to catch all of them. R. T. France, "The Formula-Quotations of Matthew 2 and the Problem of Communication," *NTS* 27 (1980-81): 233-51, has posited that Matthew envisaged a discussion among the congregation in which certain members would identify some of these allusions and other members would catch additional ones. If France is correct, this suggestion would point to another characteristic of the audience: it received the Gospel of Matthew as catalyst for ongoing conversation regarding its meaning and significance.

[60]Stendahl, *School*; Gundry, *Use of the Old Testament*; Goulder, *Midrash and Lection*.

[61]See Craig S. Keener, *A Commentary on the Gospel of Matthew* (Grand Rapids: Eerdmans, 1999), 208, 210.

transliteration of the Hebrew name Joshua. The writer leaves Aramaic words untranslated at Matthew 5:22; 6:24; 27:6 but provides translation at Matthew 27:33, 46.[62]

If, in fact, it is indisputable that the readership was Jewish, were Gentiles also a part of the audience? The many passages that speak of the Gentiles as outsiders, as those who have no relationship with God, would seem to point to a negative answer (Mt 6:7, 32; 18:16; 20:25). And yet the Gospel contains the suggestion that God is able to make Gentiles "sons of Abraham" (Mt 3:9).[63] And Matthew anticipates the inclusion of the Gentiles into the people of God (Mt 4:15-16; 8:11-12; 12:18-21; 21:43; 22:1-10; 28:18-20; possibly also 13:32; 25:1). Matthew indicates this inclusion already at the beginning of the Gospel of Matthew by reference to Jesus as "Son of Abraham," through whose "seed," or son, God would bless the Gentiles (Mt 1:1, 2, 17; cf. Gen 12:1-12; 22:15-18; 17:5); by the incorporation of Gentile women into the genealogy of Jesus the Messiah (Mt 1:2-16); and by narrating the coming of the Gentile magi and presenting them as proleptic disciples (Mt 2:1-12). These considerations, along with Matthew's strong polemic against certain Jewish groups and institutions, have led some scholars to believe that Matthew's community was originally Jewish but was increasingly admitting Gentiles, in other words, that it was a mixed community of both Jews and Gentiles.[64]

While a mixed community is possible, the evidence suggests that the implied readership is Jewish Christian.[65] The references to Gentile evangelization are expectations for the Jewish-Christian community, and the

---

[62]It is possible that the readers did not know Hebrew or Aramaic but were acquainted with a few isolated terms. On the other hand, the play on the Hebrew transliteration in Mt 1:21 and the untranslated Aramaic terms at Mt 5:22; 6:24; 27:6 occur in uniquely Matthean material, while the translations of Aramaic at Mt 27:33, 46 are found in material common to Mark and/or Luke and may indicate that the latter were part of the broader Gospel tradition; this consideration may point to the conclusion that at least some of the original audience of the Gospel of Matthew knew Hebrew and/or Aramaic.

[63]In light of other references in the Gospel of Matthew to the anticipated inclusion of Gentiles, this is probably the meaning of the phrase.

[64]E.g., France, *Evangelist and Teacher*, 108; Jack Dean Kingsbury, *Matthew*, 3rd ed. (Nappanee, IN: Evangel, 1998), 96-103. Indeed, some have gone so far as to argue that by the time the Gospel of Matthew was written Matthew's community was essentially Gentile; e.g., Neeper-Christensen, *Matthäusevangelium*; Strecker, *Der Weg*; Wolfgang Trilling, *Das Wahre Israel: Studien zur Theologie des Matthäus-Evangeliums* (München: Kösel, 1964).

[65]Thus several scholars opt for an exclusively (or nearly exclusively) Jewish-Christian audience, e.g., Hagner, *Matthew 1-13*, lxiv-lxv; Overman, *Matthew's Gospel*, 157.

mention of the inclusion of Gentiles may anticipate the evangelization of Gentiles on the part of the community.[66] In fact, most references to the evangelization or inclusion of the Gentiles picture them as being geographically far-flung and distant from the readers (Mt 2:1-12; 8:11; 24:14; 28:19), although several portray them as "coming" (Mt 2:1-12; 8:11). Matthew does not clearly indicate whether those expectations had been realized by the time the Gospel of Matthew was written. We cannot be sure whether these passages are describing a reality in the community or whether they are urging a course of action for the audience which will result in a future accomplishment of Gentile participation.[67]

The fact that the Gospel of Matthew is so Jewish and that the implied reader is a Jewish Christian raises the issue of the relationship between these Jewish-Christian readers and Judaism. In the Gospel of Matthew the religious leaders are solidly and without exception opposed to Jesus and continue to contradict the resurrection and accuse Jesus' followers of calumny into the period of the reader (Mt 28:11-15; cf. Mt 27:62-66). Presumably such a portrait, made to the implied reader, would resonate with the experience of the intended readers. Moreover, all the particular groups that constituted the religious leaders in Matthew's narrative stand together in their opposition to Jesus and his followers. The great differences that existed among these groups in Palestinian Jewish society of the middle of the first century are entirely passed over by Matthew in favor of presenting them as forming a single solid wall of opposition to Jesus.[68]

Yet chief among the opposition are the Pharisees, who appear in the Gospel of Matthew somewhat more often than in Mark or Luke; obviously a number of these references are unique to the Gospel of Matthew. This Matthean emphasis on the Pharisees has led many scholars to insist that the

---

[66]Schuyler Brown, "The Matthean Community and the Gentile Mission," *NovT* 22 (1980): 193-221, contends that disagreement may have existed in Matthew's community regarding the mission to Gentiles.

[67]Paul Foster, *Community, Law and Mission in Matthew's Gospel*, WUNT, 2/177 (Tübingen: Mohr Siebeck, 2004), 218-20.

[68]On the differences among the groups, see Marcel Simon, *Jewish Sects at the Time of Jesus* (Philadelphia: Fortress, 1967); Emil Schürer, *A History of the Jewish People in the Age of Jesus Christ*, 3 vols., ed. Geza Vermes, Fergus Miller, and Matthew Black (New York: T&T Clark, 1973–87), 2:381-414; Anthony J. Saldarini, *Pharisees, Scribes and Sadducees in Palestinian Society: A Sociological Approach* (Grand Rapids: Eerdmans, 2001). On the single wall of opposition to Jesus, see Walker, *Heilsgeschichte*, 11-16; Trilling, *Wahre Israel*, 90-91.

readers of the Gospel of Matthew were in a struggle with the Pharisees of their own day. These scholars identify such a struggle as most likely occurring after AD 70 when the temple had been destroyed and the Pharisees assumed increasing prominence in the Judaism that was taking shape in the post-war period. Indeed, we shall note below that most scholars believe this situation obtained especially in the years immediately following the Council of Jamnia (85-90), when, it is generally held, the Pharisees solidified their control of Judaism. But as we shall see, questions exist regarding such a late date for the Gospel of Matthew.

Moreover, when we compare the Gospel of Matthew with the other Synoptics we find that not only the Pharisees but also the Sadducees receive greater mention in the Gospel of Matthew. The Sadducees, who were the party of the chief priests and the temple leadership, had ceased to exist as a force in Jewish life after the destruction of the temple. In fact, the gradual shift of emphasis away from the Pharisees toward the Sadducees and the chief priests as Matthew's story moves from conflict in Galilee to the opposition that Jesus experiences in Jerusalem, and especially around the temple, points to a kind of historical verisimilitude, since in the 30s the Pharisees were dominant in Galilee and the Sadducees were prominent among the elites in Jerusalem.[69] These observations about the presentation of the Sadducees (and the chief priests) in the Gospel of Matthew warn us against easily assuming that the role of the Pharisees in Matthew's story necessarily reflects a situation in which the audience is engaged in a struggle specifically and exclusively with the Pharisaic leadership.

Actually, it is necessary to employ greater methodological precision than has sometimes been practiced as we attempt to ascertain how the implied reader of the Gospel of Matthew might serve as an index for the situation of the intended readers in their connection to the Judaism of their own day. I suggest that there is an ascending scale of significance among Matthean

---

[69]Matthew presents the Sadducees, who were historically associated with the upper echelons of the priesthood and especially with the high-priestly families, as located in Judea and usually in Jerusalem (Mt 3:7; 22:23, 34); Jesus mentions them in his teaching just before he begins his journey to Jerusalem (Mt 16:1-12). On the other hand, Matthew links the Pharisees primarily with Galilee (Mt 5:20; 9:11, 14, 34; 12:2, 14, 28, 38; 15:1, 12; 16:1, 6, 11, 12; but cf. Mt 19:3). After Jesus enters Jerusalem the Pharisees are mentioned relatively little, and almost always in some connection with the Sadducees or chief priests (Mt 21:45; 22:15 [cf. Mt 22:23]; 22:34; 27:62-66 [cf. Mt 28:11-15]; yet cf. Mt 22:41). The Pharisees play no direct role in Jesus' passion (Mt 26:1–27:55).

passages that pertain to Israel for the question of the relationship of Matthew's intended readers to Judaism.

The first level of significance involves those passages that describe the relationship between Jesus and Israel. These passages have significance, but a limited one, for the question at hand, since the implied reader identifies with Jesus in a relatively *distant* way. Insofar as the implied reader is a follower of Jesus, acknowledges Jesus as Lord, and embraces Jesus as the model for both discipleship and mission, the reader identifies in some measure with Jesus in his interactions with Israel. But the implied reader identifies with Jesus only in an indirect way since Jesus is a transcendent figure (e.g., Mt 1:20; 11:27; 28:18) who plays an utterly unique role in the narrative world of the Gospel of Matthew and inhabits a time distinct from the period of the reader.

The second level of significance pertains to those passages that describe the relationship between Israel and the (twelve) disciples of Jesus during Jesus' earthly ministry.[70] These passages have somewhat greater significance for the issue of the relationship of Matthew's intended readers to the Judaism of their own day, since the implied reader has *proximate* identification with the twelve. Like the twelve, the implied reader is a follower of Jesus, is "with" Jesus (Mt 1:21-23; 12:30; 18:20; 28:20), and frequently sees his experience mirrored in the story of the twelve.[71] Yet the difference of historical setting and the salvation-historical uniqueness in the role of the twelve over against later disciples (e.g., Mt 12:2-4; 19:28; 26:30-35, 56) creates a measure of separation between the implied reader and the twelve.

The third level of significance involves those passages that describe the disciples of the post-Easter period in relation to Israel. The implied reader has *coalescent* identification with post-Easter disciples as they are described in the Gospel of Matthew because the implied reader is in fact a member of the community of post-Easter disciples.

As to the first level, which pertains to Jesus' relationship with Israel, we see that Jesus experiences unrelenting opposition from the Pharisees, the Sadducees, and the chief priests, along with the "scribes" (γραμματεύς). The

---

[70]In the Gospel of Matthew (in contrast to Mark and Luke) Jesus' "disciples" (μαθηταί) are limited to the twelve.

[71]Note, e.g., how the five great discourses (Mt 5–7; 10; 13; 18; 24–25) are, according to the narrative, directed to the twelve and yet have significance for post-Easter Christians in general.

scribes were teachers of the law (Mt 7:28-29; 17:10-13; 23:1-7) and in the Gospel of Matthew they are almost always mentioned either with the Pharisees (Mt 5:20; 12:38; 15:1; 23:2, 13, 14, 15) or with the chief priests (Mt 2:4; 16:21; 20:18; 21:15; 26:57; 27:41).[72] Consequently they do not form a separate group in the narrative world of the Gospel of Matthew but are aligned with either the Pharisees or chief priests; they seem to constitute the teaching arms of each of those groups.[73] At the heart of the conflict between Jesus and the Pharisees, Sadducees, and chief priests is their rejection of Jesus' transcendent authority. For the Pharisees it is a denial of Jesus' transcendence especially in relation to the law and its interpretation (Mt 9:10-13; 12:9-14; 22:15-22).[74] They do not understand the true meaning of God's revelation in Scripture (Mt 12:7) and consequently refuse to believe that Jesus is its true interpreter or that he fulfills the law. Rather they are convinced that Jesus' intent is to "abolish the law and the prophets" (Mt 5:17-18).[75] For the chief priests it is a denial of Jesus' transcendence in relation to the temple (Mt 21:12-17; 26:57-69; 27:39-42), which, along with the law, served as a pillar of Judaism.[76]

But Matthew is careful to chart not only Jesus' interactions with the religious leaders but also with the people (λαός; Mt 2:4; 13:15; 15:8; 27:25) or the Jewish crowds (ὄχλοι).[77] Throughout most of the Gospel of Matthew the crowds are positively inclined toward Jesus, even serving as a buffer between him and the murderous plans of the religious leaders. Yet they never become

---

[72]Probably connected with the Pharisees also at Mt 7:29 (cf. Mt 5:20) and Mt 9:3, since these passages are found within the period of Jesus' Galilean ministry, where, as we have seen, the Pharisees dominate.

[73]The "elders" (πρεσβύτεροι) are presented as part of the council, along with the chief priests, with whom they are associated (Mt 16:21; 21:23; 26:3, 47, 57; 27:1, 3, 12, 20, 41). The reference in Mt 15:2 to the "tradition of the elders" is of a different order, alluding to the earlier authoritative teachers of the law who were responsible for the oral tradition of the Pharisees.

[74]Note how Mt 12, a passage in which Jesus attacks the Pharisees, emphasizes Jesus' transcendence by the repeated "greater than" statements (Mt 12:6, the temple; Mt 12:41, Jonah; Mt 12:42, Solomon).

[75]In light of the observation that Jesus goes on to castigate the scribes and Pharisees (Mt 5:20-48) and the "hypocrites," which seems, given the description, to refer to the Pharisees (Mt 6:1-18; cf. Mt 23:13, 15, 16, 23, 25, 27, 29), it is natural to think that the charge that Jesus intends to abolish the law and prophets comes from the Pharisees.

[76]N. T. Wright, *The New Testament and the People of God* (Minneapolis: Fortress, 1992), 224-43.

[77]The complexity of the people's relationship to Jesus is indicated by the tension between positive references to the people in Mt 1:21; 2:6; 4:23; 26:5 and the increasing hostility of the λαός toward Jesus suggested by the repeated phrase "chief priests and elders *of the people*" toward the end of the Gospel (Mt 21:23; 26:3, 47; 27:1; cf. Mt 27:25).

followers of Jesus in the sense of disciples or adherents; in fact, Jesus rebukes them as unrepentant (Mt 11:20-24) and describes them as dull of heart and heavy of hearing (Mt 13:14-15), from whom God has chosen to withhold the "secrets of the kingdom of heaven" (Mt 13:10-13). And at the end of the Gospel of Matthew the crowds are persuaded by the chief priests to appeal for Jesus' death and call down the responsibility for his execution not only on themselves but on their children (Mt 27:20-26); this responsibility, then, continues into the time of the implied reader.

As to the second level, which pertains to the relationship between the religious leaders and the twelve, we note that the Pharisees attack not only Jesus but also his disciples. Here the issue has to do with the performance of legal practices that pertain to sabbath observance (Mt 12:1-8) and purity (Mt 15:1-20), the latter discussion focusing on compliance with the "tradition of the elders." Moreover, Jesus demands of his disciples a "righteousness that exceeds that of the scribes and Pharisees" (Mt 5:20), which suggests that the Pharisees are oriented toward compliance to the letter of the law rather than the will of God that stands behind the letter as Jesus reveals that divine will through his process of fulfillment. Yet Jesus insists that the scribes and Pharisees "sit on Moses' seat," and therefore the disciples are "to practice and observe whatever they tell you," even if the disciples are not to model their lives after the Pharisees' poor example (Mt 23:1-2). This expectation of obedience on the part of the disciples (and, in this case, also the crowds) to the teaching of the Pharisees and scribes stands in tension with both the immediate context (Mt 23:4) and many passages in the broader context in which Jesus warns his disciples precisely not to embrace their teaching (Mt 12:1-14, 24-33; 15:1-20). Thus, in spite of the inclusive wording of Matthew 23:3 ("*whatever* they tell you"), context requires that we understand this demand in a qualified way, that is, "insofar as their teaching accords with the law of Moses as I have interpreted it" (cf. Mt 5:17-48; cf. Mt 7:29).[78] Matthew portrays the twelve, then, as submitting, with qualification, to the teaching of the Pharisaic scribes.

But Jesus also urges the disciples to "beware of the teaching of the Pharisees and Sadducees" (Mt 16:5-12). The teaching of the Pharisees is clear

---

[78] So also Orton, *Understanding Scribe*, 34. This implicit qualification of the demand corresponds to Matthew's practice to speak of "*some* of the scribes" in certain passages where he presents scribes in a negative light (Mt 9:3; 12:38).

enough on the basis of Matthew 12:1-8; 15:1-20; but the content of the teaching of the Sadducees is less evident. The consideration that the Greek construction indicates here a common teaching between them suggests that Jesus may have in mind their human-centered orientation expressed in their mutual request that Jesus satisfy their demand for a sign (Mt 16:1-4; we will see below that the demand for a sign represents an attempt to bring the Kingdom of God under their own control). It is arresting that Jesus speaks here of the leaven/teaching of the Pharisees *and Sadducees*, since the reference to Sadducees at this point is unique to the Gospel of Matthew; the parallel passage in Mark reads "the leaven of the Pharisees and the leaven of Herod" (Mk 8:15).[79] Among the Gospels, then, only the Gospel of Matthew warns the twelve of the teaching of the Sadducees.[80] Yet the twelve have no contact with the Sadducees throughout the narrative, nor for that matter with the Jewish crowds, but only sporadic interaction with the Pharisees.

As to the third and most significant level, which pertains to Matthew's presentation of the relationship between Israel and the post-Easter disciples, we note that conflict will rage in this period. At the transition into the post-Easter period the Pharisees raise the suspicion that Jesus' disciples intend to remove his body with a view toward falsely proclaiming that he has been raised from the dead (Mt 27:62-66), while it is the chief priests who spread the lie that the disciples have stolen his body, a lie that continues among the Jews "to this day" (Mt 28:11-15). But the post-Easter church experiences conflict not only with the chief priests but with the Pharisees and the Jewish crowds. As a result of their itinerant ministry to the towns of Israel (Mt 10:5-15, 23) they will be persecuted from town to town (Mt 10:23; 23:34) and delivered up, presumably by the Jewish crowds (Mt 10:17) or even members of their own families (Mt 10:34-39), to councils, and will be flogged in the synagogues (Mt 10:17, 34). Councils and synagogues were spheres in which the Pharisees were dominant.[81] Indeed, they will at times be put to

---

[79] Luke has "the leaven of the Pharisees" (12:1).

[80] Contrary to their historical role, Matthew does not link the Sadducees with the chief priests but rather with the Pharisees, as forming a united front in opposing his teachings. See Romeo Popa, *Allgegenwärtiger Konflikt im Matthäusevangelium: Exegetische und sozialpsychologische Analyse der Konfliktgeschichte*, NovTOA/SUNT 111 (Göttingen: Vandenhoeck & Ruprecht, 2017), 99-100, 108.

[81] Although this word (συνέδριον) will be used of the Sanhedrin in Mt 26:59, here it refers to local Jewish assemblies, linked with the synagogue, that have the power of discipline. For the

death (Mt 10:28, 38-39), even by crucifixion (Mt 23:34-35),[82] presumably by both religious leaders (Mt 23:29-35) and civil authorities to whom the religious leaders remand them (Mt 10:18).

The fact that Matthew describes the direct opposition that the church will experience in the post-Easter period as coming from the Pharisees (Mt 23:29-36; 10:24-25, whose association through "Beelzebul" connects it with opposition from the Pharisees in Mt 9:34 and Mt 12:24-27) and as centering in the synagogue (Mt 10:17; 23:34), where the Pharisees were dominant, over against the temple, where the Sadducees and the chief priests held sway, leads the implied reader to expect that in the post-Easter period opposition will come primarily from the Pharisees, although the reference to post-Easter antagonism on the part of the chief priests in Matthew 28:11-15 may indicate continuing conflict also with them. And, as we have seen, Matthew suggests that conflict will come from the people as well. Thus, the audience of the Gospel of Matthew was apparently experiencing repudiation from the people and severe conflict with the Pharisaic leadership, and possibly also, though much less likely, from the chief priests.

We can therefore draw the following provisional conclusions. On the basis of Matthew's presentation of Jesus and Judaism it is *possible* that the intended audience was in conflict with both the Pharisees and the chief priests, including scribes who occupied the teaching office for both groups. These groups continued to reject the audience's claims of Jesus' absolutely supreme transcendence and authority which challenged their customary and cherished ways of thinking about the law and the temple cult. The Pharisees considered that not only had Jesus intended to abolish the law and the prophets, but that his followers, the audience of the Gospel of Matthew, shared the same intention. And the chief priests were convinced that his followers purposed, as did Jesus, to destroy the temple or at least to disrupt it and to undermine the order that it provided for the Jewish people. For their part, the audience continues to experience the Jewish people as

---

connection between Pharisees and the synagogues in Matthew's narrative, see Mt 6:2; 12:9 (cf. Mt 12:2, 14); Mt 23:6, 34.

[82]The sense here is probably "have them crucified," presumably by the Romans (as in Acts 2:36; 4:10), since Jews in this period did not engage in crucifixion; though see Josephus, *Antiquities of the Jews* 13:380-83; *Jewish War* 97-98, where he describes the crucifixion of 800 Pharisees under the Saducean high priest Alexander Janneus around 90 BC.

unrepentant, dull of heart and heavy of hearing in the face of the proclamation of the kingdom of God and unable even to comprehend the message they preach.

On the basis of Matthew's presentation of the twelve and Judaism it is *probable* that the intended audience was in conflict with the Pharisees and the people-as-a-whole, but perhaps not with the chief priests. The Pharisees objected that the audience's observance of sabbath and purity regulations did not go far enough, for it fell short of what was required in Pharisaic oral tradition. They took exception to the audience's insistence that the law should be practiced according to Jesus' interpretation rather than the instruction of the Pharisees. Yet the audience continues to adhere to the teaching of the Pharisaic scribes insofar as it does not conflict with the instructions of Jesus.

On the basis of Matthew's presentation of the connection between post-Easter disciples and Judaism it is *extremely likely* that the audience was in conflict with the people-as-a-whole and the Pharisees. The conflict was occasioned by the audience's efforts, through itinerant travel, to evangelize the Jewish people. The people were suspicious of the audience's claims regarding the resurrection of Jesus since they, or at least many of them, believed their leaders' explanation that the resurrection was a hoax perpetrated by the followers of Jesus. In general, the audience met with persecution wherever they went. Specifically, the people frequently delivered them to the local judicial councils that were associated with the synagogues where the intended readers were flogged and on occasion perhaps even killed; at other times they were turned over to the civil authorities to give an account of their evangelistic actions and claims.

Any final conclusion we draw from these observations regarding the relation of the intended readers to Judaism should incorporate the consideration, mentioned above, that a measure of historical distance exists between the implied reader on the one hand and Matthew's presentation of the earthly Jesus and the twelve disciples on the other. The implied reader recognizes that Matthew intends that some elements of the story of Jesus and the original disciples do not reflect the situation of the implied reader but are rather to be understood as belonging to the historical past with a view that the implied reader will derive insight by attending specifically to their past-historical character. This concern for pastness we might call Matthew's "historicization."[83] Yet the implied reader also recognizes that Matthew has so presented certain features of his story as to connect directly with the experience of the implied reader who stands on this side of Matthew 28:20. This contemporary identification we might call Matthew's "contemporization." Thus, Matthew engages in both historicization and contemporization.[84]

We see historicization in Matthew's insistence that during the period of Jesus' earthly life Jesus restricted his ministry to Jews (Mt 15:21-28) and the disciples were to do the same (e.g., Mt 10:5-6; 15:24),[85] for this restriction was rendered obsolete with the climactic command to "make disciples of all nations" in the time of the implied reader (Mt 28:18-20). The Gospel of Matthew itself indicates, then, that the confinement of ministry to Israel obtained only during the period before the resurrection. As with everything Matthew includes in the Gospel of Matthew, this description of restrictive ministry has significance for the implied reader in his own situation, but only as the reader attends to its past-historical character.[86]

---

[83]I am not using "historicization" in the sense in which Walker, *Heilsgeschichte*, or Strecker, *Der Weg*, employed the term, i.e., a theological attempt on Matthew's part to isolate the "time of Jesus" from the "time of the church," along the lines of Conzelmann's threefold understanding of salvation history in Luke-Acts, into the time of Israel/the time of Jesus/the time of the church. Such periodization is problematic at least in the Gospel of Matthew (and in my judgment also within Luke-Acts), since Matthew links the time of Jesus with the time of the church as together belonging to the period of "fulfillment," as Kingsbury has argued. See Kingsbury, *Matthew: Structure, Christology, Kingdom* (Philadelphia: Fortress, 1975), 1-39.

[84]Ulrich Luz, *Studies in Matthew* (Grand Rapids: Eerdmans, 2004), 115-16. For a full-fledged examination of this combination of historicization and contemporization from a narrative-critical perspective, see David B. Howell, *Matthew's Inclusive Story: A Study of the Narrative Rhetoric of the First Gospel*, JSNTSup 42 (Sheffield: Sheffield Academic Press, 1990).

[85]On two occasions Jesus does heal Gentiles (Mt 8:5-13; 15:21-28). But these are exceptions that prove the rule. Jesus will heal Gentiles only in the face of their overwhelming faith (Mt 8:10; 15:28).

[86]E.g., this restriction may contribute to Matthew's claim that God was faithful to the promises God made to his people Israel in that the eschatological hope of the OT was directed specifically to Israel. If the Matthean Jesus had ministered indiscriminately to both Jews and Gentiles he would have at least introduced confusion and ambiguity regarding God's faithfulness to his ancient people. This confusion, in turn, may have lessened the responsibility of Israel to react positively to Jesus' proclamation of the kingdom, since the Jews may have been forgiven for thinking that real discontinuity existed between the revelation of God in their Scriptures and the practice of Jesus. Moreover, the (historically temporary) restriction may enforce the more fundamental point of the importance of timing; it is theologically significant that certain things that God ultimately desires to take place may be contrary to God's will in specific circumstances or during particular periods.

We see contemporization in Jesus' instruction regarding fasting (Mt 6:16-18). Although Jesus gives instruction about fasting to his disciples (cf. Mt 5:1-2), we learn a bit later in the narrative that the disciples did not fast and indeed were not to fast while Jesus was with them, but would fast only "after the bridegroom had been taken away," that is, after the departure of the earthly Jesus (Mt 9:14-15). Thus, the instructions regarding how followers are to fast did not obtain for the twelve during Jesus' earthly ministry, even though the instruction was given to them within the period of Jesus' earthly ministry; it pertains rather to the time of the implied reader.[87] We see that statements construed in light of the broader context of the Gospel alert the reader to the presence of historicization and contemporization in these instances.

But these examples cause us to think that such historicization and contemporization are present even when the Gospel of Matthew provides no such explicit indications as we find in the cases just cited. The upshot is that we cannot assume that every feature of Matthew's story directly reflects the contemporary situation of the audience; nor, on the other hand, can we assume that no feature of Matthew's story exists primarily to describe the situation and to speak directly to the needs of the intended audience. We must be attentive to subtleties in the broader context of the Gospel of Matthew to make a determination between historicization and contemporization. Thus Jesus' warning to the twelve regarding the leaven of the Sadducees (Mt 16:5-20) may be an example of historicization, and not descriptive of a situation in which the intended audience is in contact with the Sadducees. Passages in the Gospel of Matthew that describe the time of the implied reader make no mention of the Sadducees. And the fact that Matthew seems generally to emphasize that the Pharisees and Sadducees

---

[87]We should not assume that passages that represent contemporization are necessarily creations of the church or the evangelists that have been put into Jesus' mouth. All the Gospels indicate that Jesus expected a significant period between his resurrection and Second Coming (though perhaps not centuries, cf. Mk 13:32) and that he gave instructions during his earthly life that would pertain to this period. This is not to deny that Matthew, (as I believe) under the inspiration of the Holy Spirit (or as Matthew may have put it, the resurrected Jesus who continues to speak to his church), may have modified the traditions that came to him at points; cf. M. Eugene Boring, *Sayings of the Risen Jesus: Christian Prophecy in the Synoptic Tradition*, SNTMS 46 (New York: Cambridge University Press, 1982); Cope, *Scribe Trained*; Orton, *Understanding Scribe*, 165-76. But even when Matthew adopted the tradition he inherited his decision to include it in his Gospel could manifest his desire to address his intended audience in their situation; and thus even traditional material in the Gospel of Matthew may reflect the character and conditions of the audience.

formed a common front against Jesus during his earthly ministry might explain Matthew's mentioning the Sadducees along with the Pharisees in Matthew 16.

But we must grant that we do not always share with the original readers the ability to discern with confidence whether a passage falls under the category of historicization or contemporization, since we lack the knowledge of the contemporary situation that the original audience would have brought to their reading of the Gospel of Matthew. These considerations regarding historicization and contemporization, then, introduce an element of tentativeness into our work of reconstructing the original audience addressed in Matthew's composition, including the question of the relationship between Matthew's audience and Judaism.

Before leaving the matter of the relationship of the audience to Judaism we should consider a question that is central to that relationship and one that is debated among scholars: To what extent did Matthew's audience continue to participate in Judaistic practices, particularly synagogue worship? Did they consider themselves practicing members of the Judaistic faith (*intra muros*, "inside the walls"), or had they essentially broken ties with the synagogue and no longer considered themselves practitioners of Judaism (*extra muros*, "outside the walls")? If the former, they would think of themselves as "Christian Jews." If the latter, they would consider themselves "Jewish Christians." Scholars are divided on this question precisely because the Gospel of Matthew contains evidence for both positions.

Matthew presents several indications that his audience was *extra muros*.[88] The readers embraced the absolute transcendence and supremacy of Jesus as the Christ, so that their identity was ultimately linked to his person, and everything else in their universe of thinking, including their Jewish background, was relativized and subordinated to him.[89] Specifically, they maintained Jesus' supremacy over the great symbols and institutions of Judaism: the temple (Mt 12:6), the prophets (Mt 12:41), the kingship and

---

[88] E.g., Stanton, *Gospel for a New People*, 113-45; Donald A. Hagner, "Matthew: Apostate, Reformer, Revolutionary?" *NTS* 49 (2003): 193-209; Kingsbury, *Matthew as Story*, 154-56 and *Matthew*, 101-3; Goulder, *Midrash and Lection*, 152; Ulrich Luz, *The Theology of the Gospel of Matthew* (New York: Cambridge University Press, 1995), 14-15; Petri Luomanen, *Entering the Kingdom of Heaven: A Study on the Structure of Matthew's View of Salvation*, WUNT, 2 Reihe, 101 (Tübingen: Mohr Siebeck, 1998), 263-65.

[89] This is emphasized especially by Hagner, "Matthew: Apostate, Reformer, Revolutionary?"

the wisdom tradition (Mt 12:42), and the law (Mt 5:17-48; 11:28-30; 18:20).[90] For them, the entire history of God's dealings with his people finds its fulfillment in him (Mt 1:1-17, and the repeated "fulfillment quotations" throughout the Gospel of Matthew). Further, Matthew presents the whole religious establishment, particularly the Pharisees and their scribes, who were especially associated with the synagogues, in a consistently negative way.[91]

Moreover, several have argued that the Gospel of Matthew contains hints of separation from the synagogue, particularly Matthew's repeated reference to "their" (αὐτῶν) synagogue,[92] whereas Mark and Luke generally read "the synagogue." But this consideration seems rather inconsequential, since it may reflect Matthew's historicization; the implied reader is clearly separate from the synagogues described in the story of Jesus, both in time and probably in place, whether the intended audience was attached to synagogues or not.[93] Much more significant are indications of participation in a separate religious organizational structure. The Matthean Jesus speaks of "the church," which is understood both as the communion of Christians generally (Mt 16:18-19) and local congregations (Mt 18:15-20); this latter passage describes in sketchy fashion certain operations within the local congregation.

---

[90]In Mt 11:28-30 Jesus suggests that discipleship to him replaces relationship to Torah, since Jews often spoke of taking on themselves the yoke of the law (m. 'Abot 3:5; m. Ber. 2:2). And in Mt 18:20 the statement that "where two or three are gathered together in my name, I am there among them" echoes a sentiment among the rabbis that applied to the law (m. 'Abot 3:2, 6).

[91]We find this negative presentation throughout the Gospel of Matthew, to the point that this claim hardly requires support or specific citation. But it is interesting that, in contrast to Mark and Luke, we find in the Gospel of Matthew no passage where the Pharisees or scribes are presented positively (though cf. Mt 23:1-3a, but then immediately Mt 23:3b-8); cf. Mk 12:28-34; Lk 10:25-28. Mark and Luke describe the man who approaches Jesus for the healing of his daughter as "a ruler of the synagogue," whereas Matthew identifies him simply as "a ruler" (Mt 9:18-26; Mk 5:21-43; Lk 8:40-56). True, a scribe does try to initiate discipleship with Jesus (Mt 8:18-20), but since, in the Gospel of Matthew, discipleship must be initiated by Jesus, Jesus rebuffs him. See Jack Dean Kingsbury, "On Following Jesus: The 'Eager' Scribe and the 'Reluctant' Disciple (Mt 8:18-20)," NTS 34 (1988): 45-59.

[92]Mt 4:23; 10:17; 12:9; 13:54; 23:34 (here, speaking to the Pharisees, "your synagogues"). But cf. "their synagogue" in Mk 1:39. For a critical analysis of the role of these passages in the attempt to determine the relation of the Matthean community to Pharisaic Judaism, see Anders Runesson, "Rethinking Early Jewish-Christian Relations: Matthean Community History as Pharisaic Intergroup Conflict," JBL 117 (2008): 117-23.

[93]Note that in Mt 11:1 Matthew speaks of "their cities." The same point obtains for the reference to "their scribes" in Mt 7:29 (though cf. "the scribes" in Mk 1:22).

On the other hand, it is possible to argue that the intended audience continues to participate in Jewish religious life, even to the point of functioning as a "sect" of Judaism.[94] As we saw above, the Matthean Jesus insists that the Pharisees and scribes "sit on Moses' seat," and therefore the twelve disciples, along with the crowds, are to "do whatever they teach you and follow it" (Mt 23:2-3). Further, in Matthew 17:24-28 Jesus urges his disciples to continue to pay the temple tax, expected of all practicing Jews. Of course, both Matthew 23:2-3 and Matthew 17:24-28 pertain to the disciples who followed Jesus during his earthly ministry, and it is debatable whether these passages represent historicization or contemporization. In addition, the intended audience is actively involved in evangelization of their fellow Jews (Mt 10:16-39; 23:34), which leads to punishment in the synagogues as severe as scourging and even death. The experience of these punishments points to an intended audience that continues to submit itself to the authority of the synagogue leadership.

When all the evidence is taken into account, it seems best to conclude that the intended audience was at one and the same time both "inside the walls" and "outside the walls." The descriptions of the internal life of the Christian community are decisive in favor of a separate ecclesial structure and identity. On the other hand, the Gospel of Matthew manifests clear indications of continuing participation in the life of the Jewish community. As a Methodist, it occurred to me that this situation may be analogous to the experience of early British Methodists, who participated both in Methodist "societies" while also identifying with, and remaining active within, the Church of England. I was gratified when I came across a reference to that very analogy by the Catholic scholar Ian Boxall.[95]

If, in fact, the audience of the Gospel of Matthew participated in "churches" that had their own internal dynamics, how were these churches structured,

---

[94]E.g., Andrew Overman, *Matthew's Gospel and Formative Judaism: The Social World of the Matthean Community* (Minneapolis: Fortress, 1990); Schuyler Brown, "Matthean Community"; Anthony J. Saldarini, "Boundaries and Polemics in the Gospel of Matthew," *BibInt* 3 (1995): 239-65, and *Matthew's Christian-Jewish Community* (Chicago: University of Chicago Press, 1994); Sim, *Apocalyptic Eschatology*, 182-221, and *The Gospel of Matthew and Christian Judaism: The History and Social Setting of the Matthean Community*, SNTW (New York: T&T Clark, 1998).

[95]Ian Boxall, *Discovering Matthew: Content, Interpretation, Reception* (Grand Rapids: Eerdmans, 2014), 68. See also France, *Evangelist and Teacher*, 101; Roger Mohrlang, *Matthew and Paul: A Comparison of Ethical Perspectives* (New York: Cambridge University Press, 1984), 130-31; Popa, *Allgegenwärtiger*, 397.

and more generally, what was the character of these communities? On two occasions Jesus mentions Christian "scribes." Insofar as Matthew 13:52 speaks of a "scribe who is trained" (μαθητεύσατε, literally "discipled") in the "kingdom of heaven" who "is like the master of a household who brings out of his treasure what is new and what is old" it is clear that Jesus is referencing persons who were skilled in combining understanding of the meaning of the Old Testament Scripture ("things that are old") with insight into the revelation in Christ ("things that are new"). In a sense, everyone who is discipled in the kingdom of heaven has at least a measure of this insight or understanding; and it is possible to translate this statement, "everyone discipled to be a scribe."[96] If so, this is a reference to disciples in general and does not specify a particular group of scribes among them.[97]

But in Matthew 23:34 Jesus speaks of scribes whom, along with prophets and sages, he will send (in the post-Easter period) to the Jews and especially Jewish leaders apparently for the purpose of evangelization. Thus these scribes have an external as well as an internal role: they make use of their extraordinary insight to proclaim to Jews and Jewish leaders the true meaning of God's revelation in the Old Testament as that revelation has come to fulfillment in Jesus and they do so as part of the mission of the church to Israel.

We have just seen that in Matthew 23:34 Jesus mentions "sages" and "prophets" along with "scribes." In rabbinic literature, scribes are often also labelled "sages," which may be simply an alternative designation for scribes.[98] The New Testament describes Christian prophets whom God has chosen to be his mouthpiece in order to proclaim God's will, purposes, and plans (e.g., Acts 11:27; 13:1; 21:10; Rom 12:6; 1 Cor 12:28-29; 14:1-32; Eph 4:11). The warnings against false prophets who *come to you* in sheep's clothing," prophesying in the name of Christ (Mt 7:15-23), may suggest that such persons mirror a legitimate class of prophets ("true prophets") among the readership. If so, these persons would have responsibility for both the

---

[96]Nolland, *Gospel of Matthew*, 570-71. Such an understanding corresponds well to the context of Mt 13, as well as to additional occurrences of μαθητεύω in Matthew.

[97]Orton, *Understanding Scribe*, 137-63, believes that this notion of the Christian scribe derives from the concept of the God-inspired scribe of Jewish apocalyptic, who has insight into the realities pertaining to the eschatological age of fulfillment.

[98]Davies and Allison, *Matthew*, 3:315.

nurture of persons within the church and evangelism toward those on the outside (cf. Mt 10:41). It is therefore possible that Matthew describes two groups (scribes and prophets) within the church who were especially endowed by God with gifts of insight into the revelation of God which they were to teach within the church and to proclaim to Jewish outsiders.[99]

Even if the community that Matthew envisions contained distinct subgroups with their own ministry functions, it is clear that the community was to be characterized by a lack of hierarchy. Although Peter is the first to be called (Mt 4:18-20; cf. Mt 10:2) and Jesus gives to Peter the "keys of the kingdom" (Mt 16:18-19), meaning the authority to teach commandments that will be binding on the community and thus required for entrance into the kingdom, later in the Gospel of Matthew we learn that the entire church shares in this responsibility (Mt 18:18-20). And in 23:8-12 Jesus demands that, in contrast to the Pharisees and scribes, disciples are to reject honorific titles and even official distinctions among themselves, out of a recognition of their common relationship to Jesus, who alone possesses special status. Indeed, in the Gospel of Matthew even "apostle" is not an honorific title and refers not to a distinct office, but rather to those who go forth, sent by Jesus, on a mission (Mt 10:1-42).[100] The term refers not just to the twelve (Mt 10:2-4), but also to other "laborers" who will be sent into the white fields of harvest (Mt 9:36-38). The disciples were to consider every person within their ranks as "brother/sister" (Mt 5:22-24, 47; 7:3-5; 12:46-50; 18:15, 21, 35; 23:8; 25:40; 28:10) and of inestimable value (Mt 18:10-14).

To what extent these instructions in Matthew 23:4-8 reflect the reality of the intended audience we cannot say. It is unclear whether these statements are prescriptive in a confirmatory direction, affirming and encouraging what was characteristic of the intended readers, or whether they are prescriptive in a corrective direction, urging a different way of thinking and behavior than was the case among the intended readers. If the former, they reflect the disdain for hierarchy among the original readers. If the latter, they

---

[99] Édouard Cothenet, "Les prophètes chrétiens dans l'Évangile selon saint Matthieu," in *L'Evangile selon saint Matthieu: Rédaction et Théologie*, ed. M. Didier, BETL 29 (Glemboux: Duculot, 1972), 281-308, argues for three groups of itinerant missionaries: "prophets" are proclaimers, "the righteous" are teachers of the way of righteousness, and "the wise" are scribes who are teachers of the law.

[100] In the Gospel of Matthew the term *apostle* (ἀπόστολος) reflects, and is subordinate to, the verb *send* (ἀποστέλλω). See Mt 10:5, 16.

would suggest quite the opposite, namely that the original audience was characterized by hierarchialism and the trappings of ecclesial office, a tendency that the writer was attempting to correct.

Thus we cannot be certain how well the intended audience embodied Matthew's vision of the Christian community. But it does seem that Matthew perceived a problem among his intended readership at the point of lawlessness, or at least laxness in obedience to the commands of the law as Jesus has interpreted God's law. Apparently, some among the readership concluded that part of the purpose of Jesus' coming was to free them from obedience to "the law and the prophets." Jesus warns against a view of realized eschatology that insists that with the coming of Jesus the Messiah God's demands as expressed in the Old Testament Scriptures have been rendered passé. In order to set the matter straight, Jesus affirms that he has come "not to abolish but to fulfill the law and the prophets" (Mt 5:17), and Jesus goes on to demonstrate that his fulfilling the law and the prophets involves not a softening of the commandments but, if anything, an intensification of them in the direction of addressing underlying motive over against merely overt compliance to the letter of the law (Mt 5:21-48).

Some among the readers may have come to believe that Jesus intended to relax the demands of God in the law because of Jesus' repudiation of the hyper-rigorous Pharisaic practices toward purity and sabbath, as reflected in the Pharisee's embrace of the "tradition of the elders" (Mt 15:1-20; cf. Mt 9:10-13; 12:1-14), and Jesus' (perhaps hyperbolic) insistence that even the fifth command in the Decalogue ("Honor your father and your mother") must be set aside if it interferes with discipleship to Jesus (Mt 8:21-22; but cf. Mt 19:16-19). In addition, the intended readership may have been inclined to adopt a measure of laxness toward obedience to God's law through the influence of certain "false prophets" who, especially by their behavior, communicated that "doing the will of the Father" was irrelevant for acceptance with God and Christ (7:13-23). These persons made the Christological confession ("Lord, Lord") and were successful in various forms of ministry in the name of Jesus, which may have made their appeal to the audience all the greater;[101] but they failed to realize that judgment will depend on doing

---

[101]It seems unnecessary to conclude, as many scholars have done, that these persons were enthusiasts who substituted their charismatic activity for any real attention to obedience to divine demands. See, e.g., Gerhard Barth, "Matthew's Understanding of the Law," in *Tradition and*

the will of the heavenly Father (Mt 7:21-23). Indeed, Matthew may have included an emphasis on end-time judgment throughout his Gospel precisely to warn the readership of the dangers of repudiating the divine demands as they have been brought to fulfillment in Jesus (e.g., Mt 3:7-12; 8:11-12; 13:24-30, 47-50; 25:31-46).

WHEN WAS THE GOSPEL COMPOSED?

The clearest patristic testimony regarding the date of the composition of the Gospel of Matthew comes from Irenaeus in a passage cited above to the effect that Matthew produced his Gospel "while Peter and Paul were preaching in Rome." This would put the date of the Gospel of Matthew prior to AD 63, which is most commonly identified as the year of Peter's death. While none of the other Fathers makes explicit reference to the date of the Gospel's composition, their comments suggest that they would be in at least general agreement with Irenaeus. Yet modern scholars, with a few exceptions, date the Gospel of Matthew anywhere from the late 60s to the late 80s. The major issue is whether Matthew was written before or after the destruction of Jerusalem in AD 70, an event which produced radical changes in Jewish and early Christian life.

Several considerations point to a post-70 date. First, the Gospel of Matthew describes great conflict with the Pharisees, a situation that may reflect the adversarial relationship between Pharisees and Christians that obtained in the period around the Council of Jamnia, which was held between AD 85 and 90, under the supervision of Rabbi Johanan ben Zakkai and (somewhat later) Gamaliel II.[102] Scholars have often maintained that it was at the Council of Jamnia that the Pharisees formally established their dominance in post-war Judaism over rival groups such as the Sadducees

---

Interpretation in Matthew, 59-164; Cothenet, "Les prophètes chrétiens," 300; Eduard Schweizer, "Observance of the Law and Charismatic Activity in Matthew," *NTS* 16 (1969-70): 213-30; Jean Zumstein, *La Condition du croyant dans l'évangile selon Matthieu* (Göttingen: Vandenhoeck & Ruprecht, 1977). The repeated "Lord" may point only to the depth of their commitment to make the christological confession, and the description of their activities is intended to show the dissonance between their ministerial success and their lack of compliance to God's law. For a summary of scholarly opinion regarding these persons, see Hagner, *Matthew 1-13*, 182-83.

[102]The classic argument for the connection between Matthew and Jamnia was set forth by William D. Davies, *The Setting of the Sermon on the Mount* (New York: Cambridge University Press, 1966), 256-315, though it was anticipated by von Dobschütz, "Matthew as Rabbi and Catechist," and Kilpatrick, *Origins*, 127-28.

(who had been essentially extirpated at the time of the destruction of the temple), the Essenes, the Zealots, and Christians. Many consider that the formal break with Christians is represented by the addition of a clause to the Eighteen Benedictions, a series of prayers which were developed at Jamnia and which every Jew was to recite three times a day. This clause, the *Birkath ha-Minim*, reads: "Let Nazarenes [Christians] and *minim* [heretics] be stricken out of the book of the living, and let them not be mentioned with the righteous." This *Birkath* is attributed to Samuel the Small who produced it at the time of Gamaliel II, who himself was in charge of Jamnia from 90 until 110.[103]

Scholars often claim that Pharisees are mentioned more often in the Gospel of Matthew than in Mark or Luke, suggesting a Pharisaic dominance in the religious landscape of Judaism that may actually have obtained only after 85 with Jamnia. They frequently insist that Matthew's strong denunciations against the Pharisees, including woes against "scribes, Pharisees, and hypocrites" (23:13-36), reflect the break with Pharisaic Judaism at the time of Jamnia. And they note that twice Matthew quotes Hos 6:6 ("I desire mercy and not sacrifice;" Mt 9:13; 12:7), a passage often employed at Jamnia.[104]

Yet the Pharisees are not significantly more prominent in the Gospel of Matthew than in the other Synoptics. It is true that Mark mentions the Pharisees only 13 times compared to Matthew's 28. But the difference is diminished when we remember that the Gospel of Matthew is significantly longer than Mark. And Luke mentions the Pharisees 27 times, almost as many occurrences as we find in Matthew.

Further, it is not clear that the Pharisees assumed a dominant position in Judaism only after 70. Josephus describes the Pharisees as dominant in Galilee before the war;[105] and several recent scholars have adduced evidence that supports Josephus' claim.[106] Indeed, Matthew's emphasis on contention with the Pharisees may actually reflect a time before a formal

---

[103] *Berakot* 28b-29a.
[104] This was a favorite verse of Johanan ben Zakkai, which led von Dobschütz, "Matthew as Rabbi and Catechist," 20, to opine that Matthew may have been an erstwhile disciple of ben Zakkai.
[105] Josephus, *Jewish War* 2.8.14; *Antiquities of the Jews* 18.1.3.
[106] E.g., Martin Hengel, *Judaism and Hellenism: Studies in their Encounter in Palestine During the Early Hellenistic Period*, 2 vols. (Philadelphia: Fortress, 1981), 1:175-218; Saldarini, *Pharisees, Scribes, and Sadducees*, 102-103; Ellis Rivken, *A Hidden Revolution: The Pharisees' Search for the Kingdom Within* (Nashville: Abingdon, 1978).

schism had occurred; the fact that Matthew describes confrontation with the Pharisees and punishment in the synagogues suggests that he envisions the church in significant contact with the Pharisees, over against a scenario in which they have been excluded from the synagogue, such as we find in John (9:22; 12:42; 16:2). In fact, the New Testament provides ample evidence of Pharisaic opposition to Christians before 70.[107]

In addition, the significance of the Council of Jamnia and the *Birkath ha-Minim* for the question of the relationship between Pharisees and Christians is in real doubt. The Council may have served as little more than a point along the way in the development of formative Judaism rather than playing a decisive role.[108] And the reference to "Nazarenes" in the *Birkath* is found in only two texts of the *Cairo Geniza* and may have been added only sometime after 150.[109] Thus, the original form of the *Birkath* might not have included an explicit reference to Christians at all. In the face of these cautions regarding Jamnia, the common employment of Hos 6:6 can be explained in other ways, including coincidence, that do not require a connection with the events at Jamnia.

The second rationale for a post-70 date is that Matthew contains arguably more vivid descriptions of the destruction of Jerusalem than do the other Synoptics, thus suggesting that the Gospel of Matthew contains actual recollections of that fateful event of 70. Most notably we find this statement in the parable of the wedding banquet: "The king was enraged. He sent his troops, destroyed those murderers, and burned their city" (22:7). This

---

[107] Note especially the persecution from the Pharisee, Saul of Tarsus: 1 Cor 15:9; Gal. 1:13; Phil. 3:5-6; 1 Tim 1:13; cf. Acts 7:57–8:3; 9:1-2, 13-14, 21; 22:3-5, 19; 26:9-11.

[108] Jack P. Lewis, "Jamnia (Jabneh), Council of," *ABD*, 3:634-37.

[109] Marvin R. Wilson, *Our Father Abraham: Jewish Roots of the Christian Faith* (Grand Rapids: Eerdmans, 1989), 67-102, concludes, "The Birkat ha–Minim did not mark any direct breach between synagogue and church" (65). See also Peter Schäfer, "Die sogenannte Synode von Jabne. Sur Trennung von Juden und Christen im ersten/zweiten Jh. N. Chr.," *Judaica* 31 (1975): 54-64, 116-24; Günter Stemberger, "Die sogenannte 'Synode von Jabne' und das frühe Christentum," *Kairos* 19 (1977): 14-21; R. Kimelman, "*Birkat Ha-Minim* and the Lack of Evidence for an Anti-Christian Jewish Prayer in Late Antiquity," in *Aspects of Judaism in the Graeco-Roman World*, ed. E. P. Sanders and A. I. Baumgarten (London: SCM, 1981), 2:226-44; Steven T. Katz, "Issues in the Separation of Judaism and Christianity After 70 CE: A Reconsideration," *JBL* 103 (1984): 43-76. Note also the contention of Douglas R. A. Hare, *The Theme of Jewish Persecution of Christians in the Gospel of St. Matthew* (New York: Cambridge University Press, 1967), 54-55, that the Birkath did not involve formal repudiation at all, but rather "self-exclusion." But cf. William Horbury, "The Benediction of the Minim and early Jewish-Christian Controversy," *JTS* 33 (1988): 19-61.

description, not found in Luke's version of the parable, seems out of place in the story of the parable, and contains details of the destruction of Jerusalem, particularly its burning; consequently, many scholars have insisted that it is *vaticinia ex eventu* (after the fact).

Yet this brief statement in the parable does not actually contain many details at all, and the ones that are present, including the reference to the burning of the city, were typical of warfare during that period and in fact are found in numerous accounts of conquest in both Jewish and Roman-Hellenistic sources.[110] Thus, even excluding the Gospels' claim that Jesus had predictive power,[111] anyone living at that time could have surmised that the destruction of Jerusalem (which was clearly anticipated by Jesus and the early Christians, according to the Gospel tradition) would have involved the burning of the city. Matthew may well have included this statement in the parable of the wedding guests in order to tie this parable to the parable of the wicked tenants, which immediately precedes the parable of the wedding guests and ends with a reference to putting "those wretches to a miserable death" (Mt 21:41).

Third, it has been argued that the Gospel of Matthew contains a rather developed Christology and ecclesiology that we would expect to find toward the end of the first century rather than around the middle of the century. In terms of ecclesiology, the Gospel of Matthew includes the word "church" (ἐκκλησία; Mt 16:17; 18:17) and describes the ongoing decision making within the church regarding requirements for kingdom entrance (Mt 16:18-19) and the process of church discipline (Mt 18:15-20). Yet the epistles of Paul, certainly produced before any of our Gospels, speak abundantly of the "church," both as a local congregation and as the universal body of believers (e.g., 1 Cor 10:32; 12:28; 15:9; Gal 1:13; Phil 3:6). And Paul's epistles are replete with references to offices (e.g., Phil 1:1) and procedures (e.g., 1 Cor 5) within the church. Indeed, if anything the ecclesiology of the Gospel of Matthew appears rather primitive; we have already observed that Matthew eschews distinct offices and hierarchical structures.

---

[110] Karl Heinrich Rengstorf, "Die Stadt der Mörder (Mt 22.7)," in *Judentum, Urchristentum, Kirche: Festschrift für Joachim Jeremias*, ed. Walther Eltester, BZNW (Berlin: Töpelmann, 1960), 106-29. Gundry, *Matthew*, 599-600, traces the language of Mt 22:7 to Is 5:24-25.

[111] Found, *inter alia*, in Jesus' predictions regarding the fall of Jerusalem in Mt 24; Mark 13; and Luke 21.

In terms of Christology, Matthew avoids such human touches as Mark's descriptions of Jesus' emotions,[112] or Mark's acknowledgement of the limitations of Jesus' knowledge,[113] in favor of highlighting the dramatic and supernatural elements surrounding Jesus (e.g., 27:51-55; 28:2-6). In the Gospel of Matthew Jesus is consistently addressed with the honorific title "Lord" (κύριος) by his disciples and persons of faith, thus reflecting the exalted confession of a developed Christology.[114] And only in Matthew do we find the "Trinitarian" baptismal formula: "baptizing them in the name of the Father and of the Son and of the Holy Spirit" (Mt 28:19).

Yet we find dramatic, supernatural elements in Mark (e.g., Mk 1:11; 15:33). And it is difficult to imagine a higher Christology than we encounter in Paul's epistles (including the honorific title "Lord"), all of them presumably written before any of our Gospels, where we also find the "trinitarian" formula (e.g., 2 Cor 13:14; cf. 1 Pet 1:1-2). Moreover, Matthew 11:27// Luke 10:22, which according to the two (four)-source hypothesis belongs to Q, the earliest strata of the Gospel tradition, reflects an extremely high Christology. All of this indicates that it is likely that what we consider "high Christology" developed alongside what we would think of as a lower Christology, with the result that it is hazardous to date New Testament materials on the basis of where they stand in a neat and simple trajectory from low to high Christology.[115]

But perhaps the major reason many scholars date Matthew after AD 70 involves their embrace of the two (four)-source hypothesis, according to which Matthew used Mark as one of his principal sources. Since, according to the testimony of Irenaeus, Mark was written after the death of Peter

---

[112] E.g., cf. Mk 10:14 and Mt 19:13-14; cf. Mk 10:21 and Mt 19:16-22; but cf. Jesus' compassion (Mt 9:36; 14:14; 15:32; 20:34) and sorrowfulness (Mt 26:38).

[113] E.g., cf., Mk 5:25-34 and Mt 9:18-22; though cf. Mt 24:36 and Mk 13:32.

[114] The word κύριος could be either an exalted title of honor ("Lord") or a term indicating only mild respect ("sir"). The fact that Jesus is addressed in Mark and Luke as κύριε indiscriminately by disciples, opponents, and others suggests that in those Gospels the word (at least often) means simply "sir."

[115] Thus Larry Hurtado, *One God, One Lord: Early Christian Devotion and Ancient Jewish Monotheism* (New York: T&T Clark, 1988), and *Lord Jesus Christ: Devotion to Jesus in Earliest Christianity* (Grand Rapids: Eerdmans, 2003); Richard Bauckham, *God Crucified: Monotheism and Christology in the New Testament* (Grand Rapids: Eerdmans, 1999); Daniel Boyarin, *Border Lines: The Partition of Judeo-Christianity* (Philadelphia: University of Pennsylvania Press, 2004); Richard Hays, *Reading Backwards: Figural Christology and the Fourfold Gospel Witness* (Waco, TX: Baylor University Press, 2016).

(around 63),[116] and since it would be necessary to allow several years for Mark's Gospel to circulate in the church before Matthew would have had opportunity to encounter it and make use of it as a source, it is believed that the Gospel of Matthew could not have been written before the mid-70s, at the earliest. Yet we see that this argument is built on a series of assumptions: *If* Markan priority is correct, and *if* Mark was composed around 65 or later,[117] and *if* Matthew made use of Mark as one of his sources, and *if* it required more than five years for Mark's Gospel to reach Matthew and for Matthew thereafter to forge his Gospel, *then* it follows that the Gospel of Matthew must have been written after 70. We saw above that Markan priority and Matthew's use of Mark may be likely, but they are not sure. And although Irenaeus testified that Mark was written after the death of Peter, Clement of Alexandria insisted that Mark produced his Gospel while Peter was still alive.[118] And the necessity of several years to pass between the appearance of Mark's Gospel and Matthew's use of Mark in his own composition is a mere guess.[119] Thus while each of these claims is plausible, and perhaps even likely, none of them is certain.

On the other hand, a number of indications suggest the Gospel of Matthew may have been composed before 70. First, the Gospel of Matthew contains both accusation and instruction regarding temple activities and specifically the altar of the temple (Mt 5:23-24; cf. Mt 23:16-22). The instruction is within the Sermon on the Mount, where Jesus is giving directives to his twelve disciples, with whom the implied reader identifies. And, as we shall see later, the Sermon on the Mount is one of the five great discourses in the Gospel of Matthew, and these five discourses are especially relevant to the post-Easter reader. Yet we must allow for the possibility of historicization here; we remember that although the

---

[116] Irenaeus, *Against Heresies* 3.1.1; Eusebius, *Ecclesiastical History* 5.8.2.

[117] Although most scholars date Mark around AD 65, suggestions have ranged from the 40s well into the 70s. See Donald Guthrie, *New Testament Introduction*, 4th ed. (Downers Grove, IL: InterVarsity Press, 1990), 88-89; Christopher B. Zeichmann, "The Date of Mark's Gospel Apart from the Temple and Rumors of War: The Taxation Episode (12:13-17) as Evidence," CBQ 79 (2017): 422-37.

[118] Eusebius, *Ecclesiastical History* 2:15.1-2; 6:14.6-7. See France, *Evangelist and Teacher*, 82-83.

[119] Streeter, *Four Gospels*, 503, 523-24, declares that we must allow at least ten years between Matthew's reception of Mark and the production of his own Gospel; but Hagner, *Matthew 1–13*, lxxiv, who adopts the two (four)-source hypothesis, insists that no extended period of time is necessary between the production of Mark's Gospel and Matthew's.

command to limit ministry to Israel is also directed to the twelve disciples and is found in the second great discourse (Mt 10:5-7), yet the Gospel makes it clear that such instruction does not pertain to the time of the reader (Mt 28:18-20).[120]

Second, while the relative prominence of the Pharisees in the Gospel of Matthew may indicate a post-70 date, we note that Matthew's inclusion of several references to the Sadducees not found in the other Synoptics may point to a pre-70 date, since the Sadducees had ceased to function as a party within Judaism after the destruction of the temple.[121] But we have already mentioned Matthew's desire on theological grounds to present the various religious leaders as forming a unified wall of opposition to Jesus. This theological *Tendenz* may have led Matthew to engage in this bit of historicization; if so, the repeated mention of the Sadducees would not have direct relevance for the matter of dating.[122]

Third, Matthew 17:24-27 raises the issue of paying the "half-shekel tax," levied on Jews for the purpose of supporting the operations of the Jerusalem temple. Naturally, this tax ceased with the destruction of the temple. Those who argue for a post-70 date point out that this tax was succeeded by a fee levied on Jews by the Romans to support the temple of Jupiter in Rome,[123] and thus the passage would have relevance for a post-70 readership. But Matthew 17:24-27 intimates that the disciples, like Jesus, are free from the tax because they are "sons" of the king (God) who is worshiped in the temple. It is hard to imagine that the Matthean Jesus would suggest that his disciples are sons and daughters of Jupiter.[124]

---

[120]The point of this passage is clearly the underlying principle that integrity of relationship in the face of anger is more important than liturgical duties. It has to do with the problem of anger (Mt 5:21-22) and not specifically with the process of temple offerings. The reader would have understood and gained direction from the underlying principle whether or not the temple was still standing.

[121]The Gospel of Matthew contains seven references to the Sadducees (Mt 3:7; 16:1, 6, 11, 12; 22:23, 34), while Mark and Luke have one occurrence each (Mk 12:18; Lk 20:27).

[122]Matthew's unique references to the Sadducees are clustered in Mt 16, with the exception of Mt 22:34, which picks up on the earlier reference in Mt 22:23.

[123]Josephus, *Jewish War* 7.218.

[124]William G. Thompson, *Matthew's Advice to a Divided Community: Mt. 17:22-18:35*, AB (Rome: Biblical Institute Press, 1970), 67-68, indicated that the temple tax may have been succeeded, later, by a fee for the support of Jamnia. But, as Thompson admits, given Matthew's attitude to the Pharisaic authorities it is hard to believe that Matthew would urge his readers to contribute to the business of Jamnia.

Yet, as we shall see when we discuss the interpretation of this passage, Matthew 17:24-27 may be an "object lesson" to the readers, urging them to avoid causing a fellow disciple to stumble by insisting on their own rights.[125] The passage immediately precedes the "community discourse" and the word translated "cause offense" in Matthew 17:27 (σκανδαλίζομαι) appears also at Matthew 18:6 (with the noun form in Mt 18:7) in a passage encouraging humility and warning against doing anything that might cause one of these "little ones who believe in me" to stumble (Mt 18:6). Alternatively, the passage may be intended to communicate the general point that disciples should avoid causing unnecessary offense to Jews as they attempt to evangelize them. If, then, the passage is meant to convey the principle of non-offense, either toward other disciples or toward Jews who otherwise might be won to the gospel, the instructional point of the passage for the implied reader would not be the half-shekel tax at all, and the passage would have no bearing on the date of the Gospel of Matthew.

Fourth, Matthew 24:15-20 urges readers to "flee to the mountains" when they see the desolating sacrilege spoken by Daniel just before the destruction of Jerusalem; yet we know that just before Jerusalem's destruction Christians escaped not to the mountains but to Pella.[126] Moreover, this passage describes the desolating sacrilege as erected before the destruction of the temple, whereas we know that the placing of the Roman eagle in the temple area occurred at the destruction of the temple. If Matthew were writing after 70 would he have included these statements without altering them to fit the actual events? Of course, since this Matthean passage corresponds to its parallel in Mark, Matthew may simply be repeating the Gospel tradition he inherited, leaving it unaltered with a view toward allowing his readers to draw significance from the underlying principle.

But Matthew has not only "Pray that your flight not be in winter" (Mt 24:20) like Mark but includes the additional phrase "nor on the Sabbath." If Matthew has added "on the Sabbath," it may suggest that he was providing further instruction relevant to his readers who will need to flee from Jerusalem's devastation. Yet Matthew may have added (or

---

[125]David E. Garland, "Matthew's Understanding of the Temple Tax," in *Treasures New and Old: Recent Contributions to Matthean Studies*, ed. David R. Bauer and Mark Allan Powell, SBLSS 1 (Atlanta: Scholars, 1996), 69-98.
[126]Eusebius, *Ecclesiastical History* 3.5.

maintained) this reference to the sabbath in order to enforce the general principle that disciples, under any circumstances, should avoid causing unnecessary offense, either to other disciples who may have scruples regarding Sabbath observance (cf. Mt 18:5-14) or to Jews who might otherwise be evangelized (Mt 17:24-27).

Fifth, in Matthew 24:29 Matthew is unique in inserting the word *immediately* to the phrase "after the tribulation of those days," which has led some scholars to conclude that Matthew envisions the Second Coming of Christ occurring immediately after the destruction of the temple. Since anyone writing after 70 would know that such did not happen, the inclusion of the word *immediately* suggests that Matthew wrote before the temple's destruction.[127] Yet this conclusion assumes both that Matthew 24:29-31 is intended to describe the Second Coming and that "the tribulation of those days" refers to the destruction of the temple.[128] But as we shall see below in our **interpretation** section, it is more likely that Matthew 24:29-31 continues the description, in apocalyptic terms, of the destruction of the temple.[129]

The *terminus ad quem* for the composition of the Gospel of Matthew is clear; the Gospel of Matthew must have been written before AD 100, since both Ignatius and the writer of the *Didache* knew it. But on the basis of our analysis the *terminus a quo* is less certain. The evidence is sufficiently ambiguous and conflicting that we cannot say with confidence whether the Gospel of Matthew was composed before or after the destruction of Jerusalem. We have no compelling reason to exclude the possibility of a pre-70 date, and we have seen nothing to require a date in the late 80s or 90s. Thus, we can conclude that the Gospel of Matthew was probably composed sometime between 65 and 85. This range may seem broad, but any more

---

[127]Gundry, *Matthew*, 603-4. Donald A. Hagner, "Determining the Date of Matthew," in *Jesus, Matthew's Gospel and Early Christianity: Studies in Memory of Graham Stanton*, ed. Daniel M. Gurtner, Joel Willitts, and Richard Burridge (New York: T&T Clark, 2011), 76-92, goes so far as to say that this addition of "immediately" caused him to rethink the dating of the Gospel of Matthew and to shift from post-70 to a pre-70 position.

[128]Many scholars believe it describes the Second Coming; e.g., Floyd V. Filson, *The Gospel According to St. Matthew*, BNTC (London: Adam and Charles Black, 1960), 256; Sim, *Apocalyptic Eschatology*, 168-69; Ulrich Luz, *Matthew 21–28*, Hermeneia (Minneapolis: Fortress, 2005), 200.

[129]E.g., Jeffrey A. Gibbs, *Jerusalem and Parousia: Jesus' Eschatological Discourse in Matthew's Gospel* (St. Louis: Concordia, 2000), 178; France, *Gospel of Matthew*, 922; David E. Garland, *Reading Matthew: A Literary and Theological Commentary on the First Gospel* (New York: Crossroad, 1993), 238.

specific dating would involve a focus on one set of data to the neglect or at least downplaying of other data.[130]

WHERE WAS THE GOSPEL WRITTEN?

As we saw above, patristic testimony suggests that the Gospel of Matthew was composed in Palestine, perhaps around Jerusalem. But a critical analysis of this testimony indicates that this was probably a guess on the part of the early church, based on the Jewishness of the Gospel of Matthew and the belief of these Fathers that it was composed in Hebrew, that is, in Aramaic, which was the language of the Jewish people in Palestine.[131] Conversely, the fact that we know the Gospel of Matthew was originally composed in Greek may argue against a Palestinian origin. It will be remembered that Eusebius claimed that it originated in Caesarea,[132] a view recently reprised by Benedict T. Viviano, but with little compelling evidence.[133]

The consideration that the Gospel of Matthew presents the ministry of Jesus as exclusive to Jews (e.g., Mt 10:5; 15:24) but includes anticipation of inclusion of Gentiles (e.g., Mt 8:11; 28:18-20) may suggest that the Gospel of Matthew was composed in a location where the church was originally and perhaps still primarily Jewish but with openness to evangelistic ministry to Gentiles, and possibly contained a significant Gentile contingency within its ranks. As one canvasses the New Testament for candidates, one is struck by Syrian Antioch as a possibility. The Book of Acts indicates that the church at Antioch was composed of both Jews and Gentiles ("Hellenists"), and that the Antiochene church was committed to serious internal instruction (cf. Mt 28:20, and the five great discourses in the Gospel) as well as

---

[130]Thus also Guthrie, *Introduction*, 53-56.

[131]Patristic statements regarding the Palestinian origin of the Gospel of Matthew are consistently linked to claims regarding Jewish addressees and the Hebrew (Aramaic) language of the Gospel of Matthew.

[132]Eusebius wrote of an Aramaic Matthew, housed in the library at Caesarea, which suggests that he was not referencing our Greek Gospel of Matthew, and indeed raises suspicions that he may have been confusing the Gospel of Matthew with another gospel, written in Aramaic, which purported to come from the hand of the apostle Matthew.

[133]Benedict T. Viviano, "Where Was the Gospel According to St. Matthew Written?" *CBQ* 41 (1979): 533-46, and *Matthew and His World: The Gospel of the Open Jewish Christians: Studies in Biblical Theology*, NovTOA (Göttingen: Vandenhoeck & Ruprecht, 2007), 23. See the critique of Viviano's proposal in Davies and Allison, *Matthew*, 1:141. Among others supporting a Palestinian provenance are Julius Schniewind, *Das Evangelium nach Matthäus*, 6th ed. (Göttingen: Vandenhoeck & Ruprecht, 1953), 1-9; and Wikenhauser, *Introduction*, 195-96.

evangelistic ministry to Gentiles (Acts 11:19-26; 13:1-3; 14:21–15:5). And Galatians 2:11-21 confirms the coalescence of Jews and Gentiles in the church at Antioch. Galatians further testifies to the importance of Peter at Antioch,[134] which corresponds to the prominence given to Peter in the Gospel of Matthew.

Burnett Hillman Streeter, at least, was impressed with these observations and offered what has come to be the classic argument for Antioch on the Orontes as the provenance of the Gospel of Matthew.[135] In addition to the considerations listed above, Streeter made two further points in support of Antiochene provenance. First, an anonymous Gospel would need the support of a major church in order to gain broad acceptance in the Christian community, and Antioch early became a center of emerging Christianity.[136] The other major churches, such as Rome, Ephesus, and Alexandria are ruled out because the Jewishness of the Gospel of Matthew does not accord with the overwhelmingly Gentile complexion of these other churches.[137] Second, Streeter noted that the Gospel of Matthew was apparently the only Gospel known and used by Ignatius and the *Didache* at the beginning of the second century. Ignatius certainly wrote from Antioch and the *Didache* likely came from there.

By far the majority of scholars have followed Streeter in locating the production of the Gospel of Matthew in Antioch, or at least in Syria. And, indeed, they have identified further evidence for a Syrian provenance. For example, the claim that Jesus was to be called a "Nazarene" (Mt 2:23) reflects, some say, the practice of Syrian Christians to refer to themselves by the same appellation.[138] And Matthew alone reports that Jesus' "fame spread throughout all Syria" (Mt 4:24). And some have suggested that Matthew's

---

[134]The precise role of Peter at Antioch is not clearly indicated in Galatians, and it is questionable that he was the founder and first bishop of the church at Antioch. For patristic testimony, see Glanville Downey, *A History of Antioch in Syria from Seleucus to the Arab Conquest* (Princeton: Princeton University Press, 1961), 281-87, 583-86.

[135]Streeter, *Four Gospels*, 500-27.

[136]This reflects Streeter's "Great Church Theory." Streeter assumed that it was necessary for each of the Gospels to be connected to a major church.

[137]Streeter excluded Caesarea because it was "the port of entry of Samaria," and it was unthinkable that a Gospel that contained the admonition "enter no town of the Samaritans" (Mt 10:5) would have emerged there.

[138]Most scholars simply repeat this assertion, e.g., Boxall, *Discovering Matthew*, 73; Luz, *Theology of the Gospel of Matthew*, 18; Gerd Theissen, *The New Testament: A Literary History* (Minneapolis: Fortress, 2012), 134.

numerous references to "city" (πόλις) suggests an urban readership, and Antioch was one of the largest cities in the world.

Of course, one could raise objections. For example, Acts presents Antioch as very much under the tutelage of Paul, and yet the Gospel of Matthew bears little evidence of direct Pauline influence.[139] In addition, the fact that internal evidence does not necessarily indicate that Gentiles constituted a significant portion of the readership, but that Gentile incorporation may have been only an aspiration or expectation, undercuts the need to identify the provenance with a mixed church, such as Antioch. Moreover, the consideration that Ignatius and the *Didache* cited from the Gospel of Matthew accords with the preference given to the Gospel of Matthew throughout the early church. Their bias toward the Gospel of Matthew was not unique, although the extent of their employment of the Gospel of Matthew to the relative neglect of the other Gospels is apposite. Further, Acts 24:5 makes it clear that "Nazarene" was a Christian self-designation not limited to Syria. Then, too, the single reference to Syria in Matthew 4:24, admittedly in a passage where we would not necessarily expect it and one unique to the Gospel of Matthew, actually proves little; the very next verse mentions crowds following Jesus from the Decapolis (another uniquely Matthean passage). And while the Gospel of Matthew mentions *city* twenty-six times compared to Mark's eight, the word occurs in Luke thirty-nine times. In any case, it is precarious to infer an urban readership from the number of references to *city* within a narrative.

In light of these questions regarding Syrian Antioch other possibilities have been offered. H. Dixon Slingerland has posited that the Gospel of Matthew was produced in the Decapolis. He insists that when the Gospel of Matthew speaks of the west side of the Jordan as "beyond the Jordan" (Mt 19:1) it suggests that the writer and his community lived to the east of the Jordan.[140] Yet "beyond the Jordan" in Matthew 19:1 may refer not to the west side but to the east side of the Jordan and indicate that Jesus wished to avoid Samaritan territory as he traveled from Galilee to Jerusalem.[141]

---

[139] Indeed, Kilpatrick, *Origins*, 129-30, insisted that the author of the Gospel of Matthew did not know any of Paul's epistles.

[140] H. Dixon Slingerland, "The Transjordanian Origin of St. Matthew's Gospel," *JSNT* 3 (1979): 18-29; also Luomanen, *Entering the Kingdom*, 275-77.

[141] So, e.g., Donald A. Hagner, *Matthew 14–28*, WBC (Dallas: Word, 1995), 543.

Kilpatrick thought Tyre or somewhere else on the seacoast of Phoenicia a preferred location for the provenance of the Gospel of Matthew, since (among other things) Matthew refers to the woman from Tyre and Sidon as a "Canaanite" (Mt 15:21), and "Canaan was still current as the Semitic equivalent of Phoenicia not so long before Matthew was written."[142] But Kilpatrick's arguments regarding the use of "Canaanite" in Matthew 15:21 are convoluted and unpersuasive, and most of his additional evidence pertains to Syria more generally. S. G. F. Brandon and Sief van Tilborg have suggested Alexandria;[143] but we have little evidence for a significant Jewish-Christian community in Alexandria during the first century. And J. Andrew Overman, convinced that the story of the Gospel essentially mirrors the situation of Matthew's church, argues that Matthew's tendency to go beyond Mark in limiting Jesus' ministry to Galilee and his dominant concern with disputations with the religious leaders indicate that the Gospel of Matthew was written in the Galilean cities of Tiberius or Sepphoris, where the Sanhedrin was known to hold court.[144] But clearly Overman carries transparency to an extreme and fails to take fully into account the necessary distinction between elements within a narrative and the situation of the readership.

Finally, we saw above that ancient biographies were often written for general audiences and that several scholars, most notably Richard Bauckham, have argued that our Gospels were likely produced for all Christians and not localized to particular communities.[145] But while these arguments are suggestive, they are not decisive. We have seen that we can identify in the Gospel of Matthew certain features that seem to reflect the character and conditions of the readership. In other words, Matthew does appear to have an audience complexion in mind. Yet it seems improbable that such a sophisticated and complex Gospel, whose production would require immense human investment, would be written for just one church or even a limited number of churches in a narrow geographical compass. No doubt several house

---

[142]Kilpatrick, *Origins*, 133. Davies and Allison, *Matthew*, 2:547, list a number of possible reasons for Matthew's calling this woman a "Canaanite." The Phoenician explanation is not among them.

[143]S. G. F. Brandon, *The Fall of Jerusalem and the Christian Church* (London: SPCK, 1951), 217-43; Van Tilborg, *Jewish Leaders*, 171-72.

[144]Overman, *Matthew's Gospel*, 150-61; also Runesson, "Rethinking," 106-7; and Aaron M. Gale, *Redefining Ancient Borders: The Jewish Scribal Framework of Matthew's Gospel* (New York: T&T Clark, 2005).

[145]Bauckham, *Gospels for All Christians*.

churches, each numbering no more than fifty, existed in Antioch.[146] Although Acts tells us that "a great number became believers" (Acts 11:21) and "a great many people were brought to the Lord" (Acts 11:24) in Antioch, these terms are relative and we really do not know how large the Christian community in Antioch was.[147] It is questionable whether the number of Christians in one city, even a city as large as Antioch, would be sufficient to serve as the complete audience for a Gospel like Matthew. Thus Stanton's solution, though impossible to prove, seems the most likely, namely that the Gospel of Matthew was written to a number of churches in a broad geographical area, perhaps even an entire region.[148]

On the basis of our analysis, it seems probable that this broad geographical area was Syria, or perhaps Syria and a number of surrounding areas. I use the word *probable* advisedly for, as we have seen, none of the evidence for location is decisive.[149]

I acknowledge that our examination of the circumstances of the composition of the Gospel of Matthew, including the sources employed, the author, the audience, and the date and place of writing, has emphasized the ambiguous and often conflicting character of the evidence, which has led to tentative conclusions. In this regard, these conclusions stand at the opposite end of the spectrum from the definitive pronouncements on these matters made by some scholars. It is understandable that scholars desire to present sure answers to these questions of critical introduction. But it is a virtue to accept limitations, including limitations of knowledge. And a confident tone is no substitute for definite facts or compelling arguments. Fortunately, a robust interpretation of the Gospel of Matthew is not dependent on indubitable answers to the questions we have pursued in this chapter. Although an ability to speak confidently regarding these background issues could at points enhance our understanding of the message of the Gospel of Matthew, our experience with the Book of Hebrews happily underscores the fact that

---

[146]Graham Stanton, "Revisiting Matthew's Communities," in *SBL 1994 Seminar Papers*, ed. Eugene H. Lovering Jr. (Atlanta: Scholars, 1994), 12.

[147]Downey, *History of Antioch*, 275-76.

[148]Stanton, *Gospel for a New People*, 51-53.

[149]Several scholars share this reserve on the matter of provenance. See, e.g., Davies and Allison, *Matthew*, 1:146, who refer to their conclusion of a Syrian provenance as "an educated guess"; and Ulrich Luz, *Matthew 1-7: A Commentary* (Minneapolis: Augsburg, 1989), 92, who declares that "Antioch is not the worst of the hypotheses."

we can learn a great deal about the message of a book without sure answers to such things as the identity of the writer or the time of writing.[150] Thus we will make use of the background knowledge we have been able to ascertain, while remaining content to accept the limitations of our information.

---

[150]Scholars divide almost evenly on the question of whether Hebrews was written before or after the destruction of Jerusalem.

4

SHAPE OF COMPOSITION

IF THE CIRCUMSTANCES OF COMPOSITION that we have examined in the last chapter offer limited help in our interpretation of the Gospel of Matthew, we find that the shape of the composition, or its literary structure, is critically important for the construal of the message of Matthew's Gospel. Yet no consensus exists regarding the structure of the Gospel of Matthew. The statement from Léonard Ramaroson, made nearly fifty years ago, remains true: "Everyone agrees the plan of Matthew is masterfully constructed—but the disagreement begins with trying to discern the lines of its fine architecture."[1] The purpose of this chapter is to describe briefly some of the major proposals for the structure of the Gospel of Matthew, identifying points of strengths and weaknesses in each, and to present, in a somewhat full fashion, the structural program that will serve as the framework for our interpretation of the Gospel.

HISTORY OF INVESTIGATION INTO MATTHEW'S STRUCTURE

Matthean scholarship has generated seven major proposals for the structure of the Gospel of Matthew.[2]

---

[1]My translation. The original reads: *De l'aveu de tous, le plan de Matthieu is soigneusement construit.—Mais le désaccord commence dès qu'il s'agit de determiner les lignes de la belle architecture.* Léonard Ramaroson, "La structure du premier Evangile," *ScEs* 26 (1974): 69.

[2]For a fuller treatment of the structure of the Gospel of Matthew, see David R. Bauer, *The Structure of Matthew's Gospel: A Study in Literary Design*, JSNT 31, BLitS 15 (Sheffield: Almond, 1988).

Geographical-chronological structural proposals. From the middle of the nineteenth century until around 1930 most scholars argued that the Gospel of Matthew was constructed according to geographical or chronological development. Those scholars who accepted the priority of the Gospel of Matthew and took it to be a "life of Jesus" whose purpose was to provide a stage-by-stage reportage of Jesus' activities naturally saw the Gospel of Matthew as a chronological account of Jesus' life that gave attention also to the geographical venues where he ministered. In this regard, Lagrange is typical:

> First Part: The Origin of the Christ, his peregrinations from Bethlehem to Nazareth (I-II)
>
> Second Part: The Investiture of the Messiah, Son of God (III,1-IV,11)
>
> Third Part: The Manifestation of the Christ in Galilee (IV,12-XIII,58)
>
> Fourth Part: Preamble to the foundation of the Church, at the edge of Galilee (XIV,1-XX,16)
>
> Fifth Part: Ministry at Jerusalem (XX,17-XXV)
>
> Sixth Part: The Passion and the Resurrection (XXVI-XXVIII)[3]

But scholars who embraced Markan priority and believed that Matthew had used Mark as his principle source also adopted this geographical-chronological structure. They argued that it was the Gospel of Mark, in its role as the earliest Gospel, that provided a life of Jesus; insofar as Matthew adopted Mark's framework as the basis for his own narrative Matthew had simply incorporated the geographical-chronological structure from Mark. Thus the outline from Willoughby C. Allen and L. W. Grensted:

> i-ii. Birth and Infancy of the Messiah
>
> iii.1-iv.11. Preparation for His Ministry (=Mk. i.1-13)
>
> iv.12-xv.20. Work and Teaching in Galilee (=Mk i.14-vii.23)
>
> xv.21-xviii.35. Work outside Galilee (=Mk vii.24-ix.50)

---

[3]Marie-Joseph LaGrange, *Évangile selon Saint Matthieu*, 7th ed. (Paris: Gabalda, 1948), xxv. My translation.

xix.1-xx.34. A Journey to Jerusalem (=Mk x)

xxi-xxviii. Last days of the Messiah's Life (=Mk xi.-xvi.8)[4]

As is obvious from these two outlines, scholars who divide the Gospel of Matthew according to geographical-chronological considerations do not agree where the major breaks occur. Most identify the beginning of the Galilean ministry at Mt 4:12, but some prefer Mt 4:17 or Mt 5:1.[5] They usually identify the beginning of the journey to Jerusalem at Matthew 19:1, but sometimes at Matthew 16:13, Matthew 16:21, or Matthew 17:1.[6] And some do not separate out the journey to Jerusalem.

More recent scholars have sometimes adopted this chronological-geographical structure because of their sense of theological significance in Matthew's employment of geography,[7] or because they, like their early

---

[4] Willoughby C. Allen and L. W. Grensted, *Introduction to the Books of the New Testament*, 3rd ed. (New York: T&T Clark, 1929), 23. A similar outline with corresponding passages from Mark can be found in Willoughby C. Allen, *A Critical and Exegetical Commentary on the Gospel According to S. Matthew*, 3rd ed. ICC (Edinburgh: T&T Clark, 1912), lxiii-lxiv.

[5] Beginning at Mt 4:12, see, e.g., Hans Conzelmann and Andreas Lindemann, *Arbeitsbuch zum Neuen Testament* (Tübingen: Mohr, 1975), 251; Alfred Durand, *Évangile selon Saint Matthieu: Traduction et Commentaire* (Paris: Beauchnesne et ses Fils, 1948), 1; Erich Klostermann, *Das Matthäus-Evangelium*, 4th ed., HNT (Tübingen: Mohr, 1971); LaGrange, *Matthieu*, xxvi-xxix; Max Meinertz, *Einleitung in das Neue Testament*, 5th ed. (Paderborn: Ferdinand Schöning, 1950), 167-68; Leon Morris, *The Gospel According to Matthew*, PNTC (Grand Rapids: Eerdmans, 1992), vi; Alfred Plummer, *An Exegetical Commentary on the Gospel According to Matthew* (London: Robert Scott, 1909), lxiii; Donald Senior, *Invitation to Matthew: A Commentary on the Gospel of Matthew with Complete Text from the Jerusalem Bible* (Garden City, NY: Doubleday, 1977), 15-16; Theodor Zahn, *Introduction to the New Testament*, 3 vols. (New York: T&T Clark, 1909 [1897]), 2:541. Beginning at Mt 4:17, see Henry Martin Battenhouse, *New Testament History and Literature* (New York: Thomas Nelson, 1937), 93; Alan Hugh McNeile, *The Gospel According to Matthew: The Greek Text with Introduction, Notes, and Indices* (London: Macmillan, 1938), xii; Adolf Jülicher, *Einleitung in das Neue Testament* (Freiburg: Akademische Verlagsbuchhandlung von J. C. B. Mohr, 1894), 1865; Theodore H. Robinson, *The Gospel of Matthew*, MNTC (London: Hodder and Stoughton, 1928), xix; Eduard Schweizer, *The Good News According to Matthew* (Atlanta: John Knox, 1975), 5. Beginning at Mt 5:1, see Samuel Davidson, *An Introduction to the Study of the New Testament: Critical, Exegetical, Theological*, 3rd ed., 2 vols. (London: Kegan Paul, Trench, Trübner, 1894), 1:345; Herbert Roux, *L'Évangile du Royaume*, 2nd ed. (Geneva: Labor et Fides, 1956).

[6] Beginning at Mt 19:1, see, e.g., Battenhouse, *New Testament History*, 93; Davidson, *Introduction to the Study*, 1:345; Durand, *Saint Matthieu*, 1; LaGrange, *Saint Matthieu*, xxiii; McNeile, *Matthew*, xii; Morris, *Matthew*, vii. Beginning at Mt 16:13, see, e.g., Klostermann, *Matthäus-Evangelium*, contents page. Beginning at Mt 16:21, see, e.g., Senior, *Invitation*, 15-16. Beginning at Mt 17:1, see, e.g., Robinson, *Matthew*, ix-xx.

[7] These scholars are often impressed with studies that emphasize the theological role of geography in Mark, and are inclined to see the same, or similar, theological significance in geographical references in the Gospel of Matthew, e.g., Ernest DeWitt Burton, "The Purpose and

twentieth-century predecessors, are enamored with Matthew's adoption of Mark.[8] Although some diversity of theological conclusions among these scholars exists, advocates of the chronological-geographical structure generally emphasize Jesus' role as the Christ, the royal Son of David, who fulfills his Messianic destiny by traveling from Galilee to Jerusalem where he is rejected by the Jews, or Jewish leaders, and crucified, but vindicated by God in the resurrection.[9] Correspondingly, they suggest that the structure of the Gospel of Matthew as well as the repetition of fulfillment quotations indicate that Matthew's purpose was to assure Jewish Christians that Jesus was in fact the Christ despite his rejection by the Jews and that, consequent on the general Jewish rejection of Jesus at Jerusalem, the kingdom has now been delivered to a new people composed of Jews and Gentiles who will produce its fruit.[10]

The consideration that most recent scholars have abandoned the geographical-chronological structural program indicates that it contains significant problems. As we noted above, the nineteenth-century assumption that our Gospels, either Matthew and/or Mark, are similar to modern biographies, with their concern for strict chronological reportage and emphasis on geographical setting, is contrary to what we know of the nature and purpose of the Gospels. Moreover, it is inappropriate to ascertain the structure of one Gospel by appeal to another, as do those scholars who assume that because Matthew (presumably) made use of Mark his Gospel must share the same structural program. Further, even if Matthew did employ Mark as a source, there is every reason to believe that Matthew did more than simply repeat the structure he found in Mark. (If Matthew had been satisfied with Mark's Gospel,

---

Plan of the Gospel of Matthew," *BW* 11 (1898): 37-44, 91-101; Conzelmann and Lindemann, *Arbeitsbucht*, 251.

[8] A recent advocate of this chronological-geographical breakdown on the basis of Matthew's use of Mark is Craig A. Evans, *Matthew*, NCBC (New York: Cambridge University Press, 2012), 9-11: "Perhaps it is better to view Matthew's arrangement and structure as an expansion and adaptation of Mark's relatively simple outline of a ministry in Galilee, then a journey south to Judea and Jerusalem, and finally the Passion in Jerusalem" (9). Evans is actually a bit inconsistent, since he adopts the notion of "mixed structure," and he identifies his main divisions according to shifts in biographical emphases but divides his subunits according to the alternation between narrative and discourse, along the lines of Bacon.

[9] A recent advocate of the geographical-chronological breakdown who is explicit in connecting it with the theme of Jesus' rejection is Sebastian Mullooparambil, *Macrostructure of Matthew's Gospel* (Bangalore: Dharmaram, 2011).

[10] E.g., Meinertz, *Einleitung*, 168-69; Plummer, *Matthew*, xxv-xxxi.

why would he have produced his own?) Indeed, as we shall see below, other scholars have used Matthew's employment of Mark as the basis for emphasizing those structural features that distinguish the Gospel of Matthew from Mark's Gospel and consequently infer a completely different understanding of the structure of the Gospel of Matthew. Yet these studies have reminded us that the Gospel of Matthew is above all a story about Jesus, and they have pointed to the role of geographical setting (especially Galilee and Jerusalem) in the Gospel of Matthew.

Conceptual structural proposals. Some scholars have attempted to define the Gospel's structure according to a theme or central idea around which Matthew has organized his materials. These scholars actually deny any sort of topical arrangement or discrete divisions within the Gospel of Matthew, in favor of the notion that Matthew has constructed his Gospel around an idea or purpose within his own mind. Most of these scholars identify this central concept as Matthew's view of salvation history and insist that the whole organization of the Gospel reflects Matthew's desire to understand salvation history as consisting of three periods: Israel, Jesus, and church. These scholars differ, however, in their understanding of the specific way Matthew presents his view of salvation history and therefore in the precise structuring of the Gospel of Matthew.[11]

The primary difficulty with this approach is that it denies the basic literary principle that readers construe meaning on the basis of the narrative development of the story. The very nature of literary texts, and particularly narrative texts, is that the sequential ordering of material is crucial to the communication of sense. It may in fact be said that these scholars do not address so much the structure of the *Gospel* as the structure of Matthew's *thought*. The structure of Matthew's thought, or put another way, his theology, is a preeminently important area of inquiry, and one which we will

---

[11]Georg Strecker, *Der Weg der Gerechtigkeit* (Göttingen: Vandenhoeck & Ruprecht, 1975), and "The Concept of History in Matthew," *JAAR* 35 (1967): 219-30; Wolfgang Trilling, *Das Wahre Israel: Studien zur Theologie des Matthäus-Evangeliums* (München: Kösel, 1964); Rolf Walker, *Die Heilsgeschichte im ersten Evangelium* (Göttingen: Vandenhoeck & Ruprecht, 1967); Hubert Frankemölle, *Jahwe-Bund und Kirche Christi: Studien zur Form- und Traditionsgeschichte des "Evangeliums" nach Matthäus*, Neutestamentliche Abhandlungen/Neue Folge 10 (Münster: Aschendorff, 1974); William G. Thompson, *Matthew's Advice to a Divided Community: Mt. 17:22-18:35*, AB (Rome: Biblical Institute Press, 1970), 259-62, and "An Historical Perspective in the Gospel of Matthew," *JBL* 93 (1974): 243-62; John P. Meier, "Salvation History in Matthew: In Search of a Starting Point," *CBQ* 37 (1975): 203-13.

pursue in due time. But the theology of a document is inferred, *inter alia*, from its literary structure and is not a substitute for literary structure.

On the other hand, these scholars have pointed to an important fact regarding literary structure, namely that is not limited to linear progression of material or discrete divisions of a book, but rather also involves the dynamic interplay of themes, motifs, and other elements throughout a document. In other words, literary structure necessarily involves the identification of discrete units, but is not restricted to such identification. We must note also how various elements interact with one another throughout a book, even when such interaction transcends the movement from one block of material to another. In addition, these scholars have properly raised the question of the importance of salvation history within the Gospel of Matthew, and they have pointed to the relationship between the structure of the Gospel of Matthew and Matthew's view of salvation history.

Enumeration outlines. Some scholars offer as their structural proposal an outline of the Gospel of Matthew that does little more than list the topics discussed in sequence throughout the Gospel of Matthew. These lists are similar to tables of contents at the beginning of a book. They actually involve no real structural analysis whatsoever, and, in fact, typically reflect a dismissal of the importance of literary structure for interpretation. Thus, Donald Senior presents the following "suggested structure":

The origins of Jesus and His Mission (1:1–4:11)

Jesus: Messiah in Word and Deed (4:12–10:42)

Responding to Jesus: Rejection and Understanding (11:1–16:12)

The Journey to Jerusalem (16:13–20:34)

In the Holy City: Conflict, Death, Resurrection (21:1–28:15)

Finale (28:16–20)[12]

I have presented just the headings to Senior's outline; he includes a brief descriptive paragraph for each unit. But Senior makes no attempt to relate these units to one another, either through the headings or through his paragraph-length descriptions. He presents each as essentially separate and

---

[12]Donald Senior, *The Gospel of Matthew* (Nashville: Abingdon, 1997), 31-32.

isolated. In fact, his concern is actually Matthew's use of Mark; Senior discusses each of these units as to how they either mirror Mark or point to Matthew's redaction of Mark.

Senior explicitly dismisses the significance of literary structure for understanding the Gospel of Matthew when he insists that "It is unlikely that any single formal structure or single set of structures will suddenly unlock the master plan of the Gospel of Matthew. The composition of a narrative is more organic, more subtle, and more complex than the kind of literary design one might give to the formulation of a strategic plan or to a closely reasoned philosophical paper."[13] He then goes on to suggest that the structure of the document is not ultimately significant because of the presence of other kinds of literary features, such as characterizations and settings. Yet it does not follow that because the structure of the Gospel of Matthew may be more subtle and complex that it is not coherent and discernable, or that it is incapable of specific analysis; nor does it follow that the existence of other literary features diminishes the role played by structure for understanding. In fact, characters and settings are placed within the dynamic movement of the text, in other words its structure, which largely gives them meaning.

Similarly, in his massive commentary, John Nolland implicitly dismisses the importance of literary structure. He offers no structural discussion but presents only a topical outline of twenty-two main sections, with headings that are not even grammatically consistent.[14]

Senior and Nolland seem to assume that structure is reducible to an outline that rehearses sequential content and is therefore of marginal assistance for interpretation. Their failure to deal seriously with structure because of a limited view of structure encourages us to consider a broader understanding of structure, one that includes not only the identification of blocks of material on the basis of major themes but also organizational dynamics within the book that transcend the division of the book into discrete sections.[15]

---

[13]Senior, *Gospel of Matthew*, 30-31.
[14]John Nolland, *The Gospel of Matthew*, NIGTC (Grand Rapids: Eerdmans, 2005), 44-62. Some of his headings are nominal clauses, others participial clauses, and still others declarative statements.
[15]Others who present the structure of the Gospel of Matthew as essentially an enumerative outline include David Hill, *The Gospel of Matthew*, NCB (Grand Rapids: Eerdmans, 1972), 44-48; Schweizer, *Good News*, 5-10.

Alternating narrative-discourse pattern. The appearance in 1930 of *Studies in Matthew*, by Benjamin Wisner Bacon, marked a watershed in the history of investigation into Matthew's structure, for his view that the structure of the Gospel of Matthew is characterized by the alternation of narrative and extended speeches, or discourses, became dominant at least in the English-speaking world for the next fifty years.[16] Bacon identified five great discourses: the Sermon on the Mount (Mt 5:1–7:28); the missionary discourse (Mt 10:1-42); the parable discourse (Mt 13:1-52); the community discourse (Mt 18:1-35); and the eschatological discourse (Mt 23:1–25:46), each one ending with the formulaic statement "when Jesus had finished these sayings" (καὶ ἐγένετο ὅτε ἐτέλεσεν τοὺς λόγους) or the like. Bacon judged this formulaic saying in each case to be terminating, that is, to mark the end of one division and the beginning of the next. Accordingly, Bacon divided the body of the Gospel of Matthew (Mt 3:1–25:46) into "five books," each beginning with narrative and concluding with a great discourse. To the body of his Gospel Matthew has affixed a "preamble" (Mt 1:1–2:23) and an "epilogue" (26:1–28:20). The following is Bacon's outline:

The Preamble (1:1–2:23)

Book First. Discipleship (3:1–7:28)

    Division A. Introductory Narrative (3:1–4:25)

    Division B. The Discourse (5:1–7:28)

Book Second. Apostleship (8:1–10:42)

    Division A. Introductory Narrative (8:1–9:38)

    Division B. The Discourse (10:1-42)

Book Third. The Hiding of the Revelation (11:1–13:53)

    Division A. Introductory Narrative (11:1–12:50)

    Division B. The Discourse (13:1-53)

Book Fourth. Church Administration (14:1–18:35)[17]

---

[16] Bacon's full discussion of Matthew's structure in this book was anticipated in his earlier article, "The 'Five Books' of Moses Against the Jews," *Expositor* 15 (1918): 56-66.

[17] Bacon does not account here, or later in the book, for Mt 13:54-58.

Division A. Introductory Narrative (14:1–17:27)

Division B. The Discourse (18:1-35)

Book Fifth. The Judgment (19:1–25:46)

Division A. Introductory Narrative (19:1–22:45)

Division B. The Discourse (23:1–25:46)

Epilogue (26:1–28:20)[18]

Bacon insisted that he was not the first to identify this fivefold division in the Gospel of Matthew, citing lines of iambic verses, which Rendel Harris dated from the second century: "Matthew curbs the audacity of the Jews / Checking them in five books as it were with bridles."[19] Although Bacon argued that these lines referred to the Gospel of Matthew,[20] Harris took them to pertain not to the Gospel of Matthew but to a book of testimonies to which Papias referred.[21] Bacon cites also Godet in support of the fivefold division but, as Bacon acknowledges, Godet was not speaking of the Gospel of Matthew but just of the five discourses which he took to be the "proto-Matthew" described by Papias.[22] In my survey of the history of investigation into Matthew's structure going back to the middle of the nineteenth century I have been able to identify no one before Bacon who clearly identified a fivefold structure of the Gospel as we have it on the basis of the alternation between narrative and discourse.[23]

In fact, Bacon developed his understanding of Matthew's structure through a comparison of the Gospel of Matthew with the Gospel of Mark. Assuming Markan priority, Bacon sought to discover how Matthew differed from Mark so as to uncover Matthew's unique perspective and contribution

---

[18]Benjamin Wisner Bacon, *Studies in Matthew* (New York: Henry Holt, 1930), xxii-xxiii.
[19]Bacon, *Studies in Matthew*, xv-xvi. The translation comes from Morton S. Enslin, "'The Five Books of Matthew': Bacon on the Gospel of Matthew," *HTR* 24 (1931): 67.
[20]This is the main argument of Bacon, "Five Books of Matthew." Enslin, "Five Books," seeks to support Bacon's contention.
[21]Rendel Harris, *Testimonies* (New York: Cambridge University Press, 1920). See also Marianne Meye Thompson, "The Structure of Matthew: A Survey of Recent Trends," *SBibTheol* 12 (1982): 197-98.
[22]Frédéric Louis Godet, *Introduction to the New Testament*, 2 vols. (New York: T&T Clark, 1899), 2:182.
[23]I acknowledge that I may have overlooked an earlier espousal of this view. If so, I would be grateful for any correction.

to the New Testament. He noted that what most clearly distinguished the Gospel of Matthew from Mark was the presence of the five great discourses we have just described. He observed that Matthew had taken over most of Mark's narrative and had supplemented it with a large amount of discourse material, which he combined into five great speeches.[24]

But Bacon's purpose was not simply to track Matthew's redactional activity; he wanted to ascertain the theological motive behind Matthew's editorial work. He noted that the Bible and extrabiblical Jewish literature contained many written works divided into five parts,[25] but he saw a clear connection between "the five books of Jesus" in the Gospel of Matthew and the five books of Moses that constitute the Pentateuch. Bacon insisted that even as the five books of the Pentateuch began with narrative and concluded with teaching material—more specifically, legal instruction—so the five books of Jesus in the Gospel of Matthew commence with narrative and culminate with the teaching of legal instruction. This structural observation, connecting the Gospel of Matthew with the law of Moses in the Pentateuch, along with several specific redactional changes Matthew introduced to his Markan source,[26] led Bacon to conclude that Matthew's church was troubled by lawlessness or antinomianism. Bacon further insisted that Matthew, a converted rabbi and legalist, attempts to address this problem by presenting Jesus as a teacher, and indeed, as a new lawgiver or a new Moses, who presents a new law to his people, one that differs from that of the scribes and Pharisees only in that it requires "greater inwardness and greater emphasis on 'good works.'"[27] Matthew reinforced the urgency of submitting to this

---

[24]He also supplemented Mark with some additional narrative material, most notably the birth and infancy narrative in Mt 1:1–2:23 and augmentations to the passion and resurrection narratives in Mt 26:1–28:20. With the exception of the Sermon on the Mount, the great discourses in the Gospel of Matthew have a Markan core. But the point stands that, assuming Markan priority, even in these latter discourses Matthew seems to be responsible for combining the Markan core with the additional material from another source(s).

[25]Bacon, "'Five Books,'" 62. Among others, note the Psalms, Lamentations, the Megilloth, and 1 Enoch. See William D. Davies, *The Setting of the Sermon on the Mount* (New York: Cambridge University Press, 1966), 15-16.

[26]E.g., addition of Mt 5:17-20; alterations in Mt 19:16-22 in the direction of requiring compliance to the commandments of the law; Jesus' final statement in Mt 28:20, "teaching them to observe all that I have *commanded* you"; and the addition of the word *lawlessness* (ἀνομία) at three points (Mt 7:13-23; 13:41; 24:10-12). See Benjamin Wisner Bacon, "Jesus and the Law: A Study of the First 'Book' of Matthew," *JBL* 47 (1928): 203-31.

[27]Bacon, *Studies in Matthew*, 80.

new torah by repeated threats of apocalyptic judgment.[28] Clearly, Bacon's model emphasizes ecclesiology and (future) eschatology over Christology.

Many have adopted Bacon's views on the structure of the Gospel of Matthew. Yet differences in details exist among these scholars. Some have argued that Matthew 23:1-39 is not part of the eschatological discourse and belongs either with the preceding narrative or is a separate (sixth) discourse.[29] A few scholars have even opted for seven discourses.[30] Differences exist also over the relationship between the discourses and the surrounding narrative material. Some agree with Bacon that the discourses belong with the preceding narrative.[31] But others insist that they are linked

---

[28] Bacon, "Jesus and the Law," 205.
[29] Those who agree with Bacon that Mt 23 belongs to the eschatological discourse include Peter Fiedler, *Das Matthäus-evangelium* (Stuttgart: Kohlmammer, 2006), 342-80; Robert H. Gundry, *Matthew: A Commentary on His Handbook for a Mixed Church Under Persecution*, 2nd ed. (Grand Rapids: Eerdmans, 1994), 453; Donald Guthrie, *New Testament Introduction*, 4th ed. (Downers Grove, IL: InterVarsity Press, 1990), 59; David P. Scaer, *Discourses in Matthew: Jesus Teaches the Church* (St. Louis: Concordia, 2004), 343-93; Grant R. Osborne, *Matthew*, ZECNT (Grand Rapids: Zondervan, 2010), 41-43; Edwin D. Freed, *The New Testament: A Critical Introduction* (Belmont, CA: Wadsworth, 2001), 147-62; David A. DeSilva, *An Introduction to the New Testament: Context, Methods & Ministry Formation* (Downers Grove, IL: InterVarsity Press, 2004), 239-40. Those who insist that Mt 23 belongs to the preceding narrative material include Dale C. Allison Jr., *Studies in Matthew: Interpretation Past and Present* (Grand Rapids: Baker Academic, 2005); Raymond E. Brown, *Introduction to the New Testament* (New York: Doubleday, 1997), 172, 193-99; Karl E. Levesque, "Quelques Procédés Litteraires de Saint Matthieu," *RB* 25 (1916): 387-405; Alfred Loisy, *The Origins of the New Testament* (London: George Allen and Unwin, 1950), 26-28; John P. Meier, *Matthew*, NTM 3 (Wilmington, DE: Michael Glazier, 1980), xii; Jean Radermakers, *Au fil de l'évangile selon saint Matthieu*, 2 vols. (Louvain: Heverlee, 1972), 2:21-22; Philippe Rolland, "From the Genesis to the End of the World: The Plan of Matthew's Gospel," *BTB* 2 (1972): 155-76; David L. Turner, *Matthew*, BECNT (Grand Rapids: Baker, 2008), 10; Charles H. Talbert, *Matthew*, Paideia (Grand Rapids: Baker Academic, 2010), 6-8; Donald A. Carson, "Matthew," in *The Expositor's Bible Commentary*, ed. Frank E. Gaebelein and Walter C. Kaiser Jr., 12 vols. (Grand Rapids: Zondervan, 1984), 8:50-57. Those who consider Mt 23 a separate sixth discourse include Shirley Jackson Case, "The Origin and Purpose of the Gospel of Matthew," *BW* 34 (1909): 391; Herman Ridderbos, *Matthew's Witness to Jesus Christ: The King and the Kingdom* (New York: Association, 1958); Karl Hermann Schelkle, *Das Neue Testament: Seine literarische und theologische Geschichte*, 3rd ed. (Kevelaer, Rhineland: Butzon & Bercker, 1966), 55; Ben C. Witherington III, *Matthew*, SHBC (Macon, GA: Smyth & Helwys, 2006), 15-16.
[30] E.g., Robert G. Gromacki, *New Testament Survey* (Grand Rapids: Baker, 1974); H. Benedict Green, "The Structure of St. Matthew's Gospel," in *Studia Evangelica IV: Papers Presented to the Third International Congress on New Testament Studies Held at Christ Church, Oxford, 1965. Part I: The New Testament Scriptures*, ed. Frank L. Cross (Berlin: Akademie, 1968), 57-59.
[31] E.g., Pierre Benoit, *L'Évangile selon Saint Matthieu*, SB, 3rd ed. (Paris: Les Editions du Cerf, 1961), 7-12; Raymond Brown, *Introduction*, 172; Paul S. Minear, *Matthew: The Teacher's Gospel* (New York: Pilgrim, 1982), 12-16; Turner, *Matthew*, 10; Herman C. Waetjen, *The Origin and Destiny of Humanness: An Interpretation of the Gospel According to Matthew* (San Rafael, CA: Crystal, 1976), 33-34.

with the following narrative,[32] while others hold that they belong equally to the preceding and following narratives,[33] and still others say that they exist as separate units, set off from both the preceding and following narratives.[34] Finally, many who hold to the alternating pattern have abandoned Bacon's connection with the five books of the Pentateuch and the notion that this fivefold structure points to Jesus as a new Moses presenting Torah to his church.[35]

The problems with the Baconian structure are numerous. First, the connection between Bacon's fivefold division of the Gospel of Matthew and the five books of Moses in the Pentateuch is dubious. With the possible exception of Exodus and Deuteronomy the books of the Pentateuch do not move from narrative to a culminating legal discourse. And the discourses in the Gospel of Matthew do not, for the most part, contain legal material, while "legal issues" are discussed in Matthean passages outside the five discourses (e.g., Mt 15:1-20).[36] Moreover, the figure of Moses in Matthew is not sufficiently dominant to justify the claim that Matthew presents Jesus as a "new Moses."[37] Matthew mentions Moses only seven times (fewer than Mark or Luke), and usually incidentally as a metonym for the law (Mt 8:4; 19:7, 8; 22:24; 23:2; cf. Mt 17:3, 4). On the other hand, Matthew identifies Jesus explicitly as "Son of David" and "Son of Abraham."

---

[32]E.g., Loisy, *Origins*, 111; Radermakers, *Saint Matthieu*, 2:19-22; Rolland, "From the Genesis," 146-57.
[33]Hill, *Matthew*, 144-48; David L. Barr, "The Drama of Matthew's Gospel: A Reconsideration of Its Structure and Purpose," *TD* 24 (1976): 349-59; Christopher R. Smith, "Literary Evidences of a Fivefold Structure in the Gospel of Matthew," *NTS* 43 (1997): 544-51.
[34]E.g., Allison, *Studies in Matthew*, 137-42.
[35]Those who continue to hold to a "new Moses" Christology include Enslin, "Five Books," 389; Reginald H. Fuller, *A Critical Introduction to the New Testament* (London: Duckworth, 1971), 117; Edward Lohse, *The Formation of the New Testament* (Nashville: Abingdon, 1972), 141; Loisy, *Origins*, 113; Scaer, *Discourses in Matthew*, 25-26. Among those who have abandoned this "new Moses" Christology are Barr, "Drama," 351, 357; Brown, *Introduction*, 173-74; Guthrie, *Introduction*, 31; Talbert, *Matthew*, 8; Turner, *Matthew*; and Witherington, *Matthew*, 15-16. Austin Farrer, *St. Matthew and St. Mark* (London: Dacre, 1954), 179, insists that the alternating pattern points not to a new Pentateuch but a new Hexateuch, and finds a "new Joshua" Christology in the Gospel of Matthew.
[36]As pointed out by Davies, *Setting*, 19. Davies includes a lengthy discussion of Bacon's proposal in which he offers a number of objections.
[37]See Dale C. Allison Jr., *The New Moses: A Matthean Typology* (Minneapolis: Fortress, 1993), for a vigorous argument for the dominance of Moses typology in the Gospel of Matthew. In my judgment, one can find a Moses typology in most of the passages discussed only if one approaches the Gospel looking for it.

Second, Bacon's insistence that the structural dominance of the discourses reflects Matthew's purpose to present Jesus primarily as a teacher is contradicted by the fact that the Matthean Jesus is addressed as "teacher" or "rabbi" only by Judas (Mt 26:25, 29) or opponents or strangers (e.g., Mt 8:19; 12:38; 22:16). The disciples typically address Jesus as "Lord" (κύριε). Of course, the discourses and many other passages throughout the Gospel of Matthew indicate that teaching is one of Jesus' main activities (see, e.g., Mt 4:23; 9:35; 11:1); nevertheless, the pattern of address we have just described is perplexing if Matthew wished to present the person of Jesus primarily as teacher.

Third, we may raise a question regarding Bacon's claim that the five discourses belong structurally to the preceding narrative in each case. We have seen that many scholars link the discourses with the following narratives, and others insist that the discourses belong equally with the preceding and following narratives. In fact, B. H. Streeter, one of the first to note the significance of the concluding formula "When Jesus had finished these sayings" judged that phrase was transitional rather than terminative, that is, that it linked the discourse in each case to the succeeding material.[38] Attempts to link each of the discourses exclusively or even primarily with either the preceding or following narrative material have not been successful.[39] As we will see in the **interpretation** section below, each discourse is connected equally to the preceding and succeeding narrative, fully incorporated into the broad narrative movement of the book. But if, in fact, the discourses are embedded within the narrative framework they can no longer be determinative for structural breaks throughout the Gospel of Matthew.

Fourth, the fact that the discourses are connected with both the preceding and following narrative material, as is indicated by (among other things) the transitional character of the "concluding formula," explains why disagreement has existed regarding where the discourses begin. If, in fact, Matthew presents the discourses as entirely discrete units, markers of

---

[38] Streeter, *Four Gospels*, 262.
[39] Smith, "Literary Evidences," 544-50, attempts to support the claim that the discourses belong with the narratives that precede by identifying connections between the discourses and the preceding narratives (some more convincing than others), but his argument is weakened by the fact that he does not consider also possible links between the discourses and the following material.

structural divisions, would he not have made it clear where each discourse begins? Terence Keegan has attempted to address this problem, insisting that a number of related words tend to cluster at the beginning of each discourse.[40] But, as France has pointed out, "Keegan's 'precise and distinctive' opening formulae are hardly impressive,"[41] since the same set of terms do not appear around the beginning of each discourse, and the ones Keegan identified are found throughout the Gospel of Matthew and not specifically in the vicinity of the discourses.[42] This lack of clarity explains why disagreement exists about whether Matthew 23:1-39 is part of the eschatological discourse, or belongs with the preceding narrative unit, or constitutes a sixth discourse.

Fifth, the disagreement regarding the number of discourses weakens Bacon's claim. As we have seen, Bacon identifies five, while several other scholars have seen six or even seven. This consideration pertains to the significant objection that within Bacon's "narrative" material we find several other extended discourses, most notably Matthew 11:2-30 and Matthew 15:1-20, and possibly Matthew 23:1-39. Conversely, we will find that a narrative substructure exists in the parable discourse and the community discourse. Now, the presence of the concluding formula at the end of the five great discourses certainly sets them apart from these other discourse blocks, but it is clear that we do not have a completely clean narrative-discourse alternation in the Gospel of Matthew.

Sixth, many have objected that insofar as Bacon's model identifies Matthew 1–2 as "preamble" and Matthew 26–28 as "epilogue" it unacceptably assigns these passages to secondary status, whereas in fact the first two chapters lay a foundation that is critical for the remainder of the Gospel and the final three chapters bring it to its climax.[43] This objection is certainly

---

[40]Terence J. Keegan, "Introductory Formulae for the Matthean Discourses," *CBQ* 44 (1982): 415-30.
[41]R. T. France, *Evangelist and Teacher* (Grand Rapids: Zondervan, 1989), 142.
[42]Smith, "Literary Evidences," 542-44, acknowledges these problems with Keegan's presentation, and seeks to distil from the various terms Keegan identified the phrase "the disciples came" (προσῆλθον οἱ μαθηταί) as a sure beginning marker. But this phrase is not found at the beginning of each of the discourses (e.g., the missionary discourse), and it appears not at the beginning but in the middle of the parable discourse (Mt 13:36), which significantly weakens Smith's argument.
[43]Some advocates of the Baconian structure have recognized this problem and have attempted to treat Mt 26–28 as the climax to the Gospel of Matthew. But these attempts either fail to convincingly relate this climactic functioning to the narrative-discourse alternation or they fall into

apposite. But this critique assumes a more fundamental problem with the Baconian model, namely that Bacon's proposal diminishes both the Gospel's essential narrative character and its christological focus. The implicit recognition that the Gospel of Matthew is primarily *a story about Jesus* is exactly what causes discomfort over Bacon's diminution of the beginning and end of the narrative, both of which focus on the person of Jesus, who is the primary subject of the Gospel of Matthew throughout. Yet to emphasize the discourses as key to the Gospel's structure moves attention away from both the narrative flow and the person of Jesus to blocks of teaching which center on certain themes or ideas. Note the main headings of Bacon's outline: "Discipleship," "Apostleship," "The Hiding of the Revelation," "Church Administration," "The Judgment." A person who was unfamiliar with the Gospel of Matthew and had nothing but these structural headings would be unaware that Jesus was even mentioned in the Gospel of Matthew.[44]

Finally, we should note the problem with attempting to determine the literary structure of a document on the basis of the writer's redaction of earlier sources. While obviously one could observe the presence of great speeches within the narrative of the Gospel of Matthew without an examination of Matthew's editorial activity, it is nevertheless the case that Bacon's understanding of the structure of the Gospel of Matthew emerged from a focus on the changes and especially additions that Matthew presumably introduced into his Markan *Vorlage*. As a result, Bacon ascertained the structure of the redactional process rather than the structure of the Gospel of Matthew itself. I contend that if one examines the Gospel of Matthew on its own terms, without recourse to changes over against Mark, one will be impressed with the basic sense that this is a continuous story of Jesus, from

---

apparent contradiction, as when Reginald H. Fuller and Pheme Perkins, *Who Is This Christ? Gospel Christology and Contemporary Faith* (Philadelphia: Fortress, 1983), 83, insist that the passion is the climax to the Gospel of Matthew, while claiming that Mt 23 is a passage that characteristically comes at the end of a document. H. J. Bernard Combrink, "The Structure of the Gospel of Matthew as Narrative," *TynBul* 34 (1983): 61-90, seeks to have it both ways by introducing a confusing distinction between "macrostructures" versus "superstructures" and "textual means" versus "textual message," but in the end the reader is left wondering how the alternating structural pattern relates to the flow of the narrative toward its climax in the passion and resurrection.

[44]The same is true of headings provided by other scholars who adopt Bacon's structure, e.g., Christopher Smith, "Literary Evidences," 549, who offers the following titles to the main structural units: "The Foundations of the Kingdom," "The Mission of the Kingdom," "The Mystery of the Kingdom," "The Family of the Kingdom," and "The Destiny of the Kingdom."

beginning to end, and will expect structural divisions on the basis of the development of that story.[45]

The value of Bacon's model is that it has drawn attention to the presence of the five great discourses in the Gospel of Matthew, along with the concluding formula in each case. And in the process it has raised the question of the role of these great speeches in the macrostructure of the Gospel. Any attempt to deal with the structure of the Gospel of Matthew must include the significance of these great discourses.

Concentric structures. A few scholars have discerned a concentric or chiastic structuring of the Gospel of Matthew. Briefly put, chiasm involves the repetition of elements in inverted order, often with a central, or key, element in the center. When presented visually, chiasm takes the form of the Greek letter X, which gives it its name (see figure 4.1).

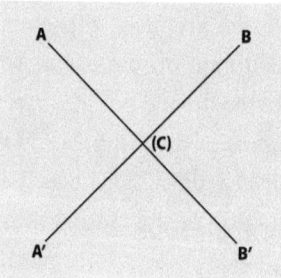

Figure 4.1 Greek letter X as shape of chiasm

Actually, chiasm does not always include a middle element. Take, for example, the chiasm in Matthew 5:48: a) evil b) good b') just a') unjust. Or take another example from a more extended passage, Hebrews 5:1-10, where the writer sets forth chiastically the qualifications for Christ's high priesthood:

a) Human sympathy required of high priests generally (Heb 5:1-3)

b) Divine appointment required of high priests generally (Heb 5:4)

---

[45]Smith, "Literary Evidences," 541-51, attempts to establish the Baconian structure on the basis of "literary criticism," which he distinguishes from "narrative criticism." But in the process he must deny the ultimately narrative character of the Gospel of Matthew; thus he states that Mt 4:17 and Mt 16:21 are "transitions in the narrative, taken as a whole, rather than in the Gospel as a whole" (550).

Shape of Composition

b') Divine appointment of Jesus the high priest (Heb 5:5-6)

a') Human sympathy of Jesus the high priest (Heb 5:7)

In such cases, the chiastic arrangement usually emphasizes the first and last elements (a and a').[46] But when a central element (c) exists in a chiasm, that element is often emphasized, and the arrangement is similar to rings going out from a center; scholars refer to this as "concentric" structure. Scholars who work with chiastic or concentric structures stress the parallelism between coordinate elements in the chiasm (between a and a' and between b and b') as well as the critical role of the central (c) element.

It so happens that most concentric proposals for the structure of the Gospel of Matthew assume the alternating pattern of the Baconian model, and thus they could be discussed under that heading. But the outstanding feature of these concentric proposals is the parallelism of coordinate passages around a critical center, and that feature warrants a separate consideration of these proposals. Two representative chiastic models are those of Peter F. Ellis and H. Benedict Green.

Ellis notes that many specific Matthean passages are characterized by symmetry, and therefore examines the Gospel of Matthew to determine if such symmetry is present in it as a whole. He observes a balance of length among the discourses, and correspondingly he finds also a balance of themes, assuming the subordination of narratives to their discourses. He pairs the discourses (and their introductory narratives) thus:

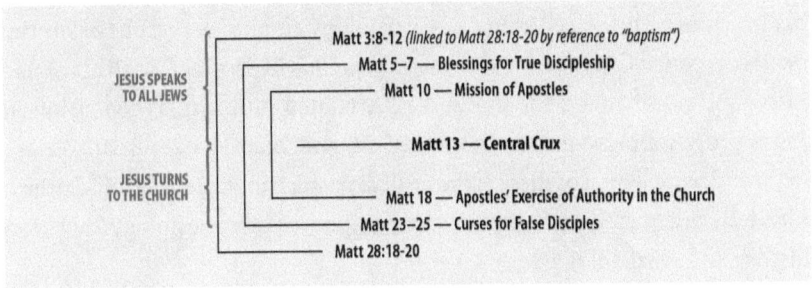

Figure 4.2 Chiastic structure of Matthew according to Ellis

---

[46] As in the case of Mt 5:48. See David R. Bauer and Robert A. Traina, *Inductive Bible Study: A Comprehensive Guide to the Practice of Hermeneutics* (Grand Rapids: Baker Academic, 2011), 118-21.

Matthew 13 forms the middle element, with the division within that chapter between Matthew 13:35 and Matthew 13:36 marking the major change in Jesus' activity in the Gospel of Matthew-as-a-whole. To quote Ellis: "Up to 13.35 Jesus speaks to all the Jews. After 13.35, as in Mk. 8.27-46, Jesus bestows the major part of his attention on the disciples, who, in contrast to the Jews, listen and understand him. Thus, in Matthew 13, Jesus turns from the pseudo-Israel which will not accept him (cf. Mt 11–12) to the church, the true Israel, which believes in him."[47]

Although Ellis sees Matthew 13 as the turning point of the Gospel of Matthew, which of course involves ecclesiology and salvation history, and specifically the shift from the Jewish nation to the church, he insists that Matthew is concerned above all with Christology. Accordingly, he considers that the book reaches its climax with the commissioning scene of 28:18-20, where Jesus appears as the Danielic Son of Man. Thus Matthew presents primarily a Son-of-Man Christology.

This chiastic model from Ellis is not convincing. Although one may note a general tendency in the Gospel of Matthew away from proclamation to the Jewish crowds toward a concentration on instruction to disciples, Matthew 13:34-36 will not bear the weight Ellis places on it. In fact, the disciples are the primary (if not the essential) audience of the Sermon on the Mount, and the sole audience of the missionary discourse; conversely, Jesus ministers to and addresses both the Jewish crowds and leaders frequently in the chapters following Matthew 13 (e.g., Mt 21:1–23:39). Moreover, Ellis is unable to justify the subordination of narrative to discourse. Indeed, his insistence on the centrality of Christology implies an emphasis on the narrative, since Christology is presented primarily through Matthew's narrative and not through the discourses. A related problem is the tension in Ellis's proposal between Matthew 13:35-36 and Matthew 28:18-20. We are left wondering which of these is the critical passage in the Gospel of Matthew. Ellis fails adequately to relate his dual emphases of ecclesiology/salvation history and Christology.

Finally, many of the parallels in Ellis's concentric arrangement are forced. For example, can Matthew 28:18-20 be paired with Matthew 3:8-12 on the basis of the reference to baptism, when "baptizing" is mentioned in Matthew 28:19

---

[47]Peter F. Ellis, *Matthew: His Mind and Message* (Collegeville, MN: Liturgical, 1974), 13.

only as part of a participial phrase which modifies the main verb "make disciples?" And does Matthew 18 have to do with the authority of the apostles in the church, or does it deal rather with community relations involving the entire body of believers? And can Matthew 23–25 properly be labelled "curses for false disciples," when Matthew 23 is addressed to both the crowds and the disciples and involves woes directed against the scribes and Pharisees, and when Matthew 24–25 contains no curses but rather instructions to be obeyed in light of end-time judgment *and reward*? For chiasm to function well, the parallels must be quite obvious and distinctive. The insistence on distinctiveness of chiastic pairing is especially pertinent in the case of the Gospel of Matthew, since it is characterized by redundancy and repetition throughout;[48] consequently, several of the repetitions that Ellis assigns to a specific parallel passage in his chiastic arrangement are found not just in that passage but throughout the Gospel of Matthew.[49]

Like Ellis, H. Benedict Green is impressed by the chiasm that characterizes smaller units in the Gospel of Matthew and explores whether in fact the entire Gospel might be thus structured.[50] But he sees the turning point not on Matthew 13 but rather Matthew 11. In a move that demonstrates that Green is dependent on redaction-critical considerations, he notes that Matthew has significantly altered Mark up to Matthew 12, after which point he follows Mark closely.[51] For Green, this observation makes Matthew 11 strategic in Matthew's redactional activity. Moreover, Green claims that Matthew 11 is a summary of the entire book, referring back to John the Baptist (Mt 11:2-19; cf. Mt 3:1-17), to Jesus' mighty acts (Mt 11:4-6, 20-24; cf. Mt 8:1-9:38), and anticipating Jesus' rejection (Mt 11:2-6, 16-24; cf. Mt 12:1-45, etc.), with a climax in the witness Jesus makes regarding himself (Mt 11:25-30). He sees the following parallels moving out from Matthew 11:

---

[48] Janice Capel Anderson, *Matthew's Narrative Web: Over and Over Again*, JSNTSup 91, LNTS 91 (Sheffield: Sheffield Academic Press, 1994).
[49] For a helpful discussion of the criteria to determine if chiasm is in fact present, see Craig A. Smith, "Criteria for Biblical Chiasms: Objective Means for Distinguishing Chiasm of Design from Accidental and False Chiasm," (PhD diss., University of Bristol, 2009).
[50] Green, "Structure," 47-59.
[51] M. Eugene Boring, "The Gospel of Matthew," in *The New Interpreter's Bible: A Commentary in Twelve Volumes*, ed. Leander E. Keck (Nashville: Abingdon, 1994-2002), 8:112-19, like Green, bases his structure on the consideration that Matthew begins to follow Mark more faithfully around Mt 12; like Green, Boring assumes Bacon's alternation between narrative and discourse. But Boring finds chiasm dominating only Mt 1–12.

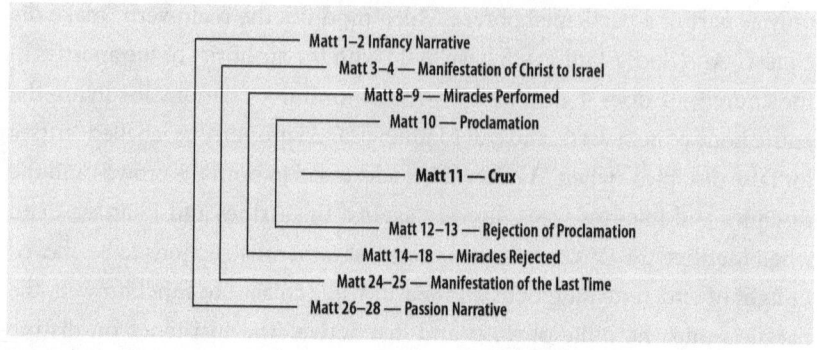

Figure 4.3 Chiastic structure of Matthew according to Green

The concentric proposal of Green is even less persuasive than that offered by Ellis. For one thing, the parallels are remarkably weak. The proclamation of Matthew 10 is made by the disciples, whereas the rejection of Matthew 12-13 is directed against Jesus; miracles do not particularly cluster in Matthew 14-18 (note, e.g., the community discourse in Mt 18), and it is unclear that any rejection there is directed specifically against Jesus' miracles; it is equally dubious that the rejection of Jesus in Matthew 19-23 pertains particularly to Jesus' teaching in the Sermon on the Mount; the "manifestations" of Matthew 3-4 and Matthew 24-25 are not coordinate, since one has to do with sphere ("to Israel"), while the other pertains to time ("the last time"). Further, as I mentioned in critique of Bacon's approach, it is methodologically problematic to base structural analysis on the (putative) changes the evangelist has made to his sources. The text invites readers to construe meaning from the Gospel itself and not from a process to which the reader has no access.

On the basis of these critiques, we can understand why almost no scholars have adopted a concentric understanding of the Gospel of Matthew.[52] Yet both Ellis and Green have directed us to the frequent use of chiasm in smaller units throughout the Gospel of Matthew,[53] and have drawn our

---

[52] Other scholars who have put forward proposals for concentric structure in the Gospel of Matthew include Charles H. Lohr, "Oral Techniques in the Gospel of Matthew," *CBQ* 23 (1961): 403-35; Combrink, "Structure"; and D. W. Gooding, "Structure Littéraire de Matthieu, XIII, 53 à XVIII, 35," *RB* 85 (1978): 227-38. This last is discussed and assessed in France, *Evangelist and Teacher*, 145-46.

[53] The prevalence of chiasm throughout the Gospel of Matthew is amply demonstrated by Paul Gaechter, *Die Literarische Kunst im Matthäus-Evangelium* (Stuttgart: Katholisches Bibelwerk,

Shape of Composition

attention to connections that serve to frame the beginning and end of Matthew's Gospel.

Biographical threefold structure. Several scholars over the years have noted the parallel formula in Matthew 4:17 (*"From that time Jesus began* [ἀπὸ τότε ἤρξατο ὁ Ἰησοῦς] to preach and to say, 'Repent for the kingdom of heaven is at hand'"*) and Matthew 16:21 (*"From that time Jesus began* [ἀπὸ τότε ἤρξατο ὁ Ἰησους] to show his disciples that he must go to Jerusalem and suffer many things from the elders and chief priests and scribes, and be killed, and on the third day be raised."*) and have suggested that these verses may mark the main divisions in the Gospel of Matthew.[54] But it is Jack Dean Kingsbury who first developed this proposal in detail and presented a sustained argument on its behalf.[55]

Kingsbury insists that the twofold formula at Matthew 4:16 and Matthew 16:21 is peculiar to the Gospel of Matthew and is distinctive, combining as it does a preposition with an adverb. The phrase "from that time" (ἀπὸ τότε) is found only four times in the New Testament, three of them in the Gospel of Matthew, and only at Matthew 4:17 and Matthew 16:21 is it used as a "fixed formula." In contrast to the other Matthean use of "from that time" (ἀπὸ τότε)

1966) and *Das Matthäus Evangelium: Ein Kommentar* (Innsbruch: Tyrolia-Verlag, 1963), esp. 13-21 where he presents his own chiastic structure for the Gospel of Matthew.

[54]Frank Bertram Clogg, *An Introduction to the New Testament*, 2nd ed. (London: University of London, 1940); Josef Dillersburger, *Matthäus: Das Evangelium des heiligen Matthäus in theologischer und heilsgeschichtler Schau*, Bd. 1: *Seine Kommen in Vilhalt (die Vorgeschichte)* (Salzburg: Otto Müller, 1953), 1:1-171; Theodor Keim, *Geschichte Jesu von Nazara* (Zurich: Füssli, 1867-74), 1:52; Marcus Dods, *An Introduction to the New Testament* (London: Hodder and Stoughton, n.d.); Edgar Krentz, "The Extent of Matthew's Prologue: Towards the Structure of the First Gospel," *JBL* 83 (1964): 409-15; Georg Kümmel, *Introduction to the New Testament*, rev. ed. (Nashville: Abingdon, 1975), 105-6; Wilbert Webster White, *Thirty Studies in the Gospel by Matthew* (S. M. Henderson, 1905); Caroline L. Palmer, *Emmanuel: Studies in the Gospel by Matthew* (Atlanta: Committee on Women's Work, PCUSA, 1947); Dean Greer McKee, "Studia Biblica VI. The Gospel According to Matthew," *Int* 3 (1949): 194-205; Frederick William Farrar, *The Message of the Books: Being Discourses and Notes on the Books of the New Testament* (New York: E. P. Dutton, 1897); Christoph Rau, *Das Matthaus-Evangelium: Enstehung, Gestalt, Essenischer Einfluss* (Stuttgart: Urachhaus, 1976); Ned B. Stonehouse, *The Witness of Matthew and Mark to Christ* (Philadelphia: Presbyterian Guardian, 1944), 129-30; Augustus H. Strong, *Popular Lectures on the Books of the New Testament* (Philadelphia: Griffith and Rowland, 1914); Ernst Lohmeyer, *Das Evangelium des Matthäus*, ed. Werner Schmauch, 4th ed. (Göttingen: Vandenhoeck & Ruprecht, 1967), 65, 264-65.

[55]Jack Dean Kingsbury, "The Structure of Matthew's Gospel and His Concept of Salvation-History," *CBQ* 35 (1973): 451-74; *Matthew: Structure, Christology, Kingdom* (Philadelphia: Fortress, 1975), 1-39; *Matthew*, 3rd ed. (Nappanee, IN: Evangel, 1998), 29-30; *Matthew as Story* (Minneapolis: Fortress, 1986), 1-93.

in Matthew 26:16, it is employed asyndetically, that is, without a connective to the preceding, such as "and" or "now," it is concerned with the chief subject of the Gospel of Matthew, Jesus, and it links thematically to the following material. Its function is to mark the beginning of a new period of time, since the word *begin* (ἄρχομαι) is used in its nonpleonastic sense of a real commencement.[56]

Over against the fivefold formula that marks the end of the great discourses, so prominent in the Baconian model, the formula of Matthew 4:17 and Matthew 16:21 is not simply transitional but thematic in that it serves as the superscription to each of the major divisions that follow. Kingsbury believes that the proposal that Matthew 4:17 and Matthew 16:21 serve as headings to the second and third major divisions of the Gospel of Matthew implies that Matthew 1:1 has a similar role in relation to the first major division (Mt 1:1–4:16). Accordingly, he argues against the claim made, for example, by Theodor Zahn that Matthew 1:1 should be understood as "book of the history of Jesus Christ,"[57] or the notion put forward by W. D. Davies that it means "The book of the 'New' Creation being wrought by Jesus Christ,"[58] in favor of understanding it as "the book of the origin of Jesus Christ," in line with the occurrence of the same word (*origin*, γένεσις) in Matthew 1:18. Indeed, insofar as Matthew 1:1 mirrors the same phrase used in the Genesis 5:1, where it introduced both a genealogy and the narrative material that followed directly from it, and Genesis 2:4, where it introduced the second creation account, that is, the origins of humanity, the phrase in Matthew 1:1 introduces the genealogy of Jesus in Matthew 1:1-17 and the narrative of the "origins" of Jesus up to Matthew 4:17, the point where Jesus begins his public ministry. Moreover, Matthew 1:1–4:16 is bound together by a concern throughout to establish a portrait of the person of Jesus for the reader that will be assumed in the remainder of the Gospel; this portrait includes Jesus' role as "Son of Abraham" (Mt 1:1, 2, 17), "Son of David" (Mt 1:1, 6, 17, 20), "Emmanuel" (Mt 1:21-23), "king of the Jews" (Mt 2:2) and "Christ"

---

[56]NT writers sometimes use *begin* (ἄρχομαι) to indicate action simply as occurring without any intention to describe commencement; in such a case the verb could properly be left untranslated. Scholars refer to this phenomenon as "pleonastic ἄρχομαι."

[57]Theodor Zahn, *Das Evangelium des Matthäus*, 3rd ed. KNT (Leipzig: A Deichert, 1910), 42; also Walter Grundmann, *Das Evangelium nach Matthäus*, 4th ed. (Berlin: Evangelische Verlagsanstalt, 1981), 61.

[58]Davies, *Setting*, 68-69.

(Mt 1:1, 16, 17; 2:4), but most of all "Son of God," since Jesus' divine sonship is indicated indirectly throughout Matthew 1:1–4:16 but comes to climactic explicit expression in the declaration from God himself at Jesus' baptism (Mt 3:17) and the temptation narrative that flows from it (Mt 4:1-10). Kingsbury argues on both grammatical and thematic grounds against major breaks at Matthew 3:1 and Matthew 4:12 in favor of the unity of Matthew 1:1–4:16. Although Jesus positions himself for public ministry in Matthew 4:12-15, his ministry begins only at Matthew 4:17.

Kingsbury insists that Matthew 4:17 serves as a heading for the whole of Matthew 4:18–16:20, since Matthew ties together the early chapters of this second major division by three summary passages that repeat from Matthew 4:17 the mention of Jesus' proclamation to Israel (Mt 4:23-25; 9:35; 11:1). This second major division moves from the proclamation proper to Israel's general rejection of the proclamation, a rejection that is described in Matthew 11:1–12:50 and is reacted to (by Jesus) in Matthew 13:1–16:20. Thus this second major division evinces a logical progression around the overarching theme of Jesus' proclamation of the kingdom to Israel.

The parallel wording of Matthew 16:21 alerts the reader that this passage marks a new beginning in the presentation of Jesus and that the remainder of the Gospel of Matthew will focus no longer on proclamation to Israel but on Jesus' suffering, death, and resurrection. Similar to the second major division, this division also contains three summary passages (Mt 16:21; 17:22-23; 20:17-19), predicting Jesus' imminent passion and resurrection, that serve to link this material to the superscription of Matthew 16:21. Here Jesus concentrates on his disciples, as the observation that the major discourses in this portion of the Gospel of Matthew are directed exclusively to them makes clear, with relatively little attention to teaching the crowds (and no reference to "preaching" to them), although, as their Messiah, he does continue to heal them. But, for the most part, Jesus' public activity in this third major division is the setting for growing conflict with the Jewish leaders and ultimately the Jewish crowds.

Kingsbury's proposal has received wide acknowledgment, and it is, along with the alternating model, one of the most commonly adopted perspectives on Matthean structure. I myself have written a monograph advocating and developing this understanding of the Gospel's structure.[59] Yet several objections have been registered.

First, some scholars have questioned the claim that Matthew 1:1 serves as a heading to the first major division. Some have insisted that if Matthew 1:1 were, in fact, a superscription for the first major division that reaches its climax in the declaration that Jesus is God's Son it would certainly contain mention of Jesus' divine sonship.[60] But Kingsbury was aware of this potential objection, and argued that Matthew makes no mention of Jesus as Son of God in Matthew 1:1 because it is important to Matthew that God be the first to express Jesus' divine sonship;[61] indeed, allowing God to be the first to make such an explicit declaration regarding Jesus is a major point in the climactic development that Matthew has created within Matthew 1:1–4:16. Certain scholars have also resisted the claim that γένεσις in Matthew 1:1 should be translated "origin," rather than "birth,"[62] with the corollary that it serves not as a superscription for Matthew 1:1–4:16 but rather to introduce either Matthew 1:2-17 or Matthew 1:2–2:23. Admittedly, the word does often mean "birth."[63] But the consideration that Matthew 1:1 is almost certainly an allusion to Genesis 2:4 and Genesis 5:1 indicates that in all probability we

---

[59]Bauer, *Structure of Matthew's Gospel*. Among the scholars who have adopted Kingsbury's threefold structure (or at least major breaks at Mt 4:17 and Mt 16:20) are Augustine Stock, *The Method and Message of Matthew* (Collegeville, MN: Michael Glazier, 1989), 6-9; Alexander Sand, *Das Evangelium nach Matthäus* (Regensburg: Verlag Friedrich Pustet, 1986); Tommy B. Slater, "Notes on Matthew's Structure," *JBL* 99 (1980): 667-70; Russell Pregeant, *Matthew*, CCT (St. Louis: Chalice, 2004), 9-11; Craig L. Blomberg, *Matthew*, NAC (Nashville: Broadman, 1992), 23-24; David E. Garland, *Reading Matthew: A Literary and Theological Commentary on the First Gospel* (New York: Crossroad, 1993), 9-10; Rudolf Schnackenburg, *The Gospel of Matthew* (Grand Rapids: Eerdmans, 2002), 1-4; Donald Verseput, *The Rejection of the Humble Messianic King: A Study of the Composition of Matthew 11-12*, EUS 291 (Frankfurt: Peter Lang, 1986), 18-21; Léopold Sabourin, *L'Évangile selon Saint Matthieu et Ses Principaux Paralleles* (Rome: Biblical Institute Press, 1978); Joachim Gnilka, *Das Matthäus-evangelium*, 2 Teile, HThKNT (Freiburg: Berder, 1988), 2:523-24; with some qualification, Craig S. Keener, *A Commentary on the Gospel of Matthew* (Grand Rapids: Eerdmans, 1999), 36-37. David Hill's cautious adoption of Kingsbury's structure and general views on salvation history and Christology in his article, "Some Recent Trends in Matthean Studies," *IBS* 1 (1979): 139-49, marks a departure from his earlier espousal of Bacon's alternating model in his commentary.

[60]E.g., Wim J. C. Weren, *Studies in Matthew's Gospel: Literary Design, Intertextuality, and Social Setting* (Leiden: Brill, 2014), 22.

[61]Kingsbury, *Structure, Christology, Kingdom*, 17.

[62]E.g., Raymond E. Brown, *The Birth of the Messiah: A Commentary on the Infancy Narratives in the Gospels of Matthew and Luke*, new ed., ABRL (New York: Doubleday, 1993), 58, 123; see Marianne Meye Thompson, "Structure," 230.

[63]BDAG, "γένεσις."

should take it in the sense of "origin," the meaning that it has in the Genesis passages. Although I think it plausible that Matthew 1:1 is a superscription for the first major division, the breakdown of the book at Matthew 4:17 and Matthew 16:21 does not depend on its serving as a heading to Matthew 1:1–4:16, since Kingsbury has adequately demonstrated the unity of Matthew 1:1–4:16 on other grounds.[64]

Second, some have denied that ἀπὸ τότε ("from that time") marks the beginning of new divisions at Matthew 4:17 and Matthew 16:21. Several have observed that the phrase occurs also at Matthew 26:16, where Matthew tells us that "from that time Judas was seeking an opportunity to betray him." If Matthew was concerned clearly to mark off main divisions with this phrase at Matthew 4:17 and Matthew 16:21, would he have included it also at this third passage?[65] But a closer examination reveals that Matthew 26:16 is really not comparable to Matthew 4:17 and Matthew 16:21. For one thing, it includes only the first two words of the formulaic saying; Matthew 4:17 and Matthew 16:21 are linked not only by this prepositional phrase, but also by the name Jesus plus the infinitive clause that follows, "Jesus began to." Moreover, Matthew 4:17 and Matthew 16:21 have Jesus, the protagonist of the narrative, as subject, whereas Judas, whose story hardly constitutes the main plotline of the Gospel of Matthew, is the subject of Matthew 26:16. And Matthew 4:17 and Matthew 16:21 are asyndetic (that is, they contain no connectives linking them with the preceding context), while Matthew 26:16 links to the preceding context by way of the connective *and* (καί).

Moreover, Neirynck has insisted that an examination of Matthew's redaction of Mark places the beginning of Jesus' ministry not at Matthew 4:17 but at Matthew 4:12,[66] and that really the whole of Matthew 4:12-17 should be seen as the beginning of the ministry of Jesus.[67] But, as I have mentioned

---

[64] Even if Mt 1:1 were taken as a heading binding together Mt 1:1–2:23 it would not be a serious problem for the broader unity of Mt 1:1–4:16, since Kingsbury grants that Mt 1:1–2:23 forms a subsection within Mt 1:1–4:16.

[65] Marianne Meye Thompson, "Structure," 231, 233; Frans Neirynck, "ΑΠΟ ΤΟΤΕ ΗΡΞΑΤΟ and the Structure of Matthew," *ETL* 64 (1988): 46-48; Donald Senior, *What Are They Saying About Matthew?*, rev. ed. (New York: Paulist, 1996), 33; Fuller and Perkins, *Who Is This Christ?*, 82.

[66] Frankemölle, *Jahwebund*, 344, argues that ἀπὸ τότε points not forward but backward to Mt 4:12-16, and that the same phrase at Mt 16:21 connects with Mt 16:13-20.

[67] Neirynck, "ΑΠΟ ΤΟΤΕ ΗΡΞΑΤΟ," 25-32, 58. Neirynck actually agrees with Kingsbury's view of the breakdown of the Gospel of Matthew to the extent that he considers the passages around Mt 4:17 and Mt 16:21 to be significant for Matthew's structure, but he understands Mt 4:17 and

before, we should identify the structure of the Gospel of Matthew on the basis of the Gospel of Matthew itself, the text that is directed to the implied reader, and not to putative redactional moves.[68] Clearly, a difference exists between Jesus positioning himself geographically for ministry (which is really preparation for ministry), as he does in Matthew 4:12, and actually beginning his activity of ministry, as he does in Matthew 4:17, which is the first time Matthew describes *Jesus' acts of ministry*. Moreover, Matthew 4:12 does not name Jesus but depends on the prior mention of "Jesus" in Matthew 4:10. Conversely, Matthew 4:17 is asyndetic, thus separating it from Matthew 4:16, but it is linked with Matthew 4:18 in that Matthew 4:18 includes the connective "now" (δε) and does not name Jesus explicitly but depends on the mention of "Jesus" in Matthew 4:17.[69]

Also, some scholars have objected that Matthew 4:17 and Matthew 16:21 cannot function as superscriptions since the material that follows in each case goes beyond what is mentioned in these headings.[70] But this objection assumes too rigid and limited an understanding of the role of the superscriptions. To claim that Matthew 4:17 and Matthew 16:21 are headings does not mean that the large units that follow in each case contain nothing at all but that which is explicitly named in the superscriptions, but only that the headings indicate the major emphasis of each division and provide a general framework for the material in the division. Kingsbury's claim that Matthew 4:17–16:20 is bound together by a major emphasis on Jesus' proclamation of the Kingdom to Israel (which includes Israel's response to that proclamation) and that Matthew 16:21–28:20 is pervaded by the necessity of Jesus' journey to Jerusalem where he will suffer, die, and be raised are supported by a close examination of the contents of each of these divisions. The consideration

---

Mt 16:21 to stand not by themselves but to belong to broader passages that mark transitions in the book. And he insists that Mt 16:13-23 is subordinate to Mt 4:12-17 in that it marks a new stage within the development of Mt 4:12–25:46.

[68] Even if one accepts a redaction-critical basis for structural determination, one will find that Neirynck's arguments on the basis of Matthew's redaction of Mk 1:14-15 are convoluted and involve a number of assumptions.

[69] Gnilka, *Matthäus-evangelium*, 1:99. See also G. M. Soares Prabhu, *The Formula Quotations in the Infancy Narrative of Matthew: An Inquiry into the Tradition History of Mt 1-2*, AnBib, 63 (Rome: Pontifical Biblical Institute, 1976), 108-35, who argues for the unity of Mt 4:12-16 and sets it apart from Mt 4:17.

[70] E.g., Weren, *Studies in Matthew's Gospel*, 22; Neirynck, "ΑΠΟ ΤΟΤΕ ΗΡΞΑΤΟ," 47; Evans, *Matthew*, 9.

that within Matthew 1:1–16:20 we find a few hints or oblique references to Jesus' death does not nullify the operative fact that Jesus' death is not a major emphasis in the earlier chapters of the Gospel but is in fact the major concern in Matthew 16:21–28:20 generally.

Third, these critiques regarding the separating function of ἀπὸ τότε at Matthew 4:17 and Matthew 16:21 lead naturally into the objection that by making a major break at Matthew 16:21 we separate the narrative of Jesus' conversations with Simon Peter (Mt 16:13-23) that surround Matthew 16:21.[71] On the surface this appears to be a weighty consideration, especially since a number of features relate Matthew 16:18-20 to Matthew 16:22-23, such as the dual naming of Simon ("Peter," Mt 16:18; "Satan," Mt 16:23), and the relationship between "rock" and "stumbling stone" (σκάνδαλον). Without question, these passages are complementary, or shall we say, contrasting. Actually, this contrast between the positive portrait of Peter in Matthew 16:18-20 and his negative portrayal in Matthew 16:22-23 corresponds nicely to the broad Matthean shift of emphasis that Kingsbury and I have identified at Matthew 16:21. The positive description of Peter in the earlier passage belongs to the generally positive description of the disciples throughout Matthew 4:17–16:20, and derives from Peter's confession regarding the identity of Jesus in Matthew 16:13-16, a confession that brings to a climax the issue of Jesus' identity that pervades Matthew 4:17–16:20. At the end of the second major division, the disciples, represented by Peter, understand that Jesus is the Christ, the Son of God. But the first explicit prediction of Jesus' suffering and death in Matthew 16:21 introduces, and indeed serves as a catalyst for, the disciples' resistance to Jesus' vocation of suffering and death that pervades the entirety of the third major division. Thus the transition from the positive to the negative portrayal of Peter in the immediately surrounding context of Matthew 16:21 accords perfectly with the flow of the narrative more generally from the second major division (issue of Jesus' identity/positive portrayal of disciples) to the third (issue of Jesus' vocation of suffering and death/negative portrayal of disciples).

---

[71]This point is mentioned by several critics, including Neirynck, "ΑΠΟ ΤΟΤΕ ΗΡΞΑΤΟ," 47-57; France, *Evangelist and Teacher*, 152; and Ian Boxall, *Discovering Matthew: Content, Interpretation, Reception* (Grand Rapids: Eerdmans, 2014), 39.

Fourth, it may be argued that Jesus proclaims the kingdom to Israel not only in Matthew 4:17–16:20 but also well into Matthew 16:21–28:20,[72] indicating that a division break at Matthew 16:21 is unjustified. But while it is true that the theme of kingdom appears often in Matthew 16:21–28:20, the operative point is that only in Matthew 4:17–16:20 does Matthew report that Jesus *preaches* the kingdom to Israel. It is never said in Matthew 16:21–28:20 that Jesus preaches (κηρύσσω);[73] the only references to this verb in the last major division are in the passive and refer to the preaching of the gospel to the world on the part of the church in the post-Easter period (Mt 24:14; 26:13).

Fifth, it has often been said that although Matthew 4:17 and Matthew 16:21 may introduce stages in Matthew's presentation of the story of Jesus they do not necessarily function as structural markers for the Gospel.[74] Yet, if the Gospel of Matthew is essentially a story about Jesus, we cannot so easily set the shape of its story of Jesus over against the shape of the Gospel itself.

Finally, some have objected that Kingsbury's proposal does not take sufficiently into account the role of the five great discourses.[75] While this criticism may be apposite for Kingsbury's earlier presentations on structure, he has addressed the role of the discourses in his later discussions.[76] Yet it is certainly true that more attention ought to be given to the function of the speeches in this threefold biographical model. I have attempted to do so in my earlier work on the structure of the Gospel of Matthew and will address this issue even more directly in the **interpretation** section below.

Additional structural offerings. It would be impossible to discuss all the structural proposals for the Gospel of Matthew that have been put forward. I have attempted to describe only those that have received significant attention in the scholarly community. But before we leave this brief history of investigation into Matthew's structure, we should note that recently several scholars have been troubled by the fact that still no consensus exists regarding the structure of the Gospel of Matthew and have attempted to overcome this "impasse." These attempts fall broadly into two categories.

---

[72]Thus, e.g., Neirynck, "ΑΠΟ ΤΟΤΕ ΗΡΞΑΤΟ," 58.
[73]Nor is the (generally) synonymous "preach the gospel" or "evangelize" (εὐαγγελίζομαι) found in Mt 16:21–28:20, but only at Mt 11:5.
[74]E.g., Barr, "Drama," 351; France, *Evangelist and Teacher*, 152; Hagner, *Matthew 1–13*, li; Thompson, "Structure," 233; Gundry, *Matthew*, 10-11.
[75]Fuller and Perkins, *Who Is This Christ?*, 82; Hagner, *Matthew 1–13*, li; Thompson, "Structure," 233.
[76]E.g., Kingsbury, *Matthew as Story*, 105-13.

Some have insisted that the structure of the Gospel of Matthew is "mixed." Both the alternating pattern of Bacon with its fivefold concluding formula and the threefold biographical model of Kingsbury with its superscriptions at Matthew 1:1; 4:17; 16:21 present important markers in the flow of the Gospel of Matthew, they say, but neither of them can claim dominance in its structure. Exactly how the two distinct views of Matthew's composition set forth by Bacon and Kingsbury can actually be correlated in the overall plan of the Gospel of Matthew these scholars do not tell us.[77] We hear only that the Gospel of Matthew resists any single "grand scheme." Thus this attempt to overcome a structural impasse is actually a structural dead end; it allows scholars to acknowledge that the Gospel of Matthew has real coherence but to abandon the attempt to ascertain what constitutes that coherence in the large.[78]

Others have tried to overcome the present impasse by focusing on the plot of the Gospel of Matthew. For example, Frank J. Matera employs Chatman's notion that plot, which involves the causal chain of events throughout a narrative, includes both "kernels" and "satellites."[79] Kernels are events that are essential to the movement of the plot and cannot be omitted without "destroying the logic of the plot." Satellites are less important events whose omission would not destroy the plot; they cluster around the kernels and develop their meaning. Matera identifies the kernels of Matthew's plot at the birth of Jesus (Mt 2:1); the beginning of Jesus'

---

[77] Two scholars who have essentially accepted Kingsbury's model but attempt to correlate Bacon's fivefold structure to it are Blomberg, *Matthew*, who accepts Mt 4:17 and Mt 16:21 as marking off major divisions but who sees the alternating narrative-discourse pattern as the key to the subdivisions; and Dan O. Via, "Structure, Christology, and Ethics in Matthew," in *Orientation by Disorientation: Studies in Literary Criticism and Biblical Literary Criticism*, ed. Richard A. Spencer (Pittsburg: Pickwick, 1980), 199-215.

[78] Proponents of this view include Brevard S. Childs, *The New Testament as Canon: An Introduction* (Philadelphia: Fortress, 1984), 64; David D. Kupp, *Matthew's Emmanuel: Divine Presence and God's People in the First Gospel*, SNTSMS 90 (New York: Cambridge University Press, 1996), 6-7; Boxall, *Discovering Matthew*, 41; France, *Evangelist and Teacher*, 153; Gundry, *Matthew*, 10-11; Senior, *Gospel of Matthew*, 31; Carl R. Holladay, *A Critical Introduction to the New Testament: Interpreting the Message and Meaning of Jesus Christ* (Nashville: Abingdon, 2005), 137-38; Udo Schnelle, *The History and Theology of the New Testament Writings* (Minneapolis: Fortress, 1994), 225; Paul J. Achtemeier, Joel B. Green, and Marianne Meye Thompson, *Introducing the New Testament: Its Literature and Theology* (Grand Rapids: Eerdmans, 2001), 95-96; Luz, *Matthew 1–7*, 42; Luke Timothy Johnson, *The Writings of the New Testament: An Interpretation*, rev. ed. (Minneapolis: Fortress, 1999), 189-90.

[79] Frank J. Matera, "The Plot of Matthew's Gospel," *CBQ* 49 (1987): 233-53. Matera draws on Chatman's discussion in *Story and Discourse*, 43-95.

ministry (Mt 4:12-17); the question of John the Baptist (Mt 11:2-6); Jesus' conversation at Caesarea Philippi (Mt 16:13-28); the cleansing of the temple (Mt 21:1-17); and the Great Commission (Mt 28:16-20). Since each of these kernels marks a turning point in Matthew's narrative, Matera infers the following "narrative blocks":

1. The coming of the Messiah (Mt 1:1–4:11)
2. The Messiah's ministry to Israel of preaching, teaching, healing (Mt 4:12–11:1)
3. The crisis in the Messiah's ministry (Mt 11:2–16:12)
4. The Messiah's journey to Jerusalem (Mt 16:13–20:34)
5. The Messiah's death and resurrection (Mt 21:1–28:15)
6. The Great Commission (Mt 28:16-20)

Several years later Warren Carter set out to affirm Matera's basic approach but to correct several details of Matera's analysis.[80] Carter identifies kernels at Matthew 1:18-25; 4:14-25; 11:2-6; 16:21-28; 21:1-7; 28:1-10 and these consequent narrative blocks:

1. God initiates the story of Jesus (Mt 1:1–4:16)
2. Jesus manifests God's saving presence in his public ministry of preaching and healing (Mt 4:17–11:1)
3. Jesus' actions reveal his identity as God's commissioned agent, necessitating a response from human beings, raising the question of whether Israel will recognize God's Messiah (Mt 11:2–16:20)
4. Jesus teaches his disciples that God's purposes for him involves his death and resurrection, an event that shapes discipleship (Mt 16:21–20:34)
5. In Jerusalem, Jesus conflicts with and is rejected by the Jewish leaders and dies at their hands (Mt 21:1–27:66)
6. God's saving purposes are not thwarted; the resurrected Jesus commissions his disciples to worldwide mission (Mt 28:1-20)

---

[80]Warren Carter, "Kernels and Narrative Blocks: The Structure of Matthew's Gospel," *CBQ* 54 (1992): 463-81.

In response, we might note that although both Matera and Carter insist that their plot analysis has significance for structure, neither delineates the precise relationship between plot and structure. In spite of France's assertion that in the Gospel of Matthew "the plot *is* the structure,"[81] a distinction must be made between plot and structure and the relationship clearly set forth.[82] According to Abrams, plot centers on "actions, as these are rendered and ordered toward achieving particular emotional and artistic effects,"[83] while structure is "the order, emphasis, and rendering of all [a work's] component materials and parts into 'a beautiful and effective whole of a determinate kind.'"[84] In other words, plot is the chainlike causal connection between events, whereas structure is the literary arrangement of materials throughout the book.

It is clear, then, that structure is both broader and deeper than plot. Structure is broader than plot in that all books, whatever their genre, have structure; indeed, structure is constitutive of all communication and is the necessary formal element that renders content understandable. But plot is limited to narrative. Structure is deeper than plot, for insofar as structure is the literary arrangement of all the material in a book it is the means by which the implied author reveals both the overall plot and the distinction between "kernels" and "satellites." Thus both Matera and Carter have necessarily yet implicitly employed structure for their analysis of plot.

We note, too, that the kernels and the correlative narrative blocks put forward by Matera, and especially Carter, largely reflect Kingsbury's breakdown of the Gospel of Matthew. Both see major turning points around Matthew 4:16 and Matthew 16:21. They add turning points around Matthew 11:2, at Matthew 21:1-17, and around Matthew 28. Insofar as the first two of these turning points center not on the actions of the protagonist, Jesus, but rather the response of Israel, they do not belong to the main narrative plot,[85]

---

[81] France, *Evangelist and Teacher*, 153, italics his.
[82] See Smith, "Literary Evidences," 411-12, for the problem of collapsing the structure of the Gospel of Matthew into plot.
[83] M. H. Abrams, *A Glossary of Literary Terms*, 5th ed. (Fort Worth, TX: Holt, Rinehart, and Winston, 1988), 139.
[84] Abrams, *Glossary*, 70.
[85] This observation leads me to suggest that it would be beneficial to differentiate between primary and secondary kernels. Primary kernels may pertain to the storyline of the protagonist, and center on his actions, while secondary kernels may pertain to subordinate yet essential storylines that focus on characters who interact with the protagonist and whose relationship with the

but rather to the intertwined yet subordinate storyline of Israel.[86] The turning point that Matera and Carter identify with the resurrection or missionary commissioning reflects the Gospel's climax,[87] which Kingsbury also sees at the end of the Gospel of Matthew.[88]

In spite of some methodological and material reservations, the articles by Matera and Carter do take seriously the ultimately narrative character of the Gospel of Matthew and helpfully raise the question of the relationship of plot, and indeed other narrative and literary features, to the book's structure. Their careful analysis of kernels and satellites suggests that the structure of the Gospel of Matthew is far more inclusive and dynamic than simply noting breaks that mark one division off from the next.

Conclusions from the history of investigation into Matthew's structure. On the basis of this critical examination of the scholarly debate regarding the Gospel's structure I remain convinced that the threefold biographical proposal offered by Kingsbury is the most viable way to understand it. Moreover, the insistence on the part of many of the scholars herein mentioned that Matthew's structure is so dynamic that it is not reducible to hard divisional breaks, however well-established these breaks may be, suggests that a fully adequate structural analysis will address not only the identification of main blocks within the Gospel of Matthew but will deal also with structural features that go beyond the division of the Gospel of Matthew into blocks. Thus any structural proposal that focuses more or less exclusively on the breakdown, or the division, of the Gospel of Matthew, falls short of addressing all the relevant issues pertaining to the Gospel's structure. Indeed, if we understand structure as the literary arrangement of materials that serves as the vehicle for the communication

---

protagonist serves at points to move the action forward. I think this would helpfully distinguish between primary and secondary causes among the events of the narrative.

[86] As correctly recognized by Kingsbury, *Matthew as Story*, 115-27; and Mark Allan Powell, "The Plot and Subplots of Matthew's Gospel," *NTS* 38 (1992): 187-204.

[87] Yet the repeated passion predictions (Mt 16:21; 17:22-23; 20:17-19) indicate that the whole of the passion and resurrection narrative functions as the Gospel of Matthew's climax.

[88] A similar attempt to identify the structure of the Gospel of Matthew on the basis of kernels is offered by Weren, *Studies in Matthew's Gospel*, 22-41. He prefers to think of these kernels as "hinges" (another word used by Chatman to describe them) that belong not just to the following material but serve to connect preceding and succeeding passages. In spite of Weren's objection to decisive structural breaks he presents quite distinct "narrative blocks," with clear beginnings and endings.

of meaning, we must broaden the scope of structural analysis to include not only linear progression, that is, breakdown, but also structural patterns that operate throughout the book. I propose that, in addition to breakdown, literary structure involves the dynamic relationships between various themes, motifs, and other elements that at times intersect with the issue of the division of the book, but also transcend, or go beyond, the matter of linear development. I refer to these organizational systems within the biblical book as structural relationships; linguists and discourse analysts call them "semantic structures."[89]

Scholars, and other readers of the Bible for that matter, often note these structural relationships in passing, but they usually fail to incorporate them into their discussion of the book's structure. These structural relationships include such devices of arrangement as repetition, contrast (association of things whose differences are stressed by the writer), comparison (association of things whose similarity is stressed by the writer), causation (movement from cause to effect), substantiation (movement from effect to cause), particularization (movement from general to particular), generalization (movement from particular to general), and climax (movement toward high point of culmination).[90] We find these structural relationships both pervading the book as a whole and present as organizing features within individual passages. An adequate structural analysis, then, will attend both to the linear development of the Gospel of Matthew and to these structural relationships that are essential to grasping adequately how Matthew has so organized the material of his Gospel to communicate his message to the reader.

Of course, in the final analysis, any structural proposal must be tested by its ability to account well for all the data of the text and to reveal the richness

---

[89]Joseph E. Grimes, *The Thread of Discourse* (Berlin: Mouton, 1975), 207-10; Eugene A. Nida, *Exploring Semantic Structures* (Munich: Wilhelm Fink, 1975), 50-65; Robert E. Longacre, *The Grammar of Discourse* (New York: Plenum, 1983), 77-149; Peter Cotterell and Max Turner, *Linguistics and Biblical Interpretation* (Downers Grove, IL: InterVarsity Press, 1989), 188-229.

[90]For a full discussion of these structural relationships, see Robert A. Traina, *Methodical Bible Study: A New Approach to Hermeneutics* (New York: Ganis & Harris, 1952; repr., Zondervan); Bauer and Traina, *Inductive Bible Study*, 79-126; Fredrick J. Long, "Major Structural Relationships: A Survey of Origins, Development, Classifications, and Assessment," *JIBS* 1 (2014): 22-59. Mark Allan Powell, *What Is Narrative Criticism?*, GBS (Minneapolis: Fortress, 1990), 32-34, dubs these relationships "narrative patterns"; yet they do not belong solely to narrative but are found in all communication.

of the message the implied author is communicating to the implied reader. I now attempt such a structural analysis of the Gospel of Matthew.

A Structural Analysis

Figure 4.4, presenting main units and subunits, helps capture the linear development of the Gospel of Matthew as I see it. If one grants that the Gospel of Matthew is essentially a story about Jesus, one should ascertain the linear development of the Gospel of Matthew by identifying those points that mark major shifts of emphasis in the presentation of Jesus. We have already noted that Matthew includes the formulaic statement in Matthew 4:17 and Matthew 16:21 that seems, in each case, to introduce in a general fashion the main emphasis of the following large division. These statements are arresting both because of their asyndetic character (with no connective linking them to the preceding) and their obviously parallel form, including in each case the ablative, or separating, preposition followed by the correlative adverb of time ("from that time" or "from then on," ἀπὸ τότε), which in turn is followed by the verb *began* (ἤρξατο) and the name Jesus, who is the subject of

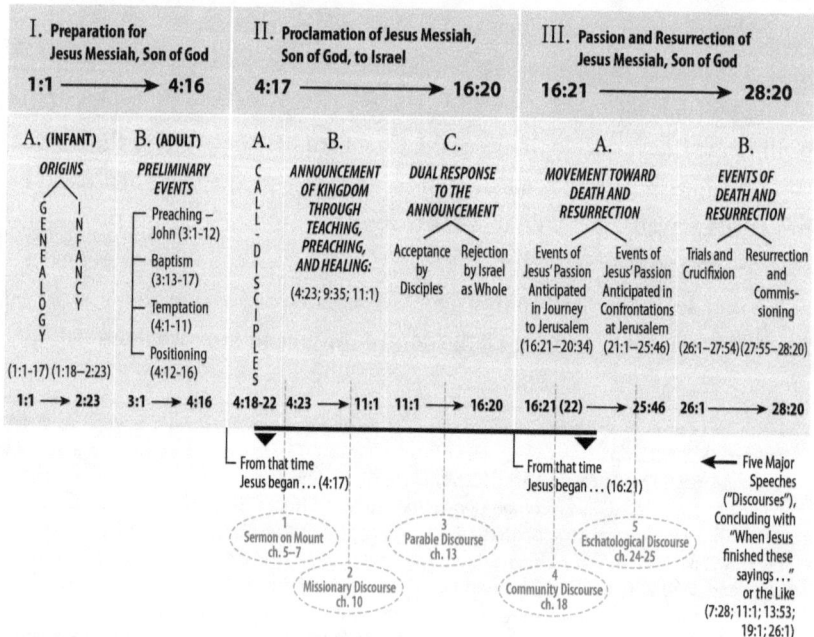

Figure 4.4 Structure of the Gospel of Matthew

the entire narrative, then a complementary infinitive. These entire statements are so distinct from the other reference to "from that time," in Matthew 26:16, referring to Judas, that it is difficult to understand why many scholars continue to point to the latter passage as undermining the significance of Matthew 4:17 and Matthew 16:21 for the structure of the Gospel of Matthew.

The identification of main units and subunits is as far as many scholars go in their structural analysis. But it is important to consider also structural features that go beyond the locating of discrete units and to observe dynamic organizational patterns that Matthew employs, along with the linear progression, to communicate the message of the book to his readers.

The first of these organizational patterns, or structural relationships, involves the broad connections of the main units within the Gospel of Matthew to one another. Matthew 1:1–4:16 serves to *prepare*, or provide background, to the remainder of the book. Moreover, Matthew 4:17–16:20 serves as the basis or cause for Matthew 16:21–28:20 in that the disciples' progressive recognition that Jesus is the Son of God in Matthew 4:17-16:20 (esp. Mt 14:33 and Mt 16:13-20) causes Jesus to show them what it means for him to be the Son of God in Matthew 16:21–28:20, that is, one who is perfectly obedient to the will of his Father, even to the point of suffering and death. And we should note that each of the three major divisions reaches a climax in the declaration that Jesus is God's Son (Mt 3:17; 16:16; 27:54); thus, Matthew structures his Gospel around a repeated climax centering on Jesus' divine sonship.

Second, we find a *repeated comparison* throughout the Gospel of Matthew between Jesus and the expectations for his disciples. Matthew 16:21–28:20 is bound together by a repeated comparison between the God-ordained destiny of Jesus (suffering-death-resurrection) and that of the disciples; this represents a more specific form of the repeated comparison that we observe more generally throughout the entire Gospel.

We should note this is not a comparison between Jesus and the disciples themselves but a comparison between Jesus and the *expectations* for the disciples. We find, for one thing, a repeated comparison between the mission of Jesus and the mission of the disciples. Thus, the geographical sphere of ministry both for Jesus (Mt 4:23; 17:22; 21:11; 26:69; 27:55) and for the disciples (Mt 28:16) is Galilee. Indeed, when Jesus begins his ministry he withdraws "into Galilee" (Mt 4:12); and in the same way when the disciples are about to begin their mission they go "into Galilee," where "Jesus had commanded them" (Mt 28:16; cf. Mt 26:32; 28:7, 10). Moreover, during the time of the earthly Jesus, both Jesus and the disciples are sent not to the Gentiles or Samaritans, but only "unto the lost sheep of the house of Israel" (Mt 10:5-6; 15:24). Further, both Jesus and (eventually) the disciples teach (Jesus: Mt 4:23; 5:2, 19; 7:29; 9:35; 11:1; 13:54; 21:23; 26:55; disciples: Mt 28:19); both Jesus and the disciples have authority to cast out demons (Jesus: Mt 8:16, 28-34; 9:32-34; 12:22-29; 15:21-28; 17:14-20; disciples: Mt 10:1, 8; 17:14-20); and both Jesus and the disciples preach the same message ("the gospel of the kingdom"; Jesus: Mt 4:23; 9:35; disciples: Mt 24:14; 26:13), namely, "the kingdom of heaven is at hand" (Mt 4:17; 10:7). In addition, the rejection of the disciple's message carries the same consequences expressed in the same language as those attending the rejection of Jesus' message ("it will be more tolerable on the day of judgment for the land of Sodom and Gomorrah than for that town," Mt 10:15; cf. Mt 11:22-24; 12:41-42). Finally, both the ministry of Jesus and that of the disciples result in persecution.[91]

For another thing, Matthew constructs a repeated comparison between the behavior of Jesus and the behavioral expectations for the disciples. The instructions of Jesus to his disciples (e.g., Mt 5:17-48; 7:12; 12:50; 22:36-40) corresponds to Jesus' activities (e.g., Mt 3:15; 4:1-11; 20:28; 26:53-56) as these are narrated by Matthew. To take just one example: Even as Jesus is the merciful one par excellence (Mt 9:27, 36; 14:14; 15:22, 25, 32; 17:15; 20:30-34), so the disciples are to be merciful (Mt 5:7; 9:13; 12:7; 18:33; 23:23).

In addition, Matthew's use of filial (family) language underscores the comparison between Jesus and the disciples in terms of their relationship to God. Both Jesus and the disciples are "Son" or "sons" of God and know God as "Father." Although the Matthean Jesus consistently differentiates between "my Father" and "your Father," the fact remains that both Jesus and the disciples are identified, respectively, as "Son" and "sons" of the "Father."[92]

---

[91]Jesus: Mt 9:1-13, 33; 12:1-4, 24-42; 15:1-21; 16:1-4, 21; 17:22-23; 20:17-19; 21:1-17, 23-27; 22:1-40; 26:3-5; 26:47–27:26, 41-45, 62-66; disciples: Mt 5:10-11; 10:16-23, 26-39; 13:21; 16:24; 20:22-23; 23:29-36; 24:9-14; 28:11-15; both: Mt 10:24-25.

[92]References to Jesus as "Son" (of God): Mt 1:21, 23, 25; 2:15; 3:17; 4:3, 6; 8:29; 11:27; 14:33; 16:16; 17:5; 21:37-38; 22:2, [42]; 24:36; 25:63; 27:40, 43, 54; 28:19. References to God as Jesus' "Father": Mt 7:21; 10:32-33; 11:25-27; 12:50; 15:13; 16:17, 27; 18:10, 14, 19, 35; 20:23; 24:36; 25:34, 41; 26:29, 39, 42, 53; 28:19. References to disciples as "sons" (of God): Mt 5:9, 45; 7:9; 9:15; 13:38; 17:25-26.

Of course, comparison involves analogy, not identity. Therefore, a measure of difference exists between Jesus and the disciples in each of these areas of analogy; for instance, Jesus' relationship of sonship to the Father is not identical in every particular to disciples' relationship of sonship. Nevertheless, Matthew wishes repeatedly to draw attention to these similarities between Jesus and the disciples.

Third, we observe a *repeated contrast* between Jesus and his opponents, especially the Jewish leaders and, to some extent, the political leaders, and increasingly the Jewish crowds.[93] This contrast takes the form of a constant yet growing conflict between them. In the process, Matthew sets forth various aspects of the difference between Jesus and these leaders.

Fourth, the Gospel of Matthew is characterized by a number of *repetitions*, which point to major themes, or motifs, that Matthew wishes to emphasize and develop throughout the Gospel. Among these are "king"/"kingdom," "fulfill"/"fulfillment," "Son of David," "Son of man," and "Christ."[94]

Fifth, we note the repetition of several elements that together function as a complex within the dynamics of the Gospel. These elements involve the repeated contrast between righteousness versus wickedness, with righteousness being the cause which results in its effect, salvation and reward, while wickedness is the cause that results in its effect, eternal condemnation.[95] This structural complex pertains to the often noted dominant themes of righteousness and judgment within the Gospel. A visual image may present it more clearly (see figure 4.5).

References to God as the disciples' "Father": Mt 5:16, 45, 48; 6:1, 4, 6, 8-9, 14, 18, 26, 32; 7:11; 10:20, 29; 13:43; 21:28-33; 23:9. Because of the verbal connection Matthew forges between Jesus as Son of God and disciples as sons of God I will consistently use the gender specific "Son/son" to describe disciples, recognizing that women are certainly included.

[93]E.g., Mt 2:1-23; 9:1-13, 33; 11:7-24; 12:1-14, 24-42; 13:10-15; 15:1-21; 16:1-12; 20:17-19, 25-28; 21:12-17; 23:1-38; 26:3-5, 47; 27:15-23, 26, 41-45, 62-66; 28:11-16.

[94]"King" or "kingdom": Mt 1:6; 2:2, 9; 3:2; 4:23; 5:19-20; 6:10, 33; 7:21; 8:11; 9:35; 11:11, 12; 12:25, 26, 28; 13:19, 24, 31, 33, 38, 41, 43-45, 47, 52; 16:19, 28; 17:25; 18:1, 3-4, 23; 19:12, 14, 23-24; 20:1, 21; 21:31, 43; 22:2; 23:13; 24:14; 25:1, 40; 26:29; 27:11, 29, 37, 42. "Fulfill" or "fulfillment," including the "fulfillment quotations," that are part of the broader pattern of fulfillment language: Mt 1:22; 2:15, 17, 23; 3:15; 4:14; 5:17; 8:17; 12:17; 13:35, 48; 21:4; 23:32; 26:54, 56; 27:9. "Son of David": Mt 1:1, 4, 17, 20; 9:27; 12:23; 15:22; 20:30-31; 21:9, 15; 22:42, 45. "Son of man": Mt 8:20; 9:6; 10:23; 11:19; 12:8, 32, 40; 13:37, 41; 16:13, 27-28; 17:9, 12, 22; 18:11; 19:28; 20:18, 28; 24:27, 30, 37, 39, 44; 25:31; 26:2, 24, 45, 64. "Christ": Mt 1:1, 16-18; 2:4; 11:2; 16:16, 20; 22:42; 23:10; 24:5, 23; 26:63, 68; 27:17, 22.

[95]Mt 5:3–7:27; 8:1–9:34; 10:5-16, 26-42; 11:2-30; 12:22-50; 13:3b-29, 36-51; 15:1-28; 16:24-28; 18:5-35; 19:16-30; 20:29-34; 21:28-32, 40-23:39; 24:3-25:46.

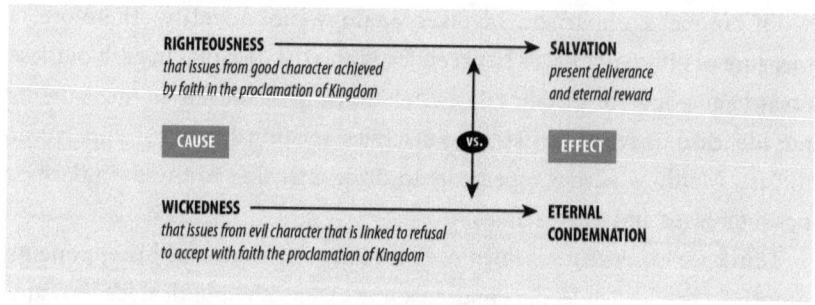

Figure 4.5 Themes of righteousness and judgment in Matthew

We note that Matthew understands righteousness as a pattern of behavior that accords with God's will and that issues from a transformed inner character, which itself is achieved by placing confidence in the proclamation of the gospel, whereas wickedness is behavior that reflects an inner corruption, which Matthew links to refusal to accept with confidence the proclamation of the kingdom.

Matthew describes this necessity of inner transformation for a life of righteousness by repeatedly employing the tree-fruit metaphor. Thus John the Baptist demands that his hearers "Bear fruit that befits repentance," warning that "even now the axe is laid to the root of the trees; every tree therefore that does not bear good fruit is cut down and thrown into the fire" (Mt 3:8, 10). And Jesus insists that his hearers will discern the essential character of people by their fruits (Mt 7:16-20; 12:33-35). Already in Matthew 3:8 John the Baptist presents good fruit as an expression of repentance, which itself is an appropriate response to the proclamation of the gospel (Mt 3:2; 4:17); and throughout the Gospel of Matthew, repentance and the experience of the blessings of the kingdom are associated with faith (Mt 8:10, 13; 9:2, 22, 28-29; 15:28; 18:6, 21, 32).[96]

Sixth, the Gospel of Matthew reaches its climax in the passion and resurrection narratives, and ultimately in the missionary commissioning (Mt 28:16-20), which is itself the only resurrection appearance to the disciples. Although Matthew 16:21 marks the beginning of the emphasis on the

---

[96]See Gerhard Barth, "Matthew's Understanding of the Law," in *Tradition and Interpretation in Matthew*, ed. Günther Bornkamm, Gerhard Barth, and Heinz Joachim Held, NTL (Philadelphia: Westminster, 1963), 112-16.

passion and resurrection that characterizes the third major division, the theme of Jesus' suffering, death, and resurrection is found in the Gospel of Matthew from almost the very beginning. During the infancy of Jesus, Herod's attempts to kill Jesus prepare the reader for the murderous actions of the religious and political leaders at the end of the Gospel, and God's effective deliverance of Jesus from Herod's hands anticipates the resurrection of Jesus (Mt 2:1-23). In Matthew 9:3 some of the scribes, hearing Jesus declare a man's sin forgiven, say within themselves that Jesus is blaspheming, which was a capital offense among the Jews (cf. Mt 26:65-66). In Matthew 9:15 Jesus speaks of himself as the bridegroom, who will be taken away from them. In Matthew 10:4 Judas is described as the one "who betrayed him." In Matthew 10:38 Jesus declares that those who do not take up their cross and follow him are unworthy of him, thus implying that he will take up his cross. Later, in the wake of a healing on the Sabbath, "the Pharisees went out and took counsel against him, how to destroy him" (Mt 12:14). In Matthew 12:40 Jesus alludes obliquely to his own death and resurrection when he declares that "as Jonah was three days and three nights in the belly of the whale, so will the Son of man be three days and three nights in the heart of the earth." And Jesus will again make reference to "the sign of Jonah" in Matthew 16:4. This brings us to Matthew 16:21, which commences the dominance of the theme of Jesus' passion and resurrection through the end of the Gospel.

The ultimate climax of the Gospel of Matthew is the missionary commissioning, not only because it culminates the resurrection narrative as the only resurrection appearance to the post-Easter disciples,[97] but also because it highlights, in a final and determinative manner, the theme of the enlargement of mission to include the Gentiles and the theme of the presence of God and Christ with their people. Throughout the Gospel of Matthew Jesus is careful to restrict his ministry and the ministry of his disciples to Jews. Accordingly, when Jesus gives instructions to the twelve regarding their ministry, he insists that they are to "go nowhere among the Gentiles, and enter no town of the Samaritans, but go rather to the lost sheep of the house of Israel" (Mt 10:5-6). And Jesus restricts his own ministry in the same

---

[97]Note how Jesus' resurrection appearance to the disciples in Galilee is not only predicted to the disciples in Mt 26:32 but also twice to the women at the tomb, the first time by the angel (Mt 28:7), the second time by Jesus himself (Mt 28:10). Thus the narrative constantly points forward to Mt 28:16-20.

way; thus when the Canaanite woman approaches him with the plea to heal her daughter Jesus at first refuses with the declaration, "I was sent only to the lost sheep of the house of Israel" (Mt 15:24). Jesus does eventually heal this woman's daughter, and on one other occasion he heals a Gentile (Mt 8:5-13), but these are exceptions that prove the rule and indicate that even during his earthly ministry the superabounding faith of a Gentile could lead Jesus to suspend, in an isolated instance, his otherwise carefully maintained restriction. But in contrast to this earlier restriction, it is only at the missionary commissioning, in the wake of his resurrection and his assumption of cosmic authority, that he commands the disciples to "make disciples of *all nations*" (Mt 28:19). Matthew has earlier given hints of the eventual inclusion of the Gentiles (Mt 4:14-16; 8:11; 10:18; 12:17-21; 24:14), which is part of the climactic character of Matthew 28:16-20, but only here do we have the breaking of the exclusion and the actual inclusion of the Gentiles.

This final passage highlights also the theme of the presence of God and Jesus with their people. Indeed, Matthew 28:16-20 forms both a climax to this theme, which is mentioned on a few earlier occasions,[98] and an inclusio with its first appearance in Matthew 1:23. The wording of Matthew 1:23 and Matthew 28:20 is parallel, with only one letter in the Greek differentiating the two prepositional phrases: "God with us" (μεθ᾽ ἡμῶν, Mt 1:23) and "I [Christ] am with you always" (μεθ᾽ ὑμῶν, Mt 28:20). This inclusio encourages us to read the promise from Jesus, God's Son (see Mt 28:19), "I am with you always," in light of Matthew 1:23, "Emmanuel, God with us," indicating that God continues to be present in the midst of his post-Easter disciples in the person of Jesus his Son.

A final word about the climax of Matthew 28:16-20 pertains to the structural role of the five great discourses. We have seen how significant are the five great speeches in the history of investigation into the structure of the Gospel of Matthew. Their structural role pertains to the climax of the missionary commissioning. Here Jesus commands the post-Easter disciples to "make disciples," not only by "baptizing" but also by "teaching them to observe all I have commanded you." Insofar as the content of the five great

---

[98]Indeed, Kupp, *Matthew's Emmanuel*, 49-108, finds this theme of divine presence in practically every passage throughout the Gospel of Matthew.

speeches, though ostensibly directed to the twelve disciples during Jesus' earthly ministry, actually centers on discipleship in general in the post-Easter period, it is natural to think that the primary referent of "all that I have commanded you" in Matthew 28:20 is the five great discourses. Moreover, we should note the verbal link between the "all" that is mentioned in the concluding formula of the last great discourse "When Jesus finished *all* these sayings" (Mt 26:1) and the mention of "all" in Matthew 28:20: "teaching them to observe *all* that I have commanded you." While we should take seriously the inclusive scope of the "all" of Matthew 28:20 and thereby understand that it incorporates everything without exception that Jesus taught throughout the Gospel of Matthew, the evidence just cited suggests that Jesus' instructions in the five great discourses form the critical core of the church's catechesis that constitutes a central part of the discipling of the nations throughout the post-Easter period.

PART TWO

INTERPRETATION

The discussion of the structure of the Gospel of Matthew leads naturally into an examination of the meaning of the text of the Gospel of Matthew, for the linear development of the Gospel and the additional structural features that we have identified will provide a framework for the interpretation. The interpretation will be informed not only by the structural analysis, but also by other conclusions reached in the orientation section above. In turn, the interpretation offered in this section will form the basis for the discussion of the theology of the Gospel of Matthew in the third part of the book.

Under ideal circumstances, and if space were unlimited, I would include conversation with the history of interpretation for each passage and would provide thorough exegetical and historical arguments for each interpretive decision with supporting evidence in the footnotes. But the character and scope of this volume require that I not present a full-fledged commentary on the text of the Gospel of Matthew but rather offer a close reading of the text (which is informed by careful exegetical and historical analysis) that will lead to conclusions regarding its theology. Consequently, I will keep footnotes in this section to a minimum.

5

INTERPRETATION OF MATTHEW 1:1-4:16

MATT 1:1–2:23. We saw above that Matthew 1:1–2:23 forms the first of two units within Matthew 1:1–4:16, and that it pertains to the origins of Jesus. Matthew presents Jesus' origins in terms of his genealogy (Mt 1:1-17) and events surrounding his infancy (Mt 1:18–2:23). The genealogy also constitutes Matthew's testimony to the person of Jesus, the first in a series of reliable witnesses to Jesus which will continue throughout Matthew 1:1–4:16, culminating in the witness from God in Matthew 3:17 and the material that flows from it in Matthew 4:1-16.

This genealogy is significant for grasping the message of the Gospel of Matthew. Ancient writers, like modern ones, typically placed that which is most important at the beginning and end of their books. And biblical writers frequently intend that genealogies should communicate a theological message over against simply presenting a family tree. The presence of theologically loaded terms (such as "Son of David" and "Christ") and concepts (such as three periods in salvation history) indicate that such is the case with the Matthean genealogy. Here Matthew offers a theological interpretation of Israel's history from the perspective of its fulfillment in Christ which will serve as the basic orientation for the story that follows.

The genealogy begins with a general heading, in which Matthew sets forth his testimony that Jesus is Christ, Son of David, Son of Abraham (Mt 1:1), which he then develops and supports in the genealogical list that follows

(Mt 1:2-16). Matthew does not base his testimony on his own authority, but substantiates it by appeal to the genealogy, which is really an appeal to the Old Testament and ultimately to God who has revealed his purposes in the Old Testament.

The genealogical list reverses the order of Matthew 1:1, by beginning with Abraham (Mt 1:2), moving to David (Mt 1:6), and concluding with "Jesus . . . who is called Christ" (Mt 1:16), thus creating a chiasm that emphasizes the first and last elements, that is, Jesus' role as Christ.[1] Matthew reinforces this emphasis by bringing the list to its climax with "Christ."[2] The climactic structure itself gives content to the title "Christ" here: Jesus is Christ as the one who has been anointed (that is, chosen and empowered) by God to bring salvation history, which began with Abraham, to its climax.[3] As the climax to Israel's history, Jesus gives meaning to the history of Israel as a whole and to individual events and persons within Israel's history.[4] In other words, he fulfills, or fills full with meaning, Israel's history as presented in the Old Testament; he reveals and embodies the significance of God's dealings with his people Israel. The whole of the Old Testament thus bears witness to Jesus the Christ, and the essential function of the Old Testament is to testify to him. By including this genealogy within his story of Jesus and by placing Jesus' name over this genealogy from Abraham through David ("The genealogy of Jesus Christ"), Matthew indicates that the whole of the Old Testament is taken up and made part of the Jesus story. This claim, introduced in the genealogy, forms the basis for the fulfillment quotations that punctuate the remainder of the Gospel of Matthew.

Here Matthew lifts up four critical points in salvation history: Abraham, David, deportation, and Christ (Mt 1:1, 17). Matthew singles out Abraham

---

[1] As I mentioned above, chiasm often emphasizes the first and last element. In this case, it is clear that Matthew emphasizes "Christ" over "Son of Abraham," which stands in the center of the chiastic arrangement, since elsewhere Matthew stresses Jesus' role as Christ but does not mention again his Abrahamic sonship.

[2] In a sense, therefore, "Son of David" and "Son of Abraham" are folded into the concept of "Christ," i.e., Jesus' messiahship includes his roles as Son of David and Son of Abraham.

[3] The meaning of *Christ* (χριστός) is "anointed one," probably referring here to the anointing of Davidic kings (see "son of David," and emphasis on kingship throughout Matthew).

[4] Matthew's genealogy reflects the "teleological" view of history that we find in the Bible as a whole, which holds that history is moving toward a goal or "telos" in which all that precedes in the historical process finds its final significance.

and David because they received promises of a "son" or "seed." In each case the promise of a son was purposeful and was central to the covenant God made with each of them.

The Old Testament links God's covenantal promise of a son to Abraham with God's purpose to bless the nations, or the Gentiles, through Abraham and specifically through his descendants/seed/son (Gen 22:18; cf. Gen 12:2-3; 17:1-8). The literal rendering of both the Hebrew word in the Masoretic Text and the Greek word in the Septuagint is *seed*, which could mean descendants or a specific son. In the context of Genesis it pertained to Isaac and his descendants, that is, the whole of Israel. But Matthew insists that it refers specifically to Jesus, suggesting that the role Israel as a whole was to play in the redemption of the nations would be realized through Jesus, who embodies in himself the purposes and function that God had in mind for the entire nation. This description of Jesus' role as Son of Abraham thus anticipates the ultimate inclusion of the Gentiles among the redeemed people of God, as Jesus will announce in the wake of his passion and resurrection in Matthew 28:18-20. Indeed, the fact that the book begins with "Son of Abraham" and concludes with the commission to "make disciples of all nations" suggests that Matthew wishes to frame his Gospel with the promise of the redemption of the Gentiles through the work of Jesus.

But Matthew also introduces here the notion that Jesus is "the Son of David," recalling the covenant God made with David, when God promised, "I will raise up your offspring [seed] after you . . . and I will establish his kingdom. . . . I will establish the throne of his kingdom forever" (2 Sam 7:12-13). The Old Testament repeatedly declares that God has designated the Davidic kings, or an ideal future Davidic king, to be the agent of God's rule over his people Israel and ultimately over the entire world (e.g., Ps 2; 89; Is 11:1-16; Jer 33:14-26; Mic 5:2-15).

Matthew links this title with "king" (Mt 1:6), thus indicating that these two designations are virtually synonymous. Yet Matthew notes that already at the beginning of the monarchy David, as king, was the father of Solomon "by the wife of Uriah" (Mt 1:6; cf. 2 Sam 11–12), thus pointing both to David's adultery ("wife") and murder ("of Uriah") and suggesting that the entire period of the monarchy (Mt 1:6-11) in which David's sons, or seed, reigned over Judah, was characterized by moral and spiritual failure. Accordingly, the monarchy ends with the punishment of Babylonian exile (Mt 1:11-12).

But the exile involved the punishment not only of the Davidic monarchy but of the entire nation, for the repetition of the phrase "and his brothers" links the whole nation (Mt 1:2) with the deportation of "Jeconiah and his brothers" (Mt 1:11).[5] Therefore, the exile points to the fact that Israel failed to function as "son of Abraham" even as the Davidic kings failed in their function as "Son of David." Jesus succeeds where Israel and the Davidic kings have failed: he is the Son of David through whom God is establishing God's own rule over his people and finally over the entire world, and he is the Son of Abraham through whom God will bring salvation to the Gentiles. In addition, the reference to the exile (the only event mentioned in the genealogy) reminds the reader that God judges his people, which forms the foundation for the theme of the judgment of Israel (e.g., Mt 3:7-10; 8:11; 21:28–22:14) and those in the church (e.g., Mt 7:15-23; 13:47-50; 24:45–25:46) that we find throughout the Gospel of Matthew.

Matthew includes the four women in the course of the genealogy (Mt 1:3, 5, 6) at least in part to support the claim that Jesus is the Son of Abraham who brings Gentiles into the community of God's people, for the four women were Gentiles who were incorporated into the Old Testament community of faith.[6] The inclusion of these Gentile progenitors suggests that God had the inclusion of the Gentiles in mind all along and that such was not a divine afterthought or an act of divine desperation in the wake of Israel's rejection of Jesus, God's Son; it suggests, too, that the possibility of Gentile inclusion is Christocentric in that it relates directly to Jesus' role as Son of Abraham.[7]

---

[5]The reference to "and his brothers" in Mt 1:11 could refer to the siblings of Jeconiah. Yet according to 1 Chron 3:16 Jeconiah had but one brother, and the fact that this phrase appears both in Mt 1:2, where it clearly describes all the sons of Jacob, i.e., of Israel, and in Mt 1:11 suggests that Matthew wishes to indicate that "and his brothers" refers here to the entire nation, which suffered the punishment of Babylonian exile.

[6]This is indubitably true of Rahab and Ruth, and almost certainly true of Tamar. Bathsheba ("the wife of Uriah") was probably a Hebrew, but by referring to her not by her given name but as Uriah's wife Matthew reminds the reader that she was married to the Hittite Uriah, and as such (in that patriarchal society) was considered to belong to the foreigners in the land.

[7]Actually, the mention of the women seems to play a dual role in the genealogy. In addition to supporting the claim that Jesus is Son of Abraham who draws Gentiles into the community of God, it also anticipates the theme of Jesus' ministry to the powerless and marginalized (e.g., Mt 11:5; 25:31-46), for insofar as Matthew links these four women to Mary (Mt 1:16, 18-25) he

The summary in Matthew 1:17, which divides the genealogy into three periods of fourteen generations each, suggests that God was purposefully and carefully working throughout salvation history to bring it to its culmination in Christ. The reference to fourteen probably represents a doubled seven, a number that Matthew employs to point toward perfection or completeness; Matthew therefore insists that Jesus perfectly fulfills the roles of Christ, Son of David, and Son of Abraham, and that God's dealings with his people Israel throughout its history have perfectly prepared for the Christ.[8]

Matthew continues his concern for the origins of Jesus when he moves from the genealogy to events surrounding Jesus' birth and infancy (Mt 1:18–2:23). Here Matthew puts forth two additional witnesses: the testimony of the angel in Matthew 1:18-25 and the testimony of the magi in Matthew 2:1-13. Matthew sets both testimonies in the context of the first struggles Jesus experiences in the Gospel, namely, the innocent challenge from Joseph (Mt 1:18-25) and the malevolent challenge from Herod (Mt 2:1-23).[9]

The description of this material in terms of two testimonies suggests a shift between Matthew 1:25 and Matthew 2:1. Whereas Matthew 1:18-25 depicts the conception and birth of Jesus, Matthew 2:1-23 deals with events surrounding Jesus' infancy. But Matthew binds this material together through the fivefold repetition of the pattern of divine (angelic) revelation through a dream leading to obedient human response (Mt 1:18-25; 2:12, 13-15, 19-20, 22). This pattern moves the action of the story along, and thus represents the propelling force of the history herein narrated. Matthew's point is clear: God is in control of this history; he exercises his sovereign control by revealing his will to righteous ones who in turn participate in God's control of history by their obedient response. God's control of the history surrounding his Messiah is thus not monergistic but synergistic, which means that in these cases God does not

---

reminds the reader that they all, like Mary, found themselves in a position of vulnerability and danger, yet assumed critical roles in the redemptive purposes of God.

[8] For a fuller treatment of these, and other, aspects of the genealogy, see David R. Bauer, "The Literary and Theological Function of the Genealogy in Matthew's Gospel," in *Treasures New and Old: Recent Contributions to Matthean Studies*, ed. David R. Bauer and Mark Allan Powell, SBLSS 1 (Atlanta: Scholars, 1996), 129-59.

[9] Joseph's initial decision to divorce Mary, which would remove the possibility of Jesus being incorporated into the Davidic line (cf. Mt 1:1-17), was the result of the righteousness of Joseph, as explicated below.

work alone but involves the participation of those obedient to his revelation.[10] God is transcendent over history but is involved in history through the mediation of angels and of humans.

Here God overcomes all obstacles, and thereby equips Jesus for his Messianic role by his adoption into the Davidic line through Joseph son of David (Mt 1:18-19) and protects him from Herod's murderous attempts (Mt 2:13-23). Yet we see God's sovereignty in the historical process most profoundly when God uses even Herod's most egregious action of murdering the Bethlehem infants to fulfil Scripture (Mt 2:17-18). This divine employment of human evil, specifically murder and attempted murder of the Christ (cf. Mt 2:4), to fulfil God's redemptive ends anticipates the ultimate expression of such divine sovereignty when God uses the crucifixion of Jesus to bring salvation to the world (Mt 20:28; 26:27-28; cf. Mt 1:21).

Another feature binding Matthew 1:18–2:23 together is the repeated fulfillment quotations, which also appear five times in the course of this segment. These quotations were not all, in their original Old Testament contexts, messianic predictions; indeed, the final and climactic one (Mt 2:23) does not explicitly appear in the Old Testament at all. But Matthew is assuming a view of salvation history according to which individual persons, events, and declarations in the Old Testament find their meaning and significance in specific events surrounding Jesus. These fulfillment quotations suggest not only that God is in control of this history, but that God has an overriding aim for this history, and that aim is to work out his purposes as set forth in Scripture.

Matthew presents the witness of the angel in Matthew 1:18-25. At the center of the angel's testimony is the essential mission and purpose of Jesus, namely to "save his people from their sins" (Mt 1:21). The *basis* of Jesus' saving activity is his role as Davidic king, for this passage emphasizes that Jesus is Son of David (that is, king, cf. Mt 1:6) by virtue of his being adopted by Joseph the descendent of David when Joseph gave to him his name.[11] Thus Jesus is the Davidic king in the sense that it is through Jesus' reign that

---

[10] *Monergism* means "working alone," while *synergism* means "working together."
[11] The naming of a child on the part of a man was an act of *de facto* adoption. See Jean Daniélou, *The Infancy Narratives* (New York: Herder and Herder, 1968), 43-52; Raymond E. Brown, *The Birth of the Messiah: A Commentary on the Infancy Narratives in the Gospels of Matthew and Luke*, new ed., ABRL (New York: Doubleday, 1993), 138-39.

God is mediating his salvation to his people. Moreover, Matthew indicates the *importance* of this saving purpose by linking it to Jesus' personal name, which God himself selects. The angel requires that Joseph name the child "Jesus," the shortened Greek form of the Hebrew יהושע, meaning "Yahweh saves." Matthew is the only New Testament writer to find significance in the name Jesus, and he does so in order to aver that this saving purpose belongs to the very essence of Jesus' being and behavior. In a sense, every time we encounter the name Jesus we are to think of his saving work.

Moreover, Matthew describes the *object* of this saving activity by the phrase "from their sins." In the Old Testament the king functioned as the agent of God's salvation of his people primarily from military and political enemies (1 Sam 9:16; 10:27; 11:3–18:30; 2 Sam 5:1–12:31; 1 Kings 20:1-43; 2 Kings 3:1-27; 18:1–19:27; 1 Chron 11:1-47; 18:1–20:8; 2 Chron 14:1-14; 20:1-35; 32:1-33). Here Matthew suggests that the fundamental problem facing the people of God is not military oppression but bondage to sin.[12] Matthew will describe the bases, nature, extent, and consequences of the sins of the people in his presentation of the religious leaders, the crowds, and (to some extent) the disciples throughout the remainder of the Gospel of Matthew. Yet Matthew portrays the fundamental character of sin in the portrayal of Herod in Matthew 2: rebellion against the rule of God that has come in Jesus, God's designated king in the line of David, which leads to the abuse of power and the destruction of others.

Furthermore, Matthew declares that the *sphere* of this saving activity is "his people," apparently synonymous with the people of God (cf. Mt 2:6). It is unclear whether this phrase refers to the nation of Israel or to the church. It probably refers to both. On the level of God's purpose, it refers (primarily) to the nation of Israel, and suggests that God intended that this Son of David should function as the Messiah-King sent specifically to the people of Israel in order to bring them wholeness and salvation (cf. Mt 2:2: "the king of the Jews;" also Mt 2:6). But the remainder of the Gospel of Matthew (beginning already in chap. 2) portrays Israel as refusing to submit to Jesus' kingship. This description of divine purpose, then, points to the faithfulness of God toward his people Israel in fulfilling his promises to them surrounding

---

[12]Contra Joel Willitts, *Matthew's Messianic Shepherd-King: In Search of 'The Lost Sheep of the House of Israel'*, BZNW (Berlin: De Gruyter, 2007), 114-34.

David and his "Son." But it also points to the stubbornness of the people of Israel as a whole in refusing to submit to this Son of David and to the sad consequence that by refusing to submit to Christ's rule most in Israel have excluded themselves from the salvation of God. On the level of actual experience, this phrase refers to true disciples within the church, for the immediate context defines "his people" as those who confess that Jesus is "Emmanuel," that is, "God with us,"[13] and thereby experience salvation from their sins.

This phrase anticipates the emphasis on Christian community that we find throughout the Gospel of Matthew and suggests that God communicates his salvation to individuals as they participate in the community of the church. Through Christ God is saving his *people*; it is precisely in the sphere of peoplehood that God is manifesting his salvation. Believers experience that salvation as they encounter within the dynamics of the Christian community the saving presence of God in the person of his Son who is Emmanuel, God with us, and who himself continues to dwell in the midst of his church "always, to the end of the age" (Mt 28:20).

Thus the *means* of this saving activity is the presence of God in the midst of his people in the person of Jesus. The notion of "God with us," taken over from the Old Testament, points to God's unlimited, overcoming power to deliver his people. This emphasis on God's presence with his people in the person of Jesus assumes the closest possible connection between God and Jesus, and it is this close personal connection that Matthew wishes to support and explicate by reference to the virginal conception.

Matthew does not describe any sexual relations between the Holy Spirit and Mary; in fact, he rules it out by calling Mary a "virgin" even after the conception. Rather, Matthew emphasizes the utterly unique character of this conception, and because it is unique it is also ultimately mysterious and inexplicable. And that is Matthew's point: The relationship between God and Jesus is absolutely unique, mysterious, and inexplicable. The consideration that a virginal conception stands outside the realm of human experience and understanding makes a profound statement about Jesus: The Jesus whose origin is thus unique and unexplainable cannot himself be fully

---

[13]Both the MT and the LXX of Is 7:14 read, "you [singular] shall call his name Emmanuel." Matthew has apparently redacted the Isaiah passage so as to suggest that it is those who experience salvation who thus consider or address him.

comprehended by human experience or understanding (cf. Mt 8:27). Of course, the fact that Jesus is conceived by the divine operation of the Holy Spirit also suggests that the essential reality about Jesus is his relationship to God as his Father, a theme Matthew develops throughout his Gospel.

Yet the claim that Jesus is "Emmanuel, God with us" raises the question of the exact nature of the relationship between Jesus and God. Is Jesus simply the representative or agent of God's saving presence, or is he in some sense God? The remainder of the Gospel of Matthew will progressively clarify this relationship, although the finally inexplicable character of the relationship will maintain the element of mystery. Even at this point, however, Jesus' conception by the Holy Spirit seems to carry ontological implications, that is, to suggest in some sense divine being.

While the witness of the angel, which focuses on the person of Jesus, stands at the center of Matthew 1:18-25, this passage also explicates the theme of discipleship by presenting Joseph as a proleptic disciple. Matthew characterizes Joseph as a "righteous man" (δίκαιος), thus introducing the theme of righteousness that occupies a central role in Matthew's understanding of discipleship.[14] Joseph's righteousness consists of his intention to divorce the impregnated Mary in conformity to the law of Moses which required that husbands put away betrothed women who lacked the marks of virginity (Deut 22:13-21).[15] But he manifested righteousness also by joining this legal compliance with mercy and love (cf. Mt 23:23; 25:37, 46). Both of these commitments anticipate this Gospel's expectations that disciples will do "the least of these commandments" (Mt 5:19), while also being merciful (Mt 5:7; 9:13; 12:7), recognizing that the entire law hangs from the central and dominant command to "love your neighbor as yourself" (Mt 22:39; cf. Mt 7:12).

We find the first conflict surrounding Jesus in Matthew 2:1-23, and it centers on Herod. Within this conflict Matthew embeds the witness of the magi, who stand in stark contrast to Herod. These magi, who are presumably members of the royal court of Babylon, the same city to which

---
[14]This Gospel repeatedly refers to disciples as "righteous" and insists that "righteousness" (δικαιοσύνη) is a chief characteristic of disciples.
[15]See Brown, *Birth of the Messiah*, 127: "Deuteronomy required the stoning of the adulteress; but in a less severe legal system the command to 'purge the evil from the midst of you' could have been met by divorcing her."

Israel had gone into exile (cf. Mt 1:11, 12, 17), are the first persons in Matthew's narrative to utter a christological confession; ironically, it is these Gentile astrologers and interpreters of dreams who proclaim to Jerusalem the birth of the "king of the Jews" (Mt 2:2).[16] Like Joseph, these magi are anticipatory disciples; they do exactly what, according to the remainder of the Gospel of Matthew, disciples are to do; for example, both the magi and the disciples worship (Mt 2:2, 11; cf. Mt 14:33; 28:9, 17) and both experience joy (Mt 2:10; cf. Mt 13:20, 44; 25:21, 23; cf. Mt 28:8). And, like the women in the genealogy, they point to the inclusion of the Gentiles, and even the most unlikely of Gentiles, since magi were regarded by the Jews as dangerous and anathema.[17]

By way of contrast, Herod is troubled at the news of the birth of the king (Mt 2:3) and resorts to deception (Mt 2:7), lying (Mt 2:8), and murder (Mt 2:16) in order to be rid of this Christ. In this way, Herod anticipates the opposition to Jesus on the part of the religious leaders later in the Gospel of Matthew; they also are troubled at Jesus' authority (Mt 9:3), take secret counsel (Mt 12:14), engage in deception and lying (Mt 19:3; 22:15; 26:60), and finally kill Jesus (Mt 26–27).[18] Already in this passage Matthew describes all Jerusalem being "with Herod" (Mt 2:3); and he mentions specifically "the chief priests and scribes of the people." Matthew allows no middle ground here: the magi worship while Herod seeks to kill him. Herod is the antidisciple.[19]

---

[16] The LXX employed the term for "magi" almost exclusively to refer to a group of magicians, astrologers, and interpreters of dreams in the Babylonian royal court (Dan 1:20; 2:2; 4:4; 5:7). Matthew does not suggest that these men were magicians, but he does present them as astrologers (Mt 2:2) and perhaps also as adept at the interpretation of dreams (Mt 2:12). I will use *magi*, the Latin transliteration of the Greek word.

[17] Thus *bShab.* 75: "The one who learns from a magus is worthy of death." The other NT references to μάγος indicate a link to false prophecy (Acts 13:6, 8; cf. Acts 8:9-12).

[18] Thus even the stages of development of Herod's opposition in this passage prefigure the development of opposition on the part of the religious authorities. Moreover, Matthew links Herod's opposition to the later opposition on the part of the religious authorities by the repetition of the same terms, e.g., Herod "assembles" (συνάγω) all the chief priests and scribes in Mt 2:4, which anticipates the repeated use of συνάγω to describe the religious leaders convening to plot Jesus' death (Mt 26:3, 57; cf. Mt 28:12), and Matthew speaks of Herod "seeking" (ζητέω) Jesus' life, even as later he will use the same word to describe the chief priests seeking to arrest Jesus (Mt 21:46), seeking an occasion to deliver him up (Mt 21:16), and seeking false witnesses against Jesus (Mt 26:59). Indeed in Mt 22:16 the Pharisees join forces with the "Herodians" to entangle Jesus.

[19] Matthew draws a contrast also between Herod and Joseph: Joseph protects the life of Jesus while Herod seeks to kill him. Matthew reinforces this contrast by the use of "secretly" (λάθρᾳ): Joseph expresses kindness by his desire to divorce Mary "secretly" (Mt 1:19), while Herod summons the

Yet Matthew 2:1-23 contains not only a contrast between Herod and the magi, but also between Herod and Jesus, and this contrast involves kingship. Both Herod and Jesus are kings (Mt 2:1-3, 6, 9). This passage develops the character of Herod's kingship: it involves self-serving attempts to maintain his own power and control leading to the destruction of others, specifically the death of his subjects. Matthew also provides here a sketch of Jesus' kingship: he is the eschatological Davidic king,[20] who will "shepherd" God's people Israel (Mt 2:6), which involves saving them from their sins (Mt 1:21); for it was the function of a shepherd to save his sheep from destruction.[21] Matthew will develop more fully the meaning of Jesus' kingship in the one other portion of the Gospel of Matthew which presents Jesus as king, namely the passion narrative, where Jesus is condemned and dies as "king of the Jews" (Mt 27:11, 29, 37, 42).[22] There we will learn that Jesus rules precisely by dying on behalf of his people. Thus, Herod rules by maintaining his own interests and destroying his subjects, while Jesus (in the broad sweep of the Gospel of Matthew) rules by giving his life for his subjects and thereby saving them. In this way, Herod's kingship represents the evil and God-opposing character of all earthly kingdoms (admittedly *in extremis*), since "all the kingdoms of the world and the glory of them" belong to the devil and he allots them on the basis of the worship of his person (Mt 4:9). Yet this portrait informs not only the Gospel's presentation of political leadership, but also of the religious leaders; for insofar as Matthew has Herod prefigure the opposition of the religious authorities Matthew suggests that the hostility Jesus will experience at their hands is a Herod-like opposition.[23]

---

magi secretly in order to effectuate his plans to murder Jesus (Mt 2:7). Matthew presents Herod as an unreliable character, so that the reader is to assume his statements are untrue; thus Herod never intended to "worship" Jesus (Mt 2:8).

[20]The repeated references to Bethlehem (Mt 2:1, 5, 6, 8) allude to Jesus' Davidic kingship, as does the insistence on Jesus' connection to the Davidic line in Mt 1:18-25.

[21]See Ps 23:4; 80:1-2; Is 31:4; 56:10-12; Jer 23:4; 31:10; 49:19; 50:6, 44; Ezek 34:5-7; Amos 3:12; Zech 10:2-3; 11:5, 8-9, 15-16; cf. Jn 10:9, 10-15. It was also the function of a shepherd to feed the sheep (Ps 23:5; Song 1:8-14; Is 3:20; 40:11; Ezek 34:2-3, 8, 23; Zech 11:16), which seems to lie behind Jesus' feeding of the crowds in Mt 14:13-21; 15:32-39. The shepherd's role included also leading the sheep (Num 27:17; 1 Kings 22:17; Ps 23:1-3; 80:1; Is 40:11; Jn 10:1-5), giving rest to the sheep (e.g., Jer 33:12), and gathering them (e.g., Nah 3:18; Zech 13:7; cf. 1 Pet 2:25).

[22]Mt 26:31 draws the connection between "shepherd" and Jesus' passion.

[23]For a fuller discussion of Mt 1:18-2:23, see David R. Bauer, "The Kingship of Jesus in the Matthean Infancy Narrative: A Literary Analysis," *CBQ* 57 (1995): 306-23.

Matt 3:1-4:16. Matthew 3:1–4:16 is distinct from that which precedes in that Matthew moves from describing events surrounding Jesus' birth and infancy to events surrounding the adult Jesus as he prepares to embark on his ministry. The events recorded here in Matthew 3:1–4:16, however, do not constitute the ministry of Jesus itself, which begins only in Matthew 4:17. This passage therefore continues the prolegomena to Jesus' ministry and serves a threefold function of preparation: (1) like Matthew 1:1–2:23 it prepares the reader for the narrative of Jesus' ministry in the remainder of the Gospel of Matthew; (2) it describes events in which Jesus himself is prepared for his ministry; and (3) it includes the account of the ministry of John, which functions to prepare the people for Jesus' ministry.

Matthew here continues his series of reliable witnesses to the person of Jesus. To the witness of Matthew himself (Mt 1:1-17), the angel (Mt 1:18-25), and the magi (Mt 2:1-23) Matthew now adds the witness of John. Matthew carefully establishes the reliability of John's witness. He preaches the same message as Jesus and the disciples (Mt 3:2; cf. Mt 4:17; 10:7).[24] He fulfills Old Testament prophecy (Mt 3:3), and he proclaims the message of God without fear, remaining uncompromised in the presence of human opposition and even deadly attacks (Mt 3:7-11; 4:11; 11:2; 14:1-12; 17:10-13).

Perhaps the most significant feature of John's reliability is that he stands in the succession of Elijah. Jesus identifies John explicitly with Elijah (Mt 11:14; 17:10-13) and with the messenger of Malachi 3:1, probably taken to be one with the coming Elijah described in Malachi 4:5-6 (cf. Mt 11:10). Moreover, the very description of John in our passage reflects the demeanor of Elijah as described in 2 Kings 1:8. It is clear that Matthew does not intend to suggest that John the Baptist was literally Elijah *redivivus*,[25] but rather that John fulfilled the function of the Elijah-like prophet who would prepare the people for the coming of the Messiah and the kingdom.

This reference to John's fulfillment of the role of Elijah suggests the essential character of his work. He is a prophet. That is the way Jesus describes him in Matthew 11:9-15, and the depiction of John's dress in our passage alludes to Zechariah 13:4, in which prophets are described as wearing the

---

[24]John also shares with Jesus and later the disciples the fate of persecution unto death, which Matthew indicates by the technical expression "deliver over" (παραδίδομαι, Mt 4:12; 10:4, 17, 19, 21; 17:22; 20:18-19; 24:9-10; 26:2, 15, 16, 21, 23, 24, 45, 46, 48; 27:2, 3, 4, 18, 26).

[25]Elijah, after all, functions as a separate character in Matthew's narrative (Mt 17:1-4).

hair of a camel. But John is "more than a prophet" (Mt 11:9). The Judaism of Jesus' day (and of Matthew's) generally accepted the notion that prophetic revelation had ceased with Malachi, some four hundred years earlier, with the result that the people lacked the advantage of this rather direct means of divine communication.[26] The appearance of John breaks the prophetic silence in order to communicate a message unique among the prophets in its transcendent significance. Thus, insofar as John is a prophet, he stands in continuity with the prophets of the Old Testament and, in some sense, represents that prophetic tradition within the narrative of the Gospel of Matthew. But insofar as John is the eschatological prophet in the succession of Elijah, he plays a unique role in salvation history. His function is to "prepare the way of the Lord" (Mt 3:3), which in the Isaiah passage herein quoted, referred to Yahweh, who in the person of Jesus is now "God with us" (Mt 1:23).

The uniqueness of John is found in his message and in his work of baptism. But we cannot finally separate these two elements, for his baptism is a "prophetic action," and thus part of the message of John itself.[27] It is at this point that we come to describe specifically the content of John's witness to Jesus.

First, John bears witness to Jesus through his fulfillment of prophecy (Mt 3:1-3). This connection with Isaiah 40:3 is obviously a Matthean construction, since John the Baptist does not himself cite this Isaianic passage. The reader, who knows the Old Testament and thus Isaiah 40:3, would recognize that the "Lord" referenced there was Yahweh. This passage, then, reinforces the close connection between Jesus and God introduced in the account of the virgin conception and especially in Matthew 1:23, where Jesus is described as "God with us." It also prepares for the honorific and indeed exalted use of κύριος ("Lord") throughout Matthew.

Second, John bears witness to Jesus through the setting of his ministry. Matthew sets the proclamation of John within the environment of the "desert," in fulfillment of Is 40:3; the evangelist thereby alludes to the Old Testament promises of God to his people regarding their return from Babylonian exile and their experience of God's great blessings on the land

---

[26]See, e.g., 1 Macc 9:27.
[27]Donald A. Hagner, *Matthew 1–13*, WBC (Dallas: Word, 1993), 46.

in which God would reestablish them (this is the subject of Isaiah 40). N. T. Wright has demonstrated that most Jews in Jesus' day believed that the return from exile had not been fully accomplished in the days of Ezra and Zerubbabel, but rather that God would fulfil his promises of return when he established his eschatological kingdom.[28] Thus, the reference in Matthew 1:11, 17 to "after the exile" anticipates this ultimate return from exilic existence. John declares that it is Jesus who will bring to full realization God's good purposes for Israel expressed in the Old Testament hope of return from exile.[29] This witness from John, then, invites the reader to consider how Jesus fulfils these hopes and how the Old Testament portrait of return and reestablishment illumines the person and work of Christ.

Third, John bears witness to Jesus through his demeanor. Both the location of his ministry, in the wilderness away from societal structures, his food, and his clothing are eloquent testimony to his rejection of comfortable and familiar social conventions in favor of challenging accepted ways of thinking and behaving. Like the poor, John depends for his diet and dress on what God provides through nature (cf. Mt 6:25-34) and anticipates Jesus who "has nowhere to lay his head" (Mt 8:20) and who insists that in associating with the poor, the disciples are aligning themselves with him (Mt 25:31-46).

Fourth, John bears witness to Jesus through his demand for a baptism of repentance. This demand implies, negatively, that the people, in their present condition, are not fit for the kingdom that God is about to inaugurate. They must become prepared through a turning of the mind away from old habits of thinking and behavior toward the new reality that God is about to usher in his kingdom.[30] This repentance involves the confessing of sins, which includes a recognition of sins and a willingness to take responsibility for them with a view toward submitting to God's process of dealing with them, and the overt act of submitting to baptism. Matthew's point is clear: racial

---

[28]N. T. Wright, *The New Testament and the People of God* (Minneapolis: Fortress, 1992), 159, 241, 268-71, 386, 399, 406, 440, 446.

[29]The theme of return from exile explains also the emphasis on John's baptizing in the Jordan River, for exiles returning from Babylonian captivity would of necessity pass through the waters of the Jordan. In submitting to baptism, then, the people were affirming and symbolically participating in God's restoration of Israel from exile.

[30]"Turning of the mind" is the basic meaning of *repentance* (μετανοέω).

descent from Abraham and membership in the Jewish community are insufficient to qualify persons to participate in the kingdom that God is about to establish in Jesus.

The demand for a baptism of repentance implies, positively, that God wishes to establish a new covenant community around the kingdom which Jesus is about to inaugurate. The question of membership in the covenant community necessarily involved the issue of sonship to Abraham, for God originally established covenant with his people on the basis of the promise he made to Abraham regarding Abraham's descendants (Gen 12:2-3; 15:1-20; 18:9-15; 22:1-19). It is therefore hardly surprising that Matthew presents some among John's hearers as taking exception to the notion that they were not truly children of Abraham, at least not in a way that really mattered. Thus, an altercation occurs between John and the religious leaders over just this issue, and John employs this altercation to develop a significant aspect of Jesus' work, namely, his role in God's activity of creating a new eschatological community, in other words, making others children of Abraham.

The reference to "children of Abraham" in Matthew 3:7-10 relates to Jesus' role as "Son of Abraham" in Matthew 1:1-17, where Jesus' Abrahamic sonship pertains to his function as the one who, in fulfillment of God's promises to Abraham regarding his son, would be the agent of God's blessings to "all nations," that is, to Gentiles. Already in Matthew 2 Jesus begins to fulfil this role when Gentile magi come to worship him and become proleptic disciples. But whereas Matthew 2 emphasizes *that* Jesus is the Son of Abraham who attracts Gentiles to the kingdom of God, Matthew 3 suggests *how* Jesus functions as Son of Abraham, namely, by making others, both Jews and Gentiles, true children of Abraham.

Finally, John bears witness to Jesus through his description of the Christ, which emphasizes the preeminence of Jesus over John. John declares that the coming one is preeminent in power and majesty. Although, according to the Old Testament, the prophets were servants/slaves of Yahweh, John the prophet is unworthy to carry Jesus' sandals, that is, to be his slave (Mt 3:11).[31]

Thus Jesus is much more than a prophet. The prophets, including John, testify to this Christ, but Jesus and his work are not simply a continuation

---

[31] To carry or unloose sandals was one of the most menial tasks a slave would perform.

of earlier prophetic revelation; Jesus represents the discontinuity that necessarily accompanies eschatological fulfillment. Through John, the last and greatest of the prophets, the prophets themselves declare the Christ's transcendence over them and their revelation. This discontinuity is found in the fully eschatological character of the baptizing work of the coming one over against John's baptism. All persons will experience the baptism of the Christ. For some it will be a baptism of the Spirit,[32] but for the rest it will be a baptism of the fire of eternal judgment.[33] Thus the Christ has the prerogative to save (baptism with the Spirit) and to judge, the very prerogatives that, according to the Old Testament, belonged to Yahweh. Moreover, this baptism with the Spirit transcends the prophetic gift of the Spirit in the preceding dispensation; for this experience of the Spirit on the part of those who will experience this baptism is transcendent in manner, measure, and scope of operation over against the functioning of the Spirit prior to the appearance of the Christ, since this is a truly eschatological reality that belongs to the coming of the end-time kingdom.

It is clear that John was not a disciple of Jesus and actually in one sense was not even in the kingdom.[34] When John confesses that he needs to be baptized by Jesus, he implies that he has not received the baptism of the Spirit which Jesus will administer as qualification for participation in the kingdom (Mt 12:28; 28:19).[35] And when Jesus announces that "he who is least in the kingdom of heaven is greater than [John]" (Mt 11:11), Jesus also implies that John is outside the kingdom. Because John's work straddles the line between the time before and after the arrival of the kingdom, John

---

[32]The pouring out of the Spirit was regarded in the OT and intertestamental Judaism as God's eschatological gift to those who would participate in his end-time kingdom, a gift making possible intimate communion with God and often associated with salvation itself; see, e.g., Joel 2:28-32.

[33]Note *unquenchable* fire; cf. the "eternal punishment" of Mt 25:46. The motif of fire emphasizes the subjective experience of torment, an emphasis we will encounter later in Matthew's description of "weeping and gnashing of teeth," e.g., Mt 8:12; 13:42, 50.

[34]It has often been suggested that Jesus might have been a disciple of John. But while Jesus was surely influenced by John and was baptized by him, no firm evidence exists that he was part of a more or less limited group of close followers. Matthew certainly does not present Jesus as a disciple of John (cf. Mt 9:14; 11:2).

[35]Matthew seems to present John as proclaiming that the baptism of the Spirit and end-time judgment will occur simultaneously (Mt 3:11-12), a connection that seems to be reinforced by John's question in Mt 11:2-3. Although John is a reliable character, certain aspects of his proclamation will be corrected by Jesus in Jesus' ministry as a whole, esp. in Mt 11:4-6.

Interpretation of Matthew 1:1–4:16

cannot be fully part of the eschatological kingdom, though he is intimately related to its coming.

Within the account of the baptism of Jesus (Mt 3:13-17) we encounter the final and climactic witness to Jesus, that from God himself (Mt 3:17). The third-person address ("This is my beloved Son") marks it as testimony, really as a confession.[36] This declaration stands as the climax to Matthew 1:1–4:16 for three reasons. First, the nature of the witness: here God himself witnesses to Jesus, over against mortals and angels in Matthew 1:1–3:12. Second, the nature of the testimony: this statement informs us that Jesus is far more than Son of Abraham or Son of David or even Christ—he is God's own Son. Finally, the progress of the narrative up to this point indicates the climactic function of Matthew 3:17. This statement stands as the culmination of several hints and indirect allusions to Jesus as Son of God. These hints begin already at the beginning of the Gospel with the genealogy. The genealogical list ends in Matthew 1:16 with an alteration in the established pattern. Whereas we would expect to see: "Joseph was the father of Jesus," we read "Joseph the husband of Mary of whom Jesus was born." The passive "was born" (ἐγεννήθη) is a circumlocution for divine activity, that is, a way of saying that Jesus was conceived and born of God, which in turn points ahead to the passive "was conceived" (γεννηθέν) in Matthew 1:20.[37] Thus, Matthew suggests that Jesus was not the natural son of Joseph, but that he is the Son of God.

The concept of Son of God appears also in Matthew 1:18-25. Here Matthew takes pains to show that Jesus is not the product of a union between Joseph and Mary. Twice we are told that the child was conceived by the Holy Spirit (Mt 1:18-20). Through the words of the prophet, Mary is called a "virgin" (Mt 1:23) even after she has conceived. And after Joseph takes Mary as his wife, he does not have sexual contact with her until she has borne Jesus (Mt 1:25). Matthew also mentions the term *son* in this section. The angel predicts that Mary will bear a "son" (Mt 1:21), and this prediction is fulfilled

---

[36] The third-person address here in Matthew is distinct from the second-person address that we find in the Markan and Lucan accounts.

[37] This is an example of the "divine passive," or "passive of divine circumlocution," which is a way of talking about the activity of God without using the name of God, perhaps out of extreme regard for the divine name. See Daniel B. Wallace, *Greek Grammar Beyond the Basics: An Exegetical Syntax of the New Testament* (Grand Rapids: Zondervan, 1996), 437-38; Maximilian Zerwick, *Biblical Greek* (Rome: Pontifical Biblical Institute, 1963), 76.

in Matthew 1:25, where the term is repeated. Even more significant, a reference to "son" appears in the prophetic quotation of Matthew 1:23: "a virgin shall conceive and bear a son." In the introduction to this quotation and in the introduction to the one other fulfillment quotation in which Matthew mentions "son" (Mt 2:15), Matthew has altered his usual wording: in these two introductory statements he has added "by the Lord." Matthew has inserted this prepositional phrase into these two passages to emphasize that God is here speaking about his own Son.[38]

I have just mentioned the fulfillment quotation of Matthew 2:15, where the Lord once again speaks through the prophet about his Son: "Out of Egypt I have called my son." This is a quote from Hosea 11:1, which originally referred to the exodus of Israel, God's son, from Egyptian bondage, and is now applied by Matthew to refer to Jesus in such a way as to link Jesus' divine sonship to that of Israel and to suggest that Jesus is Son of God as one who experiences God's protection and deliverance.

All these indications of divine sonship lead up to the declaration of Matthew 3:17. Matthew alerts us to the climactic character of Matthew 3:17 by a double "and behold" (καὶ ἰδοὺ), which he typically uses to indicate that something of special significance is about to be said or done (e.g., Mt 12:42; 28:9-10). Up to this point, the divine sonship of Jesus has been expressed through circumlocutions or statements made by God indirectly through the prophets. Now God announces unambiguously that Jesus is his Son.

Matthew has so structured this first major division of the Gospel as to bring it to a climax with the declaration of Matthew 3:17 because he wishes to show that Jesus is to be understood primarily in terms of Son of God. Matthew employs a number of christological titles throughout Matthew 1:1–4:16, including Son of David and Christ. But all of these are subordinate and supportive of the primary way in which we are to understand Jesus, and that is as Son of God.

The declaration of Matthew 3:17 itself comes from two Old Testament passages. Isaiah 42:1 speaks of the Servant of Yahweh, while Psalm 2:7 is a coronation hymn used at the enthronement of the kings of Judah. Accordingly, Matthew suggests that Jesus is Son of God in the sense that he is the Servant

---

[38] Rudolf Pesch, "Der Gottessohn im matthäischen Evengelienprolog: Beobachtungen zu den Zitationsformeln der Reflexionszitate," *Biblica* 48 (1967): 410.

who, in accordance with God's will, identifies in suffering with the people as a whole in order to deliver them through the sacrifice of himself, thus pointing to his passion, and that he is at the same time the king in the line of David who will be elevated to the throne, thus pointing to his resurrection.

Yet we must determine the meaning of "Son of God" here primarily from the climactic development leading up to Matthew 3:17 and the immediate context, especially the story of Jesus' baptism. Hence Jesus is Son of God in the sense that he has his origin in God, and thus sustains a unique, intimate, and ultimately mysterious relationship to God so that he can reveal the person and will of God his Father, and in the sense that he shares in the work of his Father by being the agent of God's salvation (Mt 1:18-25). Moreover, he is Son of God as one who experiences God's protection and deliverance, so that he himself might be the agent of God's deliverance for his people (Mt 2:15; cf. Mt 2:6; 1:20-25).

Moreover, the immediate context of Matthew 3:13-17 indicates that Jesus is Son in the sense that he perfectly obeys the will of his Father. God himself declares in Matthew 3:17 that he is "well pleased" with this Son, and Jesus submits to baptism, against the objections of John, in order "to fulfill all righteousness" (Mt 3:15).[39] Jesus submits to baptism not because he has sin to confess and repent of, but because it is God's will that Jesus identify with the people in their need so as to deliver them.[40] Ironically, in this act of identification with sinners Jesus demonstrates his righteousness, for the divine declaration of approval comes immediately in the wake of Jesus' baptism. Furthermore, Matthew explicates the obedience of Jesus Son of God in the temptation narrative that follows. Repeatedly Jesus is tempted by Satan in his capacity as Son of God (Mt 4:3, 6) and precisely in his role as Son of God refuses to yield to these temptations. Finally, Matthew 4:12 witnesses to Jesus' obedience to the will of his Father in that Jesus embarks on

---

[39]The concept of "righteousness" is significant for Matthew, the noun occurring seven times in the Gospel of Matthew. Disagreement exists as to whether Matthew uses it exclusively in an ethical sense, i.e., the ethical demand God places on persons (so Benno Przybylski, *Righteousness in Matthew and His World of Thought*, SNTMS 41 [New York: Cambridge University Press, 1980]), or sometimes also in a dynamic sense, i.e., God's eschatological saving activity on behalf of persons so that his good and just purposes are realized in them and in the world (so Hagner, *Matthew 1-13*, 56). In this passage we seem to have a combination of the two senses.

[40]For an understanding of Jesus' baptism as participation in the life of the people with a view toward their salvation, see G. R. Beasley-Murray, *Baptism in the New Testament* (Grand Rapids: Eerdmans, 1973), 45-67.

his ministry only after John, the God-appointed preparer, is removed from the scene. Jesus begins his ministry in accordance with God's timing.

Jesus is Son in this passage also as one who receives a gift from his Father: the Holy Spirit. Although Jesus was conceived by the Holy Spirit (Mt 1:18-25), it was necessary for him actually to be anointed with the Spirit; the narrative of the Gospel implies that it is only by the power of the Spirit that Jesus is able to overcome the temptations of Satan (Mt 4:1-11) and perform his ministry (e.g., Mt 12:28). And it follows that those whom Jesus will "baptize with the Holy Spirit" will possess, at least in some measure, this transcendent power to overcome temptation (Mt 6:13; 26:41) and fulfil the ministry to which Christ commissions them (Mt 10:5-42; 28:18-20).

In Matthew 3:13-4:11 Jesus encounters the two great cosmic powers: God and Satan. Both of them address Jesus as Son of God; indeed, the text suggests that Satan knows that Jesus is Son of God because, as a transcendent being, he overheard the divine declaration of Matthew 3:17, which otherwise seems to have been heard only by Jesus.[41] The Greek construction indicates that Satan recognizes that Jesus is Son of God and tempts him to express his divine sonship in ways that contradict God's will.[42]

The background of this passage is Deuteronomy 6–8, which describes the people of Israel being tempted for forty years in the wilderness and yielding to that temptation.[43] For one thing, the introductory statement that Jesus was led by the Spirit into the desert (or wilderness) to be tempted by the devil alludes to Deuteronomy 8:2. For another thing, three times Jesus responds to temptation with a quote from a passage within Deuteronomy 6–8. Jesus thus relives the experience of Israel in the wilderness but makes good where Israel failed: as Israel God's son was tempted in the wilderness and yielded to this temptation (cf. Deut 8:5), even so Jesus God's Son is tempted in the wilderness but refuses to yield, remaining completely obedient to the will of his Father.[44]

---

[41]Although the third-person address may suggest that other humans were present, the fact that later John the Baptist has reservations regarding Jesus' messiahship (Mt 11:2-6) and that up to the point of Jesus' crucifixion only the disciples (and demons) know that Jesus is Son of God indicates that human beings were not privy to this divine announcement.

[42]The Greek construction is a first-class conditional statement (note εἰ vs. ἐάν); we might in this case more precisely translate: "Since you are . . ."

[43]Birger Gerhardsson, *The Testing of God's Son (Matt 4:1-11 & Par): An Analysis of an Early Christian Midrash*, Coniectanea Biblica, New Testament Series 2:1 (Lund: Gleerup, 1966).

[44]Note that Mt 2:15 prepares for this connection between Jesus Son of God and Israel son of God.

In the first temptation (Mt 4:3-4) the devil urges Jesus to turn stones into bread, thus providing food for himself. Since it is obviously no sin for a hungry man to desire bread,[45] we must understand that it is God's will for Jesus to refuse to provide bread for himself at this stage and in this way. God's testing of Israel in the wilderness involved Israel's being "hungry" (that is, dependent only on the manna that God provided) in order that God might know what was in Israel's heart and might discipline Israel so that Israel would keep God's commandments, which involved essentially trust and obedience (Deut 8:3-6). In the same way, God will determine through this period of Jesus' hunger whether Jesus will depend not on his own resources but trust in God's provision for the basic necessities of his life. Jesus will later insist that it is God who provides bread (Mt 6:11, 26), and Jesus will be the agent of divine provision when he multiplies bread for the multitudes (Mt 14:13-21; 15:32-39). The temptation from Satan, then, is that Jesus should distrust God by taking the responsibility for his life on himself. Jesus remembers, however, that trustful submission to God's word is as necessary for true existence as food itself.

In the second temptation (Mt 4:5-7) Satan takes Jesus to the highest point of the temple and, through the remarkable method of himself quoting Scripture (Ps 91:11-12), urges Jesus to throw himself down in order that God might deliver him from death. The Old Testament presents the period of wilderness wanderings as a time of God's protection of Israel (e.g., Deut 8:4, 14-16; cf. Deut 1:31), and also presents the temple as a place of divine protection (e.g., 1 Kings 8:12-61).[46] Indeed, Matthew speaks of the "pinnacle" of the temple, a word that literally means "wing," and thus alludes to those Old Testament passages that describe God's protection in terms of abiding under his wings.[47] The tempter is thus urging Jesus to put God to the test in order to determine if God will fulfil his covenant promise of protection; in such a scenario, God becomes servant to the whims and dares of those who put him to the test. But Jesus remembers that God has forbidden such testing, since it involves a violation of divine sovereignty (Deut 6:16).

---

[45]Indeed, the legitimate need for bread is implied in the passage from Deut 8:3 which Jesus quotes in Mt 4:4: "Humans do not live by bread *alone*."

[46]See Gerhardsson, *Testing of God's Son*, 56-58.

[47]In fact, this very expression appears earlier in Ps 91: "under his wings you will find refuge" (Ps 91:4). Jesus uses the same Greek word in 23:37.

The testing of humans is a divine prerogative; humans must not take it on themselves to test God.[48] In addition, this temptation involves an urging that Jesus attempt to force God to save his life; insofar as Jesus refuses to yield to this temptation he shows that he is ready to forego this demand for divine protection and is willing to lose his life in obedience to the divine will (Mt 26:1–27:54; esp. Mt 26:36-46), which anticipates his refusal to expect God to deliver him from the cross (Mt 27:42) out of a confidence that he will experience the ultimate deliverance of the resurrection, according to God's timing and methods (Mt 12:40; 16:4, 21; 17:22-23; 20:18-19).[49]

It is remarkable that, in this second temptation, the devil quotes Scripture; but it is even more significant that, in the process of quoting Psalm 91, he implicitly interprets it by indicating that it should be understood in terms of an invitation for the human to force God's hand. Matthew presents here, then, a "devilish hermeneutic," one that interprets Scripture according to the prerogatives and power of the self over against patient trust in God and submission to God's sovereignty. It is, of course, this latter principle that lies behind Jesus' use of Scripture here.

In the third and climactic temptation (Mt 4:8-10),[50] Satan takes Jesus to a high mountain in order to offer Jesus "all the kingdoms of the world and their glory" in exchange for worshiping him. Jesus apparently believes that Satan has the ability to deliver on this offer, for otherwise the temptation would have no force for Jesus. But we should remember that according to Psalm 2 (which was quoted in Mt 3:17) God has already promised to give all the earth to his Son (Ps 2:8), and at the end of the Gospel of Matthew, Jesus, standing once again on a mountain, will declare that "all authority in heaven and on earth has been given to me [by God]" (Mt 28:18). The temptation pertains, then, to how and when Jesus will take possession of all the earth, whether it will be now and on his terms, which is tantamount to submitting to the authority of God's foe, the devil, or whether it will be in God's time and on God's terms. We note, therefore, that in all three temptations the issue is the same: How and when will Jesus appropriate these benefits that God has promised? The reference to the ministering angels (Mt 4:11) forms

---

[48]The OT repeatedly indicates that it is God who tests (e.g., Gen 22:1; Deut 13:3).

[49]Note the significance of "the third day," as the time of God's deliverance.

[50]Lk 4:5-8 presents this as the second temptation, while Matthew places it in the strategically final position.

Interpretation of Matthew 1:1–4:16

an eloquent indication that God will provide all that is needed to Jesus (and by implication to others) who resist temptation and trust in God.

Although the devil leaves Jesus (Mt 4:11), Jesus continues to be tempted throughout the Gospel of Matthew in these same ways. This is especially the case in Matthew 16:22-23 and Matthew 26:36-46, and climactically in the crucifixion, where the passersby and religious authorities employ the same terminology Satan uses here: "If you are the Son of God . . ." (Mt 27:40, 43).

The first major division of the Gospel ends with the seventh fulfillment quotation (Mt 4:12-16). The number seven has the same significance in Matthew as in the rest of the Bible: it points to completion.[51] It thus signifies here that the period of preparation is complete, and Jesus begins his ministry at just the right moment, according to God's timing.[52]

---

[51]See, e.g., Karl Heinrich Rengstorf, "ἑπτά," *TDNT* 2:627-35.
[52]We find this emphasis also in the reference to John's imprisonment: Jesus begins his ministry only after John, the forerunner of the Messiah, is removed.

6

INTERPRETATION OF MATTHEW 4:17–16:20

MATT 4:17. The ministry of Jesus begins only in Matthew 4:17, and this statement serves as a general heading to the whole second major division of the Gospel of Matthew (Mt 4:17–16:20). But the significance of Matthew 4:17 extends beyond this structural role. It also contains two major, interrelated elements. The first of these elements is the announcement that the kingdom of heaven is near.

Matthew uses "the kingdom of heaven" and "the kingdom of God" interchangeably; they mean the same thing. Matthew's general use of "the kingdom of heaven" reflects the inclination on the part of Jews of the period to avoid the use of the divine name, believing that even uttering the name of God would somehow violate its holy character. Thus they devised expedients to speak of God while avoiding the word *God*, and one of these expedients was to substitute the place where God dwelt for the divine name itself.[1]

Matthew 4:17 declares that the long-awaited rule of God has now drawn near in Jesus. But the meaning of "is near" (ἐγγίζω) is ambiguous. At this

---

[1] Thus most commentators. Though see Robert L. Mowery, "The Matthean References to the Kingdom: Different Terms for Different Audiences," *ETL* 70 (1994): 398-405. Jonathan Pennington, *Heaven and Earth in the Gospel of Matthew*, NovTSup 126 (Leiden: Brill, 2007), has taken exception to this explanation, insisting that Matthew employs "kingdom of heaven" to emphasize the transcendence of heaven over against the earthly realm. Pennington is certainly correct in noting the element of transcendence here, but the attempt to substitute the divine name can hardly be denied. See, e.g., Mt 16:19; 21:25-26.

point in the narrative it is unclear whether the kingdom is near in the sense that it is about to arrive, but has not yet appeared, or whether it is near in the sense that it is already beginning to dawn. It is only as readers move through the remainder of the Gospel of Matthew that they realize that the phrase is deliberately ambiguous in that it means both.

But the Matthean Jesus declares that it is insufficient for persons to hear the proclamation of the kingdom; they must respond. And the response is repentance. This is the second major element in Matthew 4:17. The structure of the verse indicates that repentance is made possible and necessary, or obligatory, by the proclamation of the kingdom (note "for," γάρ). The fact that Matthew 4:17 is a general heading to the second major division indicates that Matthew spells out the specific content both of the proclamation of the kingdom and of repentance by means of the declarations, commands, and actions of Jesus (in interaction with others) throughout Matthew 4:18–16:20.

Matt 4:18-22. Matthew 4:18-22 introduces the two major recipients of Jesus' ministry of proclamation: the disciples (Mt 4:18-22) and the crowds (Mt 4:23-25). It is significant that Matthew presents Jesus' first specific act of ministry as that of the calling of the disciples, for in this way Matthew indicates the supreme importance of the disciples and discipleship in the Gospel of Matthew. Indeed, Matthew 4:18-22 is presented as background or setting for the second major division and thereby suggests that we are to understand the whole of Matthew 4:23–16:20 in terms of its significance for discipleship, especially as discipleship is portrayed within Matthew 4:18-22.

Here Jesus appears on the scene and without preparation or introduction calls two sets of brothers to discipleship. These stories are parallel, both in their general structure and in many of their details.[2] This parallelism has a threefold effect: 1) it emphasizes those elements that are repeated in the two stories (such as the immediacy of the disciples' response and their abandonment of former commitments); 2) it allow us to interpret one story in light of the other (e.g., we know from Mt 4:19 that the "call" to James and John in Mt 4:21 involves the demand that they "follow" Jesus); and 3) it stresses the normative and paradigmatic character of these two episodes, suggesting that this is the way Jesus repeatedly or typically calls disciples and

---

[2]The parallelism that is present in the description of this event in Mark and Luke is heightened in the Gospel of Matthew.

implying, further, that this story points to essential characteristics of discipleship in general.

Matt 4:23–11:1. The second major division of the Gospel of Matthew contains an overarching causal movement from the announcement of the kingdom (Mt 4:23–11:1) to the dual reactions of this announcement (Mt 11:1–16:20). Moreover, Matthew 4:23 and Matthew 9:35 are essentially parallel statements that bracket the Sermon on the Mount (Mt 5:1–7:29) and the ten mighty acts of Jesus around the Sea of Galilee (8:1–9:35). These bracketing passages contain a description of Jesus' ministry in terms of teaching, preaching, and healing. Even as the ten mighty acts of Matthew 8–9 expand on the reference to healing, so the Sermon on the Mount expands on the reference to teaching.

But if Matthew intends that the Sermon on the Mount should specify the teaching activity of Jesus described in Matthew 4:23 and Matthew 9:35, it follows that Matthew is not presenting the Sermon on the Mount as one teaching episode that Jesus literally performed on a mountain, but rather as a summary or compilation of Jesus' teaching in the synagogues throughout this whole period; for Matthew 4:23 and Matthew 9:35 describe Jesus' teaching activity as constant and *in their synagogues*. It seems likely, then, that Matthew does not intend that we should take the reference to "mountain" in Matthew 5:1 so much geographically as theologically. Matthew frequently uses *mountain* to refer to a place of revelation (e.g., Mt 17:1-8; 28:16-20), and that is its significance here. But, more specifically, in this passage Matthew seems to employ the image of mountain to allude to the revelation of God and of God's will to God's people on Mount Sinai (Ex 19–40).[3] For just as Moses ascended the mountain in order to receive oracles from God to deliver to the people of Israel, so Jesus ascends the mountain in order to declare God's will for life within the newly constituted

---

[3]Terence Donaldson, *Jesus on the Mountain: A Study in Matthean Theology,* JSNTSup 8 (Sheffield: JSOT Press, 1985), takes issue with this generally recognized understanding of the role of "mountain" in the Gospel of Matthew in favor of seeing it as the place where the eschatological messianic community is constituted and as presented by Matthew in terms of the OT and Jewish notion of the new Jerusalem. But the associations of "mountain" language with the revelation of Jesus throughout the Gospel of Matthew seem more natural than the constitution of the community around the eschatological new Jerusalem, and the connections of the mountain here in Mt 5–7 with Sinai are considerable, even if we do not have a full-blown "new Moses" Christology here. Yet in a few passages (notably Mt 5:14) Donaldson's construal appears applicable.

eschatological people of God.⁴ As such, the analogy to the revelation of God on Sinai suggests that Jesus' teaching here is just as reliable in creating a life of wholeness and divine blessing, just as authoritative in representing God's will and demands, just as effective for the forming of a people into God's own community, and just as determinative for destiny on the part of those who obey or disobey the demands herein contained as was the law of Moses; indeed, it is much more so, for Jesus here brings the law of Moses to its fulfillment (Mt 5:17-20).

The consideration that the Sermon on the Mount expands Matthew's reference to Jesus' teaching in Matthew 4:23 and Matthew 9:35 further suggests that the Sermon on the Mount involves teaching rather than preaching. Indeed, both the introduction and conclusion to the Sermon on the Mount describe this speech as teaching (Mt 5:2; 7:28-29). Many scholars contend that in the New Testament no substantive difference exists between teaching (διδαχή) and preaching (κηρύγμα).⁵ And, indeed, in some New Testament writings these two terms are interchangeable (e.g., compare Lk 4:15 with Lk 4:44). Nevertheless, the Gospel of Matthew seems to distinguish between these two elements, for in Matthew preaching involves the announcement of the presence of the kingdom with the consequent call to repent and is directed only to those on the outside, whereas teaching pertains to the explication of the specific content of the presence of the kingdom and of the demand for repentance.⁶ Although Matthew intimates that sometimes Jesus "teaches" the crowds (Mt 4:23; 7:29; 9:35; 11:1; 13:54; 21:23; 22:16; 26:55), the actual content of "teaching" as Matthew presents it has primary significance for those in the kingdom, that is, for disciples (and usually post-Easter

---

⁴This analogy is suggested by the phrase "he went up on a mountain," echoing similar terminology in Ex 19:3, 12; 24:15, 18; 34:1, 4, by the phrase "he came down from the mountain," echoing Ex 34:29, and by the consideration that this discourse functions in much the same way within the Gospel of Matthew as the Sinai revelation functioned in the OT, viz., as the fundamental and formative declaration of God's will for God's people. Thus most commentators, including Donald A. Hagner, *Matthew 1-13*, WBC (Dallas: Word, 1993), 85; Robert H. Gundry, *Matthew: A Commentary on His Handbook for a Mixed Church Under Persecution*, 2nd ed. (Grand Rapids: Eerdmans, 1994), 66; Ulrich Luz, *Matthew 1-7: A Commentary* (Minneapolis: Augsburg, 1989), 224.

⁵E.g., Hagner, *Matthew 1-13*, 80.

⁶Note the use of "preach" (κηρύσσω/κηρύγμα) in Mt 3:1; 4:17, 23; 9:35; 10:7, 27; 11:1; 12:41; 24:14; 26:13.

disciples) and not for the crowds.⁷ Yet Jesus' teaching is related to preaching in that the very authority with which Jesus teaches bears witness to, and is proclamatory of, the fact that the kingdom of God has come in Jesus' person and ministry (cf. Mt 7:28-29). At this point, then, it is important to understand that the Sermon on the Mount announces the presence of the kingdom only implicitly; its primary burden is the instruction of those who have already embarked on the life of discipleship (compare Mt 4:18-22 with Mt 5:1).

This discussion raises the issue of the relationship between the crowds and the disciples. Both the crowds and the disciples hear the Sermon on the Mount. The crowds are present at both the beginning and the end (Mt 5:1; 7:28-29). But Matthew 5:1-2 indicates that Jesus directs this teaching to the disciples. Indeed, some scholars have argued that Matthew makes no real distinction between the crowds and the disciples but rather that he presents the crowds as in some sense disciples, since he describes both disciples and crowds as "following" (ἀκολουθέω) Jesus.⁸

But a careful analysis of the crowds in the Gospel of Matthew indicates that they are in no way disciples of Jesus, for they consistently fail to repent, to place faith in Jesus or the gospel, or to make the (only adequate) christological confession, namely that Jesus is the Son of God, and at the end of the Gospel they call for Jesus' crucifixion (Mt 27:15-26).⁹ In fact, in the Gospel of Matthew the disciples are essentially limited to the twelve.¹⁰ Matthew frames the Sermon on the Mount with references to the crowds in order to tie this speech into the flow of the narrative so that the speech will contribute to Matthew's presentation of the person of Jesus throughout Matthew 4:17–16:20 (which deals with Jesus' ministry to Israel) and to suggest that the life of discipleship as set forth in the Sermon on the Mount must be conducted in the context of, and to some extent for the sake of,

---

⁷This is clearly the case already in the Sermon on the Mount.

⁸E.g., Gundry, *Matthew*, 64, 66; Paul S. Minear, *Matthew: The Teacher's Gospel* (New York: Pilgrim, 1982); and to a large extent, Hagner, *Matthew 1-13*, 81. For the Matthean distinction between "following" on the part of the crowds and the disciples, see J. R. C. Cousland, *The Crowds in the Gospel of Matthew*, NovTSup 102 (Leiden: Brill, 2002), 164-68.

⁹Jack Dean Kingsbury, "The Verb AKOLOUTHEIN ('To Follow') as Index of Matthew's View of His Community," *JBL* 97 (1978): 56-73.

¹⁰Michael J. Wilkins, *Discipleship in Matthew and in his World of Thought*, 2ⁿᵈ ed. (Grand Rapids: Baker, 1995), 132-33, 166-69.

Interpretation of Matthew 4:17–16:20

those who are on the outside, a point Jesus makes within the Sermon itself (Mt 5:13-16, 43-48).[11]

The Sermon on the Mount forms the first of the five great discourses in the Gospel of Matthew and sets forth the nature of life within the kingdom. Both its position of priority and its more general content indicate that it offers foundational teaching regarding the kingdom, while the subsequent major discourses develop more specific aspects of life within the kingdom, such as mission (Mt 9:35–11:1) and community relationships (Mt 18:1-35).

When we come to the Sermon on the Mount we find that it is rather clearly structured. It is framed by an introduction (Mt 5:1-2) and conclusion (Mt 7:28-29), and its body falls neatly into three main units. The first of these units extends from Matthew 5:3 to Matthew 5:16 and deals with the character of life within the kingdom according to two aspects: the fundamental reality of life within the kingdom (blessedness by God, Mt 5:3-12); and the essential responsibilities of life within the kingdom (manifestation of good works so that God may be glorified on the part of outsiders, Mt 5:13-16).

The second main unit extends from Matthew 5:17 through Matthew 7:12 and sets forth the requirements of those in the kingdom according to their relationship to the commands of the law, necessitating an exceeding righteousness (Mt 5:17-58); their relationship to acts of piety, necessitating the absence of pretense (Mt 6:1-18); their relationship to possessions, necessitating rejection of focus on possessions in favor of orientation to divine sufficiency (Mt 6:19-34); their relationship to perceived moral failure in others, necessitating refusal to judge but commitment to discernment (Mt 7:1-6); and climactically their relationship to kindness, necessitating an active confidence in God's kindness toward them that will result in comprehensive kindness toward others.[12] The remainder of the Gospel of Matthew indicates that other relationships (such as relationship to the consummation, Mt 24–25) are also important; nevertheless, those developed in the Sermon have a kind of pride of place.

---

[11]In addition to these two purposes is a third that I mentioned above: to allow the crowds to experience the authority of Jesus' teaching activity with a view that this authority itself would function as a form of proclamation to them that the kingdom of God has come in Jesus.

[12]The concept of kindness here, though not the vocabulary, reflects the major OT theme of חסד. See H.-J. Zobel, "חסד," *TDOT* 5:44-64.

The third major unit runs from Matthew 7:13 through Matthew 7:27 and presents warnings regarding the kingdom; these warnings pertain to entrance into the kingdom (Mt 7:13-14), false prophets (Mt 7:15-23), and obedience to the demands of the Sermon on the Mount (Mt 7:24-27).[13] Figure 6.1 presents this structure graphically.

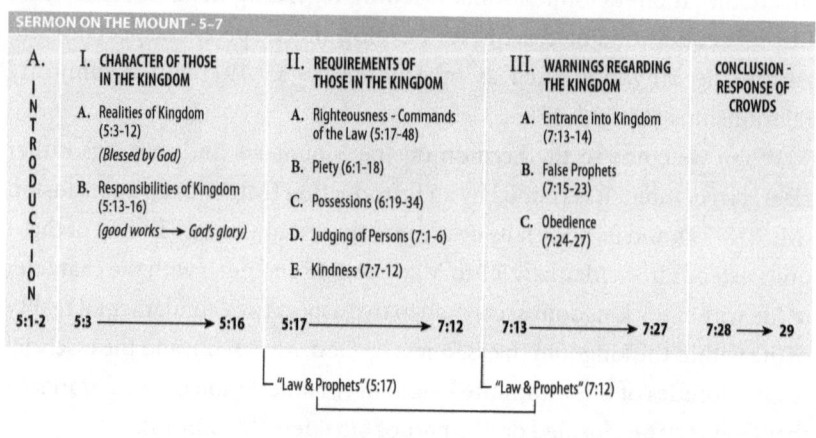

Figure 6.1 Structure of the Sermon on the Mount

We should note, too, that the body of the Sermon begins in the third person (Mt 5:3-10) and in a subtle way moves to the second person (Mt 5:11–7:20), and with equal subtleness shifts back to the third person at the end (Mt 7:21-27). This grammatical framing of third-person address corresponds to the mention of the crowds at the beginning and end and suggests that the realities of kingdom participation belong not just to the disciples who are addressed (the "you") but are open to all, including the crowds who are implicitly invited to join the disciples in the kingdom project and in this sense become disciples themselves.[14]

---

[13]For brief surveys of scholarly views regarding the structure of the Sermon on the Mount, see Graham Stanton, *A Gospel for a New People: Studies in Matthew* (New York: T&T Clark, 1992), 297-98; Craig S. Keener, *A Commentary on the Gospel of Matthew* (Grand Rapids: Eerdmans, 1999), 162-63. See also Jack Dean Kingsbury, "The Place, Structure, and Meaning of the Sermon on the Mount Within Matthew," *Int* 41 (1987): 131-43; Dale C. Allison Jr., "The Structure of the Sermon on the Mount," *JBL* 106 (1987): 423-45.

[14]Although the crowds are never said to be or to become disciples in the Gospel of Matthew (only the twelve are described as "disciples," μαθηταί), the possibility remains open throughout the Gospel of Matthew that some may become followers of Jesus (e.g., Mt 11:28-30).

The Matthean Jesus begins the Sermon on the Mount with a description of the reality of life within the kingdom in the passage that we normally label "the beatitudes." Life within the kingdom is characterized above all by "blessedness" (μακάριος), a rich Old Testament concept that carries the idea "it will be well with."[15] The Matthean Jesus frames the eight beatitudes that run in Matthew 5:3-10 with the promise "for theirs is the kingdom of heaven," thus indicating that they and the intervening promises (Mt 5:4-9) are specific aspects of kingdom blessing. The future tense in the second clauses suggests that Jesus has in mind the experience of the kingdom in its consummated form.[16] Thus the blessedness involves living now in light of the consummation; in this way the future is invading the present and ultimately determining the quality of life within the present. The employment of the passive voice, undoubtedly the divine passive, indicates that God will perform each of the acts described in the second clause.

Scholars have debated whether the first clause of each of the beatitudes describes moral/spiritual qualities that persons inculcate or difficult circumstances in which people find themselves. Thus some have suggested that the beatitudes involve the eschatological reversal of unfortunate circumstances,[17] while the majority argue that they describe the happy consequences of those who live according to the principles of the kingdom.[18] The consideration that all the descriptions of the "blessed" are presented elsewhere in the Gospel of Matthew as virtues of Jesus and expectations for the disciples speaks in favor of the latter construal, as does

---

[15] Keener, *Matthew*, 165-66. Jonathan Pennington, *The Sermon on the Mount and Human Flourishing: A Theological Commentary* (Grand Rapids: Baker Academic, 2017), 54-67, in accord with the general perspective of his volume, prefers "flourishing are those who . . ."

[16] Note also reference to inheriting the earth (Mt 5:5) and seeing God (Mt 5:8), which points to the eschaton.

[17] As in the beatitudes found in Luke's Gospel (Lk 6:20-23; cf. Lk 6:24-26). See e.g., Robert A. Guelich, *The Sermon on the Mount: A Foundation for Understanding* (Waco, TX: Word, 1982), 63-118; W. D. Davies and Dale C. Allison Jr., *The Gospel According to Saint Matthew*, ICC (New York: T&T Clark, 1997), 1:439-67.

[18] E.g., R. T. France, *The Gospel of Matthew*, NICNT (Grand Rapids: Eerdmans, 2007), 165-70; Georg Strecker, *The Sermon on the Mount: An Exegetical Commentary* (Nashville: Abingdon, 1988), and "Die Makarismen der Bergpredigt," *NTS* 17 (1970-71): 255-75; Jacques Dupont, *Les beatitudes*, 3 vols. (Paris: Gabaldi, 1969-73). Probably also John Nolland, *The Gospel of Matthew*, NIGTC (Grand Rapids: Eerdmans, 2005), 198-210; and Charles H. Talbert, *Reading the Sermon on the Mount: Character Formation and Ethical Decision Making in Matthew 5-7* (Grand Rapids: Baker Academic, 2004), 50-55. Cf. Mark Allan Powell, "Matthew's Beatitudes: Reversals and Rewards of the Kingdom," *CBQ* 58 (1996): 460-79.

the general Matthean emphasis on the causal connection between motives/behavior and reward.

The reference to persecution for the sake of righteousness (Mt 5:11-12) forms a transition to the responsibilities of the kingdom (Mt 5:13-16). Although such righteous behavior may be met with severe hostility, disciples must refuse to remain safe by trying to keep their works of righteousness private but rather they must display the life of obedience in the public realm, both for the sake of the flourishing and preservation of the world and ultimately for the glory of God among the peoples, which is the highest value in the kingdom, and the goal of Jesus' own ministry (Mt 9:7; 15:31). This dual focus on the flourishing of others and the glory of God anticipates Jesus' insistence that the whole of the law is reducible to the commands to love God and neighbor (22:34-40). The reader will catch the connection between the "mountain" on which Jesus gives this body of instruction and a city set on a "hill" (the same Greek word is employed), and will thus recognize that insofar as the community lives according to the teachings of the Sermon it functions as the eschatological Jerusalem that God is establishing to give light to the world.[19]

The great central section of the Sermon (Mt 5:17–7:12) takes up the issue of righteousness and provides an exposition of the character of the righteousness of the kingdom, in terms of the disciples' major relationships. The heading for this section is Matthew 5:17-20, which Jesus develops in an immediate sense in Matthew 5:21-48, for this passage shares with Matthew 5:17-20 a concern for disciples' relationship to the commandments of the law, and in a broader sense in Matthew 6:1–7:12.[20] Jesus' insistence that he came "not to abolish the law and the prophets but to fulfil them," may function as an answer to the charge that will be made against Matthew's audience from

---

[19]Jerusalem is the only city mentioned thus far in the narrative (Mt 2:1; cf. Mt 4:5); Bethlehem and Nazareth are villages. This is an allusion to Is 2:2-3 and Is 49:6, and probably to the notion that the eschatological Jerusalem will function as a light to the nations. See Donaldson, *Jesus on the Mountain*, 117-18. The divine passive ("set on a hill") indicates that it is positioned there by God himself and suggests that God has lit the lamp; thus it is God who intends that it should not be hidden but give light to the world and who makes this (moral) light possible.

[20]Note, e.g., the repetition of δικαιοσύνη, translated by NRSV "righteousness" in Mt 5:20 and "piety" in Mt 6:1, as well as the inclusio of "the law and the prophets" at Mt 5:17 and Mt 7:12. George A. Kennedy, *New Testament Interpretation Through Rhetorical Criticism* (Chapel Hill: University of North Carolina Press, 1984), 48-63, considers Mt 5:17-20 to be the "propositio" for the Sermon.

outsiders that Jesus and his community have dismissed the continuing relevance of the Old Testament law, or it may be an attempt to address a problem of antinomianism that will arise within the community (Mt 7:15-28).

But the antitheses of Matthew 5:21-48, some of which involve an abrogation of the command, at least in terms of its letter, may themselves raise questions regarding Jesus' adherence to the law. And thus Matthew 5:17-18 clarifies Jesus' intentions in the antitheses that follow: The reader must not understand Jesus' "but I say to you" statements as abolishing the law but rather as fulfilling the law, that is, filling the law full of meaning in the sense of teaching the will of God that lies behind the letter of the law, which is, at one and the same time, expressed in the law and (in terms of the meaning of the will of God for the eschatological community experiencing the inbreaking of God's kingdom) obscured by the law. Jesus insists that the inbreaking of the kingdom does not marginalize or reduce the role of the law but if anything intensifies it, for every *yod* remains in force until the end of the age (Mt 5:18; cf. Mt 24:34), and any attempt by disciples to mitigate "even the least of these commandments" in their own performance or in their teaching will result in being reckoned worthy of the lowest status within the kingdom. Indeed, to live according to the righteousness of the scribes and Pharisees, which is specified in the "you have heard" statements that follow, will result not in entering the kingdom (Mt 5:20) but will lead rather to guilt before God and to judgment by God (Mt 5:22-26, 29-30).

Some have found a contradiction between Jesus' statements regarding the inviolability of the law (Mt 5:17-20) and Jesus' antitheses (Mt 5:21-48). The confusion arises from the fact that Jesus insists on the law's continuing validity by citing the sanctity of the letter (every *yod* and *iota* of the law, Mt 5:18), while he proceeds to argue against a righteousness that involves a focus on compliance to the letter of the law, for the "you have heard" statements that Jesus sets over against his demands are literal quotations of the law. The solution is found in the consideration that in Matthew 5:18 Jesus is speaking metaphorically, referencing individual letters to describe careful obedience to every commandment, while in Matthew 5:21-48 he defines this careful obedience in terms of the inner disposition of the whole life, not just overt actions, to the will of God which lies behind the letter of the commandment and which comes to light in its most complete form only as Jesus engages in the process of "fulfilling" the commandment.

The antitheses of Matthew 5:21-48 reach a climax in the final antithesis, that involving love (Mt 5:43-48). The contrast between "you have heard that it was said" and "I say to you" in each case involves the principle of relational redemptiveness, or love, that is, an attitude that actively seeks the good of the other, over against overt compliance to a legal norm. This principle of love, then, that lies behind Jesus' demands throughout Matthew 5:21-42, comes to explicit expression in Matthew 5:43-48. It is no surprise that love is the key to discerning the meaning of the commandments of the law, for Jesus will later declare that love to God and neighbor are the central commands of "the law and the prophets" (Mt 22:34-40), from which all the others spring.

In Matthew 6:1-18 Jesus moves from the disciples' relationship to commandments of the law to relationship to acts of piety, both of which involve basic obligations toward God. The issue of internal attitude, which underlies Jesus' demands in Mt 5:21-48, continues in this passage. After a heading that sets forth the thesis of Mt 6:1-18, dealing with piety (or, more literally, "righteousness") in general (Mt 6:1), Jesus discusses three specific forms of piety, a movement which indicates that the principles Jesus herein puts forward are applicable not only to almsgiving, prayer, and fasting, but also to other religious acts ostensibly directed to God.

This segment contains three virtually perfectly parallel descriptions regarding almsgiving (Mt 6:2-4), prayer (Mt 6:5-6), and fasting (Mt 6:16-18). But the otherwise consistent pattern is broken in Matthew 6:7-15, where Jesus expands the section on prayer to discuss the contrast between disciples and the Gentiles and includes a model prayer.[21] In each case of the parallel pattern, Jesus draws an overarching contrast between acts done for the purpose of being seen by humans, with the consequence of having received any reward such persons will get (that is, no reward from the Father), versus acts done for the purpose of being in secret, with the consequence of receiving reward from the heavenly Father. The former characterizes the behavior of "hypocrites," probably referring specifically to the Pharisees and

---

[21]Floyd V. Filson, "Broken Patterns in the Gospel of Matthew," *JBL* 75 (1956): 227-31, drew attention to Matthew's penchant to develop symmetrical patterns only to break them.

scribes (Mt 15:6; 23:13, 23, 25, 27, 29), while the latter describes what the disciples are to do. This insistence that acts of piety be done in private rather than before humans may seem to contradict Matthew 5:13-16, but the issue in each case is one of motivation: for the glory of God (Mt 5:16), not for personal religious ostentation.

In the expansion on prayer (Mt 6:7-15) Jesus differentiates the expectations for the disciples with the practice of "the Gentiles," who think that they will be heard because of their elaborate and verbose manner of prayer. In contrast, Jesus offers a model prayer that is characterized by brevity and simplicity, similar to Jewish prayers of the period.[22] It begins with petitions that seek the honor of God and only then moves to include petitions pertaining to the needs of the pray-er. Accordingly, it is not the many words and efforts of the petitioners (thus anthropocentric and egocentric), but the petitioners' desire for the glory of God and confident relationship to God as Father (thus theocentric) that are the key to the effectiveness of prayer. The use of the plural throughout ("our"/"us") indicates that this prayer is to be offered by the community or by individuals in recognition of their role within the community.

In Matthew 6:14-15 Jesus comments on the petition regarding forgiveness, indicating that the reception of God's forgiveness places the person under obligation to extend forgiveness to others. This apparent *quid pro quo* may seem theologically problematic to some who quite naturally see an emphasis in the Gospel of Matthew on God's free, gracious act of forgiveness (e.g., Mt 9:1-2; 26:28). But it reflects the profoundly interpersonal character of the experience of divine forgiveness, in that the personal reception of God's forgiveness is intended to lead to a perspectival transformation that embraces a comprehensive framework of forgiveness involving all relationships (Mt 18:23-35); the failure of disciples to forgive others thus amounts to a repudiation of God's purpose in their forgiveness with the consequence that their own experience of forgiveness is nullified.

The placing of confidence in the goodness of God who "knows what you need before you ask him" (Mt 6:8) in matters of prayer leads to the insistence of the same kind of confidence in the "your heavenly Father [who] knows

---

[22]Jörg Frey, "Das Vaterunser im Horizont antik-judischen Betens unter besonderer Berücksichtigung der Textfunde vom Toten Meer," in *Das Vaterunser in seinen antiken Kontexten*, ed. Florian Wilk (Göttingen: Vandenhoeck & Ruprecht, 2016), 1-24.

that you need ... all these things" (Mt 6:32-33) regarding material things (Mt 6:19-34). In a sense, this section develops the petition "give us this day our daily bread" in the Lord's Prayer. Jesus deals with the disciples' relation to material possessions from two perspectives: warnings regarding greed over material excess (Mt 6:19-21) and warnings regarding worry over material necessities (Mt 6:25-34). Between these two passages Jesus articulates principles that lie behind both sets of instructions. A focus on material things is inclusive of moral corruption in that it leads to the "darkening" of the whole inner life of the person (Mt 6:23). On the other hand, orienting life to material things (either material excess or material necessities) means a servility to materialism that excludes the possibility of serving God, since both materialism and God place ultimate demands on the person (Mt 6:24). Both greed and worry involve the attempt to find security in the acquisition of material things, rather than trusting God for all one needs (Mt 6:30), which contradicts broadly God's demonstration of provision for the natural world (Mt 6:26-30) and specifically the claim that God's end-time rule has come in the ministry of Jesus (Mt 6:33; cf. Mt 4:17).

The high moral and religious standards required of the community as set forth in Matthew 5:17–6:34 lead to the question as to how disciples should respond to others in the community who appear to fall short of these standards. Such apparent failure on the part of the "brother/sister" to meet the demands of the kingdom may naturally prompt an attitude of condemnation (Mt 7:1-5). But Jesus prohibits a judgmental spirit, for such would involve usurping the role of judgment that belongs to God alone,[23] and will consequently result, in accord with divine justice, in the disciple being on the receiving end of an equally strict judgment by God. Moreover, such a judgmental spirit is inherently unjust, since it entails condemning others by a higher standard than one is apt to apply to oneself (Mt 7:3-5), a practice that blinds one to significant breaches in one's own life, thus preventing the necessary repentance of these violations (Mt 4:17).

Jesus' statement in Matthew 7:6 is notoriously difficult to relate to the surrounding passages, but it is most natural to take it as a correction to a possible false conclusion from Matthew 7:1-5, namely that one should never

---

[23] Note the divine passive, "will be judged," thus indicating that judgment is properly the action of God.

exercise critical assessment of others. Thus Matthew 7:6 qualifies Matthew 7:1-5 in that it insists that discernment of the character of others is necessary in order to avoid being responsible for the profaning of the holy things of God by those who are unworthy or unappreciative of them,[24] and to avoid the damage that may result to the disciple who ignores the necessity of such discernment, and suffers an attack which may lead to spiritual shipwreck.[25]

I mentioned above that Matthew 7:12 forms an inclusio with Matthew 5:17 and thus functions as the conclusion of the great central section of the Sermon. In Matthew 7:7-12 Jesus brings this section of the Sermon to its climax by discussing the disciples' relationship to kindness. In Matthew 7:7-11 Jesus exhorts his disciples to avail themselves of the generous kindness of the heavenly Father by confidently seeking him (in prayer) for the fulfillment of every need, while Matthew 7:12 urges disciples to extend this same sort of kindness toward others. Even as forgiveness from God leads to an attitude of forgiveness toward others and an obligation to forgive others (Mt 6:12-15), so the experience of God's kindness leads to an attitude of kindness and an obligation to show kindness toward others. Disciples' experience of receiving goodness from God leads to their extending goodness toward others.

This passage stands as the culmination to the requirements of the kingdom in Matthew 5:17–7:12 in that it describes the healthy relational environment—a circle of kindness—that makes the fulfilling of the requirements of the kingdom both possible and obligatory for disciples; the security they find in God's loving provision of every need and wholesome desire impels them to trust God (Mt 6:7-12, 19-34), glorify God (Mt 5:13-16; 7:6), orient their lives around reward from the Father (Mt 6:1-18), and extend the same kind of love toward others (Mt 5:17-48; 7:1-5).[26] Indeed, the "golden rule" of Matthew 7:12 is essentially a restating of the love command, since

---

[24] This statement may therefore allude to the principle articulated in Mt 10:11-14, where disciples are to minister only to "those who are worthy," i.e., those who are at least open to responding appropriately to the gospel.

[25] In the Gospel of Matthew, the danger to disciples is consistently understood in terms of falling away (σκανδαλίζω) or falling short, e.g., Mt 10:28; 24:9–25:30.

[26] Scholars disagree as to whether Mt 7:7-12 belongs primarily with Mt 7:1-6 (thus Talbert, *Reading the Sermon*, 131-37; Pennington, *Sermon on the Mount*, 255-68), or is separate from these earlier verses in Mt 7 (thus Luz, *Matthew 1–7*, 412-35; Guelich, *Sermon on the Mount*, 377-81). It is unclear how Mt 7:7-12 can connect specifically with Mt 7:1-6 without reading elements into Mt 7:7-12 which manifestly are not present.

Jesus describes both Matthew 7:12 and the double law commands of Matthew 22:34-40 as "the law and the prophets." The principle of love to others thus culminates both the disciples' relationship to the law (Mt 5:43-48) and the central section of the Sermon in the large.

In order to make clear that the instructions that Jesus has thus far given in the Sermon are indeed *requirements* for entrance into the consummated kingdom on the Day of Judgment, Jesus concludes the Sermon with a series of three warnings (Mt 7:13-27), contrasting those who will enter versus those who will not, dependent on their putting his instructions into practice.

We saw above that an inclusio is created around Matthew 4:23 and Matthew 9:35, thus joining the Sermon on the Mount with Jesus' ten mighty acts around the Sea of Galilee. That which links the Sermon to these ten mighty acts is a common concern in both for Jesus' *word*, his word of teaching in Matthew 5:1-7:29, and his word of deliverance (mostly in the form of healings) in Matthew 8:1-9:34, for Jesus performs most of these mighty acts with a word (Mt 8:3, 13, 16, 26, 32; 9:6, 22, 29).[27] This conjoining of the Sermon with Jesus' ten miracles in Matthew 8-9 around Jesus' word informs the reader that Jesus' teaching word is a powerful healing, delivering word, and that his delivering word is a teaching or revelatory word. Indeed, Matthew reports the mighty acts in Matthew 8:1-9:34 in such a way as to communicate instruction regarding discipleship.[28] And Matthew further reinforces the instructional character of these miracles by producing an alternation between blocks of mighty acts and teaching regarding discipleship.[29]

---

[27]Julius Schniewind, *Das Evangelium nach Matthäus*, 6th ed. (Göttingen: Vandenhoeck & Ruprecht, 1953), 37-124, notes the inclusio but labels Mt 5:1-7:29 as Messiah of Word and Mt 8:1-9:34 as Messiah of Deed.

[28]As noted, e.g., by Heinz Joachim Held, "Matthew as Interpreter of the Miracle Stories," in *Tradition and Interpretation in Matthew*, ed. Günther Bornkamm, Gerhard Barth, and Heinz Joachim Held, NTL (Philadelphia: Westminster, 1963), 165-246; and Walter T. Wilson, *Healing in the Gospel of Matthew: Reflections on Method and Ministry* (Minneapolis: Fortress, 2014). Birger Gerhardsson, *The Mighty Acts of Jesus According to Matthew*, ScrMin 5 (Lund: Gleerup, 1979), sees this connection between Jesus' healings and teaching throughout; thus, "Matthew does not really make any clear distinction between Jesus' preaching/teaching and his therapeutic activity. They belong together. The Matthean Jesus teaches when healing and heals when teaching" (23).

[29]The passages that contain teaching regarding discipleship link that teaching with themes from the surrounding miracle stories; thus, Mt 8:18-22 connects Jesus' authority to heal in the miracle stories to his authority to demand absolute allegiance expressed in the abandoning of comforts and family responsibilities, and it speaks of the cost Jesus bears in this itinerant healing ministry (cf. Mt 8:17); Mt 9:10 applies the theme of "mercy" found explicitly in Mt 9:27 and implicitly

Mt 8:1-17	Three stories of mighty acts
Mt 8:18-22	Teaching regarding discipleship
Mt 8:23-9:8	Three stories of mighty acts
Mt 9:9-17	Teaching regarding discipleship
Mt 9:18-34	Three stories containing four mighty acts[30]

These mighty works are events of deliverance, or salvation, with the word *save* (σώζω) appearing repeatedly, thereby raising the question of the relationship between this salvation from physical danger and infirmities in these chapters and the purpose of Jesus, according to the angel in Matthew 1:21, that "he will save his people from their *sins.*" Matthew clarifies this relationship in Matthew 9:1-9 where he indicates that one purpose of physical healings is to make known that "the Son of man has authority on earth to forgive sins" (Mt 9:6, 8). Salvation is thus holistic in that it includes physical deliverance as well as deliverance from sin, but it centers on the latter and is, according to Matthew 1:21, ultimately concerned with reconciliation with God.[31] Accordingly, insofar as Matthew emphasizes the role of faith (Mt 8:2-3, 10, 13; 9:2, 22, 28; cf. Mt 8:26) in these stories of physical deliverance, he suggests that salvation from sin also comes about through faith.

With the missionary discourse (Mt 9:35–11:1) we move from the announcement made by Jesus (4:23–9:35) to the announcement made by his disciples. Matthew begins by presenting the cause, or basis, for Jesus' instructing his disciples for mission: The compassion of Jesus, which points both to Jesus' loving concern for the Jewish crowds (cf. Mt 23:37) and the crowd's vulnerable condition before tormenting oppression. This passage seems to be dependent especially on Ezekiel 34:1-16, where God bemoaned that the religious leaders ("shepherds of Israel") were not caring for the people, who were "scattered, because there was no shepherd," and therefore God declared "I myself will be the shepherd of my sheep" (Ezek 34:15).

---

throughout all the stories; and Mt 9:14-17 applies the joy of salvation in all these surrounding stories to the issue of fasting and to the newness of the kingdom expressed in these transcendent acts of deliverance.

[30] The intercalation of the healing of the woman with an issue of blood into the raising of the ruler's daughter (Mt 9:18-26) results structurally in one narrative containing two mighty acts.

[31] Which Matthew describes in terms of "sonship" to God and knowing God as Father. See Wilson, *Healing*, 139-59.

Matthew is thus suggesting that Jesus is assuming the role that God had designated for himself.[32] The primary danger to the sheep here is cosmic evil,[33] manifested in sickness, demon possession, death (Mt 8:1–9:35; 10:1, 8), and especially sin (Mt 1:21-23; 4:17; 10:7). He is the kingly shepherd (Mt 2:6) who delivers Israel from these torments and will finally be stricken because of his shepherding care (Mt 26:31). Yet Jesus is unable to address these needs alone, and thus he dispatches his disciples. But because they, by themselves, are unequal to the task of liberating Israel from these ills and preparing the people for the impending harvest of God's judgment,[34] they are to "pray to the Lord of the harvest," probably referring to Jesus himself,[35] to send additional laborers into the harvest, a prayer that will be answered beyond the storyline of Matthew's narrative itself, when they "make disciples of all nations" (Mt 28:19), including Israel.

Matthew 10:1-4 provides background for the speech Jesus is about to give.[36] Here we learn that those he instructs in mission are "his twelve disciples," a number which suggests that these twelve are a group formed in analogy to the twelve tribes of Israel in the Old Testament (cf. Mt 19:28). Matthew subtly shifts the nomenclature from "disciples" to "apostles," the only time this designation appears in the Gospel of Matthew, suggesting that their "apostolic" role has to do with their being sent out to exercise authority over the powers of evil they will encounter in their mission.

Although we are told that Jesus "sent out" these twelve (Mt 10:5), we observe that, in contrast to Mark and Luke, Matthew does not say that the twelve actually went out and returned. Indeed, Matthew never describes any

---

[32]In Ezek 34:23-24 God promises that he will set over Israel "one Shepherd, my servant David," who will feed them. But God does not give to this Davidic figure authority to gather the sheep or rescue them. God leaves those tasks for himself (Ezek 34:11-13).

[33]For the notion of cosmic evil in the Synoptics, see James G. Crossley, "Jesus, Healings and Mark 2:1-12: Forgiveness, a Release, or Bound Again to the Great Satan?," in *Evil in Second Temple Judaism and Early Christianity*, ed. Chris Keith and Loren T. Stuckenbruck, WUNT 2/417 (Tübingen: Mohr Siebeck, 2016), 86-100.

[34]In the Gospel of Matthew "harvest" language consistently refers to end-time judgement (Mt 3:12; 13:30, 37-43).

[35]That Jesus is "Lord of the harvest" is suggested by the considerations that "Lord" regularly refers to Jesus in the Gospel of Matthew, and that it is Jesus who sends forth the disciples for mission (Mt 10:5, 23; 23:34; 28:18-20). Cf. Dorothy Jean Weaver, *Matthew's Missionary Discourse: A Literary Critical Analysis*, JSNTSup 38 (Sheffield: Sheffield Academic Press, 1990), 79, 187-88.

[36]My understanding of the structure of Mt 9:35–11:1 agrees generally with that of Weaver, *Missionary Discourse*, 71-126.

such ministry on the part of the disciples in the remainder of the narrative.[37] On the contrary, they appear disinclined to "feed" the sheep of Israel (Mt 14:15; 15:33) and are (in spite of Jesus' protestations) incapable of healing (Mt 17:14-21). These considerations suggest that Matthew means "he sent them out by charging them"; thus, at this point the sending out is the charge, that is, the instructions he is about to give. Jesus will commission his disciples to go out only at the end of the Gospel of Matthew (Mt 28:18-20). Indeed, for the most part the instructions and description of ministry that follow pertain to the post-Easter period (Mt 10:18-23, 26-39), as do the instructions in all of the five great discourses, although the limitation of ministry to Israel has the historicizing function of reminding us that Jesus gave these instructions during his earthly ministry when such limitation was appropriate (compare Mt 10:5-6; 15:24 with Mt 28:19-20). The missionary discourse, then, pertains to the ministry to the Jewish nation that will be part of the mission to all the nations that Jesus authorizes in Matthew 28:18-20.[38]

The discourse itself moves from a description of the activities of ministry (Mt 10:5-15) to the responses to the ministry (Mt 10:16-42), although Matthew

---

[37] Weaver, *Missionary Discourse*, 129-53.

[38] For the major views regarding the relationship of the missionary discourse, and particularly the restriction of Mt 10:5-6 to the Great Commission of Mt 28:16-20, see Axel von Dobbeler, "Die Restitution Israels und die Bekehrung der Heiden: Das Verhältnis von Mt 10,5b.6 und Mt 28,18-20 unter dem Aspekt der Komplementarität. Erwägungen zum Standort des Matthäusevangeliums," ZNW 91 (2004): 19-44. Von Dobbeler argues that the restrictive command of 10:5-6 and the demand of universal mission in 28:16-20 both remain in force in that the mission in chap. 10 pertains to Israel while the Great Commission pertains to Gentiles, and that both are to continue until the end. Von Dobbeler insists that Matthew calls for a "restitution of Israel," which involves Jews' embracing obedience to their law as Jesus has brought it to fulfillment; this constitutes not conversion but an affirmation of the faith that has always been theirs. But according to Von Dobbeler, Matthew looks to the conversion of the Gentiles through a process of discipleship, since it involves for them a turning away from paganism to the faith of Israel as Jesus has fulfilled it. Thus according to this view, Matthew envisages two separate missions. But this ingenious solution fails to persuade, since in Matthew's Gospel disciples are to be made of Jews as well as Gentiles, and since both the restricted command of 10:5-6 and the universal commission of 28:18-20 are directed to the same group: the twelve [eleven] disciples. Either they are not to go to the ἔθνη (28:19) or they are to go and make disciples of the ἔθνη (28:19); these are mutually exclusive alternatives. A much better solution is that 10:5-6 reflects the limited scope of mission that was appropriate during Jesus' earthly ministry, but was to be followed by a subsequent universal mission on the part of the now reconstituted Israel. See Anton Vögtle, "Das christologische und ekklesiologische Anliegen von Mt 28,18-20," *Studia Evangelica* 2 (1964); Georg Strecker, *Der Weg der Gerechtigkeit* (Göttingen: Vandenhoeck & Ruprecht, 1975), 33, 117-118; Joachim Gnilka, *Das Matthäus-evangelium*, 2 Teile, HThKNT (Freiburg: Berder, 1988), 1:362-63.

10:13-15 is transitional, in that it introduces in a general way the matter of response. Jesus gives much more attention to the negative (Mt 10:16-39) than to the positive (Mt 10:40-42) response, suggesting that the overwhelming reaction will be repudiation.[39] Still, Jesus brings the discourse to its climax with a description of those who accept the message, since such is the goal and desired result. Throughout this section Jesus indicates a close, virtually inextricable, connection between response to the disciples' message and treatment of the disciples themselves, both positive and negative.

The reader discerns a clear comparison, or analogy, between the announcement made earlier by Jesus (Mt 4:23–9:35) and that made by the disciples in this passage. Matthew links the ministry of Jesus with that of the disciples by several parallels: Jesus gives the disciples authority "to heal every disease and every infirmity" (Mt 10:1; cf. the same phraseology in Mt 9:35; 4:23); they are to preach that "the kingdom of heaven is at hand," even as did Jesus (cf. Mt 4:17), and, according to Matthew 10:8, they are to "heal the sick" (cf. Mt 8:5-17; 9:1-8, 20-26), "cleanse lepers" (cf. Mt 8:1-4), and "cast out demons" (also Mt 10:1; cf. Mt 8:16, 28-34; 9:32-33). Of all Jesus' major acts of ministry in the preceding chapters the only one missing from this list is teaching, since Jesus will give the disciples authority to teach only at the end of the Gospel of Matthew after they have been instructed in the meaning and necessity of Jesus' suffering and death (Mt 28:20). Thus, the first portion of the missionary discourse, which involves acts of ministry (Mt 10:5-15), compares the performance of the ministry of the disciples with Jesus' performance of ministry in the preceding chapters.

The second portion of the discourse, though, compares the responses to the disciples (Mt 10:16-42), which are mostly negative, with the responses to Jesus' ministry by Israel in Matthew 11:1–16:20, where we learn that all groups within Israel, except the disciples, reject Jesus' proclamation of the gospel. Thus whereas Matthew 10:5-16 recalls Jesus' acts of ministry in the previous chapters, Mathew 10:16-42 anticipates the rejection of Jesus in the following chapters. This missionary discourse, then, forms a bridge between Jesus'

---

[39]Additional reasons for the greater attention here to the negative response are 1) the surprising character of this negative response, given the redemptive nature of the ministry described; and 2) the danger to the ministers that such a negative response poses, a danger that involves both life and limb (Mt 10:19-22, 28, 38-39) but especially the possibility of falling away in the face of it (Mt 10:32-33, 35-39).

proclamation of the kingdom and the responses to that proclamation, and is thus fully embedded in the ministry of Jesus. All of this emphasizes the close connection between the ministry of the earthly Jesus and that of the (post-Easter) disciples, in terms of content, character, and results.[40]

Matt 11:1–16:20. When we move from the announcement of the kingdom by both Jesus and the disciples in 4:18–11:1 to the dual responses to that announcement in 11:1–16:20, we see that Matthew begins with a catalogue of responses in 11:1–12:50, where he indicates that the two major sub-groups within Israel, the Jewish crowds (11:2-24) and the religious leaders (12:1-45), repudiate Jesus' proclamation of the kingdom; only the disciples (Mt 11:25-30; 12:46-50) accept it.[41] Matthew 11:2-24 sets forth the bases and significance of the unbelief of the crowds, alternating between the reasons for the crowd's repudiation of the gospel and the salvation-historical significance of that rejection.

Surprisingly, Matthew begins his analysis of the reasons for the crowd's repudiation by reintroducing John the Baptist (Mt 11:2-6), who hears in prison about "the deeds of the Christ" (Mt 11:2) and consequently asks Jesus if he is "the one to come, or shall we look for another?" The deeds that cause this consternation are Jesus' works of healing, exorcisms, and resuscitations (Mt 4:23-25; 8:1–9:34). John's preaching had emphasized apocalyptic judgment (Mt 3:1-12) but contained no mention of these kinds of deeds that have been occupying Jesus. Thus John represents disappointed expectations of apocalypticism; John assumed that the coming of the kingdom would involve immediately executed judgment. When Jesus answers by citing Isaiah 35:5-6 and Isaiah 61:1, which catalog the very deeds that Jesus has been doing, he is implicitly urging John to see from the Scriptures that God's kingdom is characterized primarily by salvation rather than judgment (even though the rest of the Gospel of Matthew indicates that judgment is also involved).

John is not a member of the Jewish crowds nor does he repudiate the gospel, but the fact that Matthew positions this passage at the beginning of his presentation of the response of the crowds, and the consideration that the crowds were devoted to John and were drawn to his message (Mt 3:5; 11:7-10; 21:27), indicate that such disappointed expectations lie behind the

---

[40] As I mentioned above, the primary focus of this passage is on the post-Easter ministry of disciples.
[41] See David R. Bauer, "The Major Characters of Matthew's Story: Their Function and Significance," *Int* 46 (1992): 363-66.

crowd's rejection of the ministry of Jesus. The positive characterization of John throughout the Gospel of Matthew leads the reader to conclude that John accepted Jesus' explanation and is among those who are blessed because they do not take offense (Mt 11:6).

This indirect conversation with John leads Jesus to talk with the crowds about John the Baptist, and to make the salvation-historical point that an inextricable connection exists between prophetic revelation, of which John was a part and in fact the climax, and himself. For John was the Elijah-like messenger who was sent to prepare the way before him (Mt 11:7-15). Thus to accept the prophets is to embrace Jesus' own message, with the dark corollary that to reject Jesus' message is to reject also the prophets.

Jesus proceeds to give a further reason for the rejection of his message by the greater part of Israel: an irrational commitment not to believe (Mt 11:16-19). The people reject John because of his asceticism and reject Jesus because of his lack of asceticism. When Jesus declares that "wisdom is justified by her deeds," he suggests that the ministries of John and Jesus produce the kind of wholeness and human flourishing that the Old Testament and Judaism insisted wisdom produced, even though the crowds in their irrationality fail to see it.

Jesus goes on to talk about the salvation-historical significance of the crowd's rejection of his mighty works (Mt 11:20-24). When Jesus accuses the crowds of failure to repent in the face of these mighty works he implies that these deeds proclaim the presence of the kingdom (see Mt 4:17), but that the crowds refuse to allow these works to fulfill their proclamatory potential, even though their persuasive power would have convinced the most wicked cities of the past and present. In the process Jesus utters the principle that with greater revelation goes greater responsibility to accept it, with the risk of greater degree of judgment.

The final reason for this rejection of the gospel is theological; God has chosen to hide the meaning of this revelation from the "wise and understanding," but to "reveal it to babes" (Mt 11:25-26). The "wise and understanding" refer primarily to the Jewish crowds (though certainly the religious authorities would also be included),[42] while "the babes" allude to the disciples

---

[42]The phrase "at that time" links Mt 11:25-26 to the preceding passage, which describes the rejection of the cities where his mighty works were performed.

(see Mt 13:10-17).[43] Those who depend on their own human wit and understanding, which reflects the thinking and values of culture unaffected by God's revelation, will never understand the saving mysteries of the kingdom.[44] But those who, like babes, have no illusion regarding the ultimacy of their own patterns of thinking will find that God reveals to them these mysteries in the proclamation of the gospel.

But the revelation of the gospel is intimately linked to the person of Jesus himself. For the first time in the Gospel of Matthew Jesus explicitly, though indirectly, refers to himself as Son of God, who alone knows the Father and is known by the Father, and exclusively reveals the Father (Mt 11:27). Since the knowledge of the Father is possible only through him, Jesus issues an invitation directed toward the crowds, and indeed toward all, to come to him (Mt 11:28-30), which he specifies as assuming his "yoke." Insofar as Jewish teachers often used this language for submission to the law,[45] Jesus is indicating that the role that had been played by the law is now assumed by the process of transformative learning that comes through discipleship. Such discipleship will result in "rest" to those who are chafing under burdens, perhaps a reference to the burdensome demands imposed by the Pharisees (cf. Mt 23:4), but more likely to the life-struggles associated with cosmic evil experienced by those who are outside the saving benefits offered by discipleship in the kingdom, for this passage is followed immediately by sabbath controversies (Mt 12:1-14), in the course of which Jesus declares that he is the "Lord of the sabbath" (Mt 12:8) who brings wholeness through the healings he performs on the sabbath (Mt 12:9-14). Yet Jesus' rest comes paradoxically through the adoption of a new burden and yoke, that is, the rigorous demands that Jesus describes throughout the Gospel of Matthew. But they are "light" and "easy," because disciples have the help that comes from presence of God in the person of his Son, who continues to dwell with them (Mt 1:21-23; 28:20).[46]

Matthew 12:1-45 describes the bases, issue, and results of the rejection on the part of the religious leaders. In terms of bases, the religious authorities

---

[43]Matthew otherwise describes disciples as "little ones" (Mt 10:42; 18:6) and urges them to become like children (Mt 18:2-6).

[44]The insistence that God hides his revelation from those who depend on their own thinking is an oft-repeated OT principle; see Keener, *Matthew*, 347.

[45]Davies and Allison, *Matthew*, 2:289-90.

[46]This help from Jesus stands in contrast to the lack of assistance on the part of the Pharisees who lay burdens on others but "will not move them by their finger" (Mt 23:4).

are ignorant of the meaning of God's revelation in the prophets (Mt 12:7), especially regarding God's prioritizing of mercy over ritual compliance. Behind this misreading is the second basis: the essential evil of their hearts (Mt 12:33-37). The issue is their rejection of the transcendent authority and preeminence of Jesus; Jesus tells them that "something greater" than the temple (Mt 12:6), the prophets (Mt 12:41), and the kingship, and perhaps also the wisdom tradition (Mt 12:42), is present.

And Matthew presents a threefold result to their repudiation of the gospel. Their rejection of Jesus' ministry will lead to a moral and spiritual bondage to sin and evil that exceeds their slavish condition before the gospel came to them (Mt 12:43-45); they make themselves vulnerable to the removal of the possibility of forgiveness in that their accusation that Jesus casts out demons by collaboration with the devil constitutes a blasphemy against the Holy Spirit who is the actual agent of Jesus' exorcisms (Mt 12:22-32); and they will consequently experience eschatological condemnation (Mt 12:33-42). In contrast to the religious leaders, disciples are described as the very family of Jesus insofar as they do the will of the Father (Mt 12:46-50).

Throughout the remainder the second major division (Mt 13:1–16:20), Jesus responds both to the rejection of the crowds and religious authorities and to the acceptance on the part of the disciples. This reaction starts with the parable discourse (Mt 13:1-52), where Jesus begins by going out of the house and teaching the crowds in parables (Mt 13:1-3) but eventually leaves the crowds and goes into the house so as to teach only his disciples (Mt 13:36). Thus Matthew 13:3-35 contains parables addressed to the Jewish crowds, with the disciples present,[47] whereas Matthew 13:36-52 contains parables addressed solely to the disciples.[48]

The parable of the soils points to the significance of the ministry of Jesus and of the disciples, and describes the significance of the various responses

---

[47]That the disciples are present is indicated by Mt 13:10-23, and by the explanation of the parable of the weeds given to the disciples in Mt 13:36-43.

[48]Jack Dean Kingsbury, *The Parables of Jesus in Matthew 13: A Study in Redaction-Criticism* (London: SPCK, 1969). This understanding of the structure of Mt 13:1-52 must account for the complication that Mt 13:1-35 contains material other than parables addressed to the Jewish crowds, since Mt 13:10-23 is not parable, nor is it directed to the Jewish crowds. But Mt 13:10-17 deals with the issue of Jesus speaking to the Jewish crowds in parables (the whole passage is an answer to the question posed in Mt 13:10), and Mt 13:18-23 is an explanation of the parable of the soils which was addressed to the crowds.

to this ministry (Mt 13:3-23). The parable opens with the activity of the sower, and everything that follows is a result of his sowing. In Matthew 13:19 Jesus declares that the seed represents "the word of the kingdom," which refers to the preaching regarding the kingdom proclaimed by both Jesus and the disciples (Mt 4:17; 10:7). The consideration that this proclamation is made by both Jesus and the disciples indicates that the sower represents them both: Jesus, as he ministers during his earthly life, and the disciples, as they minister especially after the resurrection of Jesus (Mt 28:18-20).

The seed that falls on the path represents the Jewish crowds, who "hear and do not understand" (compare Mt 13:4, 19-20 with Mt 13:13, 15). They are without understanding not because they lack the ability to comprehend or are ignorant,[49] but because the demand to submit to God's rule as it has come in Jesus is so far from their thinking, values, and commitments that, according to God's decree, it does not make sense to them (Mt 11:25-26). Insofar as the seeds that fall on other soils lead to the beginning of a plant, they represent those who accept the yoke of discipleship. Still, many who begin the life of discipleship will fall away because of persecution (Mt 13:5-6, 20-21; cf. Mt 24:9-13) and worry over material necessities and the deception of wealth (Mt 13:7, 22; cf. Mt 6:19-35). Even as the crowds constitute the flesh-and-blood example of the path-like soil within the narrative of the Gospel of Matthew, so the disciples form the flesh-and-blood example of the good soil whose plant bears the fruit of righteousness, for the good soil represents those who "hear and understand" (Mt 13:23; cf. Mt 13:10-17).

The parables of the weeds, mustard seed, and yeast address the tension that exists in Jesus' preaching of the kingdom. The parable of the weeds (Mt 13:24-30, 36-43) deals with the issue of the continuing presence of evil and evil-producing persons in the world, even after the announcement of the kingdom, while the parables of the mustard seed and leaven (Mt 13:31-33) deal with the issue of the present (apparent) smallness and weakness of God's kingdom in relation to its future greatness.

If Jesus directed the first four parables of Matthew 13 to the crowds, with the disciples present, he addresses the last three parables to the disciples

---

[49]In Mt 13:10-17 Jesus describes the crowds as seeing and hearing, and as having ears and eyes. Indeed, Matthew otherwise notes that the crowds "follow" (ἀκολουθέω) Jesus (Mt 4:25; 8:1; 12:15; 14:13; 19:2; 20:29; 21:9), a term which, as applied to the crowds, does not involve discipleship, but rather points to the fact that the crowds were with Jesus and experienced his ministry.

alone. The first two of these parables, the treasure and the pearl (Mt 13:44-46), are twin parables. In each case, the finding of a thing of great value causes the man to go and sell as that he has in order to purchase it. Thus the future, consummated kingdom is of such superior value that everything a disciple has is worthless in relation to it, but the only way to possess the kingdom is to sacrifice all for it.[50]

The story of the dragnet culminates the parables of Matthew 13. Like the parable of the weeds, the issue here is the presence together of the evil and the righteous until the separation of the Day of Judgment. But Jesus speaks this parable only to the disciples, not to the crowds; and the evil and good exist together not in the world, but in a smaller sphere within the world (a net cast into the sea). Here, then, Jesus addresses the problem of the evil and the righteous within the church.[51] Certain persons will attach themselves to the church who are not true disciples, and Jesus affirms here, as he does elsewhere in the Gospel of Matthew, that there will be a judgment of the church on the last day. In light of this judgment, those in the church should not assume that they will necessarily escape God's judgment; rather, they should examine their lives to be sure they are good fish, that is, those who are sacrificing all for the kingdom (Mt 13:44-46), the righteous who do the will of the Father (Mt 13:8, 23, 24, 43).

According to this passage, parabolic speech is judgmental, in that it hides saving revelation from the Jewish crowds because they have already rejected Jesus' proclamation of the gospel (Mt 13:10-17; cf. Mt 11:25-26), but reveals more and more of the saving mysteries of the kingdom to the disciples because they have accepted Jesus' proclamation (Mt 13:10-17, 51-52). Indeed, here Jesus withdraws not only revelation from the Jewish crowds while

---

[50]Since these parables are addressed solely to the disciples, who are already entering the kingdom in its realized form, the demand of these parables is to do all possible to possess the consummated kingdom that is yet to come.

[51]In spite of the wording of Mt 13:47, "the kingdom of heaven is like a net," the net does not represent the kingdom, but the church. The parable of the weeds has already indicated that the kingdom does not necessarily represent the first thing mentioned in a parable, since the "man who sowed good seed in his field" does not represent the kingdom (Mt 13:24), but "the Son of Man" (Mt 13:37). Moreover, in Matthew's theology the kingdom represents the sphere where God's will is perfectly performed, and thus does not contain "bad fish." Although the church is not synonymous with the kingdom, it is the community in which God exercises his rule in a special way, and the church is uniquely called to bear witness in the world to the kingdom of God. Of course, this parable goes on to describe the Great Assize that will inaugurate the end-time kingdom.

granting it to the disciples, but he withdraws himself from them (Mt 13:36), while offering himself exclusively to the disciples (Mt 13:36).

In this way, the parable discourse serves as a microcosm for the whole of Matthew 13:1–16:20, for throughout this material Jesus reacts to the negative response of the Jewish crowds by repeatedly withdrawing from them, while he reacts to the positive response of his disciples by revealing himself to them, finally drawing from them the confession that he is "the Christ, the Son of the living God" (Mt 16:16). Twice within these chapters Matthew tells us that Jesus "withdrew" (ἀναχωρέω) from the crowds (Mt 14:13; 15:21), and finally, using a stronger term (καταλείπω), that he "left" them (Mt 16:4), each time in the wake of rejection or opposition.

Moreover, throughout Matthew 13:53–16:20 the hostility between Jesus and Israel, and particularly the religious leaders, continues. In the process, Matthew presents four additional reasons why the greater part of Israel has rejected Jesus' message. First, many were "put off" by his ordinariness. In Matthew 13:53-59 Jesus is rebuffed in his hometown of Nazareth. The people in the small village have heard of his "wisdom and his mighty works,"[52] yet far from celebrating his success and fame they were offended, even as were the Pharisees (Mt 15:12), but in the case of the Nazarene townspeople it was the scandal of the familiar or the ordinary. The text suggests that they, like John the Baptist, were expecting something more unusual or spectacular, according to their own set of anticipations, and, as Jesus had warned John, they "took offense at him" (Mt 13:57; cf. Mt 11:6). It is unlikely that Matthew is concerned to inform the reader only of the reaction of Nazareth; rather, in this section dealing with *Israel's* response we are to see this hometown repudiation as paradigmatic for Israel in the large. Yet the concern of this passage is not only with Christology but also discipleship, for when Jesus utters the proverb about a prophet in his own country he is speaking not only about himself, but his disciples, whom he elsewhere compares to the prophets (Mt 5:11-12; cf. Mt 10:41), who will be rejected in their prophetic role (Mt 23:34). They, like Jesus, can expect repudiation by intimates (Mt 10:21, 35-38; 24:12).

Second, Matthew indicates that the greater part of Israel has rejected Jesus because he has exposed their lawlessness. This is the reason given for

---

[52]Nazareth had a population of perhaps five hundred; see Stanton, *Gospel for a New People*, 93.

the execution of John the Baptist at the hands of Herod (Mt 14:1-12), and Jesus will later draw a comparison between his rejection and death and that of John (Mt 17:10-13). Jesus has insisted on a "righteousness that exceeds that of the scribes and Pharisees" (Mt 5:20) and he excoriates the leaders for thinking evil in their hearts (Mt 9:4), "condemning the guiltless" (Mt 12:7), blaspheming against the Holy Spirit (Mt 12:31), "making void the word of God" (Mt 15:6), neglecting the most significant matters of the law (justice, mercy, and faith; Mt 23:23), extortion (Mt 23:25), and murder (Mt 23:29-36).

Third, this rejection stems from the Pharisees' desire to nullify the Word of God by their human tradition (Mt 15:1-20). The Pharisees and scribes accuse Jesus' disciples of "transgressing the tradition of the elders"[53] by eating with unwashed hands. But Jesus retorts that it is actually they who transgress God's Word by appeal to their tradition, for they allow persons to avoid the command to honor father and mother by officially declaring that their possessions have been dedicated to God, with the implication that since these possessions technically no longer belong to them they have nothing to offer in parental support.

Manifestly, Jesus is not objecting to tradition as such, for the Scriptures, the "commandment of God," are tradition (παράδοσις), that is, revered truth that has been passed down. Rather, it is a matter of competing tradition, divine versus human. These "precepts of humans" (Mt 15:9) provide an opportunity for persons to circumvent the divine will revealed in God's Word out of self-serving motives. As in Matthew 9:10-13 and Matthew 12:1-8, Jesus insists that, according to the Scriptures, a morality that involves love and honoring others trumps ritualism, especially when such ritualism interferes with redemptive actions toward others. Yet this error regarding the nature of transgression is not essentially a matter of cognitive confusion, but rather stems from a heart that is far from God (Mt 15:8); and it is from the heart, and not from ceremonial or ritual violation, that all manner of uncleanness springs (Mt 15:10-20).

Finally, rejection of Jesus results from his refusal to acquiesce to the demand from the religious leaders for a sign (Mt 16:1-4; cf. Mt 12:38-40). Their

---

[53]The "tradition of the elders" refers to oral tradition that eventually found its way into the Mishnah. Although not accepted by other sects, such as the Essenes or Sadducees, the Pharisees believed it went back, in terms of its origins, to the time of Moses, and was almost as authoritative as the written Scriptures. See Davies and Allison, *Matthew*, 2:520.

desire for a sign is expressive of an "evil and adulterous generation," for it arises out of a desire to have the kingdom of God that Jesus proclaims on their own terms, with the consequence that the rule of God would be transmogrified into their own rule. They wish to determine the sign; and we learn later, at the cross, that the sign they ultimately demand is that Jesus come down from the cross (Mt 27:40). Jesus declares that a sign will be given to them, but one determined by God, that is, the sign of Jonah, which refers to the resurrection. Yet when the religious leaders are confronted with the empty tomb in Matthew 28:11-15 they reject this sign and contrive lies to hide it.

To emphasize the surprising and appalling character of this repudiation and hostility toward Jesus on the part of his own people, Matthew reports, by way of contrast, the worship and superabounding faith on the part of the Gentile woman from Tyre who implores healing for her daughter (Mt 15:21-28). Her distance from the blessings that were promised to Israel is indicated by the fact that she is a "Canaanite," thus belonging to a people who, according to the Old Testament, were to be destroyed from the land. Nevertheless, in spite of resistance from the disciples (Mt 15:23) and especially from Jesus (Mt 15:24-26) she perseveres and validates Jesus' declaration in 11:21 that the people of Tyre would be more receptive of the kingdom than Israelite cities.

The general drift of Matthew 13:53–16:20 involves Jesus withdrawing from a recalcitrant Israel and revealing himself to the receptive disciples, but Matthew here qualifies this broad schema, both on the side of Israel and on the side of the disciples. Although Matthew reports that Jesus repeatedly withdraws from Israel, Matthew also describes Jesus as being with Israel for a significant portion of these chapters.[54] Jesus does, in fact, heal and teach the crowds in these chapters (Mt 14:14, 34-36; 15:10-20, 29-31). And twice Jesus feeds the crowds (Mt 14:14-21; 15:32-39). In all of this Jesus fulfills the role that God has assigned to himself and to his appointed Davidic "prince" in Ezekiel 34, namely, to shepherd Israel by feeding them, healing their sick, binding up their crippled, and strengthening their weak (Ezek 34:3, 13-15, 23-24).[55] As long as he is in the midst of Israel Jesus shepherds the people.

---

[54]Thus, Jesus moves constantly back and forth, repeatedly withdrawing from Israel and moving back among Israel (compare Mt 14:13a with Mt 14:13b; compare Mt 15:21 with Mt 15:29).

[55]The references to "feed them on the mountains of Israel," and "upon the mountain heights of Israel shall be their pasture," and "they shall feed on the mountains of Israel" connect with the

But Matthew qualifies not only Jesus' repeated removal from Israel within these chapters, but also the generally favorable attitude of Jesus toward his disciples. Jesus must warn the disciples to "beware of the leaven of the Pharisees and Sadducees" (Mt 16:5-12), suggesting that the disciples were vulnerable to the anthropocentric and egocentric orientation of the teaching of these persons who had just demanded that Jesus perform a sign of their own choosing (Mt 16:1-4). When Jesus couches this warning in the image of "leaven," the disciples express anxiety over their lack of bread, forgetting that the feedings of Jesus demonstrated his ability to meet every need. Consequently, Jesus dubs them "men of little faith" (ὀλιγόπιστοι, Mt 16:8), the same epithet he had cast at Peter when Peter sinks in the wake of Jesus' behest to come to him walking on the water (Mt 14:31).

Yet despite their weak faith and lack of understanding regarding aspects of Jesus' teaching (Mt 15:15-16; Mt 16:8-11),[56] the disciples recognize that Jesus is the Son of God. At the climax to this second major division of the Gospel of Matthew Jesus raises with his disciples explicitly the matter of his identity, an issue that has become increasingly prominent throughout Matthew 4:17–16:20.[57] Jesus actually poses two questions. The first involves the opinion of human beings: "Who do human beings say the Son of Man is?" Since Matthew 8:20 Jesus has frequently referred to himself as the "Son of Man," either in open settings when speaking to the religious leaders or Jewish crowds (with his disciples also present, Mt 8:20; 9:6; 11:19; 12:8, 32, 40), or in speech to his disciples when he is describing his activity in the world at large (Mt 10:23; 13:37, 41). It is thus a public designation and therefore appropriate for the question regarding general opinion. When the disciples respond by listing John the Baptist, Elijah, Jeremiah, or one of the prophets, it is clear that the bottom line is that Jesus is a prophet, for John is depicted as a prophet (Mt 3:1-12; 11:9-14; 21:26), and indeed in some sense as Elijah (Mt 17:1-8; compare Mt 3:4 with 2 Kings 1:8). The reader recalls that Herod Antipas had already given this answer at Matthew 14:1-2, as Herod tried to

---

mention of the mountain in Mt 15:29-39; and the reference to "lie down in good grazing land" connects with Jesus' command to have the crowds sit down on the grass/ground in both feedings.

[56]Jeanine K. Brown, *The Disciples in Narrative Perspective: The Portrayal and Function of the Matthean Disciples*, SBLAcBib 9 (Leiden: Brill, 2002), 59-120.

[57]Matthew 11:1–16:20 is punctuated with three questions regarding Jesus' identity (Mt 11:3; 12:23; 13:55) and two representative answers (Mt 14:2, 33).

find explanation for Jesus' mighty works. But this answer is wrong, for John the Baptist and Jeremiah bear witness to Jesus (Mt 2:17; 3:1-12) and Elijah talks with him (Mt 17:3-4), and Jesus has demonstrated that he is much more than a prophet (Mt 12:41).

When Jesus asks his disciples for their identification, Peter responds, "You are the Christ, the Son of the living God." This is entirely the correct answer, since Jesus responds with a blessing, and since this insight comes from divine revelation (Mt 16:17), it thus expresses God's own point of view regarding Jesus (Mt 3:17).

In making this confession, Peter is speaking on behalf of the disciple circle. For one thing, Jesus directs both questions to the disciples, and the disciples together answer the first question. Moreover, the disciples had already declared Jesus to be Son of God in the second boat scene at Matthew 14:33 when Jesus came to them walking on the water; the disciples' declaration there formed an answer to the question they shouted at the first boat scene, "What sort of man is this, that even winds and sea obey him?" (Mt 8:27). In addition, the revelation from the Father that stands behind Peter's confession at Matthew 16:16 has been given to all the disciples (Mt 11:25-27; 13:10-17).

Indeed, throughout the Gospel of Matthew Peter often functions as representative spokesman for the disciple circle, and his actions are also representative of the disciples. Jack Dean Kingsbury has demonstrated that most of the things Matthew says of Peter he says also of the disciple circle.[58] And many scholars have noted this representative function of the character of Peter in this Gospel.[59] Others have insisted that Matthew presents Peter as the "chief rabbi," who has unique authority to serve as the "guarantor" of Jesus' teachings within the church.[60] Against this view is Jesus' repudiation

---

[58]Jack Dean Kingsbury, "The Figure of Peter in Matthew's Gospel as a Theological Problem," *JBL* 98 (1979): 69-83.

[59]E.g., Georg Strecker, *Der Weg der Gerechtigkeit* (Göttingen: Vandenhoeck & Ruprecht, 1975), 205; Rolf Walker, *Die Heilsgeschichte im ersten Evangelium* (Göttingen: Vandenhoeck & Ruprecht, 1967), 118; Pheme Perkins, *Peter: Apostle for the Whole Church* (Minneapolis: Fortress, 2000), 70-71; and, with some modification, R. T. France, *Matthew: Evangelist and Teacher* (Grand Rapids: Zondervan, 1989), 244-46.

[60]E.g., Reinhart Hummel, *Die Auseindersetzung zwischen Kirche und Judentum im Matthäusevangelium* (München: Kaiser, 1963); Günther Bornkamm, "Authority to Bind and Loose in the Church in Matthew's Gospel," *Perspective* 11 (1970): 37-50; Ulrich Luz, *Matthew in History: Interpretation, Influence and Effects* (Minneapolis: Fortress, 1985), 67-70; and (tentatively) Raymond

in Matthew 23:8-12 of special offices within the church, especially "rabbi" or teacher, in favor of the functioning of the whole body of the church under the authority of Jesus. And, according to Matthew 28:20, all the disciples will have the authority to teach. It is true that Peter was the first to be called to discipleship, and accordingly, in the list of disciples he is dubbed "first" (πρῶτος). He thus has a kind of "salvation-historical primacy," to use Kingsbury's expression, in that he was the first of the reconstituted people of God around Jesus, but he does not possess a teaching primacy.

Jesus responds to this confession with promises to Peter (16:18-19). Having changed Simon's name to Peter (πέτρος), Jesus declares that he will build his church "on this rock" (πέτρα). Since in the cause (Peter's confession) Peter represents the disciple circle, it is natural to infer that Peter represents the disciple circle in this effect of Jesus' responsive promise. Thus, Jesus gives the promise to all the disciples insofar as they make the christological confession of Matthew 16:16; yet Simon's nickname marks him as the one who actually uttered the solemn confession at this critical moment and his name forever reminds the church of Jesus' transcendent promise.[61] Accordingly, it is the embracing of the christological confession that constitutes the rock on which the church will be built.[62] The image of rock alludes to the permanence and stability of the church in the face of tremendous onslaught (cf. Mt 7:24-27).

Peter has just declared that Jesus is the Son of the *living* God; now Jesus insists that the gates of Hades, the abode of the dead, which in this passage represents death, shall not prevail against the church. The church will storm the gates of Hades so as to render the power of death incapable of swallowing or even substantially harming the church. Jesus then moves from the permanence of the church to the power of the church. He promises to give to Peter "the keys of the kingdom of heaven," that is, the power to open or shut the kingdom, with the consequence that whatever he binds or looses on earth will therefore likewise be bound or loosed by God.[63] The Jewish-Christian readers of the Gospel of Matthew would recognize that this language of binding and

---

E. Brown, Karl P. Donfried, and John Reumann, eds., *Peter in the New Testament* (Minneapolis: Augsburg, 1973), 83-107.

[61]For a careful treatment of Peter in this passage, properly balancing the attention given specifically to Peter with Peter's representative function, see Wilkins, *Discipleship*, 185-98.

[62]For a history of interpretation into the meaning of "this rock," see Luz, *Matthew in History*, 57-63.

[63]Both the divine passive and the use of *heaven* as a metonym for God indicate that God is the subject of the binding and loosing in the second clauses.

loosing was used by Jewish teachers to refer to the binding (that is, requiring) or loosing (that is, not requiring) of commandments on persons.[64]

Again, Peter is representative of the disciples,[65] who are themselves, as is often the case in the Gospel of Matthew, representatives of post-Easter disciples in general.[66] Accordingly, in Matthew 18:18, Jesus will make this same promise to the church, although there Matthew refers to dynamics within local congregations, whereas here in Matthew 16:18-19 the whole church, that is, the universal body of Christ, is in view. Thus Jesus will give to the entire church the authority to declare what is required and what is not required for entrance into the kingdom, and God himself will validate and act on these decisions. Manifestly, the authority to declare what is required and not required does not include the possibility of contradicting the teaching of Jesus. The law continues in force, and Jesus is its true interpreter (Mt 5:17-48). The judicial decisions of the church may involve adapting and applying the commands of Jesus to new situations which the church will continually encounter in the period between the resurrection and the parousia (Mt 28:18-20),[67] with the assurance that such ecclesial decisions will be binding.[68]

---

[64] Friedrich Büchsel, "δέω, λύω," *TDNT*: 2:60-61. Among the rabbis, note, e.g., *b. Sanh* 38. This is also the sense of "loose" (λύω) in Mt 5:19.

[65] Throughout the Gospel of Matthew Peter is representative of the disciples in both their positive and negative characteristics. Robert H. Gundry, *Peter: False Disciple and Apostate According to Saint Matthew* (Grand Rapids: Eerdmans, 2015), focuses on the negative characterization of Peter and isolates these negative characterizations from corresponding negative characterizations of the disciples, and consequently arrives at the unlikely conclusion that Matthew presents Peter as a kind of antidisciple. See earlier Arlo J. Nau, *Peter in Matthew: Discipleship, Diplomacy, and Dispractice* (Collegeville, MN: Liturgical, 1992).

[66] Note 1) that the five great discourses (Mt 5–7, 10, 13, 18, 24–25) are directed to the twelve, and yet these discourses focus on concerns of post-Easter Christians in general, so that what Jesus says to the disciples is really being said to the post-Easter church; 2) the twelve are constantly presented as struggling with the kinds of issues and experiences that would be especially relevant to the Christians in the post-Easter church (e.g., Mt 14:28-32; 16:5-12; 19:27-29; 26:30-46; 24:1–25:30); 3) both the twelve and post-Easter disciples are called "disciples"—the noun form used of the twelve in Matthew's narrative, the verb form of post-Easter disciples (Mt 28:19, cf. Mt 13:52; 27:57); 4) at the end of the Gospel of Matthew Jesus promises the eleven to be with them until "the end of the age," thus suggesting he is speaking to them as representatives of the entire church throughout the period culminating in his parousia. See Ulrich Luz, "The Disciples in the Gospel According to Matthew," in *The Interpretation of Matthew*, ed. Graham Stanton (Philadelphia: Fortress, 1983), 98-128.

[67] The "binding and loosing" on the part of the rabbis involved just such application vis-à-vis the law.

[68] As such, this applicatory function may be part of "teaching them to observe all I have commanded you" in Mt 28:20. See Jn 16:12-16 for a similar provision for the post-Easter future.

Yet in contrast to these great and transcendent promises regarding the future (after Jesus' resurrection), for the present the disciples are not so much as to tell anyone that Jesus is the Christ (Mt 16:20). This command to silence leads naturally to the third major division.

7

INTERPRETATION OF MATTHEW 16:21-28:20

WE HAVE JUST OBSERVED that at the conclusion to the second major division (Mt 4:17–16:20) the disciples know that Jesus is the Christ, the Son of God; yet Jesus charges them to tell no one that he is the Christ. The reader naturally wonders why the disciples are to keep Jesus' messiahship and divine sonship a secret. That riddle is solved in the third major division, in which Jesus demonstrates to his disciples the necessity for his passion, death, and resurrection. The logic of the narrative, then, makes clear that the disciples were not to proclaim that Jesus is the Christ because they did not yet know what it meant for him to be the Christ, Son of God, namely, that he is Son of God as one who is perfectly obedient to the will of his Father, even to the point of suffering and death, leading finally to resurrection glory.

Matt 16:21. The third major division begins with a general heading in Matthew 16:21 that encapsulates the interrelated themes that unite Matthew 16:22–28:20: Jesus' journey to Jerusalem, where he will suffer, die, and be raised; and Jesus' showing his disciples the necessity for this journey, which draws out the significance for them of Jesus' journey, with its suffering and death. Actually, Matthew 16:21 has a twofold structural function: This verse is not only a superscription to this division, it is also the first of three passion predictions (with Mt 17:22-23 and Mt 20:18-20) that will punctuate the early chapters of this third major division and tie these early chapters to the events of passion and resurrection in Matthew 26–28.

Matt 16:22–20:34. The role of Matthew 16:21 as a passion prediction, necessarily given at a particular point in Jesus' ministry, prompts Peter's response to this utterance in Matthew 16:22-23. This passage begins the movement toward Jesus' passion and resurrection (Mt 16:22–25:46) that will be followed by the events of passion and resurrection (Mt 26:1–28:20). It also sets the stage for the repeated resistance on the part of the disciples to Jesus' commitment to the cross throughout the remainder of the book.

When Jesus calls Peter "Satan," that is, tempter, and orders him to "get behind me," recalling the words that Jesus directed to the devil in Matthew 4:10 (the command "depart" [ὕπαγε] is found in both passages), the reader understands that the vocation Jesus just described in Matthew 16:21 is a struggle for him and that he is tempted to avoid this God-ordained path, an impression that is reinforced by Jesus' insistence that Peter is a "hindrance" or "stumbling stone" to him. This negative description of Peter stands in stark contrast to the positive portrait in Matthew 16:16-19: there Peter was the object of blessing, while here he is the object of reprimand; there he was called "Peter," associated with the rock of building, while here he is called "Satan" and "a stone of stumbling" (σκάνδαλον); there Peter represented the viewpoint of God over against humans (Mt 16:17), while now he is on the side of humans. The change turns entirely on the passion prediction of Matthew 16:21, where Jesus for the first time in the Gospel of Matthew explicitly teaches his disciples about his suffering and death. And, consequently, this altercation marks a new stage in the characterization of the disciples; from this point to the end of the book they will be portrayed, above all, as resistant to Jesus' commitment to the cross.

Jesus responds to this altercation with Peter by addressing all the disciples regarding the necessity of their own self-denial and cross-bearing (Mt 16:24-28), thereby suggesting that Peter was representing the entire disciple circle in his rebuke.[1] The nature of this response to the disciples indicates, further, that behind the rebuke directed against Jesus' passion was the

---

[1] The constant alternation in the surrounding verses between Peter and the disciples indicates that Peter is representative of them throughout. Thus Jesus poses a question to all the disciples (Mt 16:15), which Peter answers (Mt 16:16-18), to which Jesus responds with a charge to the entire disciple circle (Mt 16:20); then Jesus makes an announcement to the entire disciple circle (Mt 16:21), leading to Peter's reaction (Mt 16:22-23), to which Jesus responds with instruction to the entire disciple circle (Mt 16:24-28).

suspicion in the minds of the disciples that this destiny of Jesus would involve them in the same kind of vocation.

In fact, Matthew 16:24 encapsulates the vocation of disciples even as Matthew 16:21 encapsulates the vocation of Jesus, but here Jesus supports their vocation with arguments, for the disciples require to be persuaded (Mt 16:25-28). Yet what is true for them is true for "anyone," the indefinite subject repeated throughout, thus indicating that the twelve are representative of those who will be made disciples through them in the post-Easter period (Mt 28:18-20).

According to Matthew 16:24, the desire to come after Jesus can be realized only by self-denial and cross-bearing. The phrase "come after me" recalls Jesus' invitation to the crowds to assume the yoke of discipleship in Matthew 11:28, while "follow me" brings to mind Jesus' calling of the first set of disciples in Matthew 4:19, again suggesting a commensurability between the twelve and others who will be made disciples. These two phrases, pertaining to discipleship to Jesus, form an inclusio around "deny themselves" and "take up their cross," indicating that self-denial and cross-bearing constitute the specific content of coming after Jesus and following him. Self-denial means saying "no" to the self,[2] and specifically denying claims that the self places on one, even as Peter's denial of Jesus will involve his rejecting relationship with Jesus and the claims that Jesus (in this case rightly) had on him (Mt 26:34, 35, 70, 72, 75). Matthew has not yet made any mention of Jesus' cross; the first references to cross (here and earlier in Mt 10:38) pertain to the cross of the disciples, thereby emphasizing the participation of the disciples in the destiny of Jesus. As will become clear, the essential meaning of Jesus' taking up his cross in the Gospel of Matthew is complete submission to the will of God even to the point of suffering and death in humble service toward others. Thus discipleship is constituted by assuming the same orientation toward God.

Jesus supports these requirements for discipleship by insisting that, paradoxically, the desire to save what is involved in one's physical life will result in its opposite, the loss of all that typically belongs to the flourishing of life, whereas the losing of one's life will result in its opposite, the finding of a kind of life that one did not have before (Mt 16:25). For those who may be

---

[2] Heinrich Schlier, "ἀρνέομαι," *TDNT* 1:469.

reluctant to pay such a heavy price for this new form of life, Jesus insists that the life he is talking about is of inestimably more value than all that a person has (Mt 16:26). In Matthew 16:27-28 Jesus climactically places these decisions that one makes concerning life in the present within the context of end-time judgement, describing in Matthew 16:27 the immense cosmic and personal significance of the Day of Judgment, and in Matthew 16:28 its certainty, implying that the coming of Jesus' kingly rule over the world in the form of his own exaltation ("the Son of man coming in his kingdom),[3] which some of the disciples will soon witness,[4] offers assurance that this cosmic rule that he will enter upon at his resurrection (Mt 28:18) will culminate in end-time eschatological judgment. I take Matthew 16:28, then, to refer to Jesus' exaltation at the point of his resurrection, since the Gospel of Matthew differentiates between the kingdom of Jesus and the kingdom of God. Jesus enters into his kingdom at his exaltation, and his exaltation is the basis for the assurance of his parousia.[5]

This reference to the glorification of Jesus, which involves his exaltation that culminates in eschatological return, leads to a visionary anticipation of that glorification at the transfiguration (Mt 17:1-13). The reference to "six days" (cf. Ex 24:16), the appearance of Moses and Elijah, both of whom had experiences with God on Sinai, or Horeb (Ex 24:1–32:14; 1 Kings 19:4-18), the mention of tabernacles, and the bright, overshadowing cloud all bring to mind God's revelation on Sinai and suggest that even as God revealed his glory on Mt. Sinai (see esp. Ex 24:15-18) so now he is revealing on the Mount of Transfiguration the glory that his Son will manifest when he is raised

---

[3]See, e.g., Mt 13:41-42, where Jesus distinguishes between the kingdom of the Son of Man, which involves his present rule over the world (i.e., the cosmic rule that he will assume at the exaltation, 28:18), and the kingdom of the Father, which will come in its consummated form only after "all causes of sin and all evildoers" will have been removed from his realm (Mt 13:43). Moreover, in distinction from Mark, at his trial the Matthean Jesus answers the high priest's question regarding his divine sonship by declaring "from now on" (ἀπ' ἄρτι) you will see the Son of Man seated at the right hand of Power and coming on clouds of heaven" (Mt 26:64; cf. Mk 14:62), thus pointing not to his return but to his exalted rule beginning with his resurrection. Matthew indicates that Jesus' rule over the world in the period after his resurrection will culminate in his ushering in the end-time kingdom of God with his parousia by describing the Son of Man "sitting on his glorious throne" in final judgment over the nations (Mt 25:31). For the major ways in which Mt 16:28 has been interpreted, see Donald A. Carson, "Matthew," in *The Expositor's Bible Commentary*, ed. Frank E. Gaebelein and Walter C. Kaiser Jr., 12 vols. (Grand Rapids: Zondervan, 1984), 8:380-81.
[4]Jesus speaks of "some," because Judas will not survive to see it (Mt 27:5). He may also have in mind his transfiguration, which three of the disciples will witness, and which serves as an anticipation of his resurrection glory.
[5]So rightly R. T. France, *The Gospel of Matthew*, NICNT (Grand Rapids: Eerdmans, 2007), 640-41.

Interpretation of Matthew 16:21–28:20 199

from the dead. The divine voice also recalls Sinai, though here it testifies not to God's law but to God's Son, as did the heavenly voice at Matthew 3:17. Yet, here, in contrast to 3:17, the voice adds "listen to him." The disciples need to hear this demand, since they are resistant to Jesus' words regarding his passion. As they come down from the mountain, Jesus forbids them to say anything about the transfiguration until after his resurrection, suggesting that they will not understand its true significance, and in fact will misunderstand it, unless they construe it through the prism of his passion, in analogy to the rejection and death of John (Mt 17:9-13).

Peter's desire to build three booths on the mount of transfiguration betokens a desire to bask in the glory that was experienced there, but in Matthew 17:14-21 Jesus and his disciples confront their obligation to ongoing human need. Although Jesus had given the disciples "authority over unclean spirits, to cast them out" in Matthew 10:1 the nine disciples could not exorcise the demon from the epileptic boy, leading Jesus to allude implicitly to his passion at the hands of "a faithless (ἄπιστος) and perverse generation." This expression refers to the Jewish crowds (e.g., Mt 11:16; 24:34) and especially to the religious leaders (Mt 12:39, 41, 42, 45; 16:4; 23:36), but it is prompted at this point by the failure of the disciples. Here, then, Jesus draws a connection between the "weak faith" (ὀλιγόπιστος, Mt 17:20) behind the disciples' inability to fulfill the ministry Jesus had given to them and the faithlessness (ἄπιστος) of this murderous generation. This connection (by no means identification) points to the seriousness of the weakness of faith on the part of the disciples. When Jesus instructs his disciples about the unimaginable power of a faith "like a grain of mustard seed," he makes clear that ὀλιγόπιστος involves not amount of faith ("little faith") but quality of faith, that is, faith contaminated by an element of doubt (cf. Mt 14:31).

The segment that began in Matthew 16:21 with the first passion prediction culminates in the second passion prediction at Matthew 17:22-23, thus forming an inclusio.[6] At this point Matthew informs us that Jesus and

---

[6]As I mentioned above, Mt 16:21 plays a dual structural role. On the one hand, it serves as a superscription for the whole of Mt 16:22–28:20, and thus relates equally to the whole of the third major division. On the other hand, its connection with Peter's response in Mt 16:22-23 indicates that Matthew wants us to construe it also as a specific passion prediction delivered at a particular point; it is in this latter capacity that Matthew joins it with Mt 16:22–17:23 to form a segment. This employment of a single passage to fulfill two structural roles is not unique in the Gospel of Matthew; we saw above that Mt 5:17-20 is the heading specifically for the antitheses in

his company have moved south from Caesarea Philippi (Mt 16:13) to Capernaum, thereby connecting this passion prediction with the theme of Jesus' journey to Jerusalem, as he did also in Matthew 16:21 and will do again at Matthew 20:18-20.

Although redaction critics have construed Matthew 17:24-27 as instruction to the members of Matthew's church regarding their paying a certain type of tax within their own setting, we have seen that these critics have had difficulty identifying exactly which tax within the situation of Matthew's community this passage might be intended to address. Moreover, the primary issue of the passage is not whether the *disciples* pay the tax but whether *Jesus* pays it. Indeed, if we read this passage in terms of its narrative function, we see that Matthew links it with the community discourse that immediately follows by way of an inclusio around the image of "king" (Mt 17:24; 18:23-25) and by the repetition of "cause offense" (σκανδαλίζω/ σκάνδαλον; Mt 17:27; 18:6, 7, 8, 9). Therefore, within the story of the Gospel of Matthew, this passage sets forth the principle that even as Jesus does not insist on his rights in the matter of the payment of the tax, the "sons" of the kingdom should not insist on their "rights" when the exercise of these rights might give offense to those on the outside, so as to prevent them from accepting the proclamation of the kingdom.[7]

Jesus moves on, then, to apply this very principle to relationships within the community (Mt 18:1-35). Life within the kingdom requires a childlike humility (Mt 18:1-4), in the sense that even as children did not have "rights" that they could enforce in their relations with others, so disciples are to forego the exercise of their rights in favor of doing that which is good for others in the community, as does Jesus who gave up his rights as "Lord" and "king" to be served in order "to serve and to give his life as a ransom for many" (Mt 20:28). For disciples, this means doing all possible to avoid exercising their rights in such a way as to cause others in the community to fall away from the faith, since God, like a protective father, will severely judge those who destroy the faith of his vulnerable children ("little ones"),

---

Mt 5:21-48, and more broadly for the whole central section of the Sermon, which extends from Mt 5:17 to Mt 7:12.

[7] As argued, rightly, by David E. Garland, "Matthew's Understanding of the Temple Tax," in *Treasures New and Old: Recent Contributions to Matthean Studies*, ed. David R. Bauer and Mark Allan Powell, SBLSS 1 (Atlanta: Scholars, 1996).

for even one of these is supremely valuable in his sight (Mt 18:5-15). Disciples are to manifest this childlike humility in active reconciliation and unlimited forgiveness of an erring "brother/sister" (Mt 18:16-35), since God will not forgive, but rather judge, those who do not forgive their brother/sister in the face of their unimaginably abundant forgiveness by God.

In the course of this discussion regarding forgiveness Jesus addresses the process of dealing with sin within the community. Here sin is understood primarily as violation against others in the church;[8] an attitude of forgiveness is to pervade any process of dealing with an offending fellow disciple. Jesus insists that everything should be done to maintain the integrity of a just and loving process,[9] including avoidance of unnecessary public censure (cf. Mt 1:19) through initial private confrontation and "evidence confirmed by two or three witnesses" (Mt 18:16). And all is to be done to "gain the brother/sister" (Mt 18:15), that is, to restore such a one to full obedient discipleship. Yet, if the process is unsuccessful in that the erring disciple refuses to heed even the gathered assembly, the disciple is to be excluded from the community, for the sake of the witness of a purified church to the world (Mt 5:13-16), but also for the sake of the erring disciple. Treating such a one as "a Gentile and tax collector" (Mt 18:17) may involve excluding them precisely in order to place them within the sphere of redemption, since at the end of the Gospel of Matthew Jesus will commission the eleven to "make disciples of all nations" (or Gentiles, ἔθνος), and Jesus has already called a "tax collector" to discipleship and initiated meal fellowship with others of the same maligned vocation (Mt 9:9-13).[10]

As the church conducts this difficult task of discipline, it can be assured that whatever it binds (decision to impose punitive sanction) will be bound (that is, confirmed) by God, and whatever it looses (decision not to punish) will be loosed (also confirmed) by God,[11] so long as even the work of the two

---

[8] Even as Mt 18:5-14 warns regarding sinning against a fellow disciple ("little ones"), so Mt 8:15-35 instructs regarding what to do when a fellow disciple ("brother/sister") sins against us.

[9] In contrast to the unjust proceedings directed against Jesus at the end of the Gospel of Matthew (Mt 26:57–27:26).

[10] This redemptive use of the "ban" recalls 1 Cor 5:3-5, even as avoiding causing offense to others in the church by insisting on one's freedom in Christ from certain legal obligations recalls Paul's discussion of meat offered to idols in 1 Cor 8:1-12; 10:23-30; Rom 14:1-15:13.

[11] General agreement exists that the language of binding and loosing was employed by the rabbis not only in terms of declaring something forbidden or permitted, as we saw in the treatment of Mt 16:19, but also the judicial implementation of such decisions in declaring persons guilty

or three witnesses is pursued with prayer for divine direction and confirmation (Mt 18:18-19). Jewish teachers insisted that where two or three were gathered to study Torah God himself would be present.[12] Now Jesus declares that where two or three are gathered to apply Jesus' teachings regarding matters of church discipline, Jesus, who is "Emmanuel, God with us" (Mt 1:23), will be present to guide and help (Mt 18:20).[13]

Even as the community discourse applies Jesus' vocation of self-denial and cross-bearing, which is to be shared by the disciples, to matters of relationships within the churches, so Matthew 19:1–20:34 proceeds to explore how this cruciform vocation informs a series of other relationships. Some have found in this series an example of "household codes" (*Haustafeln*), common in Graeco-Roman and Hellenistic Jewish circles (and found elsewhere within the New Testament; see Col 3:18–4:1; Eph 5:21–6:9; 1 Pet 2:18–3:7; cf. 1 Tim 2:1-15; Tit 2:1-10).[14] Yet the correspondence between Matthew 19:1–20:34 and these household codes breaks down at several points and can be maintained only by straining the data of the text. It is preferable simply to accept the series as Matthew offers it, without attempting to impose a framework from outside. The unity of this segment is established by an inclusio of healing in the midst of "great crowds" at Matthew 19:2 and Matthew 20:29-34, and by the repeated application to a variety of relationships of an attitude of self-denial and cross-bearing in obedience to God and service to others that radically contradicts self-centered ways of thinking.

Jesus challenges self-focused attitudes about relationship to the wife by maintaining that marriage is permanent and that no cause for divorce, save that of πορνεία, or sexual infidelity, is valid (Mt 19:3-12).[15] Jesus bases his teaching on the principle that marriage and divorce must be viewed from

---

or not guilty of an offense that might result in exclusion from the community. But cf. William G. Thompson, *Matthew's Advice to a Divided Community: Mt. 17:22-18:35*, AB (Rome: Biblical Institute Press, 1970), 188-94.

[12]m. Abot 3:2´3.3. W. D. Davies and Dale C. Allison Jr., *The Gospel According to Saint Matthew*, ICC (New York: T&T Clark, 1997), 2:789-90; Craig S. Keener, *A Commentary on the Gospel of Matthew* (Grand Rapids: Eerdmans, 1999), 455-56.

[13]Hubert Frankemölle, *Jahwe-Bund und Kirche Christi: Studien zur Form- und Traditionsgeschichte des "Evangeliums" nach Matthäus*, Neutestamentliche Abhandlungen/Neue Folge 10 (Münster: Aschendorff, 1974), 29-36.

[14]Michael H. Crosby, *House of Disciples: Church, Economics, and Justice in Matthew* (Maryknoll, NY: Orbis, 1988), 110, 263; Warren Carter, *Households and Discipleship: A Study of Matthew 19-20*, JSNTSup 103 (Sheffield: Sheffield Academic Press, 1994).

[15]For an extensive discussion of the meaning of πορνεία here, see Keener, *Matthew*, 466-69.

the perspective of God's purpose, set forth in the creation account, rather than in terms of human desire to separate which stems from a hardness of heart. In permitting divorce, the Mosaic law concedes this hardness of heart, but such hardness has no place in the kingdom, which promises salvation from sins (Mt 1:21) and therefore expects purity of heart (Mt 5:8). Such commitment to the wife involves a denial of the interests of the self in favor of the kind of complete obedience to the will of God in the service of others that is at the center of what it means for Jesus to take up his cross and for the disciples to do the same. Radical obedience to God in this area means that it would be better not to marry, even by adopting the shameful role of a eunuch for the sake of the kingdom, than to divorce contrary to God's purpose.

Jesus challenges self-focused, hierarchical attitudes about relationship to children in Matthew 19:13-15. The humble spirit implicit in self-denial and taking up the cross makes plain that childlike humility characterizes God's kingdom (Mt 18:4). This consideration affords the highest status to children, who otherwise had no position or status and were thus considered a bother or interruption. They must be given priority.

Jesus challenges self-centered ways of thinking about relationship to possessions in the episode concerning the rich young man in Matthew 19:16-30. Discipleship requires the rejection of the security of present possessions in favor of sacrificing all for the sake of those in need. Such an attitude,[16] which renders a person "perfect"[17] in the sense of completely fulfilling the command

---

[16] The willingness to sacrifice all for the sake of those in need is required of all who would be disciples (Mt 19:23-27), though actual self-dispossession is not required of all, since elsewhere the Gospel of Matthew assumes the continuing possession of property on the part of disciples (Mt 5:42; 6:2-14) and speaks of a "rich man . . . who was a disciple of Jesus" and possessed a tomb (Mt 27:57-60). Jesus required dispossession in the case of this man apparently because he was especially personally vested in his possessions.

[17] In Mt 5:48 Jesus had insisted on perfection, or completeness, in terms of the *scope* of love; here Jesus insists on perfection in terms of completeness in the *depth* of love, an attitude of truly costly sacrifice. This man had fulfilled "you shall love your neighbor as yourself" in terms of the letter of the commandments in the first tablet of the Decalogue, so long as the prohibition against covetousness was omitted (Mt 19:18-19), but not in terms of radical sacrifice for the good of the other, which involves the will of God that lies behind the letter and transcends it. See David R. Bauer, "Perfection of Disciples in Matthew's Gospel: An Examination of a Central Concept in Matthean Kingdom Ethics," in *Kingdom Rhetoric: New Testament Explorations in Honor of Ben Witherington III*, ed. T. Michael W. Halcomb, (Eugene, OR: Wipf & Stock, 2013), 3-20; Rudolf Schnackenburg, "Die Vollkommenheit des Christen nach den Evangelien," *GuL* 32 (1959): 420-33.

"you shall love your neighbor as yourself" (Mt 19:19), is necessary for the realization of eternal life (Mt 19:16), entrance into the kingdom (Mt 19:23-24), and salvation (Mt 19:25). It is a monetary application of taking up one's cross, in analogy to Jesus who gave up all, even his very life, for the sake of those who desperately need the benefits of his sacrificial act (Mt 20:28). Yet those who abandon possessions, and also family, for the sake of discipleship (cf. Mt 4:18-22) will be more than compensated in the "new world" with rule and with transcendent forms of these forfeited treasures (Mt 19:27-29).

This talk about compensation and reward leads to the parable of the laborers in the vineyard, in which Jesus challenges self-focused ways of thinking about the receiving of compensation (Mt 19:30–20:16). Jesus gives this parable in response to Peter's statement in Matthew 19:27, which assumes a compensation mentality: the notion that God is under obligation to reward each one on the basis of one's sacrifice and labor in strict correlation to the sacrifice and labors of others for the kingdom. The parable is a specific elaboration of the chiastic saying about the first being last and the last first (Mt 19:30; 20:16) that frames the parable (inclusio), which describes workers who were hired first (and worked throughout the day, bearing its heat) being paid last, while those who were hired last (and worked for only one hour in the cool of the evening) were paid first. And all of them together received the same pay. The parable teaches that when it comes to compensation God does not operate on the basis of human assumptions regarding fairness and equity, but rather for him justice (δίκαιος) involves delight in giving freely, more than deserved.[18] God will reward as he promised. But, in his generosity, he may give to some more than they deserve. Those who believe they do not benefit fully in this exceeding generosity have no basis for ill-feeling toward the Father; rather, they are invited to share his vision of generous goodness.

Finally, Jesus addresses self-focused, hierarchical, attitudes to position (Mt 20:17-34). On the heels of Jesus' last and most complete passion prediction (Mt 20:17-19) the mother of James and John requests, on their behalf, the chief places of honor and dominion (cf. Mt 19:28), on the right hand and the left in Jesus' kingdom. The angry response of the rest of the disciples

---

[18]The language of justice is found at the beginning (Mt 20:4) and end (Mt 20:13) of his dealings with the laborers.

demonstrates that they shared this interest in honor and status and were angry at James and John for getting their request to Jesus ahead of them. Jesus indicates that his kingship is not about honor, as humans generally understand it, but about suffering (Mt 20:22-23); the reader will recall this statement when, toward the end of the Gospel of Matthew, those who are crucified with Jesus are said to be at his right and at his left (Mt 27:38). Jesus insists that in the kingdom the issue of position and status is turned on its head. In contrast to the thinking of the Gentiles, who will finally kill him (compare Mt 20:25 with Mt 20:19), it is those who most abjectly reject positions of honor and status in favor of humble submission to the needs of others who will have the greatest status in the kingdom, for this is the essential model of Jesus' whole life, culminating in his death; he came "not to be served, but to serve, and to give his life a ransom for many" (Mt 20:28). Jesus goes on to exemplify this claim in Matthew 20:29-34, when two blind men appeal to him in his kingly role as Son of David. In contrast to the impatient crowds who order these men to be silent, Jesus asks them, "What do you want me to do for you?" (Mt 20:32) and humbly serves them by complying with their request.

Matt 21:1-25:46. In Matthew 16:21-20:34 Jesus is on the journey to Jerusalem, but in Matthew 21:1 he enters the environs of Jerusalem. From this point to Matthew 25:46 the events of Jesus' passion are anticipated in his activity in Jerusalem. Matthew 21:1-27 describes the initial actions of Jesus in the city; this royal Son of David claims the city in the form of his triumphal entry in Matthew 21:1-11, and he claims the temple in his act of cleansing the temple and the subsequent dispute regarding this act in Matthew 21:12-27.[19]

In the triumphal entry Jesus combines royal prerogative and humility, thus affirming his rightful rule, but clarifying its character. Jesus' act of commandeering of the donkey with her colt and the acquiescence of the objecting stranger demonstrates Jesus' kingly authority over animals and humans (Mt 21:2-3). And Jesus accepts the trappings of a royal entrance, including the spreading of branches and garments and the hailing of the people, who ascribe to him salvation and blessing (Mt 21:9). All of this, in the context of approaching Passover, would suggest to the Jewish-Christian

---

[19]The references to Jesus entering the city (Mt 21:10) and entering the temple (Mt 21:12) point to the two spheres of his activity in these initial days in Jerusalem.

implied reader the fervor surrounding the appearance of a religious-revolutionary conqueror. But Jesus' choice of animal is not a mighty steed, symbolizing military authority and brutal conquest, but a donkey with her foal, thus fulfilling the prophecy of Zechariah 9:9 which speaks of a king who comes in humility (Mt 21:5). The Jewish crowds, who followed him from Galilee (Mt 20:29), announce to a perplexed Jerusalem that this Son of David is "the prophet Jesus" (Mt 21:11). Here the reader recalls the inadequacy of identifying Jesus as a prophet, since confessing him to be a prophet represents not the revelation from God that Jesus is his Son, but the "flesh-and-blood" opinion of human beings (Mt 16:13-14, 17). This inability to recognize the divine truth that Jesus is Son of God (Mt 16:15-17; 3:17) will result, the next time the crowd shouts in assembly, in a much different cry: "Let him be crucified," "His blood be upon us and our children" (Mt 27:22, 25).

Jesus claims authority over the temple by overturning the tables and seats of those who sold doves and changed money in the temple for the sacrifices offered by those who came to worship at the Passover, and declaring that those who had responsibility for the temple had thus transformed this "house of prayer" into a "den of robbers"; thereby Jesus indicates that the temple had become defiled (Mt 21:12-13). The forcefully disruptive character of Jesus' actions points to the destruction of this defiled temple (Mt 23:38; 24:1-2; 26:61; 27:40). Yet, for now, Jesus reclaims the temple for God by teaching and healing the blind and lame, thereby making it the place of God's truth and of the salvation of those who had heretofore been excluded from the temple and the worship and service of God that it represented (Mt 21:14). In response, the children cry out, "Hosanna to the Son of David," as the crowds had done earlier. But, unlike the crowds, they do not add "the prophet," for insofar as they share the humility of Jesus (Mt 18:1-5; 19:13-15) these "babes" have been given understanding from the Father (Mt 21:15-16; cf. Mt 11:25). In contrast, the chief priests and elders, leaders of the temple who now in Jerusalem take over from the Pharisees the role of Jesus' antagonists, are as ignorant of the meaning of the Scriptures as were the Galilean Pharisees (Mt 21:16; cf. Mt 12:5). The reason becomes clear: after Jesus teaches his disciples the necessity of faith in prayer in the midst of this kind of opposition (Mt 21:18-22), the chief priests return to the scene and reveal their anthropocentric and egocentric concern to maintain their own control and standing with the people over against any interest in the truth regarding the divine origin of Jesus' authority (Mt 21:23-27).

Jesus continues his teaching in the temple with three parables in which he accuses the religious leaders of the following: 1) hypocrisy that renders them farther from the kingdom than the morally despicable tax collectors and prostitutes (Mt 21:28-32); 2) a long history of killing the prophets, culminating in the murder of God's own Son out of a desire to control the vineyard, that is, God's people Israel, for their own benefit (Mt 21:33-46); and 3) selfish and ungrateful refusal to accept God's invitation to the wedding feast, that is, the messianic banquet of the kingdom (Mt 22:1-14). In the process, Jesus declares that God will take his kingdom from them and also from the people, insofar as they are under the tutelage of such leaders,[20] and give it to a "nation" that will yield to God the kind of obedience that God desires.[21]

These three parables spoken by Jesus to the religious leaders are followed by three questions posed by the religious leaders to Jesus, designed "to entangle him in his talk" and thus shame him before the people (Mt 22:15-40). Their purpose is to dissuade the multitudes from the conviction that Jesus is a prophet, and thereby make possible the leaders' arrest of Jesus (Mt 21:46). By his answers Jesus not only deftly escapes their rhetorical-theological traps but offers insight into the nature of the kingdom. We learn that, despite the countercultural character of the kingdom that rejects the ultimacy of the social structures of this present world (Mt 4:18-22; 10:34-39), life in the kingdom involves fulfilling the obligation to pay taxes (Mt 22:15-22) and thus offer support for the proper functions of government. We learn, too, that the resurrection life will involve an existence that transcends and

---

[20] That the kingdom will be taken from Israel, and not just the leaders, is indicated by the fact that God will give the kingdom not to another set of leaders, but to a "nation" (ἔθνος), a word that often means "Gentile" in the Gospel of Matthew, and certainly corresponds to "all nations" in Mt 28:19. Moreover, in the parable of the marriage feast it is not only the leaders who reject the invitation, but all to whom the invitation is offered; those who will consequently be killed are the "murderers," who in the Gospel of Matthew include the Jewish crowds (Mt 27:23, 25). Also, the declaration that the invitations will now go to others who were not invited at the first (Mt 22:8-10) corresponds to "the kingdom will be ... given to another nation." Finally, in Mt 8:12 Jesus has already spoken of the eschatological exclusion of "the sons of the kingdom"; cf. Mt 15:14.

[21] As mentioned above, in the Gospel of Matthew "fruit" always refers to repentant obedience that stems from a life transformed by placing faith in the proclamation of the gospel.

therefore relativizes the most intimate relationships persons enjoy in the present (Mt 22:23-33). And we learn that every command of God in Scripture is an expression of love to God and love to neighbor (Mt 22:34-40), which provides the basic structure to Matthean ethics.

Finally, Jesus turns the tables and poses to the Pharisees the question regarding the role of "Son of David" in Messianic expectations, thus clarifying the acclaim of Davidic sonship that the crowds shouted in Matthew 21:15. In a manner typical of rabbinic discussions, Jesus places all the Old Testament passages that suggest the Messiah will be Son of David over against Psalm 110:1, in which David calls him "Lord," in an attempt to make sense of the whole. Thus, Jesus does not here deny that the Christ is David's Son, but indicates that his lordship over David renders him more than Son of David. The reader recalls that, according to God's point of view, Jesus is above all Son of God (Mt 3:17; 17:5). This final joust with the Pharisees convinces them of the inadvisability to engage him further in debate, and it therefore marks the end of any discussion with the religious leaders.

The climax of Jesus' attack on the religious leaders, therefore, is not directed to the leaders themselves, but takes the form of warning to the Jewish crowds and the disciples to avoid the dangers posed by these leaders (Mt 23:1-39), even though the leaders are rhetorically addressed in the woes.[22] In Matthew 23:1-12 Jesus describes the general demeanor of the "scribes and Pharisees" as hypocritical in that they "preach but do not practice" (Mt 23:3); as rigorous in placing heavy legal demands on others while, unlike Jesus (Mt 11:28-30), doing nothing to ease their burden (Mt 23:4); and as anthropocentric rather than theocentric, in that they perform both their acts of righteousness and religious professional duties for the sake of appearance before humans with a view toward self-aggrandizement (Mt 23:5-7). At this point Jesus explicitly draws a contrast between the behavior of these religious leaders and his disciples: the latter must not insist on titles or positions of status, but assume the egalitarianism of "brothers," recognizing that the only status among them is the anti-status attitude of humility (Mt 23:8-12; cf. Mt 18:4).

The seven woes against the "scribes and Pharisees, hypocrites" that follow develop this general description of their demeanor described in Matthew 23:1-12

---

[22]This didactic purpose of Mt 23 is emphasized by David E. Garland, *The Intention of Matthew 23*, NovTSup 52 (Leiden: Brill, 1979), 37-63.

and add additional problematic behaviors. Jesus lambasts them for creating unrealistic and improper demands for others to enter the kingdom with the result that such persons become morally and spiritually more corrupt than the religious leaders themselves (Mt 23:13-15); Jesus insists that their theological perception is hopelessly distorted, making ridiculous distinctions regarding oaths (Mt 23:16-23) and inverting major and minor commandments of the law (Mt 23:23-24).[23] Jesus accuses them of focusing on outward appearance of righteousness while ignoring their inward corruption (Mt 23:25-28); and Jesus describes them as being one with their fathers in murdering the prophets and righteous ones since they themselves will kill those whom Jesus will send to them (Mt 23:29-36), so that on them "may come all the righteous blood."

The remainder of the Gospel of Matthew indicates that the crowds do not heed the warnings of Jesus regarding these religious leaders, but rather are seduced to join them, since at Matthew 27:25 the cry of the crowds, "His blood be upon us," essentially repeats Jesus' words here. Indeed, Jesus declares that the murderous reception of his envoys will spell judgment not just for the religious leaders but for the nation as a whole ("Jerusalem"), declaring that the temple will be forsaken, the divine passive suggesting, "by God," pointing ahead to the rending of the veil of the temple at Matthew 27:51. And Jesus himself leaves the temple at this point, never to return (Mt 24:1). Moreover, the people will be bereft of his saving presence as well, unless and until they cry out, "Blessed is he who comes in the name of the Lord."[24] This is the last statement Jesus speaks to the Jewish crowds in the Gospel of Matthew (Mt 23:37-39).

Accordingly, Jesus addresses the eschatological discourse of Matthew 24-25 to his disciples alone (Mt 24:1, 3). The eschatological discourse is notoriously

---

[23] Thus Jesus implies that some commandments are more significant than others, that is, a structure exists within the law.

[24] The most likely construal is that any future salvific visitation of Jesus to Israel is contingent on acceptance by Israel of Jesus' messiahship. This passage holds out the possibility of such acceptance, but nowhere in the Gospel of Matthew is any confidence expressed that such acceptance will take place. See France, *Gospel of Matthew*, 884-85; Jeffrey A. Gibbs, *Jerusalem and Parousia: Jesus' Eschatological Discourse in Matthew's Gospel* (St. Louis: Concordia, 2000), 123-25; David L. Turner, *Israel's Last Prophet: Jesus and the Jewish Leaders in Matthew 23* (Minneapolis: Fortress, 2015), 327-29; Dale C. Allison Jr., "Matthew 23:39 = Luke 13:35b as a Conditional Prophecy," *JSNT* 18 (1983): 75-84. Allison's study is especially helpful because of his compelling analysis of the Greek sentence.

resistant to straightforward structural analyses, and any structural proposal must address difficulties that the proposal itself raises.[25] The key, then, is to adopt an understanding of the structure that raises the fewest problems.

The most satisfying way to understand the eschatological discourse is to see it as an answer to the questions posed by the disciples in Matthew 24:3, but with the recognition that Jesus' answer corrects two false premises lying behind the questions from the disciples. The first false premise is that the destruction of the temple will coincide with "the close of the age." Jesus is thus careful in his answer to separate these two events, while still indicating a deep connection between them. The second false premise is that Christ's coming (parousia) and "the close of the age" will be presaged by a sign. Jesus will indicate that although signs will hearken the approach of the destruction of the temple, the end of the age will occur suddenly, with no signs. Jesus' answer thus contains predictions and corollary instructions regarding the *destruction of Jerusalem* and the *parousia*.

The eschatological discourse breaks down into two main units. In the first main unit, Matthew 24:4-14, Jesus discusses the significance of observed phenomena for the timing of the end. He begins by describing phenomena surrounding the destruction of Jerusalem (Mt 24:4-8),[26] which are just the "beginning of birth pangs" (Mt 24:8), or the messianic woes that many Jews believed would occur before the coming of the Messiah. Because of the experience and the news of these troublesome events, disciples may become alarmed to the point that they will be vulnerable to messianic pretenders who will take advantage of these tidings. These "false Christs" will be as seductive ("take heed") as they are dangerous, for in attracting persons to themselves they will be drawing such persons away from the truth of Jesus. Nevertheless, "the end (τέλος) is not yet" (Mt 24:6).

---

[25]For a survey of scholarly investigation into the eschatological discourse, see George R. Beasley-Murray, *Jesus and the Last Days* (Peabody, MA: Hendrickson, 1993). And for a brief survey of structural analyses, see Alistair I. Wilson, *When Will These Things Happen: A Study of Jesus as Judge in Matthew 21-25* (Carlisle, UK: Paternoster, 2004), 77-80, 133-39.

[26]Many commentators have noted that the phenomena Jesus describes here are known to have occurred just before the destruction of the temple. E.g., Joachim Gnilka, *Das Matthäus-evangelium*, 2 Teile, HThKNT (Freiburg: Berder, 1988), 2:315-17; Craig L. Blomberg, *Matthew*, NAC (Nashville: Broadman, 1992), 356; France, *Gospel of Matthew*, 899-905; Keener, *Matthew*, 567-70, although Keener believes they may not be limited to this period. I agree with Hagner, *Matthew 14-28*, WBC (Dallas: Word), 690-92, that this description of events which were otherwise associated with the destruction of Jerusalem implies that Matthew is referencing this time period.

In Matthew 24:9-14 Jesus describes those phenomena that will characterize the period between the destruction of Jerusalem and the close of the age. These are not "signs," but rather conditions that will be experienced throughout the entire period before the end. These conditions involve especially distress for the community, including "tribulation," or extreme persecution, in all nations where disciples find themselves proclaiming the gospel (Mt 24:9, 14). This external struggle will lead to dysfunction within the community, so that many will stumble away from discipleship, and many false prophets will arise in the church so as to deceive disciples into embracing wickedness and, as a corollary, abandoning love (Mt 24:11-12; cf. Mt 7:15-23; 22:37-40). Therefore, Jesus reminds them that only "those who endure to the end will be saved" (Mt 24:13; cf. Mt 10:22). This description reaches a climax in Matthew 24:14 with the assurance that when the gospel has been preached to all nations "then the end (τέλος) will come" (cf. Mt 24:6).

In Matthew 24:15–25:46 Jesus moves from this general description of associated phenomena to a specific discussion of the two stages of the eschatological development: the destruction of the temple (Mt 24:15-35) and the parousia (Mt 24:36–25:46).

The first sign heralding the destruction of Jerusalem is the "desolating sacrilege" described in Daniel 9:27 (Mt 24:15). This event indicates the imminence of the city's destruction, and therefore immediate flight is essential (Mt 24:16-20). At this time too, tribulation will become exponentially intensified; yet here, in distinction to Matthew 24:9, the tribulation is directed against all the inhabitants of Jerusalem by the Romans, though also perpetrated by Jews against Christians as the latter flee.[27] It is now Jewish disciples of Jesus, and not the Jewish people in general, who are "the elect" (Mt 22:14), for whose sake these days of extreme anguish for all Jews will be shortened. Here both false Christs (cf. Mt 24:5) and false prophets (cf. Mt 24:11) will appear with "signs and wonders." They will insist that the Christ is hiding in remote areas. But Jesus' hearers are not to believe it. And in support of that admonition Jesus introduces the parousia into this section

---

[27] They should pray that the flight will not be "on a sabbath," since this would cause them to stand out as disciples of Jesus who, in obedience to Jesus' counsel of urgency here, would not have scruples about fleeing on the sabbath, as would Jews in general, and in fleeing the city they would be seen as political traitors. See Graham Stanton, *A Gospel for a New People: Studies in Matthew* (New York: T&T Clark, 1992), 192-206.

that deals generally with the destruction of the temple in order to make the point that the (re)appearance of Christ will not be surreptitious in the wilderness but will be manifest as a cosmic event (Mt 24:27).[28]

The second sign is heavenly portents that immediately precede "the sign of the Son of Man in heaven" (Mt 24:29-31). The image of the disruption of the cosmos (Mt 24:29) does not indicate the destruction of the natural order, but, as in the Old Testament, describes a theophany, that is, a powerful divine visitation that marks a radical transformation in the political or more general ordering of life.[29] If we take "in heaven" (Mt 24:30) not with the verb "appear" but with the noun "Son of Man," then we would read, "then will appear the sign of the heavenly Son of Man."[30] This third and last sign is then the coming of the Son of Man itself.

The phrase "Son of Man coming (ἐρχόμενον) on the clouds of heaven with power and great glory" strongly echoes Daniel 7:13-14, where the Son of man comes "with clouds of heaven" not to earth but to the throne of God to receive dominion and glory. As we saw in our discussion of Matthew 16:28, this language pertains to Jesus' exaltation and to the manifestations of the dominion, or rule, of this exalted one on the earth, which may be made known at any time between his resurrection and parousia. Thus, "the sign of the Son of Man" refers to the manifestation of Jesus' exaltation and rule in the destruction of Jerusalem. Later in the eschatological discourse his "coming" will refer to the manifestation of his exalted rule at the parousia (Mt 24:44); but here it describes the manifestation of his exalted rule at the destruction of the temple.

The phrase often translated "all the tribes of the earth" (Mt 24:30) should be rendered "all the tribes of the land," since it is an allusion to Zechariah 12:10-14, referring to the mourning of the families of Israel because of the one "they have pierced." This is Matthew's way of saying that the destruction of Jerusalem is punishment for Israel's part in the murder of Jesus. The language of Matthew 24:31 is extremely allusive, and its meaning comprehensible only

---

[28] France, *Gospel of Matthew*, 917-18.
[29] J. Richard Middleton, *A New Heaven and a New Earth: Reclaiming Biblical Eschatology* (Grand Rapids: Baker Academic, 2014), 109-128; France, *Gospel of Matthew*, 921-22; N. T. Wright, *The New Testament and the People of God* (Minneapolis: Fortress, 1992), 280-338.
[30] Thus Gibbs, *Jerusalem and Parousia*, 198-99; France, *Gospel of Matthew*, 925-26; contra David E. Garland, *Reading Matthew: A Literary and Theological Commentary on the First Gospel* (New York: Crossroad, 1993), 238-39.

in light of intertextual connections.[31] If we keep both context and these intertextual connections in mind, we may conclude that the destruction of Jerusalem will lead the exalted Christ to harness the power of his angels to assist the church in the evangelization of the nations so as to gather to himself those so evangelized, who are now the "elect" ones, a role that had previously been filled by Israel.[32]

In Matthew 24:32-35 Jesus moves from the question, "What is the sign?" to answer the question, "When will this be?" Disciples will know when the destruction of Jerusalem is approaching (Mt 24:32-35), for the predictions that Jesus has given about that event (Mt 24:4-8, 15-28) function like the appearance of tender branches and leaves on a fig tree (Mt 24:32). Jesus therefore says to them, "when you see all these things, you know that he is near" (Mt 24:33).

But, by contrast, disciples will *not* know the time of the parousia (Mt 24:36-46). "No one knows the day or the hour," not the angels or even the Son, but the Father only (Mt 24:36), even as those in the days of Noah "did not know until the flood came" (Mt 24:39) and swept them away in the midst of their routine activities. Jesus tells them "you do not know on what day your Lord is coming" (Mt 24:42), for "the Son of Man is coming at an hour you do not expect" (Mt 24:44). The master of the servant "will come on a day when he does not expect him and at an hour he does not know" (Mt 24:50). Yet disciples are to "know" the significance of their not knowing the time of the parousia (Mt 24:43), namely, that they must be constantly prepared for his coming, remaining faithful (Mt 24:45) by wakefully watching (Mt 24:42; 25:13).

Such wakefulness does not involve obsessing about the end, but rather being careful that, within the rhythms of ongoing daily life which include slumbering and sleeping (Mt 25:5), one lives each moment in light of the coming judgment (Mt 24:38–25:30). And Jesus develops specifically what it means to live in light of the parousia by way of three parables, each of which involves a contrast between those who are prepared for the judgment that may come at any moment, and those who are not (Mt 24:45–25:30).

The parable of the unfaithful servant warns that what seems like a long wait for the parousia may evoke spiritual and ethical apathy, and therefore

---

[31] See esp. Deut 30:4 LXX; Zech 2:10; Ps 147:2.
[32] For a helpful interpretation of this entire paragraph, see France, *Gospel of Matthew*, 920-28.

one should not succumb to the notion that because Christ has not yet come one should treat others as though he will not come at all (Mt 24:45-51). The parable of the ten virgins (Mt 25:1-13) warns that the unexpected timing of the appearance of the "bridegroom" means that one cannot safely put off preparedness until some indefinite later point, but must be ready every day to meet Christ with the "oil" of a life of constant obedience (cf. Mt 22:11-14; 7:21-23). And the parable of the talents indicates that preparedness involves being intentional and zealous to return to the Lord the value of every opportunity he has given out of a recognition that he will require account of the stewardship of these opportunities (Mt 25:14-30). As in the parable of the unfaithful servant, this parable teaches that Christ's positive assessment of the faithfulness of disciples will result not in blissful languor, but in greater and more authoritative responsibility in the eschaton (Mt 24:47; 25:21, 23) and that a negative assessment will result in the horrible punishment of being cut in pieces and cast into outer darkness (Mt 24:51; 25:30).

The theme of judgment that pervades Matthew 24–25 comes to a climax in the "apocalyptic discourse" of the judgment of the nations in Matthew 25:31-46.[33] This passage expands on the brief description of Jesus' second coming in Matthew 16:27, for here also we have reference to "glory" and "the angels," and Jesus the king is once again pictured as "repaying every person for what that person has done." Here Jesus assumes the role of judging the nations, which, according to the Old Testament, belonged to Yahweh (e.g., Joel 3:1-16).

This passage has been the subject of a great deal of scholarly debate, particularly over the question of who are the sheep and the goats, and who are "the least of these my brethren?"[34] Some have insisted that Matthew portrays the sheep and goats as non-Christian pagans (perhaps including non-Christian Jews) and that "the least of these my brethren" represent the poor and disenfranchised in general, or all Christian disciples in their poor and marginalized condition. We can immediately rule out the notion that the "the least of these my brethren" pertains to the poor in the world in general,

---

[33]So Stanton, *Gospel for a New People*, 221-30, identifies the genre of this passage.
[34]For the history of interpretation of this passage, see Sherman W. Gray, *The Least of My Brothers Matthew 25:31-46: A History of Interpretation*, SBLDS 114 (Atlanta: Scholars, 1989); Ulrich Luz, "The Final Judgment (Mt 25:31-46): An Exercise in 'History of Influence' Exegesis," in *Treasures New and Old: Recent Contributions to Matthean Studies*, ed. David R. Bauer and Mark Allan Powell, SBLSS 1 (Atlanta: Scholars, 1996), 271-310.

since Jesus consistently uses "brothers/sisters" to describe his disciples (Mt 12:48; 28:10).

The context requires that we construe this passage as the judgment of the nations with special reference to the judgment of persons in the church, who by the end of the age will be found among the nations of the world (Mt 24:14; 28:18), for 1) the immediately preceding material, which reaches a climax in this passage, is concerned with the judgment of those in the church (Mt 24:36–25:30); 2) by focusing on the sheep and the goats and addressing only the sheep and the goats, the passage leads the implied reader, who is a disciple, to identify with them and their destiny;[35] 3) both the sheep and the goats address Jesus as "Lord," and in the Gospel of Matthew only persons who have faith in Jesus or who count themselves among his followers so address him,[36] while those on the outside never address him in this fashion; 4) elsewhere in the Gospel of Matthew only disciples are said to "enter the kingdom" (Mt 5:3, 10, 20; 6:33; 7:21; 11:11; 13:11, 43, 52; 18:1, 3, 4; 19:23, 24; 25:1-13; 26:29), or even more strongly, as this passage suggests, "inherit the kingdom," that is, rule as kings (Mt 19:28; 24:45; 25:21, 23);[37] 5) in the preceding chapter Jesus talked about the withholding of food from fellow Christians as the basis of judgment for those in the church (Mt 24:45; cf. Mt 25:42, 44); and 6) this passage links with Jesus' earlier demand that those in the church will be judged on the basis of their care toward fellow Christians in their vulnerability (Mt 18:1-14). Thus, those in the church will be judged by their expression of active love toward those who are most needy among their Christian brothers/sisters, in whom they encounter Jesus himself as he identifies with them in their suffering and helplessness.[38]

The function of the eschatological discourse is not to satisfy inquisitiveness regarding the future but rather to provide paraenesis to the readers of the Gospel of Matthew as they meet with persecutions and tribulations in

---

[35]In narrative-critical terms, the "least of my brothers/sisters" functions basically as background. See Ulrich Luz, *Matthew 1-7: A Commentary* (Minneapolis: Augsburg, 1989), 274-76.

[36]We find this phenomenon in the immediate context (Mt 25:12, 20, 22). Admittedly, it is possible that Matthew assumes that at the end all will recognize him as "Lord."

[37]See France, *Gospel of Matthew*, 962-63.

[38]The reference to "brothers/sisters" indicates that they are disciples, see Mt 12:46-50. The term translated "least" (ἐλάχιστοι) should be taken in its true superlative sense, as the NRSV properly renders it, and as used elsewhere in Matthew (Mt 5:19), rather than meaning "the lesser ones," i.e., the "little ones" who constitute the church as a whole (e.g., Mt 10:42; 18:6); contra Stanton, *Gospel for a New People*, 215-16.

the future. Central to the discourse is the exhortation to disciples to remain faithful (Mt 24:45; 25:21, 23) by watching (Mt 24:42; 25:13) in the midst of the persecution and tribulation that is coming, and thus endure to the end. This will result in their eschatological deliverance (Mt 24:13), which involves entering into eternal life (Mt 25:46), and even, in some sense, ruling in the kingdom.[39] In this regard, they are to be *like* Jesus, as he is presented in the following chapters, for in Matthew 26–28 Jesus remains faithful by "watching" in the midst of his persecution and affliction (Mt 26:38, 41), with the result that he is delivered from the grave and granted resurrection life, which for him involves obtaining "all authority in heaven and on earth."

But insofar as the disciples are to remain faithful by watching and thus be assured of resurrection reward at the end, they are to be *unlike* Israel, as Matthew presents Israel in the preceding material (Mt 21–23). For in these earlier chapters Matthew portrays Israel as disobedient and faithless, and thus as experiencing the judgmental consequences of exclusion from the kingdom (Mt 23:13), with no hope of sharing in its rule (Mt 21:43), but rather the destiny of hell (Mt 23:33).

Matthew thereby establishes a comparison between the expectations for the disciples in the discourse and Jesus' performance and experience in the following chapters, and a contrast between the expectations for the disciples in the discourse and Israel's performance and experience in the preceding chapters. Israel thus serves as a negative model for the kind of faithfulness by watching that is expected of the disciples, according to the discourse, while Jesus serves as a positive model for them.

Matthew forges an explicit connection between the description of faithless Israel in Matthew 21–23 and the warning to disciples regarding faithlessness in the eschatological discourse through his expansion of the parable of the marriage feast; the parable proper pertains to faithless Israel (Mt 22:1-10), but the expanded scene within the wedding hall describes a false disciple who has been granted admittance into the wedding feast as a guest, but who lacks the wedding garment of righteousness and is thus cast into "outer darkness," with "weeping and gnashing of teeth" (Mt 22:11-14; cf. Mt 25:30). Matthew forges such a connection also within the discourse when in Matthew 24:51 he describes the unfaithful disciple as being

---

[39] As mentioned above, this is the meaning of "inherit the kingdom."

punished "with the hypocrites," thus linking this unfaithful disciple with the repeated characterization of the religious leaders of Israel as hypocrites in the immediately preceding chapters (Mt 22:18; 23:13, 23, 25, 27, 28, 29). On the other hand, Matthew forges an explicit connection between the description of faithful Jesus in Matthew 26–28 and the exhortation to faithfulness by watching in the eschatological discourse through his portrait of Jesus in the Garden of Gethsemane (Mt 26:36-46), with the twice-repeated phrase "watch *with me*" (Mt 26:38, 41).

Matt 26:1–28:20. Immediately following the eschatological discourse we come to Jesus' passion and resurrection (Mt 26–28). The passion narrative runs throughout Matthew 26:1–27:54, and includes three storylines—the disciples, Judas, and the religious leaders—all interweaving with the primary story concerning Jesus. After establishing the setting (Mt 26:1-16), Matthew describes a series of scenes that together propel the plot to the climax of Jesus' crucifixion in Matthew 27:27-54.

In Matthew 26:1-2 Jesus for the first time predicts exactly when he will be killed ("after two days"), the (religious) context of his death ("the Passover"), and the method of his demise ("crucified"). Yet the reader questions how this prediction will be realized, since the "chief priests and elders," who are to be responsible for Jesus' death (Mt 16:21; 20:18-19), decide not to take action during the feast, lest such action create a disturbance with the crowds that will threaten the peaceful *status quo* with the Romans (Mt 26:3-5). Matthew will provide the answer to this conundrum in the form of the connivance of Judas (Mt 26:14-16).

But before he does so, Matthew tells the story of Jesus in the house of Simon (Mt 26:6-13), where an unnamed woman expends costly oil to prepare Jesus for burial by anointing Jesus' head (Mt 26:12), an act that recalls the anointing of kings in the Old Testament. In this deed, then, the woman affirms that Jesus is king and is about to manifest his kingship through his death. When the disciples, mindful of Jesus' earlier insistence on giving to the poor (Mt 6:2-4; 19:21; 24:34-44), object on the practical grounds that the oil could have been sold and given to the poor, Jesus alerts the disciples that the extraordinary events that are about to occur, which will have ultimate significance for the entire world even unto the end of the age (Mt 26:13; cf. Mt 24:14; 28:20), require at this moment a radical alteration of normally acceptable, and even demanded, practices. Indeed, this is the only burial anointing that Jesus' body will receive; when Jesus is buried the disciples will be nowhere to be found so as to perform such a duty. This is the first of several instances here at the end of the Gospel of Matthew in which women outperform the disciples in insight and duties that typically belong to disciples.

Yet the woman stands in contrast specifically to Judas. She extravagantly gives over significant material resources to affirm and solemnize Jesus' death, while Judas refuses to follow Jesus in his way of the cross but profits from it for a paltry thirty pieces of silver (Mt 26:14-16).[40] Judas, who is no longer called a "disciple," but simply "one of the twelve" now colludes with Jesus' enemies so they can "arrest Jesus by stealth" (Mt 26:4). And, in fact, Judas' collusion is so successful that the religious leaders are able to do what they had thought would be impossible, to kill him "during the feast" (Mt 26:5), thus unwittingly fulfilling Jesus' prediction that he would be crucified at the Passover (Mt 26:2).

At the Last Supper (Mt 26:20-29) Jesus explains the significance of the surrounding events in two movements, each beginning with the phrase "as they were eating" (Mt 26:21, 26). In the first movement (Mt 26:21-25) Jesus divulges his betrayal at the hands of Judas, demonstrating that he has "superhuman" knowledge of events about which he has not been informed. He insists that such betrayal is both a part of God's plan for him as set forth in Scripture (probably an allusion to Ps 41:9) and yet an act of human evil that will be met with horrendous consequences for the perpetrator (Mt 26:24).

In the second movement (Mt 26:26-29) Jesus divulges the meaning of his death. According to Exodus 12:26 the explanation of the significance of the Passover was to center on the exodus, but Jesus transforms its meaning so that it is centered on him. The bread, which had represented the hasty departure from Egypt that was orchestrated by God, becomes now a symbol of his body that is about to be offered to God as a sacrifice on the cross. And the cup now represents "the blood of the covenant," recalling not only the blood of the Passover lamb applied to the portals that brought redemption from death for the Israelites on the first Passover in Egypt (Ex 12:21-27), but

---

[40] A reference to Zech 11:12-13, where an ungrateful Israel reckons the wages, or value, of the shepherd God will appoint over his people, at "thirty shekels of silver."

Interpretation of Matthew 16:21–28:20

even more so the sprinkling of the blood of the animal sacrifices on the people of Israel at Sinai which sealed them as God's covenant people (Ex 24:5-8). Insofar as Jesus' blood is poured out for "many," it points to the establishment of a new covenant people constituted of Jews and Gentiles (cf. Mt 8:11-12; 10:23) gathered not around Sinai but around Jesus. Whereas the blood of the Passover sacrifice effected a political deliverance from Egyptian bondage, the shedding of this blood will produce "forgiveness of sins," that is, a kind of reconciliation with God that effectively addresses violations that have ruptured relationship with God. But the salvific effects of his sacrifice pertain not only to the present life but extend into the world to come. For this meal "with" his disciples (Mt 26:18) points ahead to an eschatological "with-ness" of intimacy with Christ around the wine of his blood at the messianic banquet in his Father's kingdom (Mt 26:29).

But in the meantime Jesus and his disciples will confront the excruciating test of the cross. On the basis of the testimony of Zechariah 13:7, Jesus accurately predicts the falling away of the disciples and the denial on the part of Peter with a precision that demonstrates his perfect knowledge of these future events (Mt 26:31). For their part, the disciples wrongly express confidence in their own resolve never to fall away or deny. The language Jesus uses to predict the failing performance of the disciples is strong; when he speaks of their "falling away" (σκανδαλίζω) the reader recalls that in the Gospel of Matthew this word means a stumbling away from actual or potential discipleship. And Peter's denial recalls the warning of Jesus in Matthew 10:32, where Jesus insists that those who deny him before people will find that he will deny them before his Father. Yet Jesus will not allow this failure, with its egregious consequences, to have the final word, for he, in the power of his resurrection, will restore them as his "brethren" (Mt 28:10) by his act of going before them into Galilee (Mt 26:32; 28:16-20). In the end, then, final success will be achieved not by their own resolve, but by his presence with them as the resurrected one.

For his part, Jesus refuses to depend on his own resources as he looks ahead to his testing (Mt 26:36-46). In Gethsemane he is in extreme anxiety over the events that are about to befall him; apparently it is especially unnerving for him that, as Son of God, he will soon experience the sense of being forsaken of his Father's delivering presence (Mt 27:43, 46, 50). For

Jesus, the great challenge is the struggle over submission to the will of God in the face of the cross that God has determined he should endure. In three prayers corresponding to the three temptations he will experience on the cross Jesus expresses to God his desire to avoid the suffering of the cross (Mt 26:39), asking that, if it is possible, that is, according to God's will, the cup of suffering might pass without his drinking it. Nevertheless, his prayer is finally for God's will to be done.

The three disciples who witnessed his glory on the Mount of Transfiguration (Mt 17:1-8) now accompany Jesus at this moment of his greatest anguish. These are also the three disciples who expressed the most confidence about sharing Jesus' fate. Although Jesus charges them to "watch with me," they repeatedly fall asleep. The fervency of spirit that James and John manifested when they confidently announced that they were able to drink his cup (Mt 20:22-23), or the determination of Peter when he insisted "I will not deny you" (Mt 26:35), is no match for the weakness of the flesh, unless these disciples, aware of that weakness, direct their resolve not to their own inner resources but to a constant dependence on God in prayer.

As Jesus is still speaking to the three disciples his arrest is at hand (Mt 26:47-56). Judas, apparently aware of Jesus' isolated location, guides the motley forces sent from the chief priests and elders so they can arrest him "by stealth" (cf. Mt 26:4), away from the potentially riotous crowds who still harbor some support for the man they consider to be a promising Davidic revolutionary (Mt 21:9-11). When one of the disciples draws a sword and severs the ear of the slave of the high priest Jesus takes the opportunity to distance himself from all such violence and to utter the principle that "all who take the sword will perish by the sword" (Mt 26:52), a warning directed to those who had come "with swords and clubs" (Mt 26:47), in other words, a caution against the kind of armed revolution that would eventually lead to the destruction of Jerusalem.

In fulfillment of the prediction of Jesus at Matthew 26:31, "all the disciples forsook him and fled" (Mt 26:56). Later, it will be Simon of Cyrene, not Simon Peter, who "takes up" the cross and follows Jesus (Mt 27:32).[41] And the positions on the right and left of Jesus, which James and John requested (Mt 20:20-24), are occupied not by these brothers, but by two robbers (Mt 27:38).

---

[41] The word "take up" (αἴρω) is also used in Mt 16:21.

The trials before the Sanhedrin (Mt 26:57-75) and Pilate (Mt 27:1-26) are generally parallel, each describing Jesus' silence before false charges, with a question from the leader of the trial, which Jesus answers with "so you have said" (σὺ εἶπας/σὺ λέγεις), which in turn leads to condemnation. Jesus is thus condemned before the two great power structures within the narrative of the Gospel of Matthew, the religious establishment of the temple authorities and the political establishment of Rome, represented by Pilate.

The trial before the Sanhedrin is illegitimate, in that the "whole council" was seeking false testimony against Jesus (an implicit acknowledgement of his innocence). At first they were unable to find two or more false witnesses who agreed, so as to meet the legal standard that any conviction must be established by two or three witnesses (Deut 17:6; 19:15). Yet finally two came forth who claimed that Jesus said that he was able to destroy the temple and rebuild it in three days (Mt 26:61). The reader knows that although Jesus predicted the destruction of the temple (Mt 24:1-2) and in his public teaching vaguely implied he would be raised from the dead after three days (Mt 12:40; 16:4), this testimony is also false in that Jesus never said that he was able to destroy the temple and build it in three days.[42] This testimony is ironic, for although the witnesses believe they are giving false testimony, the substance of it is true. The exalted Son of Man will come in judgment against the city, and its temple, to destroy it as punishment for its rejection of the gospel (Mt 24:15-28; 22:7; 23:38), and he, as resurrected one, will be the locus of God's presence among his people, which was the function of the temple (Mt 1:23; 18:20; 28:20).

The testimony that Jesus had said he was able to destroy the temple and build it in three days leads the high priest to press Jesus to declare whether or not he is "the Christ." Since, according to the Old Testament, the temple would be built by the Son of David, who was also "son of God,"[43] and since Jesus had obliquely referred to himself as Son of God in the parable of the wicked tenants, which he spoke to the religious leaders (Mt 21:33-43), the notion that Jesus was able to build the temple leads the high priest to insist that Jesus answer the question regarding his divine sonship.

---

[42] It is unclear how these false witnesses would have known of this prediction by Jesus. Possibly Matthew wants us to understand that Jesus spoke Mt 24:2 in a public setting (see Mt 24:3; but cf. Mt 24:1), or that Judas had divulged that prediction to his new confederates.

[43] When God established covenant with David in 2 Sam 7:12-14 God declared that David's "seed," or son, who would also be God's Son, would build the temple.

As long as the false witnesses are giving their perjured testimony, Jesus remains silent. But when the high priest poses the question regarding Jesus' divine sonship Jesus finally answers. The fact that Jesus breaks his silence only when he is confronted with the truth of his divine sonship suggests one reason why he remained silent all along: Jesus, who has been the sole of integrity and truthfulness throughout the narrative will not dignify this false testimony with an answer, thus showing utter disdain for all untruth (see, e.g., Mt 5:33-37). But another reason also commends itself. Here, in his silence, Jesus assumes the role of the Suffering Servant of Isaiah, who, according to Isaiah 53:7 "was oppressed, and he was afflicted, yet he opened not his mouth."[44] Although at his arrest Jesus declared that by his simply speaking the word God would send more than twelve legions of angels, that is, seventy-two thousand (Mt 26:54), Jesus will not even so much as say a word to defend himself. He is thus the one who rejects the resources at his disposal so as to "trust in God" (Mt 27:43).

In answer to the question from the high priest, Jesus declares, "so you have said." It is an affirmative answer that nevertheless places the responsibility for the answer on the person who has asked the question. Jesus essentially says, "Yes, but I am agreeing with it according to how *I* understand it, and not necessarily how *you* mean it."[45] Jesus goes on to place the whole matter in perspective when he declares that "from now on" they will see, or experience, the Son of Man in his exalted rule over the earth (Mt 28:18).

For this affirmative answer Jesus is condemned on the charge of blasphemy, which is ironic, since when Jesus implicitly acknowledges that he is Son of God he is assuming God's point of view regarding himself (Mt 3:17). Indeed, it is the members of the council who are the blasphemers, since blasphemy is understood here as making a claim about oneself that does not accord with reality and serves to dishonor God, or bring God down.[46] But that is exactly the meaning of hypocrisy, and it is precisely the religious leaders who are the prime examples of hypocrisy, according to the Gospel

---

[44]Matthew associates Jesus with the Suffering Servant on other occasions as well; see esp. Mt 8:17 and Is 53:4; Mt 12:18-21 and Is 42:1-4; and Mt 27:57-60 and Is 53:9.

[45]For a detailed discussion of this answer, see David R. Catchpole, "The Answer of Jesus to Caiaphas," *NTS* 17 (1971): 212-26.

[46]Since, as we have seen, the notion that Jesus is Son of God derives from the (false) accusation regarding the destruction of the temple, the charge of blasphemy may involve too, the dishonoring of God by dishonoring his holy place.

of Matthew.[47] Moreover, when they declare that Jesus "deserves death" (Mt 26:66), the reader knows it is actually they who deserve death, for such was the sentence for false testimony (Deut 19:16-21).

Since the Sanhedrin did not have authority to carry out capital punishment (so Jn 18:31), they deliver Jesus to Pilate, the governor (Mt 27:1-2). At this point Matthew takes the opportunity to report the death of Judas (Mt 27:3-14), who expresses remorse to the chief priests and elders and confesses to them that he has "sinned in betraying innocent blood." Even though priests had the duty to mediate for sin among the people these priests refuse to take any action on Judas' behalf or to accept the responsibility that manifestly was theirs, casting all the onus on the shoulders of Judas; thereby they demonstrate that there is no honor among conspirators. This is the kind of "community" that those who reject the way of Jesus create for themselves. And in the end Judas, the betrayer, experiences the utter despair that characterizes suicide.[48] The meticulous care on the part of the religious leaders to act lawfully regarding the fine points of disposal of "blood money" contrasts sharply with their murderous actions in shedding innocent blood and confirms Jesus' earlier accusation that they "strain out a gnat and swallow a camel" (Mt 23:24).[49]

The issue before Pilate is Jesus' role as "king of the Jews." Jesus answers Pilate's question with the same response he made to the high priest, "you have said so" (σὺ λέγεις).[50] Clearly, in the ears of those present this claim would have meant that Jesus was a revolutionary bent on insurrection against Rome. Indeed, Matthew suggests that such was the charge the religious leaders were leveling against Jesus in their testimony here (Mt 27:12-13). Again, before these false charges Jesus remains silent (Mt 27:14).

Yet Pilate seeks desperately to release Jesus, since he is unconvinced by these charges (Mt 27:15-23). Pilate recognizes that the leaders had delivered

---

[47] Accordingly, Matthew describes those at the cross who falsely accuse Jesus of wishing to destroy the temple and build it in three days as "blaspheming" (Mt 26:65, βλασφημέω).

[48] This is the way the great majority of commentators have interpreted the event. But cf. Catherine Sider Hamilton, "The Death of Judas in Matthew: Matthew 27:9 Reconsidered," JBL 137 (2018): 419-37.

[49] Jesus had directed this charge against the Pharisees, while here in Mt 27:3-10 the "chief priests and elders" are in view. But Matthew largely disregards the differences between the various groups of religious leaders, presenting them as a united front against Jesus.

[50] The only difference between this response and Mt 26:64 is the use of the present tense here over against the aorist in Jesus' response to the high priest.

Jesus up not because of any legitimate complaint, but out of "envy" over Jesus' popularity with and potential control over the Jewish crowds. And Pilate's wife urges him to "have nothing to do with this righteous man," because of a dream that she takes as a warning from God.[51] God thus seeks to correct Israel's folly through a dream to a Gentile woman.

But when the crowds witness Jesus' rejection of the role of a revolutionary Messiah they are easily persuaded to shift their support away from Jesus and to the chief priests and elders; and it is their cry that ultimately causes Pilate to yield. He, like the religious leaders, wants to avoid a "riot" (θόρυβος, Mt 27:24; cf. Mt 26:5),[52] and, like them, in the words "see to it yourselves" (Mt 27:24; cf. Mt 27:4) he refuses to take responsibility for his part in the death of an innocent man, even though he had official duty to carry out justice by protecting the righteous and punishing miscreants like Barabbas. But "all the people" (a designation Matthew uses for the crowds and religious leaders now joined together) are eager to take the responsibility that Pilate seeks to evade, crying out "His blood be on us and on our children" (Mt 27:25). This phrase is full of irony, since Jesus intended that his "blood of the covenant" (Mt 26:28), like the blood thrown on the people at Sinai (Ex 24:8), would establish the people in true covenant with their God but now in their obduracy they are excluding themselves from the benefits of his blood (cf. 23:35).

In the wake of Jesus' condemnation before the Sanhedrin the members of that body revile and mock Jesus, calling on him to "prophesy to us," a truly ironic statement, since Jesus had indeed prophesied exactly what at that point was happening to him (Mt 26:67-68). Now, in the wake of his condemnation by Pilate the soldiers mock him as "king of the Jews," giving him cheap and tawdry imitations of royal accoutrements (Mt 27:27-31). With additional irony, when they place a wreath of thorns on his head they are actually expressing the true nature of his kingship, for Jesus reigns as one who dies on behalf of his people; the wreath of thorns is his crown, and the cross is his throne, replete with the placard of his rule mounted above his head on the crossbeam.

---

[51] In Matthew, messages through dreams always come from God (Mt 1:18–2:23).
[52] Thus, Pilate and the Sanhedrin will put Jesus to death to avoid an insurrectionist revolution, while the crowds wish to see Jesus put to death because he refused the role of an insurrectionist Messiah.

Jesus had been condemned as both "Son of God" (Mt 26:57-75) and as "King of the Jews" (Mt 27:11-26); now he dies in both capacities. This double significance frames the crucifixion scene in that it is expressed by soldiers at the beginning and the end. In Matthew 27:27-31 the soldiers (ironically) hail him as "king of the Jews," and at the end the Roman centurion and those soldiers with him keeping watch over Jesus declare, "Truly this was the Son of God." Moreover, three times at the crucifixion Jesus is said to be "king of the Jews/Israel" (Mt 27:29, 37, 42), and three times to be "Son of God" (Mt 27:40, 43, 54).

The religious leaders and the passersby call on Jesus to demonstrate his divine sonship by means of a sign, recalling the temptation by Satan in the wilderness (Mt 27:40; cf. Mt 4:3, 6). But Jesus refuses to vindicate his divine sonship in this manner. Jesus leaves vindication of his sonship to God. Accordingly, the signs come not from Jesus but God (Mt 27:51-53).[53]

Matthew emphasizes that Jesus dies as obedient Son of God, as he confronts in this experience of the cross his last and greatest temptation. Indeed, this event is the climax of earlier temptations throughout the Gospel of Matthew. Even as Jesus' experience in the wilderness (Mt 4:1-1) involved three temptations, so Jesus is here tempted three times (Mt 27:39-40, 41-43, 44). The point of that earlier temptation was to achieve the good that God desired his righteous Messiah to have by grasping for it himself rather than waiting for God to grant it to him in God's own way and time. So here, Jesus is tempted to achieve deliverance from death by coming down from the cross, but he waits for God to grant to him deliverance from death by raising him from the dead three days later. Even as the religious leaders had tempted Jesus to give them a sign from heaven (Mt 12:38-40; 16:1-4) so now they are tempting him to do the same, only at this point they are designating the sign they have in mind, namely to come down now from the cross (Mt 27:42). And even as Peter assumed the role of Satan in tempting Jesus to construe his divine sonship by avoidance of suffering and death (Mt 16:22-23), so now Jesus is being tempted to dictate to God how God will vindicate Jesus' sonship, namely by delivering him from the necessity of death. Jesus remains totally cognizant of the painful sense of being

---

[53]Note the (divine) passive voice throughout, and the consideration that the first of these signs, that of the rending of the curtain of the temple, is torn from "top to bottom," whereas human hands would have necessarily torn it from bottom to top.

forsaken by God in terms of the absence of God's deliverance, uttering the cry that stands at the beginning of Psalm 22 (Ps 22:1) while maintaining the confidence of ultimate deliverance expressed at the end of that very psalm (Ps 22:22-31).[54] Thus Jesus refuses to yield to these temptations, putting his faith in God to deliver him (Mt 27:43) and to vindicate his claim to being Son of God as God sees fit.

Matthew emphasizes, too, that because Jesus dies as obedient Son his death is able to atone for sin. Here Jesus pours out his blood for the forgiveness of sins, in analogy to the pouring of the blood of animal sacrifices on the people at Sinai so as to bring Israel into covenant relationship with God (Mt 26:28); this image points to release from the guilt of sin. Here Jesus gives his life a ransom for many (Mt 20:28), recalling the sacrifice of the Passover lamb that effected Israel's deliverance from Egyptian slavery; this image points to freedom from the existential bondage to sin. It is here that Jesus saves his people from their sins (Mt 1:23), even as God had anointed Davidic kings to deliver his people from their enemies; this image points to freedom from the destructive power of sins. Although the language of blood sacrifice is sometimes used in this Gospel, Matthew employs this cultic language metaphorically, to point to the relational reality of reconciliation. It is through the obedience of Jesus Son of God throughout his entire life, that is, the sacrifice of his will, culminating in his obedience at the cross,[55] that Jesus is able to effect an atonement that brings others into a relationship of sonship to God.

The salvific aspect of Jesus' death is developed in Matthew 27:51-53. The point of this odd passage with its apocalyptic features, such as the earthquake and the opening of tombs, is that in the death of Jesus the saints who died before the coming of the kingdom in Jesus will find their freedom from the grave, and in his resurrection they will find their resurrection. In other words, the death and resurrection of Jesus are retroactive in their atoning power.[56]

---

[54]Stanley E. Porter, *Sacred Tradition in the New Testament: Tracing Old Testament Themes in the Gospels and Epistles* (Grand Rapids: Baker Academic, 2016), 156-74. The Matthean passion narrative is replete with allusions to Psalm 22 but alludes to other OT passages as well, e.g., Ps 69:22.

[55]Birger Gerhardsson, "Gottes Sohn als Diener Gottes: Messias, Agape, und Himmelsherrscaft nach dem matthäusevangelium," *StTheol* 27 (1973): 73-106.

[56]The inclusion of this assurance may address the problem of the fate of the righteous ones who lived and died before Christ. Heb 9:15 may speak to the same concern; cf. Harold W. Attridge, *Hebrews*, Hermeneia (Philadelphia: Fortress, 1989), 255.

Matthew insists, too, that Jesus' death is presence-producing. Here God rends the curtain of the temple (Mt 27:51), indicating that God's presence is departing the temple and therefore that the temple is about to be destroyed (Mt 23:37–24:2; 26:61; 27:40).[57] Matthew insists that Jesus now replaces the temple as the dwelling place of God among God's people (Mt 1:23; 18:20; 28:20). Indeed, the perfect tense of the verb "was crucified," which we might more literally render "is crucified" (Mt 28:5), indicates that the resurrected Christ who continues to be present with his church (Mt 28:20) bears the marks of his crucifixion; he is present precisely as crucified one.

Matthew also emphasizes that Jesus' death is universalizing. The fact that it is Gentile guards who confess Jesus to be the Son of God points to the reality that his death provides salvation not only to Jews but to the "many" (Mt 20:28; 26:28), that is, to Gentiles (Mt 8:11). We note here the irony: the Gentile centurion and soldiers with him, who actually crucified Jesus, confess Jesus, while the chief disciple denies him (Mt 26:69-75). The issue is confession versus denial in the face of the cross. This points, therefore, to the inclusion of the unlikely outsider, and the weakness and possible failure of the privileged insider.[58]

Thus this declaration from the centurion that Jesus is Son of God, which culminates the passion narrative, brings the third major division to its initial climax. Here the point of view of the Gentile guards accords with the point of view of God (Mt 3:17) and the point of view of the disciples, or the church (Mt 16:16), regarding Jesus. Now, as they consider the cross, the most unlikely join the confession of the church that Jesus is God's Son.

But the death of Jesus is not the end of the Gospel of Matthew. The formalized predictions that punctuate the early chapters of this third major division have indicated that the climax to the third major division, and indeed to the Gospel of Matthew, includes the complex of Jesus'

---

[57] See France, *Gospel of Matthew*, 1080, for the major views regarding the meaning of the rending of the curtain. The allusions here to Mt 23:38; 26:61; 27:40, along with Matthew's emphasis on Jesus as the presence of God among his people, which had been the role of the temple, indicate that this event points to God's departure from the temple, thereby rendering it purposeless and good for nothing but to be destroyed (Mt 21:18-20). Thus David M. Gurtner, *The Torn Veil: Matthew's Exposition of the Death of Jesus*, SNTSMS 139 (New York: Cambridge University Press, 2007), 97-202.

[58] Near the beginning of the Gospel of Matthew the Gentile magi announce to Israel at the birth of Jesus that Jesus is "king of the Jews" (Mt 2:2); now, at almost the end of the Gospel, Gentile soldiers announce to Israel, and in a sense to the world, that Jesus is the "Son of God" (Mt 27:54).

passion *and* resurrection. These are two aspects of a single overarching reality. It is not surprising, then, that Matthew includes reference to Jesus' resurrection within the crucifixion scene itself (Mt 27:51-53) and that he begins the resurrection narrative (Mt 27:55–28:20) with repeated references to Jesus' crucifixion.[59]

The resurrection narrative contains contrasting responses to Jesus, and especially to his resurrection, presented in alternating blocks between Jesus' followers and his opponents.[60]

Mt 27:55-61	The women and Joseph of Arimathea
Mt 27:62-66	The chief priests and Pharisees
Mt 28:1-10	The women
Mt 28:11-15	The chief priests and Pharisees (and guards)
Mt 28:16-20	The disciples

On the one hand, this alternating pattern forms a chiasm around Matthew 28:1-10 and thereby indicates the centrality of the resurrection within the passage. On the other hand, this pattern, along with the predictions about Jesus meeting his disciples in Galilee (Mt 28:7, 10), points also to the climactic encounter between Jesus and his disciples in Matthew 28:16-20. This indicates the prime importance of that encounter and leaves the reader at the end of the Gospel of Matthew with the question as to how the disciples, who react in an ambiguous fashion to the appearance of the resurrected Christ in Matthew 28:17, will respond to Jesus' announcement in Matthew 28:18-20.

The women form the link between Jesus' passion and resurrection and serve as the only witnesses to the three events of the death of Jesus (Mt 27:55-56), his burial (Mt 27:61), and the happenings surrounding his resurrection at the empty tomb (Mt 28:1-10). Although Matthew does not call these women "disciples," he informs us that they "followed" Jesus from Galilee and "ministered" to him, even as the angels ministered to Jesus in

---

[59]The reference to the women (Mt 27:55-56), to Jesus' burial (Mt 27:57-61), and to the sealing of the tomb (Mt 27:62-66), all of which play a key role in the resurrection account, link Mt 27:55-66 to the events of Mt 28:1-20 and form with Mt 28 a coherent segment.

[60]Even the actions of the chief priests and Pharisees in Mt 27:62-66 are in response to the predictions of Jesus regarding his resurrection.

the wake of his temptation in Matthew 4:11, thereby suggesting that they were the agents of God's provision for Jesus throughout his ministry.

Likewise, Matthew does not label Joseph a "disciple" (μαθητής) of Jesus but rather describes him as a man who was discipled to Jesus,[61] employing the same verb that will appear at Matthew 28:19 when Jesus demands that the eleven "make disciples" of all nations. Matthew thereby links Joseph with those who will be made disciples.[62] Insofar as Joseph buries the body of Jesus, which Matthew considers to be the proper duty of disciples,[63] while the disciples are nowhere to be found, Joseph fulfills the role of a disciple better than the twelve.

Moreover, Joseph's actions point to his sacrifice. In asking Pilate for the body of a man condemned for insurrection against Rome, Joseph was risking not only his status and considerable wealth, but also his life. In this act, along with offering his own pricey tomb for Jesus' burial,[64] Joseph demonstrates how a rich man can enter the kingdom even as a camel enters through a needle's eye (Mt 19:24), namely by considering his property (and his life) not his own but yielding it to the service of Christ.

In this story of Joseph, Matthew begins his *apologia* for the actual bodily resurrection of Jesus. The consideration that Joseph lays Jesus in a "new tomb" indicates that his body was alone present, and the women could therefore not have been confused later about the absence of his body on the basis of miscounting the number of bodies in the tomb. And the consideration that the women observed the sepulcher in which Joseph placed the body indicates that they could not have misidentified the tomb on Sunday morning.

While Joseph is careful to maintain the sanctity of the sabbath by arranging for the burial of Jesus "in the evening," before the onset of the sabbath at nightfall, the chief priests and Pharisees have no scruples regarding the posting of a guard on the sabbath (Mt 27:62-66), thus pointing to their hypocrisy regarding sabbath observance (cf. Mt 12:1-14). This is an

---

[61] Although the NRSV indicates that Joseph "was a disciple of Jesus," the noun *disciple* does not appear in the passage, but rather the verb *be discipled*; thus the statement should be rendered, "who was discipled to [or perhaps, by] Jesus."

[62] See also Raymond E. Brown, *The Death of the Messiah: A Commentary on the Passion Narrative in the Four Gospels*, 2 vols., ABRL (New York: Doubleday, 1994), 2:1223-25.

[63] Matthew is careful to note that the disciples of John bury his body (Mt 14:12).

[64] Keener, *Matthew*, 694.

ironic admission on their part that Jesus does bring about a radical revision of the character of sabbath observance (cf. Mt 12:1-14). In their response to Jesus' prediction regarding his resurrection on the third day, they secure the tomb with some sort of sealant and post a guard, for fear the disciples will steal his body.[65] In this way, Matthew continues his defense for the bodily resurrection. They refer to Jesus as an "imposter," really a deceiver who leads the people astray (πλανάω), thus recalling for the reader Jesus' warnings regarding "false Christs" who will attempt to lead them astray (Mt 24:11, 24). This raises the question as to who the real deceivers are, a question that will be answered in the deceptive cover-up orchestrated by these very religious leaders in Matthew 28:11-15.

When the women arrive at the tomb very early on the first day of the week, they witness an earthquake and the angel rolling away the stone, apparently for the benefit of their seeing into the empty tomb, for Jesus has already been raised (Mt 28:1-3, cf. Mt 28:6). Insofar as the angel sends the women to tell Jesus' disciples that he is risen, they became the first to proclaim his resurrection (Mt 28:7-8). And when they leave the tomb, they encounter Jesus and instinctively worship him, thereby becoming the first to see the resurrected Jesus and to worship the exalted Lord (Mt 28:9). They are also the first to teach what Jesus commanded, for Jesus gives to them the responsibility of communicating his demand that the disciples meet him in Galilee (Mt 28:10; cf. Mt 28:20).

This teaching from the women to Jesus' disciples stands in contrast to the "teaching" that the religious leaders give to the guards when they instruct them to spread lies regarding both the empty tomb and the post-Easter disciples (Mt 28:11-15).[66] The religious leaders, who had asked for a sign from heaven (Mt 12:38-42; 16:1-4), now reject the sign of the resurrection that God offers, the "sign of the prophet Jonah." Every deed of the religious leaders in this passage is an attempt to deceive the people regarding the ultimate action of God on their behalf. For their part, the guards forget their fear at the events surrounding the empty tomb (Mt 28:4) and choose the easy path of

---

[65] While most commentators conclude that the leaders successfully petitioned Pilate to post Roman guards, France, *Gospel of Matthew*, 1094, 1103-6, has argued that Pilate refused their request and that Jewish guards who were beholden to the religious leaders were dispatched.

[66] The word translated by the NRSV as "directed" (Mt 28:15) is διδάσκω, meaning "teach," the same term employed in Mt 28:20.

payment and protection (cf. Mt 7:13-14), serving as a foil not only for the disciples in the next passage, but also for those who will be made disciples.

In obedience to the command of Jesus through the women (Mt 28:10) and with confidence in Jesus' promise that he will meet them (Mt 26:32; 28:7) the disciples go to Galilee (Mt 28:16).[67] Throughout the Gospel, Matthew has consistently described the disciples as "the twelve." The reference here to "the eleven disciples" reminds the reader of the absence of Judas, who has repudiated in a fundamental way the perspective of Jesus and thus falls away so as not to return, thereby serving as a warning to disciples of the dangerous possibility of apostasy. But the number also points to the presence of Peter, who failed under pressure, but repents,[68] returns, and is reinstated, thereby serving as an example of hope for those who likewise deny Jesus under pressure.

Even as Jesus positioned himself geographically just before the beginning of his ministry by withdrawing "into Galilee" (Mt 4:12, εἰς τὴν Γαλιλαίαν), so Matthew now employs the same phrase to describe the disciples as they are about to embark on their mission. This correspondence indicates that the ministry that the disciples are about to undertake is, like that of the earthly Jesus, eschatological, in that it is the fulfillment of Scripture (cf. Mt 4:14-16), and is therefore transcendent, of an entirely different order than what is otherwise done in the world. The mountain is here, as typically in the Gospel of Matthew, the place of revelation, for the resurrected Jesus reveals himself to his post-Easter disciples.

This revelation meets with a twofold response. On the one hand, the disciples "worship" him, indicating a sense of indescribable awe and a recognition of his ultimate glory, and indeed, deity, for only God may be worshiped (Mt 4:10). The consideration that the disciples (Mt 14:33) and others (Mt 2:2, 11; 8:2; 9:18; 15:25; 20:20) had worshiped him prior to his resurrection points to continuity between the earthly Jesus and the exalted Christ in terms of his worth, glory, and dignity, in spite of the obvious differences between Jesus in his preresurrection and resurrection states.[69]

---

[67]For a more detailed exegesis of Matt 28:16-20, see David R. Bauer, "The Theme of Mission in Matthew's Gospel from the Perspective of the Great Commission," *AJ*, forthcoming.

[68]The fact that Peter accedes to Jesus' command here and is reinstated, in that he is commissioned along with the rest, indicates that his going out and weeping bitterly (Mt 26:75) is an act of repentance.

[69]Although some of these preresurrection instances involve paying homage in the process of making a request, the notion of worship is nevertheless present. See BDAG, "προσκυνέω."

Yet, "some doubted." Clearly this statement refers to the eleven, for according to the narrative only the eleven are present here. The question as to whether all the disciples, or only some of them, doubt is secondary to the fundamental claim that post-Easter discipleship is characterized by both worship and doubt. The word translated "doubt" here (διστάζω) is found only once more in the New Testament, in Matthew 14:31, where it is also linked with worship. There it is used in the sense of weakness of faith (ὀλιγόπιστος) in the power of the Jesus who beckons and commands that prevents one from making use of all the resources in Jesus for fulfilling successfully Jesus' demand (cf. Mt 14:22-30).[70] This element of uncertainty in the reality and power of the resurrected Jesus fits the present context well: Jesus is about to send them out on a global mission where they will encounter the same kind of opposition to them that had just done Jesus in (Mt 28:11-15).

In response to this doubt Jesus makes the claim of universal authority in Matthew 28:18. The notion of "authority" (ἐξουσία) in the Gospel of Matthew includes both capability and legitimacy, that is, the right and ability to act,[71] in other words, "all rightful power." Jesus had exercised various forms of authority throughout the Gospel of Matthew, for example, the authority to forgive sins (Mt 9:8) or the authority to cast out demons (Mt 12:28), and certainly the "all authority" here must include all these components of authority. But the observation that this declaration in Matthew 28:18 leads to a commission to his disciples that transcends what Jesus had earlier demanded of them suggests that the authority described here goes beyond what Jesus had possessed earlier. The (divine) passive voice "has been given," indicates that this authority has been given by God, and the dominant role of the resurrection in this context suggests that God granted this all-inclusive authority to Christ at that point.[72] Jesus, who refused to grasp all rule, power, and authority on the mountain when he was tempted by the devil (Mt 4:8-10) now, on this mountain, declares that he has been granted by God all authority everywhere, not just on earth, but also "in heaven." This language

---

[70]See I. P. Ellis, "But Some Doubted," *NTS* 14 (1968): 574-80.
[71]BDAG, "ἐξουσία."
[72]Otto Michel, "The Conclusion of Matthew's Gospel: A Contribution to the History of the Easter Message," in *The Interpretation of Matthew*, ed. Graham Stanton (Philadelphia: Fortress, 1983), 33-38.

reflects the enthronement of the Son of Man, described in Daniel 7:13-14 and thus informs "Son of Man" references earlier in the Gospel of Matthew. But this passage transcends the Danielic vision in several ways,[73] and Jesus does not refer to himself here as "Son of Man," but as Son of God (Mt 28:19).

Because "all authority" everywhere has been given to Jesus, therefore all persons everywhere are to be brought under his sovereign authority by way of discipleship. The main verb in Matthew 28:19-20a is "make disciples" (μαθητεύσατε), preceded by an aorist participle ("go") and followed by two present participles. Most translations correctly take the preceding participle as indicating "attendant circumstance"; it is thus coordinate with the imperative "make disciples" but also somewhat subordinate to the command of the main verb. Thus the making of disciples involves the disciples going to the nations; this stands over against the Old Testament prophetic expectation that the nations would come to Jerusalem and learn of the Lord there (e.g., Is 2:2-4; Mic 4:1-5). It also stands in contrast to the restrictive scope of the ministry of Jesus (Mt 15:24) and of the disciples earlier in the Gospel of Matthew (Mt 10:5-6, "*go nowhere* among the Gentiles"). The word "nations" (ἔθνη) could mean "Gentiles," but here it should be understood as all the people groups of the world, including Jews. Israel is now one nation among the others.

The two present participles "baptizing" and "teaching" develop the ways in which disciples are to be made. "Baptizing" describes the initiatory aspect of making disciples. The only reference to baptism in the Gospel of Matthew has been to the baptizing work of John the Baptist, which included the baptism of Jesus himself (Mt 3:1-17). Surely, then, our understanding of baptism here is to be informed by that earlier description. Yet since John described his baptism as preparatory for the coming one, we must acknowledge also some discontinuity between John's baptism and Christian baptism. Since Matthew does not develop the meaning of Christian baptism, we infer that he expected his readers to bring knowledge of the meaning and significance of Christian baptism to their construal of this reference. We note, too, that "name" is singular, though followed by the three names, "Father, Son, and Holy Spirit," suggesting a fundamental unity among them.

---

[73]David R. Bauer, *The Structure of Matthew's Gospel: A Study in Literary Design*, JSNT 31 (Sheffield: Almond, 1988), 111-12.

Jesus has made disciples of the twelve by, among other things, teaching them.[74] This observation supports the notion that "teaching," along with the coordinate participle "baptizing," constitutes specific content to making disciples. They are to make disciples of Jesus, not of themselves, for they are not to teach their own instructions but only his. And they are not to be selective, teaching only what is agreeable and acceptable but "all" that he has taught. It is likely that the five great discourses form the critical mass of this catechetical instruction, for all of them, in content, pertain to matters relevant to post-Easter disciples in general and not just to the twelve during Jesus' earthly ministry. The reference to "all" here connects with the formula at the end of the final great discourse, "When Jesus had finished all these sayings" (Mt 26:1). Yet we must take the inclusive scope seriously, and not restrict the range of Jesus' teaching to just these five passages, but include all that Jesus taught, both by word and by example.[75]

The Matthean Jesus supports the command of Matthew 28:19-20a with the promise of Matthew 28:20b. They will be able to fulfil this mission because Jesus will be with them to the end of the age. This reference to "with" forms an inclusio with Matthew 1:23, "Emmanuel, God with us," indicating that God himself continues to dwell with his disciples (church) in the person of his Son. In the Old Testament the promise of God to be "with" his people or their leader(s) involved deliverance or salvation, but sometimes help to fulfill the humanly impossible charge he was giving; this is the meaning of the term here (e.g., Ex 3:12; 4:12; Josh 1:5, 9; Jud 6:16). Given such exigencies as described in Matthew 28:11-15 they will require divine assistance.

The Gospel of Matthew ends, then, with Jesus in the midst of his post-Easter disciples, promising to remain with them until the eschaton. Accordingly, Matthew does not include an account of ascension. Although Matthew has earlier suggested that Jesus would be absent between the resurrection and parousia (e.g., Mt 9:15), Matthew does not want the reader to think of this period as a time of Jesus' absence but of his presence. It is precisely the presence of Jesus that characterizes above all else Christian existence in the time of the reader.

---

[74] We noted above that the verb *make disciples* (μαθητεύσατε) is found in Mt 27:57. It appears also in Mt 13:52, where it points to the role of learning.
[75] Note, e.g., the wording of Mt 16:21: "Jesus began to *show* his disciples."

PART THREE

REFLECTION

Our interpretation of the Gospel of Matthew will serve as the basis for a synthetic treatment of some of the major theological issues presented in the Gospel of Matthew, namely Christ, God, salvation history and eschatology, and discipleship. Some of these topics will involve the discussion of subtopics; for example, the chapter on discipleship will include also ecclesiology and mission, and the chapter on salvation history will attend also to the topic of the kingdom. Then, too, the dynamic, interrelated character of Matthew's theology renders it impossible to separate completely these various aspects of theology. Christology, for example, necessarily bleeds over into matters of discipleship and eschatology.

8

JESUS: THE CHRISTOLOGICAL TITLES

SCHOLARS HAVE OFTEN treated the Christology of the Gospels by focusing on christological titles, such as "Son of Man," or "Son of David."[1] And yet interpreters have increasingly realized that such titles, while important, cannot capture all the relevant meaning of the evangelists' presentation of Jesus.[2] Accordingly, I examine here Matthew's employment of major christological titles, and in the next chapter treat some of the other significant aspects of Matthew's Christology.

SON OF GOD

Of all the christological titles Matthew employs, Son of God is the most central.[3] As we have seen, the structure of the Gospel of Matthew emphasizes Jesus' divine sonship in that each of the three major divisions reaches a climax in the declaration that Jesus is God's Son (Mt 3:17; 16:16; and

---

[1]E.g., Vincent Taylor, *The Names of Jesus* (London: Macmillan, 1953); Ferdinand Hahn, *The Titles of Jesus in Christology: Their History in Early Christianity* (New York: World, 1969); Oscar Cullmann, *The Christology of the New Testament*, rev. ed., NTL (Philadelphia: Westminster, 1963). See also the many works of Jack Dean Kingsbury, who emphasizes the role of christological titles.

[2]Leander E. Keck, "Toward the Renewal of New Testament Christology," *NTS* 32 (1986): 368-70. With regard to this matter as it relates specifically to the Gospel of Matthew, see Mogens Müller, "The Theological Interpretation of the Figure of Jesus in the Gospel of Matthew: Some Principal Features in Matthean Christology," *NTS* 45 (1999): 157-73.

[3]For a thorough treatment of the importance of this title in the Gospel of Matthew, see Jack Dean Kingsbury, *Matthew: Structure, Christology, Kingdom* (Philadelphia: Fortress, 1975), 40-83.

Mt 27:54; 28:19). Moreover, God himself, who is the ultimate reality in the narrative world of the Gospel of Matthew, declares twice that Jesus is his Son (Mt 3:17; 17:5), and it is the only title that involves explicitly Jesus' relationship with God. In addition, it is the only title that expressly connects Christology with discipleship, since not only is Jesus repeatedly said to be Son of God and to know God as Father, but the disciples are likewise described as "sons of God," who is their "Father."

In spite of its dominance in the Gospel of Matthew, this title seems not to have had much currency in Jewish messianic expectations of the period. According to the Old Testament, the son of David (a favorite messianic designation for the Messiah among Jews) was also God's son (2 Sam 7:14; 1 Chron 17:12-13; 22:10; Ps 2:7-8; 89:26-27). But the only references within contemporary Jewish sources to the Messiah being Son of God are contained in a few fragments from Qumran.[4] Yet the considerations that the messianic hope of the time was consistently linked to an ideal Davidic king, who in the Old Testament is described as son of God, and that some New Testament passages assume a connection between Messiah and Son of God (e.g., Mk 14:61) suggest that the notion that the Messiah was Son of God was not entirely alien to Judaism. Yet this sparsity of background requires that we derive the meaning of Son of God for Matthew from within the Gospel itself.

Jesus is Son of God as one whose origin is in God. According to Matthew 1:18, 20, Jesus has been conceived (γεννάω) by the Holy Spirit, and Matthew points to the divine activity in Jesus' conception by the use of the divine passive in Matthew 1:16. Although some have denied that this passage involves Jesus' divine sonship at all,[5] the notion of conception belongs to the semantic range

---

[4] 4QFlor 1:10-14 applies 2 Sam 7:11-14 to the Messiah; 1QSa 2:11-12 could be read as God begetting the Messiah (though the text is damaged); and 1QpsDan A^a (4Q246) reads, "he shall be hailed as the Son of God, and they shall call him Son of the Most High." According to Joseph A. Fitzmyer, "The Contribution of Qumran Aramaic to the New Testament," *NTS* 20 (1973): 391-94, this probably refers to the Messiah, although, once again, the text is damaged. See Martin Hengel, *Son of God* (London: SCM, 1986), 39-54, for this concept within Judaism.

[5] John Nolland, "No Son of God Christology in Matthew 1:18-25," *JSNT* 62 (1996): 3-12; David D. Kupp, *Matthew's Emmanuel: Divine Presence and God's People in the First Gospel*, SNTSMS 90 (New York: Cambridge University Press, 1996), 172; Donald J. Verseput, "The Role and Meaning of the 'Son of God' Title in Matthew's Gospel," *NTS* 33 (1987): 532; contra Kingsbury, *Matthew: Structure, Christology, Kingdom*, 43-44; Rudolf Pesch, "Der Gottessohn im matthäischen Evangelienprolog: Beobachtungen zu den Zitationsformeln der Reflexionszitate," *Biblica* 48 (1967): 395-420.; and Daniel J. Harrington, *The Gospel of Matthew*, SP (Collegeville, MN: Liturgical, 1991), 36-40.

of sonship.[6] Insofar as the virginal conception is outside the capacity of human understanding, it suggests that Jesus' relationship of Son to the Father is ultimately mysterious and beyond the reach of full human comprehension.

Jesus' divine sonship is mediated through the infusion of the Holy Spirit. Insofar as Jesus' conception is by means of the Holy Spirit, the Spirit is the middle element between the Father and Jesus that makes this sonship possible. Jesus' intimate relationship with the Father is grounded in the operation of the Holy Spirit. Matthew will emphasize the role of the Spirit in Jesus' intimate relationship of sonship later at the baptism where the divine declaration that Jesus is God's Son comes immediately in the wake of Jesus' baptism with the Spirit (Mt 3:16-17), thereby suggesting that the entire ministry of Jesus Son of God is due to the power of the Spirit (e.g., Mt 12:28). And at the end of the Gospel of Matthew Jesus as Son is part of a unity that includes the Father and the Holy Spirit (Mt 28:19).

Jesus is Son of God by virtue of his being Son of David. We have noted above that the notion of divine sonship is associated in the Old Testament with Davidic (messianic) sonship. Matthew makes the same connection by linking Jesus' divine conception to the naming of Jesus by Joseph "Son of David" (Mt 1:20-21). Moreover, the confession by God of Jesus' divine sonship in Matthew 3:17; 17:5 echoes Psalm 2:7, a passage that was associated with the coronation of Davidic kings. And later "Son of God" will be linked with "Christ" (Mt 16:16; 26:63) and "King of Israel" (Mt 27:42). The allusion to Psalm 2:7 is especially significant, because the verses that immediately follow in the Psalm speak of the dominion of this Davidic king over the nations and indicate that Jesus is Son of God through whom God establishes his rule over Israel and finally over the nations.

And yet Jesus Son of God transcends the role typically ascribed to the Davidic king. In Matthew 22:41-46 Jesus raises the issue of the sonship of the Messiah, when he asks the Pharisees "What do you think of the Christ, whose son is he?"[7] The ensuing discussion reveals that, in Jesus' view,

---

[6] As suggested by the repeated use of γεννάω in Mt 1:1-17, where Matthew uses it to support the notion that Jesus is *Son* of David and *Son* of Abraham. As we saw above, Mt 1:18-25 is the beginning of the development of the theme of Jesus' divine sonship in Mt 1:18–4:16 toward its climax in the declaration from God at Mt 3:17.

[7] Matthew's version of this account introduces the contrast between two types of sonship more than does Mark, which reads, "How can the scribes say that the Christ is the son of David?" (Mk 12:35-37).

although Jesus is Son of David he is more than Son of David; the consideration that this passage is leading toward the climax of the Gospel of Matthew where Jesus will die as God's Son (Mt 26:63; 27:40, 43) and be confessed as "Son of God" (Mt 27:54) makes plain that his Davidic sonship must be understood in terms of the transcendent category of Son of God.[8]

The role of Jesus' sonship is to save his people from their sins. One way in which Jesus Son of God transcends the role of Son of David is by effectively dealing with the people's sins. For while Davidic kings delivered the people from military and political oppression, never does the Old Testament speak of a king as saving the people from their sins. But that is the nature of Jesus' divine sonship. In dealing with the sin problem, Jesus reconciles the people to God and thus establishes right relationship between them and God.[9] Jesus does this by making them "sons of the Father,"[10] even as he is the Son of the Father.

Moreover, Matthew insists that the death of Jesus as obedient Son atones for sins (Mt 27:27-54), for at the cross he pours out his blood for the forgiveness of sins (Mt 26:28) and gives his life "as a ransom for many" (Mt 20:28). According to Matthew 1:21 this salvation is to be directed toward his people Israel who were God's son in a sense (Mt 2:15), but potentially, according to God's purpose, may become God's son in a fuller sense through Jesus Son of God. Later, in the wake of the rejection of Jesus, Son of God, by the greater part of Israel, this sonship to God will be realized by a new "nation" (Mt 21:43), which does not repudiate, as Israel did, this relationship of sonship by rejecting the one who can effect it, namely God's own Son (Mt 21:36-39; 22:1-10). Indeed, Jesus, as Son, is "the stone," the "head of the corner," on which this new nation will be built (Mt 21:42; cf. Mt 22:2; 16:16-18).

As Son, Jesus is the locus of God's presence among his people. In his capacity as Son, Jesus is "Emmanuel, God with us" (Mt 1:23). In context, this presence of God in the person of his Son is the means God employs to effect salvation from sin, that is, to make operative the benefits of Jesus' atoning work. But when Matthew has Jesus promise at the conclusion of the Great Commission that he as "Son" (Mt 28:19) will be "with you always" (Mt 28:20), Matthew indicates that in his Son God himself will be present to enable the

---

[8]Verseput, "Son of God," 545-46.
[9]This anticipates the claim made below that the essence of Jesus' divine sonship is intimate, personal relationship with the Father.
[10]See Mt 5:9, 16, 45, 48; 6:1, 4, 6, 8-9, 14, 18, 26, 32; 7:9, 11; 9:15; 10:20, 29; 13:38, 43; 17:25-26; 23:9.

post-Easter church to fulfill its mission of making disciples of all nations, in spite of internal (Mt 28:17) and external (Mt 28:11-15) challenges.

Some have taken this statement in Matthew 1:23 to be a predication, thereby indicating that Jesus is God himself, that is, that he is God who dwells among us.[11] In fact, the phrase allows for an identification of Jesus, as Son, with God, but it does not require it. The emphasis on Jesus' role here as the agent of salvation suggests a functional rather than an ontological focus. On the other hand, Jesus' conception by the Holy Spirit has ontological implications, and, as we shall see below, throughout Matthew's narrative Jesus assumes roles that, according to the Old Testament, belonged to Yahweh.

Jesus is Son of God as one who has a relation of personal intimacy with the Father. Insofar as "only the Father knows the Son and only the Son knows the Father" they share a personal relationship which is utterly unique. Although this mutual relationship is exclusive, it is communicable to others, but only by the Father and Son themselves. Thus the "Son reveals the Father" (Mt 11:27) and the Father reveals the Son. Indeed, no one can know that Jesus is the Son, or know what is involved in his divine sonship and thus participate in this relationship to God the Father, except as the Father reveals the Son (Mt 3:17; 16:16-17; 27:51-54) and the Son reveals the Father. This revelation consists not only in the cognitive perception that God is the Father of Jesus, or that Jesus is the Son, but rather in the personal experience of knowing God as Father, and in the sharing, in some sense, that filial fellowship which is enjoyed between the Father and the Son. Moberly rightly says, "This is the basic premise of Jesus' ministry. Jesus seeks to enable others to enter into the relationship with God as Father which he himself enjoys."[12]

Knowledge between the Father and the Son is used here in the sense of personal relationship that expresses itself in actions.[13] Thus this relationship

---

[11] J. C. Fenton, "Matthew and the Divinity of Jesus: Three Questions Concerning Matthew 1:20-23," in *Studia Biblica 1978. Papers on the Gospels*, ed. E. A. Livingstone (Sheffield: JSOT Press, 1979), 79-82; Donald A. Hagner, *Matthew 1–13*, WBC (Dallas: Word, 1993), 21; contra Murray J. Harris, *Jesus as God: The New Testament Use of Theos in Reference to Jesus* (Grand Rapids: Baker, 1992), 256-58. John Nolland, *The Gospel of Matthew*, NIGTC (Grand Rapids: Eerdmans, 2005), 102, wisely states that the rejection of a clear predication here does not express a "low Christology" but an "imprecise Christology" at this point.

[12] R. W. L. Moberly, *The Bible, Theology, and Faith: A Study of Abraham and Jesus*, CSCD (New York: Cambridge University Press, 2000), 208.

[13] Rudolf Bultmann, "γινώσκω," *TDNT* 1:679-719, describes it as "a personal fellowship, in which each is decisively determined by the other in his own existence." He sees the word employed

between the Father and the Son is characterized above all by mutual responsiveness to that which the other requires from the relationship. In his capacity as Father God is responsive to the desires of the Son (e.g., Mt 18:19-20), even in a case where such responsiveness might contradict the Father's will (Mt 26:53). And the Son, in his obedience and especially in the submission of his will, is responsive to the dominant role played by the Father. The Father gives to the Son all that the Son needs and properly desires (Mt 7:9-11); and the Son gives to the Father trust and obedience.

Part of the mutual responsiveness within this interpersonal relationship, then, is that *the Father grants all things to the Son*. Accordingly, Matthew 11:27 begins with the declaration that all things have been given to the Son by the Father, which involve especially the authority that the Son exercises in his pre-Easter ministry, that is, "the deeds of the Christ" (Mt 11:2, 20-24; 9:8). Hence, Jesus as Son of God is one who consistently exercises preternatural power (e.g., Mt 8:27; 14:22-33). And yet, when Jesus declares in Matthew 28:18 that "all authority in heaven and on earth has been given to me" we are led to think that the Son has now been given dimensions of authority that he did not have prior to his resurrection.[14] Thus, according to Matthew 11:27, the Father had given Jesus all authority according to the parameters of Jesus' earthly existence, but with the resurrection Jesus' capacity for the exercise of authority has boundlessly expanded, and the Father is responsive to this greater capacity on the part of the Son.[15]

But the other aspect of this mutual responsiveness is that Jesus is Son of God as one who perfectly obeys the will of his Father. In fact, this is the dimension of Jesus' divine sonship that Matthew stresses more than any other. When God confesses Jesus as his Son it is because God is "well pleased" with him (Mt 3:17). Indeed, the divine confession comes in the wake of Jesus' baptism which Jesus undertook "to fulfill all righteousness" (Mt 3:15). And immediately on the heels of this confession Jesus is tempted by the devil in

---

here in essentially a Johannine sense. One can recognize the legitimacy of Bultmann's insights without accepting his notion of Gnostic provenance. See also, Ernst Dieter Schmitz, "Knowledge," in *The New International Dictionary of New Testament Theology*, ed. Colin Brown, 4 vols. (Grand Rapids: Zondervan, 1974-79), 2:392-409.

[14]Note, among other things, that as a consequence of this authority ("therefore") Jesus commissions the disciples to do things that he had not previously authorized and had even previously forbidden them (compare Mt 28:19 with Mt 10:5-6).

[15]Moberly, *Bible, Theology, and Faith*, 207.

the wilderness in his role as "Son of God," and refuses to yield to these temptations. In fact, Jesus is repeatedly tempted, or tested, throughout the Gospel of Matthew, and these temptations reach their climax in the greatest temptation of all, the cross, where Jesus, as Son of God, once again refuses to yield to temptation and dies as one who trusts in God to deliver him (Mt 27:43), which is presented by Matthew as the essence of righteousness.[16]

Son of David, Shepherd, King

We have seen that "Son of God" is closely related to the promise God made to David regarding David's "seed" or "son." But "Son of David" is a title in its own right. It is especially frequent in the Gospel of Matthew, appearing twelve times, eight of which are peculiar to it. Moreover, Matthew links "Son of David" to the images of shepherd and king.

In the Gospel of Matthew Jesus is the Messiah-king sent specifically to Israel to grant them wholeness and salvation, but who, in the wake of Israel's rejection of their shepherd-king, offers salvation to his new people, the church. Already in Matthew 1:1 is Jesus declared the Son of David, and that claim is supported by demonstrating, through the genealogy, that Jesus is in the line of David (Mt 1:1-17). By adding the designation "the king" to the mention of David in the genealogy (Mt 1:6) Matthew gives notice to the reader that "Son of David" and "king" are associated concepts. But according to Matthew 1:18-25 the point is not that Jesus is in the bloodline of David, for Jesus is not the biological son of Joseph. Rather, Jesus is Son of David by adoption, at the behest of the divine command, and therefore Jesus has been appointed and commissioned by God to function as the Son of David. This function involves saving his people from their sins (Mt 1:21). Insofar as "his people" refers to the people of Israel (Mt 2:2, 6; 27:37, 42) this Son of David has been chosen by God to bring salvation to the Jews. But insofar as this salvation will be realized by those who confess that he is "Emmanuel, God with us" (Mt 1:23) this Son of David will actualize his saving rule over those who make that confession, namely his church, composed of both Jews and Gentiles.

---

[16]It is ironic that the religious leaders are those who proclaim Jesus' righteousness, by citing a combination of Ps 22:8 and Wis 2:18, which refer to the faith or confidence in God on the part of the righteous sufferer.

Throughout the remainder of the Gospel, Matthew develops Jesus' Davidic sonship along two closely related lines: 1) as a shepherd-king who heals; and 2) as a shepherd king who reigns by dying on behalf of his people. In both cases, he is the agent of God's salvation to God's people.

Matthew 2 and Matthew 27 describe Jesus as the shepherd-king who brings salvation to his people by dying on their behalf. By repeating the term *king* (Mt 2:2, 3, 9; cf. also "rulers/ruler" in Mt 2:6) Matthew 2:1-12 orients the reader to the issue of Jesus' kingship, and by emphasizing Bethlehem Jesus' kingship is related to David (Mt 2:1, 6, 8, 16). Herod rules by destroying his subjects (Mt 2:16-18); Jesus, by contrast, is to rule by shepherding God's people (Mt 2:6; cf. 2 Sam 5:2).[17] In this context shepherding clearly involves his "saving them" (Mt 1:21). Matthew is here drawing on Ezekiel 34, which portrays God as the shepherd of his people who will "save" his flock (Ezek 34:22) by setting over them "one shepherd, my servant David" (Ezek 34:23), who shall be "prince among them" (Ezek 34:24). Matthew specifies *how* Jesus is the shepherd king who saves his people from their sins in the one other passage that describes Jesus' kingship, namely Matthew 27:11-54. Here Jesus, the shepherd (Mt 26:31), rules as "king of the Jews" or "king of Israel" (Mt 27:37, 42; cf. Mt 27:11, 27-31) by dying on behalf of his people. Yet he also extends his saving rule beyond ethnic Israel, for here he "gives his life as a ransom for *many*" (Mt 20:28) since his blood is "poured out for *many* for the forgiveness of sins" (Mt 26:28).

Moreover, Matthew employs the title "Son of David" to explicate Jesus' role as the shepherd-king who heals. Indeed, after the infancy narrative (Mt 1–2) the title appears exclusively in the context of Jesus' healings. On two occasions Jesus' healings lead persons to speak of him as "Son of David" (Mt 12:23; 21:15). In addition, three times persons in need of healing cry out, "Have mercy upon me [us], Son of David" (Mt 9:27; 15:22; 20:30-31), and Jesus heals them as an expression of his mercy. In each of these instances the petitioner addresses Jesus also as "Lord" (κύριος), thereby implying confidence or faith in Jesus' transcendent power and submission to his lordly rule. Also in each case the petitioner demonstrates earnestness by realizing healing through the overcoming of

---

[17] Mt 2:6 actually combines 2 Sam 5:2, pertaining to David himself, with Mic 5:2, a "messianic" passage that describes a future Davidic king.

obstacles.[18] Thus these persons seriously embrace Jesus as Son of David and as a consequence experience the blessings of his rule.

These passages play a double role in the Gospel of Matthew. On the one hand, they explicate the meaning of Jesus' Davidic sonship. In linking the Son of David to healing, Matthew is drawing once again on the image of the shepherd in Ezekiel 34:1-24, where God is pictured as a shepherd who "will bind up the crippled and strengthen the weak" (Ezek 34:16), and who, as we saw above, will set over this flock "one shepherd, my servant David" (Ezek 34:23), who also "will be prince among them" (Ezek 34:24).[19] This Son of David rules, then, by being the viceroy, or agent, of God's salvation over God's flock. In the Gospel of Matthew, healing is a form of salvation, in that it overcomes the oppressive power of cosmic evil expressed in sickness and demon possession (note the use of "save" [σώζω] in Mt 9:21, 22), but such physical healing also bears witness to Jesus' authority to save from sin (Mt 9:1-8; cf. Mt 1:21). I might mention, too, that insofar as Ezekiel 34 describes this Davidic shepherd as taking up God's role of feeding the sheep, Matthew's portrait of the feedings of the five thousand and four thousand may also present Jesus as the Son of David who fulfills Ezekiel 34 by caring for the flock, providing them all they need for continuous well-being and wholeness.[20]

On the other hand, these passages point to the guilt of Israel in rejecting Jesus as the healing Son of David. As Kingsbury has pointed out, it is the "no accounts" of Jewish society (the sick, the blind, the demon possessed, all

---

[18]This is the case in all these healings, with the possible exception of Mt 9:27-32, although here the description of these *blind* men following him probably points in the same direction.

[19]This role of Ezek 34 is recognized and developed by Wayne S. Baxter, "Healing and the 'Son of David': Matthew's Warrant," *NovT* 48 (2006): 36-50; and by Lidija Novakovic, *Messiah: The Healer of the Sick*, WUNT 2 (Tübingen: Mohr Siebeck, 2003). Novakovic also appeals to a Davidic construal of Is 42:1-4 and Is 53:4, as does Michael F. Bird, *Jesus Is the Christ* (Downers Grove, IL: InterVarsity Press, 2012), 69-70. Cf. Joel Willitts, *Matthew's Messianic Shepherd-King: In Search of 'The Lost Sheep of the House of Israel,'* BZNW (Berlin: De Gruyter, 2007), who objects to an almost exclusive focus on Ezekiel and points to Jer 23:1-6 and Jer 50:6. Attempts to find a background in traditions regarding Solomon's exorcisms have faltered on a number of grounds, including the observation that the healings of Jesus Son of David in the Gospel of Matthew are directed primarily toward the blind. See, e.g., Dennis C. Duling, "The Therapeutic Son of David: An Element in Matthew's Christological Apologetic," *NTS* 24 (1977-78): 392-410; Romeo Popa, *Allgegenwärtiger Konflikt im Matthäusevangelium: Exegetische und sozialpsychologische Analyse der Konfliktgeschichte*, NovTOA/SUNT 111 (Göttingen: Vandenhoeck & Ruprecht, 2017), 66.

[20]Compare Mt 14:13-21; 15:32-39 with Ezek 34:13-14, 23-24.

who were unclean and not allowed to enter the temple,[21] and children), and on one occasion a Gentile (indeed a "Canaanite") who appeal to Jesus as Son of David and are thereby healed, whereas the crowds respond with doubt (Mt 12:23) and the religious leaders react with anger (Mt 21:15) and blaspheming (Mt 12:22-32).[22] Insofar as all these healings that were performed on Jews involve restoring of sight to the blind Matthew draws a contrast between the physically blind who nevertheless see that Jesus is the Son of David and experience the blessings of the end-time kingdom, and the crowds and religious authorities of Israel who "see but do not see" for "their eyes they have closed" (Mt 13:13, 15).[23]

It is true that on the occasion of Jesus' triumphal entry the crowds acclaim Jesus as the Son of David who brings salvation ("Hosanna," Mt 21:9). But in doing so they show that they do not truly understand the nature of his kingship. For they go on to describe this Son of David as "the prophet Jesus from Nazareth" (Mt 21:11), and in the Gospel of Matthew to confess Jesus as a prophet represents the opinion of "human beings" rather than the revelation of God and is therefore an entirely inadequate response to the person of Jesus (Mt 16:13-17). They do not perceive that only as one understands this Son of David in terms of his transcendent role as Son of God (Mt 22:21-46), who suffers and dies in obedience to his Father and in the service of others, can one embrace his Davidic sonship rightly. They construe his Davidic sonship along the lines of a swaggering, conquering military deliverer, a political insurrectionist like the Davidic Messiah portrayed in the Psalms of Solomon, who violently mows down all opposition to achieve military and political hegemony for Israel over the nations.[24] They miss entirely the significance of his riding into Jerusalem not on a mighty steed but on an ass, in fulfillment of Zechariah's prophecy about a "humble" king (Mt 21:1-5).

In just one other passage does Matthew describe Jesus as a king, the scene of the judgment of the nations in Matthew 25:31-46. Although most

---

[21]See Dennis C. Duling, "Matthew's Plurisignificant 'Son of David' in Social Science Perspective: Kinship, Kingship, Magic, and Miracle," *BTB* 22 (1992): 112-13.
[22]Jack Dean Kingsbury, "The Title 'Son of David' in Matthew's Gospel," *JBL* 95 (1976): 591-602.
[23]James M. Gibbs, "Purpose and Pattern in Matthew's Use of the Title 'Son of David,'" *NTS* 10 (1963): 446-64.
[24]See esp. *Pss.Sol.* 17–18. This passage contains the earliest explicit reference in extant Jewish literature to the Messiah as the Son of David. The book is a Pharisaic document produced around 50 BC.

commentators do not identify a connection between Jesus' kingship here and his Davidic sonship throughout the Gospel of Matthew, the consideration that this pericope, like other passages that Matthew uses to explicate Jesus as kingly Son of David, draws on the language of Ezekiel 34 (see esp. Ezek 34:17-24) indicates that Matthew may be making some connection between Jesus as end-time sovereign judge and his role as Son of David. If so, Matthew may consider that Jesus fulfills the role of the Davidic scion in Psalm 2, to which Matthew has already alluded in Matthew 3:17; for Psalm 2:7, which lies behind Matthew 3:17, is immediately followed by the king's judgment on "the nations" (Ps 2:8-11). But even if this judgment scene does allude to Jesus' Davidic sonship, it is at the periphery of Matthew's Son-of-David Christology.

Although Son of David is a significant christological category, it does not stand at the center of Matthew's Christology, as some scholars have claimed.[25] It is consistently subordinated to "Son of God." The Matthean Jesus sees it as deficient unless supplemented by the transcendent category of Son of God (Mt 22:41-46). In addition, it pertains specifically to Jesus' relationship to David, rather than to his relationship to God, the ultimate reality in the narrative world of the Gospel of Matthew. Finally, in contrast to "Son of God," the disciples never confess that Jesus is Son of David; such is done only by supplicants and (in an inadequate sense) by the crowds.[26]

Christ

The word rendered "Christ" (χριστός) means "anointed [with oil],"[27] and was typically used in the Old Testament for Davidic kings who were anointed at the point of their accession.[28] Consequently, the notion of "Christ" or "Messiah" was closely linked with "Son of David" and by extension "Son of God" (2 Sam 7:12-16), and we find that linkage in the Gospel of Matthew as well. Matthew employs the title sixteen times, eleven of which are unique to his Gospel.

---

[25]So, e.g., Anders Suhl, "Der Davidssohn im Matthäus-Evangelium," *ZNTW* 59 (1968): 57-81; Christoph Burger, *Jesus als Davidssohn: Eine Traditionsgeschichtliche Untersuchung* (Göttingen: Vandenhoeck & Ruprecht, 1970).
[26]See Kingsbury, *Matthew: Structure, Christology, Kingdom*, 102.
[27]As does the Hebrew term משיח, which lies behind the Septuagint's χριστός.
[28]E.g., 2 Sam 19:21; 22:51; 23:1; Ps 2:2; 18:50; 20:6; 89:38, 51; 132:10, 17. It is also used of priests (e.g., Lev. 4:5, 16; 6:22; 2 Macc 1:10) and even metaphorically for Israel (Ps 28:8; 84:9; 105:15; Hab 3:13; Lam 4:20).

We encounter this title at the very first verse of the Gospel of Matthew, where on first glance it seems to be part of a proper name, "Jesus Christ." But the genealogy that follows indicates that Matthew is employing it as a title. Indeed, the structure of the genealogy gives specific content to the meaning of "Christ." Insofar as the genealogy, which is a theological interpretation of Israel's history, reaches its climax in Jesus "who is called Christ" (Mt 1:16), it suggests that Jesus as Christ has been anointed (that is, chosen and empowered) by God to bring salvation history, which began with Abraham, to its climax or full realization, that is, its fulfillment. Hence, the genealogy functions as the theological basis for the fulfillment quotations throughout the Gospel of Matthew and suggests that each of the fulfillment quotations implicitly bears witness to and develops in specific ways the notion of Jesus as Christ. The genealogy indicates more specifically that Jesus as Christ brings to fulfillment all that God had in mind for the Son of Abraham and Son of David; thus, Matthew incorporates these titles within the more general rubric of "Christ."

Matthew 2:4 links the title "Christ" both to "Son of David" (Mt 2:1-2, 5-6) and to the fulfillment of prophecy (Mt 2:5-6). Herod is the first person in the narrative to call Jesus "Christ," even as Pilate will be the last (Mt 27:17, 22). For both Herod and Pilate the title has a nationalistic political character that threatens the stability of their own rule.[29] Both Herod and Pilate thus construe this Christ as a political disruptor who must be removed. But when Matthew indicates that "all Jerusalem" joins Herod in being "troubled" (Mt 2:3) and describes the "chief priests and scribes" as serving Herod by announcing to him where in the Scriptures the Christ is to be born, but, in contrast to the magi, not going themselves to Bethlehem to worship him, the evangelist suggests that Israel, too, shares Herod's views regarding this "Christ" and is resistant to Jesus' messianic role. They prefer Herod's rule, as violent and oppressive as it is (Mt 2:16-18), to that of a Christ whom God has signaled by the star that has "come forth out of Jacob" (Mt 2:2; cf. Num 24:17) and announced by Gentile magi (Mt 2:1-2). All this anticipates their later antagonism to Jesus' messiahship.

Although not using the title "Christ" explicitly, John the Baptist proclaims Jesus' messiahship; for the expression "the coming one" (Mt 3:11) is John's

---

[29]Note that Jesus as Christ is "king" (Mt 2:2) and "ruler/governor" (ἡγεμών, Mt 2:6), even as Herod is "king" (Mt 2:1, 3, 9) and Pilate is "governor" (Mt 27:11, 14, 15, 21, 27).

manner of talking about Jesus as "the Christ."[30] Even as the genealogy presented Jesus the Christ as the climax to salvation history, thereby giving meaning and significance to the salvation history that preceded Christ, so John declares that Jesus as Christ stands at the climax of history as end-time judge. To him is given the divine prerogatives of salvation and judgment (Mt 3:11-12). This Christ is also the fulfillment of the work of John the Baptist (Mt 3:2, 11), who was a prophet—indeed the last and greatest of the prophets. As such Jesus as Christ is exponentially greater than both the work and the person of John the Baptist. By extension, therefore, this Christ is transcendently superior to all the prophets.

For John, then, Jesus is the Christ as one who will execute apocalyptic judgment: both the end-time pouring out of the Spirit on the blessed and fiery punishment on the condemned (Mt 3:12). But this role of Jesus as Christ, while accurate, is incomplete. For the "deeds" of the Christ involve healing, exorcisms, and raising the dead, which Matthew describes as typical of Jesus' ministry (Mt 11:2). All these activities fulfill the Scriptures that anticipate a Messiah who will not only judge but will break the power of cosmic evil that manifests itself in sickness, death, disease, and demon possession (Mt 11:4-6; cf. Is 35:5-6; 61:1). The occupation of Jesus with these mighty acts of mercy, along with the correlative slowness of Jesus to realize the messianic expectations surrounding end-time judgment, is the reason why some in Israel fall away from embracing him as their Messiah (Mt 11:6).

These mighty acts, however, lead the disciples to confess Jesus as "the Christ, the Son of the living God" (Mt 16:16). In this confession "Christ" is not only linked to "Son of God," but is defined by it, to the point that to speak properly of Christ is to speak of him as Son of God.[31] Yet Jesus immediately forbids the disciples to tell anyone that he is the Christ (Mt 16:20) because they possess an inadequate understanding of "Christ," one that would be propagated in the minds of those to whom the announcement at

---

[30]Note that Matthew directly connects "the coming one" from John's mouth with "the Christ" in Mt 11:2. In Matthew, John announces that Jesus is "the coming one" (ὁ ἐρχόμενος, 3:11), whereas in Mark, John announces that "after me comes one who is mightier than I" (Mk 1:7). This connection between "Christ" and "the coming one" also reinforces the centrality of fulfillment in Matthew's conception of Jesus as Christ.

[31]Thus, when Jesus cautions the disciples not to announce publicly the confession they just made, which included both "Christ" and "Son of God," he charges them simply to tell no one that he was "the Christ."

this point would be made. The disciples have confessed Jesus as Christ, Son of God, on the basis of his powerful deeds, which is not wrong in itself, but it is incomplete; it involves the fundamental misconstrual that "Christ" involves essentially spectacular displays of power, with the corollary that it excludes all suffering (Mt 16:22-23). The disciples are to tell no one that Jesus is the Christ, the Son of God, until it has been made clear to them the he is Christ as one who suffers and dies in fulfillment of the Scriptures (Mt 16:21; 26:54).

The process whereby Jesus progressively corrects and clarifies the notion of "Christ" continues in the explicit discussion with the religious authorities regarding the nature of messiahship (Mt 22:41-46). When Jesus poses the question, "What do you think of the Christ, whose Son is he?" he implies that the key to understanding messiahship is to get the question of sonship straight. Jesus engages in a rabbinic form of argument known as *haggadah*, in which an apparent contradiction between two passages, or sets of passages, is discussed in such a way that the truth of each is affirmed. Here Jesus implicitly sets all the passages that present the Christ as Son of David over against Psalm 110:1, which seems to contradict this understanding. Jesus hereby affirms that the Messiah is the Davidic ruler but insists that such an understanding must be supplemented and interpreted by the more fundamental reality that he is the Son of God as one who perfectly obeys the will of his Father, which means for him suffering and death followed by resurrection glory.

Yet the Christ has an authority and superior station above his disciples that excludes all forms of hierarchialism among his followers (Mt 23:10). His followers are all on the same level, as they together stand below him who is their teacher or guide, that is, the one who alone has authority to direct their lives (Mt 23:10, καθηγητής). But this authority and superior station of the Christ is one of humility; he will be exalted through the humiliation of the cross (Mt 23:11-12).

In this passage, Jesus implicitly acknowledges his messiahship. He does the same in Matthew 24:5, 23-24 when he warns of "false Christs" who come in his name, though they have an entirely different agenda from his own, expressed in the dazzling display of signs and wonders. Such an agenda has great human appeal, but it leads persons astray from the way of God (cf. Mt 16:23) and will result in the destruction of the nation, exactly the opposite of what these Christ pretenders promise (Mt 24:15-28).

At the trial before the Sanhedrin the high priest actually accuses Jesus of being such a "Christ" as Jesus has described in Matthew 24. Trying to tie Jesus to the (false) testimony that Jesus claimed he had the authority to perform the miraculous sign of destroying the temple and rebuilding it in three days, Caiaphas requires that Jesus come straight as to whether he is "the Christ, the Son of the living God" (Mt 26:63). Jesus' circumlocutionary answer ("you have said so," Mt 26:64) is an attempt to confirm his messiahship *in the way he understands it*, while rejecting it in the way the high priest takes it, that is, according to typical Jewish expectations of one who will win over popular opinion through spectacular displays of power so as to "lord it over them" and "exercise authority over them" (Mt 20:25).

It is precisely because Jesus rejects such expectations that the Jewish crowds finally reject him as their Messiah. The notion of a royal Messiah who resists the display and accolades associated with human power is ridiculous to the crowds. They show the depth of their hostility to this kind of a Christ when they respond to Pilate's offer to release to them "Jesus who is called Christ" with the insistence that a criminal be granted to them instead (Mt 27:15-21). And they show their hostility even more when they respond to Pilate's question, "What shall I do with Jesus who is called Christ?" with the cry, "Let him be crucified" (Mt 27:22). Indeed, they acknowledge that refusing to be the kind of Messiah they want is an evil that is worthier of crucifixion than is gross criminality (Mt 27:23).

Lord

In the world in which the Gospel of Matthew emerged the word that is often translated in our English Bibles "Lord" (κύριος) had a variety of uses, all of which appear in this Gospel. Sometimes it is a term of respect directed toward a social superior and means simply "sir" (e.g., Mt 27:63). As a variant of this use, it occasionally refers to a master in a master/slave relationship (Mt 10:24-25; 25:18-26), or the owner of a house or vineyard in an employer/employee relationship (Mt 21:40; 13:27; 24:45-51), or a king in a sovereign/client relationship (Mt 18:23-34). And, finally, it is sometimes a title for deity.[32] Indeed, the Jews of Jesus' day often translated or read the divine name "Yahweh," which they considered too sacred to speak, as κύριος ("Lord"), and this is possibly the way the Septuagint typically translated "Yahweh."[33]

All these uses are straightforward and thus raise no questions. But the Gospel of Matthew, like most other New Testament books, employs this term as a christological title. In fact, the term *Lord* is applied to Jesus much more often in the Gospel of Matthew than in any of the other Gospels; and consequently, most of the occurrences of "Lord" as it pertains to Jesus are unique to the Gospel of Matthew. In addition, Matthew is particularly intentional in his employment of this title for Jesus, since he uses it repeatedly in connection with Jesus' transcendent authority, such as his power to heal (e.g., Mt 9:27; 15:22) or to calm the forces of nature (Mt 8:25; 14:30). In this Gospel only disciples, or those who approach Jesus in faith for healing, address him as "Lord,"[34] while his opponents and others who are not followers of Jesus typically address him as "teacher" or "Rabbi."[35] Indeed, in the Gospel of Matthew disciples always call him "Lord"; they never refer to him in any other way. Such a distinction is unknown in the other Gospels.

This careful and discriminating application of "Lord" on the part of Matthew indicates that the title is meant to acknowledge Jesus' superior authority and that it is a confessional title such as would be used by the Christians in Matthew's audience in their devotion and worship of the risen Christ. And the consideration that Matthew uses this same term often to refer to the God of the Old Testament has led some scholars, notably Günther Bornkamm, to insist that it "has the character of a divine

---

[32] As in Mt 1:21, 22, 24; 2:13, 15; 3:13; 4:7, 10; 5:33; 11:25; 21:9, 42; 22:37, 44; 23:39; 27:10; 28:2.

[33] Larry Hurtado, *Lord Jesus Christ: Devotion to Jesus in Earliest Christianity* (Grand Rapids: Eerdmans, 2003), 108-11; Joseph A. Fitzmyer, "The Semitic Background of the New Testament Kyrios-Title," in *A Wandering Aramean: Collected Aramaic Essays*, ed. Joseph A. Fitzmyer, SBLMS 25 (Missoula, MT: Scholars, 1979), 115-43; George Howard, "The Tetragram and the New Testament," *JBL* 96 (1977): 63-83; Albert Pietersma, "Kyrios or Tetragram: A Renewed Quest for the Original Septuagint," in *Studies in Honor of John W. Wevers on His Sixty-Fifth Birthday*, ed. Albert Pietersma and Claude Cox (Mississauga, Ontario: Benben, 1984): 85-101.

[34] Including unacceptable or illegitimate disciples, i.e., those who consider themselves disciples, who make the Christological confession, even though they will be judged by Christ to be deficient and unworthy to enter the consummated kingdom (Mt 7:21-23; 25:11; possibly also Mt 25:44).

[35] A comparison of Mt 26:22 with Mt 26:25 reveals the difference. The disciples ask Jesus, "Is it I, Lord?" But Judas, by this time no longer a disciple, asks "Is it I, Rabbi?"

Name of majesty."[36] Indeed, Bornkamm saw "Lord" as one of the central titles for Jesus in the Gospel of Matthew, and certain other scholars have insisted that it is the chief christological title for Matthew.[37] Yet it is doubtful that "Lord" plays such a dominant role, since it is never used in a confessional formula; in contrast to "Son of God" or "Son of David," never does anyone say "You [or he is] are Lord."[38] And Kingsbury has shown that "Lord" is consistently subordinated to other titles in its use throughout the Gospel of Matthew.[39]

Nevertheless, we cannot doubt its importance. Jesus frequently refers to himself as "Lord" (Mt 7:21-22; 9:38; 12:8; 24:42; 25:11; and probably Mt 21:3). The title pertains both to the time of the earthly Jesus,[40] to the period between his resurrection and Second Coming (Mt 9:38), and to his parousia (Mt 7:21, 22; 24:42; 25:11, 37, 44). The main question this christological title poses is its relationship to the designation "Lord" as applied to God, which itself prompts the issue of Jesus' divine status in the Gospel of Matthew.

On the one hand, Matthew draws a close connection between Jesus as "Lord" and God as "Lord." At the beginning of the ministry of John the Baptist Matthew quotes Isaiah 40:3: "Prepare the way of the Lord, make his paths straight" (Mt 3:3). The readers of the Gospel of Matthew recognize that the "Lord" of Isaiah 40:3 is Yahweh, and that Matthew is clearly applying it to Jesus. When supplicants cry out to Jesus, "Lord, have mercy on me [us]" (Mt 7:21, 22; 24:42; 25:11, 37, 44) they are employing the same phrase repeatedly directed to Yahweh in the Psalms (Ps 6:2; 9:13; 25:16; 26:11; 27:7; 30:10; 31:9; 41:4, 10; 51:1; 57:1; 86:1). When Jesus heals those who appeal to him as "Lord," we remember that, according to Psalm 103:3 it is Yahweh the Lord who "heals all your diseases" (cf. Ps 103:3). When Jesus declares that he is "Lord of the sabbath" (Mt 12:8) the reader naturally asks who can be Lord over the sabbath except the one who established the sabbath? Peter implores

---

[36] Günther Bornkamm, "End-Expectation," in *Tradition and Interpretation in Matthew*, ed. Günther Bornkamm, Gerhard Barth, and Heinz Joachim Held, NTL (Philadelphia: Westminster, 1963), 42.
[37] E.g., Hubert Frankemölle, *Jahwe-Bund und Kirche Christi: Studien zur Form- und Traditionsgeschichte des "Evangeliums" nach Matthäus*, Neutestamentliche Abhandlungen/Neue Folge 10 (Münster: Aschendorff, 1974); Wolfgang Trilling, *Das Wahre Israel: Studien zur Theologie des Matthäus-Evangeliums* (München: Kösel, 1964), 21-26.
[38] In this regard, Matthew's use stands in contrast to Paul (e.g., Rom 10:9; 1 Cor 12:3; Phil 2:11).
[39] Jack Dean Kingsbury, "The Title 'Kyrios' in Matthew's Gospel," *JBL* 94 (1975): 250-54.
[40] Mt 8:2, 6, 8, 21, 25; 9:28; 12:8; 14:28, 30; 15:22, 25, 27; 16:22; 17:4, 15; 18:21; 20:30, 31, 33; 21:3; 22:43, 44, 45; 26:22.

Jesus as Lord to bid him come to Jesus on the water (Mt 14:28) immediately after Jesus has spoken of himself using the self-identification of Yahweh in the Old Testament "It is I"/"I am" (ἐγώ εἰμί, Mt 14:27).[41] When we read the Canaanite woman's appeal to Jesus, "Lord, help me" (Mt 15:25), we recognize that the very same phrase appears in Psalm 108:26 LXX, referring to Yahweh. And when Jesus is addressed as "Lord" at the judgment he is assuming the role of end-time judge that the Old Testament assigns exclusively to Yahweh (Mt 7:21, 22; 25:11, 37, 44).

On the other hand, at a few points Matthew differentiates between the lordship of Christ and the lordship of Yahweh. Thus Jesus addresses his Father as "Lord" (Mt 11:25). And Jesus himself draws a distinction between Yahweh who is "Lord," and the Christ who is David's "Lord" (Mt 22:41-46). And although Jesus is "Lord" as end-time judge, the standard of his judgment is "the will of my Father" (Mt 7:21-22).

Therefore, Jesus' lordship cannot be collapsed into the lordship of Yahweh. Jesus as Lord is separate from Yahweh as Lord. Yet Matthew associates Jesus as Lord with Yahweh as Lord and at several points virtually identifies the two. Thus, κύριος is a "divine Name of Majesty,"[42] which indicates that Jesus "is of exalted station who wields divine authority."[43] This goes far beyond what the Jews were prepared to grant to their Messiah (Mt 22:41-46). It is a title that, at one and the same time, both links Jesus with Yahweh of the Old Testament and distinguishes Jesus from him.

Son of Man

This discussion of "Son of Man" will function as a bridge between the treatment of christological titles and a consideration of other descriptions of Jesus, beyond Christological titles, that illumine Matthew's presentation of Jesus. "Son of Man" serves well such a transitional role, for although it is a favorite self-designation for Jesus it is not, strictly speaking, a title, in that it does not

---

[41]Cf. Ex 3:14; Deut 32:39; Is 41:4; 43:10. See, e.g., Donald A. Hagner, *Matthew 14–28*, WBC (Dallas: Word), 423; Joachim Gnilka, *Das Matthäus-evangelium*, 2 Teile, HThKNT (Freiburg: Berder, 1988), 2:13; David L. Turner, *Matthew*, BECNT (Grand Rapids: Baker, 2008), 372-73; Robert H. Gundry, *Matthew: A Commentary on His Handbook for a Mixed Church Under Persecution*, 2nd ed. (Grand Rapids: Eerdmans, 1994), 299. But cf. Paul Gaechter, *Das Matthäus Evangelium: Ein Kommentar* (Innsbruch: Tyrolia-Verlog, 1963), 483; Nolland, *Gospel of Matthew*, 601.
[42]Bornkamm, "End-Expectation," 42.
[43]Kingsbury, "The Title 'Kyrios,'" 255.

contribute any insight into the identity of Jesus.[44] Accordingly, no one in the Gospel of Matthew comes to discover that Jesus is "Son of Man," nor does anyone ever confess that he is "Son of Man." In fact, no one other than Jesus even refers to him as "Son of Man." Rather, Jesus' role as Son of Man raises the question of his identity but does not answer it; the answer to the identity of Jesus Son of Man is properly that he is "Son of God" (Mt 16:13-17).

Yet the fact that "Son of Man" is not a title does not render it insignificant for Matthew's presentation of Jesus. The consideration that Matthew includes several references to Son of Man that are not found in the other Gospels (Mt 13:37, 41; 16:13, 28; 19:28; 24:30; 25:31; 26:2), and that these unique occurrences tend to emphasize the exaltation and rule of the Son of Man as described in Daniel 7:13-14, suggests that Matthew is intentional in the employment of this term. As we shall see, it serves as a vehicle to highlight and to probe certain aspects of Jesus' destiny, according to the will and purpose of God (Mt 26:45, 54).

The term "Son of Man" means essentially "this man," or "this human being."[45] It thus fits well Jesus' adoption of it as a self-designation referring to his specific destiny. Although the term appears in several Old Testament books, its employment in the Gospel tradition seems to stem from Daniel 7:13-14, where "one like a son of man" comes with the clouds of heaven to "the ancient of days" [God] and is presented before him, at which time he "was given dominion and glory and kingdom, that all peoples, nations, and languages should serve him." In the Danielic context, this personage represents "the saints of the Most High" (Dan 7:22) who are vindicated by God after suffering oppression (Dan 7:25-27). But this corporate image is narrowed when, at the end of the passage, the masculine singular is employed: "His dominion is an everlasting dominion which will not pass away; and his kingdom is one which will not be destroyed" (Dan 7:14 NASB).[46] The

---

[44]Jack Dean Kingsbury, *Matthew as Story* (Minneapolis: Fortress, 1986), 96-98, offers a detailed argument against Son of Man as a title. Others who reject its role as a title are Barnabas Lindars, *Jesus Son of Man: A Fresh Examination of the Son of Man Sayings in the Gospels in Light of Recent Research* (Grand Rapids: Eerdmans, 1983), 115-16, and Ulrich Luz, "The Son of Man in Matthew: Heavenly Judge or Human Christ," *JSNT* 48 (1992): 3-21. Contra R. T. France, *Matthew: Evangelist and Teacher* (Grand Rapids: Zondervan, 1989), 288-92.

[45]Carston Colpe, "ὁ υἱὸς τοῦ ἀνθρώπου," *TDNT* 8:400-20.

[46]Chrys C. Caragounis, *The Son of Man: Vision and Interpretation*, WUNT 38 (Tübingen: Mohr, 1986), 61-81, argues that in Daniel 7 the Son of Man does not represent the nation of Israel at all

first-century *Similitudes of Enoch* and *4 Ezra* use this Danielic language to speak of a preexistent Messianic figure who will exercise judgment on the nations. Yet it is unclear how widely this Messianic conception was in vogue among the Jews at the time of Jesus or even of Matthew. And scholars disagree regarding the extent to which Matthew's portrayal of Jesus as Son of Man was influenced by the *Similitudes* or even Daniel.[47]

Yet scholars generally agree that the Son-of-Man sayings in the Gospel of Matthew fall into three groups: 1) earthly ministry, 2) passion and resurrection, and 3) future coming, including judgment.[48] The "Son of Man" thus reflects the three stages, or tiers, of Jesus' destiny. As Kingsbury has demonstrated, in all three tiers "Son of Man" functions as a public designation, in that every one of these sayings is either spoken to those who are on the outside, that is, not part of the disciple circle, or spoken to disciples so as to inform them about matters that pertain to those on the outside.[49] For example, when Jesus speaks to the disciples regarding the coming judgment performed by the Son of Man (Mt 13:41; 16:27, 28; 19:28; 24:30; 25:31), he is describing an event that will be manifest to the entire world.

---

but rather a single supernatural "transcendental" figure. Certainly, the flow of the Danielic passage moves in this direction.

[47] For the view that Matthew was dependent on the *Similitudes*, see Johannes Theisohn, *Der Auserwählte Richter*, SUNT (Göttingen: Vandenhoeck & Ruprecht, 1974), 158-200; and Leslie W. Walck, *The Son of Man in the Parables of Enoch and Matthew*, JCT 9 (New York: T&T Clark, 2011). But most scholars are not persuaded; see France, *Evangelist and Teacher*, 290; Luz, "Son of Man," 8; Maurice Casey, *The Solution to the Son of Man Problem* (New York: T&T Clark, 2007), 82-115. While no one denies that Matthew was aware of Daniel 7:13-14 in connection with Son of Man, since echoes of Daniel 7 are more pronounced in Matthew's version of the Son of Man sayings at Mt 26:64 and Mt 24:30 than in the other synoptics and Matthew alone speaks of the "kingdom" of the Son of Man (Mt 13:41; 16:28), great disagreement exists regarding just how specifically Matthew is drawing the attention of the reader to these Danielic apocalyptic themes. R. T. France, *The Gospel of Matthew*, NICNT (Grand Rapids: Eerdmans, 2007), 396-97, argues for strong apocalyptic influence from Daniel; contra Luz, "Son of Man," 8-9; Douglas R. A. Hare, *The Son of Man Tradition* (Minneapolis: Fortress, 1990), 180-82.

[48] For earthly ministry, see Mt 8:20; 9:6; 11:19; 12:8, 32; 13:37; 16:13; for passion and resurrection, see Mt 12:40; 17:9, 12, 22; 20:18, 28; 26:2, 24, 45; and for future coming, see Mt 10:23; 13:41; 16:27, 28; 19:28; 24:27, 30, 37, 39, 44; 25:31; 26:64.

[49] Kingsbury, *Matthew: Structure, Christology, Kingdom*, 114-18, and *Matthew as Story*, 100-101. A comparison with Mark and Luke points to this emphasis on the public nature of "Son of Man." Thus the Matthean Jesus makes a distinction between "Who do human beings say the *Son of Man* is" and "Who do you say *I* am?" (Mt 16:13, 15), while Mark and Luke have "I" in both questions. And a comparison between Mt 10:32 and its parallel in Mk 8:38 and Lk 9:26 reveals the same: here the Matthean Jesus, warning his disciples, says "Whoever acknowledges *me* before humans, *I* also will deny before my Father," whereas Mark and Luke employ "Son of Man."

But the pattern of Son-of-Man sayings is not only tiered and public, but also dialectical, in that within the first two tiers (earthly vocation, and passion and resurrection) these sayings reflect a combination of weakness and supreme strength. The earthly Son of Man experiences weakness in the form of homelessness (Mt 8:20), accusation of blasphemy and wrongdoing (Mt 9:6; 11:19; 12:8 [cf. Mt 12:2], 32), and opposition from Satan (Mt 13:37), but he demonstrates supreme strength in that he has authority to heal the sick and to forgive sins (Mt 9:1-8), determine what is acceptable sabbath practice (Mt 12:1-8), declare persons beyond the veil of forgiveness (Mt 12:32), and demand that persons follow him as disciples even if that means abandoning allegiance to God's law (Mt 8:21-22). And the Son of Man not only endures the weakness of condemnation, suffering and death at the hands of humans, but supreme strength in his resurrection from God.

While the first two tiers are characterized by this mixture of weakness and strength, the third tier is unqualified strength, for the Son of Man who had been homeless now has a "kingdom" (Mt 16:28); he who had been challenged by Satan now destroys "the sons of the evil one" (Mt 13:41); he who had been accused of blasphemy now sits at the right hand of God (Mt 26:64); he who had been condemned for wrongdoing (Mt 20:18) is now the judge of his attackers (Mt 16:27; 25:31; 26:64). Thus the third tier culminates the theme of strength in the first two tiers but reverses the weakness in those tiers. As Luz points out, Matthew's presentation of Jesus as Son of Man emphasizes that this kind of suffering and deprivation are joined in the same person with resurrection and cosmic authority.[50]

Jesus' role as Son of Man, however, has significance not only for Jesus, but also for those on the outside, and for his disciples. As those on the outside witness in Jesus Son of Man this grand dialectic of the weakness of deprivation, insult, condemnation, and suffering with the strength of transcendent authority and resurrection they must decide what this dialectic means regarding the identity of this Son of Man and their embrace or rejection of him. They must answer for themselves the question: "Who do humans beings say the Son of Man is?" (Mt 16:13). Yet in the end it is this Son of Man who will exercise judgmental decision regarding them (Mt 16:27).

---

[50]Luz, "Son of Man," 17-18.

As far as the disciples are concerned, the experience of Jesus Son of Man is paradigmatic for their own existence. As Jesus Son of Man is homeless (Mt 8:20), so they have left everything, including houses, to follow Jesus (Mt 19:27, 29). As this Son of Man is accused of wrongdoing (Mt 9:1-8), so are they (Mt 12:2; 15:2). As this Son of Man must contend against the activity of his enemy, the devil (Mt 13:24-30, 37), so must they struggle with "the sons of the evil one" (Mt 13:38-42). As the Son of Man must suffer and be crucified (Mt 17:22-23; 20:18-19; 26:2), so must they (Mt 10:38; 16:24-26). And yet, as Jesus Son of Man has authority to heal and forgive sins (Mt 9:1-8), so these "men" (Mt 9:9) also have the authority to heal (Mt 10:1, 8) and to forgive sins (Mt 18:15-35). As Jesus Son of Man is raised from the dead, so also these who have lost their lives will find resurrection life (Mt 16:25; 25:46). As Jesus Son of Man sits on his throne as judge, so they will "sit on twelve thrones, judging the twelve tribes of Israel" (Mt 19:28).

Nevertheless, Jesus is unique as Son of Man, and therefore this designation pertains only to Jesus, and not to them.[51] They do not reign over their own kingdom (Mt 13:41; 16:27; 25:31), nor do they have authority to call others to follow them at the expense of repudiating commandments in the law of God (Mt 8:20-22), nor can they determine proper sabbath observance (Mt 12:8), nor can they judge others in the community (Mt 7:1). They do not "sow good seed" in the field of the world, but rather are those who are sown by the one Son of Man (Mt 13:24-30, 37-43).

---

[51]Contra Margaret Pamment, "The Son of Man in the First Gospel," *NTS* 29 (1983): 116-29. See also T. W. Manson, *The Teaching of Jesus: Studies of Its Form and Content* (New York: Cambridge University Press, 1945), 227-28, for the notion that "Son of Man" has a corporate aspect in that it fulfills the concept of the righteous remnant.

9

JESUS: ADDITIONAL ASPECTS OF CHRISTOLOGY

IN THE PROCESS OF EXPLORING how the various major titles function within the Gospel of Matthew we have already encountered dimensions of Matthew's presentation of Jesus that go beyond the titles. Nevertheless, it will be helpful to conclude with brief discussions of some additional aspects of Matthew's Christology.

PROPHET

A number of characters in Matthew's narrative construe Jesus as a prophet. Herod Antipas concludes that Jesus can perform mighty acts because Jesus is John the Baptist (whom the people hold to be a prophet) *redivivus* (Mt 14:1-5). We are told that the general opinion of "human beings" is that Jesus is a prophet (Mt 16:13-14). When Jesus enters Jerusalem, the crowds hail him as "the prophet Jesus from Nazareth" (Mt 21:11). And we are later told that the crowds "held him to be a prophet" (Mt 21:46). And in the wake of his condemnation by the Sanhedrin, the members of that body slap Jesus and say, "Prophesy to us, you Christ" (Mt 26:68).

Noteworthy about this catalog is that each of the characters or character groups who proclaim Jesus as a prophet is, from the point of view of Matthew, unreliable. Herod is a murderer (Mt 14:8-11); the Jewish crowds ultimately call out for Jesus' death (Mt 27:21, 25); and the members of the Sanhedrin, like Herod, are murderers, and at any rate are speaking ironically in that they do not themselves believe that Jesus is really a prophet. In fact, from Matthew's point of view, to consider Jesus to be a prophet is to misconstrue his identity. That Jesus is a prophet is the perspective of humans who have not received the revelation of God, while the only correct answer to the question of Jesus' identity is that he is "Son of God," for this insight comes from God and receives a blessing from God (Mt 16:13-17; cf. Mt 3:17; 17:5). Matthew indicates that because the crowds confessed that Jesus was a prophet and did not embrace the truth of his divine sonship, thus reflecting the point of view of humans which stands over that of God (Mt 16:17, 23), they ultimately turn on Jesus and demand his destruction.

Matthew insists that the prophets preceded Jesus and bore testimony to him. Accordingly, Jesus declares that "all the prophets and the law" prophesied until (and through) John, thus implying that the time of the prophets ended with John (Mt 11:13). Their role was to prepare for Jesus. Thus Jesus is the fulfillment of the prophets.[1]

And Jesus transcends the prophets. John the Baptist, the last and greatest of the prophets, who is himself "more than a prophet" (Mt 11:9-15), is unworthy to be Christ's slave (Mt 3:11). Jesus is "something greater than Jonah" (Mt 12:41). The prophet Elijah fades away before Jesus on the Mount of Transfiguration (Mt 17:1-5). And the parable of the wicked tenants differentiates between the prophets whom God repeatedly sent to Israel and Jesus as God's Son, in that the Son has a much higher status and a relationship with God that is of a transcendent character (Mt 21:33-41). Yet, in this parable, the Son shares the function of the prophets in relationship to Israel, namely, to gather from Israel a harvest of obedience that properly belongs to God and will be rendered to God.

Therefore, Matthew differentiates Jesus from the prophets. But he also relates Jesus to the prophets in three ways. For one thing, even as the prophets predicted the future accurately, so Jesus divulges the future according to God's plan.[2] Moreover, even as the prophets, along with the law, proclaimed truly God's will and ways, so does Jesus, for Jesus repeatedly appeals to "the law and prophets," or to various statements from the prophets, indicating that his message corresponds to theirs (e.g., Mt 5:17-19; 7:12; 9:13;

---

[1] Mt 1:22; 2:5, 15, 17, 23; 3:3; 4:14; 5:17; 8:17; 12:17; 13:17, 35; 21:4.
[2] Mt 10:16-23; 12:40; 16:4, 21, 27-28; 17:13, 22-23; 20:18-19; 21:41; 22:7; 23:29–25:46; 26:1, 20-25, 30-35.

11:7; 13:14; 15:6; 22:40). Finally, even as the prophets "came in the way of righteousness" (Mt 21:32), were rejected, persecuted and killed by their fellow Israelites to whom they were sent (Mt 5:11-12; 14:1-12; 17:10-13; 23:29-37), so also Jesus will suffer at their hands (Mt 17:12; 21:33-41). It is this correspondence of rejection that Jesus has in mind when he, repudiated in his hometown of Nazareth, utters the aphorism about a prophet not being without honor except in his own country (Mt 13:57).

But Matthew actually describes two sets of prophets who share Jesus' message and (in part) his vocation. Just as the Old Testament prophets preceded Jesus and bore witness to him during the time of preparation, so Jesus, after his resurrection, will send (Christian) prophets who will bear witness to him (e.g., 10:42). And as the prophets who preceded Jesus were rejected and persecuted unto death for their proclamation of "the way of righteousness" that was fulfilled in Jesus, so also these Christian prophets will suffer the same fate (Mt 23:29-37). Thus two groups of prophets stand on either side of Jesus, both bearing witness to him by their proclamation and by their rejection. Hence, even though Jesus participates in certain prophetic functions, he is not so much a prophet as the one to whom the prophets point.

TEACHER

Because of the preponderance of teaching material in the Gospel of Matthew, as evidenced, *inter alia*, by the five great discourses, and the several times that Jesus is described as "teaching" (Mt 4:23; 5:2; 7:29; 9:35; 11:1; 13:54; 21:23; 26:55), one may be forgiven for thinking that Matthew presents Jesus, above all, as teacher.[3] Yet it is a fact worthy of note that disciples, or persons of faith, never address Jesus as teacher, but, as we saw above, as "Lord," thereby acknowledging their submission in faith to his exalted status and divine authority. Only his opponents or those who fail to become disciples call Jesus "teacher" (διδάσκαλος, Mt 9:11; 12:38; 17:24; 19:16; 22:16, 24, 36; 26:18).[4]

---

[3] See, e.g., Samuel Byrskog, *Jesus the Only Teacher: Didactic Authority and Transmission in Ancient Israel, Ancient Judaism and the Matthean Community* (Stockholm: Almqvist & Wiksell, 1994), who speaks of "didactic Christology."
[4] Mt 8:19 is no exception, because this scribe, who attempts to initiate discipleship, is rebuffed by Jesus. See Jack Dean Kingsbury, "On Following Jesus: The 'Eager' Scribe and the 'Reluctant' Disciple (Mt 8:18-20)," *NTS* 34 (1988): 45-59.

Twice Judas, having relinquished his discipleship by betraying Jesus, addresses Jesus as "Rabbi," a term that had come to mean a teaching scribe, and thus a synonym of "teacher." Yet in Matthew 23:8 Jesus acknowledges his role as "teacher" of the disciples, and he indirectly does the same in an aphoristic saying in Matthew 10:24.

All of this suggests that although Jesus functions as a teacher, he is more than a teacher. And, consequently, to identify him as a teacher by addressing him as such is not simply to underestimate his status but to misconstrue his essential being and significance.

Yet the reader of the Gospel of Matthew recognizes the importance of teaching within the ministry of Jesus. In the Gospel of Matthew, teaching is essentially guidance in the ways and will of God, which involves at least implicit demand.[5] This guidance may be either accurate or inaccurate (e.g., Mt 5:19, 9). Most of the actual teaching of Jesus that Matthew presents is directed to the disciples; this is the case, for example, with all five great discourses. Nevertheless, Matthew frequently speaks of Jesus "teaching" the crowds (Mt 9:35; 11:1; 13:54; 26:55), yet in such cases the disciples are always present. Moreover, insofar as Matthew records this teaching to the crowds, we note that such teaching is pertinent primarily to "insiders," that is, to disciples, rather than to those on the outside, for such teaching expresses the principles of the kingdom that Jesus calls persons to enter through discipleship.[6]

Insofar as such teaching expresses the reality and ways of the kingdom it contains implicitly the proclamation that the kingdom of God has come in Jesus. Hence, Jesus' teaching the crowds is a form of preaching to them, a way of announcing the kingdom by describing its character and implementation. Thus, for instance, the crowds respond to the Sermon on the Mount by a recognition of the authority of Jesus, the teacher (Mt 7:28-29). Their experience of Jesus' teaching activity raises implicitly for them the "Jesus question": who is he, and what is his role in relation to the kingdom about which he teaches?

---

[5] This aspect is emphasized in Mt 28:20, "teaching them to observe all that I have *commanded* you." See also Mt 5:17-48.

[6] Thus David E. Garland, *The Intention of Matthew 23*, NovTSup 52 (Leiden: Brill, 1979), has demonstrated that this discourse, which is directed to the "crowds and to the disciples" (Mt 23:1) contains virtually exclusively instruction for Christian discipleship.

Jesus and Moses

In our discussion of the structure of the Gospel of Matthew, we saw that B. W. Bacon insisted that his fivefold division of the Gospel of Matthew corresponds to the five books of Moses in the Pentateuch, and that therefore Matthew presents Jesus as a new Moses who delivers a new law to his people. Although most recent scholars who have adopted Bacon's structure for the Gospel of Matthew do not consider "new Moses" to be a major christological category, certain other interpreters throughout the years, notably Dale C. Allison, have found additional connections between Jesus and Moses.[7]

Thus Herod's attempts to kill the infant Jesus, which are related to the infanticide of male children in Bethlehem (Mt 2:1-12, 16-18), recall Pharaoh's murder of the Israelite infants, which involved the attempted destruction of Moses (Ex 1-4). Even as God delivered the infant Moses from death at the hands of Pharaoh, so God delivers Jesus from death at the hands of Herod. The unexpected phrase "those who sought the child's life are dead" in Matthew 2:20 aligns with the angelic announcement to Moses in Exodus 4:19, when he, like Jesus in Matthew's story, is required to return to the land of Egypt so as to deliver his people Israel. Jesus' fasting for forty days and forty nights (Mt 4:2) reminds the readers that Moses was forty days and forty nights on Mount Sinai (Ex 34:28; Deut 9:9, 18). Jesus' ascent to the mountain to proclaim the Sermon on the Mount (Mt 5:1) may correspond to Moses' ascent to Mount Sinai where he received the law with a view to proclaiming it to the people (Ex 24–31). The ten mighty works of Jesus in Matthew 8–9 may recall the ten miracles (in this case, plagues) that Moses performed at the court of Pharaoh (Ex 7–12). The shining of Jesus' face on the Mount of Transfiguration (Mt 17:2) may correspond to the brightness of Moses' countenance as he descended Mount Sinai (Ex 34:29-35). The heavenly voice on the Mount of Transfiguration, with the addition to the divine announcement made in Matthew 3:17 of "listen to him" (Mt 17:5), may allude to Moses' command in Deuteronomy 18:15-16, "The Lord God will raise up a prophet like me from among your brethren—him you shall heed—just as you desired of the Lord your God at Horeb." And the Great Commission of Matthew 28:18-20, when Jesus, in his last appearance within the story

---

[7] Dale C. Allison Jr., *The New Moses: A Matthean Typology* (Minneapolis: Fortress, 1993). See also Wayne S. Baxter, "Mosaic Imagery in the Gospel of Matthew," *TJ* 20 (1999): 69-83.

of Matthew, commissions the eleven to make disciples of all nations may bring to mind Moses at the end of his life, when he commissioned Joshua to lead the people into the land of Canaan, with the promise of divine presence, where they would conquer the nations living there (Deut 31–34).

Clearly, some of these points of connection are more compelling than others. And in certain of these cases, as well as others he cites, Allison finds it necessary to bolster alleged Mosaic parallels with appeal to intertestamental Jewish literature which may or may not reflect the reservoir of background knowledge that the implied reader of the Gospel of Matthew would have possessed. Nevertheless, it is undeniable that at points (especially in Mt 1:18–2:23) Matthew has told the story of Jesus so as to correspond with that of Moses.[8] In addition to these possible parallels, Matthew mentions Moses explicitly seven times, though these do not so much concern the person of Moses himself, but are metonymic for the law.[9]

Matthew includes certain correspondences between Jesus and Moses in order to contribute to his broader claim that Jesus brings to fulfillment the whole history of Israel. The personage who, along with David and Abraham, is the most prominent in that history, and who, along with David and Abraham (and, of course, Noah), participated in the establishment of a covenant, was Moses. Matthew speaks within the genealogy of the role of David and Abraham in the history of Israel that has been brought to fulfillment in Jesus. But the constraints of the genealogy do not allow mention of Moses. Consequently, Matthew may have included these parallels in order to make the point that Jesus fulfills the role of Moses, even as the genealogy (and other passages throughout the Gospel of Matthew) indicate that Jesus fulfills the roles of David, and to a lesser extent, Abraham.

Jesus and Wisdom

It is appropriate to say something about the claim that Matthew 11:19 and Matthew 11:28-30 present Jesus as Wisdom incarnate, a theme that, it is

---

[8]See, e.g., Raymond E. Brown, *The Birth of the Messiah: A Commentary on the Infancy Narratives in the Gospels of Matthew and Luke*, new ed., ABRL (New York: Doubleday, 1993), 110-19; Anton Vögtle, "Die matthäische Kindheitsgeschichte," in M. Didier, *L'Évangile selon Matthieu: Rédaction et Théologie*, vol 29, BETL (Leuven: Peeters, 1972), 153-83.

[9]In two instances, Matthew reads "God said" where the Markan parallel has "Moses" (compare Mt 15:4 with Mk 7:10; and Mt 22:31 with Mk 12:6). In the context of both passages the Matthean Jesus emphasizes the difference between divine revelation and human thinking.

alleged, can be found elsewhere in the Gospel (especially Mt 23:34, 37), though these passages in Matthew 11 serve as the anchor to the argument.[10] As for Matthew 11:19, some insist that Matthew has altered the traditional saying that he found in Q and is known to us from Luke 7:35, "Wisdom is justified by all her children." By changing "children" to "deeds," it is said, Matthew has linked the deeds of wisdom to the "deeds of the Christ" (Mt 11:2) and consequently has identified Jesus with wisdom. And since wisdom is frequently personified in the Old Testament and intertestamental Jewish literature and is sometimes presented as preexistent (e.g., Prov 3:19; 8:3-36; Sir 24), some scholars who see wisdom Christology in this passage find also indication that Matthew presents Jesus as preexistent.[11] But although a connection exists with Matthew 11:2, the most immediate referent for the deeds of wisdom here are the deeds of Jesus *and* John the Baptist (Mt 11:17-19). And that which is "justified" here is not so much Jesus himself as it is the proclamation of the kingdom that is implicit in his mighty works (Mt 11:20-24).

Many of the same scholars discern a wisdom Christology also in Matthew 11:25-27, where, they claim, the theme of the unknowability of wisdom to any but God stands behind the unknowability of the Son to anyone except the Father (cf. Prov 30:3-4, 18-19). This hypothesis suffers from the observation that Matthew does not mention wisdom explicitly here, and the points of connection are vague.

The same cannot be said for Matthew 11:28-30, where Jesus employs two or three phrases that pertain to wisdom in Sirach 24; 51. But on closer examination one finds that the connections are not exact, and that much that stands at the center of Matthew 11:28-30 has nothing to do with these connections to wisdom. The passage echoes certain statements from Sirach, but these statements do not determine the meaning of Matthew 11:28-30 or the significance of Jesus as presented herein. The connections between

---

[10]See, e.g., Jack M. Suggs, *Wisdom, Christology, and Law in Matthew's Gospel* (Cambridge, MA: Harvard University Press, 1970); Cecilia Deutsch, "Wisdom in Matthew: Transformation of a Symbol," *NovT* 32 (1990): 13-47; Ben C. Witherington III, *Matthew*, SHBC (Macon, GA: Smyth & Helwys, 2006), 16-21.

[11]E.g., Robert G. Hamerton-Kelly, *Pre-Existence, Wisdom, and the Son of Man: A Study of the Idea of Pre-Existence in the New Testament*, SNTSMS 21 (New York: Cambridge University Press, 1973); and Felix Christ, *Jesus Sophia: Die Sophia-Christologie bei den Synoptikern* (Zurich: Zwingli-Verlag, 1970), 100-19.

wisdom and Matthew 23:34, 37 are even more tenuous. For critiques of the claim of wisdom Christology in these passages and elsewhere in the Gospel of Matthew, see the extended discussions by Graham Stanton, Marshall Johnson, R. T. France, and especially Simon Gathercole.[12]

Jesus and the Servant of Yahweh

Matthew's passion narrative makes a number of allusions to the Servant Songs of Isaiah, some of which I mentioned in the **interpretation** section above. Jesus' silence at his trials (Mt 26:62-63; 27:12) alludes to the Servant who "opened not his mouth" (Is 53:7), where the Servant assumes the role of the poor, righteous sufferer. Matthew alone mentions that Joseph of Arimathea, who laid Jesus in his tomb, was a "rich man" (Mt 27:57), thus drawing the connection with Isaiah 53:9: "They made his grave with . . . a rich man in his death." When, at the Last Supper, Jesus declares, "This is my blood . . . which is poured out for many for the forgiveness of sins" (Mt 26:28), he is alluding to Isaiah 53:10, "he makes himself an offering for sin," and to Isaiah 53:12, "he bore the sins of many." This reference to "many" in Isaiah 53:12 also lies behind the "many" in the Jesus' ransom saying at Matthew 20:28. But we find allusions to the Servant also outside of the passion narrative. When Jesus speaks of the "necessity" of his suffering and death, according to God's will as expressed in Scripture,[13] he is in all likelihood referencing Isaiah 53:10, "It was the will of the Lord to bruise him." And most interpreters hear an echo of Isaiah 42:1, along with Psalm 2:2, in the declaration from God at Matthew 3:17, "This is my beloved son, in whom I am well pleased."[14]

But the most obvious allusions to the Suffering Servant are the two fulfillment quotations that explicitly cite the Servant Songs. In Matthew 8:17 we learn that Isaiah 53:4, "He took our infirmities and bore our diseases," is

---

[12]Graham Stanton, "Salvation Proclaimed: X. Matthew 11:28-30: Comfortable Words?," *ExpTim* in 94 (1982-83): 3-9; Marshall D. Johnson, "Reflections on a Wisdom Approach to Matthew's Christology," *CBQ* 36 (1974): 44-64; R. T. France, *Matthew: Evangelist and Teacher* (Grand Rapids: Zondervan, 1989), 302-6; Simon Gathercole, *The Pre-existent Son: Recovering the Christologies of Matthew, Mark, and Luke* (Grand Rapids: Eerdmans, 2006), 193-209.

[13]In Mt 16:21, the first passion prediction, Jesus declares that he "must" suffer, die, and be raised. The term "must" (δεῖ) refers to that which is necessary to fulfill God's will, as the appearance of the same word at Mt 26:54.

[14]See the detailed discussion of the allusions behind Mt 3:17 in W. D. Davies and Dale C. Allison Jr., *The Gospel According to Saint Matthew*, ICC (New York: T&T Clark, 1997), 1:336-39.

fulfilled in Jesus' ministry of physical healing. Although this language in Isaiah can be taken to refer to physical infirmities and diseases, the context (of which Matthew was certainly aware) indicates that it is employed metaphorically for spiritual infirmity, that is, sin.[15] Matthew, then, is using this scriptural quotation to form a connection between Jesus' physical healings and his work of saving from sin, a link that he will make again in Matthew 9:1-9, 21-22 when he speaks of the healing of the woman as an act of salvation (σώζω; cf. Mt 1:21). The saving from sin and physical healings are not identical, but they are profoundly connected in that both involve the breaking of the power of cosmic evil that manifests itself in broken relationship to God as well as physical distress.

The second fulfillment quotation that features a Servant Song is Matthew 12:17-21, which comes on the heels of the first mention of the conspiracy on the part of the religious leaders to kill Jesus (Mt 12:14) and Jesus' consequent withdrawing from them and ordering those whom he heals not to make him known (Mt 12:15-16). We find the connection between the quotation and the narrative context in Matthew 12:19-20, where the Servant will realize his vocation of bringing righteous victory to the weak and vulnerable and hope to the Gentiles (Mt 12:18-21) by refusing to "wrangle or cry aloud" or letting his voice be heard in the streets. This passage explains, then, Jesus' repeated practice in these chapters of "withdrawing" (Mt 13:53; 15:21; 16:4) in the face of opposition and of attempting, in some measure, to keep his mighty acts a secret (Mt 8:4; 9:30; but cf. Mt 11:4-6): both are intended, at least in part, to avoid a premature confrontation that would compromise Jesus' ability to bring redemption to the weak and vulnerable and the realization of salvation to Gentiles. All of this is an expression of obedience to God and is accomplished through God's Spirit (Mt 12:18; cf. Mt 3:13-17). Even as the fulfillment quotation of Matthew 8:17 illumines the significance of Jesus' physical healings, so this quotation explains certain actions of Jesus whose purpose would otherwise remain obscure.

The motif of the "Servant of Yahweh," then, explains, clarifies, and gives depth to significant components of Jesus' actions and especially to his vocation of suffering, death, and resurrection. Moreover, it places these

---

[15]Note reference to "transgressions" and "iniquities" (Is 53:5), "gone astray" (Is 53:6), and "transgression" (Is 53:8).

actions and vocation within the framework of the fulfillment of Scripture and obedience to the will of God.

Jesus as "God with Us"

In the examination of the structure of the Gospel of Matthew we observed the key role played by the notion of the presence of Jesus as "God with us."[16] I noted that the Gospel of Matthew is framed by an inclusio around the theme of "with-ness," to coin a term,[17] since at the beginning of the Gospel of Matthew we learn that Jesus is "Emmanuel, God with us" (Mt 1:23), which has its parallel at the very end of the Gospel of Matthew where Jesus promises, "I will be with you always" (Mt 28:20). But Matthew 28:20 not only brackets Matthew 1:23, it also serves as the climax of a number of references to the presence of Jesus among his people. A most notable reference, and one that directly relates to Matthew 1:23 and Matthew 28:20, is found within the community discourse at Matthew 18:20: "Where two or three are gathered together in my name, there am I in the midst of them." Hubert Frankemölle has demonstrated that in the LXX ἐν μέσῳ ("in the midst") is equivalent to μετά ("with").[18] Thus Matthew places this theme of Jesus as God with us in the midst of his people at the beginning, middle, and end of the book.

In Matthew 1:23, Jesus, whose name means "Yahweh is salvation," is God's soteriological or salvational, presence with his people. The Old Testament often speaks of God's with-ness in terms of salvation or deliverance, but almost exclusively construes this divine salvation in terms of deliverance from military or political enemies, or from material want (that is, material blessings).[19] The reference here is to salvation from sins (Mt 1:21). This implies that the greatest problem facing God's people is sin, that is, broken relationship with God. God is powerfully present in Jesus, his Son, to

---

[16]For detailed treatments of this theme in Matthew, see David D. Kupp, *Matthew's Emmanuel: Divine Presence and God's People in the First Gospel*, SNTSMS 90 (New York: Cambridge University Press, 1996), and Hubert Frankemölle, *Jahwe-Bund und Kirche Christi: Studien zur Form- und Traditionsgeschichte des "Evangeliums" nach Matthäus*, Neutestamentliche Abhandlungen/Neue Folge 10 (Münster: Aschendorff, 1974).

[17]This is the English equivalent of the German *Mitsein*.

[18]Frankemölle, *Jahwe-Bund*, 30-32.

[19]E.g., Ex 3:12; Deut 20:1; Josh 22:31; Judg 2:18; 1 Sam 17:37; 2 Chron 36:23; Ezra 1:3; Ps 91:15 (90:15 LXX); Is 8:8-10 (where "Emmanuel" is employed); Is 41:10; 43:5.

accomplish reconciliation of the people to God in the sense that through Jesus God makes them "sons" who know or relate to God as "Father."

This passage also relates divine presence to peoplehood, for it is "his people" who will call his name "Emmanuel." This means, on the one hand, that God manifests his saving presence specifically among his *people*, that is, within the community. God mediates salvation to persons as they participate within the dynamics of the community in which Jesus continues to dwell (Mt 28:20). Indeed, Matthew never speaks of Jesus as God's presence being with "you" in the singular; it is always of matter of "you" in the plural or "them" (i.e., disciples).

But this concern to relate divine presence to peoplehood also means that it has significance for determining who, in fact, are God's people. In this passage, God's people are defined by those who declare that Jesus is "Emmanuel, God with us." The immediate context indicates that the people of Israel are in view (Mt 2:2, 6), suggesting that the purpose of this divine presence is that God would thereby mediate salvation to his people Israel. But the broader context of the Gospel of Matthew, beginning already with Matthew 2:3-6 and developing progressively throughout the book, indicates that the greater part of Israel rejects Jesus as God's Son and thus fails to confess that Jesus is "Emmanuel, God with us," thereby excluding themselves from the salvation that is promised in Matthew 1:21-23. It is the church, represented narratively by the disciples who confess that Jesus is God's Son, that experiences this divine presence (Mt 20:20, cf. Mt 28:16). Thus, the christological category of Jesus as God's presence has ecclesiological implications.

The notion of Jesus as "God with us" also raises the question of what this phrase might mean for the divine status of Jesus. In itself the statement is somewhat ambiguous in this regard. It could mean only that Jesus functions as the mediator of God's salvation. On the other hand, it might suggest that Jesus is himself God and that God is therefore personally present with his people in Jesus. The decision as to whether Matthew here attributes divine status to Jesus turns on the way in which the evangelist portrays Jesus in the remainder of the Gospel of Matthew, a matter I shall discuss in the final section of this chapter.

In Matthew 18:20 the phrase pertains to Jesus' ecclesial presence. As individual congregations of even the smallest size go about the difficult task of church discipline, deciding whether or not to expel members accused of errant behavior,[20] Jesus declares that, in answer to their prayer, God will adopt whatever they decide as the standard for inclusion or exclusion of such persons within the kingdom at the Great Assize (Mt 18:18-19). They can be assured that their decision reflects the will of God because in such deliberations, conducted within the sphere of Jesus' power and authority ("my name"), Jesus is in the midst of them. Commentators have long noted the parallel with the rabbinic statement associated with Hananaiah ben Teradyon in *m. 'Aboth* 3:2: "If two sit together and the words between them are of Torah, then the Shekinah is in the midst of them."[21] If, as most likely, the Matthean Jesus is drawing on such a rabbinic notion that was circulating already in the first century,[22] this passage speaks of the presence of God in the person of Jesus among those who are poring over both the Old Testament Scriptures, as explicated by Jesus, and the commandments of Christ (Mt 13:52, "things new and old"; cf. Mt 28:20) in order to discern the divine will regarding a particular disciplinary matter that was not specifically addressed in either the Old Testament Scriptures or the teachings of Jesus that had been passed on to them. The Jesus who is God-with-us as the one who continues in the post-resurrection period to speak to his people (Mt 28:18-20) directs them so they can hear God's own will for this new situation which now confronts them.

Insofar as this passage describes the circumstances of the post-Easter church, it makes clear that the reality of Jesus' God-with-us presence pertains not solely, or even primarily, to the physical presence of Jesus with his twelve disciples but involves his post-resurrection spiritual presence among his people. And insofar as this passage describes proceedings within individual congregations, it makes clear that the promise of Jesus' presence

---

[20]Mt 18:15-20 is the only passage in Matthew that deals with ecclesial process, thus the mention of presence suggests both the importance and difficulty of this responsibility of church discipline.

[21]See Hermann L. Strack and Paul Billerbeck, *Kommentar zum Neuen Testament aus Talmud und Midrasch*, 10e Aufl., 6 Bände (Munich: Beck, 1994), 1:794-95.

[22]Scholars disagree as to whether this rabbinic statement recorded in the Mishnah expresses earlier teaching that was known at the time of Jesus and the writing of Matthew, or whether it was produced as a response to Mt 18:20 in order to counter Matthew's claims regarding Christ here. Even if the latter is the case, it gives evidence that Mt 18:20 was understood by certain Jewish Christians as claiming that the presence of God's Shekinah-glory abides in the person of Jesus and is manifest as Christians reflect on their sacred writings. See Richard Hays, *Reading Backwards: Figural Christology and the Fourfold Gospel Witness* (Waco, TX: Baylor University Press, 2016), 45-46.

pertains not only to the universal church, but also to local assemblies. Moreover, even as Matthew 1:23 reflects those Old Testament passages that speak of the divine promise "I will be with you" in terms of *salvation*, so Matthew 18:20 reflects Old Testament passages that employ this notion to describe God's presence as *empowerment*, the ability to perform those divine demands that are humanly impossible but can be accomplished through the help that comes from God.[23]

Jesus' God-with-us presence as empowerment lies also behind the climactic promise of presence in Matthew 28:20. Jesus has just given to the eleven the impossible task to "make disciples of all nations," rendered all the more difficult because the same kind of opposition which had been directed against Jesus is now aimed, with some success, against the disciples (Mt 28:11-15). These are the disciples who, earlier in the narrative, proved unable to exercise the authority that Jesus had given to them to heal and cast out demons even within Israel while Jesus was physically present with them (Mt 17:14-21) and who retreated in the presence of need rather than even attempting to help (Mt 15:21-28, 32-39).

The promise at the end of Matthew 28:20 substantiates the missionary commission of Matthew 28:19-20 in two ways. It insists that the power of God in the person of Jesus his Son alone makes possible the realization of the demands of the commission, for this Jesus has now been granted "all authority in heaven and on earth" (Mt 28:18). And it therefore also gives encouragement to the post-Easter church to pursue this operation of worldwide evangelization.

But it is possible that the causal nexus works also in the opposite direction. As the church engages in this global missionary activity the result will be an experience of the presence of God in the person of his Son Jesus that would otherwise remain unrealized. If so, this would reflect a third major usage of "I am with you" in the Old Testament, namely divine presence in terms of blessing.[24] The presence of God among God's people, the spring

---

[23]E.g., Ex 3:11-12; Num 14:42-43; Deut 1:42; Josh 1:5; 7:12; Judg 6:16; 1 Sam 18:12; 2 Chron 25:7; Hag 2:4-5.

[24]E.g., Gen 21:22; 26:24, 28; 31:5; 39:2-3, 21, 23; Deut 2:7; Josh 6:27; 1 Sam 16:18; 18:12, 18, 28; 2 Sam 7:3; 1 Kings 11:38; 2 Kings 18:7; 1 Chron 11:9; 17:2; 22:11, 16, 18; 2 Chron 1:1; Job 29:5. Although most of these OT passages describe material blessings, the blessings associated with the presence of Jesus who is God with us are given specific description throughout the Gospel of Matthew, e.g., 5:3-11; 13:16; 24:46.

of blessing and wholeness which had been located in the temple, is now encountered in the person of Jesus.[25] But disciples experience this presence not in Jerusalem or even as they stay in Galilee, but as they "go and make disciples of all nations."

Even as Matthew 1:23 speaks of soteriological with-ness, and Matthew 18:20 refers to ecclesial with-ness, Matthew 28:20 describes missional with-ness. And insofar as Matthew 28:20 brings to a climax these earlier forms of God's presence in Jesus, it may indicate that, to some extent at least, these earlier types of with-ness exist for the sake of the global mission of the church. If so, the purpose of the saving presence is not simply that members of the church might themselves experience salvation, but that such an experience of salvation will be the basis for their serving as the agents of salvation to the nations of the world (Mt 5:43-48; 9:35–11:1; 24:14). And, accordingly, the purpose of the ecclesial presence is not exhausted by the experience of communal wholeness that results from a healthy handling of church discipline, but rather such presence equips the church to witness to the world through its own purity, peace, and love (Mt 5:3-16).

But we find in Matthew also eschatological with-ness, for Jesus declares that a "new" level of intimacy with him who is God with us will be experienced only at the eschatological messianic banquet, of which the Lord's Supper is an anticipation (Mt 26:29; cf. Mt 26:18, 20). Yet both missional and eschatological with-ness are provisional, dependent on "watching with me," that is, joining with Jesus in total dependence on God in the face of the temptation that is implicit in persecution and tribulation (Mt 26:38, 40).

Jesus and God

Every aspect of Christology that we have treated pertains, at least to some extent, to Jesus' relationship to God, whether Son of God, or Christ who has been anointed by God, or Son of David who ushers in the kingdom of God, or the Servant of Yahweh. Hence one aspect of Christology begs to be explored, namely the identification of Jesus with God. We noted that the issue is prompted by the designation, early in the Gospel of Matthew, of Jesus as "God with us" (Mt 1:23). In what sense, then, is Jesus God with us?

---

[25]Kupp, *Matthew's Emmanuel*, 88-108.

Jesus: Additional Aspects of Christology

We have already observed that Matthew repeatedly applies to Jesus the title "Lord" (κύριος), the same designation that he employs in several passages to refer to the God of the Old Testament. And we saw, too, that in several instances Matthew describes Jesus as "Lord" in the same way in which the Old Testament speaks of Yahweh as Lord. At this point I will discuss several additional passages in which Matthew seems to associate Jesus with the person of God.

First, Matthew sometimes attributes to Jesus functions that belonged to Yahweh in the Old Testament. Thus in Matthew 3:11 John declares that the coming one will "baptize you with the Holy Spirit," recalling that in the Old Testament it is God who pours out his Spirit (e.g., Is 44:3; Ezek 39:29; Joel 2:28-30 [LXX 3:1-2]). The words of Jesus have power to determine a person's destiny (Mt 7:24-27), recalling the same claim made regarding the words of God in Deuteronomy 11:26-32; 30:1-20. Matthew 8:27 reports that Jesus stilled the sea, so that "even the winds and sea obey him," recalling what is said of God in Psalm 107:29, "He made the storm be still, / and the waves of the sea were hushed." In Matthew 11:28-29 Jesus promises to give "rest," consistently a function of Yahweh in the Old Testament.[26] In Matthew 23:39 Jesus declares that often he wished to gather Jerusalem's children "under his wings," an expression regularly used of God in the Scriptures (e.g., Ex 19:4; Deut 32:11; Ps 17:8; 36:7; 63:7; 91:4). In Matthew 24:35 Jesus insists that, in contrast to heaven and earth, "my words will not pass away," reminiscent of Isaiah 40:8, "The grass withers, the flower fades; / but the word of our God will stand forever." When Jesus describes the coming of the Son of Man "and all his angels with him" (Mt 25:31), he echoes what is said regarding the coming of God in Zechariah 14:5: "The Lord will come, and all his holy ones with him."

Second, Matthew often attributes to Jesus a God-like status or function. Thus John the Baptist, whom Jesus dubs the greatest human who ever lived (Mt 11:11), declares that he is unworthy to be his slave (Mt 3:11). John also implies the sinlessness of Jesus, since John declares that Jesus has no need to submit to a baptism of repentance (Mt 3:14). In Matthew 5:21-48 Jesus sets his own commands over against the wording of God's law. Similarly, discipleship to Jesus trumps observance of the law (Mt 8:22). Jesus exercises

---

[26]E.g., 2 Sam 7:11; 1 Chron 22:9, in both passages the same word, ἀναπαύσω, occurs; also Is 14:3.

control over nature (Mt 17:27) and has prerogative over creation (Mt 21:3). Jesus appears to have something approaching a God-like knowledge, for he is aware of things about which he has not been informed (Mt 17:25),[27] and he knows specifics of the future that could not be deduced on the basis of empirical observation (Mt 26:3-5, 21-25, 34, 46-47). And Jesus implies equality, and perhaps unity with the Father, when he commands baptism in the one name (ὄνομα) of "the Father, Son, and Holy Spirit." (Although to talk about this as "trinitarian" is anachronistic, in that to do so implies a level of reflection about the relationship between the Father, Son, and Spirit that Matthew has not pursued.)

Yet perhaps the strongest indicator of Jesus' deity in the Gospel of Matthew is that Jesus is worshiped (προσκυνέω).[28] Although προσκυνέω can signify homage paid to a king or patron, as we saw, in several places in the Gospel of Matthew it must refer to the worship of Jesus which is appropriate to deity (Mt 14:32; 28:9, 17); and these instances suggest that its use on other occasions where the notion of homage would be possible may contain overtones of the worship of Jesus as divine.[29] When Jesus declares in Matthew 4:10, quoting Deuteronomy 6:13, "You shall worship the Lord your God and him only shall you serve," he himself suggests that for anyone but God to accept worship would be not only to countenance blasphemy but to commit blasphemy.

Yet Matthew portrays Jesus also as possessing attributes that belong to human beings over against God. For example, Jesus is tempted by the devil (Mt 4:1-10); he is hungry (Mt 4:2); he depends on angels ministering to him (Mt 4:11); he gives thanks to God (Mt 11:25; 15:36); and he prays to the Father (Mt 14:23; 19:13). And it is the Father, not Jesus, who has the prerogative to determine who will occupy seats of authority in the coming kingdom (Mt 20:23). Nor does Jesus know the day or the hour of the coming of the Son of Man (Mt 24:36); this is knowledge reserved for the Father. Moreover,

---

[27]Note that Matthew is careful to indicate that Jesus spoke to Simon before the latter had an opportunity to divulge to Jesus the conversation with the collectors of the tax.

[28]The Gospel of Matthew is the only synoptic Gospel that speaks of the worship of Jesus, with the exception of one likely Lucan reference to the worship of the risen Jesus (Lk 24:52), although Mark uses προσκυνέω once to describe reverence paid to Jesus by the Gerasene demoniac (Mk 5:6). For a detailed argument that Matthew's use of προσκυνέω points to Jesus' deity, see Joshua E. Leim, *Matthew's Theological Grammar: The Father and the Son*, WUNT 2/402 (Tübingen: Mohr Siebeck, 2015).

[29]Hays, *Reading Backwards*, 44-45, 53; Larry Hurtado, *Lord Jesus Christ: Devotion to Jesus in Earliest Christianity* (Grand Rapids: Eerdmans, 2003), 337-38.

Matthew gives no indication of Jesus' preexistence, although he says nothing that would necessarily preclude it.[30]

In sum, then, Matthew gives several indications, most significantly the worship of Jesus, that Jesus is divine as well as human. Jesus' relationship to God is characterized by both equality and subordination. This is not to suggest that Matthew offers the clear and explicit portrayal of the deity of Jesus that we find in the Gospel of John, nor that Matthew communicates anything like a worked-out Chalcedonian Christology. But his presentation of Jesus, with its indirect suggestions of deity, served as an understandable foundation for later christological conceptualizations.

Indeed, Matthew's portrait of Jesus does not focus on ontology, that is, issues pertaining to his being. Any ontological claims must be inferred from Jesus' actions and relationships, both to God and to other persons. Rather, Matthew presents Jesus' association with God in functional and relational terms. The primary claims Matthew wishes to make about Jesus are that he functions with divine authority and that he is perfectly obedient to the will of his Father.

---

[30]Contra Gathercole, *Pre-existent Son*, 214-20, who argues that Jesus' statement in Mt 23:37 points to his preexistence; since, according to Matthew's narrative, Jesus had not visited Jerusalem before, Jesus must be referring to his attempts to gather Jerusalem's children throughout Israel's history. Most commentators, however, believe that Mt 23:37 contains a hint that Jesus had ministered in Jerusalem previously, though unrecorded by this Gospel. See, e.g., Robert H. Gundry, *Matthew: A Commentary on His Handbook for a Mixed Church Under Persecution*, 2nd ed. (Grand Rapids: Eerdmans, 1994), 473; Pierre Bonnard, *L'Évangile selon saint Matthieu* (Geneva: Labor et Fides, 2002), 342; R. T. France, *The Gospel of Matthew*, NICNT (Grand Rapids: Eerdmans, 2007), 883; Hagner, *Matthew 14-18*, 680.

10

GOD

IN ONE WAY, it is strange that treatments of the theology of Matthew generally give no separate attention to Matthew's presentation of God. God is, after all, the ultimate reality in the narrative world of the Gospel of Matthew and is the final arbiter of what is true and untrue, and of what is right and wrong. Matthew indicates this determinant role of God at the very beginning of his Gospel; immediately after giving his own testimony about Jesus, the evangelist supports this testimony by appeal to the genealogy, which is actually an appeal to the God who reveals his purposes and will through the history of God's people Israel, as recorded in the Scriptures. In other words, the reliability of the narrator is dependent on his agreement with God as God has expressed his point of view in the Scriptures. And, as we shall see momentarily, Matthew emphasizes in the early chapters that the history he records moves along according to the will and purpose of God set forth in the Scriptures. God is Lord not only of creation (e.g., Mt 6:25-33; 19:4), but also of history, and particularly the history that Matthew reports in the Gospel of Matthew.

But, on the other hand, it is in some ways understandable that interpreters of Matthew give little specific attention to the theological significance of God, for in large measure God remains hidden behind his intermediaries, who, in a sense, front for him. The main "front" for God is, of course, Jesus. But, as we shall see, there are also other ways in which God communicates and acts indirectly into the world of the Gospel of Matthew.

These initial considerations actually lead us to the first thing that we might say regarding Matthew's portrait of God, namely that God is both transcendent and immanent. That God is transcendent, that is, "wholly other," requires no argument. Matthew emphasizes God's transcendence by his lavish use of the divine passive, which, as we saw above, is a way of talking about God without using the name "God," so as to avoid violating the sacredness of God's name by uttering it unnecessarily.[1] The name of God, which is the manifestation of his person to the world, and thus identified with his person in the closest possible way, is holy (Mt 6:9). Matthew expresses God's transcendence also by repeatedly substituting "heaven" for the name of God, which may, like the divine passive, be a means of talking about God without using the name "God," so sanctifying his name. But Pennington has demonstrated that when Matthew uses "heaven" in relation to God he does so in order to emphasize the great gulf separating the transcendent realm of God from the mundane sphere of this world. Indeed, when speaking of "heaven" as the place where God dwells Matthew typically employs the plural, so as to set it off from the sky, making it clear that God stands over and above every aspect of this world, even the heights.[2] The earth is but the "footstool" of God (Mt 5:35).

Yet God, as transcendent one, is also immanent, that is, active in the world. The transcendent God becomes immanent especially in Jesus, who is "God with us." When interpreted in light of the broader context of the Gospel of Matthew, this phrase has overtones of deity; yet it is actually Jesus' humanity that makes this revelation of God accessible to "us." At any rate, as we saw above, Matthew emphasizes the functional and relational aspects of Jesus' role as "God with us."

This reality of God-with-us in Jesus is accomplished through the Holy Spirit. While in the Book of Acts the Holy Spirit is the means whereby the exalted Christ is operative in the world, and especially among his people,[3] in the Gospel of Matthew the Spirit is the means whereby God is operative

---

[1] Hans Bietenhard, "ὄνομα," *TDNT*, 5:242-83.
[2] Jonathan Pennington, *Heaven and Earth in the Gospel of Matthew*, NovTSup 126 (Leiden: Brill, 2007), 125-351, notes that Matthew typically employs the singular when referring to the sky or when he pairs "heaven and earth" by way of contrast. But when Matthew uses this term in conjunction with the Father or the kingdom he always employs the plural.
[3] E.g., Alan J. Thompson, *The Acts of the Risen Lord Jesus: Luke's Account of God's Unfolding Plan*, NSBT (Downers Grove, IL: InterVarsity Press, 2011), 129-32.

in *Jesus*.[4] And the Holy Spirit is operative in Jesus to make God present to his people in Jesus, both as Jesus is physically "with" his disciples throughout his ministry, and as Jesus will be "with" his post-Easter disciples in a way that transcends physical presence. The Holy Spirit is the means of the accomplishment of God's purposes in him. The Holy Spirit is in Jesus inherently, on the basis of the Spirit's participation in the conception of Jesus and is thus part of the essential personhood of Jesus. But the Spirit also comes on Jesus, as it were, from the outside, at his baptism, a descent on him which Jesus himself witnesses, thereby emphasizing the externality of the reception,[5] thus complementing the interiority of the Spirit implied by the virgin conception.

The Spirit is not only the source of moral empowerment over temptation for Jesus (Mt 4:1-10), but also the one who leads Jesus to the place of testing (Mt 4:1), even as God "led" Israel into the wilderness to "test" Israel (Deut 8:2). Thus this level of temptation comes only after Jesus has been baptized with the Spirit. The Holy Spirit, then, operates within Jesus according to the prompting of God. The Holy Spirit is the agent of God's acting in Jesus. This is why the sin against the Holy Spirit involves the charge pertaining to what *Jesus* is doing. The accusation by the Pharisees that Jesus casts out demons by the prince of demons, which is the substance of the sin against the Holy Spirit, is an attack on the operative power within Jesus.

Although the transcendent God becomes immanent primarily in the person and work of Jesus, God is also actively involved in the historical process, but in an even more indirect way than he is active through his Spirit in the person of Jesus. Matthew sets forth this activity in history most prominently in the first major division (Mt 1:1-4:16), and these chapters are foundational to God's activity throughout the remainder of the Gospel of Matthew.[6] In other words, at the beginning of the Gospel, Matthew presents a pattern of God's operation in the world according to which the reader is expected to construe the rest of the narrative. Here the activity of God in the world takes two forms.

---

[4]R. W. L. Moberly, *The Bible, Theology, and Faith: A Study of Abraham and Jesus*, CSCD (New York: Cambridge University Press, 2000), 197-98.
[5]Matthew is careful to note that Jesus "saw" the Spirit descending on him (Mt 3:16).
[6]Thus David D. Kupp, *Matthew's Emmanuel: Divine Presence and God's People in the First Gospel*, SNTSMS 90 (New York: Cambridge University Press, 1996), 56-63, though Kupp limits this foundational role to Mt 1–2.

The first way in which God invades history is through "the angel of the Lord," who appears five times in Matthew 1:18–2:23 (Mt 1:20; 2:12, 13, 19, 22).[7] The angel betokens God's transcendence, since the angel is the mediating voice between God and the persons addressed, and even more so since the angel speaks here only through dreams. In the Gospel of Matthew, no one actually sees or converses with an angel, with the exception of the women at the tomb in Matthew 28:1-7.[8]

God orchestrates events through the activity of his angel. By this means God reveals his will to his righteous ones, and in their responsive obedience they bring about the accomplishment of God's will on the plane of history. But angels play no significant role in the narrative after Matthew 2, because after Matthew 3:1 the revelation of God comes not through the voice of angels in dreams, but through the voice of Jesus. It is only when the voice of Jesus is essentially silenced that an angelic revelation through a dream reoccurs (Mt 27:19).

Yet the dream-revelations in Matthew 1:18–2:23 do have a continuing impact on the reader's sense of God's immanent activity throughout the rest of the narrative. By his response to the dream-revelation in fearful circumstances, Joseph anticipates Jesus' perfect obedience to the will of God throughout the Gospel of Matthew and illumines how Jesus' compliance to God's will, even in the midst of fearful opposition, realizes God's redemptive purposes. In the Gospel of Matthew, only Joseph and Jesus are described as "righteous" (δίκαιος, Mt 1:19; 27:19).

By their response to the dream revelation, the magi foreshadow how disciples will participate in the realization of God's purposes as they obey the divine revelation that will come to them through Jesus, and, unlike the case of the magi, no longer through angels; for disciples, Jesus will be the voice through whom God speaks. The Gentile magi prepare especially for those who will become disciples through the post-Easter process of discipling the

---

[7] Although Matthew does not mention the angel explicitly in Mt 2:12 and Mt 2:22, the repetition of "dream" and the presence of the pattern throughout indicate that the angel was involved in these instances as well.

[8] The exceptional character of this angelic revelation, not in a dream but face to face, points to the significance of this event: it is precisely *not* a vision, but the making known by full sensory experience of an actual event. The point is that it is God, through his angel, who is revealing the empty tomb to the women. See Kristian A. Bendoraitis, *Behold the Angels Came and Served Him: A Compositional Analysis of Angels in Matthew*, LNTS 523 (New York: T&T Clark, 2015), 186-99.

nations. Like the magi, they will come from afar (cf. Mt 8:11) to worship Jesus and effect God's purposes by refusing to accede to the demands of powerful and manipulative tyrants but instead obey the voice of God that comes to them through the continuing speaking of the exalted Christ (Mt 28:18-20).

The second way in which Matthew presents God as effectively involved in the course of history is through the fulfillment quotations that, like the angelic dreams, cluster in the first major division (Mt 1:22-23; 2:5-6, 15, 17-18, 23; 3:3, 15).[9] Seven of the twelve fulfillment quotations that punctuate the whole of the Gospel of Matthew are found here. These quotations are spoken directly to the implied reader, and through these fulfillment quotations Matthew indicates to the reader that God is, to use Hays's term, "scripting" the Jesus story, and really the entire time of fulfillment. In other words, God is implementing his plan and purposes, which he has made known in the Scriptures, in the events surrounding Jesus.[10] The stereotyped fulfillment quotations actually represent only about a fifth of the Old Testament quotations Matthew includes throughout his Gospel,[11] and therefore they are representative of a much wider scriptural framework that pervades the Gospel of Matthew and that suggests that all the events herein reported accord, at least at some level, with the will and purpose of God.

And yet the way in which that divine will and purpose play out in the narrative is complicated, because it confronts the dynamic realities of human decision and human history. The complication from human history is represented in Matthew 2:20-22, where the divine intention, enunciated by the angel, for the holy family to "go to the land of Israel" (Mt 2:20) is altered because of the enthronement of Archelaus over Judea. The quotation of Matthew 2:23 marks fulfillment, but only through this circuitous path.

And we encounter the complication from human decision when we see that God's purposes, as set forth in Scripture, are fulfilled not only by the

---

[9]It is true that Mt 2:5-6 and Mt 3:3 lack the typical introductory formula, but they function in the same way as the other quotations that have the formula and should therefore be included with them.

[10]Richard Hays, *Reading Backwards: Figural Christology and the Fourfold Gospel Witness* (Waco, TX: Baylor University Press, 2016), 37-38.

[11]According to Donald Senior, the Gospel of Matthew includes 61 OT quotations. See Donald Senior, "The Lure of the Formula Quotations: Re-assessing Matthew's Use of the Old Testament with the Passion Narrative as a Test Case," in *The Scriptures in the Gospels*, ed. Christopher Mark Tuckett, BETL 131 (Leuven: Leuven University Press, 1977), 90, cited by Hays, *Reading Backwards*, 38.

obedient response to the revelation of God on the part of obedient ones, but also by the outrageous, evil act of the murder of the Bethlehem infants (Mt 2:16-18). Here God uses the most wicked intentions of Herod ultimately to fulfill God's plan. God does not work in spite of Herod's evil infanticide, but through it, even as later God will use the human evil of Christocide to achieve his ultimate good purposes of redemption (Mt 20:28; 26:28). This is not monism, according to which God works out his purposes in history ultimately on his own without any authentic human involvement. Persons act not from predetermined divine fiat, but from the deep intentions of their own hearts (Mt 7:15-19; 12:33-37; 15:17-20; 23:26); accordingly, God will judge them on the basis of their decisions, which mirror their inner life.[12] But God sovereignly uses all actions, including even those, like the murder of infants, of which he does not approve (e.g., Mt 5:21-22; 15:19; 26:52), somehow to fulfill his purposes.

The discussion thus far has shown not only that God is effectively, though indirectly, active in history, and especially the Christ history, but also that God reveals himself, and particularly his purposes and will. In addition to God's revelation through Jesus, through angelic communication, and through the witness of Scripture, God reveals his ways and will also in nature and even in the typical ordering of human life, as the parables make clear.[13] Indeed, God prompts the first christological confession in the Gospel of Matthew by way of the appearance of a star (Mt 2:1, 9-10). But these insights into God's ways and purposes that come through nature and human life must be interpreted by Scripture (Mt 2:1-13) or by the teaching of Jesus (Mt 12:10-14), in other words, "treasures . . . new and old" (Mt 13:52); otherwise, they remain a mystery (Mt 13:35).

Among the things that God reveals about himself is that, as the transcendent one, he is the ultimate reality in the world, and therefore devotion to him must be exclusive. God is alone to be worshiped and served (Mt 4:10). But the formal act of worship is not the same as rendering the kind of service which God demands; that is a matter of intimacy of heart, of oneness with God in fellowship and will (Mt 15:8-9).

---

[12]Note, e.g., that in the same breath Jesus declares that Judas' betrayal fulfills Scripture and that Judas will be horrifically punished for his crime (Mt 27:24).

[13]In nature: Mt 7:15-23; 13:3-23, 24-30, 31-33; 24:32-35. In human life: Mt 7:9-11, 24-27; 13:44-50; 17:24-27; 18:10-14, 31-35; 21:28-32, 33-46; 22:1-14; 24:42-51; 25:1-30.

Division of loyalty to God is impossible (Mt 6:24). The desire to be praised by humans excludes the possibility of reward from the Father (Mt 6:1-18). Serving God and material possessions are also mutually exclusive (Mt 6:24). Indeed, one can know God as Father only by forsaking relationship with earthly fathers (Mt 4:21; cf. the repetition of "your [heavenly] Father" in Mt 5:1–7:29).

God reveals also that he is good. In the Gospel of Matthew this means that he is committed to making possible for others (including even plants and animals) the satisfying experience of realizing their full and proper purpose as God intended it (what Pennington calls "flourishing"). Indeed, only God is good (Mt 19:16-17), and all human "goodness" pales in comparison to the goodness of God, and certainly is inadequate to achieve eternal life, which is made possible only by the gracious power of God (Mt 19:25-26). God is the Lord of all creation (Mt 6:26-30; 10:29), and as such not only gives to creatures what they need, but is extravagant, providing beauty as well as sustenance (Mt 6:28-30). Yet God is primarily concerned with persons (Mt 6:26-30; 10:30-31), in that he numbers the hairs of their head (Mt 10:30). He delights in generosity (Mt 20:1-16), and therefore gives "good things" to those who ask him (Mt 7:7-11). And God provides for all, regardless of their moral behavior, out of a deep love for them (Mt 5:43-45).

God has directed his attentive goodness especially to Israel, his "son" (Mt 2:15; 15:24), for he is "the God of Israel" (Mt 15:31). But God welcomes all into the kingdom, on the basis of faith (Mt 8:10-11), especially after the "children" have been fed from the table, that is, after the offer of the salvation of the kingdom has been made to Israel (Mt 15:22-28), and in the wake of Israel's rejection of his Son (Mt 21:33–22:10). Thus, God is especially desirous to restore all persons to right relationship with himself, since that relationship has been ruptured by "sins" (Mt 1:21; 20:28; 26:28), and to do so through the forgiveness of sins (Mt 6:9-15; 9:2-6; 12:31; 26:28), thereby making persons "sons" to whom he is "Father."

Accordingly, God focuses his loving and active care on these sons of the Father. Those who are not his children do not recognize God as a generous giver, and therefore live in anxiety (Mt 6:32) or with a sense that they must struggle to gain God's attention (Mt 6:7). But the very fact that God knows what his children need means that he is anxious to give it to them (Mt 6:8, 32).

Nevertheless, God expects that they should ask him in prayer, with faith (Mt 17:20-21; 21:20-22); insofar as they do so, no good and proper thing will be impossible for them (Mt 19:26; 7:11, cf. Mt 26:39-44), including the overcoming of temptation (Mt 26:41). God is especially responsive to the united prayer of the community that gathers in the name of Jesus, even if small in number (Mt 18:19). And God exercises particular care toward the weak and vulnerable among his children; their angels have most intimate access to God's throne and behold his face (Mt 18:11).

God reveals also that he is characterized by wrath, which is the divine response to the repudiation of God's purposes and will (Mt 7:21), centered in the double command to love God with all one's being and to love one's neighbor as oneself (Mt 22:34-40). God is judge (Mt 5:21-22), who is capable of executing great and drastic punishment (Mt 5:22), insofar as he can destroy both soul and body in hell (Mt 5:29-30; 10:28; 18:7-10 [note the divine passive]). God's verdict will be based, at least in part, on the testimony of Jesus before the judgment seat of God, which itself reflects persons' public embrace or disavowal of Jesus (Mt 10:32-33). Yet God not only judges sin but rewards righteousness (Mt 5:46; 6:1, 4, 6). God will humble the exalted and exalt the humble (Mt 23:12).

God will also execute judgment on Israel in the form of the destruction of Jerusalem, including the temple (Mt 21:41; 22:1-10; maybe also Mt 24:2 with possible divine passive). In response to Israel's murderous rejection of his Son, God will destroy the nation and give the kingdom of God to others (Mt 21:33–22:14). But even those who answer the invitation to enter the kingdom will be judged by God if they are not clothed in righteousness (Mt 22:11-14).

Yet God's judgment begins even now in terms of his decree of understanding. God has decreed that those who depend on their own (human) wit and understanding will experience a kind of darkening of the mind, unable to comprehend the saving mysteries of the kingdom, while to those who, like infants, are open to the radically alternative perspective of the preaching of the kingdom, God will grant saving knowledge (Mt 11:25-26).

At all three of these levels of judgment (final, destruction of Jerusalem, present darkening/enlightenment) God has given to Jesus the authority to judge (e.g., Mt 7:21-23; 13:10-17; 25:31-46). The most economical way to understand the relationship between passages that describe God as judge and those that describe Jesus in the same terms is that God has given to Jesus authority to execute God's own judgment (Mt 11:27; 28:20). All of this, of course, has to do with eschatology, a matter to which we now turn.

11

SALVATION HISTORY AND ESCHATOLOGY

SALVATION HISTORY AND ESCHATOLOGY BELONG together because they both have to do with God's activity throughout history. Salvation history pertains to the development of God's redemptive work in history, while eschatology pertains to the culmination of that redemptive work.

Actually, eschatology intersects with salvation history at two levels. On one level, the Christ event brings to culmination, or fulfillment, God's previous dealings with Israel and inaugurates God's end-time rule. Thus the Christ event, which includes the time of the church when Jesus continues to dwell in the midst of his people, is "inaugurated eschatology." This inaugurated eschatology involves the initial coming of the end-time kingdom of God in the person and ministry of Jesus, and the experience of salvation that is associated with the kingdom in its present manifestation. On another level, the eschaton, or what Matthew calls "the end of the age," is the point at which God will bring to final culmination the entire historical process. We may therefore dub this event, and all that pertains to it, "consummated eschatology." This consummated eschatology involves the coming of the end-time kingdom of God in its full, future sense, and the experience of salvation, and judgment, that is associated with the kingdom in its future manifestation. The broad topic of "salvation history and eschatology" breaks down, then, into three specific areas: fulfillment, the kingdom of heaven/God, and the consummation.

Fulfillment

It is a truism that all the Gospels consider Jesus and the kingdom that he inaugurates to be the fulfillment of God's past dealings with his people Israel. But the theme of fulfillment is more prominent in the Gospel of Matthew than in the others. No other Gospel begins with a genealogy describing Jesus as the culmination of Israel's history through Abraham and David.[1] And no other Gospel contains a discrete set of Old Testament quotations that are introduced with a formula that speaks explicitly of fulfillment.

Matthew introduces the notion of fulfillment in the genealogy (Mt 1:1-17). Because the genealogy narrates the action of Abraham (literally, "he begat") and those of his named descendants, the narrative world of the Gospel of Matthew begins with Abraham and includes the history of Israel. Matthew thereby brings the entire history of Israel prior to Jesus into the story of Jesus and makes it part of Jesus' story. Matthew reinforces this incorporation of the story of Israel into the Jesus story by the way he designates the genealogy. Insofar as it is "the book of the genealogy of Jesus Christ," that which is contained in the genealogy is ultimately about Jesus; Israel's history is really his history. The structure of the genealogy also serves to incorporate Abraham and David, and all the others who are named, into the story of Jesus. The chiasm in this passage—Christ, David, Abraham (Mt 1:1)/Abraham, David, Christ (Mt 1:2, 6, 16)—brackets Abraham and David with Christ, and thereby subordinates them, and all the other generations herein mentioned, to "Jesus, who is called Christ."

This genealogy is therefore not a bare record of physical lineage. In fact, Matthew 1:18-25 makes clear that it does not involve the physical lineage of Jesus at all, since Jesus is not the biological son of Joseph. Rather, the genealogy is a theological interpretation of the history of Israel from the perspective of the fulfillment of that history in "Jesus, who is called Christ" (Mt 1:16).

Insofar as Matthew brings the genealogical list to a climax in the birth of Jesus, who is called Christ, he makes the central claim that Jesus brings the whole history of Israel to its fulfillment as its τέλος, or goal, in whom Abraham, and David, and the entire history for that matter finds their

---

[1] The Gospel of Luke does include a genealogy, but it traces Jesus' lineage finally to Adam, betokening a primary interest in Jesus' relationship to humanity rather than to Israel (Lk 3:23-38). Admittedly, Luke has a significant concern to demonstrate that Jesus is the fulfillment of the OT Scriptures, but the interest is not as prominent in Luke as in Matthew.

ultimate significance. As we saw in the discussion of this passage in the **interpretation** section above, Jesus brings to realization, in a way that Israel never did, the divine purpose related to the Abrahamic covenant, namely that in Abraham's "seed," that is, the people of Israel, "all the nations of the earth will be blessed" (Gen 22:18). In the broad sweep of the Old Testament this purpose was to be achieved when all the nations would stream to Jerusalem and learn of the Lord there (Is 2:1-4; Mic 4:1-8). But Israel's disobedience to God's covenant law resulted not in the nations coming to Jerusalem for instruction in the ways of Yahweh but rather in Israel's humiliating journey to Babylon in exile (Mt 1:11). With Israel, then, the promise of blessing toward the nations was left unfulfilled.

Similarly, Jesus brings to fulfillment, in a way the Davidic kings never did, the divine purpose implicit within the Davidic covenant, namely that God would establish David's "seed" to reign over Israel forever. In the broad sweep of the Old Testament this purpose was to involve a humble recognition by these kings that they would be the agent of God's own rule over Israel and finally over the nations (e.g., Ps 2; Zech 9:9-17). But the moral and religious failure of the Davidic kings led to the end of the kingship with the Babylonian exile. With the house of David, then, the promise of rule over God's people and God's world was left unfulfilled.

But the history to which the genealogy bears witness prepares for the fulfillment in Jesus not only negatively, in terms of failure, but also positively, in terms of anticipation and foreshadowing. Thus, the mention of women who were either Gentiles or associated with Gentiles in the land (in the case of Bathsheba) points to the fact that God, who exercised sovereign control over the prehistory of the Messiah, according to the genealogy,[2] was revealing through this prehistory that at the time of fulfillment the Messiah would be instrumental in the incorporation of Gentiles into the people of God.

The sole mention of a sibling, namely Zerah (Mt 1:3), points in the same direction. For it recalls the story of the birth of Perez and Zerah, twins in the womb of Tamar (Gen 38:27-30). Zerah appeared to be the firstborn, but because of a reversal within the birth process, Perez surprisingly turned out

---

[2]Note the three-times-fourteen schema of salvation history culminating in Christ, according to Mt 1:17.

to be the firstborn. No careful reader could miss Matthew's point: This unexpected reversal in the birth of these twins within the prehistory of the Messiah foreshadows the surprising reversals that characterize the ministry of Jesus. It is precisely Gentile magi who announce to Jerusalem the birth of "the king of the Jews" (Mt 2:2); the kingdom of God will be taken away from Israel and given to a nation that will be composed of both Jews and believing Gentiles (Mt 21:43; cf. Mt 8:11; 28:19).

In addition to the mention of "Son of Abraham," the reference to "and his brothers" at Matthew 1:2; 11 indicates that Jesus brings to fulfillment the history of the entire people of Israel. The purpose of this phrase is to point to the lateral or expansive implications of the genealogy over against seeing in it a concern only for the direct line of individuals from Abraham through David to Jesus; in other words, it indicates that in the genealogy the whole people of Israel are in view and not simply those individuals expressly mentioned in the list. For in Matthew 1:2 the phrase refers to all twelve of the sons of Jacob, or Israel, at the time of the establishment of the covenant with the patriarchs. And in Matthew 1:11 it refers again to the entire people, not just to the siblings of Jeconiah, since the people as a whole went into exile. Thus, the whole history of Israel is, in fulfillment, concentrated in Jesus. In a sense, Jesus is Israel, for he embodies the divine purposes expressed in Israel's history.

Clearly, Matthew did not come to the conclusion that Jesus is Christ, Son of David, and Son of Abraham, on the basis of the number of generations derived from the genealogical records in the Old Testament or in the more immediate family line of Jesus.[3] The three-times-fourteen schema is imposed by Matthew, through the omission of three generations from David to Jeconiah. And even the genealogy itself does not contain fourteen generations in each of the three blocks.[4] Rather, Matthew has come to the conclusion that Jesus is Christ, Son of David, Son of Abraham, to whom the Old Testament, read properly, bears witness on the basis of the Jesus

---

[3] For a discussion of the development of the genealogy for the post-biblical period, see Raymond E. Brown, *The Birth of the Messiah: A Commentary on the Infancy Narratives in the Gospels of Matthew and Luke*, new ed., ABRL (New York: Doubleday, 1993), 86-90.

[4] Mt 1:2-5 includes fourteen names, but only thirteen generations, and we can find fourteen generations in the second and third blocks only by counting Jeconiah twice, or by including Mary as a generation. See Raymond Brown, *Birth of the Messiah*, 81-84.

history. And, having come to that conclusion, he has massaged some of the data from the genealogical lists of the Old Testament to express that theological conviction. This conclusion is confirmed by an examination of the fulfillment quotations.

In at least the majority of cases, the fulfillment quotations do not influence the reporting of the events to which Matthew applies them, as though Matthew were creating or radically reshaping his account of the events in the Jesus history to correspond to the Old Testament passages.[5] But rather Matthew selects the quotations, and at points modifies them, on the basis of the events. Thus the events themselves prompt consideration of the Old Testament fulfillment. On the other hand, Matthew has so transmitted the Old Testament passages he cites, not only the fulfillment quotations, but also other quotations and allusions throughout the Gospel of Matthew, so as to draw out their deeper significance for the fulfillment of the Christ event. For this reason, Gundry has referred to Matthew as a "targumist."[6] Thus the Jesus history brought to Matthew's mind the fulfillment of certain Old Testament passages. And Matthew employs these passages in order to show how the Jesus history illumines the Old Testament passages cited, and, conversely, how the Old Testament passages that are cited illumine the Jesus history.

Although Matthew sometimes translates Old Testament passages into Greek in such a way as to highlight their fulfillment in Jesus, Matthew never rips them out of their original context so as to make them say something that was foreign to their original meaning.[7] Yet he sometimes recognizes a fuller meaning in these passages that may transcend the intention of the original authors, a significance that has now become plain in light of the Jesus history.[8] Indeed, a careful analysis of Matthew's citation of these passages reveals that he typically wishes to reference elements in the context

---

[5]Thus, rightly, R. T. France, *Matthew: Evangelist and Teacher* (Grand Rapids: Zondervan, 1989), 176-81.
[6]Robert H. Gundry, *The Use of the Old Testament in St. Matthew's Gospel with Special Reference to the Messianic Hope*, NovTSup 18 (Leiden: Brill, 1967), 172-74. This allusion refers to the tendency on the part of those responsible for the *Targumim* to allow their understanding of the deeper significance of OT passages to influence their translation of these passages into Aramaic.
[7]Contra C. F. D. Moule, *The Origin of Christology* (New York: Cambridge University Press, 1977), 127-32.
[8]So Gundry, *Use of the Old Testament*, 205-34; and France, *Evangelist and Teacher*, 181-85.

of these Old Testament passages so that the reader will apply these contextual insights to the Jesus history Matthew is reporting, a process known as "metalepsis."[9]

Thus far, I have discussed how Matthew describes Jesus' fulfillment of the history of Israel. But Matthew is also concerned about how this fulfillment affects the status of Israel. Without question, at the beginning of the Gospel of Matthew Israel is the people of God, as has been the case since the calling of Abraham (Gen 12:1-3; 15:1-21; 18:1-33; 22:15-20; Mt 1:1; 22:32). Jesus is the Son of David, the "king of the Jews" (Mt 2:2). God, through the Scriptures, speaks of "my people Israel" (Mt 2:6). It is the Jewish crowds who are "sheep without a shepherd," to whom Jesus ministers and, through his instructions, to whom he sends his disciples (Mt 9:35–11:1); Israel is the flock that he feeds (Mt 14:13-21; 15:32-39; cf. Ezek 34:1-24). Throughout most of the Gospel of Matthew, Jesus speaks disparagingly of the Gentiles, portraying them as outsiders (Mt 5:47; 6:7-8, 32; 18:17; 20:25). He has been sent "only to the lost sheep of the house of Israel" (Mt 15:24), and the disciples are likewise to restrict their ministry to Israel (Mt 10:5-6).

Yet from the very beginning we see indications that fulfillment of Scripture involves the inclusion of the Gentiles. We have already noted the presence of Gentile women in the genealogy. In Matthew 4:12 Jesus positions himself for ministry by relocating to Galilee, in fulfillment of Isaiah 9:1-2, which speaks of "Galilee of the Gentiles," where "the people who sat in darkness have seen a great light" (Mt 4:14-16). Matthew 12:17-21 quotes Isaiah 42:1-4, which declares that the Servant will "proclaim justice to the Gentiles," and "in his name will the Gentiles hope." Accordingly, Jesus himself declares that "many will come from east and west, and sit with Abraham, Isaac, and Jacob in the kingdom" (Mt 8:11). All of this leads to the Great Commission, where Jesus commands his disciples to "make disciples of all nations" (Mt 28:19).

But Matthew explicitly cites Isaiah not only to point to the eventual inclusion of the Gentiles, but also to mark the obduracy and self-exclusion of "this generation" of Israel (Mt 13:14-15, citing Is 6:9-10; 15:7-9, citing Is 29:13). Accordingly, Jesus declares not only that "many will come from east and

---

[9] See esp. Richard Hays, *Reading Backwards: Figural Christology and the Fourfold Gospel Witness* (Waco, TX: Baylor University Press, 2016), 38-43.

west, and sit with Abraham, Isaac, and Jacob in the kingdom," but also that "the sons of the kingdom will be cast into outer darkness" (Mt 8:11). Thus by the end of the Gospel of Matthew we know that "the kingdom of God will be taken away from you [Israel as an ethnic entity] and given to a nation producing the fruits of it" (Mt 21:43), that the invitation to the marriage feast will be offered to others (Mt 22:8-10). In fulfillment of the Scriptures, a shift of peoplehood has occurred. Israel, as an ethnic entity, is no longer the people of God; that role now belongs to the church (Mt 16:18), composed of believing Jews and Gentiles.

Scholars have debated whether Matthew envisions any future restoration of the people of Israel. Some believe, primarily on the basis of Matthew 23:39, that Matthew adopts the position that "all Israel will be saved" (cf. Rom 11:26) before or at the parousia,[10] while others insist that Matthew holds out no hope for Israel's salvation.[11] Indeed, a few scholars have argued that the command to "make disciples of all nations" in Matthew 28:19 does not include Israel, since the word translated "nations" (ἔθνη) is frequently used in Matthew to refer to "Gentiles" (Mt 4:15; 6:32; 10:5, 18; 12:18, 21; 20:19, 25). Yet the word does mean "nations" in several Matthean passages, especially toward the end of the Gospel (Mt 21:43; 24:7, 9, 14; 25:32), and statements like Matthew 10:23 and Matthew 23:34-35 indicate that Matthew envisions a continuing ministry to Jews. But a continuing mission to Israel does not necessarily imply a wholesale repentance on the part of the people. In fact, Matthew does not give a clear indication regarding the future of Israel. It is probably best to take Matthew 23:39 as holding out the possibility of the restoration of a large portion of Israel, but contingent on their genuine repentance, which, as we saw, Matthew considers at best a possibility.

The key to this change in peoplehood is Jesus as the fulfillment of Israel and of God's dealings with Israel. If Jesus is Israel, in the sense that the entire history of Israel and the purposes that God had for Israel are embodied in him, then oneness with him, which Matthew describes as being

---

[10]E.g., Adolf Schlatter, *Der Evangelist Matthäus*, 5th ed. (Stuttgart: Calwer, 1959), 691; Craig S. Keener, *A Commentary on the Gospel of Matthew* (Grand Rapids: Eerdmans, 1999), 558-59; Robert H. Gundry, *Matthew: A Commentary on His Handbook for a Mixed Church Under Persecution*, 2nd ed. (Grand Rapids: Eerdmans, 1994), 474.

[11]E.g., David E. Garland, *The Intention of Matthew 23*, NovTSup 52 (Leiden: Brill, 1979), 208-9; Douglas R. A. Hare, *Matthew*, IBC (Louisville: John Knox, 1993), 272-73; Ulrich Luz, *Matthew 21-28*, Hermeneia (Minneapolis: Fortress, 2005), 163.

"with him," constitutes participation in the eschatological people of God. In such a context, claiming racial lineage to Abraham, with its corollary of ethnic identity, is nothing but presumption, for God is able, through Jesus Son of Abraham (Mt 1:1-17) to "raise up children to Abraham" even from stones (Mt 3:9).

Yet Matthew attends not only to Jesus' fulfillment of Israel, but also to his fulfillment of the law. When Jesus declares in Matthew 5:17 that he has come to "fulfill the law and the prophets," he suggests that, outside of their fulfillment in him, they are incomplete. Moreover, insofar as Jesus speaks not only of fulfilling the prophets, but fulfilling the law, he suggests that the law functions as prophecy, for the notion of fulfillment properly has to do with prophecy. Indeed, Jesus says as much in Matthew 11:13: "For all the prophets *and the law* prophesied until John." In fact, Matthew considers that the whole of the Old Testament prophesies regarding Jesus; thus, according to Matthew 13:34-35 the Writings (the Psalms) are also prophecy that he fulfills.[12]

The law itself implicitly prophesies that the coming one will fulfill the law in the way Jesus does bring it to fulfillment, especially in the antitheses of Matthew 5:21-48. Thus, Jesus implies that his fulfillment of the commands in the antitheses represents the law's own perspective in that the law testifies regarding itself of the need for Jesus' fulfillment in order for the law to function, certainly at the time of the eschatological coming of the kingdom, as the vehicle that fully expresses God's will. Both the structure of the antitheses, reaching a climax in Jesus' demand of an all-inclusive love, and Jesus' explicit declaration that the whole of the law and the prophets is an expression of the dual love commands (Mt 22:34-40) indicate that a major aspect of Jesus' fulfillment of the law is the recognition of a structure within the law, namely that the law has a center that finds expression in all the commands—and that center is love (Mt 5:43-48; 19:16-22).

But Jesus fulfills not only the law, but also the Old Testament institutions of Sabbath and temple. Matthew immediately follows Jesus' promise to give "rest" to those who take up the yoke of discipleship with Sabbath controversies, in the course of which Jesus declares that he is "lord of the Sabbath"

---

[12] Note that the formulaic introduction mentions "the prophet," although the quotation comes from Ps 78:2.

(Mt 12:8); Matthew thereby indicates that Jesus fulfills the role that had hitherto been played by the Sabbath. In the process, Jesus redefines Sabbath rest; the relief from labor (Mt 11:28) that was associated with the Sabbath is achieved by taking on oneself Jesus' yoke and burden (Mt 11:30), which means being actively involved as the agent of wholeness or rest for others as was Jesus when he healed on the Sabbath day (Mt 12:9-14).

And the same passage suggests that Jesus fulfills the temple. The Pharisees charge that, in plucking grain on the Sabbath, the disciples are acting unlawfully (Mt 12:1-2). Jesus responds by talking about the temple. He insists that the temple, like the Sabbath (Mt 12:9-14), exists to provide merciful help to persons (Mt 12:3-4) and that the Old Testament itself testifies that the temple sanctifies labor on the Sabbath day (Mt 12:5; cf. Num 28:9-10), especially work that mercifully satisfies human need (Mt 12:7). Because Jesus is "greater than the temple" (Mt 12:6), the presence of God dwells in him (Mt 1:23) in a way that far transcends the presence of God in the temple. Consequently, if the temple sanctified labor on the Sabbath, how much more does Jesus' presence sanctify Sabbath-day labor that is undertaken to satisfy human need.

Clearly, then, fulfillment centers on the person of Jesus, who is God-with-us. And because the Jesus who walked the shores of Galilee and taught his disciples is the same Jesus who continues to be with his church "to the end of the age" (Mt 28:20), the period of fulfillment spans both the time of the earthly Jesus and the time of Jesus' exaltation and reign after his resurrection. Matthew therefore divides salvation history into two periods: the period of preparation and the period of fulfillment, which is, of course, the period of the kingdom.[13]

Yet within the period of fulfillment we find a stepped development in the manifestation of the kingdom. The time of fulfillment, or the kingdom, begins with the birth of Jesus, in that he is "God with us" from the beginning (Mt 1:23). Nevertheless, before Jesus begins his public ministry the kingdom is announced by John the Baptist, but is not yet fully available to persons, including John himself (Mt 3:14; 11:11). In Jesus' earthly ministry the power of the kingdom is manifested by conquest over cosmic evil (e.g., Mt 12:24-32),

---

[13]See Jack Dean Kingsbury, *Matthew: Structure, Christology, Kingdom* (Philadelphia: Fortress, 1975), 31-39, for a vigorous argument in favor of this twofold conception of salvation history in the Gospel of Matthew.

yet the benefits of the kingdom are limited to Israel. After the resurrection, God gives to Jesus authority that he did not possess heretofore, and on the basis of that newly acquired level of authority Jesus makes the blessings of the kingdom available to "all nations"; and Jesus promises that his disciples will experience the presence of "God with us" in a way that transcends their association with him during his earthly ministry (Mt 28:20). But the fullest manifestation of fulfillment is the consummated kingdom that God will establish through Jesus at the parousia (Mt 26:29). Matthew, then, presents the time of fulfillment, and the coming of the kingdom, in the dynamic terms of ever greater degrees of manifestation. It is to the matter of this kingdom that we now turn.

Kingdom

The prominence of the theme of the kingdom of heaven/God in the Gospel of Matthew is generally recognized. Statistically, the term *king* (βασιλεύς) occurs in the Gospel of Matthew thirty-four times, almost as many as in all the other Gospels combined; "kingdom" (βασιλεία) appears fifty-six times, compared to eighteen times in Mark, forty-four times in Luke (which is longer), and only four times in John. Structurally, we have seen that the heading to the second major division references the kingdom: "From that time Jesus began to preach, saying 'repent, for the kingdom of heaven is at hand'" (Mt 4:17). This passage indicates that the announcement of the kingdom is the substance of Jesus' preaching in the Gospel of Matthew. Indeed, this announcement of the kingdom is made not only by Jesus, but also by John the Baptist (Mt 3:2) and the disciples (Mt 10:7).

In the Old Testament, the phrase "kingdom of God" does not appear, although we find "kingdom of Yahweh" in 1 Chronicles 28:5 and 2 Chronicles 13:8, and in 1 Chronicles 29:11 David declares, "Thine is the kingdom." But the Old Testament is replete with references to God as "king" or to God as reigning. In addition, the Old Testament frequently mentions God's "throne." According to the Old Testament, God reigns over both creation and history, and his rule, as it pertains to history, is centered especially on Israel, in that God reigns over Israel, and, through Israel or Israel's king, God reigns over the nations. This divine reign emphasizes God's power both to save and to destroy by judgment. And yet the condition of the world and especially the circumstances of Israel's life in the world sometimes brought into question the claim of God's rule. This situation obtained particularly at the time of the exile, and it was primarily in the context of that disappointment that the notion of the future reign of God developed, a theme we find especially in Isaiah (e.g., Is 24:21-23; 33:22; 52:7) and Daniel (e.g., Dan 2:34-45; 7:1-28).[14]

But even after Judah returned from exile disappointment was pervasive. Many of the promises God had made through the prophets regarding the dominion of Yahweh over Israel and the nations and the great blessings that would attend that reign did not materialize.[15] And the righteous continued to suffer and the evil continued to prosper. The Jews of the period dealt with this tension in a variety of ways, and different conceptualizations of the kingdom of God developed. But for many Jews, the conviction that the promises of God could not fail to realize led to a hope that God would eventually usher in his end-time kingdom. In the intertestamental period, this hope took shape especially in the apocalyptic movement. The extent of the influence of apocalypticism in first-century Judaism is debated, but eschatological elements associated with apocalypticism are found in several strands of first-century Judaism, and these are assumed by the New Testament as the Jewish background pertaining to the coming of the kingdom.

At the risk of oversimplification and overgeneralization, we may say that the concept of the kingdom in Jewish apocalypticism involved the following. All history falls into two periods: the present evil age and the age to come. During the present evil age, God remains sovereign as the Lord of creation and history, but he has chosen not to manifest his sovereign rule, but for the moment to keep it hidden. This results in a situation in which the world is in bondage to evil and the evil one. God is ultimately sovereign, but, in the sphere of human life especially, seems in large part to be absent. Bondage to this cosmic evil is expressed in sickness, death, demon possession, human sinfulness and injustice, political and military oppression of God's people Israel, and (in the thinking of many Jews) illegitimate worship in the temple.

---

[14]See Charles H. H. Scobie, *The Ways of Our God: An Approach to Biblical Theology* (Grand Rapids: Eerdmans, 2003), 106-7, 121-24.
[15]This disappointment is represented in such books as Ezra, Nehemiah, Haggai, and Malachi.

The present evil age will be followed by the age to come, which many groups believed God would usher in through his Messiah.[16] The age to come will bring the complete victory and rule of God. This victory of God will involve, negatively, the destruction of the enemies of God, including cosmic evil and persons who do evil (both inside and outside Israel); positively, it will involve the deliverance of the people of God, specifically freedom from bondage to cosmic evil and from military and political oppression. In anticipation of the age to come, God's faithful ones orient their lives to this coming reign by committing to righteousness and devotion.[17]

The Gospels, and the Gospel of Matthew in particular, assume this framework of history, but with two differences. For one thing, Matthew adopts an "elongation" of the age of the kingdom, so that the kingdom comes in two phases (inaugurated and consummated) over against a single, sudden emergence, as was presupposed among the Jews. In addition, the coming of the kingdom in Jesus does not involve Israel's deliverance from foreign military and political dominance.

Coming to the Gospel of Matthew, we note that "the kingdom of heaven" and "the kingdom of God" are used interchangeably; they mean the same thing. Matthew alone of all the New Testament writers speaks of "the kingdom of heaven," using it thirty-three times; on only four occasions does he use "the kingdom of God" (Mt 12:28; 19:24; 21:31, 43).[18] Matthew declares that the long-awaited rule of God has now drawn near in the person of Jesus

---

[16] Not always was the kingdom of God linked closely with the Messiah; moreover, a number of different conceptions of the Messiah existed in first-century Judaism, although certain broad lines are discernible. See N. T. Wright, *The New Testament and the People of God* (Minneapolis: Fortress, 1992), 307-20; William Horbury, *Messianism Among Jews and Christians: Twelve Biblical and Historical Studies* (New York: T&T Clark, 2003), 35-122.

[17] For discussions pertaining to this background, see Kingsbury, *Matthew: Structure, Christology, Kingdom*, 133-37; N. T. Wright, *New Testament and the People of God*, 280-338, and *Jesus and the Victory of God* (Minneapolis: Fortress, 1996), 198-226; Emil Schürer, *A History of the Jewish People in the Age of Jesus Christ*, 3 vols., ed. Geza Vermes, Fergus Miller, and Matthew Black (New York: T&T Clark, 1973–1987), 2:488-554.

[18] An explanation for the inclusion of this phrase in just these four passages is that Matthew employs "kingdom of heaven" when addressing the disciples or the crowds, but "kingdom of God" when addressing the religious leaders, as argued by Mowery, "Matthean References." But this is not the case in Mt 19:24 or Mt 22:2. In my judgment, there is no clear pattern. Matthew may include "kingdom of God" on a few occasions to make it clear to any (Gentile) reader who may not be acquainted with "kingdom of heaven" that the phrase means "kingdom of God" and is used interchangeably with it. See esp. Mt 19:23, 24 where Jesus employs the two expressions side by side. The phrase "kingdom of heaven" was not in use among Gentiles but is found in Jewish writings.

(Mt 3:2; 4:17; 10:7). But, as I mentioned above in the interpretation of Matthew 4:17, the meaning of "is at hand" is ambiguous. Scholars have long debated whether the kingdom is near in the sense that it is about to arrive, but has not yet appeared, or is near in the sense that it is just now arriving. A survey of its use in Matthew reveals that it means both.[19] The kingdom has already arrived in the eschatological ministry of Jesus in which he breaks the power of evil through his work of proclamation, healing, raising the dead, and casting out demons. Thus in Matthew 12:28 Jesus declares, "the kingdom of heaven has come upon you," employing the aorist tense of the verb. The "sons of the kingdom" are those who participate in the kingdom now, who are the good plants sown in the world by the Son of Man (Mt 13:24, 38); they are even now "sons of the Father who is in heaven" (Mt 5:45), and thus have privileges as "sons" of the king (Mt 17:24-27). But alongside these passages that speak of the presence of the kingdom stand others indicating that the kingdom is future in the sense that it is yet to be fully manifested, or consummated, at the parousia (e.g., Mt 6:10; 13:43; 25:34). Most of Matthew's references to "entering" the kingdom refer to admission into the kingdom in its consummated form (Mt 5:20; 7:21; 18:8, 9; 19:17, 23, 24; 25:10, 21, 23).[20] Thus, the kingdom is both "already" and "not yet."

The parables of Matthew 13, and especially the weeds, mustard seed, and leaven, illustrate these two dimensions of the kingdom and present implicit instruction as to how persons are to relate to the already and not yet of the kingdom. The parables of the mustard seed and leaven portray both continuity and discontinuity between the present and future manifestations of the kingdom. According to these parables, the kingdom develops from conflict and apparent insignificance toward greatness and expansion in its

---

[19]On the kingdom not yet arrived, see Johannes Weiss, *Jesus' Proclamation of the Kingdom of God*, ed. Richard H. Hiers and D. Larrimore Holland (Philadelphia: Fortress, 1971 [1892]). On the kingdom just now arriving, see C. H. Dodd, *The Parables of the Kingdom*, rev. ed. (New York: Scribner's, 1961). Most scholars hold that the kingdom is both "not yet" and "already arriving," e.g., George Eldon Ladd, *The Presence of the Future* (Grand Rapids: Eerdmans, 1974); and George R. Beasley-Murray, *Jesus and the Kingdom of God* (Grand Rapids: Eerdmans, 1986).

[20]Yet it is well not to make too much of a distinction between entering the kingdom in its present manifestation (that is, participating in the kingdom now) and entering the kingdom at the end, for participation in the kingdom now is prerequisite for entering it at the end, and some references to entering the kingdom pertain to the kingdom in its present manifestation (Mt 22:12; 23:14), and others are ambiguous, so that it is unclear whether the present or future kingdom is in view (Mt 7:13; 18:3).

consummated form. Those who participate in the kingdom in its present smallness and apparent weakness will participate in the final glory of the kingdom. The delay in the arrival of the future manifestation of the kingdom (Mt 24:48; 25:5) is due to God's desire to provide an opportunity for the evangelization of the nations.[21]

A survey of this concept of the kingdom in the Gospel of Matthew reveals also the radical character of God's kingdom. It constantly stands over against typical human ways of thinking and valuing and accepted cultural norms. Although of necessity some connection must exist between generally accepted notions of what is true and false, or right and wrong, and the proclamation of the kingdom (for otherwise the proclamation of the kingdom would have no starting point with persons, no initial moral appeal),[22] nevertheless, at deep levels of human thinking and valuing the kingdom is radically subversive.

Already in the beatitudes the kingdom turns the notion of wellbeing on its head; it is the "poor in spirit," those who "mourn," and "those who are persecuted" who are blessed. Whereas persons in general understand status in terms of positions of honor (Mt 20:21; 23:5-7), in the kingdom status belongs to those who assume the role of children (Mt 18:4), who especially in that culture had no position whatsoever.[23] Whereas persons in general understand greatness in terms of the exercise of power and authority so as to enforce one's own prerogatives over others, in the kingdom greatness belongs to those who cast aside such authority in favor of humble service for the sake of others (Mt 20:24-28). Whereas persons in general understand power in terms of might, manipulation, and the prerogatives of office (Mt 2:1-18; 22:15-18; 26:51), in the kingdom the power of God is made manifest in human weakness (Mt 26–27). Whereas persons in general understand security in terms of their attempts to establish their own security (Mt 6:19-21; 19:16-22), in the kingdom one gains one's life in the process of

---

[21] Thus according to Mt 13:29-30 the servants are not to gather the weeds now "lest in gathering the weeds you root up the wheat along with them," but rather "let both grow together *until the harvest*"; and Mt 13:32, "so that birds of the air may come and make nests in its branches"; cf. Mt 24:14; 28:19.

[22] This principle stands behind Jesus' practice of communicating truths about the kingdom through parables, slices of life from nature or human relationships.

[23] Thomas Wiedemann, *Adults and Children in the Roman Empire* (New Haven: Yale University Press, 1989).

losing it, that is, security is achieved through the giving up of the search for it (Mt 16:25-26). The kingdom challenges even generally held views about justice and fairness (Mt 20:1-16).

But Jesus declares that it is not enough for persons to hear the proclamation of the kingdom, they must respond (Mt 7:24-27) in repentance (μετανοέω, Mt 3:2, 8, 11; 4:17; 11:20, 21; 12:41). The basic meaning of repentance is the changing of the mind,[24] and in the Gospel of Matthew it signifies the reorientation of the whole person, beginning with that person's thinking. Specifically, its connection to the proclamation of the gospel indicates that it involves a profound reorientation to the one ultimate reality that God's kingdom has now drawn near in Jesus. As such, repentance is just as radical as is the kingdom to which it is the response.

Indeed, repentance is radical in two ways. It is radical in terms of its comprehensiveness, for repentance involves reorientation at each point at which the kingdom challenges accepted ways of thinking and valuing. It is therefore also radical in its continuousness, for constantly the kingdom challenges the perspectives of this age, and at each new point of challenge persons are called on to repent. Matthew points to the continuous character of this repentance by employing the present imperative of "repent" in the key passages Matthew 3:2 and Matthew 4:17, which may be literally rendered, "be repenting." Matthew demonstrates the continuous nature of repentance also through his characterization of the disciples; the disciples repeatedly confront new ways in which the kingdom challenges their patterns of thinking and behaving and are expected, in each case, to conform to the perspective of the kingdom (e.g., Mt 16:22-23; 19:13-15; 20:17-28).

Specifically, the repentance that is requisite for participation in the kingdom now and for entrance into the kingdom that is to come is manifested by a spirit of humility (Mt 5:3; 18:3, 19:14), a willingness to bear persecution for the sake of Jesus (Mt 5:10-11), and especially a righteousness that exceeds that of the scribes and Pharisees (Mt 5:20); such righteousness constitutes the will of the Father (Mt 6:10; 7:21; 12:50; 21:31; 26:42). This righteousness is summed up in the double love command (Mt 22:34-40), which is the "law and the prophets" as Jesus has brought them to fulfillment through his teaching (Mt 5:17-48) and through his example of submission

---

[24]BDAG, "μετανοιέω"; J Behm, "μετανοέω, μετανοία," *TDNT*, 4:989-1008.

to the will of God in self-sacrificial service to others, which is the way of the cross (Mt 10:38; 16:24). Those who bear these fruits of repentance possess the kingdom (Mt 5:3, 10; 19:14), which means that the kingdom is properly theirs.

For its part, Israel refuses to meet the announcement of the kingdom with repentance, and therefore Israel no longer possesses the kingdom, although Israel did possess it previously. Israel was considered "sons of the kingdom" (Mt 8:11), and, indeed, Jerusalem was "the city of the great king" (Mt 5:35). In other words, on the basis of Israel's special relationship to God as God's "son" (Mt 2:11) it was to be assumed that Israel would experience the kingdom (Mt 19:29; 25:34). But now "the kingdom of God will be taken away from [them]" (Mt 21:43) because they have failed to yield, through God's Son, the fruit of righteousness that belongs to God (Mt 21:33-41) and that is made possible by embracing "the gospel of the kingdom" (Mt 4:23; 9:35).

Yet Matthew speaks not only of "the kingdom of God," but also of the kingdom of Jesus, the Son of Man (Mt 13:41; 16:28; 20:21). In fact, Jesus is central both to the kingdom of God and to the kingdom of the Son of Man. In what sense, then, does Jesus rule, and how does the kingdom of Jesus the Son of Man relate to the kingdom of God?

We know that Jesus has been king all along (Mt 2:2; 21:4-5), in that it is through Jesus that God is beginning to exercise God's end-time rule. Through his ministry, Jesus serves, as it were, as God's viceroy in the kingdom of God. Yet the kingly rule of Jesus gains greater clarity through the passion and resurrection. Jesus' crucifixion is a kind of coronation, with the wreath of thorns his crown and the cross his throne. It is a coronation that displays the very essence of Jesus' rule: total obedience to the will of his Father manifested in humble service toward others. Yet it is at the resurrection that Jesus actually assumes total royal authority as ruler of the universe (Mt 28:18; 22:41-45). It is at that point that Jesus enters into his own kingdom, the kingdom of the Son of Man (Mt 16:28).

The kingdom of the Son of Man, then, is this world, viewed from the perspective of Christ's reign over the world (Mt 13:24, 27, 38). In the parable of the weeds Jesus repeatedly refers to the field, which represents "the world" (Mt 13:38) as belonging to the householder (Mt 13:24, 27), the Son of Man (Mt 13:37); indeed, he refers to this world as "his kingdom" (Mt 13:41). One of the main ways in which the Son of Man exercises his rule within this world is by "planting" and causing to grow true disciples who bear the fruit of righteousness, who are, in other words, "sons of the kingdom [of God]" (Mt 13:24-27, 38-39). Through reigning in this way over his kingdom, the world, the Son of Man causes the kingdom of God to increase and expand in the world (Mt 13:31-33). This marks the intersection between the kingdom of the Son of Man and the kingdom of God in the time between the resurrection and the parousia.

But Christ's reign in this world, while real, is not absolutely manifested, since the enemy (the devil) continues to be operative within the world, sowing his own plants, the "sons of the evil one," who do his bidding in the world, and continuing to command "the kingdoms of the world" (Mt 4:8). Yet this situation is temporary, since at the culmination of the period of the kingdom of the Son of Man this Son of Man will exercise his sovereignty in a way that he had deliberately decided not to do heretofore, namely by sending his angels to remove from his kingdom "all causes of sin and evildoers," in other words, "the sons of the evil one," and to cast them into a fiery furnace (Mt 13:41-42). The "sons of the kingdom [of God]" alone will remain, and at that time the kingdom of the Son of Man, which is this world now purged of evil, will become the kingdom of God in its consummated form. The Son of Man will therefore share the reign of God in the consummated kingdom of God (Mt 13:43). Accordingly, Matthew presents the consummation in terms of the judgment that God will exercise through Jesus the Son of Man, who will sit on his throne (Mt 25:31), and therefore occupy the highest position in the consummated kingdom of God. All of this leads naturally to our examination of Matthew's presentation of the consummation.

THE CONSUMMATION

The coming of the kingdom of God in the birth and ministry of Jesus inaugurates the time of fulfillment. Consequently, the entirety of the story of Jesus in the Gospel of Matthew is eschatological—it depicts "the end times." Nevertheless, Matthew gives a great deal of attention to events that are future in relation to the earthly ministry of Jesus.

Matthew employs two terms, especially, to depict these events. In four passages, all within the eschatological discourse (Mt 24:3, 27, 37, 39),

Matthew uses "parousia" (παρουσία) to signify the appearance of Jesus at "the end of the age" to render universal judgment.²⁵ Moreover, in eight passages Matthew speaks of "the coming (ἔρχομαι) of the Son of Man" (Mt 10:23; 16:27, 28; 24:30, 44; 25:31; 26:64), and four of these occurrences are unique to Matthew (Mt 10:23; 16:28; 24:30; 25:31). Scholars are in virtually unanimous agreement that these references allude to Daniel 7:13-14: "And behold, with the clouds of heaven there came one like a son of man, and he came to the Ancient of Days and was presented before him. And to him was given dominion and glory and kingdom, that all peoples, nations, and languages should serve him; his dominion is an everlasting dominion, which shall not pass away, and his kingdom one that shall not be destroyed."

One notes the appearance of a number of details from Daniel 7:13-14 in the Matthean Son-of-Man passages, such as "clouds of heaven" (Mt 24:30; 26:64), "glory" (Mt 16:27; 24:30; 25:31), and "kingdom" (Mt 16:28; cf. "throne," Mt 25:31). And in two additional passages Matthew includes language that mirrors Daniel 7:13-14: certainly in Matthew 19:28 (note "the Son of Man sitting on his glorious throne") and possibly in Matthew 28:18.²⁶ As we saw above, in Daniel 7 "the Ancient of Days" refers to God and "one like a son of man" refers to "the saints of the Most High," that is, to Israel, or more precisely the righteous remnant within Israel (Dan 7:18, 22, 27), who have suffered oppression from their enemies and are now vindicated (Dan 7:19-27). Thus Jesus is applying to himself the role that belonged to Israel in Daniel 7. Even as the Danielic persecuted son of man "comes" to God "on clouds of heaven" and receives from God "an everlasting kingdom" and "authority," with the result that "all nations" should serve him, so also Jesus, having been persecuted unto death, comes to God and is granted glory (Mt 16:27; 24:30; 25:31) and sovereign rule (Mt 16:28; 19:28; 25:31; 26:64; cf. Mt 22:41-45) over the nations (Mt 28:18).

If we take the intertextual connections seriously, we will see that this language refers not to Jesus the Son of Man coming to earth, but rather to his coming to God so as to receive from God "all authority." In other words, it pertains to Jesus' exaltation, which in the Gospel of Matthew is related

---

²⁵Albert Oepke, "παρουσία, πάρειμι," *TDNT*, 5:858-71.
²⁶The key connection here involves the Danielic son of man being given glory (ἐδόθη αὐτῷ ἐξουσία), essentially the same phrase as in Mt 28:18. In both Dan 7:13 and Mt 28:18 the phrase is followed by reference to "all the nations" (πάντα τὰ ἔθνη).

especially to his resurrection (Mt 28:18). Such a construal is confirmed especially by Matthew 26:64, where the Matthean Jesus declares to the high priest, "*from now on* [ἀπ' ἄρτι] you will see the Son of Man seated at the right hand of Power and coming on the clouds of heaven" (NRSV).[27] Since Matthew employs this language of the coming of the Son of Man to describe the destruction of Jerusalem (Mt 10:23; 16:28; 24:30) as well as Jesus' second coming in judgment over the world (Mt 16:27; 19:28; 24:44; 25:31), it follows that Matthew uses the image of the coming of the Son of Man to describe both the *inauguration* of Jesus' universal authority and rule at the point of his exaltation (Mt 28:18; cf. Mt 26:64) and the *manifestations* of his authoritative judgmental work in the world at the destruction of Jerusalem and at his parousia.[28] Thus the destruction of Jerusalem is the beginning of the end, and the parousia is the culmination of the end.[29] The consummation pertains specifically to the parousia. Therefore, we turn now to consider the coming of the Son of Man in judgment at the parousia.

In contrast to "false Christs and false prophets" who will entice followers with the suggestion that Christ's end-time appearance will be secretive or isolated (Mt 24:24-26), Matthew emphasizes that the parousia is a cosmic event of epic proportions (Mt 24:27). To that end Matthew mentions repeatedly "glory" (Mt 16:27; 19:28; 25:31), that is, "divine, heavenly radiance,"[30] and the role of the angels (Mt 13:38-43; 16:27; 25:31), which points to Jesus' transcendence and the comprehensiveness involved in the gathering of the peoples of the world. At his arrest Jesus refused to call on God for help from the angels, though God had made more than seventy-two thousand available to him at his behest (Mt 26:53-54), but now the Son of Man calls into service this unfathomably mighty, cosmic power.

Likewise, the parousia has been carefully planned and orchestrated by the Father. Matthew suggests that the Father has set a predetermined day and

---

[27]Matthew is the only Gospel that contains this statement. Mark lacks ἀπ' ἄρτι (cf. Mk 14:62) and Luke lacks reference to his coming in clouds of glory (cf. Lk 22:69).

[28]Most English versions introduce confusion by translating both παρουσία and ἔρχομαι in Mt 24 as "coming."

[29]This construal of the Matthean use of "the coming of the Son of Man" is developed especially by France, *Evangelist and Teacher*, 290-92, 314-16, and *Gospel of Matthew*, 396-98. See also Carson, "Matthew," 380-81, who, in comment on the coming of the Son of Man in Mt 16:28 insists that "Christ's kingly rule is exhibited after the resurrection in a host of ways," including the destruction of Jerusalem and the parousia.

[30]Gerhard Kittel, "δόξα," *TDNT*, 2:233-53.

hour for its occurrence (Mt 24:36) and has already designated who will sit at Jesus' right and left hand in the coming kingdom (Mt 20:21-23). Yet the parousia will occur at a time entirely unexpected (Mt 24:37–25:13); to drive this point home, Matthew indicates that even those who will be at the center of the action, the Son and the angels, do not know the time of its occurrence, but only the Father (Mt 24:36).

The parousia will involve primarily judgment. Although Jesus declares that he will repay each person for what that person has done (Mt 16:27), the Son of Man will pass judgment ultimately on the basis of the moral and spiritual condition of the heart (Mt 3:3-10; 5:19-20, 28; 15:8, 18, 19; 18:35; 22:37; 24:48), with a recognition that both speech (Mt 12:33-37) and deeds (Mt 3:7-10; 7:15-20; 15:10-20) necessarily express what is within. He will thus consider motivation (Mt 6:1-18). Moreover, Matthew portrays the last judgment (probably figuratively) as a court scene, in which other persons (Mt 5:25-26; 12:41-42) and Jesus himself (Mt 10:32-33) will plead either for or against the "defendant" who stands before the judgment bar. Further, the judgment will involve separation into two discrete camps (Mt 25:31-46), and this clean separation will obtain for both the judgment of the world (Mt 13:24-30, 36-43) and the church (Mt 13:47-50). Matthew envisions no third alternative; it will be a matter of either "life" or "destruction" (e.g., Mt 7:13-14; 12:37; 25:46).

Matthew's portrayal of the future state emphasizes embodied existence. Thus Jesus speaks of the "whole body" being thrown into hell (Mt 5:29-30), and he describes persons being thrown into the fire with two hands, two feet, two eyes, or, conversely, of "entering life" maimed, lame, or with one eye (Mt 18:8-9). His disciples should fear only the one who can "destroy both soul and body in hell" (Mt 10:28), the "soul" (ψυχή) referring to one's essential being (cf. Mt 11:29; 16:25-26; 26:38).[31]

Like the rest of the New Testament, the Gospel of Matthew does not think in terms of disembodied immortality but rather envisions resurrection (Mt 22:23-33). Yet resurrection existence will involve an altered state, since Jesus describes the resurrected ones as being "like the angels in heaven," in the sense that earthly human needs and desires, and even present human

---

[31] Eduard Schweizer, "ψυχή," *TDNT*, 9:639-40. Dorothy Jean Weaver, *Matthew's Missionary Discourse: A Literary Critical Analysis*, JSNTSup 38 (Sheffield: Sheffield Academic Press, 1990), 109, rightly understands the phrase, "soul and body" as referring to the "totality of the human being."

relationships, will be transcended (Mt 22:34). When Matthew describes the future condition of the righteous ("they will shine like the sun," Mt 13:43) in much the same terms as his description of Jesus on the Mount of Transfiguration ("his face shown like the sun," Mt 17:2), which foreshadows Jesus' resurrection, Matthew suggests that Jesus' resurrection body is a prototype of theirs (cf. Phil 3:21; 1 Cor 15:20-23).

As for the blessed, they will be rewarded for the righteousness and the good they have done (Mt 5:46-48; 6:1-18; 10:41-42) with entrance into the future kingdom (Mt 5:19; 25:34-40, 46), and authority to share, in some measure, Christ's rule over the world.[32] But Jesus indicates, too, that entrance will be on the basis of faith (Mt 8:10-13; cf. 22:28-32).[33] Thus Matthew makes a subtle, but real, connection between faith and works of righteousness. As far as "reward" goes, any "fruit" of righteousness that disciples produce is due ultimately to the operation of the "word of the kingdom" that God through Jesus graciously sows into the heart (Mt 13:3-9, 18-23; cf. Mt 13:24-30, 36-44). Entering the coming kingdom, then, is possible only "with God" (Mt 19:26).

Moreover, Matthew describes degrees of status and degrees of reward in the coming kingdom. Some will be (or will be called), "great" or "greatest" in the future kingdom (Mt 5:19; 18:4; cf. Mt 20:26), while others will be "least" in the kingdom (Mt 5:19; 11:11). The ones who are great excel in those areas that are required for entrance into the kingdom, while they who are least do no more than meet the basic threshold requirements for admittance. Likewise, some will have greater abundance of reward (Mt 25:14-30); indeed, Jesus urges persons to "store up treasure" in heaven (Mt 6:20; 19:21). Since "heaven" is the sphere where God dwells, that is, where God reigns completely and immediately,[34] this means confidently investing the resources of

---

[32]As I mentioned above, this is the meaning of "inherit the kingship" in Mt 25:34. See also Mt 24:47; 25:21, 23; and Jesus' description of those who follow him sitting "on twelve thrones judging the twelve tribes of Israel" (Mt 19:28). The specific meaning of 19:28 is much disputed, but the sense of eschatological judgment or rule on the part of Jesus' followers is clear. See Hanna Roose, "Sharing in Christ's Rule: Tracing a Debate in Earliest Christianity," *JSNT* 27 (2004): 123-48.

[33]Contra Anders Runesson, *Divine Wrath and Salvation in Matthew: The Narrative World of the First Gospel* (Minneapolis: Fortress, 2016), 136-42, who notes that Matthew never makes a direct connection between πίστις and acquittal at the Last Judgment. I would argue that the Gospel of Matthew makes an indirect, though important, connection.

[34]Thus Mt 5:34 describes heaven as "the throne of God;" cf. also Mt 6:10.

one's life in those things that accord with God's purposes and will, knowing that such investment is secure and is awaiting its acquisition.

Matthew describes the reward of the righteous as "life," and, indeed "eternal life" (Mt 7:14; 19:16, 22; 25:46) construed as salvation (Mt 19:25), since it involves fleeing from "the wrath to come" (Mt 3:7). In Matthew, "life" clearly signifies full, vibrant existence that participates in the essence of God (cf. Mt 16:16, "the *living* God"; also Mt 22:32). "Eternal" indicates that such life is ongoing, without end. Yet Matthew does not conceive of the age to come as a nonworldly, ethereal existence (he never speaks, e.g., of "going to heaven"), but rather as taking place in a restored or regenerated creation (Mt 19:28, παλιγγενεσίᾳ). Jesus does say that "heaven and earth will pass away" (Mt 24:35; 5:18), but in light of the eschatological promise of Matthew 5:5 that "the meek shall inherit the earth,"[35] the passing away of heaven and earth apparently refers not to the annihilation of the earth but to the destruction of the cosmos *as we know it*, with the corollary of a restored, or reconstituted earth.[36]

Finally, Matthew describes the coming kingdom as a messianic wedding banquet (Mt 22:1-4), signifying joyous, lavish celebration in community. And that community includes Abraham, Isaac, and Jacob (Mt 8:11). Although such Old Testament worthies could not experience all the blessings of the present kingdom that are available now to disciples (Mt 13:16-17), they will participate in the kingdom that is to come, experiencing their freedom from the tomb and resurrection through the death and resurrection of Jesus, which are retroactive in their atoning effects (Mt 27:51-53).[37]

As for the condemned, Matthew emphasizes the extremity of their punishment. He describes it in the most excruciating terms. "Gehenna," which

---

[35] Although Jesus is alluding to Ps 37:11, where γῆ refers to the "land" (of Israel), here in Mt 5:5 it signifies the entire earth, since Matthew does not envision the kingdom in any way localized to the land of Israel, and since every other occurrence of this word in the Gospel of Matthew (with the possible exception of Mt 27:45) refers to the entire earth.

[36] See N. T. Wright, *New Testament and the People of God*, 320-338, and *The Resurrection of the Son of God* (Minneapolis: Fortress, 2003), 129-398, for a detailed argument that such was the view in Judaism and in earliest Christianity. See also David M. Russell, *The "New Heavens and New Earth": Hope for the Creation in Jewish Apocalyptic and the New Testament*, SBibApL 1 (Philadelphia: Visionary, 1996), 149-52.

[37] Whatever might be said regarding the resurrection of the saints in this passage, we can observe three things: 1) it is making a theological point (which does not rule out, in itself, its historicity); 2) it describes the resurrection of those who died before Jesus' crucifixion; and 3) the resurrection of the saints is linked causally to Jesus' death and resurrection. See Donald A. Hagner, *Matthew 14–28*, WBC (Dallas: Word), 846-53.

originally referred to the Valley of Hinnom south of Jerusalem, had long been associated in Judaism with the place of punishment.[38] But Matthew twice adds to this designation the phrase "of fire" (Mt 5:22; 18:9); indeed, he mentions punishment by fire repeatedly (Mt 3:10, 11, 12; 7:19; 13:40, 42, 50; 18:8; 25:41). It would have been better for the condemned to have been drowned with a millstone (Mt 18:6).[39] They will be "cut in pieces" (Mt 24:51), "delivered to the torturers" (Mt 18:34), and cast "into outer darkness," indicating absolute separation and isolation (Mt 8:12; 22:13). Consequently, there will be "weeping and gnashing of teeth" (Mt 8:12; 13:42, 50; 22:13; 24:51; 25:30). Whereas the kingdom to which the righteous go has been prepared for them from the foundation of the world (Mt 25:34), the cursed will be sentenced to "the eternal fire prepared for the devil and his angels" (Mt 25:41; cf. Mt 8:29); in other words, God did not design it for human existence, and thus it affords no provision for humanity. Matthew contrasts the fate of the wicked to the "life" that the righteous will experience (e.g., Mt 7:13-14; 25:46), yet he will not speak of the punishment of the cursed as "death," which is the antipode to life; he thereby suggests that death would be a welcome relief that will not be afforded them. Even as the reward of the righteous is "eternal" (Mt 19:16, 29; 25:46), so also the torment of the condemned is "eternal" (Mt 18:8; 25:46), and the fire is "unquenchable" (Mt 3:12).

But we find elements in the Gospel of Matthew that soften somewhat this harsh picture. This horrendous punishment pertains to those who have directly refused "the word of the kingdom" (Mt 13:19) or "the gospel of the kingdom" (Mt 4:23; 9:35; 24:14), either by rejecting the gospel on hearing it, or refusing to live according to it after taking on themselves the yoke of discipleship.[40] In fact, Matthew indicates that not only are there degrees of reward, as we saw above, but also degrees of judgment. For judgment will be "more tolerable" for those who did not have access to the extent of revelation that was enjoyed by those who heard the gospel from Jesus and saw Jesus' mighty works (Mt 10:15; 11:20-24; 12:41-42). Thus Jesus

---

[38] W. D. Davies and Dale C. Allison Jr., *The Gospel According to Saint Matthew*, ICC (New York: T&T Clark, 1997), 1:514-15.

[39] Keener, *Matthew*, 448, notes that "drowning represents a Roman punishment more horrifying to Jewish hearers than crucifixion and only rarely tolerated among them."

[40] Rejecting the gospel: Mt 10:14-15; 11:20-24; 13:24-30, 36-40; 23:29-36; refusing to live according to it: Mt 5:17-48; 7:1-5, 15-27; 10:32-33; 13:47-50; 18:1-14, 23-35; 22:11-14; 24:45–25:13.

makes allowance for what can reasonably be expected of persons, given their circumstances of hearing. Indeed, the reference to *"more* tolerable" judgment for those who had less revelation implies that God will show at least some measure of tolerableness even toward those who experienced the greatest revelation.[41] Then too, Jesus encourages disciples to pray for forgiveness from God (Mt 6:12), who extends great forgiveness (Mt 18:23-35). And, finally, Matthew suggests that Jesus the judge is one with the compassionate and merciful Christ, who represents the God of love (Mt 5:45; 6:26-30; 10:29-31).

---

[41]To be sure, the point of these statements is that more severe punishment that will come to those who have the advantage of greater revelation. Nevertheless, the formulation of these statements implies a level of tolerableness for all who will be judged.

12

DISCIPLESHIP

THUS FAR IN THIS VOLUME we have considered the character of the Gospel of Matthew, which must inform our approach to its study, and we have progressed through the text of the Gospel of Matthew, offering an interpretation of larger portions as well as certain key passages, which in turn has led to a synthesis of some of the major theological themes in the Gospel of Matthew. Now, in this final chapter, we turn our attention to the matter of discipleship, which is of supreme interest to the implied reader of the Gospel of Matthew, since this reader is a disciple of Jesus in the post-Easter period.

But the forming of disciples is also a major concern for the implied author. For if Jesus is the primary subject of the Gospel of Matthew, the nurturing of discipleship among the readers is its primary purpose. From beginning to end, Matthew attends to the significance of this story of Jesus for those readers who have attached themselves to Jesus as adherents. For this reason, Matthew brings his Gospel to culmination with the promise that Jesus will be with his disciples "until the end of the age," thus indicating that the existence of the post-Easter church is determined by the presence of the same Jesus who has dominated the narrative of the Gospel of Matthew.

Not surprisingly, then, Michael Wilkins insists that the Gospel of Matthew is "at least in part a manual on discipleship."[1] Yet the term *manual* may be a

---

[1] Michael J. Wilkins, *Discipleship in the Ancient World and Matthew's Gospel*, 2nd ed. (Grand Rapids: Baker, 1995), 172.

bit misleading, because (as Wilkins knows) discipleship is not a matter of adopting a set of principles or formulas. Rather, Matthew wishes to inculcate discipleship through the total impact of the Gospel of Matthew. Nevertheless, it is possible to describe certain aspects of Matthew's view of discipleship through the way Matthew presents Jesus' teaching regarding discipleship, as well as the way Matthew describes Jesus as a model for disciples, the disciples as characters within the narrative, and the negative foils to discipleship, such as the crowds and the religious and political leaders. We will examine both the character of discipleship and the mission of disciples.

THE CHARACTER OF DISCIPLESHIP

Although the word *discipleship* is not found in the Gospel of Matthew, nor anywhere in the New Testament for that matter, Matthew offers a robust portrait of the nature and experience of discipleship. The following are a few of the major characteristics.

Discipleship must be initiated by Jesus. A key passage for grasping Matthew's theology of discipleship is Matthew 4:18-22, which presents the calling of the two sets of brothers to discipleship. Here a number of the major aspects of discipleship are introduced, to be developed throughout the remainder of the Gospel of Matthew.[2] Thus in this passage we note that the two sets of brothers do not simply decide to become disciples and thus approach Jesus; rather, Jesus approaches them without warning or any prior connection, so far as this narrative is concerned, and calls them.[3] The intended readers would have regarded this initiation by Jesus as surprising, for the normal procedure involved the would-be disciple approaching the rabbi.[4] This is also Jesus' method in the calling of Matthew (Mt 9:9), the only other account of a specific person embarking on discipleship. Matthew 8:18-20 is not exception, since Jesus seems to rebuff the scribe who attempts to

---

[2]Rudolf Bultmann, *The History of the Synoptic Tradition*, rev. ed. (Oxford: Blackwell, 1972), 28, 56, recognized this scene as presenting discipleship in an idealized and paradigmatic fashion within the synoptic tradition. Of course, I am treating it in terms of its function within the Gospel of Matthew.

[3]It has been common for scholars to assume some sort of earlier (nonrecorded) encounter and even to offer imaginative speculations; but to do so is to miss the point Matthew attempts to make.

[4]See Donald A. Hagner, *Matthew 1–13*, WBC (Dallas: Word, 1993), 76-77; Craig S. Keener, *A Commentary on the Gospel of Matthew* (Grand Rapids: Eerdmans, 1999), 150; R. T. France, *The Gospel of Matthew*, NICNT (Grand Rapids: Eerdmans, 2007), 146-47.

initiate discipleship.[5] This procedure does not suggest some sort of limited election, according to which only a few divinely preselected persons can possibly become disciples, for later in the Gospel of Matthew Jesus calls all persons to discipleship (Mt 11:28-30).[6] And Jesus will declare that "many" (πόλλοι) are called, the word πόλλοι being a Semitic idiom for "all" (Mt 22:14; cf. Mt 22:9-10).[7]

This method of inaugurating discipleship implies that discipleship begins with Jesus, and that the character of discipleship is such that it is both an initial and an ongoing response to Jesus' gracious initiative. It implies, too, that discipleship is a transcendent, divine reality, since it is offered and made possible by Jesus, the Son of God (Mt 3:17), who has been conceived by the Holy Spirit (Mt 1:18, 20) and is "God with us." It further implies that the calling to discipleship is in analogy to the calling of Old Testament prophets,[8] for this unexpected summoning is analogous to the calling of Old Testament prophets and reminiscent especially of the calling of Elisha in 1 Kings 19:19-21.[9] In calling these prophets God was bringing them into the sphere of his rule and work in distinct ways, laying a special claim on them. The calling to discipleship, then, involves a personalizing of the general claim that God through Jesus now exercises over the world as a whole through his end-time rule.[10]

Discipleship involves submitting to the authority of Jesus. Again in Matthew 4:18-22 Jesus appears unexpectedly on the scene, utters the radical demand, and the brothers respond "immediately." A gap exists between the cause, Jesus' summons, and the effect of their response.[11] The reader naturally

---

[5]See especially Jack Dean Kingsbury, "On Following Jesus: The 'Eager' Scribe and the 'Reluctant' Disciple (Mt 8:18-20)," *NTS* 34 (1988): 45-59.

[6]Note the same word of summons, "come" (δεῦτε), in both passages.

[7]E.g., Joachim Gnilka, *Das Matthäus-evangelium*, 2 Teile, HThKNT (Freiburg: Berder, 1988), 2:242.

[8]E.g., David Hill, *The Gospel of Matthew*, NCB (Grand Rapids: Eerdmans, 1972), 106. See Norman Habel, "The Form and Significance of the Call Narrative," *ZAW* 77 (1965): 297-333; Klaus Baltzer, "Considerations Regarding the Office and Calling of the Prophet," *HTR* 61 (1968): 567-91; Warren Carter, "Matthew 4:18-22 and Matthean Discipleship: An Audience-Oriented Perspective," *CBQ* 59 (1997): 66-67.

[9]So almost all commentators. But this kind of prophetic calling is found repeatedly throughout the historical and prophetic books of the OT; see, e.g., Jer 1:4-12; Amos 7:14-15; Jon 1:1.

[10]This is confirmed in Mt 28:18-20, where Jesus' declaration of all-inclusive authority is followed by the command to "make disciples of all nations," implying that discipling involves bringing persons under Jesus' sovereign rule.

[11]Richard A. Edwards, "Uncertain Faith: Matthew's Portrait of the Disciples," in *Discipleship in the New Testament*, ed. Fernando F. Segovia (Philadelphia: Fortress, 1985), 53.

wonders why they acquiesce so readily to Jesus' call, particularly since it means leaving everything behind. As the reader progresses through the rest of the narrative and encounters repeated references to the authority of Jesus (Mt 5:17-48; 7:29; 9:6, 8; 21:23-27; cf. Mt 8:23-27; 9:18-26) the answer becomes plain: Although these men had no previous encounter with Jesus nor had yet heard his teaching or witnessed his mighty works, they recognized and responded to the authority of his person, that is, his rightful, absolute claim, as limited as their perception of his authority certainly was at this initial point. Indeed, throughout the entire narrative, for all their faults the disciples never waver in their acknowledgment of and submission to Jesus' authority. They are often slow to understand (e.g., Mt 15:16; 16:11) and weak in faith (e.g., Mt 14:31; 17:20), but their fault is a frailty of the flesh and not a rebellion of the spirit (Mt 26:41); indeed, not once do the disciples resist Jesus' authority or disobey his command.

Discipleship entails genuine cost. Simon and Andrew abandoned the security of vocation ("nets") and James and John left behind the security of property ("boat") and family ("father"). Nor is this the only passage where Matthew describes such relinquishment. The disciple who wishes first to go and bury his father is told to "Follow me and leave the dead to bury their own dead" (Mt 8:22). And Jesus insists that he has come "to set a man against his father, and a daughter against her mother, and daughter-in-law against her mother-in-law, and a man's foes will be those of his own household" (Mt 10:35-36). And Jesus declares that his family are not his mother and brothers, but his disciples who do the will of his Father (Mt 12:46-50). And Peter speaks for the entire disciple circle when he says, "We have left everything and followed you," which, Matthew suggests, includes houses, family members, and lands (Mt 19:27-29). Discipleship to Jesus is sufficiently radical and comprehensive that it necessarily entails the rejection of all the securities of the former life, whether material, vocational, or relational. In the narrative of the Gospel of Matthew, the embarking on discipleship involves a radical interruption; it does not allow life to move on as usual. Thus Matthew left behind his seat at the tax office (Mt 9:9), and Jesus demands the rich young man sell his possessions and give to the poor (Mt 19:21).

Yet Matthew modifies these severe demands of abandonment in two ways. For one thing, Matthew uses multivalent language in that he employs "father" in a way so as to suggest that a kind of exchange happens, so that those who embark on discipleship obtain more than they lose. It is through leaving their earthly father that the disciples can know God as their "heavenly Father," for repeatedly in the Sermon on the Mount, which follows almost immediately Matthew 4:18-22, Jesus describes God in exactly that way to these men (Mt 5:16, 45, 48; 6:1, 4, 6, 8, 9, 14, 15, 18, 26, 32; 7:11; cf. Mt 5:9; 7:9). Throughout the Gospel of Matthew only disciples, and Jesus, are said to know or address God as Father, and only they, along with Jesus, are "sons" of the Father.

But Matthew also indicates that such abandonment does not entail a complete repudiation of things that have here been left behind. Rather, Jesus insists on the continuing obligation to care for parents (Mt 15:3-9; 19:19) and declares that commitment to the wife is so sacrosanct that divorce is not to be pursued, except in the case of sexual infidelity (Mt 5:32; 19:3-9). Moreover, disciples are to use their material resources for alms (Mt 6:2-4) and to provide food to the hungry and clothes to the naked (Mt 25:31-46).[12] Thus Matthew insists that discipleship involves, if anything, more profound care for family, and a detachment from social and economic structures that is manifested by making use of them for the sake of the kingdom. It is not a matter, then, of simple abandonment, but through abandonment a realignment, so that these things are taken up and become part of discipleship. Discipleship is not the *main* thing; it is the *only* thing. And all these relationships that properly belong to life are taken up and made part of discipleship. Paradoxically, it is because these relationships are not deemed ultimate that they are given the kind of proper seriousness that God intends they should have.

Discipleship means embarking on mission. Jesus links the call to discipleship with the promise to make them fishers of people (Mt 4:19). Insofar as this promise is directed to fishermen, Jesus establishes a profound connection between the former life and the life of discipleship. Thus, not only does discipleship effect a significant rupture with the previous life, but at another level the skills and experiences of the former life may somehow be woven into the mission of disciples. When Jesus declares that he will

---

[12]Carter, "Matthew 4:18-22," 69-73, has helpfully explored this tension between abandonment of these things and continuing involvement with them, employing insights from the sociological category of "voluntary marginals."

make (ποιέω) them fishers of people he indicates that they do not possess inherently such skills or inclinations, and that Jesus will enable them for this mission. Matthew thereby implies that a major goal of Jesus' discipling the twelve throughout the narrative is to equip them for their mission. More specifically, Jesus will equip them through instruction in Matthew 10:5-42 and through the promise of his presence in Matthew 28:18-20.

I mentioned above that Matthew utilizes multivalence in his use of "father" language within Matthew 4:18-22. But he employs multivalence also in speaking about the abandonment of "nets." It is through the abandoning of one kind of net that they take up another, for later Jesus will compare the mission activity of the church to a "net which was thrown into the sea" (Mt 13:47-50).[13] Yet this passage not only points forward to Matthew 13:47 but also alludes to Jeremiah 16:16: "Behold, I am sending for many fishers, says the Lord, and they shall catch them."[14] The verses immediately preceding Jeremiah 16:16 speak of deliverance (Jer 16:14-15), while the following verses describe judgment (Jer 16:17-18). Consequently, commentators divide over whether the imagery of Matthew 4:18-22 points to a mission of salvation or judgment.[15] But the connection with Matthew 13:47-50 suggests that it designates both: The ministry of the disciples will mean judgment for some ("bad fish") and salvation for others ("good fish"). The paradigmatic character of Matthew 4:18-22, which I mentioned above, indicates that all disciples are commissioned for ministry, including those who will be made disciples by the disciples (Mt 28:19).

Discipleship involves the creation of a community around the person of Jesus. It is hardly an accident that the first calling to discipleship involves two sets of brothers, for in this way Matthew makes it clear that discipleship could never be a purely individual matter, but necessarily assumes community. In a sense, Matthew 4:18-22 marks the beginning of the church

---

[13]Matthew uses different terms for "net" in these passages, but that difference is due to the variation of settings, in that the imagery of Mt 13:47-50 requires a dragnet. The concept of "net" is constant throughout.
[14]The same word for "fishers" (ἁλιεῖς) appears in both the Matthean passage and the LXX of Jer 16:16. Matthew picks up the word "send" (ἀποστέλλω) in Mt 10:5, cf. ἀπόστολοι in Mt 10:2.
[15]Mission of salvation: Gundry, *Matthew*, 62; W. D. Davies and Dale C. Allison Jr., *The Gospel According to Saint Matthew*, ICC (New York: T&T Clark, 1997), 1:398. Mission of judgment: Gnilka, *Matthäus-evangelium*, 1:101; France, *Gospel of Matthew*, 147. Some, e.g., Hagner, *Matthew 1-13*, 77, and David L. Turner, *Matthew*, BECNT (Grand Rapids: Baker, 2008), 136, doubt that it alludes specifically to Jer 16:16.

(Mt 16:18; 18:18).[16] The centrality of community relations for discipleship is indicated by the considerations that Matthew gives over one of the five great discourses exclusively to this issue (Mt 18), and that the Sermon on the Mount, which follows almost immediately and sets forth the principles and essential character of life within the kingdom, emphasizes relationships between Christians, described in terms of "brothers/sisters" (Mt 5:22, 23, 24, 47; 7:3, 4, 5). Indeed, the calling of the first disciples in Matthew 4:18-22 is a presupposition for the Sermon on the Mount; the mention of "brothers/sisters" there would be indecipherable without this earlier passage.

Even as Matthew employs multivalent language when he speaks of "father" and "net," he does so also in his reference to "brothers," for although these men were physical brothers their answer to Jesus' summons to discipleship rendered them brothers in an additional and transcendent way. Here we have the creation of an alternative family, which is more genuine and existentially real than biological ties (Mt 12:46-50), and more enduring, for the kingdom creates divisions that can rupture family bonds and turn erstwhile loving relationships into murderous hostility (Mt 10:21-22, 34-39). Disciples' submission to the authority of Jesus is lived out in the dual spheres of mission to the world and community within the church.

It is appropriate at this point to say something regarding Matthew's view of the church. It is often noted that the Gospel of Matthew is the only Gospel that explicitly mentions "the church" (Mt 16:18; 18:17). But the importance of the church in the Gospel of Matthew goes beyond these references.

On the one hand, Matthew has an extraordinarily high ecclesiology. In Matthew 16:18 Jesus declares that he, in his capacity as "Son of the living God" (Mt 16:16), will build his church on the solid rock of the confession of his divine sonship. Yet "this rock" is not the confession in itself as an abstraction, but the confession as it is embraced by Jesus' followers, even as Peter was embracing the confession at that moment.

In the Gospel of Matthew, the image of "built on a rock" signifies endurance in the face of mighty forces that destroy everything that is not built on such a rock (Mt 7:24-28). Far from succumbing to the power of death, the most comprehensive and ruinous power humans know, and therefore

---

[16] I say, "in a sense," because the future tense of Mt 16:18 suggests that the "church" is a post-Easter phenomenon. Matthew 4 is certainly the beginning of the Christian, or more precisely, messianic community.

the one that represents those destructive forces that put an end to every human life and all human institutions, the church will render this power against the church absolutely ineffective, and will do so by breaking down that which makes this power of death potent, its "gates."[17] All of this is a poetic and poignant way of saying that the church is the only human institution that will never be in any danger of passing out of existence, no matter what the threat, precisely because it is not merely a human institution.

Manifestly, Jesus is here speaking of the church as the global community of his disciples, not of individual congregations, as the singular "my church" makes clear. Jesus addresses issues pertaining to the church as local congregations in Matthew 18. The quality of the universal church extends to individual congregations, particularly the essential experience of the presence of God himself in the person of his Son, described in terms of the global church in Matthew 28:20 and in terms of local congregations in Matthew 18:20. But the assurance of ongoing existence pertains only to the global church; Matthew does not suggest that individual Christian congregations or entities are immune to destruction (cf. Rev 1-3).

Moreover, Jesus gives to Peter the "keys of the kingdom," with the result that whatever he binds or looses on earth will likewise be bound or loosed by God in heaven (Mt 16:19). Here Peter represents the church insofar as it embraces the christological confession Peter has just enunciated, so that whatever behavior the church decides will be required or not required for entrance into the kingdom, pertaining to matters that Jesus did not explicitly address in his earthly teaching, will be upheld by God and made the basis for the divine decisions at the Last Judgment. But the most impressive claim that Matthew makes about the church is that the saving presence of God abides in the church in the person of God's Son, Jesus, who is God with *us* (Mt 1:23; 28:20; cf. Mt 18:20). This means, then, that God through Jesus mediates salvation to persons through the dynamic of their participation in the church.

---

[17]Ultimately, the power of death among humans is resident in death's finality, its capacity to keep those imprisoned by it from ever escaping. Accordingly, when Jesus wishes to talk about destroying the power of death, which represents destructive powers in general, he does so by the image of breaking down the gates that keep people in and thereby make death's power great. For the major views in the history of interpretation on the meaning of "gates of Hades," see Davies and Allison, *Matthew*, 2:630-32.

But balancing this high ecclesiology is also a realistic view of the church. Thus, as important as is participation in the life of the church, Jesus warns that disciples must look to their own life and behavior and not think that simply because they are part of the church they will be vindicated on the Day of Judgment. In the parable of the dragnet, the "net which was thrown into the sea and gathered fish of every kind" represents the church, which contains both good and bad fish; these will be separated at the Last Judgment (Mt 13:47-50).[18] And Jesus gives several parables in the eschatological discourse that describe the judgment of individuals in the church (Mt 24:45–25:30), most notably the parable of the virgins, through which Jesus makes the point that individual disciples cannot depend on the righteousness or the preparedness of others in the church to compensate for their own lack on the Day of Judgment (Mt 25:1-13).[19]

Discipleship involves "following" Jesus. Although Matthew sometimes speaks of the crowds "following" (ἀκολουθέω) Jesus, in the sense that they are present to experience his ministry (Mt 4:25; 8:1; 12:15; 14:13; 19:2; 20:29; 21:9), this language pertains especially to discipleship. In fact, in many passages in this Gospel "following" is practically a designation for discipleship. The disciples follow Jesus in the sense of being "with" Jesus (e.g., Mt 9:15; 12:30; 26:38-40) as those who accompany him and witness his powerful salvation (e.g., Mt 9:19), side with him against his opponents (e.g., Mt 9:10-17; 12:1-8) and consequently share his experience of persecution (e.g., Mt 5:10-12; 10:24-25; 12:1-8), learn from him (e.g., Mt 5:1–7:27; 15:12-20; 19:23–20:16), and orient their lives according to his example (e.g., Mt 16:24; 20:25-28). Yet the primary significance of "following" Jesus pertains to Jesus' demand that they "come after" him on the journey to Jerusalem where he will suffer, die, and be raised (Mt 16:21–28:20); here they walk behind him, so that he becomes model, motivation, and forerunner of their own destiny. Thus the language of Matthew 4:18-22 anticipates that fateful journey. While this description pertains to the twelve disciples within the narrative of the Gospel, Matthew widens this notion of following to include not just the twelve, but

---

[18]Jack Dean Kingsbury, *The Parables of Jesus in Matthew 13: A Study in Redaction-Criticism* (London: SPCK, 1969), 117-25; Arland J. Hultgren, *The Parables of Jesus: A Commentary* (Grand Rapids: Eerdmans, 2000), 303-8.

[19]On this theme, see the thorough and enlightening study in Daniel Marguerat, *Le Jugement dans L'Évangile de Matthieu*, La Monde de la Bible (Geneva: Labor et Fides, 1981), 409-475.

all who will accept the yoke of discipleship in the future. Thus "if *anyone* wishes to come after me . . ." (Mt 16:24; cf. Mt 11:28-30). All of this implies an emphasis on commitment to the person of Jesus himself, not ultimately to his teachings or to a doctrine about him, as important as these things are in their own place, and as they necessarily function as aspects of following him.

Discipleship involves the experience of salvation from sin. This characteristic of discipleship pertains to the very purpose of Jesus, "to save his people from their sins" (Mt 1:21). This salvation includes forgiveness, and, indeed, forgiveness is at its center (Mt 9:1-9; 6:12; 26:28), since salvation involves relationship to God as "sons" of the heavenly Father (Mt 5:45), and violations of proper relationship with God, or "debts" (Mt 6:12; 18:32, 34) against God, must therefore be addressed.

But this salvation experienced by disciples includes also moral transformation. The presence of God's end-time rule is the basis for the possibility of repentance (Mt 3:1-12; 4:17: "repent, *for* the kingdom of heaven is at hand"), which has its "fruit" in righteousness (Mt 3:8). It is the "good" tree that bears the "fruit" of righteousness (Mt 3:10; 7:17-20; 12:33-37), and such "fruit" is possible only as the result of the operation of "the word of the kingdom" on the heart (Mt 13:3-9, 18-23). All of this is the work of God, for salvation is possible only from God (Mt 19:25-26). Salvation from sin involves a divine moral transformation of which a life of righteousness, that is, obedience to the will of God as expressed in the law, as the law is brought to fulfillment by Jesus, is the necessary fruit (Mt 5:17-48; 22:34-40). Insofar as the disciple has any goodness it is due to the work of God in Jesus, so much so that Matthew can declare that any good disciples (those who bear "fruit," Mt 13:26) have been sown in the world by the Son of Man (Mt 13:24-30, 36-40). Therefore, when God judges persons according to their deeds (Mt 16:27), so that their deeds are the basis for either reward or punishment, it is actually (for those who have heard the gospel) a judgment based finally on persons' reception or rejection of the gospel. Thus it is disciples' acceptance of the gospel that alone produces goodness that is acceptable to God and properly rendered to God (Mt 21:33-41), which is the basis for acquittal and reward.

MISSION OF DISCIPLES

The fact that the Gospel of Matthew reaches a climax in Jesus' commission to the eleven to "make disciples of all nations" (Mt 28:19) suggests that mission is a major, if not *the* major, feature of discipleship. Although this concern for the mission of disciples is present, both implicitly and explicitly throughout the Gospel of Matthew (e.g., Mt 5:13-16; 13:3-9; 17:14-21), it is centered particularly in the missionary discourse of Matthew 9:35–11:1.[20]

Insofar as the missionary discourse serves the dual role of address to the twelve during Jesus' earthly ministry and instruction to the post-Easter reader, we must consider what is said about the mission of disciples here in light of the broader context of the Gospel of Matthew to determine what, and how, this description regarding mission pertains to the post-Easter readers. The Gospel of Matthew does not present all post-Easter disciples in Matthew's audience as the kind of itinerant missionaries that are described here, as Schweizer argued.[21] Matthew's portrait of discipleship includes many sedentary or fixed aspects, for instance, caring for parents (Mt 15:1-6; 19:19) and dealing with issues that arise within the dynamics of local congregations (Mt 18:15-20; 7:15-20). In fact, the Gospel of Matthew suggests that certain members of the community are designated for specialized evangelistic functions (e.g., Mt 7:15-23; 10:41-42; 23:34). Yet in some sense all disciples are to be involved in worldwide evangelization (Mt 28:18-20). This leads us, then, to derive principles regarding mission that are to be put into practice according to the various ways members of Matthew's church(es) view their specific role in mission, which *in some fashion* and *to some extent* pertains to all of them by virtue of being members of the community that is sent out.

The mission of disciples is compassion-motivated. The compassion of Jesus toward the crowds is the impetus for his sending out the disciples (Mt 9:36). Jesus is referencing the Jewish crowds at this point, which is

---

[20]Of course, the missionary commissioning (28:18-20) plays a significant role in this presentation as well. I have suggested a number of ways in which the missionary commissioning informs Matthew's concept of mission in my treatment of this passage within the interpretation section above. See also David R. Bauer, "The Theme of Mission in Matthew's Gospel from the Perspective of the Great Commission," *AJ*, forthcoming.

[21]Eduard Schweizer, *Matthäus und seine Gemeinde* (Stuttgart: Katholisches Bibelwerk, 1974); cf. Jack Dean Kingsbury, "The Verb *AKOLOUTHEIN* ('To Follow') as Index of Matthew's View of His Community," *JBL* 97 (1978): 56-73.

entirely understandable given the salvation-historical framework with which Matthew is operating. But the implied reader of the Gospel of Matthew, standing on this side of the Great Commission (Mt 28:18-20), would recognize that this compassion is ultimately directed toward all who have need, including Gentiles, who are mentioned later in this discourse (Mt 10:18).

The word "compassion" (σπλαγχνίζομαι, noun σπλαγχνόν) originally had to do with the entrails, or bowels, and then derivatively with deep-seated feelings.[22] It did not originally mean "pity"; that sense is found consistently for the first time in the New Testament. An analysis of its use in the New Testament reveals that it means essentially deep emotional feeling, particularly merciful love in the presence of need. In the Gospel of Matthew, it is used only of Jesus (and God).[23] And Matthew underscores Jesus' compassion, since this is the only emotion Matthew ascribes to Jesus, with the exception of "sorrowful and troubled" in Matthew 26:36-37. Hence, the mission of discipleship stems from the very deepest emotions of Jesus. It is an expression of Jesus' profound pity.

More specifically, we find here an emphasis on *number*. The numbers are great ("the harvest is plentiful," Mt 9:37), and Jesus could not minister to them himself. Consequently, Jesus sends out his disciples to do that which he did not have the capacity to do himself, given the limitations of his own individual personhood. Thus, along with the high Christology and transcendent claims Matthew makes throughout his Gospel regarding Jesus, he acknowledges the limitations of Jesus. Given the nature of the task that God and Jesus have sovereignly set for themselves, they need the disciples, that is, the church, to fulfill the task so as to satisfy the compassionate longing of Jesus. This challenge offered by "numbers" is intensified with the broader post-Easter demand to "make disciples of all nations" (Mt 28:19).

Matthew emphasizes also the *miserable condition* of the crowds (Mt 9:36). These crowds are vulnerable to harassment or torment because they are

---

[22]Helmut Köster, "σπλαγχνόν, κτλ.," *TDNT*, 7:248-59. I am aware of the caution against the "root fallacy," issued by James Barr, *The Semantics of Biblical Language* (London: SCM, 1983), 100-16. I refer to etymology here only for illustrative purposes; in this case, the history of the use of the word corresponds to its specific sense as employed in the NT.

[23]Also Mt 14:14; 15:32; 18:27; 20:34. This is true in the NT generally with the exception of Lk 10:33; although the noun σπλαγχνόν is sometimes used of Christians (Col 3:12; Phil 2:1; 1 Jn 3:17; cf. Eph 4:32; 1 Pet 3:8).

unable to help themselves,[24] and bereft of help from anyone else, since they are "lost sheep," outside the protection of a shepherd (Mt 10:6; 15:24). Although this reference to "sheep without a shepherd" may be part of Matthew's broad indictment against the Jewish authorities (e.g., Mt 15:14; 23:2-7, 13-28; cf. Ezek 34:1-10), in this case the authorities would be unable to offer assistance in any final sense, even if they wished. For the enemy that threatens is cosmic evil: sickness, death, uncleanness, and demon possession (Mt 10:8). And when Jesus declares that "the harvest is plentiful" (Mt 9:37) he suggests that they are vulnerable especially to eschatological judgment, since in the Gospel of Matthew "harvest" (θερισμός, Mt 13:30, 39) and harvest imagery (Mt 3:11-12; 13:41) always refers to the final judgment. This is an existential human predicament, not limited to Israel (Mt 8:5-13; 15:21-28). The only effective help is the operative announcement of the end-time kingdom (Mt 10:7). The mission of discipleship, then, stems from an informed and sympathetic consideration of the vulnerable condition of persons on the outside, especially their vulnerability to the destructive power of cosmic evil. These are persons in ultimate need because they are in ultimate bondage to ultimately destructive forces.

The mission of discipleship involves an eschatological ministry according to the authority given by Jesus. It includes the performance of various acts of ministry, all of them *eschatological*. Like the same ministry acts done by Jesus, these involve breaking the power of the devil by binding him so as to enter into his house and plunder his goods (Mt 12:28). This points to the ultimacy of the mission of disciples over against any inclination to trivialize it.

But this ministry is also *proclamatory*. The announcement of the kingdom is the primary thing, as it was in the ministry of Jesus (Mt 4:17) and indeed of John the Baptist (Mt 3:2). The fact that Jesus mentions the preaching of the kingdom first, and then describes miracles, such as healing and raising the dead, suggests that the function of the latter, at least in large measure, is to serve the purpose of the announcement of the kingdom,[25] as is the case in the ministry of Jesus (Mt 9:1-9; 11:2-6, 20-24). These acts proclaim the inbreaking of the kingdom now, and announce the ultimate restoration and

---

[24]The word translated "helpless" (ῥίπτω) means "thrown down" (cf. Mt 13:50; 27:5), like an injured sheep. See BDAG, "ῥίπτω."
[25]Hagner, *Matthew 1–13*, 270.

salvation of creation, including the resurrection body, in the eschaton (Mt 19:28; 22:23-33).

These eschatological acts are performed *according to the authority* given by Jesus (Mt 10:1). We saw above that "authority" (ἐξουσία) involves both the right to act and the ability to act, that is, legitimate power. Disciples have the same authority to perform these acts of ministry as did Jesus, but of course in their case it is derived authority. Matthew's pastoral purpose is clear. The opposition to their ministry that Jesus describes in Matthew 10:16-39 will lead to temptations to doubt, discouragement, fear, and giving in to intimidation. The recognition that they have authority to pursue such a mission will lead to courage in the face of danger (Mt 10:26-33), boldness in the face of opposition (Mt 10:17-23, 27-28, 34-39), assurance of right in the face of accusation (Mt 10:17-18, 24-25), and confidence of ultimate victory in the face of weakness and apparent failure (Mt 10:13-15, 26-28).

The mission of disciples involves apostleship. The twelve disciples are identified by name, and by number, for the first time in Matthew 10:2-4, at the introduction to the missionary discourse, where they are dubbed "apostles" (ἀπόστολοι), literally, "sent ones." In fact, this is the only occurrence of the word *apostle* in the whole of the Gospel of Matthew, and it comes immediately before Matthew's declaration that Jesus "sent out" (ἀποστέλλω) these twelve (Mt 10:5). In the Gospel of Matthew, there is no office or status of "apostle"; indeed, there are to be no distinct offices that offer rank at all (Mt 23:8-11). The subtle shift in nomenclature from "disciples" to "apostles" here indicates that disciples function as "sent ones." All of this points to the centrality of mission, of being sent out, in discipleship, and suggests that mission is, in large measure, the raison d'être for discipleship.

The word ἀπόστολος carried a robust sense in the world of the Gospel of Matthew. It generally involved serving as the agent for the one who commissioned the ἀπόστολος. It is as if the sender himself were present. This reinforces the notion that, in their ministry, disciples share the authority of Jesus.[26] It also emphasizes that this mission is under the command or charge of Jesus (Mt 10:5). In fact, since in the Gospel of Matthew the disciples do not go out or come back, as in Mark and Luke (cf. Mk 6:12, 30; Lk 9:6, 10),

---

[26]Karl Heinrich Rengstorf, "ἀπόστολος, *TDNT*, 1:407-46; Keener, *Matthew*, 313-15.

the "sending out" of Matthew 10:5 may be the charge itself. This implies that they are given authority only to do what Jesus herein commands, and to do it in the way in which he commands.

The mission of discipleship involves the refusal to gain financially from ministry. Thus Jesus utters the principle of Matthew 10:8, "You received without paying, give without pay." It is unclear whether Jesus means that they have received freely from God or that they have received from himself.[27] The reader may justly think of both. Both God and Jesus become the model of generous, uncompensated ministry.

The mission of discipleship involves the renunciation of earthly or material security. The ability to depend entirely on God and Jesus for the provisions of the mission is an implication both of the authority that Jesus has bestowed and the fact that he has sent them as his agents. But it is also an implication of the presence of the kingdom or rule of God which they proclaim (Mt 10:7). In this case, the very demeanor or character of the ministry corresponds to, and in fact embodies, the announcement itself; the manner of the ministry is itself an expression of the message they proclaim. And the ability of disciples to survive and thrive while being so exclusively dependent on God for even basic physical needs will validate the message.

The demand that the disciples are not to receive payment for ministry performed may suggest that they are to make careful plans for their own provisions. But Jesus insists that they leave behind all the necessities one typically associates with travel. They are not to take even the smallest change, nor money belts for protection against robbery, nor bag for carrying food from home or accumulating food along the way, nor an extra set of clothes to protect against thieves who often stripped victims (see Lk 10:30), nor even the humblest shoes, and no staff as protection against brigands and animals.[28] These usual measures that accord with "common

---

[27] Commentators are divided on this point, with those who opt for God including Paul Gaechter, *Das Matthäus Evangelium: Ein Kommentar* (Innsbruch: Tyrolia-Verlag, 1963), 324; Davies and Allison, *Matthew*, 2:171; and those who opt for Jesus including Pierre Bonnard, *L'Evangile selon saint Matthieu* (Geneva: Labor & Fides, 2002), 144; Schlatter, *Matthäus*, 331; and Walter Grundmann, *Das Evangelium nach Matthäus*, 4. Aufl., TheolHand, 1 (Berlin: Evangelische Verlagsanstalt, 1981), 290.

[28] Although Mark and Luke also prohibit many of these items (cf. Mk 6:8-9; Lk 9:3; 10:4), Matthew goes beyond Mark. Mark allows "sandals" (σανδάλιον), presumably rather than the potentially more substantial ὑπόδημα; and while Luke, like Matthew, forbids a staff, Mark allows it. Both

sense" do not apply in the kingdom where God, not human resources, is the ultimate reality, even in an area so concrete as everyday physical needs and typically essential protections.

Matthew substantiates these prohibitions with the maxim, "The laborer deserves his food" (Mt 10:10). Paul appeals to this dominical saying as a basis for the principle that those who minister should expect to earn a living from those to whom they minister (1 Cor 9:14; 1 Tim 5:18),[29] and Luke employs it in connection with accepting what hosts provide (Lk 10:7). On the basis of these parallels some interpreters conclude that Matthew also has in mind the expectation of provision from those who benefit from their ministry.[30] But according to Matthew 9:37-38 it is "the Lord of the harvest" who sends out "laborers into *his* harvest." Thus Matthew suggests that it is the Lord Jesus who will provide for all the necessities of disciples as they minister.

The mission of discipleship involves priorities based on the prospect of results. If disciples are not to plan carefully for their own provisions, they are to be intentional and "meticulous"[31] on entering a town to determine who in that town is "worthy," that is, most likely to "receive you or listen to your words," and to stay with such persons. The decision of lodging, then, is based on the likelihood of ministerial results, not on considerations of material comfort; for when Jesus instructs disciples to stay with that worthy person "until you depart," he suggests that they are not to change residence in search of greater comfort or better food.[32]

The mission of discipleship involves an acceptance of the limits of ministry. Rejection of the message leads the disciple to move on (Mt 10:12-15). The shaking of dust from the feet is a sign of total abandonment, and thus a final testimony against those who have been resistant, and functions thereby as a further warning to them (cf. Mt 23:37-39). But this gesture was performed also by those who shook off the dust of pagan

---

Mark and Luke forbid "bread"; perhaps Matthew considered the matter of food covered with mention of "bag."
[29]Although Paul chose not to take advantage of this provision (1 Cor 9:12-18; 1 Thess 2:1-12; cf. Acts 18:1-4; 20:34-35).
[30]E.g., Craig L. Blomberg, *Matthew*, NAC (Nashville: Broadman, 1992), 171; Carson, "Matthew," 245.
[31]This is the meaning of ἐξετάζω, "find out" (NRSV). See BDAG, "ἐξετάζω."
[32]While it is important to avoid uncritically reading one Gospel into another, in this case Lk 10:7 makes explicit the point that Matthew seems to be making implicitly.

soil as they entered Jewish territory, thus suggesting such dust represented a kind of defilement.[33]

Indeed, the reference to "Sodom and Gomorrah" (Mt 10:15) might recall the danger that residing too long in Sodom posed to Lot (Gen 19:1-29), and thereby suggest that continuing to stay among those who refuse the gospel may involve a danger of spiritual defilement and loss on the part of the disciple. Note a similar danger is mentioned in Matthew 7:6. But a further reason is suggested in Matthew 9:37 and Matthew 10:23: the combination of the great extent of need and the shortness of time requires disciples to minister to as many as possible.

And yet this concern to direct ministry toward the best prospects for results must be balanced by Jesus' teaching in the parable of the soils (Mt 13:3-9, 18-23). There, the sower, who represents both Jesus and the disciples,[34] sows "the word of the kingdom" with liberal abandon, not considering beforehand the quality of the soil but sowing indiscriminately. And in the Gospel of Matthew generally, it is those who at first blush would seem most unworthy, such as tax collectors and prostitutes, who enter the kingdom before those who would be expected to have the greatest spiritual and religious sensitivity (e.g., Mt 21:28-32).

The mission of discipleship involves vulnerability to persecutors. When Jesus declares that he sends disciples out "as sheep in the midst of wolves" (Mt 10:23), he indicates that disciples assume the vulnerable condition of the sheep to whom they have been sent; the harassed and helpless "sheep without a shepherd" (Mt 9:36) have now become threatening wolves. This is the outcome of the ministry of Jesus: The Jewish crowds to whom he ministers finally turn on him and demand his crucifixion (Mt 27:22-26).

In fact, much of this description of the persecution of disciples mirrors the experience of Jesus (cf. Mt 10:24-25). They, like Jesus (and John the Baptist) will be "delivered up" (παραδίδωμι, Mt 10:17), a word that, when used of persons, always carries within the Gospel of Matthew the idea of being persecuted unto death.[35] And they will be delivered up "to councils" (συνέδριον), the same word that is used of the Sanhedrin that condemned

---

[33]See, e.g., Hagner, *Matthew 1–13*, 273; Keener, *Matthew*, 320.

[34]The seed is "the word of the kingdom," that is, the preaching that "the kingdom of heaven is at hand," a word sown both by Jesus (Mt 4:17) and the disciples (Mt 10:7).

[35]Mt 4:12; 5:25; 10:4; 17:22; 20:18-19; 24:9-10; 25:15; 26:2, 15-16, 21, 23-25, 45-46, 48; 27:2, 4, 18, 26.

Jesus to death (Mt 26:59). They will be "flogged" (μαστιγόω) in the synagogues, even as Jesus was flogged (Mt 20:19; cf. Mt 27:26); this flogging *in the synagogues* suggests rejection by the religious community and accusation that they are enemies of God. They will be dragged before "governors" (ἡγεμών) and "kings" (βασιλεύς), even as Jesus was pursued by king Herod (Mt 2:1-23) and condemned by Pilate the governor (Mt 27:2, 11, 14, 15, 21, 27). This suggests rejection by society and its institutions. In all of this, the same "Spirit" that was active in Jesus' ministry (Mt 12:28) will speak through these disciples (Mt 10:20).[36] But, in addition, the disciples will be delivered up and hated by family (Mt 10:21, 35-36), thus suggesting rejection by intimates. And they will be "hated by all," indicating total rejection, the "tyranny of the absolute majority." Jesus insists that this persecution is inevitable, since it belongs to the very essence of discipleship to him (Mt 10:25), and is persistent, even "to the end" (Mt 10:23). Insofar as Matthew repeatedly draws a comparison between the disciples and Jesus, he suggests that the most profound experience of oneness with Jesus, of experiencing Jesus' presence with them, is found in this commonality of persecution that attends mission (see Mt 28:19-20).

But the sovereignty of God and the authority of Jesus is operative not only in meeting the physical needs of disciples in their mission, but also in so using human persecution as to achieve the divine purposes for the mission. Such persecution will provide an opportunity to witness to governors, kings, and Gentiles that otherwise these disciples would never have (Mt 10:18; cf. Mt 10:6). They will "confess" Jesus (Mt 10:32-33) in quarters that otherwise would have been closed to them. We find an implicit contrast of purpose here. The purpose of the persecutors is to quiet the disciples, to put an end to the message, but the persecution serves rather as a means to further the message.

The vulnerability to persecution must lead the disciple to "beware" of humans (Mt 10:16). This involves recognizing the reality of the danger persecutors pose and doing what they can to avoid unnecessary persecution (Mt 10:16, "wise as serpents"). Yet disciples should not fear what humans can do to them (Mt 10:26), for the real danger is not that of physical death, since

---

[36]This is the only reference in the Gospel of Matthew to the activity of the Holy Spirit in the lives of disciples.

all have to die anyway and God's loving care is operative through death (Mt 10:28-31), but of cowering so as to deny Jesus before them (Mt 10:32-33), or of somehow incurring guilt by the way they respond to these persecutors (Mt 10:16, "innocent as doves"), leading to their own eternal demise (Mt 10:37-39).

Yet not all will reject and persecute (Mt 10:40-42). That which makes all this vulnerability to persecution worthwhile is that some will respond positively so as to experience the same eschatological reward as the disciples themselves. Even as the rejection of the message is expressed in mistreatment toward the messengers, so the acceptance of the message is expressed in kindness toward the messengers. And even as disciples experience profound oneness with God and with Jesus, who is "God with us," through persecution, so also that oneness is operative in the positive response to the disciples' message, for those who receive the messengers thereby also receive Jesus and God (Mt 10:40). And, as far as Matthew is concerned, the experience of such oneness between humans and God is the ultimate good for humankind and the final purpose of this Gospel.

BIBLIOGRAPHY

Abel, Ernest L. "Who Wrote Matthew?" *NTS* 17 (1970-71): 138-52.

Abrams, M. H. *A Glossary of Literary Terms*. 5th ed. Fort Worth, TX: Holt, Rinehart, and Winston, 1988.

Achtemeier, Paul J., Joel B. Green, and Marianne Meye Thompson. *Introducing the New Testament: Its Literature and Theology*. Grand Rapids: Eerdmans, 2001.

Allen, Willoughby C. *A Critical and Exegetical Commentary on the Gospel According to S. Matthew*. ICC. Edinburgh: T&T Clark, 1912.

Allen, Willoughby C. and L. W. Grensted. *Introduction to the Books of the New Testament*. 3rd ed. New York: T&T Clark, 1929.

Allison, Dale C., Jr. *Jesus of Nazareth: A Millenarian Prophet*. Minneapolis: Fortress, 1998.

———. "Matthew 23:39 = Luke 13:35b as a Conditional Prophecy." *JSNT* 18 (1983): 75-84.

———. *The New Moses: A Matthean Typology*. Minneapolis: Fortress, 1993.

———. "The Structure of the Sermon on the Mount." *JBL* 106 (1987): 423-45.

———. *Studies in Matthew: Interpretation Past and Present*. Grand Rapids: Baker Academic, 2005.

Anderson, Janice Capel. *Matthew's Narrative Web: Over and Over Again*. JSNTSup 91. LNTS 91. Sheffield: Sheffield Academic Press, 1994.

———. "Matthew: Gender and Reading." *Semeia* 28 (1983): 3-27.

Attridge, Harold W. *Hebrews*. Hermeneia. Philadelphia: Fortress, 1989.

Augustine. *Harmony of the Gospels*. In *Nicene and Post Nicene Fathers*. Edited by Philip Schaff. Reprint, Peabody, MA: Hendrickson, 1994.

Bacon, Benjamin Wisner. "The 'Five Books' of Moses Against the Jews." *Expositor* 15 (1918): 56-66.

———. "Jesus and the Law: A Study of the First 'Book' of Matthew." *JBL* 47 (1928): 203-31.

———. *Studies in Matthew*. New York: Henry Holt, 1930.

Bailey, James L. "Genre Analysis." In *Hearing the New Testament: Strategies for Interpretation*, edited by Joel B. Green. Grand Rapids: Eerdmans, 1995.

Bailey, James L. and Lyle D. Vander Broek. *Literary Forms in the New Testament*. Louisville: Westminster John Knox, 1992.

Balch, David L. ed. *Social History of the Matthean Community: Cross-Disciplinary Approaches*. Minneapolis: Fortress, 1991.

Baltzer, Klaus. "Considerations Regarding the Office and Calling of the Prophet." *HTR* 61 (1968): 567-91.

Barr, David L. "The Drama of Matthew's Gospel: A Reconsideration of Its Structure and Purpose." *TD* 24 (1976): 349-59.

Barr, James. *The Semantics of Biblical Language*. London: SCM, 1983.

Barth, Gerhard. "Matthew's Understanding of the Law." In *Tradition and Interpretation in Matthew*, edited by Günther Bornkamm, Gerhard Barth, and Heinz Joachim Held, 112-16. NTL. Philadelphia: Westminster, 1963.

Battenhouse, Henry Martin. *New Testament History and Literature*. New York: Thomas Nelson, 1937.

Bauckham, Richard. "For Whom Were the Gospels Written?" In *The Gospels for All Christians: Rethinking the Gospel Audiences*, edited by Richard Bauckham, 9-48. Grand Rapids: Eerdmans, 1998.

———, ed. *The Gospels for All Christians: Rethinking the Gospel Audiences*. Grand Rapids: Eerdmans, 1998.

———. *God Crucified: Monotheism and Christology in the New Testament*. Grand Rapids: Eerdmans, 1999.

———. "John for Readers of Mark." In *The Gospels for All Christians: Rethinking the Gospel Audiences*, edited by Richard Bauckham, 147-71. Grand Rapids: Eerdmans, 1998.

Bauer, David R. "The Kingship of Jesus in the Matthean Infancy Narrative: A Literary Analysis." *CBQ* 57 (1995): 306-23.

———. "The Literary and Theological Function of the Genealogy in Matthew's Gospel." In *Treasures New and Old: Recent Contributions to Matthean Studies*, edited by David R. Bauer and Mark Allan Powell, 129-59. SBLSS 1. Atlanta: Scholars, 1996.

———. "The Major Characters of Matthew's Story: Their Function and Significance." *Int* 46 (1992): 357-67.

———. "Perfection of Disciples in Matthew's Gospel: An Examination of a Central Concept in Matthean Kingdom Ethics." In *Kingdom Rhetoric: New Testament*

Explorations in Honor of Ben Witherington III, edited by T. Michael W. Halcomb, 3-20. Eugene, OR: Wipf & Stock, 2013.

———. "Streeter Versus Farmer: The Present State of the Synoptic Problem as Argument for a Synchronic Emphasis in Gospel Interpretation." *JIBS* 6 (2019): 7-27.

———. *The Structure of Matthew's Gospel: A Study in Literary Design*. JSNT 31. Sheffield: Almond, 1988.

———. "The Theme of Mission in Matthew's Gospel from the Perspective of the Great Commission." *AJ*, forthcoming.

Bauer, David R. and Robert A. Traina. *Inductive Bible Study: A Comprehensive Guide to the Practice of Hermeneutics*. Grand Rapids: Baker Academic, 2011.

Baxter, Wayne S. "Healing and the 'Son of David': Matthew's Warrant." *NovT* 48 (2006): 36-50.

———. "Mosaic Imagery in the Gospel of Matthew." *TJ* 20 (1999): 69-83.

Beare, Francis Wright. *The Gospel According to Matthew*. San Francisco: Harper & Row, 1981.

Beasley-Murray, George R. *Baptism in the New Testament*. Grand Rapids: Eerdmans, 1973.

———. *Jesus and the Kingdom of God*. Grand Rapids: Eerdmans, 1986.

———. *Jesus and the Last Days*. Peabody, MA: Hendrickson, 1993.

Behm, J. "μετανοέω, μετάνοια." *TDNT*, 4:989-1008.

Bendoraitis, Kristian A. *Behold the Angels Came and Served Him: A Compositional Analysis of Angels in Matthew*. LNTS 523. New York: T&T Clark, 2015.

Benoit, Pierre. *L'Évangile selon Saint Matthieu*. 3rd ed. Paris: Les Editions du Cerf, 1961.

Benoit, Pierre and M.-E. Boismard. *Synopse des quartres Evangiles en français, Tome II*. Paris: le Cerf, 1972.

Bietenhard, Hans. "ὄνομα." *TDNT*, 5:242-83.

Bird, Michael F. *Jesus Is the Christ: The Messianic Testimony of the Gospels*. Downers Grove, IL: InterVarsity Press, 2012.

Blomberg, Craig L. *Matthew*. NAC. Nashville: Broadman, 1992.

Bockmuehl, Markus. *Seeing the Word: Refocusing New Testament Studies*. Grand Rapids: Baker, 2006.

Bonnard, Pierre. *L'Evangile selon saint Matthieu*. Paris: Labor et Fides, 2002.

Booth, Wayne. *The Rhetoric of Fiction*. Chicago: University of Chicago Press, 1961.

Boring, M. Eugene. "The Gospel of Matthew." In *The New Interpreter's Bible: A Commentary in Twelve Volumes*, edited by Leander E. Keck, 8:112-19. Nashville: Abingdon, 1994–2002.

———. *Sayings of the Risen Jesus: Christian Prophecy in the Synoptic Tradition*. SNTMS 46. New York: Cambridge University Press, 1982.

Bornkamm, Günther. "Authority to Bind and Loose in the Church in Matthew's Gospel." *Perspective* 11 (1970): 37-50.

———. "End-Expectation." In *Tradition and Interpretation in Matthew*, edited by Günther Bornkamm, Gerhard Barth, and Heinz Joachim Held. NTL. Philadelphia: Westminster, 1963.

———. *Jesus of Nazareth*. New York: Harper & Row, 1960.

———. "The Stilling of the Storm in Matthew." In *Tradition and Interpretation in Matthew*, edited by Günther Bornkamm, Gerhard Barth, and Heinz Joachim Held, 52-57. NTL. Philadelphia: Westminster, 1963.

Boxall, Ian. *Discovering Matthew: Content, Interpretation, Reception*. Discovering Biblical Texts. Grand Rapids: Eerdmans, 2014.

Boyarin, Daniel. *Border Lines: The Partition of Judeo-Christianity*. Philadelphia: University of Pennsylvania Press, 2004.

Brandon, S. G. F. *The Fall of Jerusalem and the Christian Church*. London: SPCK, 1951.

Brown, Jeanine K. *The Disciples in Narrative Perspective: The Portrayal and Function of the Matthean Disciples*. SBLAcBib 9. Leiden: Brill, 2002.

Brown, Raymond E. *The Birth of the Messiah: A Commentary on the Infancy Narratives in the Gospels of Matthew and Luke*. New ed. ABRL. New York: Doubleday, 1993.

———. *The Death of the Messiah: A Commentary on the Passion Narrative in the Four Gospels*. 2 vols. ABRL. New York: Doubleday, 1994.

———. *Introduction to the New Testament*. New York: Doubleday, 1997.

Brown, Raymond E., Karl P. Donfried, and John Reumann, eds., *Peter in the New Testament*. Minneapolis: Augsburg, 1973.

Brown, Schuyler. "The Matthean Community and the Gentile Mission." *NovT* 22 (1980): 193-221.

Büchsel, Friedrich. "δέω, λύω." *TDNT*, 2:60-61.

Bultmann, Rudolf. "γινώσκω." *TDNT*, 1:679-719.

———. "The Gospels (Form)." In *Twentieth Century Theology in the Making*, edited by Jaroslav Pelikan, 1:86-92. London: Fontana, 1969.

———. *The History of the Synoptic Tradition*. Rev. ed. Oxford: Blackwell, 1972.

———. *Jesus and the Word*. New York: Scribner's, 1934.

Burger, Christoph. *Jesus als Davidssohn: Eine Traditionsgeschichtliche Untersuchung*. Göttingen: Vandenhoeck & Ruprecht, 1970.

Burridge, Richard A. "About People, by People, for People: Gospel Genre and Audiences," in *The Gospels for All Christians: Rethinking the Gospel Audiences*, edited by Richard Bauckham, 113-45. Grand Rapids: Eerdmans, 1998.

———. *What Are the Gospels? A Comparison with Graeco-Roman Biography*. 2nd ed. Grand Rapids: Eerdmans, 2004.

Burton, Ernest DeWitt. "The Purpose and Plan of the Gospel of Matthew." *BW* 11 (1898): 37-44, 91-101.

Butler, Benjamin C. *The Originality of St. Matthew*. New York: Cambridge University Press, 1951.

Byrskog, Samuel. *Jesus the Only Teacher: Didactic Authority and Transmission in Ancient Israel, Ancient Judaism and the Matthean Community*. Stockholm: Almqvist & Wiksell, 1994.

Caragounis, Chrys C. *The Son of Man: Vision and Interpretation*. WUNT 38. Tübingen: Mohr, 1986.

Carson, Donald A. "Matthew." In *The Expositor's Bible Commentary*, edited by Frank E. Gaebelein and Walter C. Kaiser Jr., 8:1-599. Grand Rapids: Zondervan, 1984.

Carter, Warren. *Households and Discipleship: A Study of Matthew 19-20*. JSNTSup 103. Sheffield: Sheffield Academic Press, 1994.

———. "Kernels and Narrative Blocks: The Structure of Matthew's Gospel." *CBQ* 54 (1992): 463-81.

———. "Matthew 4:18-22 and Matthean Discipleship: An Audience-Oriented Perspective." *CBQ* 59 (1997): 66-67.

———. *Matthew: Storyteller, Interpreter, Evangelist*. Peabody, MA: Hendrickson, 1996.

Case, Shirley Jackson. "The Origin and Purpose of the Gospel of Matthew." *BW* 34 (1909): 391.

Casey, Maurice. *The Solution to the Son of Man Problem*. New York: T&T Clark, 2007.

Catchpole, David R. "The Answer of Jesus to Caiaphas." *NTS* 17 (1971): 212-26.

Chapman, John. *Matthew, Mark and Luke: A Study in the Order and Interrelation of the Synoptic Gospels*. London: Longmans, Green, 1937.

Chatman, Seymour. *Story and Discourse: Narrative Structure in Fiction and Film*. Ithaca, NY: Cornell University Press, 1978.

Childs, Brevard S. *The New Testament as Canon: An Introduction*. Philadelphia: Fortress, 1984.

Christ, Felix. *Jesus Sophia: Die Sophia-Christologie bei den Synoptikern*. Zurich: Zwingli-Verlag, 1970.

Chung, Yonghan. "A Postcolonial Reading of the Great Commission (Matt 28:16-20) with a Korean Myth." *ThTo* 72 (2015): 276-88.

Clark, Kenneth W. "The Gentile Bias in Matthew." *JBL* 66, no. 2 (1947): 165-72.

Clogg, Frank Bertram. *An Introduction to the New Testament*. 2nd ed. London: University of London, 1940.

Colpe, Carston. "ὁ υἱὸς τοῦ ἀνθρώπου." *TDNT*, 8:400-420.

Combrink, H. J. Bernard. "The Structure of the Gospel of Matthew as Narrative." *TynBul* 34 (1983): 61-90.

Conzelmann, Hans, and Andreas Lindemann, *Arbeitsbuch zum Neuen Testament*. Tübingen: Mohr, 1975.

Cope, O. Lamar. *Matthew: A Scribe Trained for the Kingdom of Heaven*. CBQMS 5. Washington, DC: Catholic Biblical Association of America, 1976.

Cothenet, Édouard. "Les prophètes chrétiens dans l'Évangile selon saint Matthieu." In *L'Evangile selon saint Matthieu: Rédaction et Théologie*, edited by M. Didier, 281-308. BETL 29. Glemboux: Duculot, 1972.

Cotterell, Peter and Max Turner. *Linguistics and Biblical Interpretation*. Downers Grove, IL: InterVarsity Press, 1989.

Cousland, J. R. C. *The Crowds in the Gospel of Matthew*. NovTSup 102. Leiden: Brill, 2002.

Crosby, Michael H. *House of Disciples: Church, Economics, and Justice in Matthew*. Maryknoll, NY: Orbis, 1988.

Crossan, John Dominic. *The Historical Jesus: The Life of a Mediterranean Jewish Peasant*. San Francisco: Harper, 1991.

Crossley, James G. "Jesus, Healings and Mark 2:1-12: Forgiveness, a Release, or Bound Again to the Great Satan?" In *Evil in Second Temple Judaism and Early Christianity*, edited by Chris Keith and Loren T. Stuckenbruck, 86-100. WUNT 2/417. Tübingen: Mohr Siebeck, 2016.

Cullmann, Oscar. *The Christology of the New Testament*. Rev. ed. NTL. Philadelphia: Westminster, 1963.

Culpepper, R. Alan. *The Anatomy of the Fourth Gospel: A Study in Literary Design*. Philadelphia: Fortress, 1983.

Daniélou, Jean. *The Infancy Narratives*. New York: Herder and Herder, 1968.

Davidson, Samuel. *An Introduction to the Study of the New Testament: Critical, Exegetical, Theological*. 3rd ed. 2 vols. London: Kegan Paul, Trench, Trübner, 1894.

Davies, W. D. and Dale C. Allison Jr. *The Gospel According to Saint Matthew*. 3 vols. ICC. New York: T&T Clark, 1988-1997.

Davies, William D. *The Setting of the Sermon on the Mount* (New York: Cambridge University Press, 1966), 15-16.

deSilva, David A. *An Introduction to the New Testament: Context, Methods & Ministry Formation.* Downers Grove, IL: InterVarsity Press, 2004.

Deutsch, Cecilia. "Wisdom in Matthew: Transformation of a Symbol." *NovT* 32 (1990): 13-47.

Dibelius, Martin. *From Tradition to Gospel.* London: James Clarke, 1971 [1919].

Dillersburger, Josef. *Matthäus: Das Evangelium des heiligen Matthäus in theologischer und heilsgeschichtler Schau, Vol. 1: Seine Kommen in Vilhalt (die Vorgeschichte).* Salzburg: Otto Müller, 1953.

Dodd, C. H. *The Parables of the Kingdom.* Rev. ed. New York: Scribner's, 1961.

Dods, Marcus. *An Introduction to the New Testament.* London: Hodder and Stoughton, n.d.

Donaldson, Terence. *Jesus on the Mountain: A Study in Matthean Theology.* JSNTSup 8. Sheffield: JSOT Press, 1985.

Downey, Glanville. *A History of Antioch in Syria from Seleucus to the Arab Conquest.* Princeton: Princeton University Press, 1961.

Duling, Dennis C. "Matthew's Plurisignificant 'Son of David' in Social Science Perspective: Kinship, Kingship, Magic, and Miracle." *BTB* 22 (1992): 112-13.

———. "The Therapeutic Son of David: An Element in Matthew's Christological Apologetic." *NTS* 24 (1977-78): 392-410.

Dunn, James D. G. *Jesus Remembered.* Christianity in the Making. Grand Rapids: Eerdmans, 2003.

Dupont, Jacques. *Les beatitudes.* 3 vols. Paris: Gabaldi, 1969-73.

Durand, Alfred. *Évangile selon Saint Matthieu: Traduction et Commentaire.* Paris: Beauchnesne et ses Fils, 1948.

Edwards, Richard A. "Uncertain Faith: Matthew's Portrait of the Disciples." In *Discipleship in the New Testament,* edited by Fernando F. Segovia, 47-61. Philadelphia: Fortress, 1985.

Ellis, I. P. "But Some Doubted." *NTS* 14 (1968): 574-80.

Ellis, Peter F. *Matthew: His Mind and Message.* Collegeville, MN: Liturgical, 1974.

Enslin, Morton S. "'The Five Books of Matthew': Bacon on the Gospel of Matthew." *HTR* 24 (1931): 67.

Eusebius. *Ecclesiastical History.* Translated by C. F. Cruse. Peabody, MA: Hendrickson, 1998.

Evans, Craig A. *Matthew.* NCBC. New York: Cambridge University Press, 2012.

Farmer, William R. *Jesus and the Gospel: Tradition, Scripture, and Canon.* Philadelphia: Fortress, 1982.

———. *The Synoptic Problem: A Critical Analysis.* New York: Macmillan, 1964.

Farrar, Frederick William. *The Message of the Books: Being Discourses and Notes on the Books of the New Testament*. New York: E. P. Dutton, 1897.

Farrer, Austin. *St. Matthew and St. Mark*. London: Dacre, 1954.

Fenton, J. C. "Matthew and the Divinity of Jesus: Three Questions Concerning Matthew 1:20-23." In *Studia Biblica 1978. Papers on the Gospels*, edited by E. A. Livingstone, 79-82. Sheffield: JSOT Press, 1979.

Fiedler, Peter. *Das Matthäus-evangelium*. Stuttgart: Kohlhammer, 2006.

Filson, Floyd V. "Broken Patterns in the Gospel of Matthew." *JBL* 75 (1956): 227-31.

———. *The Gospel According to St. Matthew*. BNTC. London: Adam and Charles Black, 1960.

Fitzmyer, Joseph A. "The Contribution of Qumran Aramaic to the New Testament." *NTS* 20 (1973): 391-94.

———. "The Semitic Background of the New Testament Kyrios-Title." In *A Wandering Aramean: Collected Aramaic Essays*, edited by Joseph A. Fitzmyer, 115-43. SBLMS 25. Missoula, MT: Scholars, 1979.

Foster, Paul. *Community, Law and Mission in Matthew's Gospel*. WUNT 2/177. Tübingen: Mohr Siebeck, 2004.

France, R. T. "The Formula-Quotations of Matthew 2 and the Problem of Communication." *NTS* 27 (1980–81): 233-51.

———. *The Gospel of Matthew*. NICNT. Grand Rapids: Eerdmans, 2007.

———. *Matthew: Evangelist and Teacher*. Grand Rapids: Zondervan, 1989.

Frankemölle, Hubert. *Jahwe-Bund und Kirche Christi: Studien zur Form- und Traditionsgeschichte des "Evangeliums" nach Matthäus*. Neutestamentliche Abhandlungen/Neue Folge 10. Münster: Aschendorff, 1974.

Freed, Edwin D. *The New Testament: A Critical Introduction*. Belmont, CA: Wadsworth, 2001.

Frey, Jörg. "Das Vaterunser im Horizont antik-judischen Betens unter besonderer Berücksichtigung der Textfunde vom Toten Meer." In *Das Vaterunser in seinen antiken Kontexten*, edited by Florian Wilk, 1-24. Göttingen: Vandenhoeck & Ruprecht, 2016.

Frickenschmidt, Dirk. *Evangelium als Biographie: Die vier Evangelien im Rahmen antiker Erzahlkunst*. Tübingen: Francke, 1997.

Fuller, Reginald H. *A Critical Introduction to the New Testament*. London: Duckworth, 1971.

Fuller, Reginald H. and Pheme Perkins. *Who Is This Christ? Gospel Christology and Contemporary Faith*. Philadelphia: Fortress, 1983.

Gaboury, Antonio. *La Structure des Evangiles synoptique*. Paris: Desclée, 1970.
Gadamer, Hans-Georg. *Truth and Method*. New York: Crossroad, 1988.
Gaechter, Paul. *Das Matthäus Evangelium: Ein Kommentar*. Innsbruch: Tyrolia-Verlog, 1963.
———. *Die Literarische Kunst im Matthäus-Evangelium*. Stuttgart: Katholisches Bibelwerk, 1966.
Gale, Aaron M. *Redefining Ancient Borders: The Jewish Scribal Framework of Matthew's Gospel*. New York: T&T Clark, 2005.
Garland, David E. *The Intention of Matthew 23*. NovTSup 52. Leiden: Brill, 1979.
———. "Matthew's Understanding of the Temple Tax." In *Treasures New and Old: Recent Contributions to Matthean Studies*, edited by David R. Bauer and Mark Allan Powell, 69-98. SBLSS 1. Atlanta: Scholars, 1996.
———. *Reading Matthew: A Literary and Theological Commentary on the First Gospel*. New York: Crossroad, 1993.
Gaston, Lloyd. "The Messiah of Israel as Teacher of the Gentiles: The Setting of Matthew's Christology." *Int* 29 (1975): 24-40.
Gathercole, Simon. *The Pre-existent Son: Recovering the Christologies of Matthew, Mark, and Luke*. Grand Rapids: Eerdmans, 2006.
Gerhardsson, Birger. "Gottes Sohn als Diener Gottes: Messias, Agape, und Himmelsherrscaft nach dem matthäusevangelium." *StTheol* 27 (1973): 73-106.
———. *The Mighty Acts of Jesus According to Matthew*. ScrMin 5. Lund: Gleerup, 1979.
———. *The Testing of God's Son (Matt 4:1-11 & Par): An Analysis of an Early Christian Midrash*. Coniectanea Biblica. NT Series 2:1. Lund: Gleerup, 1966.
Gibbs, James M. "Purpose and Pattern in Matthew's Use of the Title 'Son of David.'" *NTS* 10 (1963): 446-64.
Gibbs, Jeffrey A. *Jerusalem and Parousia: Jesus' Eschatological Discourse in Matthew's Gospel*. St. Louis: Concordia, 2000.
———. *Matthew 1:1–11:1*. ConcC. St. Louis: Concordia, 2006.
Gnilka, Joachim. *Das Matthäus-evangelium*. 2 Teile. HThKNT. Freiburg: Berder, 1988.
Godet, Frédéric Louis. *Introduction to the New Testament*. 2 vols. New York: T&T Clark, 1899.
Goodacre, Marc. *The Case Against Q: Studies in Markan Priority and the Synoptic Problem*. New York: T&T Clark, 2002.
Gooding, D. W. "Structure Littéraire de Matthieu, XIII, 53 à XVIII, 35." *RB* 85 (1978): 227-38.
Goulder, M. D. *Midrash and Lection in Matthew*. London: SPCK, 1974.

Gray, Sherman W. *The Least of My Brothers Matthew 25:31-46: A History of Interpretation.* SBLDS 11. Atlanta: Scholars, 1989.

Green, H. Benedict. "The Structure of St. Matthew's Gospel." In *Studia Evangelica IV: Papers Presented to the Third International Congress on New Testament Studies Held at Christ Church, Oxford, 1965. Part I: The New Testament Scriptures,* edited by Frank L. Cross, 57-59. Berlin: Akademie, 1968.

Green, Joel B. "Narrative and New Testament Interpretation: Reflections on the State of the Art." LTQ 39 (2004): 162-63.

Grimes, Joseph E. *The Thread of Discourse.* Berlin: Mouton, 1975.

Gromacki, Robert G. *New Testament Survey.* Grand Rapids: Baker, 1974.

Grundmann, Walter. *Das Evangelium nach Matthäus.* 4th ed. Berlin: Evangelische Verlagsanstalt, 1981.

Guelich, Robert A. *The Sermon on the Mount: A Foundation for Understanding.* Waco, TX: Word, 1982.

Gundry, Robert H. *Matthew: A Commentary on His Handbook for a Mixed Church Under Persecution.* 2nd ed. Grand Rapids: Eerdmans, 1994.

———. *Peter: False Disciple and Apostate According to Saint Matthew.* Grand Rapids: Eerdmans, 2015.

———. *The Use of the Old Testament in St. Matthew's Gospel with Special Reference to the Messianic Hope.* NovTSup 18. Leiden: Brill, 1967.

Gurtner, David M. *The Torn Veil: Matthew's Exposition of the Death of Jesus.* SNTSMS 139. New York: Cambridge University Press, 2007.

Guthrie, Donald. *New Testament Introduction.* 4th ed. Downers Grove, IL: InterVarsity Press, 1990.

Habel, Norman. "The Form and Significance of the Call Narrative." ZAW 77 (1965): 297-333.

Hadas, Moses and Morton Smith. *Heroes and Gods: Spiritual Biographies in Antiquity.* London: Routledge & Kegan Paul, 1965.

Hagner, Donald A. "Determining the Date of Matthew." In *Jesus, Matthew's Gospel and Early Christianity: Studies in Memory of Graham Stanton,* edited by Daniel M. Gurtner, Joel Willitts, and Richard Burridge, 76-92. New York: T&T Clark, 2011.

———. *Matthew 1-13,* WBC. Dallas: Word, 1993.

———. *Matthew 14-28.* WBC Dallas: Word, 1995.

———. "Matthew: Apostate, Reformer, Revolutionary?" NTS 49 (2003): 193-209.

Hahn, Ferdinand. *The Titles of Jesus in Christology: Their History in Early Christianity.* New York: World, 1969.

Hamerton-Kelly, Robert G. *Pre-Existence, Wisdom, and the Son of Man: A Study of the Idea of Pre-Existence in the New Testament*. SNTSMS 21. New York: Cambridge University Press, 1973.

Hamilton, Catherine Sider. "The Death of Judas in Matthew: Matthew 27:9 Reconsidered." *JBL* 137 (2018): 419-37.

Hare, Douglas R. A. *Matthew*. IBC. Louisville: John Knox, 1993.

———. *The Son of Man Tradition*. Minneapolis: Fortress, 1990.

———. *The Theme of Jewish Persecution of Christians in the Gospel of St. Matthew*. New York: Cambridge University Press, 1967.

Harrington, Daniel J. *The Gospel of Matthew*. Sacra Pagina. Collegeville, MN: Liturgical, 1991.

Harris, Murray J. *Jesus as God: The New Testament Use of Theos in Reference to Jesus*. Grand Rapids: Baker, 1992.

Harris, Rendel. *Testimonies*. New York: Cambridge University Press, 1920.

Hays, Richard. *Reading Backwards: Figural Christology and the Fourfold Gospel Witness*. Waco, TX: Baylor University Press, 2016.

Held, Heinz Joachim. "Matthew as Interpreter of the Miracle Stories." In *Tradition and Interpretation in Matthew*, edited by Günther Bornkamm, Gerhard Barth, and Joachim Held, 165-246. NTL. Philadelphia: Westminster, 1963.

Hengel, Martin. *Judaism and Hellenism: Studies in Their Encounter in Palestine During the Early Hellenistic Period*. 2 vols. Philadelphia: Fortress, 1981.

———. *Son of God*. London: SCM, 1986.

———. *Studies in the Gospel of Mark*. Philadelphia: Fortress, 1985.

Hill, David. *The Gospel of Matthew*. NCB. Grand Rapids: Eerdmans, 1972.

———. "Some Recent Trends in Matthean Studies." *IBS* 1 (1979): 139-49.

Hirsch, E. D., Jr. *Validity in Interpretation*. New Haven: Yale University Press, 1967.

Holladay, Carl R. *A Critical Introduction to the New Testament: Interpreting the Message and Meaning of Jesus Christ*. Nashville: Abingdon, 2005.

Holtzmann, Heinrich Julius. *Die Synoptischen Evangelien: Ihr Ursprung und Geschichtlicher Charakter*. Leipzig: Wilhelm Enselmann, 1863.

Horbury, William. "The Benediction of the Minim and early Jewish-Christian Controversy." *JTS* 33 (1988): 19-61.

———. *Messianism Among Jews and Christians: Twelve Biblical and Historical Studies*. New York: T&T Clark, 2003.

Howard, George. "The Tetragram and the New Testament." *JBL* 96 (1977): 63-83.

Howell, David B. *Matthew's Inclusive Story: A Study of the Narrative Rhetoric of the First Gospel*. JSNTSup 42. Sheffield: Sheffield Academic Press, 1990.

Hultgren, Arland J. *The Parables of Jesus: A Commentary.* Grand Rapids: Eerdmans, 2000.

Hultgren, Stephen. *Narrative Elements in the Double Tradition: A Study of Their Place Within the Framework of the Gospel Narrative.* Berlin: De Gruyter, 2002.

Hummel, Reinhart. *Die Auseindersetzung zwischen Kirche und Judentum im Matthäusevangelium.* München: Kaiser, 1963.

Hurtado, Larry. *Lord Jesus Christ: Devotion to Jesus in Earliest Christianity.* Grand Rapids: Eerdmans, 2003.

———. *One God, One Lord: Early Christian Devotion and Ancient Jewish Monotheism.* New York: T&T Clark, 1988.

Irenaeus. *Against Heresies.* Vol. 1 in *Ante-Nicene Fathers*, edited by Alexander Roberts and James Donaldson. 10 vols. Reprint, Peabody, MA: Hendrickson, 1994.

Jerome. *On Illustrious Men.* Vol. 3 in *Nicene and Post-Nicene Fathers*: Series 2, edited by Philip Schaff. 14 vols. Reprint, Peabody, MA: Hendrickson, 1894.

———. *Preface to the Four Gospels.* Vol. 6 in *Nicene and Post-Nicene Fathers*: Series 2, edited by Philip Schaff and Henry Wace. 14 vols. Reprint, Peabody, MA: Hendrickson, 1994.

Johnson, Luke Timothy. *The Writings of the New Testament: An Interpretation.* Rev. ed. Minneapolis: Fortress, 1999.

Johnson, Marshall D. "Reflections on a Wisdom Approach to Matthew's Christology." *CBQ* 36 (1974): 44-64.

Josephus. *Antiquities of the Jews.* In *The Works of Flavius Josephus.* Translated by William Whiston. Vol. 1. Grand Rapids: Baker, 1974.

———. *Jewish War.* In *The Works of Flavius Josephus.* Translated by William Whiston. Vols. 2-4. Grand Rapids: Baker, 1974.

Jülicher, Adolf. *Einleitung in das Neue Testament.* Freiburg: Akademische Verlagsbuchhandlung von J. C. B. Mohr, 1894.

Käsemann, Ernst. "The Problem of the Historical Jesus." In *Essays on New Testament Themes*, edited by Ernst Käsemann, 15-47. Philadelphia: Fortress, 1982.

Katz, Steven T. "Issues in the Separation of Judaism and Christianity After 70 CE: A Reconsideration." *JBL* 103 (1984): 43-76.

Keck, Leander E. "Toward the Renewal of New Testament Christology." *NTS* 32 (1986): 368-70.

Keegan, Terence J. "Introductory Formulae for the Matthean Discourses." *CBQ* 44 (1982): 415-30.

Keener, Craig S. *A Commentary on the Gospel of Matthew.* Grand Rapids: Eerdmans, 1999.

———. *The Historical Jesus of the Gospels.* Grand Rapids: Eerdmans, 2009.

---. "Introduction." In *Biographies and Jesus: What Does It Mean for the Gospels to Be Biographies?* edited by Craig S. Keener and Edward T. Wright, 1-45. Lexington, KY: Emeth, 2016.

Keim, Theodor. *Geschichte Jesu von Nazara.* 3 vols. Zurich: Füssli, 1867–74.

Kennedy, George A. *New Testament Interpretation Through Rhetorical Criticism.* Chapel Hill: University of North Carolina Press, 1984.

Kilpatrick, G. D. *The Origins of the Gospel According to St. Matthew.* Oxford: Clarendon, 1946.

Kimelman, R. "*Birkat Ha-Minim* and the Lack of Evidence for an Anti-Christian Jewish Prayer in Late Antiquity." In *Aspects of Judaism in the Graeco-Roman World*, edited by E. P. Sanders and A. I. Baumgarten, 2:226-44. London: SCM, 1981.

Kingsbury, Jack Dean. "The Developing Conflict Between Jesus and the Jewish Leaders in Matthew's Gospel: A Literary-Critical Study." *CBQ* 49 (1987): 57-73.

---. "The Figure of Jesus in Matthew's Story: A Literary-Critical Probe." *JSNT* 21 (1984): 3-36.

---. "The Figure of Peter in Matthew's Gospel as a Theological Problem." *JBL* 98 (1979): 69-83.

---. *Matthew.* 3rd ed. Nappanee, IN: Evangel, 1998.

---. *Matthew as Story.* Minneapolis: Fortress, 1986.

---. *Matthew: Structure, Christology, Kingdom.* Philadelphia: Fortress, 1975.

---. "On Following Jesus: The 'Eager' Scribe and the 'Reluctant' Disciple (Mt 8:18-20)." *NTS* 34 (1988): 45-59.

---. *The Parables of Jesus in Matthew 13: A Study in Redaction-Criticism.* London: SPCK, 1969.

---. "The Place, Structure, and Meaning of the Sermon on the Mount Within Matthew." *Int* 41 (1987): 131-43.

---. "Reflections on 'the Reader' of Matthew's Gospel." *NTS* 34 (1988): 458-59.

---. "The Structure of Matthew's Gospel and His Concept of Salvation-History." *CBQ* 35 (1973): 451-74.

---. "The Title 'Kyrios' in Matthew's Gospel." *JBL* 94 (1975): 250-54.

---. "The Title 'Son of David' in Matthew's Gospel." *JBL* 95 (1976): 591-602.

---. "The Verb *AKOLOUTHEIN* ('To Follow') as Index of Matthew's View of His Community." *JBL* 97 (1978): 56-73.

Kittel, Gerhard, "δόξα." *TDNT*, 2:233-53.

Klostermann, Erich. *Das Matthäus-Evangelium.* 4th ed. HNT. Tübingen: Mohr, 1971.

Köster, Helmut. "σπλαγνόν, κτλ." *TDNT*, 7:248-59.

Krentz, Edgar. "The Extent of Matthew's Prologue: Towards the Structure of the First Gospel." *JBL* 83 (1964): 409-15.

———. *The Historical-Critical Method*. GBS. Philadelphia: Fortress, 1975.

Kuist, Howard Tillman. *These Words upon Thy Heart: Scripture and the Christian Response*. Richmond: John Knox, 1947.

Kümmel, Werner Georg. *Introduction to the New Testament*. Rev. ed. Nashville: Abingdon, 1975.

———. *The New Testament: The History of the Investigation of Its Problems*. Nashville: Abingdon, 1972.

Kupp, David D. *Matthew's Emmanuel: Divine Presence and God's People in the First Gospel*. SNTSMS 90. New York: Cambridge University Press, 1996.

Kürzinger, Josef. "Das Papiaszeugnis und die Erstgestalt des Matthäusevangeliums." *BZ* 4 (1960): 19-38.

Lachman, Karl. "De ordine narrationum in evangeliis synopticis." *Theologische Studien und Kritiken* (1835): 570-90; English translation: N. H. Palmer, "Lachmann's Argument," *NTS* 13 (1967): 368-78.

Ladd, George Eldon. *The Presence of the Future*. Grand Rapids: Eerdmans, 1974.

LaGrange, Marie-Joseph. *Évangile selon Saint Matthieu*. 7th ed. Paris: Gabalda, 1948.

Leim, Joshua E. *Matthew's Theological Grammar: The Father and the Son*. WUNT 2/402. Tübingen: Mohr Siebeck, 2015.

Levesque, Karl E. "Quelques Procédés Litteraires de Saint Matthieu." *RB* 25 (1916): 387-405.

Lewis, Jack P. "Jamnia (Jabneh), Council of," *ABD*, 3:634-37.

Licona, Michael R. "Viewing the Gospels as Ancient Biographies Resolves Many Perceived Contradictions." In *Biographies and Jesus: What Does It Mean for the Gospels to Be Biographies?* edited by Craig S. Keener and Edward T. Wright, 323-28. Lexington, KY: Emeth, 2016.

Lightfoot, Robert Henry. *History and Interpretation in the Gospels*. London: Hodder and Stoughton, 1935.

Lindars, Barnabas. *Jesus Son of Man: A Fresh Examination of the Son of Man Sayings in the Gospels in Light of Recent Research*. Grand Rapids: Eerdmans, 1983.

Lohmeyer, Ernst. *Das Evangelium des Matthäus*, edited by Werner Schmauch. 4th ed. Göttingen: Vandenhoeck & Ruprecht, 1967.

Lohr, Charles H. "Oral Techniques in the Gospel of Matthew." *CBQ* 23 (1961): 403-35.

Lohse, Edward. *The Formation of the New Testament*. Nashville: Abingdon, 1972.

Loisy, Alfred. *The Origins of the New Testament*. London: George Allen and Unwin, 1950.

Long, Fredrick J. "Major Structural Relationships: A Survey of Origins, Development, Classifications, and Assessment." *JIBS* 1 (2014): 22-59.

Longacre, Robert E. *The Grammar of Discourse*. New York: Plenum, 1983.

Luomanen, Petri. *Entering the Kingdom of Heaven: A Study on the Structure of Matthew's View of Salvation*. WUNT 2. Tübingen: Mohr Siebeck, 1998.

Luz, Ulrich. "The Disciples in the Gospel According to Matthew." In *The Interpretation of Matthew*, edited by Graham Stanton, 98-128. Philadelphia: Fortress, 1983.

———. "The Final Judgment (Mt 25:31-46): An Exercise in 'History of Influence' Exegesis." In *Treasures New and Old: Recent Contributions to Matthean Studies*, edited by David R. Bauer and Mark Allan Powell, 271-310. SBLSS 1. Atlanta: Scholars, 1996.

———. *Matthew 1-7: A Commentary*. Minneapolis: Augsburg, 1989.

———. *Matthew 21-28*. Hermeneia. Minneapolis: Fortress, 2005.

———. *Matthew in History: Interpretation, Influence and Effects*. Minneapolis: Fortress, 1985.

———. "The Son of Man in Matthew: Heavenly Judge or Human Christ." *JSNT* 48 (1992): 3-21.

———. *Studies in Matthew*. Grand Rapids: Eerdmans, 2004.

———. *The Theology of the Gospel of Matthew*. New York: Cambridge University Press, 1995.

MacEwen, Robert. *Matthean Posteriority: An Exploration of Matthew's Use of Mark and Luke as a Solution to the Synoptic Problem*. LNTS 501. New York: T&T Clark, 2015.

Malina, Bruce J., and Jerome H. Neyrey. *Calling Jesus Names: The Social Value of Labels in Matthew*, Foundations and Facets Social Facets. Sonoma, CA: Polebridge, 1988.

Manson, T. W. *The Sayings of Jesus*. 2nd ed. London: SCM, 1949.

———. *The Teaching of Jesus: Studies of its Form and Content*. New York: Cambridge University Press, 1945.

Marguerat, Daniel. *Le Jugement dans L'Évangile de Matthieu*. La Monde de la Bible Geneva. Geneva: Labor et Fides, 1981.

Martin, Ralph P. *New Testament Foundations: A Guide for Christian Students*. Grand Rapids: Eerdmans, 1975.

Massaux, Edouard. *The Influence of the Gospel of St. Matthew in the Christian Literature Before St. Irenaeus*, edited by A. J. Bellinzoni. Macon, GA: Mercer, 1990.

Matera, Frank J. "The Plot of Matthew's Gospel." *CBQ* 49 (1987): 233-53.

McKee, Dean Greer. "Studia Biblica VI. The Gospel According to Matthew." *Int* 3 (1949): 194-205.

McKenzie, Steven L. and John Kaltner, eds. *Recent Approaches to Biblical Criticism and Their Applications*. Louisville: Westminster John Knox, 2013.

McKnight, Edgar V. "Presuppositions in New Testament Study." In *Hearing the New Testament: Strategies for Interpretation*, edited by Joel B. Green, 278-300. Grand Rapids: Eerdmans, 1995.

———. *What Is Form Criticism?* GBS. Philadelphia: Fortress, 1969.

McNeile, Alan Hugh. *The Gospel According to Matthew: The Greek Text with Introduction, Notes, and Indices*. New York: Macmillan, 1938.

Meier, John P. *Law and History in Matthew's Gospel*. Rome: Biblical Institute Press, 1976.

———. *A Marginal Jew: Rethinking the Historical Jesus*. 5 vols. ABRL. New York: Doubleday, 1987-2015.

———. *Matthew*. NTM 3. Wilmington, DE: Michael Glazier, 1980.

———. "Salvation History in Matthew: In Search of a Starting Point." *CBQ* 37 (1975): 203-13.

———. *The Vision of Matthew: Christ, Church, and Morality in the First Gospel*. New York: Paulist, 1979.

Meinertz, Max. *Einleitung in das Neue Testament*. 5th ed. Paderborn: Ferdinand Schöning, 1950.

Menken, M. J. J. *Matthew's Bible: The Old Testament Text of the Evangelist*. BETL 173. Leuven: Peeters, 2004.

Metzger, Bruce M. *The Canon of the New Testament*. Oxford: Clarendon, 1987.

Meynet, Roland. *Le fait synoptique reconsidéré*. Rome: Gregorian and Biblical Press, 2014.

Michel, Otto. "The Conclusion of Matthew's Gospel: A Contribution to the History of the Easter Message." In *The Interpretation of Matthew*, edited by Graham Stanton, 33-38. Philadelphia: Fortress, 1983.

Middleton, J. Richard. *A New Heaven and a New Earth: Reclaiming Biblical Eschatology*. Grand Rapids: Baker Academic, 2014.

Minear, Paul S. *Matthew: The Teacher's Gospel*. New York: Pilgrim, 1982.

Moberly, R. W. L. *The Bible, Theology, and Faith: A Study of Abraham and Jesus*. CSCD. New York: Cambridge University Press, 2000.

Mohrlang, Roger. *Matthew and Paul: A Comparison of Ethical Perspectives*. New York: Cambridge University Press, 1984.

Morgenthaler, Robert. *Statistik des neutestamentlichen Wortschatzes*. Zurich: Gotthelf, 1958.

Morris, Leon. *The Gospel According to Matthew*. PNTC. Grand Rapids: Eerdmans, 1992.

Moule, C. F. D. *The Birth of the New Testament*. 3rd ed. London: A. and C. Black, 1981.

———. *The Origin of Christology*. New York: Cambridge University Press, 1977.

Moulton, James Hope and Nigel Turner. *A Grammar of New Testament Greek*. Repr., New York: T&T Clark, 2000.

Mowery, Robert L. "The Matthean References to the Kingdom: Different Terms for Different Audiences." *ETL* 70 (1994): 398-405.

Müller, Mogens. "The Theological Interpretation of the Figure of Jesus in the Gospel of Matthew: Some Principal Features in Matthean Christology." *NTS* 45 (1999): 157-73.

Mullooparambil, Sebastian. *Macrostructure of Matthew's Gospel*. Bangalore: Dharmaram, 2011.

Nau, Arlo J. *Peter in Matthew: Discipleship, Diplomacy, and Dispractice*. Collegeville, MN: Liturgical, 1992.

Neirynck, Frans. "ΑΠΟ ΤΟΤΕ ΗΡΞΑΤΟ and the Structure of Matthew." *ETL* 64 (1988): 46-48.

Nepper-Christensen, Poul. *Das Matthäusevangelium: Ein juden-christliches Evangelium?* Aarhus: Universitetsforlaget, 1958.

Neyrey, Jerome H. *Honor and Shame in the Gospel of Matthew*. Louisville: Westminster John Knox, 1998.

Nida, Eugene A. *Exploring Semantic Structures*. Munich: Wilhelm Fink, 1975.

Nolland, John. *The Gospel of Matthew*. NIGTC. Grand Rapids: Eerdmans, 2005.

———. "No Son of God Christology in Matthew 1:18-25." *JSNT* 62 (1996): 3-12.

Novakovic, Lidija. *Messiah: The Healer of the Sick*. WUNT 2. Tübingen: Mohr Siebeck, 2003.

Oepke, Albert. "παρουσία, πάρειμι." *TDNT*, 5:858-71.

Orchard, J. B. *Matthew, Luke, and Mark*. Manchester: Koinonia, 1977.

Orton, David E. *The Understanding Scribe: Matthew and the Apocalyptic Ideal*. New York: T&T Clark, 1989.

Osborne, Grant R. *Matthew*. ZECNT. Grand Rapids: Zondervan, 2010.

Overman, Andrew. *Matthew's Gospel and Formative Judaism: The Social World of the Matthean Community*. Minneapolis: Fortress, 1990.

Palmer, Caroline L. *Emmanuel: Studies in the Gospel by Matthew*. Atlanta: Committee on Women's Work, PCUSA, 1947.

Pamment, Margaret. "The Son of Man in the First Gospel." *NTS* 29 (1983): 116-29.

Pennington, Jonathan. *Heaven and Earth in the Gospel of Matthew.* NovTSup 126. Leiden: Brill, 2007.

———. *The Sermon on the Mount and Human Flourishing: A Theological Commentary.* Grand Rapids: Baker Academic, 2017.

Perkins, Pheme. *Peter: Apostle for the Whole Church.* Minneapolis: Fortress, 2000.

Perrin, Norman. *What is Redaction Criticism?* GBS. Philadelphia: Fortress, 1969.

Pesch, Rudolf. "Der Gottessohn im matthäischen Evangelienprolog: Beobachtungen zu den Zitationsformeln der Reflexionszitate." *Biblica* 48 (1967): 395-420.

Peterson, Norman. "Can One Speak of a Gospel Genre?" *Neotestamentica* 28 (1994): 137-58.

Pietersma, Albert. "Kyrios or Tetragram: A Renewed Quest for the Original Septuagint." In *Studies in Honor of John W. Wevers on His Sixty-Fifth Birthday*, edited by Albert Pietersma and Claude Cox, 85-101. Mississauga, Ontario: Benben, 1984.

Plummer, Alfred. *An Exegetical Commentary on the Gospel According to Matthew.* London: Robert Scott, 1909.

Popa, Romeo. *Allgegenwärtiger Konflikt im Matthäusevangelium: Exegetische und sozialpsychologische Analyse der Konfliktgeschichte.* NovTOA/SUNT 111. Göttingen: Vandenhoeck & Ruprecht, 2017.

Porter, Stanley E. *Sacred Tradition in the New Testament: Tracing Old Testament Themes in the Gospels and Epistles.* Grand Rapids: Baker Academic, 2016.

Powell, Mark Allan. *Jesus as a Figure in History: How Modern Historians View the Man from Galilee.* Louisville: Westminster John Knox, 1998.

———. "Matthew's Beatitudes: Reversals and Rewards of the Kingdom." *CBQ* 58 (1996): 460-79.

———, ed., *Methods for Matthew.* New York: Cambridge University Press, 2009.

———. "The Plot and Subplots of Matthew's Gospel." *NTS* 38 (1992): 187-204.

———. *What Is Narrative Criticism?* GBS. Minneapolis: Fortress, 1990.

Prabhu, G. M. Soares. *The Formula Quotations in the Infancy Narrative of Matthew: An Inquiry into the Tradition History of Mt 1-2.* AnBib 63. Rome: Pontifical Biblical Institute, 1976.

Pregeant, Russell. *Matthew.* CCT. St. Louis: Chalice, 2004.

Przybylski, Benno. *Righteousness in Matthew and His World of Thought.* SNTMS. New York: Cambridge University Press, 1980.

Radermakers, Jean. *Au fil de l'évangile selon saint Matthieu.* 2 vols. Louvain: Heverlee, 1972.

Ramaroson, Léonard. "La structure du premier Evangile." *ScEs* 26 (1974): 69.

Rau, Christoph. *Das Matthaus-Evangelium: Enstehung, Gestalt, Essenischer Einfluss.* Stuttgart: Urachhaus, 1976.
Reicke, Bo. *The Roots of the Synoptic Gospels.* Philadelphia: Fortress, 1986.
Renan, Ernst. *Life of Jesus.* London: Kegan Paul, 1893 [1863].
Rengstorf, Karl Heinrich. "ἀπόστολος," *TDNT,* 1:407-46
———. "Die Stadt der Mörder (Mt 22.7)." In *Judentum, Urchristentum, Kirche: Festschrift für Joachim Jeremias,* edited by Walther Eltester, 106-29. BZNW. Berlin: Töpelmann, 1960.
———. "ἕπτα," *TDNT,* 2:627-35.
Resseguie, James L. *Narrative Criticism of the New Testament: An Introduction.* Grand Rapids: Baker, 2005.
Rhoads, David and Donald Michie. *Mark as Story: An Introduction to the Narrative of a Gospel.* Philadelphia: Fortress, 1982.
Ridderbos, Herman. *Matthew's Witness to Jesus Christ: The King and the Kingdom.* New York: Association, 1958.
Rist, John M. *On the Independence of Matthew and Mark.* New York: Cambridge University Press, 1978.
Rivken, Ellis. *A Hidden Revolution: The Pharisees' Search for the Kingdom Within.* Nashville: Abingdon, 1978.
Robinson, J. Armitage. *The Study of the Gospels.* London: Longmans, Green, 1902.
Robinson, James M. *A New Quest for the Historical Jesus.* London: SCM, 1959.
Robinson, Theodore H. *The Gospel of Matthew.* MNTC. London: Hodder and Stoughton, 1928.
Rohde, Joachim. *Rediscovering the Teaching of the Evangelists.* NTL. Philadelphia: Westminster, 1968.
Rolland, Philippe. "From the Genesis to the End of the World: The Plan of Matthew's Gospel." *BTB* 2 (1972): 155-76.
Roose, Hanna. "Sharing in Christ's Rule: Tracing a Debate in Earliest Christianity." *JSNT* 27 (2004): 123-48.
Roux, Herbert. *L'Évangile du Royaume.* 2nd ed. Geneva: Labor et Fides, 1956.
Runesson, Anders. *Divine Wrath and Salvation in Matthew: The Narrative World of the First Gospel.* Minneapolis: Fortress, 2016.
———. "Rethinking Early Jewish-Christian Relations: Matthean Community History as Pharisaic Intergroup Conflict." *JBL* 117 (2008): 117-23.
Russell, David M. *The "New Heavens and New Earth": Hope for the Creation in Jewish Apocalyptic and the New Testament.* SBibApL 1. Philadelphia: Visionary, 1996.

Sabourin, Léopold. *L'Évangile selon Saint Matthieu et Ses Principaux Paralleles.* Rome: Biblical Institute Press, 1978.

Saldarini, Anthony J. "Boundaries and Polemics in the Gospel of Matthew." *BibInt* 3 (1995): 239-65.

———. *Matthew's Christian-Jewish Community.* Chicago: University of Chicago Press, 1994.

———. *Pharisees, Scribes and Sadducees in Palestinian Society: A Sociological Approach.* Grand Rapids: Eerdmans, 2001.

Sand, Alexander. *Das Evangelium nach Matthäus.* Regensburg: Verlag Friedrich Pustet, 1986.

Sanders, E. P. *Jesus and Judaism.* Philadelphia: Fortress, 1985.

———. *The Tendencies of the Synoptic Tradition.* New York: Cambridge University Press, 1969.

Sanders, E. P. and Margaret Davies. *Studying the Synoptic Gospels.* London: SCM, 1989.

Scaer, David P. *Discourses in Matthew: Jesus Teaches the Church.* St. Louis: Concordia, 2004.

Schäfer, Peter. "Die sogenannte Synode von Jabne. Sur Trennung von Juden und Christen im ersten/zweiten Jh. N. Chr." *Judaica* 31 (1975): 54-64, 116-24.

Schelkle, Karl Hermann. *Das Neue Testament: Seine literarische und theologische Geschichte.* 3rd ed. Kevelaer, Rhineland: Butzon & Bercker, 1966.

Schille, Gottfried. "Bemerkungen zur Formgeschichte des Evangeliums. II. Das Evangelium des Matthäus als Katechismus." *NTS* 4 (1957/58): 101-68.

Schlatter, Adolf. *Der Evangelist Matthäus,* 5th ed. Stuttgart: Calwer, 1959.

Schleiermacher, Friedrich. "Über die Zeugnisse des Papias von unsern beiden ersten Evangelien." *Theologische Studien und Kritiken* 5 (1892): 735-68.

Schlier, Heinrich. "ἀρνέομαι." *TDNT,* 1:469.

Schmidt, Karl Ludwig. *Der Rahmen der Geschichte Jesu.* Berlin: Trowitzsch und Sohn, 1919.

Schmitz, Ernst Dieter. "Knowledge." In *The New International Dictionary of New Testament Theology,* edited by Colin Brown, 2:392-409. Grand Rapids: Zondervan, 1974-79.

Schnackenburg, Rudolf. "Die Vollkommenheit des Christen nach den Evangelien." *GuL* 32 (1959): 420-33.

———. *The Gospel of Matthew.* Grand Rapids: Eerdmans, 2002.

Schnelle, Udo. *The History and Theology of the New Testament Writings.* Minneapolis: Fortress, 1994.

Schniewind, Julius. *Das Evangelium nach Matthäus.* 6th ed. Göttingen: Vandenhoeck & Ruprecht, 1953.
Schürer, Emil. *A History of the Jewish People in the Age of Jesus Christ.* Edited by Geza Vermes, Fergus Miller, and Matthew Black, 3 vols. New York: T&T Clark, 1973–87.
Schweitzer, Albert. *The Quest of the Historical Jesus: A Critical Study of Its Progress from Reimarus to Wrede.* New York: Macmillan, 1968 [1906].
Schweizer, Eduard. *The Good News According to Matthew.* Atlanta: John Knox, 1975.
———. *Matthäus und seine Gemeinde.* Stuttgart: Katholisches Bibelwerk, 1974.
———. "Observance of the Law and Charismatic Activity in Matthew." *NTS* 16 (1969-70): 213-30.
———. "ψυχή." *TDNT*, 9:639-40.
Scobie, Charles H. H. *The Ways of Our God: An Approach to Biblical Theology.* Grand Rapids: Eerdmans, 2003.
Senior, Donald. *The Gospel of Matthew.* Nashville: Abingdon, 1997.
———. *Invitation to Matthew: A Commentary on the Gospel of Matthew with Complete Text from the Jerusalem Bible.* Garden City, NY: Doubleday, 1977.
———. "The Lure of the Formula Quotations: Re-assessing Matthew's Use of the Old Testament with the Passion Narrative as a Test Case." In *The Scriptures in the Gospels*, edited by Christopher Mark Tuckett. BETL 131. Leuven: Leuven University Press, 1977.
———. *What Are They Saying About Matthew?* Rev. ed. New York: Paulist, 1996.
Shuler, Philip L. *A Genre for the Gospels: The Biographical Character of Matthew.* Philadelphia: Fortress, 1982.
Sim, David C. *Apocalyptic Eschatology in the Gospel of Matthew.* SNTSMS 88. New York: Cambridge University Press, 1996.
———. *The Gospel of Matthew and Christian Judaism: The History and Social Setting of the Matthean Community.* SNTW. New York: T&T Clark, 1998.
———. "Matthew's Use of Mark: Did Matthew Intend to Supplement or to Replace His Primary Source?" *NTS* 57 (2011): 176-92.
Simon, Marcel. *Jewish Sects at the Time of Jesus.* Philadelphia: Fortress, 1967.
Slater, Tommy B. "Notes on Matthew's Structure." *JBL* 99 (1980): 667-70.
Slingerland, H. Dixon. "The Transjordanian Origin of St. Matthew's Gospel." *JSNT* 3 (1979): 18-29.
Smith, Christopher R. "Literary Evidences of a Fivefold Structure in the Gospel of Matthew." *NTS* 43 (1997): 544-51.

Smith, Craig A. "Criteria for Biblical Chiasms: Objective Means for Distinguishing Chiasm of Design from Accidental and False Chiasm." PhD diss., University of Bristol, 2009.

Soulen, Richard N. and R. Kendall Soulen. *Handbook of Biblical Criticism*, 3rd ed. Louisville: Westminster John Knox, 2001.

Stanton, Graham. "The Fourfold Gospel." *NTS* 43 (1997): 341.

———. *A Gospel for a New People: Studies in Matthew*. New York: T&T Clark, 1992.

———. "Revisiting Matthew's Communities." In *SBL 1994 Seminar Papers*, edited by Eugene H. Lovering Jr., 9-23. Atlanta: Scholars, 1994.

———. "Salvation Proclaimed: X Matthew 11:28-30: Comfortable Words?" *ExpTim* 94 (1982-83): 3-9.

Stein, Robert H. *The Synoptic Problem: An Introduction*. Grand Rapids: Baker, 1987.

Stemberger, Günter. "Die sogenannte 'Synode von Jabne' und das frühe Christentum." *Kairos* 19 (1977): 14-21.

Stendahl, Krister. *The School of St. Matthew and Its Use of the Old Testament*. Philadelphia: Fortress, 1968.

Sternberg, Meir. *The Poetics of Biblical Narrative: Ideological Literature and the Drama of Reading*. Bloomington: Indiana University Press, 1987.

Stock, Augustine. *The Method and Message of Matthew*. Collegeville, MN: Michael Glazier, 1989.

Stoldt, H.-H. *History and Criticism of the Marcan Hypothesis*. New York: T&T Clark, 1980.

Stonehouse, Ned B. *The Witness of Matthew and Mark to Christ*. Philadelphia: Presbyterian Guardian, 1944.

Storr, Gottlob Christian. *Über den Zweck der evangelischen Geschichte und der Briefe Johannes*. Tübingen: Heerbrandt, 1786.

Strack, Hermann L. and Paul Billerbeck. *Kommentar zum Neuen Testament aus Talmud und Midrasch*. 10e Aufl. 6 Bände. Munich: Beck, 1994.

Strecker, Georg. "The Concept of History in Matthew." *JAAR* 35 (1967): 219-30.

———. "Die Makarismen der Bergpredigt." *NTS* 17 (1970-71): 255-75.

———. *The Sermon on the Mount: An Exegetical Commentary*. Nashville: Abingdon, 1988.

———. *Der Weg der Gerechtigkeit*. Göttingen: Vandenhoeck & Ruprecht, 1975.

Streeter, Burnett Hillman. *The Four Gospels: A Study of Origins*. New York: Macmillan, 1924.

Strong, Augustus H. *Popular Lectures on the Books of the New Testament*. Philadelphia: Griffith and Rowland, 1914.

Suggs, Jack M. *Wisdom, Christology, and Law in Matthew's Gospel.* Cambridge, MA: Harvard University Press, 1970.

Suhl, Anders. "Der Davidssohn im Matthäus-Evangelium," *ZNTW* 59 (1968): 57-81.

Talbert, Charles H. *Matthew.* Paideia. Grand Rapids: Baker Academic, 2010.

———. *Reading the Sermon on the Mount: Character Formation and Ethical Decision Making in Matthew 5–7.* Grand Rapids: Baker Academic, 2004.

———. *What Is A Gospel?: The Genre of the Canonical Gospels.* Philadelphia: Fortress, 1977.

Tannehill, Robert C. *The Narrative Unity of Luke-Acts: A Literary Interpretation, Volume One: The Gospel According to Luke.* Philadelphia: Fortress, 1986.

Taylor, Vincent. *The Formation of the Gospel Tradition.* New York: Macmillan, 1960.

———. *The Gospel According to St. Mark: The Greek Text with Introduction, Notes, and Indexes.* New York: Macmillan, 1952.

———. *The Names of Jesus.* New York: Macmillan, 1953.

Tertullian. *Against Marcion.* Vol. 3 in *Ante-Nicene Fathers,* edited by Alexander Roberts and James Donaldson. 10 vols. Reprint, Peabody, MA: Hendrickson, 1994.

Theisohn, Johannes. *Der Auserwählte Richter.* SUNT. Göttingen: Vandenhoeck & Ruprecht, 1974.

Theissen, Gerd. *The New Testament: A Literary History.* Minneapolis: Fortress, 2012.

Thompson, Alan J. *The Acts of the Risen Lord Jesus: Luke's Account of God's Unfolding Plan.* NSBT. Downers Grove, IL: InterVarsity Press, 2011.

Thompson, Marianne Meye. "The Structure of Matthew: A Survey of Recent Trends." *SBibTheol* 12 (1982): 197-98.

Thompson, William G. "An Historical Perspective in the Gospel of Matthew." *JBL* 93 (1974): 243-62.

———. *Matthew's Advice to a Divided Community: Mt. 17:22-18:35.* AB. Rome: Biblical Institute Press, 1970.

———. "Reflections on the Composition of Mt 8:1-9:34." *CBQ* 33 (1971): 365-88.

Traina, Robert A. *Methodical Bible Study: A New Approach to Hermeneutics.* New York: Ganis & Harris, 1952; repr., Grand Rapids: Zondervan, 2002.

Trilling, Wolfgang. *Das Wahre Israel: Studien zur Theologie des Matthäus-Evangeliums.* München: Kösel, 1964.

Turner, David L. *Israel's Last Prophet: Jesus and the Jewish Leaders in Matthew 23.* Minneapolis: Fortress, 2015.

———. *Matthew.* BECNT. Grand Rapids: Baker, 2008.

Uspensky, Boris. *A Poetics of Composition: The Structure of the Artistic Text and Typology of a Compositional Form.* Berkeley, CA: University of California, 1973.

Van Tilborg, Sjef. *The Jewish Leaders in Matthew*. Leiden: Brill, 1972.

Vanhoozer, Kevin J. "The Reader in New Testament Interpretation." in *Hearing the New Testament: Strategies for Interpretation*, edited by Joel B. Green, 301-28. Grand Rapids: Eerdmans, 1995.

Vermes, Geza. *Jesus in the Jewish World*. London: SCM, 2010.

Verseput, Donald. *The Rejection of the Humble Messianic King: A Study of the Composition of Matthew 11-12*. EUS 291. Frankfurt: Peter Lang, 1986.

———. "The Role and Meaning of the 'Son of God' Title in Matthew's Gospel." *NTS* 33 (1987): 532.

Via, Dan O. "Structure, Christology, and Ethics in Matthew." In *Orientation by Disorientation: Studies in Literary Criticism and Biblical Literary Criticism*, edited by Richard A. Spencer, 199-215. Pittsburg: Pickwick, 1980.

Viviano, Benedict T. *Matthew and His World: The Gospel of the Open Jewish Christians: Studies in Biblical Theology*. NovTOA. Göttingen: Vandenhoeck & Ruprecht, 2007.

———. "Where Was the Gospel According to St. Matthew Written?" *CBQ* 41 (1979): 533-46.

Vögtle, Anton. "Das Christologische und ekklesiologische Anliegen von Mt 28,18-20." In *Studia Evangelica* 2. Texte und Untersuchungen 87. Berlin: Akademie-Verlag, 1964.

———. "Die matthäische Kindheitsgeschichte," in M. Didier, *L'Évangile selon Matthieu: Rédaction et Théologie*, 153-83. Vol 29. BETL. Leuven: Peeters, 1972.

Von Dobbeler, Axel. "Die Restitution Israels und die Bekehrung der Heiden: Das Verhältnis von Mt 10,5b.6 und Mt 28,18-20 unter dem Aspect der Komplementarität. Erwägungen zum Standort des Matthäusevangeliums." *ZNW* 91 (2004): 19-44.

Von Dobschütz, Ernst. "Matthew as Rabbi and Catechist." In *The Interpretation of Matthew*, edited by Graham Stanton, 19-29. Philadelphia: Fortress, 1983.

Votaw, Clyde Weber. "The Gospels and Contemporary Biographies." *AmJT* 19 (1915): 45-73; reprinted (with an introduction by John Reumann) as *Gospels and Contemporary Biographies in the Graeco-Roman World*. Philadelphia: Fortress, 1970.

Waetjen, Herman C. *The Origin and Destiny of Humanness: An Interpretation of the Gospel According to Matthew*. San Rafael, CA: Crystal, 1976.

Walck, Leslie W. *The Son of Man in the Parables of Enoch and Matthew*. JCT 9. New York: T&T Clark, 2011.

Walker, Rolf. *Die Heilsgeschichte im ersten Evangelium*. Göttingen: Vandenhoeck & Ruprecht, 1967.

Wallace, Daniel B. *Greek Grammar Beyond the Basics: An Exegetical Syntax of the New Testament*. Grand Rapids: Zondervan, 1996.

Wainwright, Elaine M. *Towards a Feminist Critical Reading of the Gospel According to Matthew*. BZRG 60. Berlin: deGruyter, 1991.

Watson, Francis, "Toward a Literal Reading of the Gospels." In *The Gospels for All Christians: Rethinking the Gospel Audiences*, edited by Richard Bauckham, 195-217. Grand Rapids: Eerdmans, 1998.

Weaver, Dorothy Jean. *Matthew's Missionary Discourse: A Literary Critical Analysis*. JSNTSup 38. Sheffield: Sheffield Academic Press, 1990.

Weiss, Christian Hermann. *Die evangelische Geschichte*. 3 vols. Leipzig: Breitkopf und Härtel, 1838.

Weiss, Johannes. *Jesus' Proclamation of the Kingdom of God*, edited by Richard H. Hiers and D. Larrimore Holland. Philadelphia: Fortress, 1971 [1892].

Wenham, John. *Redating Matthew, Mark, and Luke: A Fresh Assault on the Synoptic Problem*. Downers Grove, IL: InterVarsity Press, 1992.

Weren, Wim J. C. *Studies in Matthew's Gospel: Literary Design, Intertextuality, and Social Setting*. Leiden: Brill, 2014.

White, Wilbert Webster. *Thirty Studies in the Gospel by Matthew*. S. M. Henderson, 1905.

Wiedemann, Thomas. *Adults and Children in the Roman Empire*. New Haven: Yale University Press, 1989.

Wikenhauser, Alfred. *Introduction to the New Testament*. New York: Herder and Herder, 1958.

Wilke, Christian Gottlob. *Der Urevangelist, oder exegetisch kritische Untersuchung über das Verwandtschaftsverhältnis der drei ersten Evangelien*. Dresden: Gerhard Fleischer, 1838.

Wilkins, Michael J. *Discipleship in the Ancient World and Matthew's Gospel*. 2nd ed. Grand Rapids: Baker, 1995.

Willitts, Joel. *Matthew's Messianic Shepherd-King: In Search of 'The Lost Sheep of the House of Israel*. BZNW. Berlin: De Gruyter, 2007.

Wilson, Alistair I. *When Will These Things Happen?: A Study of Jesus as Judge in Matthew 21–25*. Carlisle, UK: Paternoster, 2004.

Wilson, Marvin R. *Our Father Abraham: Jewish Roots of the Christian Faith*. Grand Rapids: Eerdmans, 1989.

Wilson, Walter T. *Healing in the Gospel of Matthew: Reflections on Method and Ministry*. Minneapolis: Fortress, 2014.

Witherington, Ben C. III. *Matthew*. SHBC. Macon, GA: Smyth & Helwys, 2006.

Wright, N. T. *Jesus and the Victory of God*. Minneapolis: Fortress, 1996.

———. *The New Testament and the People of God*. Minneapolis: Fortress, 1992.

———. *The Resurrection of the Son of God*. Minneapolis: Fortress, 2003.

Yamasaki, Gary. *Watching a Biblical Narrative: Point of View in Biblical Exegesis*. New York: T&T Clark, 2007.

Yarbrough, Robert W. "The Date of Papias: A Reassessment." *JETS* (1983): 181-91.

Zahn, Theodor. *Das Evangelium des Matthäus*. 3rd ed. KNT. Leipzig: A Deichert, 1910.

———. *Geschichte des neutestamentlichen Kanons. II. Urkunden und Belege zum ersten und dritten Band, 1 Hälfte*. Erlangen und Leipzig: A Deichert, 1890.

———. *Introduction to the New Testament*. 3 vols. New York: T&T Clark, 1909 [1897].

Zeichmann, Christopher B. "The Date of Mark's Gospel Apart from the Temple and Rumors of War: The Taxation Episode (12:13-17) as Evidence." *CBQ* 79 (2017): 422-37.

Zerwick, Maximilian. *Biblical Greek*. Rome: Pontifical Biblical Institute, 1963.

Zobel, H.-J., "חסד," *TDOT*, 44-64.

Zumstein, Jean. *La Condition du croyant dans l'évangile selon Matthieu*. Göttingen: Vandenhoeck & Ruprecht, 1977.

AUTHOR INDEX

Abel, Ernest, 58, 98
Abrams, M. H., 125
Achtemeier, Paul J., 123
Allen, Willoughby C., 52, 96, 97
Allison, Dale C., Jr., 14, 27, 47, 50, 55, 56, 58, 77, 89, 92, 93, 105, 106, 168, 169, 183, 188, 202, 209, 263, 264, 266, 307, 314, 316, 323
Anderson, Janice Capel, 39, 113
Attridge, Harold W., 226
Augustine, 43, 44
Bacon, Benjamin Wisner, 32, 55, 102, 103, 104
Bailey, James L., 9
Balch, David L., 39
Baltzer, Klaus, 311
Barr, David L., 106
Barr, James, 320
Barth, Gerhard, 32, 79, 132, 176, 253
Battenhouse, Henry Martin, 97
Bauckham, Richard, 18, 21, 22, 34, 60, 61, 84, 92
Bauer, David R., 4, 25, 37, 39, 46, 87, 95, 111, 118, 127, 143, 149, 181, 200, 203, 214, 231, 233, 319
Baumgarten, A. I., 82
Baxter, Wayne S., 245, 263
Beare, Francis Wright, 55, 56
Beasley-Murray, George R., 157, 210, 297
Behm, J., 299
Bendoraitis, Kristian A., 278
Benoit, Pierre, 46, 105
Bietenhard, Hans, 277
Billerbeck, Paul, 270
Bird, Michael F., 245
Black, Matthew, 64
Blomberg, Craig L., 118, 123, 210, 324
Bockmuehl, Markus, 26
Boismard, M.-E., 46
Bonnard, Pierre, 275, 323
Booth, Wayne, 37
Boring, M. Eugene, 73, 113
Bornkamm, Günther, 27, 32, 132, 176, 191, 252, 253, 254
Boxall, Ian, 1, 76, 90, 121, 123
Boyarin, Daniel, 84
Brandon, S. G. F., 92
Brown, Colin, 242
Brown, Jeanine, 190
Brown, Raymond E., 39, 105, 106, 118, 144, 147, 192, 229, 264, 288
Brown, Schuyler, 64, 76
Büchsel, Friedrich, 193
Bultman, Rudolf, 12, 16, 29, 30, 241, 242, 310
Burger, Christoph, 247
Burridge, Richard A., 10, 13, 14, 15, 18, 20, 21, 22, 23, 49, 88
Burton, Ernest DeWitt, 97
Butler, Benjamin C., 45
Byrskog, Samuel, 261
Caragounis, Chrys C., 255
Carson, Donald A., 105, 198, 303, 324
Carter, Warren, 34, 124, 125, 126, 202, 311, 313
Case, Shirley Jackson, 105
Casey, Maurice, 256
Catchpole, David R., 222
Chapman, John, 45
Chatman, Seymour, 36, 38, 39, 123, 126
Childs, Brevard S., 123
Christ, Felix, 265
Chung, Yonghan, 39
Clark, Kenneth W., 57
Clogg, Frank Bertram, 115
Colpe, Carston, 255
Combrink, H. J. Bernard, 109, 114
Conzelmann, Hans, 72, 97, 98
Cope, O. Lamar, 55, 73
Cothenet, Édouard, 78, 80
Cotterell, Peter, 127

Cousland, J. R. C., 166
Cox, Claude, 252
Crosby, Michael H., 202
Cross, Frank L., 105
Crossan, John Dominic, 27
Crossley, James G., 178
Cullmann, Oscar, 237
Culpepper, R. Alan, 36
Daniélou, Jean, 31, 144
Davidson, Samuel, 97
Davies, Margaret, 46
Davies, W. D., 14, 23, 47, 50, 55, 56, 58, 77, 80, 89, 92, 93, 104, 106, 116, 169, 183, 188, 202, 266, 307, 314, 316, 323
deSilva, David A., 105
Deutsch, Cecilia, 265
Dibelius, Martin, 12, 16, 30
Didier, M., 78, 264
Dillersburger, Josef, 115
Dirk, Frickenschmidt, 13
Dodd, C. H., 297
Dods, Marcus, 115
Donaldson, Terence, 164, 170
Donfried, Karl P., 192
Downey, Glanville, 90, 93
Duling, Dennis C., 245, 246
Dunn, James D. G., 28
Dupont, Jacques, 169
Durand, Alfred, 97
Edwards, Richard A., 311
Ellis, I. P., 232
Ellis, Peter F., 111, 112, 113, 114
Eltester, Walther, 83
Enslin, Morton S., 103, 106
Eusebius, 2, 43, 49, 50, 52, 53, 85, 87, 89
Evans, Craig A., 98, 120
Farmer, William R., 32, 43, 44, 45, 46
Farrar, Frederick William, 115
Farrer, Austin, 106
Fenton, J. C., 241
Fiedler, Peter, 105
Filson, Floyd V., 88, 172
Fitzmyer, Joseph A., 238, 252
Foster, Paul, 64
France, R. T., 3, 43, 48, 50, 51, 53, 58, 62, 63, 76, 85, 88, 108, 114, 121, 122, 123, 125, 169, 191, 198, 209, 210, 212, 213, 215, 227, 230, 255, 256, 258, 266, 275, 289, 303, 310, 314
Frankemölle, Hubert, 58, 99, 119, 202, 253, 268
Freed, Edwin D., 105
Frey, Jörg, 173
Fuller, Reginald H., 106, 109, 119, 122

Gaboury, Antonia, 46
Gadamer, Hans-Georg, 26
Gaebelein, Frank E., 105
Gaechter, Paul, 51, 114, 254, 323
Gale, Aaron M., 92
Garland, David E., 87, 88, 118, 200, 208, 212, 262, 291
Gaston, Lloyd, 58
Gathercole, Simon, 266, 275
Gerhardsson, Birger, 158, 159, 176, 226
Gibbs, James M., 246
Gibbs, Jeffrey A., 46, 88, 209, 212
Gnilka, Joachim, 118, 120, 179, 210, 254, 311, 314
Godet, Frédérick Louis, 103
Goodacre, Marc, 48
Gooding, D. W., 114
Goulder, M. D., 3, 21, 55, 62, 74
Gray, Sherman W., 214
Green, H. Benedict, 105, 111, 113, 114
Green, Joel B., 9, 26, 33, 48, 123
Grensted, L. W., 96, 97
Grimes, Joseph E., 127
Gromacki, Robert G., 105
Grundmann, Walter, 116, 323
Guelich, Robert A., 169, 175
Gundry, Robert H., 24, 49, 50, 51, 56, 62, 83, 88, 105, 122, 123, 165, 166, 193, 254, 275, 289, 291, 314
Gurtner, David M., 88, 227
Guthrie, Donald, 12, 85, 89, 105, 106
Habel, Norman, 311
Hadas, Moses, 13
Hagner, Donald A., 49, 51, 52, 63, 74, 80, 85, 88, 91, 122, 151, 157, 165, 166, 210, 241, 254, 275, 306, 310, 314, 321, 325
Hahn, Ferdinand, 237
Halcomb, T. Michael W., 203
Hamerton-Kelly, Robert G., 265
Hamilton, Catherine Sider, 223
Hare, Douglas R. A., 82, 256, 291
Harrington, Daniel J., 238
Harris, Murray J., 241
Harris, Rendel, 103
Hays, Richard, 84, 270, 274, 282, 290
Held, Heinz Joachim, 32, 132, 176, 253
Hengel, Martin, 1, 2, 14, 49
Hill, David, 101, 118, 311
Hirsch, E. D., Jr., 38
Holladay, Carl R., 123
Holtzmann, Heinrich Julius, 45
Horbury, William, 82, 296
Howard, George, 252

Author Index

Howell, David B., 72
Hultgren, Arland J., 317
Hultgren, Stephen, 46, 52
Hummel, Reinhart, 19, 191
Hurtado, Larry, 84, 252, 274
Irenaeus, 3, 43, 44, 50, 52, 53, 80, 84, 85
Jerome, 43, 53
Johnson, Luke Timothy, 123
Johnson, Marshall D., 266
Josephus, 28, 70, 81, 86
Jülicher, Adolf, 97
Kaiser, Walter C., Jr., 105
Käsemann, Ernst, 27
Katz, Steven T., 82
Keck, Leander E., 113, 237
Keegan, Terence J., 108
Keener, Craig S., 20, 23, 24, 62, 118, 168, 169, 183, 202, 210, 229, 291, 307, 310, 322, 325
Keim, Theodor, 115
Keith, Chris, 178
Kennedy, George A., 47, 170
Kilpatrick, G. D., 3, 19, 21, 49, 55, 59, 80, 91, 92
Kimelman, R., 82
Kingsbury, Jack Dean, 11, 12, 20, 33, 36, 38, 61, 63, 72, 74, 75, 115, 116, 117, 118, 119, 121, 122, 123, 125, 126, 166, 168, 184, 191, 192, 237, 238, 245, 246, 247, 253, 254, 255, 256, 261, 293, 296, 311, 317, 319
Kittel, Gerhard, 303
Klostermann, Erich, 97
Köster, Helmut, 320
Krentz, Edgar, 26, 115
Kuist, Howard Tillman, 4
Kümmel, Werner Georg, 10, 43, 45, 55, 115
Kupp, David D., 48, 123, 134, 238, 268, 272, 278
Kürzinger, Josef, 51
Lachman, Karl, 44, 45
Ladd, George Eldon, 297
LaGrange, Marie-Joseph, 12, 45, 96, 97
Leim, Joshua E., 274
Levesque, Karl E., 105
Lewis, Jack P., 82
Licona, Michael R., 24
Lightfoot, Robert Henry, 30, 32
Lindars, Barnabas, 255
Lindemann, Andreas, 97, 98
Livingstone, E. A., 241
Lohmeyer, Ernst, 115
Lohr, Charles H., 114
Lohse, Edward, 106
Loisy, Alred, 105, 106
Long, Fredrick J., 127

Longacre, Robert E., 127
Luomanen, Petri, 74, 91
Luz, Ulrich, 14, 19, 34, 72, 74, 88, 90, 93, 123, 165, 175, 191, 192, 193, 214, 215, 255, 256, 257, 291
MacEwen, Robert, 47
Malina, Bruce J., 40
Manson, T. W., 51, 258
Marguerat, Daniel, 57, 317
Martin, Ralph P., 52
Massaux, Edouard, 1
Matera, Frank J., 123, 124, 125, 126
McKee, Dean Greer, 115
McKenzie, Steven L., 40
McKnight, Edgar V., 26, 29, 30
McNeile, Alan Hugh, 97
Meier, John P., 27, 58, 99, 105
Meinertz, Max, 97, 98
Menken, M. J. J., 56
Metzger, Bruce M., 3
Meynet, Roland, 48
Michel, Otto, 232
Michie, Donald, 36
Middleton, J. Richard, 212
Miller, Fergus, 64
Minear, Paul S., 3, 21, 105, 166
Moberly, R. W. L., 241, 242, 278
Mohrlang, Roger, 76
Morgenthaler, Robert, 15
Morris, Leon, 97
Moule, C. F. D., 50, 55, 289
Moulton, James Hope, 50
Mowery, Robert L., 162, 296
Müller, Mogens, 237
Mullooparambil, Sebastian, 98
Nau, Arlo J., 193
Neirynck, Frans, 119, 120, 121, 122
Nepper-Christensen, Poul, 57
Neyrey, Jerome H., 39, 40
Nida, Eugene A., 127
Nolland, John, 49, 56, 77, 101, 169, 238, 241, 254
Novakovic, Lidija, 245
Oepke, Albert, 302
Orchard, J. B., 46
Orton, David E., 56, 68, 73, 77
Osborne, Grant R., 105
Overman, Andrew, 63, 76, 92
Palmer, Caroline L., 115
Pamment, Margaret, 258
Pennington, Jonathan, 57, 162, 169, 175, 277, 282
Perkins, Pheme, 109, 119, 122, 191

Perrin, Norman, 32
Pesch, Rudolf, 156, 238
Peterson, Norman, 14
Pietersma, Albert, 252
Plummer, Alfred, 97, 98
Popa, Romeo, 69, 76, 245
Porter, Stanley E., 226
Powell, Mark Allan, 27, 35, 36, 37, 39, 40, 87, 126, 127, 143, 169, 200, 214
Prabhu, G. M. Soares, 120
Pregeant, Russell, 118
Przybylski, Benno, 157
Radermakers, Jean, 105, 106
Ramaroson, Léonard, 95
Rau, Christoph, 115
Reicke, Bo, 46
Renan, Ernst, 10
Rengstorf, Karl Heinrich, 83, 161, 322
Resseguie, James L., 35, 36, 37, 38
Reumann, John, 11, 192
Rhoads, David, 36
Ridderbos, Herman, 105
Rist, John M., 46
Rivken, Ellis, 81
Robinson, J. Armitage, 51
Robinson, James M., 27
Robinson, Theodore H., 97
Rohde, Joachim, 33
Rolland, Phillippe, 105, 106
Roose, Hanna, 305
Roux, Herbert, 97
Runesson, Anders, 75, 92, 305
Russell, David M., 306
Sabourin, Léopold, 118
Saldarini, Anthony J., 64, 76, 81
Sand, Alexander, 118
Sanders, E. P., 27, 46, 82
Scaer, David P., 105, 106
Schäfer, Peter, 82
Schaff, Philip, 44
Schelkle, Karl Hermann, 105
Schille, Gottfried, 21
Schlatter, Adolf, 12, 45, 291, 323
Schleiermacher, Friedrich, 51
Schlier, Heinrich, 197
Schmidt, Karl Ludwig, 12, 30
Schmitz, Ernst Dieter, 242
Schnackenburg, Rudolf, 118, 203
Schnelle, Udo, 123
Schniewind, Julius, 89, 176
Schürer, Emil, 64, 296
Schweitzer, Albert, 26, 27, 30

Schweizer, Eduard, 80, 97, 101, 304, 319
Scobie, Charles H. H., 295
Segovia, Fernando F., 311
Senior, Donald, 97, 100, 101, 119, 123, 280
Shuler, Philip L., 13
Sim, David C., 34, 57, 76, 88
Simon, Marcel, 64
Slater, Tommy B., 118
Slingerland, H. Dixon, 91
Smith, Christopher R., 106, 107, 108, 109, 110, 125
Smith, Craig A., 113
Smith, Morton, 13
Soulen, Kendall, 26
Soulen, Richard N., 26
Spencer, Richard A., 123
Stanton, Graham, 2, 19, 21, 23, 34, 47, 58, 74, 88, 93, 168, 187, 193, 211, 214, 215, 232, 266
Stein, Robert H., 43, 48
Stemberger, Günter, 82
Stendahl, Krister, 21, 55, 56, 62
Sternberg, Meir, 37
Stock, Augustine, 118
Stoldt, H.-H., 45, 46
Stonehouse, Ned B., 115
Storr, Gottlob Christian, 44
Strack, Hermann L., 270
Strecker, Georg, 58, 63, 72, 99, 169, 179, 191
Streeter, Burnett Hillman, 19, 24, 32, 34, 45, 46, 49, 52, 85, 90, 107
Strong, Augustus H., 115
Stuckenbruck, Loren T., 178
Suggs, Jack M., 257
Suhl, Anders, 247
Talbert, Charles H., 13, 105, 106, 169, 175
Tannehill, Robert C., 36
Taylor, Vincent, 16, 30, 31, 237
Tertullian, 52
Theisohn, Johannes, 256
Theissen, Gerd, 90
Thompson, Alan J., 277
Thompson, Marianne Meye, 103, 118, 119, 122, 123
Thompson, William G., 99, 202
Traina, Robert A., 4, 25, 37, 111, 127
Trilling, Wolfgang, 63, 64, 99, 253
Tuckett, Christopher Mark, 280
Turner, David L., 2, 105, 106, 209, 254, 314
Turner, Max, 127
Turner, Nigel, 50
Uspensky, Boris, 36, 38
Van Tilborg, Sjef, 58, 92
Vander Broek, Lyle D., 9

Author Index

Vanhoozer, Kevin J., 33
Vermes, Geza, 27, 64
Verseput, Donald, 118, 238, 240
Via, Dan O., 123
Viviano, Benedict T., 89
Vögtle, Anton, 179
Von Dobbeler, Axel, 179
Von Dobschütz, Ernst, 2, 3, 21, 47, 55, 80, 81
Votaw, Clyde Weber, 10, 11
Waetjen, Herman C., 105
Wainwright, Elaine M., 39
Walck, Leslie W., 256
Walker, Rolf, 57, 64, 72, 99, 191
Wallace, Daniel B., 155
Watson, Francis, 22, 61
Weaver, Dorothy Jean, 178, 179, 304
Weiss, Christian Hermann, 45
Weiss, Johannes, 27, 297
Wenham, John, 45
Weren, Wim J. C., 118, 120, 126
White, Wilbert Webster, 115
Wiedemann, Thomas, 298
Wikenhauser, Alfred, 49, 89
Wilk, Florian, 173
Wilke, Christian Gottlob, 45
Wilkins, Michael J., 166, 192, 309, 310
Willitts, Joel, 88, 145, 245
Wilson, Alistair I., 210
Wilson, Marvin R., 82
Wilson, Walter T., 176, 177
Witherington, Ben C., III, 105, 106, 203, 265
Wright, Edward T., 24
Wright, N. T., 27, 67, 152, 212, 296, 306
Yamasaki, Gary, 38
Yarbrough, Robert W., 49
Zahn, Theodor, 3, 12, 45, 97, 116
Zeichmann, Christopher B., 85
Zerwick, Maximilian, 155
Zobel, H.-J., 167
Zumstein, Jean, 80

SCRIPTURE INDEX

OLD TESTAMENT

Genesis
2:4, *116, 118*
5:1, *116, 118*
12:1-3, *290*
12:1-12, *63*
12:2-3, *141, 153*
15:1-20, *153*
15:1-21, *290*
17:1-8, *141*
17:5, *63*
18:1-33, *290*
18:9-15, *153*
19:1-29, *325*
21:22, *271*
22:1, *160*
22:1-19, *153*
22:15-18, *63*
22:15-20, *290*
22:18, *141, 287*
26:24, *271*
26:28, *271*
31:5, *271*
38:27-30, *287*
39:2-3, *271*
39:21, *271*
39:23, *271*

Exodus
1-4, *263*
3:11-12, *271*
3:12, *234, 268*
3:14, *254*
4:12, *234*
4:19, *263*
7-12, *263*
12:21-27, *218*
12:26, *218*
19-40, *164*
19:3, *165*
19:4, *273*
19:12, *165*
24-31, *263*
24:1-32:14, *198*
24:5-8, *219*
24:8, *224*
24:15, *165*
24:15-18, *198*
24:16, *198*
24:18, *165*
34:1, *165*
34:4, *165*
34:28, *263*
34:29, *165*
34:29-35, *263*

Numbers
14:42-43, *271*
24:17, *248*
27:17, *149*
28:9-10, *293*

Deuteronomy
1:31, *159*
1:42, *271*
2:7, *271*
6-8, *158*
6:13, *274*
6:16, *159*
8:2, *158, 278*
8:3, *159*
8:3-6, *159*
8:4, *159*
8:5, *158*
8:14-16, *159*
9:9, *263*
9:18, *263*
11:26-32, *273*
13:3, *160*
17:6, *221*
18:15-16, *263*
19:15, *221*
19:16-21, *223*
20:1, *268*
22:13-21, *147*
30:1-20, *273*
30:4, *213*
31-34, *264*
32:11, *273*
32:39, *254*

Joshua
1:5, *234, 271*
1:9, *234*
6:27, *271*
7:12, *271*
22:31, *268*

Judges
2:18, *268*
6:16, *271*

1 Samuel
9:16, *145*
10:27, *145*
11:3-18:30, *145*
16:18, *271*
17:37, *268*
18:12, *271*
18:18, *271*
18:28, *271*

Scripture Index

2 Samuel
5:1-12:31, *145*
5:2, *244*
7:3, *271*
7:11, *273*
7:11-14, *238*
7:12-13, *141*
7:12-14, *221*
7:12-16, *247*
7:14, *238*
11-12, *141*
19:21, *247*
22:51, *247*
23:1, *247*

1 Kings
8:12-61, *159*
11:38, *271*
19:4-18, *198*
19:19-21, *311*
20:1-43, *145*
22:17, *149*

2 Kings
1:8, *150, 190*
3:1-27, *145*
18:1-19:27, *145*
18:7, *271*

1 Chronicles
3:16, *142*
11:1-47, *145*
11:9, *271*
17:2, *271*
17:12-13, *238*
18:1-20:8, *145*
22:9, *273*
22:10, *238*
22:11, *271*
22:16, *271*
22:18, *271*
28:5, *294*
29:11, *294*

2 Chronicles
1:1, *271*
13:8, *294*
14:1-14, *145*
20:1-35, *145*
25:7, *271*
32:1-33, *145*
36:23, *268*

Ezra
1:3, *268*

Job
29:5, *271*

Psalms
2, *141, 160, 247, 287*
2:2, *247, 266*
2:7, *156, 239, 247*
2:7-8, *238*
2:8, *160*
2:8-11, *247*
6:2, *253*
9:13, *253*
17:8, *273*
18:50, *247*
20:6, *247*
22, *226*
22:1, *226*
22:8, *243*
22:22-31, *226*
23:1-3, *149*
23:4, *149*
23:5, *149*
25:16, *253*
26:11, *253*
27:7, *253*
28:8, *247*
30:10, *253*
31:9, *253*
36:7, *273*
37:11, *306*
41:4, *253*
41:9, *218*
41:10, *253*
51:1, *253*
57:1, *253*
63:7, *273*
69:22, *226*
78:2, *292*
80:1, *149*
80:1-2, *149*
84:9, *247*
86:1, *253*
89, *141*
89:26-27, *238*
89:38, *247*
89:51, *247*
91, *159, 160*
91:4, *159, 273*
91:11-12, *159*
91:15, *268*
103:3, *253*
105:15, *247*
107:29, *273*
108:26, *254*
110:1, *208, 250*
132:10, *247*
132:17, *247*
147:2, *213*

Proverbs
3:19, *265*
8:3-36, *265*
30:3-4, *265*
30:18-19, *265*

Song of Solomon
1:8-14, *149*

Isaiah
2:1-4, *287*
2:2-3, *170*
2:2-4, *233*
3:20, *149*
5:24-25, *83*
6:9-10, *290*
7:14, *146*
8:8-10, *268*
9:1-2, *290*
11:1-16, *141*
14:3, *273*
15:7-9, *290*
24:21-23, *295*
29:13, *290*
31:4, *149*
33:22, *295*
35:5-6, *181, 249*
40, *152*
40:3, *151, 253*
40:8, *273*
40:11, *149*
41:4, *254*
41:10, *268*
42:1, *156, 266*
42:1-4, *222, 245, 290*
43:5, *268*
43:10, *254*
44:3, *273*
49:6, *170*
52:7, *295*
53:4, *222, 245, 266*
53:5, *267*

53:6, *267*
53:7, *222, 266*
53:8, *267*
53:9, *222, 266*
53:10, *266*
53:12, *266*
56:10-12, *149*
61:1, *181, 249*

Jeremiah
1:4-12, *311*
16:14-15, *314*
16:16, *314*
16:17-18, *314*
23:1-6, *245*
23:4, *149*
31:10, *149*
33:12, *149*
33:14-26, *141*
49:19, *149*
50:6, *149, 245*
50:44, *149*

Lamentations
4:20, *247*

Ezekiel
34, *189, 244, 245, 247*
34:1-10, *321*
34:1-16, *177*
34:1-24, *245, 290*
34:2-3, *149*
34:3, *189*
34:5-7, *149*
34:8, *149*
34:11-13, *178*
34:13-14, *245*
34:13-15, *189*
34:15, *177*
34:16, *245*
34:17-24, *247*
34:22, *244*
34:23, *149, 244, 245*
34:23-24, *178, 189, 245*
34:24, *244, 245*
39:29, *273*

Daniel
1:20, *148*
2:2, *148*
2:34-45, *295*
4:4, *148*

5:7, *148*
7, *255, 256, 302*
7:1-28, *295*
7:13, *302*
7:13-14, *212, 233, 255, 256, 302*
7:14, *255*
7:18, *302*
7:19-27, *302*
7:22, *255, 302*
7:25-27, *255*
7:27, *302*
9:27, *211*

Hosea
6:6, *81, 82*
11:1, *156*

Joel
2:28-30, *273*
2:28-32, *154*
3:1-16, *214*

Amos
3:12, *149*
7:14-15, *311*

Jonah
1:1, *311*

Micah
4:1-5, *233*
4:1-8, *287*
5:2, *244*
5:2-15, *141*

Habakkuk
3:13, *247*

Haggai
2:4-5, *271*

Zechariah
2:10, *213*
9:9, *206*
9:9-17, *287*
10:2-3, *149*
11:5, *149*
11:8-9, *149*
11:12-13, *218*
11:15-16, *149*
11:16, *149*
12:10-14, *212*

13:4, *150*
13:7, *149, 219*
14:5, *273*

Malachi
3:1, *150*
4:5-6, *150*

APOCRYPHA

Wisdom of Solomon
2:18, *243*

Sirach
24, *265*
51, *265*

1 Maccabees
9:27, *151*

2 Maccabees
1:10, *247*

NEW TESTAMENT

Matthew
1-2, *108, 120, 244, 278*
1-7, *93, 123, 165, 175, 215*
1-12, *113*
1-13, *49, 51, 52, 63, 80, 85, 122, 151, 157, 165, 166, 241, 310, 314, 321, 325*
1:1, *14, 61, 63, 116, 117, 118, 119, 123, 131, 139, 140, 243, 286, 290*
1:1-2, *61*
1:1-17, *14, 17, 19, 56, 75, 116, 139, 143, 150, 153, 239, 243, 286, 292*
1:1-2:23, *102, 104, 119, 139, 150*
1:1-3:12, *155*
1:1-4:11, *124*
1:1-4:16, *5, 14, 116, 117, 118, 119, 124, 129, 139, 141, 143, 145, 147, 149, 151, 153, 155, 156, 157, 159, 161, 278*
1:1-11:1, *46*
1:1-16:20, *121*
1:2, *63, 116, 140, 142, 286, 288*
1:2-5, *288*
1:2-16, *63, 140*

Scripture Index

1:2-17, *118*
1:2-2:23, *118*
1:3, *142, 287*
1:4, *61, 131*
1:5, *142*
1:6, *61, 116, 131, 140, 141, 142, 144, 243, 286*
1:6-11, *141*
1:11, *142, 148, 152, 287, 288*
1:11-12, *142*
1:12, *148*
1:16, *117, 140, 142, 155, 238, 248, 286*
1:16-18, *131*
1:17, *61, 63, 116, 117, 131, 140, 143, 148, 152, 287*
1:18, *116, 238, 311*
1:18-19, *144*
1:18-20, *155*
1:18-25, *124, 142, 143, 144, 147, 149, 150, 155, 157, 158, 238, 239, 243, 286*
1:18-2:23, *17, 62, 139, 143, 144, 149, 224, 264, 279*
1:18-4:16, *239*
1:19, *148, 201, 279*
1:20, *61, 66, 116, 131, 155, 238, 279, 311*
1:20-21, *239*
1:20-23, *241*
1:20-25, *157*
1:21, *62, 63, 67, 130, 144, 149, 155, 177, 203, 240, 243, 244, 245, 252, 267, 268, 282, 318*
1:21-23, *62, 66, 116, 178, 183, 269*
1:22, *131, 252, 260*
1:22-23, *19, 280*
1:23, *130, 134, 151, 155, 156, 202, 221, 226, 227, 234, 240, 241, 243, 268, 271, 272, 293, 316*
1:24, *252*
1:25, *130, 143, 155, 156*
2, *62, 145, 153, 244, 279*
2:1, *123, 143, 149, 170, 244, 248, 281*
2:1-2, *248*
2:1-3, *149*
2:1-8, *17*
2:1-12, *63, 64, 244, 263*
2:1-13, *143, 281*
2:1-18, *298*

2:1-23, *131, 133, 143, 147, 149, 150, 326*
2:2, *61, 116, 131, 145, 148, 227, 231, 243, 244, 248, 269, 288, 290, 300*
2:3, *148, 244, 248*
2:3-6, *269*
2:4, *67, 117, 131, 144, 148, 248*
2:5, *149, 260*
2:5-6, *248, 280*
2:6, *67, 145, 149, 157, 178, 243, 244, 248, 269, 290*
2:7, *148, 149*
2:8, *148, 149, 244*
2:9, *61, 131, 149, 244, 248*
2:9-10, *281*
2:10, *148*
2:11, *18, 148, 231, 300*
2:12, *143, 148, 279*
2:13, *252, 279*
2:13-15, *143*
2:13-23, *144*
2:15, *130, 131, 156, 157, 158, 240, 252, 260, 280, 282*
2:16, *148, 244*
2:16-18, *244, 248, 263, 281*
2:17, *131, 191, 260*
2:17-18, *144, 280*
2:19, *279*
2:19-20, *143*
2:20, *263, 280*
2:20-22, *280*
2:22, *143, 279*
2:23, *90, 131, 144, 260, 280*
3, *153*
3-4, *114*
3:1, *15, 117, 165, 273, 279*
3:1-3, *151*
3:1-12, *17, 181, 190, 191, 318*
3:1-17, *36, 113, 233*
3:1-4:16, *150*
3:1-25:46, *102*
3:2, *57, 61, 131, 132, 150, 249, 294, 297, 299, 321*
3:3, *150, 151, 253, 260, 280*
3:3-10, *304*
3:4, *190*
3:5, *181*
3:7, *65, 86, 306*
3:7-10, *58, 142, 153, 304*
3:7-11, *150*
3:7-12, *57, 80*

3:8, *132, 299, 318*
3:8-12, *112*
3:9, *63, 292*
3:10, *132, 307, 318*
3:11, *153, 248, 249, 260, 273, 299, 307*
3:11-12, *154, 249, 321*
3:12, *178, 249, 307*
3:13, *252*
3:13-17, *155, 157, 267*
3:13-4:11, *158*
3:14, *273, 293*
3:15, *57, 130, 131, 157, 242, 280*
3:16, *278*
3:16-17, *239*
3:17, *117, 129, 130, 139, 155, 156, 157, 158, 160, 191, 199, 206, 208, 222, 227, 237, 238, 239, 241, 242, 247, 260, 263, 266, 311*
4, *315*
4:1, *278*
4:1-1, *225*
4:1-10, *117, 274, 278*
4:1-11, *130, 158*
4:1-16, *139*
4:2, *263, 274*
4:3, *130, 157, 225*
4:3-4, *159*
4:4, *159*
4:5, *62, 170*
4:5-7, *159*
4:6, *130, 157, 225*
4:7, *252*
4:8, *301*
4:8-10, *160, 232*
4:9, *149*
4:10, *19, 120, 196, 231, 252, 274, 281*
4:11, *150, 160, 161, 229, 274*
4:12, *97, 117, 119, 120, 130, 150, 157, 231, 290, 325*
4:12-15, *117*
4:12-16, *119, 120, 161*
4:12-17, *119, 120, 124*
4:12-11:1, *124*
4:12-25:46, *120*
4:14, *131, 260*
4:14-16, *19, 134, 231, 290*
4:14-25, *124*
4:15, *291*
4:15-16, *63*

4:16, *115, 120, 125*
4:17, *57, 97, 110, 115, 116, 117, 118, 119, 120, 121, 122, 123, 128, 129, 130, 132, 150, 162, 163, 165, 174, 178, 180, 182, 185, 294, 297, 299, 318, 321, 325*
4:17-11:1, *124*
4:17-16:20, *5, 120, 121, 122, 129, 162, 163, 165, 166, 167, 169, 171, 173, 175, 177, 179, 181, 183, 185, 187, 189, 190, 191, 193, 195*
4:18, *120*
4:18-19, *54*
4:18-20, *78*
4:18-22, *163, 166, 204, 207, 310, 311, 313, 314, 315, 317*
4:18-16:20, *117, 163*
4:19, *163, 197, 313*
4:21, *163, 282*
4:21-48, *18*
4:23, *61, 67, 75, 107, 129, 130, 131, 164, 165, 176, 180, 261, 300, 307*
4:23-25, *117, 163, 181*
4:23-9:35, *180*
4:23-11:1, *164*
4:23-16:20, *163*
4:24, *90, 91*
4:25, *185, 317*
5-7, *3, 19, 66, 164, 169, 193*
5:1, *97, 164, 166, 263*
5:1-2, *73, 166, 167*
5:1-7:27, *317*
5:1-7:28, *102*
5:1-7:29, *164, 176, 282*
5:2, *130, 165, 261*
5:3, *32, 167, 215, 299, 300*
5:3-10, *168, 169*
5:3-12, *167*
5:3-16, *272*
5:3-7:27, *131*
5:4-9, *169*
5:5, *169, 306*
5:6, *57*
5:7, *16, 130, 147*
5:8, *169, 203*
5:9, *130, 240, 262, 313*
5:10, *57, 215, 300*
5:10-11, *130, 299*
5:10-12, *317*

5:11-12, *170, 187, 261*
5:11-7:20, *168*
5:13-16, *167, 170, 173, 175, 201, 319*
5:14, *164*
5:16, *131, 167, 173, 240, 313*
5:17, *79, 131, 167, 170, 175, 200, 260, 292*
5:17-18, *67, 171*
5:17-19, *260*
5:17-20, *104, 165, 170, 171, 199*
5:17-48, *19, 57, 58, 68, 75, 130, 175, 193, 262, 299, 307, 312, 318*
5:17-58, *167*
5:17-6:34, *174*
5:17-7:12, *170, 175*
5:18, *171, 306*
5:19, *130, 147, 193, 215, 262, 305*
5:19-20, *61, 131, 304*
5:20, *57, 65, 67, 68, 170, 171, 188, 215, 297, 299*
5:20-48, *67*
5:21-22, *86, 281, 283*
5:21-26, *57*
5:21-42, *172*
5:21-48, *79, 170, 171, 172, 200, 273, 292*
5:22, *62, 63, 283, 307, 315*
5:22-24, *78*
5:22-26, *171*
5:23, *315*
5:23-24, *62, 85*
5:24, *315*
5:25, *325*
5:25-26, *304*
5:28, *304*
5:29-30, *57, 171, 283, 304*
5:32, *313*
5:33, *252*
5:33-37, *222*
5:34, *305*
5:35, *57, 62, 277, 300*
5:42, *203*
5:43-45, *282*
5:43-48, *167, 172, 176, 272, 292*
5:45, *130, 131, 240, 297, 308, 313, 318*
5:46, *62, 283*
5:46-48, *305*
5:47, *57, 58, 78, 290, 315*

5:48, *110, 111, 131, 203, 240, 313*
6:1, *57, 131, 170, 172, 240, 283, 313*
6:1-18, *57, 58, 62, 67, 167, 172, 175, 282, 304, 305*
6:1-7:12, *170*
6:2, *70*
6:2-4, *172, 217, 313*
6:2-14, *203*
6:4, *131, 240, 283, 313*
6:5-6, *172*
6:6, *131, 240, 283, 313*
6:7, *57, 58, 63, 282*
6:7-8, *290*
6:7-12, *175*
6:7-15, *172, 173*
6:8, *173, 282, 313*
6:8-9, *131, 240*
6:9, *277, 313*
6:9-15, *282*
6:10, *61, 131, 297, 299, 305*
6:11, *159*
6:12, *308, 318*
6:12-15, *175*
6:13, *158*
6:14, *131, 240, 313*
6:14-15, *173*
6:15, *313*
6:16-18, *73, 172*
6:18, *131, 240, 313*
6:19-21, *174, 298*
6:19-34, *167, 174, 175*
6:19-35, *185*
6:20, *305*
6:23, *174*
6:24, *50, 63, 174, 282*
6:25-33, *276*
6:25-34, *152, 174*
6:26, *131, 159, 240, 313*
6:26-30, *174, 282, 308*
6:28-30, *282*
6:30, *174*
6:32, *57, 58, 63, 131, 240, 282, 290, 291, 313*
6:32-33, *174*
6:33, *57, 61, 131, 174, 215*
7, *175*
7:1, *258*
7:1-5, *174, 175, 307*
7:1-6, *167, 175*
7:3, *315*
7:3-5, *78, 174*

Scripture Index

7:4, *315*
7:5, *315*
7:6, *174, 175, 325*
7:7-11, *175, 282*
7:7-12, *175*
7:9, *130, 240, 313*
7:9-11, *242, 281*
7:10, *193*
7:11, *131, 240, 283, 313*
7:12, *57, 130, 147, 167, 170, 175, 176, 200, 260*
7:13, *168, 193, 297*
7:13-14, *168, 231, 304, 307*
7:13-23, *104*
7:13-27, *57, 176*
7:14, *306*
7:15-19, *281*
7:15-20, *304, 319*
7:15-23, *77, 142, 168, 211, 281, 319*
7:15-27, *307*
7:15-28, *171*
7:16-20, *132*
7:17-20, *318*
7:18, *193*
7:19, *307*
7:21, *57, 61, 130, 131, 215, 253, 254, 283, 297, 299*
7:21-22, *253, 254*
7:21-23, *80, 214, 252, 283*
7:21-27, *168*
7:22, *253, 254*
7:24-25, *193*
7:24-27, *168, 192, 273, 281, 299*
7:24-28, *315*
7:27, *168*
7:28-29, *16, 67, 165, 166, 167, 262*
7:29, *67, 68, 75, 130, 165, 261, 312*
8-9, *17, 164, 176, 263*
8:1, *185, 317*
8:1-4, *180*
8:1-17, *177*
8:1-9:1, *16*
8:1-9:34, *17, 33, 131, 176, 181*
8:1-9:35, *178*
8:1-9:38, *113*
8:2, *231, 253*
8:2-3, *177*
8:3, *176*
8:4, *106, 267*

8:5-13, *58, 72, 134, 321*
8:5-17, *180*
8:6, *253*
8:8, *253*
8:10, *72, 132, 177*
8:10-11, *282*
8:10-13, *305*
8:11, *57, 61, 64, 89, 131, 134, 142, 227, 280, 288, 290, 291, 300, 306*
8:11-12, *63, 80, 219*
8:11-13, *57*
8:12, *154, 207, 307*
8:13, *132, 176, 177*
8:14-17, *54*
8:15-35, *201*
8:16, *130, 176, 180*
8:17, *131, 176, 222, 260, 266, 267*
8:18-20, *75, 261, 310, 311*
8:18-22, *176, 177*
8:19, *107, 261*
8:19-20, *37*
8:20, *16, 131, 152, 190, 256, 257, 258*
8:20-22, *258*
8:21, *253*
8:21-22, *79, 257*
8:22, *16, 273, 312*
8:23-27, *312*
8:23-9:8, *177*
8:25, *252, 253*
8:26, *176, 177*
8:27, *147, 191, 242, 273*
8:28-34, *130, 180*
8:29, *130, 307*
8:32, *176*
9:1-2, *173*
9:1-8, *180, 245, 257, 258*
9:1-9, *177, 267, 318, 321*
9:1-13, *130, 131*
9:2, *132, 177*
9:2-6, *282*
9:3, *67, 68, 133, 148*
9:4, *188*
9:6, *131, 176, 177, 190, 256, 257, 312*
9:7, *170*
9:8, *177, 232, 242, 312*
9:9, *49, 54, 55, 258, 310, 312*
9:9-13, *201*
9:9-17, *177*

9:10, *176*
9:10-11, *17*
9:10-13, *67, 79, 188*
9:10-17, *317*
9:11, *65, 261*
9:12-13, *16*
9:13, *17, 81, 130, 147, 260*
9:14, *65, 154*
9:14-15, *73*
9:14-17, *177*
9:15, *130, 133, 234, 240, 317*
9:15-17, *16*
9:18, *231*
9:18-22, *84*
9:18-26, *75, 177, 312*
9:18-34, *177*
9:19, *317*
9:20-26, *180*
9:21, *245*
9:21-22, *267*
9:22, *132, 176, 177, 245*
9:27, *17, 61, 130, 131, 176, 244, 252*
9:27-32, *245*
9:28, *177, 253*
9:28-29, *132*
9:29, *176*
9:30, *267*
9:32-33, *180*
9:32-34, *130*
9:33, *130, 131*
9:34, *65, 70*
9:35, *61, 107, 117, 130, 131, 164, 165, 176, 180, 261, 262, 300, 307*
9:35-11:1, *167, 177, 178, 272, 290, 319*
9:36, *84, 130, 319, 320, 325*
9:36-38, *78*
9:37, *320, 321, 325*
9:37-38, *324*
9:38, *253*
10, *3, 19, 66, 114, 179*
10:1, *130, 178, 180, 199, 258, 322*
10:1-4, *178*
10:1-42, *78, 102*
10:2, *54, 78, 314*
10:2-4, *54, 55, 78, 322*
10:3, *49*
10:4, *133, 150, 325*

10:5, *57, 58, 78, 89, 90, 178,*
   179, 291, 314, 322, 323
10:5-6, *72, 130, 133, 179, 233,*
   242, 290
10:5-7, *86*
10:5-15, *69, 179, 180*
10:5-16, *131, 180*
10:5-42, *158, 314*
10:6, *321, 326*
10:7, *130, 150, 165, 178, 185,*
   294, 297, 321, 323, 325
10:8, *130, 178, 180, 258, 321,*
   323
10:10, *324*
10:11-14, *175*
10:12-15, *324*
10:13-15, *322*
10:14-15, *307*
10:15, *57, 130, 307, 325*
10:16, *78, 326, 327*
10:16-23, *130, 260*
10:16-39, *76, 180, 322*
10:16-42, *179, 180*
10:17, *69, 70, 75, 150, 325*
10:17-18, *322*
10:17-23, *322*
10:18, *57, 70, 134, 291, 320, 326*
10:18-23, *179*
10:19, *150*
10:19-22, *180*
10:20, *131, 240, 326*
10:21, *150, 187, 326*
10:21-22, *315*
10:22, *211*
10:23, *69, 131, 178, 190, 219,*
   256, 291, 302, 303, 325, 326
10:24, *262*
10:24-25, *70, 130, 251, 317, 322,*
   325
10:25, *326*
10:26, *326*
10:26-28, *322*
10:26-33, *322*
10:26-39, *130, 179*
10:26-42, *131*
10:27, *165*
10:27-28, *322*
10:28, *57, 70, 175, 180, 283,*
   304
10:28-31, *327*
10:29, *131, 240, 282*
10:29-31, *308*

10:30, *282*
10:30-31, *282*
10:32, *219, 256*
10:32-33, *130, 180, 283, 304,*
   307, 326, 327
10:34, *69*
10:34-39, *69, 207, 315, 322*
10:35-36, *312, 326*
10:35-38, *187*
10:35-39, *180*
10:37-39, *327*
10:38, *133, 197, 258, 300*
10:38-39, *70, 180*
10:40, *327*
10:40-42, *180, 327*
10:41, *78, 187*
10:41-42, *305, 319*
10:42, *183, 215*
11, *113, 265, 288*
11-12, *112, 118*
11:1, *16, 75, 107, 117, 130, 165,*
   261, 262
11:1-12:50, *117*
11:1-16:20, *164, 180, 190*
11:2, *125, 131, 150, 154, 181, 242,*
   249, 265
11:2-3, *154*
11:2-6, *113, 124, 158, 181, 321*
11:2-19, *3, 113*
11:2-24, *181*
11:2-30, *108, 131*
11:2-16:12, *124*
11:2-16:20, *124*
11:3, *190*
11:4-6, *113, 154, 249, 267*
11:5, *122, 142*
11:6, *182, 187, 249*
11:7-10, *181*
11:7-15, *182*
11:7-24, *131*
11:9, *151*
11:9-14, *190*
11:9-15, *150, 260*
11:10, *150*
11:11, *57, 61, 131, 154, 215, 273,*
   293, 305
11:12, *57, 61, 131*
11:13, *260, 292*
11:14, *150*
11:16, *199*
11:16-19, *182*
11:16-24, *113*

11:17-19, *265*
11:19, *131, 190, 256, 257, 264,*
   265
11:20, *299*
11:20-24, *57, 68, 113, 182, 242,*
   265, 307, 321
11:21, *299*
11:22-24, *130*
11:25, *206, 252, 254, 274*
11:25-26, *182, 185, 186, 283*
11:25-27, *130, 191, 265*
11:25-30, *113, 181*
11:27, *66, 84, 130, 183, 241, 242,*
   284
11:28, *197, 293*
11:28-29, *273*
11:28-30, *75, 168, 183, 208, 264,*
   265, 266, 311, 318
11:29, *304*
11:30, *293*
12, *67, 113*
12-13, *114*
12:1-2, *293*
12:1-4, *130*
12:1-8, *17, 68, 69, 188, 257, 317*
12:1-14, *68, 79, 131, 183, 229,*
   230
12:1-45, *113, 183*
12:1-50, *16*
12:2, *65, 70, 257, 258*
12:2-4, *66*
12:3-4, *293*
12:4, *17*
12:5, *57, 206, 293*
12:6, *67, 74, 184, 293*
12:7, *17, 67, 81, 130, 147, 184,*
   188, 293
12:8, *131, 183, 190, 253, 256,*
   257, 258, 293
12:9, *70, 75*
12:9-14, *67, 183, 293*
12:10-14, *281*
12:14, *17, 65, 70, 133, 148, 267*
12:15, *185, 317*
12:15-16, *267*
12:17, *131, 260*
12:17-21, *134, 267, 290*
12:18, *267, 291*
12:18-21, *58, 63, 222, 267*
12:19-20, *267*
12:21, *291*
12:22-29, *19, 130*

Scripture Index

12:22-32, *184, 246*
12:22-50, *17, 131*
12:23, *61, 131, 190, 244, 246*
12:24-27, *70*
12:24-32, *293*
12:24-33, *68*
12:24-42, *130, 131*
12:25, *131*
12:26, *131*
12:28, *57, 65, 131, 154, 158, 232, 239, 296, 297, 321, 326*
12:30, *32, 66, 317*
12:31, *188, 282*
12:32, *131, 190, 256, 257*
12:33-35, *132*
12:33-37, *58, 184, 281, 304, 318*
12:33-42, *184*
12:36-37, *57*
12:37, *304*
12:38, *65, 67, 68, 107, 261*
12:38-40, *188, 225*
12:38-42, *230*
12:39, *199*
12:40, *131, 133, 160, 190, 221, 256, 260*
12:41, *67, 74, 165, 184, 191, 199, 260, 299*
12:41-42, *130, 304, 307*
12:42, *67, 75, 156, 184, 199*
12:43-45, *16, 184*
12:45, *199*
12:46-50, *78, 181, 184, 215, 312, 315*
12:48, *215*
12:50, *130, 299*
13, *3, 19, 66, 77, 112, 113, 184, 185, 186, 297, 317*
13:1-3, *184*
13:1-35, *184*
13:1-52, *16, 102, 184*
13:1-16:20, *117, 184, 187*
13:3, *131*
13:3-9, *305, 318, 319, 325*
13:3-23, *185, 281*
13:3-35, *184*
13:4, *185*
13:5-6, *185*
13:7, *185*
13:8, *186*
13:10, *184*
13:10-13, *68*
13:10-15, *131*

13:10-17, *183, 184, 185, 186, 191, 283*
13:10-23, *184*
13:11, *215*
13:13, *185, 246*
13:14-15, *68, 290*
13:15, *67, 185, 246*
13:16-17, *306*
13:17, *260*
13:18-23, *184, 305, 318, 325*
13:19, *131, 185, 307*
13:19-20, *185*
13:20, *148*
13:20-21, *185*
13:21, *130*
13:22, *185*
13:23, *185, 186*
13:24, *57, 131, 186, 297, 300*
13:24-27, *301*
13:24-28, *57*
13:24-30, *32, 80, 185, 258, 281, 304, 305, 307, 318*
13:26, *318*
13:27, *251, 300*
13:29-30, *298*
13:30, *178, 321*
13:31, *57, 131*
13:31-33, *185, 281, 301*
13:32, *298*
13:33, *57, 131*
13:34-35, *292*
13:34-36, *112*
13:35, *112, 131, 260, 281*
13:35-36, *112*
13:36, *108, 112, 184, 187*
13:36-40, *307, 318*
13:36-43, *184, 185, 304*
13:36-44, *305*
13:36-52, *184*
13:37, *131, 186, 190, 255, 256, 257, 258, 300*
13:37-43, *178, 258*
13:38, *130, 131, 240, 297, 300*
13:38-39, *301*
13:38-42, *258*
13:38-43, *303*
13:39, *321*
13:40, *307*
13:41, *104, 131, 190, 255, 256, 257, 258, 300, 321*
13:41-42, *198, 301*
13:42, *154, 307*

13:43, *131, 186, 198, 215, 240, 297, 301, 305*
13:43-45, *131*
13:44, *57, 148*
13:44-46, *186*
13:44-50, *281*
13:45, *57*
13:47, *57, 131, 186, 314*
13:47-50, *57, 80, 142, 304, 307, 314, 317*
13:48, *131*
13:50, *154, 307, 321*
13:51-52, *186*
13:52, *55, 57, 77, 131, 193, 215, 234, 270, 281*
13:53, *16, 267*
13:53-59, *187*
13:53-16:20, *187, 189*
13:54, *75, 130, 165, 261, 262*
13:54-58, *102*
13:55, *190*
13:56, *157*
13:57, *187, 261*
14-18, *114, 275*
14-28, *91, 210, 254, 306*
14:1-2, *190*
14:1-5, *259*
14:1-12, *17, 150, 188, 261*
14:2, *190*
14:8-11, *259*
14:12, *229*
14:13, *185, 187, 189, 317*
14:13-21, *149, 159, 245, 290*
14:14, *84, 130, 189, 320*
14:14-21, *189*
14:15, *179*
14:22-30, *232*
14:22-33, *242*
14:23, *274*
14:27, *254*
14:28, *253, 254*
14:28-32, *193*
14:28-33, *54*
14:30, *252, 253*
14:31, *190, 199, 232, 312*
14:32, *274*
14:33, *18, 129, 130, 148, 190, 191, 231*
14:34-36, *189*
15:1, *65, 67*
15:1-6, *62, 319*

15:1-20, *68, 69, 79, 106, 108, 188*
15:1-21, *130, 131*
15:1-28, *17*
15:2, *67, 258*
15:3-9, *313*
15:4, *264*
15:6, *57, 173, 188*
15:8, *67, 188, 304*
15:8-9, *281*
15:9, *188*
15:10-11, *16*
15:10-20, *188, 189, 304*
15:12, *65, 187*
15:12-20, *317*
15:13, *130*
15:14, *207, 321*
15:15-16, *190*
15:16, *312*
15:17-20, *281*
15:18, *304*
15:19, *281, 304*
15:21, *92, 187, 189, 267*
15:21-28, *58, 72, 130, 189, 271, 321*
15:22, *17, 61, 130, 131, 244, 252, 253*
15:22-28, *282*
15:23, *189*
15:24, *72, 89, 130, 134, 179, 233, 282, 290, 321*
15:24-26, *189*
15:25, *130, 231, 253, 254*
15:27, *253*
15:28, *72, 132*
15:29, *189*
15:29-31, *189*
15:29-39, *190*
15:31, *170, 282*
15:32, *84, 130, 320*
15:32-39, *149, 159, 189, 245, 271, 290*
15:33, *179*
15:36, *274*
16, *74, 86*
16:1, *65, 86*
16:1-4, *69, 130, 188, 190, 225, 230*
16:1-12, *65, 131*
16:4, *133, 160, 187, 199, 221, 260, 267*
16:5-12, *68, 190, 193*

16:5-20, *73*
16:6, *65, 86*
16:8, *190*
16:8-11, *190*
16:11, *65, 86, 312*
16:12, *65, 86*
16:13, *97, 131, 200, 255, 256, 257*
16:13-14, *206, 259*
16:13-16, *121*
16:13-17, *246, 255, 260*
16:13-18, *18*
16:13-20, *17, 119, 129*
16:13-23, *120, 121*
16:13-28, *124*
16:13-20:34, *124*
16:15, *196, 256*
16:15-17, *206*
16:16, *129, 130, 131, 187, 191, 192, 227, 237, 239, 249, 306, 315*
16:16-17, *241*
16:16-18, *196, 240*
16:16-19, *196*
16:16-20, *54*
16:17, *83, 130, 191, 196, 206, 260*
16:18, *121, 291, 315*
16:18-19, *75, 78, 83, 193*
16:18-20, *121*
16:19, *57, 131, 162, 201, 316*
16:20, *118, 131, 194, 196, 249*
16:21, *67, 97, 110, 115, 116, 117, 119, 120, 121, 122, 123, 125, 126, 128, 129, 130, 132, 133, 160, 195, 196, 197, 199, 200, 217, 220, 234, 250, 260, 266*
16:21-28, *124*
16:21-20:34, *124, 205*
16:21-28:20, *5, 120, 121, 122, 129, 197, 199, 201, 203, 205, 207, 209, 211, 213, 215, 217, 219, 221, 223, 225, 227, 229, 231, 233, 317*
16:22, *253*
16:22-23, *54, 121, 161, 196, 199, 225, 250, 299*
16:22-17:23, *199*
16:22-25:46, *196*
16:22-28:20, *195, 199*
16:23, *121, 251, 260*

16:24, *130, 197, 300, 317, 318*
16:24-26, *258*
16:24-28, *196*
16:25, *197, 258*
16:25-26, *299, 304*
16:25-28, *197*
16:26, *198*
16:27, *130, 198, 214, 256, 257, 258, 302, 303, 304, 318*
16:27-28, *57, 131, 198, 260*
16:28, *131, 198, 212, 255, 256, 257, 300, 302, 303*
17:1, *97*
17:1-4, *150*
17:1-5, *260*
17:1-8, *54, 164, 190, 220*
17:1-13, *198*
17:2, *263, 305*
17:3, *106*
17:3-4, *191*
17:4, *106, 253*
17:5, *130, 208, 238, 239, 260, 263*
17:9, *131, 256*
17:9-13, *199*
17:10-13, *67, 150, 188, 261*
17:12, *131, 256, 261*
17:13, *260*
17:14-20, *130*
17:14-21, *179, 199, 271, 319*
17:15, *17, 130, 253*
17:20, *199, 312*
17:20-21, *16, 283*
17:22, *129, 131, 150, 256, 325*
17:22-23, *117, 126, 130, 160, 195, 199, 258, 260*
17:24, *200, 261*
17:24-27, *54, 55, 57, 62, 86, 87, 88, 200, 281, 297*
17:24-28, *76*
17:25, *131, 274*
17:25-26, *130, 240*
17:27, *87, 200, 274*
18, *3, 19, 66, 113, 114, 315, 316*
18:1, *57, 131, 215*
18:1-4, *200*
18:1-5, *206*
18:1-14, *215, 307*
18:1-35, *102, 167, 200*
18:2-6, *183*
18:3, *215, 297, 299*
18:3-4, *57, 131*

Scripture Index

18:4, *203, 208, 215, 298, 305*
18:5-14, *88, 201*
18:5-15, *201*
18:5-35, *57*
18:6, *87, 132, 183, 200, 215, 307*
18:7, *87, 200*
18:7-10, *283*
18:8, *200, 297, 307*
18:8-9, *304*
18:9, *200, 297, 307*
18:10, *130*
18:10-14, *78, 281*
18:11, *131, 283*
18:14, *130*
18:15, *78, 201*
18:15-20, *75, 83, 270, 319*
18:15-35, *258*
18:16, *63, 201*
18:16-35, *201*
18:17, *58, 62, 83, 201, 290, 315*
18:18, *193, 315*
18:18-19, *202, 270*
18:18-20, *78*
18:19, *130, 283*
18:19-20, *242*
18:20, *66, 75, 202, 221, 227, 268, 269, 270, 271, 272, 316*
18:21, *78, 132, 253*
18:21-22, *54*
18:23, *57, 131*
18:23-25, *200*
18:23-34, *251*
18:23-35, *17, 173, 307, 308*
18:27, *320*
18:31-35, *281*
18:32, *132, 318*
18:33, *130*
18:34, *307, 318*
18:35, *78, 130, 304*
19-20, *202*
19-23, *114*
19:1, *15, 16, 91, 97*
19:1-29, *17*
19:1-20:34, *202*
19:2, *185, 202, 317*
19:3, *65, 148*
19:3-9, *313*
19:3-12, *202*
19:4, *276*
19:7, *106*
19:8, *106*
19:12, *57, 131*

19:13, *274*
19:13-14, *84*
19:13-15, *203, 206, 299*
19:14, *57, 131, 299, 300*
19:16, *204, 261, 306, 307*
19:16-17, *282*
19:16-19, *79*
19:16-22, *84, 104, 292, 298*
19:16-30, *203*
19:17, *297*
19:18-19, *203*
19:19, *204, 313, 319*
19:21, *32, 217, 305, 312*
19:22, *306*
19:23, *57, 215, 296, 297*
19:23-24, *131, 204*
19:23-27, *203*
19:23-20:16, *317*
19:24, *57, 215, 229, 296, 297*
19:25, *204, 306*
19:25-26, *282, 318*
19:26, *283, 305*
19:27, *54, 204, 258*
19:27-29, *193, 204, 312*
19:28, *66, 131, 178, 204, 215, 255, 256, 258, 302, 303, 305, 306, 322*
19:29, *258, 300, 307*
19:30, *204*
19:30-20:16, *204*
20:1, *57, 131*
20:1-15, *16*
20:1-16, *282, 299*
20:4, *204*
20:13, *204*
20:16, *204*
20:17-19, *117, 126, 130, 131, 204*
20:17-28, *299*
20:17-34, *204*
20:18, *67, 131, 256, 257*
20:18-19, *150, 160, 217, 258, 260, 325*
20:18-20, *195, 200*
20:19, *58, 205, 291, 326*
20:20, *231, 269*
20:20-24, *220*
20:21, *131, 298, 300*
20:21-23, *304*
20:22-23, *130, 205, 220*
20:23, *130, 274*
20:24-28, *298*

20:25, *57, 58, 63, 205, 251, 290, 291*
20:25-28, *131, 317*
20:26, *305*
20:28, *130, 131, 144, 200, 204, 205, 226, 227, 240, 244, 256, 266, 281, 282*
20:29, *185, 206, 317*
20:29-34, *202, 205*
20:30, *253*
20:30-31, *17, 61, 131, 244*
20:30-34, *130*
20:31, *253*
20:32, *205*
20:33, *253*
20:34, *84, 320*
21-23, *216*
21-25, *210*
21-28, *88, 291*
21:1, *205*
21:1-5, *246*
21:1-7, *124*
21:1-11, *205*
21:1-17, *124, 125, 130*
21:1-27, *205*
21:1-23:39, *112*
21:1-27:66, *124*
21:1-28:15, *124*
21:2-3, *205*
21:3, *253, 274*
21:4, *131, 260*
21:4-5, *300*
21:5, *206*
21:9, *61, 131, 185, 205, 246, 252, 317*
21:9-11, *220*
21:10, *205*
21:11, *129, 206, 246, 259*
21:12, *205*
21:12-13, *206*
21:12-17, *67, 131*
21:12-27, *205*
21:14, *206*
21:15, *61, 67, 131, 208, 244, 246*
21:15-16, *206*
21:16, *148, 206*
21:18-20, *227*
21:18-22, *206*
21:20-22, *283*
21:23, *58, 67, 130, 165, 261*
21:23-27, *130, 207, 312*
21:23-23:39, *37*

21:25-26, *162*
21:26, *190*
21:27, *181*
21:28-32, *58, 207, 281, 325*
21:28-33, *131*
21:28-43, *16*
21:28-22:14, *142*
21:31, *57, 131, 296, 299*
21:32, *57, 62, 261*
21:33-41, *260, 261, 300, 318*
21:33-43, *221*
21:33-46, *207, 281*
21:33-22:10, *282*
21:33-22:14, *283*
21:36-39, *240*
21:37-38, *130*
21:40, *251*
21:41, *83, 260, 283*
21:42, *240, 252*
21:43, *57, 63, 131, 216, 240, 288, 291, 296, 300*
21:45, *65*
21:46, *148, 207, 259*
22, *83*
22:1-4, *306*
22:1-10, *63, 216, 240, 283*
22:1-14, *207, 281*
22:1-40, *130*
22:1-45, *3*
22:2, *57, 130, 131, 240, 296*
22:7, *83, 221, 260*
22:8-10, *207, 291*
22:9-10, *311*
22:11-14, *214, 216, 283, 307*
22:12, *297*
22:13, *307*
22:14, *211, 311*
22:15, *65, 148*
22:15-18, *298*
22:15-22, *67, 207*
22:15-40, *207*
22:16, *107, 148, 165, 261*
22:18, *217*
22:21-46, *246*
22:23, *65, 86*
22:23-33, *208, 304, 322*
22:24, *106, 261*
22:31, *264*
22:32, *290, 306*
22:34, *65, 86, 305*
22:34-40, *172, 176, 208, 283, 292, 299, 318*

22:36, *261*
22:36-40, *57, 130*
22:37, *252, 304*
22:37-40, *211*
22:39, *147*
22:41, *65*
22:41-45, *300, 302*
22:41-46, *239, 247, 250, 254*
22:42, *61, 131*
22:43, *253*
22:44, *252, 253*
22:45, *61, 131, 253*
23, *105, 109, 113, 208, 209, 262, 291*
23-25, *113*
23:1, *262*
23:1-2, *68*
23:1-3, *75*
23:1-7, *57, 67*
23:1-12, *208*
23:1-36, *58*
23:1-38, *131*
23:1-39, *3, 105, 108, 208*
23:1-25:46, *102*
23:2, *67, 106*
23:2-3, *76*
23:2-7, *321*
23:3, *68, 75, 208*
23:4, *68, 183, 208*
23:4-8, *78*
23:5, *62*
23:5-7, *208, 298*
23:6, *70*
23:8, *78, 262*
23:8-11, *322*
23:8-12, *192, 208*
23:9, *131, 240*
23:10, *131, 250*
23:11-12, *250*
23:12, *283*
23:13, *57, 67, 131, 173, 216, 217*
23:13-15, *209*
23:13-28, *57, 321*
23:14, *67, 297*
23:15, *67*
23:16, *67*
23:16-22, *62, 85*
23:16-23, *209*
23:23, *67, 130, 147, 173, 188, 217*
23:23-24, *209*
23:23-26, *57*

23:24, *223*
23:25, *67, 173, 188, 217*
23:25-28, *209*
23:26, *281*
23:27, *67, 173, 217*
23:28, *217*
23:29, *67, 173, 217*
23:29-35, *70*
23:29-36, *70, 130, 188, 209, 307*
23:29-37, *261*
23:29-25:46, *260*
23:32, *131*
23:33, *216*
23:34, *69, 70, 75, 76, 77, 178, 187, 265, 266, 319*
23:34-35, *70, 291*
23:36, *199*
23:37, *177, 265, 266, 275*
23:37-39, *209, 324*
23:37-24:2, *227*
23:38, *206, 221, 227*
23:39, *209, 252, 273, 291*
24, *83, 251, 303*
24-25, *3, 19, 66, 113, 114, 167, 209, 214*
24:1, *209, 221*
24:1-2, *206, 221*
24:1-25:30, *193*
24:2, *221, 283*
24:3, *209, 210, 221, 301*
24:4-8, *210, 213*
24:4-14, *210*
24:5, *131, 211, 250*
24:6, *210, 211*
24:7, *291*
24:8, *210*
24:9, *211, 291*
24:9-10, *150, 325*
24:9-13, *185*
24:9-14, *130, 211*
24:9-25:30, *175*
24:10-12, *104*
24:11, *211, 230*
24:11-12, *211*
24:12, *187*
24:13, *211, 216*
24:14, *64, 122, 130, 131, 134, 165, 211, 215, 217, 272, 291, 298, 307*
24:15, *33, 211*
24:15-20, *87*

Scripture Index

24:15-28, *213, 221, 251*
24:15-35, *211*
24:15-25:46, *211*
24:16-20, *211*
24:20, *57, 87*
24:23, *131*
24:23-24, *250*
24:24, *230*
24:24-26, *303*
24:27, *131, 212, 256, 301, 303*
24:29, *88, 212*
24:29-31, *88, 212*
24:30, *131, 212, 255, 256, 302, 303*
24:31, *212*
24:32, *213*
24:32-35, *213, 281*
24:33, *213*
24:34, *171, 199*
24:34-44, *217*
24:35, *273, 306*
24:36, *84, 130, 213, 274, 304*
24:36-46, *213*
24:36-25:30, *215*
24:36-25:46, *211*
24:37, *131, 256, 301*
24:37-25:13, *304*
24:38-25:30, *213*
24:39, *131, 213, 256, 301*
24:42, *213, 216, 253*
24:42-51, *281*
24:43, *213*
24:44, *131, 212, 213, 256, 302, 303*
24:45, *213, 215, 216*
24:45-51, *214, 251*
24:45-25:13, *307*
24:45-25:30, *213, 317*
24:45-25:46, *142*
24:47, *214, 305*
24:48, *298, 304*
24:50, *213*
24:51, *214, 216, 307*
25:1, *57, 131*
25:1-13, *214, 215, 317*
25:1-30, *281*
25:5, *213, 298*
25:10, *297*
25:11, *252, 253, 254*
25:12, *215*
25:13, *213, 216*
25:14-30, *214, 305*

25:15, *325*
25:18-26, *251*
25:20, *215*
25:21, *148, 214, 215, 216, 297, 305*
25:22, *215*
25:23, *148, 214, 215, 216, 297, 305*
25:30, *214, 216, 307*
25:31, *131, 198, 255, 256, 257, 258, 273, 301, 302, 303*
25:31-46, *57, 80, 142, 152, 214, 246, 283, 304, 313*
25:32, *291*
25:34, *130, 297, 300, 305, 307*
25:34-40, *305*
25:37, *147, 253, 254*
25:40, *78, 131*
25:41, *130, 307*
25:42, *215*
25:44, *215, 252, 253, 254*
25:46, *147, 154, 205, 216, 258, 304, 305, 306, 307*
26-27, *148, 298*
26-28, *17, 108, 195, 216, 217*
26:1, *16, 135, 234, 260*
26:1-2, *217*
26:1-16, *217*
26:1-27:54, *160, 217*
26:1-27:55, *65*
26:1-28:20, *104, 196*
26:2, *131, 150, 218, 255, 256, 258, 325*
26:3, *67, 148*
26:3-5, *130, 131, 217, 274*
26:4, *218, 220*
26:5, *67, 218, 224*
26:6-13, *217*
26:12, *217*
26:13, *122, 130, 165, 217*
26:14-15, *55*
26:14-16, *17, 217, 218*
26:15, *150*
26:15-16, *325*
26:16, *116, 119, 129, 150*
26:18, *219, 261, 272*
26:20, *272*
26:20-25, *260*
26:20-29, *218*
26:21, *150, 218, 325*
26:21-25, *218, 274*
26:22, *252, 253*

26:23, *150*
26:23-25, *325*
26:24, *131, 150, 218, 256*
26:25, *107, 252*
26:26, *218*
26:26-29, *218*
26:27-28, *144*
26:28, *173, 224, 226, 227, 240, 244, 266, 281, 282, 318*
26:29, *107, 130, 131, 215, 219, 272, 294*
26:30-35, *66, 260*
26:30-46, *193*
26:31, *149, 178, 219, 220, 244*
26:31-35, *54*
26:32, *130, 133, 219, 231*
26:34, *197, 274*
26:35, *197, 220*
26:36-37, *320*
26:36-46, *160, 161, 217, 219*
26:37-45, *54*
26:38, *84, 216, 217, 272, 304*
26:38-40, *317*
26:39, *130, 220*
26:39-44, *283*
26:40, *54, 272*
26:41, *158, 216, 217, 283, 312*
26:42, *130, 299*
26:45, *131, 150, 255, 256*
26:45-46, *325*
26:46, *150*
26:46-47, *274*
26:47, *67, 131, 220*
26:47-56, *220*
26:47-27:26, *130*
26:48, *150, 325*
26:51, *298*
26:52, *220, 281*
26:53, *130, 242*
26:53-54, *303*
26:53-56, *130*
26:54, *131, 222, 250, 255, 266*
26:55, *130, 165, 261, 262*
26:56, *66, 131, 220*
26:57, *67, 148*
26:57-69, *67*
26:57-75, *221, 225*
26:57-27:26, *17, 201*
26:59, *69, 148, 326*
26:60, *148*
26:61, *206, 221, 227*
26:62-63, *266*

26:63, *131, 239, 240, 251*
26:64, *131, 198, 223, 251, 256, 257, 302, 303*
26:65, *223*
26:65-66, *133*
26:66, *223*
26:67-68, *224*
26:68, *131, 259*
26:69, *129*
26:69-75, *227*
26:70, *197*
26:72, *197*
26:75, *197, 231*
27, *244*
27:1, *67*
27:1-2, *223*
27:1-26, *221*
27:2, *150, 325, 326*
27:3, *67, 150*
27:3-10, *17, 55, 58, 223*
27:3-14, *223*
27:4, *150, 224, 325*
27:5, *198, 321*
27:6, *63*
27:6-10, *57*
27:9, *131, 223*
27:10, *252*
27:11, *131, 149, 244, 248, 326*
27:11-26, *225*
27:11-54, *244*
27:12, *67, 266*
27:12-13, *223*
27:14, *223, 248, 326*
27:15, *248, 326*
27:15-21, *251*
27:15-23, *131, 223*
27:15-26, *166*
27:17, *131, 248*
27:18, *150, 325*
27:19, *279*
27:20, *67*
27:20-26, *68*
27:21, *248, 259, 326*
27:22, *131, 206, 248, 251*
27:22-26, *325*
27:23, *207, 251*
27:24, *224, 281*
27:25, *58, 67, 206, 207, 209, 224, 259*
27:26, *131, 150, 325, 326*
27:27, *248, 326*
27:27-31, *224, 225, 244*

27:27-54, *36, 217, 240*
27:29, *131, 149, 225*
27:32, *220*
27:33, *63*
27:37, *131, 149, 225, 243, 244*
27:38, *205, 220*
27:39-40, *225*
27:39-42, *67*
27:40, *161, 189, 206, 225, 227, 240*
27:41, *67*
27:41-43, *225*
27:41-45, *130, 131*
27:42, *131, 149, 160, 225, 239, 243, 244*
27:43, *161, 219, 222, 225, 226, 240, 243*
27:44, *225*
27:45, *306*
27:46, *50, 63, 219*
27:50, *219*
27:51, *209, 227*
27:51-53, *225, 226, 228, 306*
27:51-54, *241*
27:53, *57, 62*
27:54, *129, 225, 227, 238, 240*
27:55, *129*
27:55-56, *228*
27:55-61, *228*
27:55-66, *228*
27:55-28:20, *228*
27:57, *193, 234, 266*
27:57-60, *203, 222*
27:57-61, *228*
27:57-75, *54*
27:61, *228*
27:62-66, *17, 19, 58, 64, 69, 130, 131, 228, 229*
27:63, *251*
28, *125, 179, 228*
28:1, *37*
28:1-3, *230*
28:1-7, *279*
28:1-10, *124, 228*
28:1-20, *124, 228*
28:2, *252*
28:4, *230*
28:5, *227*
28:6, *230*
28:7, *130, 133, 228, 231*
28:7-8, *230*
28:8, *148*
28:9, *148, 230, 274*

28:9-10, *156*
28:10, *78, 130, 133, 215, 219, 228, 230, 231*
28:11-15, *17, 19, 55, 58, 64, 65, 69, 70, 130, 189, 228, 230, 232, 234, 241, 271*
28:11-16, *131*
28:12, *148*
28:15, *230*
28:16, *129, 130, 231, 269*
28:16-20, *124, 132, 133, 134, 164, 179, 219, 228*
28:17, *148, 228, 241, 274*
28:18, *66, 160, 198, 215, 222, 232, 242, 271, 300, 302, 303*
28:18-20, *53, 63, 72, 86, 89, 112, 141, 158, 178, 179, 185, 193, 197, 228, 263, 270, 280, 311, 314, 319, 320*
28:19, *64, 84, 112, 130, 134, 154, 178, 193, 207, 229, 233, 238, 239, 240, 242, 288, 290, 291, 298, 314, 319, 320*
28:19-20, *179, 233, 234, 271, 326*
28:20, *15, 19, 62, 66, 72, 89, 104, 134, 135, 146, 180, 183, 192, 193, 217, 221, 227, 230, 234, 240, 262, 268, 269, 270, 271, 272, 284, 293, 294, 316*

Mark
1:1, *49*
1:7, *249*
1:11, *84*
1:14-15, *120*
1:22, *75*
1:23-27, *32*
1:39, *75*
2:1-12, *178*
2:13-14, *49, 54*
3:13-19, *54*
4:26-29, *32*
5:6, *274*
5:21-43, *75*
5:25-34, *84*
5:35-39, *54*
6:8-9, *323*
6:12, *322*
6:30, *322*
7:10, *264*
8:15, *69*
8:38, *256*

Scripture Index

9:40, *32*
10:14, *84*
10:21, *32, 84*
12:6, *264*
12:18, *86*
12:28-34, *75*
12:35-37, *239*
13, *83*
13:32, *73, 84*
14:61, *238*
14:62, *198, 303*
15:33, *84*

Luke
1:1, *50*
1:1-4, *2, 14*
2:41-51, *11*
2:52, *11*
3:23-38, *56, 286*
4:5-8, *160*
4:15, *165*
4:44, *165*
5:27-28, *54*
6:20, *32*
6:20-23, *169*
6:24-26, *169*
7:35, *265*
8:40-56, *75*
9:3, *323*
9:6, *322*
9:10, *322*
9:26, *256*
10:4, *323*
10:7, *324*
10:22, *84*
10:25-28, *75*
10:30, *323*
10:33, *320*
13:35, *209*
20:27, *86*
21, *83*
22:69, *303*
24:52, *274*

John
10:1-5, *149*
10:9, *149*
10:10-15, *149*
16:12-16, *193*
18:31, *223*

Acts
1:13-14, *54*

1:21-26, *1*
2:36, *70*
4:10, *70*
7:57-8:3, *82*
8:9-12, *148*
9:1-2, *82*
9:13-14, *82*
9:21, *82*
11:19-26, *90*
11:21, *93*
11:24, *93*
11:27, *77*
13:1, *77*
13:1-3, *90*
13:6, *148*
13:8, *148*
14:21-15:5, *90*
16:10-17, *2*
18:1-4, *324*
20:5-15, *2*
20:34-35, *324*
21:1-18, *2*
21:10, *77*
22:3-5, *82*
22:19, *82*
24:5, *91*
26:9-11, *82*
27:1-28:16, *2*

Romans
10:9, *253*
11:26, *291*
12:6, *77*
14:1-15:13, *201*

1 Corinthians
5, *83*
5:3-5, *201*
8:1-12, *201*
9:12-18, *324*
9:14, *324*
10:23-30, *201*
10:32, *83*
12:3, *253*
12:28, *83*
12:28-29, *77*
14:1-32, *77*
15:9, *82, 83*
15:20-23, *305*

2 Corinthians
13:14, *84*

Galatians
1:13, *83*
2:11-21, *90*

Ephesians
4:11, *77*
4:32, *320*
5:21-6:9, *202*

Philippians
1:1, *83*
2:1, *320*
2:11, *253*
3:6, *83*
3:21, *305*

Colossians
2:14, *2*
3:12, *320*
3:18-4:1, *202*

1 Thessalonians
2:1-12, *324*

1 Timothy
1:13, *82*
2:1-15, *202*
5:18, *324*

Titus
2:1-10, *202*

Hebrews
5:1-3, *110*
5:1-10, *110*
5:4, *110*
5:5-6, *111*
5:7, *111*
9:15, *226*

1 Peter
1:1-2, *84*
2:18-3:7, *202*
2:25, *149*
3:8, *320*

1 John
3:17, *320*

Revelation
1-3, *316*

Finding the Textbook You Need

The IVP Academic Textbook Selector
is an online tool for instantly finding the IVP books
suitable for over 250 courses across 24 disciplines.

ivpacademic.com

www.ingramcontent.com/pod-product-compliance
Lightning Source LLC
Chambersburg PA
CBHW051250300426
44114CB00011B/967